Games, Economic Dynamics,
and Time Series Analysis

Institut für Höhere Studien – Institute for Advanced Studies
IHS-Studies No. 2

Games, Economic Dynamics, and Time Series Analysis

A Symposium in Memoriam Oskar Morgenstern
Organized at the Institute for Advanced Studies, Vienna

Edited by
M. Deistler, E. Fürst, and G. Schwödiauer

Springer-Verlag Berlin Heidelberg GmbH

1982

ISBN 978-3-7908-0271-9

ISBN 978-3-7908-0271-9 ISBN 978-3-662-41533-7 (eBook)
DOI 10.1007/978-3-662-41533-7

International Journal of Game Theory

Contents

Part I
Game Theory as a Tool of Economic Analysis

Games, Economic Dynamics, and Time Series Analysis. 1982 ©Physica-Verlag, Wien–Würzburg

Part I: Game Theory as a Tool of Economic Analysis

Introduction

By G. Schwödiauer

Although nowadays game-theoretical models are fruitfully applied in various fields, ranging from political science to biology, the discovery and first developments of game theory were intimately related to problems of economic theory. John v. Neumann himself was well aware of the fundamental questions raised by the theoretical economists of the Austrian and the Lausanne schools of thought and perceived the potential usefulness of his then new theory of games of strategy for dealing with some basic conceptual problems of the economic theory of his age. In the very year 1928 when von Neumann's paper appeared, Oskar Morgenstern published a book on the presuppositions and possibilities of economic forecasting in which he pointed out some of the formidable consequences of „rational expectations“ or "theory absorption“ on the part of the economic agents for economic forecasting and policy making. He then gave the now famous example of Sherlock Holmes and Professor Moriarty trying to outguess each other which was later shown to be equivalent to a two-person zero-sum game solvable only in mixed strategies. Morgenstern pursued these problems further in a book on the limits of economic policy and in his seminal paper on perfect foresight and economic equilibrium. He was not able then to solve all the puzzles thrown up but he immediately recognized, as the only economist of his time, the relevance of v. Neumann's game theory when it was brought to his attention. In fact, it was this recognition which eventually made him accept an offer to teach at Princeton, and it was his wish to write an introduction to game theory for his fellow economists which brought about his collaboration with v. Neumann on the paradigmatic "Theory of Games and Economic Behavior“. It is more than likely that without Oskar Morgenstern's intervention game theory would have remained in oblivion for a considerable length of time.

In some sense, however, game-theoretic modelling had not been so completely new or even alien to economic analysis as it seemed to appear to some of v. Neumann's and Morgenstern's contemporaries. Cournot had discovered the Nash non-cooperative equilibrium in pure strategies in the context of oligopoly theory ninety years before v. Neumann's pioneering contribution, and Edgeworth's contract curve and Böhm-Bawerk's notion of "marginal pairs“ proved to be just special cases of cores of (cooperative) market games. Here, the theory of games provided a unifying mathematical framework for the analysis of oligopolistic competition and allocation in multilateral market systems. Economists working in these fields found themselves often in the position of Moliere's bourgeois gentilhomme who had spoken prosa all his life without being aware of it. Edgeworth had even already discovered that the introduction of capacity constraints in a price-setting duopoly may lead to the non-existence of a non-cooperative equilibrium in pure price strategies (a la Bertrand) – in which case the novel contribution of game theory proper has been the notion of mixed, i.e. probabilistic, strategies. In the present volume, a survey on the applications of these more "classical" concepts of non-cooperative equilibrium and core in a general-equilibrium setting is given by *Tatsuro Ichiishi*'s paper. *Reinhard Selten* and *Werner Güth* study the problem of entry into an oligopolistic market for which pure strategy equilibrium points always exist. By applying a procedure developed by Harsanyi and Selten they select one of the equilibrium points as the solution to the market entry game; it is characterized by the property that each player inside the market has lower entry costs than any player outside the market. The concept of non-cooperative equilibrium is also applied in *Karl Borch*'s contribution which shows that the conventional sampling approach to the problem of auditing of accounts may be inappropriate under realistic circumstances, i.e., when the auditor is confronted with an intelligent opponent. He demonstrates that modelling the problem as a non-cooperative, so-called inspector's game should be a more promising approach.

The problem of attribution of value of some joint enterprise to its participating members or contributing factors of production was a central theme of Austrian economics. Various "schemes of attribution" had been developed on a rather ad hoc basis by the representatives of the Austrian school and other marginalist economists. The theory of cooperative games has followed this tradition in offering several "rules of fair division" or "solutions to the bargaining problem" justifying them, however, axiomatically. The most prominent among the game-theoretical valuation concepts is the Shapley value which gives each player the mathematical expectation of his marginal contributions to the worth of the all-player coalition if all permutations of the set of players (i.e., all possible sequences of players joining the grand coalition) are considered equally probable. In his paper, *Michael Maschler* gives an intuitively very attractive and constructive justification of the Shapley value. *Joachim Rosenmüller* employs a generalized concept of value to study welfare properties of certain classes of taxation policies in economies with public goods and production. While for non-cooperative games there exists one generally accepted solution concept, viz., the Nash equilibrium, a multitude of solution concepts have been proposed for cooperative games and have been applied in various contexts. The reasons for this situation are mainly, as *John C. Harsanyi* argues in his paper, that cooperative solution theories have typically not made explicit the assumptions about the bargaining processes underlying them, and, moreover, have not always made clear the distinction between "outcome-selection models" (like, e.g., Nash's solution to the bargaining problem and other valuation concepts or arbitration schemes) on the one hand and "outcome-retention models" (like the core or the von Neumann-Morgenstern solution) on the other hand. *Harsanyi* pleads for making explicit all assumptions about the bargaining preceding the players' joint acceptance of an outcome of the game by modelling the negotiation phase as a non-cooperative bargaining game. If this game has several non-cooperative equilibria one can be selected by means of the theory developed by Harsanyi and Selten.

It is a frequent misunderstanding to conceive of possible practical applications of game theory as typically consisting in giving advice to some real-life economic agent how to behave rationally in a situation where important variables are controlled by other agents. It is clear that a rational solution to a problem of cooperation and fair division can reasonably be proposed only to the whole group of players concerned. However, also in decision-making problems that are non-cooperative games because the agents are not able to make binding commitments one could only advise a player to choose an equilibrium strategy if one can expect the other participants to behave "rationally" by adopting the "matching" equilibrium strategies (only in two-person zero-sum games a "rational" player cannot be harmed by an irrational opponent). Thus, more promising addressees of advice based on game-theoretical considerations are perhaps the policy-making agents who set the rules of the game, i.e., who possess the power of shaping the institutions which govern the allocation of economic resources. In this view, the main problem of optimum institutional economic policy would be the design of institutions, i.e. "game forms", which given the individual preferences yield non-cooperative equilibria that are "socially" desirable (or desirable according to the planners' criteria). *David Schmeidler* gives a selective survey of recent results on the design of allocation rules which under conditions of informational decentralization and strategic behavior of economic agents in neoclassical environments yield Walrasian competitive allocations as equilibrium points. To regard socio-economic institutions as part of the rules of the game is however just one way of looking at institutions. Institutions may also be regarded as endogenous, as being part of the solution to the game rather than of the exogenously given rules. It appears that this was the view taken by von Neumann and Morgenstern when they interpreted their concept of a solution as describing a stable "standard of behavior". *Simeon M. Berman* and *Andrew Schotter* in a similar spirit regard an institution or convention for a repetitive social situation as a non-cooperative equilibrium point of the respective supergame and apply this idea to a simple recurrent public goods provision problem.

It was not possible, of course, to cover all important applications of game theory in economics in this conference. There are, e.g., many problems that have arisen in the debate on the microfoundations of macroeconomics which are of a game-theoretical nature or are amenable to game-theoretical analysis. I may only mention the problem of "manipulable" rationing schemes for fix-price economies, the concept of conjectural non-Walrasian equilibria, or the work of Shubik, Shapley, and Dubey on monetary institutions. The relevance of a game-theoretical approach to the problem of optimum macro-economic policy-making in the presence of "rational expectations" is touched upon, however, in this volume in the paper by *Gregory C. Chow* contained in Part III.

Games, Economic Dynamics, and Time Series Analysis. 1982 ©Physica-Verlag, Wien–Würzburg

Non-Cooperation and Cooperation

By *T. Ichiishi*, Iowa City[1])[2])

1. Preliminary Discussion

1.1 Introduction

The purpose of this paper is to survey the development of two strands in game theory over the past three decades, and show how some of the game-theoretical concepts and tools have provided mathematical foundations for economic analysis.

One strand, represented by the Nash equilibrium of a game in normal form, studies an equilibrium concept for a society in which everybody behaves non-cooperatively. The other strand, represented by the core of a game in characteristic function form, studies the stable outcomes of a society in which everybody is aware of what he can do by co-operating with other members. Each strand has supplied basic mathematical tools applicable to a broad class of economic models. The standard model of the pure exchange economy is used here to illustrate these applications: the existence theorems of a competitive equilibrium and of a core allocation.

The paper then surveys the present author's recent works which synthesize the above two strands: A general model of society and a new solution concept (called here a social coalitional equilibrium) are presented. When the models is suitable specified, it describes-non-cooperative behavior of the members, and the social coalitional equilibrium is reduced to the Nash equilibrium. Given another extreme specification, the model is reduced to a cooperative game without sidepayments, and the set of social coalitional equilibria corresponds precisely to the core. Two applications of the social coalitional equilibrium existence theorem are then discussed. First, the theorem serves as a tool to prove the existence of an equilibrium of a new general equilibrium model with production. The new model reflects the discussions developed over the past half century under the title: theory of the firm. Second, it gives an answer to the welfare question on the Nash equilibrium.

The basic ingredients are presented in Sections 2.1 – 2.3, 3.1 – 3.3, and 4.1 – 4.4.

---

[1]) Many thanks to Ivar Ekeland, Prem Prakash and David Schmeidler for their comments and discussions on the earlier draft of this paper. Not all their suggestions have, however, been followed, and the author is solely responsible for any criticisms of this paper, in particular as regards its organization and its presentation. Section 4.4. was added shortly after the International Conference on Game Theory, Oberwolfach, March 2–8, 1980. Thanks are due to many participants in the Conference for stimulating discussions on the issue treated in Section 4.4; in particular to Pradeep Dubey, Werner Güth and Stef H. Tijs. The author's research is supported in part by U.S. National Science Foundation Grant SES 8104387 (formerly, SES-7806123).

[2]) *T. Ichiishi*, University of Iowa, Iowa City, IA, 52242, U.S.A.

Every effort has been made to make the exposition self-contained, given some mathematical background summarized in the Appendix. In all the theorems, strategy sets are assumed to be subsets of Euclidean spaces, but one can easily generalize the results to the case in which strategy sets are subsets of locally convex topological vector spaces. Sections 2.4 and 3.4 are historical notes. There, evolution of the relevant concepts is surveyed, and more recent results stated. Readers who do not want to bother with games with infinitely many players can skip the paragraphs 4, 5, 8 of Section 2.4, and the paragraphs 5 – 8, 12 of Section 3.4. The mathematical definitions and notation used throughout the paper are given in Section 1.2, and the model of the pure exchange economy is formulated in Section 1.3.

1.2 Basic Notation

Given a set A,

$\#A \equiv$ the cardinality of A.

Given a positive integer k,

$R^k \equiv$ the k-dimensional Euclidean space;

$R^k_+ \equiv$ the non-negative orthant of R^k.

For any $x, y \in R^k$, and any $A \subset R^k$,

$x \cdot y \equiv$ the Euclidean inner product of x and $y \equiv \sum_{i=1}^{k} x_i y_i$;

$\|x\| \equiv$ the Euclidean norm of $x \equiv \sqrt{x \cdot x}$;

co$A \equiv$ the convex hull of A.

$R \equiv R^1$;

$R_+ \equiv R^1_+$.

A positive integer n will be interpreted as the number of *players* throughout this paper. A set of players is called a *coalition.*

$N \equiv \{1,2,\ldots,n\}$, interpreted as the set of players;

$\mathcal{N} \equiv 2^N \setminus \{\phi\}$, interpreted as the family of non-empty coalitions.

For every $j \in N$,

$$e^j \equiv (\underbrace{0,\ldots,1}_{j},\ldots,0) \in R^n.$$

For every $S \in \mathcal{N}$,

$$\chi_S \equiv \sum_{j\in S} e^j;$$

$$\Delta^S \equiv \text{co}\,\{e^j \mid j \in S\};$$

$$\mathring{\Delta}^S \equiv \{\sum_{j\in S} \alpha_j e^j \mid \sum_{j\in S} \alpha_j = 1. \quad \forall i \in S: \alpha_i > 0\}.$$

Let X be a convex subset of R^k, and $f\colon X \to R$ a function. The function f is called *quasi-concave in* X, if for every $r \in \boldsymbol{R}$, the set $\{x \in X \mid f(x) \geqslant r\}$ is convex, or equivalently, if for any $x, y \in X$ and any t in the unit interval $[0,1]$, it follows that $f(tx + (1-t)y) \geqslant \text{Min}\,[f(x), f(y)]$. The function f is called *concave in* X, if for any $x, y \in X$ and any $t \in [0,1]$, $f(tx + (1-t)y) \geqslant tf(x) + (1-t)f(y)$.

Given two sets X, Y, a point-to-set function F from X to the subsets of Y is called a *correspondence from* X *to* Y, and is denoted by $F: X \to Y$. No ambiguity is caused. The *graph* of a correspondence F is the set $\{(x, y) \in X \times Y \mid y \in F(x)\}$, and is denoted by $\text{Gr}\,F$. Let X, Y be a metric space, a compact metric space, respectively, and $F: X \to Y$ a correspondence. The correspondence F is called *upper semi-continuous at* x (in brief, *u.s.c. at* x), if for any sequence $\{x^q\}_q$ in X converging to x and for any sequence $\{y^q\}_q$ in Y converging to y for which $y^q \in F(x^q)$ for every q, it follows that $y \in F(x)$. The correspondence F is called *upper semi-continuous in* X (in brief, *u.s.c. in* X), if it is u.s.c. at every point of X. The correspondence F is called *lower semi-continuous at* x (in brief, *l.s.c. at* x), if for any sequence $\{x^q\}_q$ in X converging to x and for any $y \in F(x)$, there exists a sequence $\{y^q\}_q$ in Y converging to y such that $y^q \in F(x^q)$ for every q. The correspondence F is called *lower semi-continuous in* X (in brief, *l.s.c. in* X), if it is l.s.c. at every point of X. [In the seventh paragraph of Section 3.4, some related concepts, such as V-upper semi-continuity, will be introduced. For a correspondence F from a metric space X to a compact metric space Y for which $F(x)$ is closed in Y for every $x \in X$, V-upper semi-continuity, H-upper semi-continuity, and the present concept of upper semi-continuity are all equivalent. For a correspondence F from a metric space X to a metric space Y for which $F(x)$ is totally bounded in Y for every $x \in X$, V-lower semi-continuity, H-lower semi-continuity, and the present concept of lower semi-continuity are all equivalent.].

1.3 Pure Exchange Economy

The model of the pure exchange economy with l types of commodities and m consumers is reviewed. A *commodity bundle* is a point x in $\boldsymbol{R}^l$; it describes the quantity x_h of each commodity $h = 1, \ldots, l$. The i-th consumer is characterized by a triple $(X^i, \precsim_i, \omega^i)$ of his consumption set X^i, his preference relation $\precsim_i$, and his initial endowment vector ω^i. The *consumption set* X^i is a subset of $\boldsymbol{R}^l$, and is interpreted as the set of all commodity bundles with which he can physically survive; the set X^i characterizes the "physical needs" of the consumer i. Suppose he chooses a bundle $x^i \in X^i$. If $x^i_h > 0$ ($x^i_h < 0$, resp.), then he demands (supplies, resp.) $|x^i_h|$ – units of the commodity h. The *preference relation* $\precsim_i$ is a binary relation on X^i. The statement $[x^i \precsim_i x^{i'}]$ is interpreted as: The commodity bundle $x^{i'}$ is at least as desirable as the commodity bundle x^i to the consumer i. The relation $\precsim_i$, therefore, characterizes the "taste" of the consumer i. Given x^i, $x^{i'} \in X^i$, denote by $[x^i \succ_i x^{i'}]$ the negation of $[x^i \precsim_i x^{i'}]$. The preference relation $\precsim_i$ is called *complete*, if for any $x^i, x^{i'} \in X^i$, it follows that $x^i \precsim_i x^{i'}$ or $x^{i'} \precsim_i x^i$; completeness means that the consumer i has a strong opinion on the commodity bundles. It is called *transitive*, if for any $x^i, x^{i'}, x^{i''} \in X^i$ for which $x^i \precsim_i x^{i'}$ and $x^{i'} \precsim_i x^{i''}$, if follows that $x^i \precsim_i x^{i''}$; transitivity means that the consumer is rational. It is called *closed*, if for any $x^i \in X^i$, the sets $\{\xi^i \in X^i \mid \xi^i \precsim_i x^i\}$ and $\{\xi^i \in X^i \mid x^i \precsim_i \xi^i\}$ are both closed in X^i; closedness means that his comparison of commodity bundles is smooth. It is called *weakly convex,* if for any $x^i \in X^i$, the set $\{\xi^i \in X^i \mid x^i \precsim_i \xi^i\}$ is convex; weak convexity means diminsihing marginal rate of substitution. It is called *convex,* if for any $x^i, x^{i'} \in X^i$ for which $x^i \succ_i x^{i'}$, and for any real number t for which $0 < t < 1$, it follows that $tx^i + (1-t)x^{i'} \succ_i x^{i'}$. A commodity bundle $x^i \in X^i$ is called a *non-satiation point,* if there exists $x^{i'} \in X^i$ such that $x^{i'} \succ_i x^i$. A numerical function u^i: $X^i \to R$ *represents* the preference relation $\precsim_i$, if for any $x^i, x^{i'} \in X^i$, $x^i \precsim_i x^{i'}$ if and only if $u^i(x^i) \leqslant u^i(x^{i'})$. A consumer whose preference relation is representable by a numerical function behaves *as though* he were trying to maximize this function. Sometimes, such a numerical function is called a *utility function.* Proof of the following theorem (1.3.1) can be found in *Debreu* [1959, (1), 56–59]:

Theorem 1.3.1. Let X^i be the consumption set of the consumer i, and $\precsim_i$ his preference relation. Assume X^i is a connected subset of R^l. Then, there exists a continuous numerical function on X^i which represents $\precsim_i$, if and only if $\precsim_i$ is complete, transitive and closed.

The *initial endowment vector* ω^i is a point in R^l, and is interpreted as the commodity bundle the consumer i holds initially. A *pure exchange economy* is now characterized by a list of specified data, $E \equiv \{X^i, \precsim_i, \omega^i\}_{i=1}^m$.

Besides the exogenous data E, economists identify the behavioral pattern of the economic agents, and also the mechanism at the "meeting place" that coordinates their behavior. Consumer behavior in accordance with a given pattern leads to economic outcomes, usually characterized by particular values of appropriate endogenous variables. Economic theorists formulate the outcomes in terms of a suitable solution concept, and try to understand them by deducing the properties of the solution.

The solution concept with the greatest importance and longest history is the competitive equilibrium: Each consumer i observes a price vector $p \in R^l_+ \setminus \{O\}$ in the market. His own budget set $\gamma^i(p, p \cdot \omega^i) \equiv \{\xi^i \in X^i \mid p \cdot \xi^i \leqslant p \cdot \omega^i\}$ is therefore determined, and within this constraint he chooses individualistically the commodity bundle that satisfies him the most. An equilibrium price vector is then determined in the market, so that the total demand cannot exceed the total supply. Let $L \equiv \{1, \ldots, l\}$. By the price-wealth homogenuity, one may restrict the price vector domain to $\{p \in R^l_+ \mid \sum_{h=1}^{l} p_h = 1\}$. which will be, by abuse of notation, denoted by Δ^L throughout this paper. Thus, a *competitive equilibrium* of a pure exchange economy E is a pair $((x^{i*})_{i=1}^m, p^*)$ of members of $\prod_{i=1}^m X^i$ and Δ^L such that 1) x^{i*} is a maximal element of $\{\xi^i \in X^i \mid p^* \cdot \xi^i \leqslant p^* \cdot \omega^i\}$ with respect to $\precsim_i$, for every i; and 2) $\prod_{i=1}^m x^{i*} \leqslant \sum_{i=1}^m \omega^i$. It is a solution concept based upon a non-cooperative behavior of the consumers and upon the market mechanism. In Section 2.3, however, its existence problem will be discussed as a particular case of the existence problem of a certain non-cooperative solution concept which does not specifically involve the market mechanism. Another solution concept for $\mathcal{E}$, based upon a cooperative behavior, will be discussed in Section 3.3.

Certain dynamic economies can be analyzed within the framework of the above static model $\mathcal{E}$. One characterizes a commodity not only by its physical properties and the place where it is available, but also by the date when it will be available and (in the case of uncertainty about the future) the elementary event that will be realized. The commodity h, for example, is defined as coffee ice-cream which will be available in Yokohama in 77 days when it is snowing. The above definition of competitive equilibrium allows for this dynamic interpretation, but one should keep in mind that all the futures markets (and also all the contingent markets in the presence of uncertainty) are assumed to exist.

2. Non-Cooperative Behavior

2.1 Nash Equilibrium of a Game in Normal Form

Given the set N of players, a game in normal form specifies a strategy set and a utility function for each player. For the player j, denote by X^j the set of all strategies available to him, and define $X \equiv \prod_{j \in N} X^j$. It is postulated that his preference relation is represented by a utility function, $u^j: X \times X^j \to \mathbf{R}$. The intended interpretation is that when all the players have chosen their strategies $x \equiv (x^1, \ldots, x^n) \in X$, the player j enjoys his utility level $u^j(x, \xi^j)$ when he changes his strategy from x^j to $\xi^j \in X^j$. Here the player j passively expects the others not to change their strategies. Another (more static) interpretation is that the j-th player's utility level is $u^j(x, \xi^j)$ when he chooses ξ^j and all the others choose $(x^1, \ldots, x^{j-1}, x^{j+1}, \ldots, x^n)$; in the latter case, u^j is assumed to be independent of x^j. Thus, the player i influences the player j through j's utility function u^j, and *vice versa.* A *game in normal form* is now defined as a list of specified data, $\{X^j, u^j\}_{j \in N}$.

Within the present framework, one can postulate cooperative behavior of the players, and hence the associated solution concept. The framework is, however, too general to yield clear-cut theorems on cooperative behavior. In this generality, a type of non-cooperative behavior has been extensively studied, which is summarized by the following solution concept. A *Nash equilibrium* of a game in normal form $\{X^j, u^j\}_{j \in N}$ is an n-tuple of strategies $x^* \equiv (x^{1*}, \ldots, x^{n*}) \in X$, such that for every $j \in N$, $u^j(x^*, x^{j*}) \geqslant u^j(x^*, \xi^j)$ for all $\xi^j \in X^j$. The real number $u^j(x^*, x^{j*})$ is the utility level that the player j currently enjoys, and there is no incentive for him to change by himself his strategy x^{j*} in equilibrium.

Theorem 2.1.1. Let $\{X^j, u^j\}_{j \in N}$ be a game in normal form. Assume for every $j \in N$, X^j is a non-empty, convex, compact subset of a Euclidean space, u^j is continuous in $X \times X^j$, and $u^j(x, \cdot)$ is quasi-concave in X^j given any $x \in X$. Then, there exists a Nash equilibrium of the game.

A complete proof of a more general theorem (2.2.1) will be given later. At this moment, it would be useful to look at a special case, customarily called a *bimatrix game.*

Suppose $n = 2$, and X^1 and X^2 are finite, say $X^j = \{1, \ldots, m_j\}$. Suppose $u^j((x^1, x^2), \xi^j)$ does not depend upon x^j (see the second interpretation of the game above), and define: $a_{pq} \equiv u^1((p', q), p)$, $b_{pq} \equiv u^2((p, q'), q)$ for $p, p' \in X^1$ and $q, q' \in X^2$. Then, the game $\{X^j, u^j\}_{j=1,2}$ reduces to the bimatrix game,

$$\begin{pmatrix} (a_{11}, b_{11}) & \cdots & (a_{1m_2}, b_{1m_2}) \\ \vdots & & \vdots \\ (a_{m_1 1}, b_{m_1 1}) & \cdots & (a_{m_1 m_2}, b_{m_1 m_2}) \end{pmatrix},$$

in which the 1-st player's (the 2nd player's, resp.) payoff is a_{pq} (b_{pq}, resp.) when the 1st chooses a pure strategy $p \in X^1$ and the 2nd chooses a pure strategy $q \in X^2$, and the Nash equilibrium reduces to the *equilibrium* of the bimatrix game. In general, equilibrium with pure strategy may not exist. But when one extends the domain of strategies from X^j to the $(m_j - 1)$-dimensional simplex (the set of the mixed strategies) – a convex, compact subset of a Euclidean space – and the payoff functions to bilinear forms in mixed strategies, then equilibrium does exist.

2.2 Social Equilibrium of an Abstract Economy

An abstract economy is formulated by introducing the concept of "feasibility" to a game in normal form. Let N be the set of players, X^j the strategy set for the player j, and define: $X \equiv \prod_{j \in N} X^j$. The feasible strategy correspondence of the player j is a correspondence $F^j: X \to X^j$. When all the players have chosen their strategies $x \in X$, feasibility of the j-th player's strategies is restricted to the subset $F^j(x)$ of X^j. It is postulated that his preference relation is respresented by a utility function, u^j: Gr $F^j \to R$. Thus, the other players influence the player j 1) indirectly by restricting j's feasible strategies to $F^j(x)$; and 2) directly by affecting j's utility level u^j. An *abstract economy* is a list of specified data, $\{X^j, F^j, u^j\}_{j \in N}$. It should be emphasized, however, that an abstract economy is *not* a game, in spite of its mathematical generality: No player can individually play this "game," since the player j must know the others' strategies in order to know his own feasible strategy set $F^j(x)$, but the others cannot determine their feasible strategies without knowing j's strategy. Thus, an abstract economy is a *meta-game*, and it is useful only as a mathematical tool to establish existence theorems in various applied contexts; see Section 2.3 below.

A non-cooperative solution concept, Nash equilibrium of a game in normal form, can readily be extended in the present general setup. A *social equilibrium* of an abstract economy $\{X^j, F^j, u^j\}_{j \in N}$ is an n-tuple of strategies $x^* \equiv (x^{1*}, \ldots, x^{n*}) \in X$, such that for every $j \in N$, 1) $x^{j*} \in F^j(x^*)$, and 2) $u^j(x^*, x^{j*}) \geqslant u^j(x^*, \xi^j)$ for all $\xi^j \in F^j(x^*)$. The condition (1) says x^{j*} is feasible, and the condition (2) says he cannot find a feasible strategy to bring about a higher utility level than the current level $u^j(x^*, x^{j*})$. Again, he passively expects the others to keep their strategies $(x^{1*}, \ldots, x^{j-1*}, x^{j+1*}, \ldots, x^{n*})$.

Theorem 2.2.1. Let $\{X^j, F^j, u^j\}_{j\in N}$ *be an abstract economy. Assume for every* $j \in N$, X^j *is a non-empty, convex, compact subset of a Euclidean space,* F^j *is both u.s.c. and l.s.c. in* X, $F^j(x)$ *is non-empty and convex for every* $x \in X$, u^j *is continuous in* Gr F^j, *and* $u^j(x, \cdot)$ *is quasi-concave in* $F^j(x)$ *given any* $x \in X$. *Then, there exists a social equilibrium of the abstract economy.*

Proof of (2.2.1). given $j \in N$ and $x \in X$, denote by $\Phi^j(x)$ the set of solutions of the following maximization problem: Maximize $u^j(x, \xi^j)$, subject to $\xi^j \in F^j(x)$. All the conditions for the Maximum Theorem (A.1) are satisfied, and so the correspondence $\Phi^j: X \to X^j$, $x \mapsto \Phi^j(x)$, is u.s.c. For each $x \in X$, $\Phi^j(x)$ is clearly non-empty. To show that it is convex, choose any $\xi^{j(0)}, \xi^{j(1)} \in \Phi^j(x)$, any $t \in [0, 1]$, and define: $\xi^{j(t)} \equiv (1-t)\,\xi^{j(0)} + t\,\xi^{j(1)}$. Convexity of $F^j(x)$ implies $\xi^{j(t)} \in F^j(x)$. By quasi-concavity of $u^j(x, \cdot)$, $u^j(x, \xi^{j(t)}) \geq \text{Min}\,[u^j(x, \xi^{j(0)}), u^j(x, \xi^{j(1)})]$. Therefore $\xi^{j(t)} \in \Phi^j(x)$. Now, define a correspondence $\Phi: X \to X$, by $\Phi(x) \equiv \Phi^1(x) \times \ldots \times \Phi^n(x)$. The correspondence Φ satisfies all the conditions for Kakutani's Fixed-Point Theorem (A.4). A fixed point of Φ is easily shown to be a social equilibrium of the abstract economy. Q.E.D.

Note that (2.1.1) is included in (2.2.1): Just set $F^j(x) \equiv X^j$ for all $x \in X$.

2.3 Competitive Equilibrium of a Pure Exchange Economy

The Social Equilibrium Existence Theorem (2.2.1) serves as a mathematical tool to prove the existence of equilibria for a wide class of economic models in which non-cooperative behavior of the agents is postulated. The purpose of this section is to show how (2.2.1) can be applied to prove the existence of a competitive equilibrium of a pure exchange economy $\{X^i, \precsim_i, \omega^i\}_{i=1}^m$ (formulated in Section 1.3). For each consumer i, denote by $\gamma^i: \Delta^L \times \boldsymbol{R} \to X^i$, his budget set correspondence: $\gamma^i(p, w^i) \equiv \{x^i \in X^i \mid p \cdot x^i \leq w^i\}$. Proof of the following lemma (2.3.1) can be found in *Debreu* [1959, (1), 63–65].

Lemma 2.3.1. Let X^i *be a consumption set of the consumer i, and* $(p, w^i) \in \Delta^L \times \boldsymbol{R}$ *a price-wealth pair. Assume that* X^i *is a convex, compact subset of* $\boldsymbol{R}^l$, *and* $\text{Min}\,\{p \cdot x^i \mid x^i \in X^i\} < w^i$. *Then,* γ^i *is both u.s.c. and l.s.c. at* (p, w^i).

Theorem 2.3.2. Let $\mathcal{E} \equiv \{X^i, \precsim_i, \omega^i\}_{i=1}^m$ *be a pure exchange economy. Assume for every i,* X^i *is a non-empty, convex compact subset of* $\boldsymbol{R}^l$, $\precsim_i$ *is complete, transitive, closed, weakly convex, and* $\text{Min}\,\{p \cdot x^i \mid x^i \in X^i\} < p \cdot \omega^i$ *for each* $p \in \Delta^L$. *Then, there exists a competitive equilibrium of* $\mathcal{E}$.

Proof of (2.3.2). First, an abstract economy is constructed from $\mathcal{E}$. Let $n = m + 1$. The i-th consumer is now called the i-th player $(1 \leq i \leq m)$, and the additional player (the n-th player) is called a "market participant." For i: $1 \leq i \leq m$, his consumption set X^i remains to be his strategy set. Define $X^n \equiv \Delta^L$. The market participant controls the price vector. By (1.3.1), $\precsim_i$ is represented by a continuous utility function, $v^i: X^i \to \boldsymbol{R}$. Weak convexity of $\precsim_i$ is equivalent to quasi-concavity of v^i. Given $((x^i)_i, p) \in \prod_{j\in N} X^j$, define

$F^j((x^i)_i, p) \equiv \gamma^i(p, p \cdot \omega^i)$ for every $j = 1, \ldots, m$; $F^n((x^i)_i, p) \equiv \Delta^L$;
$u^j(((x^i)_i, p), \xi^j) \equiv v^j(\xi^j)$ for every $j = 1, \ldots, m$; $u^n(((x^i)_i, p), \xi^n) \equiv \xi^n \cdot \sum_{i=1}^{m} (x^i - \omega^i)$.
By (1.3.1) and (2.3.1), the abstract economy $\{X^j, F^j, u^j\}_{j \in N}$ satisfies all the assumptions in (2.2.1), and therefore, has a social equilibrium $((x^{i*})_i, p^*) \in \prod_{i=1}^{m} X^i \times \Delta^L$. It is straightforward to see from the social equilibrium condition that x^{i*} is a maximal element of $\gamma^i(p^*, p^* \cdot \omega^i)$ with respect to $\precsim_i$ for every $i = 1, \ldots, m$. It is also clear that $p^* \cdot \sum_{i=1}^{m} (x^{i*} - \omega^i) \leq 0$. Thus, since $u^n(((x^{i*})_i, p^*), p) \leq u^n(((x^{i*})_i, p^*), p^*)$ for every $p \in \Delta^L$, one concludes: $p \cdot \sum_{i=1}^{m} (x^{i*} - \omega^i) \leq 0$ for every $p \in \Delta^L$. In particular, the inequality is true for $p = (\underbrace{0, \ldots, 1}_{h}, \ldots, 0)$, so $\sum_{j=1}^{m} (x_h^{i*} - \omega_h^i) \leq 0$. This is true for every $h \in L$. Thus, $\sum_{i=1}^{m} (x^{i*} - \omega^i) \leq O$. Q.E.D.

2.4 Notes

Consider the bimatrix game given in Section 2.1. When $a_{pq} + b_{pq} = 0$ for all $(p, q) \in \{1, \ldots, m_1\} \times \{1, \ldots, m_2\}$, the game is called a *zero-sum two-person game.* Here the two players have a direct conflict of interest, since one's gain is equivalent to the other's loss. Let $X^j \equiv \{x^j \in R_+^{m_j} \mid \sum_{r=1}^{m_j} x_r^j = 1\}$, $j = 1,2$. A point in the simplex X^j is interpreted as a mixed strategy, i.e., a probability on the pure strategies $\{1, \ldots, m_j\}$, $j = 1,2$. When the two players choose mixed strategies $(x^1, x^2) \in X^1 \times X^2$, the expected payoff of the player 1 (of the player 2, resp.) is $\sum_{p,q} a_{pq} x_p^1 x_q^2$ ($- \sum_{p,q} a_{pq} x_p^1 x_q^2$, resp.). *Von Neumann* [1928] initiated game theory by establishing the *Minimax Principle* for this class of games: *Given any $m_1 \times m_2$ matrix $((a_{pq}))$ of real numbers, it follows that* $\operatorname{Max}_{x^1 \in X^1} \operatorname{Min}_{x^2 \in X^2} \sum_{p,q} a_{pq} x_p^1 x_q^2 = \operatorname{Min}_{x^2 \in X^2} \operatorname{Max}_{x^1 \in X^1} \sum_{p,q} a_{pq} x_p^1 x_q^2$. The left-hand side of this equality is the maximal security level that the player 1 can achieve, and the corresponding interpretation of the right-hand side for the player 2. This number is called the *value* of the game. Strategies (x^{1*}, x^{2*}) for which $\sum_{p,q} a_{pq} x_p^{1*} x_q^{2*}$ is the value are called *optimal strategies.* The following lemma (2.4.1) of *von Neumann/Morgenstern* [1947, 95–96] relates the Minimax Principle to the equilibrium existence theorem (a special case of (2.1.1)).

Lemma 2.4.1. Let X, Y be any sets, and $f: X \times Y \to R$ a bounded function. Then, $\operatorname{Max}_{x \in X} \operatorname{Inf}_{y \in Y} f(x, y) = \operatorname{Min}_{y \in Y} \operatorname{Sup}_{x \in X} f(x, y)$, *if and only if there exists $(x^*. y^*) \in X \times Y$ such that for any $(x, y) \in X \times Y$, $f(x, y^*) \leq f(x^*, y^*) \leq f(x^*, y)$.*

The pair (x^*, y^*) of (2.4.1) is called a *saddle point* of f. Now, apply (2.4.1) to the above zero-sum two-person game. $(X = X^1, Y = X^2, f(x, y) = \sum_{p,q} a_{pq} x_p y_q)$. Then the Minimax Principle is equivalent to the existence of a saddle point. It is straightforward to check that a saddle point is in this case equivalent to a Nash equilibrium, whose existence is guaranteed in (2.1.1). Remark that (x^1, x^2) are optimal strategies, if and only if the pair is a saddle point.

Nash [1950, 1951] introduced an n-person non-cooperative game, and established the special case of (2.1.1) defined by: $X^j = \{x^j \in R_+^{m_j} \mid \sum_{h=1}^{m_j} x_h^j = 1\}$,

$u^j(x, \xi^j) = \sum_{h_1=1}^{m_1} \ldots \sum_{h_n=1}^{m_n} a^j_{h_1 \ldots h_n} x^1_{h_1} \ldots x^{j-1}_{h_{j-1}} \xi^j_{h_j} x^{j+1}_{h_{j+1}} \ldots x^n_{h_n}$, given a payoff function on the pure strategies, $a^j \colon \prod_{i \in N} \{1, \ldots, m_i\} \to R, (h_1, \ldots, h_n) \mapsto a^j_{h_1 \ldots h_n}$, for every $j \in N$. The preceding paragraph showed how *Nash* [1950, 1951] generalizes the pioneering work of *von Neumann* [1928]. The impact of *Nash* [1950, 1951], however, boils down to the shift in attention from the Minimax concept (such as the optimal strategies) to the equilibrium concept (e.g., the Nash equilibrium); it is only with the latter concept that game theorists could advance the n-person non-cooperative theory with the full generality of $n > 2$. The equilibrium concept was actually introduced first by *Cournot* [1838].

Theorem (2.1.1) is based strongly upon the assumption that each u^j is continuous *jointly* in x and ξ^j; otherwise, upper semi-continuity of Φ^j (see the proof of (2.2.1)) does not follow. For a partial relaxation of the joint continuity assumption, see *Nikaidô/Isoda* [1955]. *Debreu* [1952] formulated the abstract economy and established (2.2.1); actually, his main theorem is more general than (2.2.1). Motivated by a work of *Mas-Colell* [1974], *Shafer/Sonnenschein* [1975] established a social equilibrium existence theorem for an abstract economy in which players' preference relations may not be complete or transitive.

There are two extensions of (2.2.1) to the situation in which infinitely many players may exist. One extension ((2.4.2) below) is trivially included in *Prakash/Sertel* [1974]. (Their work will be commented on in the last paragraph of this section.)

Theorem 2.4.2. Let $\{X^a, F^a, u^a\}_{a \in A}$ be an abstract economy with the (possibly infinite) player set A. Assume for each $a \in A$, X^a is a non-empty, convex, compact subset of a locally convex topological vector space, $F^a \colon X \to X^a$ is both u.s.c. and l.s.c. in $X \equiv \prod_{a \in A} X^a$ endowed with the product topology, $F^a(x)$ is non-empty and convex for every $x \in X$, $u^a \colon \mathrm{Gr}\, F^a \to R$ is continuous, and $u^a(x, \cdot)$ is quasi-concave in $F^a(x)$ given any $x \in X$. Then, there exists a social equilibrium of the abstract economy.

The other extension, due to *Schmeidler* [1973], exploits the measure space structure of the player set. Note that in the abstract economy constructed from a given pure exchange economy (see the proof of (2.3.2)), the utility function u^n of the market participant depends only on $(\sum_{i=1}^{m} x^i, \xi^n)$, rather than on $(((x^i)_{i=1}^m, p), \xi^n)$. Therefore, the following formulation of a result in *Schmeidler* [1973] will prove useful: Let $(A, \mathcal{A}, \nu)$ be a probability measure space of players. Besides A, there is an additional player, "atom," denoted by b. Let $X(a)$ (Y, resp.) be the strategy set for the player $a \in A$ (for the player b, resp.), and assume $X(a) \subset R^l$. Given the correspondence $X: A \to R^l$, $a \mapsto X(a)$, denote by L_X the set of integrable selections of X; i.e., the set of integrable functions $f: (A, \mathcal{A}, \nu) \to R^l$ such that $f(a) \in X(a)$, ν-a.e. in A. Define $\int X \equiv \{\int_A f\, d\nu \mid f \in L_X\}$. The feasible strategy correspondence of the player $a \in A$ (of the player b, resp.) is a correspondence $F(a, \cdot, \cdot): (\int X) \times Y \to X(a)$ (a correspondence $G: (\int X) \times Y \to Y$, resp.). It is postulated that the preference relation of the player $a \in A$ (of the player b, resp.) is represented by a utility function, $u(a, \cdot, \cdot, \cdot): (\int X) \times Y \times X(a) \to R$ (by a utility function, v: $(\int X) \times Y \times Y \to R$. resp.). An *abstract economy* is a list of specified data, $((A, \mathcal{A}, \nu), \{b\}, \{X(a)\}_{a\in A}, Y, \{F(a,\cdot)\}_{a\in A}, G, \{u(a,\cdot)\}_{a\in A}, \mathrm{v})$. A *social equilibrium* of a given abstract economy is a pair (f^*, y^*) of members of L_X and Y, such that 1) ν-a.e. in A, $f^*(a) \in F(a, \int f^* d\nu, y^*)$ and $u(a, \int f^* d\nu, y^*, f^*(a)) \geqslant u(a, \int f^* d\nu, y^*, \xi^a)$ for all $\xi^a \in F(a, \int f^* d\nu, y^*)$; and 2) $y^* \in G(\int f^* d\nu, y^*)$ and $\mathrm{v}(\int f^* d\nu, y^*, y^*) \geqslant \mathrm{v}(\int f^* d\nu, y^*, \eta)$ for all $\eta \in G(\int f^* d\nu, y^*)$. A correspondence $\Gamma: (A, \mathcal{A}, \nu) \to R^l$ is called integrably bounded, if there exists an integrable function $f: (A, \mathcal{A}, \nu) \to R_+$ such that $[x \in \Gamma(a)]$ implies $[\|x\| \leqslant f(a)]$, ν-a.e. in A. Denote by $\mathcal{B}(R^l)$ the Borel σ-algebra generated by the open subsets of R^l.

Theorem 2.4.3. Let $((A, \mathcal{A}, \nu), \{b\}, \{X(a)\}_{a\in A}, Y, \{F(a,\cdot)\}_{a\in A}, G, \{u(a,\cdot)\}_{a\in A}, \mathrm{v})$ *be the abstract economy constructed above. There exists a social equilibrium of the abstract economy, if* 1) $(A, \mathcal{A}, \nu)$ *is an atomless probability measure space;* 2) X *is integrably bounded;* $\mathrm{Gr}\, X \in \mathcal{A} \otimes \mathcal{B}(R^l)$; *and* $X(a)$ *is non-empty and closed in* R^l, ν-a.e. *in* A; 2′) Y *is a non-empty, convex, compact subset of a locally convex topological vector space;* 3) $\mathrm{Gr}\, F(\cdot, w, y) \in \mathcal{A} \otimes \mathcal{B}(R^l)$ *for every* $(w, y) \in (\int X) \times Y$; $F(a, \cdot, \cdot)$ *is both u.s.c. and l.s.c., and is non-empty-valued,* ν-a.e. *in* A; 3′) G *is both u.s.c. and l.s.c., and is non-empty- and convex-valued;* 4) $u(\cdot, w, y, \cdot): \mathrm{Gr}\, X \to R$ *is measurable for every* $(w, y) \in (\int X) \times Y$; $u(a, \cdot, \cdot, \cdot); (\int X) \times Y \times X(a) \to R$ *is continuous,* ν-a.e. *in* A; 4′) $\mathrm{v}: (\int X) \times Y \times Y \to R$ *is continuous; and* $\mathrm{v}(w, y, \cdot)$ *is quasi-concave in* Y *for every* $(w, y) \in (\int X) \times Y$.

It should be noted that the convexity assumptions are dropped from the atomless part.

Arrow/Debreu [1954] established (2.3.2). Their method of proof is reproduced here; i.e., to construct the abstract economy given a more specific economic model, and apply (2.2.1). They also relaxed the boundedness assumption on the consumption sets X^i's of (2.3.2) in the following way: Assume each consumption set X^i is closed, and is bounded from below; i.e., there exists $b^i \in X^i$ such that $X^i \subset \{b^i\} + R^l_+$. Then, the set of attainable states $A(\{1, \ldots, m\}) \equiv \{(x^i)_i \in \prod_{i=1}^m X^i \mid \sum_{i=1}^m x^i \leqslant \sum_{i=1}^m \omega^i\}$ is compact. Define $K^{(q)} \equiv \{x \in R^l \mid \|x\| \leqslant q\}$, and for a given economy $\mathcal{E}$, consider the sequence of truncated economies $\{\mathcal{E}^{(q)}\}_{q=1,2,\ldots}$, defined by: $\mathcal{E}^{(q)} \equiv \{X^i \cap K^{(q)}, \precsim_i, \omega^i\}_{i=1}^m$. Apply (2.3.2) to $\mathcal{E}^{(q)}$ for all q sufficiently large, and obtain a competitive equilibrium $((x^{i,(q)})_{i=1}^m, p^{(q)})$ of $\mathcal{E}^{(q)}$. Since the sequence $\{((x^{i,(q)})_i, p^{(q)})\}_q$ of equilibria lies in a compact set $A(\{1, \ldots, m\}) \times \Delta^L$, it has a convergent subsequence. It is easy to check that the limit of the subsequence is a competitive equilibrium of $\mathcal{E}$. Thus,

Theorem 2.4.4. Let $\mathrm{E} \equiv \{X^i, \precsim_i, \omega^i\}_{i=1}^m$ *be a pure exchange economy. Under the same assumptions as in (2.3.2), except that* [X^i *is bounded*] *is relaxed to* [X^i *is bounded from below*], *there exists a competitive equilibrium of* E.

Further works were done on the existence of competitive equilbria during the 1950's, in particular by David Gale, Hukukane Nikaidô, Gerard Debreu, Lionel W. McKenzie: These works are unified in *Debreu* [1959]. *Mas-Colell* [1974] strengthened the competitive equilibrium existence theorem, by dropping the completeness and the transitivity assumptions on the preference relations.

Aumann [1964] formulated a model of pure exchange with an atomless measure space of consumers, and then subsequently established a competitive equilibrium existence theorem in *Aumann* [1966]. Let $(A, \mathcal{A}, \nu)$ be an atomless probability measure space of consumers. Each consumer a is characterized by a triple $(X(a), \precsim_a, \omega(a))$ of his consumption set (a subset of $\boldsymbol{R}^l$), his preference relation on $X(a)$, and his initial endowment (a point of $\boldsymbol{R}^l$). The function ω: $(A, \mathcal{A}, \nu) \to \boldsymbol{R}^l$, $a \mapsto \omega(a)$ is assumed to be integrable. A competitive equilibrium is a pair (f^*, p^*) of members of L_X and Δ^L, such that 1) $f^*(a)$ is a maximal element of $\{x \in X(a) \mid p^* \cdot x \leqslant p^* \cdot \omega(a)\}$ with respect to $\precsim_a$, ν-a.e. in A; and 2) $\int f^* d\nu \leqslant \int \omega\, d\nu$. Now introduce a fictitious "market participant"; call him the player b. Just as *Arrow/Debreu* [1954] used (2.2.1) to prove (2.3.2), one can use (2.4.3) to supply an alternative proof of the existence theorem of *Aumann* [1966]. Note that the (weak) convexity assumption on $\precsim_a$ is dropped here. The convexity assumption on $X(a)$ is not explicit in (2.4.3), but is usually used to establish lower semi-continuity of the budget set correspondence, $p \mapsto \{x \in X(a) \mid p \cdot x \leqslant p \cdot \omega(a)\}$. See (2.3.1), and also the assumption (3) of (2.4.3). *Yamazaki* [1978] dropped the convexity assumption on $X(a)$, and supplied a sufficient condition under which the budget set correspondence is l.s.c., ν-a.e. in A.

Some other works related to the non-cooperative solution concepts:

1) *Schmeidler* [1980] gave a new interpretation of the competitive equilibrium as a Nash equilibrium of a certain game in normal form. His work is significant, particularly because *Arrow/Debreu* [1954]'s game-theoretical interpretation of the competitive equilibrium (see the proof of (2.3.2)) is based only upon a meta-game rather than upon a game (see the first paragraph of Section 2.2).
2) *Moulin* [1979] proposed the concept of *reversible point* for a two-person game in normal form and characterized such points. The reversible points are the strategy bundles such that there exists an (infinitesimal) move in strategy, which is the best when each player behaves individualistically, but is bad from cooperative point of view. He also extended his analysis to a three-person game.
3) *Prakash/Sertel* [1974] generalized the abstract economy to the situation in which the utility and also the feasible strategy set of a player depend not only upon the others' choice of strategies but also upon the others' feasible strategy sets (e.g., upon the enemy's capabilities). Their logic for the existence theorem goes deep (beyond fixed-point theorems for topological vector spaces).

3. Cooperative Behavior

3.1 Core of a Sidepayment Game

Given the set N of players, and hence the set $\mathcal{N}$ of non-empty coalitions of players, a cooperative game explicitly formulates what each coaliton can achieve by the cooperation of its members. The simplest game of this class would be a *game in characteristic function form with sidepayments* (or simply, a *sidepayment game*) defined as a function, v: $\mathcal{N} \to \boldsymbol{R}$. The intendeed interpretation is that v(S) is the maximal total payoff of the coalition S that the members of S can bring about by their cooperation regardless of the actions of the players outside S.

A sidepayment game v is a special case of a game in normal form. Indeed, given a sidepayment game v, the associated game in normal form can be constructed as follows: For each player j, the strategy set X^j is the union of mutually disjoint sets $X^{j,S}$, with respect to the S's for which $S \ni j$. If $x^j \in X^{j,S}$, then the player j cooperates with the members in S. Define: $u^j(x, \xi^j) \equiv -\infty$, if for the coalition S for which $\xi^j \in X^{j,S}$, there exists $i \in S$ such that $x^i \notin X^{i,S}$. Also, let $u^j(x, \xi^j)$ be independent of $(x^i)_{i \in N \setminus S}$, where S is the coalition for which $\xi^j \in X^{j,S}$. Now, the required game is such that $\{(u^j(x, x^j))_{j \in S} \mid \forall j \in S: x^j \in X^{j,S}\} = \{(u_j)_{j \in S} \mid \sum_{j \in S} u_j \leqslant \mathrm{v}(S)\}$ for every $S \in \mathcal{N}$. The associated game in normal form is, however, too cumbersome to work with. One usually discards the strategy sets and the utility functions, and studies directly the function v.

An important cooperative solution concept is now given: The *core* of a sidepayment game v is the set $C(\mathrm{v})$ of all $u \in \boldsymbol{R}^n$ such that 1) $\sum_{j \in N} u_j \leqslant \mathrm{v}(N)$, and 2) it is not true that there exists $S \in \mathcal{N}$ for which $\sum_{j \in S} u_j < \mathrm{v}(S)$. The condition (1) is the feasibility of the payoff vector u via the grand coalition N, and the condition (2) is the stability of u, i.e., no coalition can improve upon u. The core $C(\mathrm{v})$ is the set of solutions of the 2^n linear inequality system: $-\chi_N \cdot x \geqslant -\mathrm{v}(N)$, and $\chi_S \cdot x \geqslant \mathrm{v}(S)$ for all $S \in \mathcal{N}$. Therefore, the logic for non-emptiness of $C(\mathrm{v})$ is included in the following theorem (3.1.1), which can be proved by a straightforward application of the Minkowski-Farkas Lemma: *Given a* $k \times n$ *matrix* A *and a* $k \times 1$ *matrix* b*, there exists an* $n \times 1$ *matrix* x *such that* $Ax = b$ *and* $x \geqslant O$*, if and only if for every* $1 \times k$ *matrix* λ *for which* $\lambda A \geqslant O'$*, it follows that* $\lambda b \geqslant 0$. For a proof of the Minkowski-Farkas Lemma, see, e.g., *Nikaidô* [1968, p. 38]; or one can supply a simple proof by a direct application of the separation theorem on convex sets.

Theorem 3.1.1. Let $\{p^1, \ldots, p^k\} \subset \boldsymbol{R}^n$ *and* $\{c_1, \ldots, c_k\} \subset \boldsymbol{R}$*. There exists* $x \in \boldsymbol{R}^n$ *satisfying* $p^1 \cdot x \geqslant c_1, \ldots, p^k \cdot x \geqslant c_k$*, if and only if for every set* $\{\lambda_1, \ldots, \lambda_k\}$ *of non-negative real numbers for which* $\sum_{i=1}^{k} \lambda_i p^i = O$*, it follows that* $\sum_{i=1}^{k} \lambda_i c_i \leqslant 0$.

A subfamily $\mathcal{B}$ of $\mathcal{N}$ is called *balanced,* if there exists an indexed set $\{\lambda_S \mid S \in \mathcal{B}\}$ of non-negative numbers such that $\sum_{S \in \mathcal{B}} \lambda_S \chi_S = \chi_N$. Note that $\sum_{S \in \mathcal{B}} \lambda_S \chi_S = \chi_N$, if and only if $\sum_{S \in \mathcal{B}: S \ni j} \lambda_S = 1$ for every $j \in N$. The set $\{\lambda_S \mid S \in \mathcal{B}\}$ is called the *associated balancing coefficients.* A sidepayment game v is called *balanced,* if for every balanced family $\mathcal{B}$

with the associated balancing coefficients $\{\lambda_S \mid S \in \mathcal{B}\}$, it follows that $\sum_{S \in \mathcal{B}} \lambda_S \, v(S) \leqslant v(N)$.

The following theorem (3.1.2) says that a sidepayment game has a non-empty core if and only if it is balanced.

Theorem 3.1.2. Let v: $\mathcal{N} \rightarrow R$ *be a sidepayment game. The core of* v *is non-empty, if and only if for every indexed set of non-negative numbers* $\{\lambda_S \mid S \in \mathcal{N}\}$ *for which* $\sum_{S \in \mathcal{N}} \lambda_S \chi_S = \chi_N$, *it follows that* $\sum_{S \in \mathcal{N}} \lambda_S \, v(S) \leqslant v(N)$.

Proof of (3.1.2). By (3.1.1), $C(v) \neq \phi$, if and only if for every set $\{\lambda'_S \mid S \in \mathcal{N}\} \cup \{\mu\}$ of non-negative numbers for which $\sum_{S \in \mathcal{N}} \lambda'_S \cdot \chi_S + \mu(-\chi_N) = \mathbf{0}$, it follows that $\sum_{S \in \mathcal{N}} \lambda'_S \, v(S) + \mu(-v(N)) \leqslant 0$. If $\mu = 0$, then $\lambda'_S = 0$ for all $S \in \mathcal{N}$, so the last inequality is automatically satisfied. If $\mu > 0$, define: $\lambda_S \equiv \lambda'_S / \mu$, and the above condition reduces to the required condition of the theorem. Q.E.D.

3.2 Core of a Non-Sidepayment Game

The concept of the "total payoff, $v(S)$," of the coalition S in a sidepayment game v is sometimes hard to interpret, when the behavior, cooperative or non-cooperative, is ultimately motivated by the individual pursuit of maximal satisfaction. A more general game is presented here to overcome this difficulty. For each coalition S, define: $R^S \equiv \{x \in R^n \mid \forall j \notin S: x_j = 0\}$. A *game in characteristic function form without sidepayments* (or simply, *a non-sidepayment game*) is a correspondence, $\tilde{V}$: $\mathcal{N} \rightarrow R^n$, such that $\tilde{V}(S) \subset R^S$ for every $S \in \mathcal{N}$. The intended interpretation is that $u \in \tilde{V}(S)$ if and only if cooperation of the members in S can bring about the utility allocation $(u_i)_{i \in S}$ to the members of S. As an equivalent definition, a *non-sidepayment game* is a correspondence V: $\mathcal{N} \rightarrow R^n$, such that $[u, v \in R^n, \forall i \in S: u_i = v_i]$ implies $[u \in V(S)$ if and only if $v \in V(S)]$ for every $S \in \mathcal{N}$. Clearly, $V(S)$ is a cylinder based on $\tilde{V}(S)$; i.e., $V(S) = \{u \in R^n \mid (u_i \, \delta_{iS})_{i \in N} \in \tilde{V}(S)\}$, where $\delta_{iS} = 1$ if $i \in S$; and $\delta_{iS} = 0$ if $i \notin S$. The second definition of a non-sidepayment game will be adopted throughout the present paper.

Just as in the second paragraph of Section 3.1, one can regard a non-sidepayment game as a special case of a game in normal form. Again, however, it is easier to work directly with the attainable utility allocations, $V(S)$

The *core* of a non-sidepayment game V is the set $C(V)$ of all $u \in R^n$ such that 1) $u \in V(N)$, and 2) it is not true that there exist $S \in \mathcal{N}$ and $u' \in V(S)$ such that $u_j < u'_j$ for every $j \in S$. The condition (1) is the feasibility of the utility allocation u via the grand coaliton N, and the condition (2) is the stability of u. The most successful theorem for non-emptiness of the core (Theorem 3.2.2) below) can be proved by an application of the following variant of a fixed-point theorem:

Theorem 3.2.1. Let $\{C_S\}_{S \in \mathcal{N}}$ *be a family of closed subsets of* Δ^N, *indexed by the mem-*

bers of $\mathcal{N}$, *such that for each* $T \in \mathcal{N}$, $\Delta^T \subset \bigcup_{S \subset T} C_S$. *Then, there exists a balanced collection* $\mathcal{B}$ for which $\bigcap_{S \in \mathcal{B}} C_S \neq \phi$.

Proof of (3.2.1). Denote by $I(x)$ the collection $\{S \in \mathcal{N} \mid C_S \ni x\}$, and define a correspondence G: $\Delta^N \to \Delta^N$ by: $G(x) \equiv \text{co}\,\{(1/\#S)\,\chi_S \mid S \in I(x)\}$. It is trivial to check that G is u.s.c., and is non-empty- and convex-valued. So is a constant correspondence F, defined by $F(x) \equiv \{(1/n)\,\chi_N\}$. Choose any $x \in \Delta^N$ and any $p \in R^n$ such that $p \cdot x \leqslant p \cdot y$ for every $y \in \Delta^N$. The subset T of N for which $x \in \overset{\circ}{\Delta}{}^T$ is uniquely determined, and for this set T, $p \cdot x = p \cdot y$ for every $y \in \Delta^T$. By the present assumption, there exists $S \in I(x)$ such that $S \subset T$; i.e., there exists $(1/\#S)\,\chi_S \in G(x)$ such that $p \cdot (1/n)\,\chi_N \geqslant p \cdot (1/\#S)\chi_S$. Thus, all the conditions for Ky Fan's Theorem (A.5) are satisfied, and there exists $x^* \in \Delta^N$ such that $F(x^*) \cap G(x^*) \neq \phi$, i.e., $(1/n)\,\chi_N \in G(x^*)$. Therefore, $I(x^*)$ is balanced. Needless to say $\bigcap_{S \in I(x^*)} C_S \ni x^*$. Q.E.D.

It should be noted that if $C_S = \phi$ for every S for which $\#S \geqslant 2$, then the above theorem (3.2.1) is reduced to the K-K-M Theorem (A.2).

A non-sidepayment game V is called *balanced,* if for every balanced subfamily $\mathcal{B}$ of $\mathcal{N}$, it follows that $\bigcap_{S \in \mathcal{B}} V(S) \subset V(N)$. Essentially the balancedness condition is sufficient (but not necessary) for non-emptiness of the core of V.

Theorem 3.2.2. Let V: $\mathcal{N} \to R^n$ *be a non-sidepayment game, and define* $b \in R^n$ *by* $b_j \equiv \text{Sup}\,\{u_j \in R \mid u \in V(\{j\})\}$, *for each* $j \in N$. *The core of* V *is non-empty, if* 1) $V(S) - R^n_+ = V(S)$, *for every* $S \in \mathcal{N}$; 2) *there exists* $M \in R$ *such that for every* $S \in \mathcal{N}$, $[u \in V(S) \cap [\{b\} + R^n_+]]$ *implies* $[u_i < M$ *for every* $i \in S]$; 3) $V(S)$ *is closed in* R^n *for every* $S \in \mathcal{N}$; *and if* (4) V *is balanced.*

Proof of (3.2.2). Without loss of generality, one may assume $b = O$. Given the positive number M of the present assumption (2), define $D^S \equiv \text{co}\,\{-M\,n\,e^j \mid j \in S\}$ for every $S \in \mathcal{N}$. The function τ: $D^N \to R$, defined by $\tau(y) \equiv \text{Max}\,\{r \in R \mid y + r\,\chi_N \in \bigcup_{S \in \mathcal{N}} V(S)\}$, is continuous by the Maximum Theorem (A.1). Also is continuous, therefore, the function f: $\Delta^N \to R^n$, defined by $f(y) \equiv y + \tau(y)\,\chi_N$. Define $C_S \equiv \{y \in D^N \mid f(y) \in V(S)\}$. Since C_S is the inverse image under f of a closed set $V(S)$, it is closed. (See Figure 1.) One claims: $[S, T \in \mathcal{N}, D^T \cap C_S \neq \phi]$ implies $[S \subset T]$. This is trivial, if $T = N$. So, assume $\#T < n$, and take any $y \in D^T \cap C_S$. On the one hand, $\sum_{j \in T} y_j = -Mn$, so there exists $t \in T$ for which $y_t \leqslant -Mn/\#T < -M$. Since $f(y) \in R^n_+$, $y_t + \tau(y) \geqslant 0$. Therefore, $\tau(y) > M$. On the other hand, $f(y) \in V(S)$, so for every $j \in S$, $y_j + \tau(y) < M$. Thus, $y_j < 0$ for every $j \in S$, from which $S \subset T$, and the claim has been proved. All the conditions for (3.2.1) are now satiesfied; there exists a balanced collection $\mathcal{B}^*$ and a point $y^* \in D^N$ such that $y^* \in \bigcap_{S \in \mathcal{B}^*} C_S$. So, $f(y^*) \in \bigcap_{S \in \mathcal{B}^*} V(S) \subset V(N)$. By the definition of τ, $f(y^*)$ is on the frontier of $\bigcup_{S \in \mathcal{N}} V(S)$, and in view of the assumption (1), it cannot be improved upon by any coalition. Thus, $f(y^*) \in C(V)$. Q.E.D.

The assumption (1) of the above theorem is customarily called the *comprehensiveness* condition. The assumption (3) can be replaced by a weaker condition: $V(N)$ is closed in R^n.

At this point, it would be useful to introduce one more concept: A *coalition structure* is a partition of N; it describes which coalitons are formed and coexist. Not all the coalition structures may be admissible (e.g., from the legal point of view), so denote by $\mathcal{T}$ the family of admissible coalition structures. A *generalized non-sidepayment game* is a pair $(V, \mathcal{T})$ of a non-sidepayment game and a family of admissible coalition structures. The *core* of $(V, \mathcal{T})$ it the set of all pairs (u^*, T^*) of members of R^n and $\mathcal{T}$ such that 1) $u^* \in V(T)$ for every $T \in \mathcal{T}^*$, and 2) it is not true that there exist $S \in \mathcal{N}$ and $u' \in V(S)$ such that $u_j < u'_j$ for every $j \in S$. Exactly the same argument as in the above proof of (3.2.2) (except that the statement $[\bigcap_{S \in \mathcal{B}^*} V(S) \subset V(N)]$, be replaced by the statement $[\bigcap_{S \in \mathcal{B}^*} V(S) \subset \bigcup_{T \in \mathcal{T}} \sum_{T \in T} \tilde{V}(T)]$, where $\tilde{V}(T) \equiv V(T) \cap R^T$) establishes that: *The core of a generalized non-sidepayment game* $(V, \mathcal{T})$, *is non-empty, if the conditions* (1) – (3) of (3.2.2) *are satisfied, and if the game* $(V, \mathcal{T})$ *is balanced; i.e., for every balanced family* $\mathcal{B}$, $\bigcap_{S \in \mathcal{B}} V(S) \subset \bigcup_{T \in \mathcal{T}} \sum_{T \in T} \tilde{V}(T)$.

Finally, a sidepayment game can be considered as a special case of a non-sidepayment game. Indeed, given a sidepayment game v, the associated non-sidepayment game V is defined by: $V(S) \equiv \{u \in R^n \mid \sum_{j \in S} u_j \leqslant v(S)\}$. In this case, it is straightforward to check

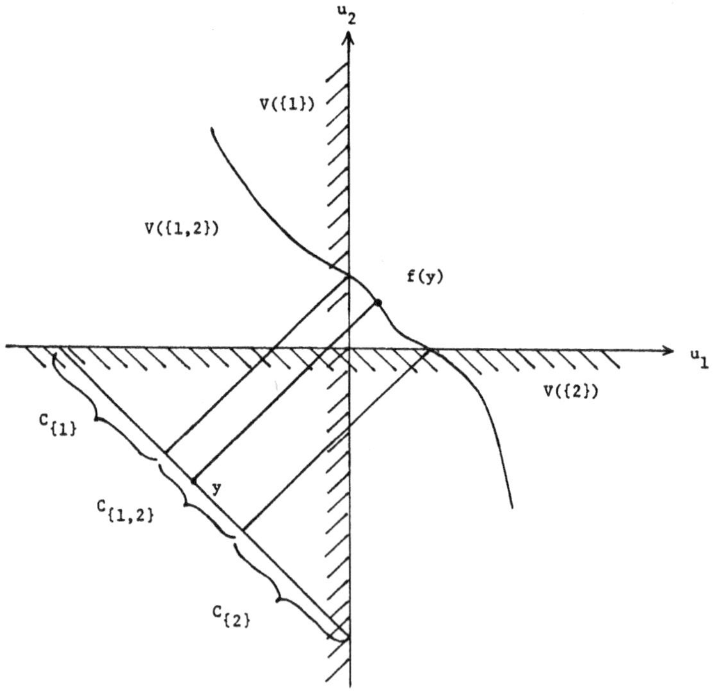

Fig. 1

that the core $C(\mathrm{v})$ of v (defined in the third paragraph of Section 3.1) and the core $C(V)$ of V (defined in the third paragraph of the present section) are identical, and that the conditions (1) – (3) of (3.2.2) are automatically satisfied. Call the balancedness condition on v (defined in the paragraph (3.1.2)) the B-Sh condition, and call the balancedness condition on V (defined in the paragraph preceding (3.2.2)) the Sc condition. Then, in this case, the B-Sh condition and the Sc condition are equivalent. Indeed, if the Sc condition is satisfied, then $C(V) \neq \phi$, by (3.2.2). Since $C(V) = C(\mathrm{v})$, the B-Sh condition holds true, by (3.1.2). On the other hand, assume the B-Sh condition, choose a balanced family $\mathcal{B}$ with the associated balancing coefficients $\{\lambda_S \mid S \in \mathcal{B}\}$, and take any $u \in \bigcap_{S \in \mathcal{B}} V(S)$. For each $S \in \mathcal{B}$, $\sum_{j \in S} u_j \leqslant \mathrm{v}(S)$. Then, $\sum_{j \in N} u_j = \sum_{j \in N} (\sum_{S \in \mathcal{B}: S \ni j} \lambda_S) u_j = \sum_{S \in \mathcal{B}} \lambda_S \sum_{j \in S} u_j \leqslant$ $\leqslant \sum_{S \in \mathcal{B}} \lambda_S \mathrm{v}(S) \leqslant \mathrm{v}(N)$. Therefore, $u \in V(N)$, and the Sc condition has been proved.

3.3 Core Allocation of a Pure Exchange Economy

Let $\mathcal{E} \equiv \{X^j, \precsim_j, \omega^j\}_{j \in N}$ be a pure exchange economy with n consumers (formulated in Section 1.3, with the change that $m = n$ here), in which each preference relation $\precsim_j$ is represented by a utility function u^j. A type of cooperative behavior of the consumers in $\mathcal{E}$ can be summarized by the associated non-sidepayment game V: $\mathcal{N} \to \boldsymbol{R}^n$, defined by: $V(S) \equiv \{u \in \boldsymbol{R}^n \mid \exists (x^i)_{i \in S} \in \prod_{i \in S} X^i \text{: } \sum_{i \in S} x^i \leqslant \sum_{i \in S} \omega^i, \text{ and for every } i \in S\text{: } u_i \leqslant u^i(x^i)\}$.

A *core allocation* of $\mathcal{E}$ is an allocation which gives rise to a member of the core of the associated game V. Actually, one can give its definition without resorting to the derivative concept, utility function, (hence without resorting to V): A *core allocation* of $\mathcal{E}$ is an n-tuple of commodity bundles $(x^{1*}, \ldots, x^{n*}) \in \prod_{j \in N} X^j$, such that 1) $\sum_{j \in N} x^{j*} \leqslant \sum_{j \in N} \omega^j$, and 2) it is not true that there exist $S \in \mathcal{N}$ and $(x^i)_{i \in S} \in \prod_{i \in S} X^i$ such that $\sum_{i \in S} x^i \leqslant \sum_{i \in S} \omega^i$ and $x^i \succ_i x^{i*}$ for every $i \in S$. The purpose of this section is to show how (3.2.2) can be applied to prove the existence of a core allocation of $\mathcal{E}$.

Lemma 3.3.1. Let $\mathcal{E} \equiv \{X^j, \precsim_j, \omega^j\}_{j \in N}$ be a pure exchange economy, in which each preference relation $\precsim_j$ is represented by a utility function u^j: $X^j \to \boldsymbol{R}$. If X^j is a convex subset of $\boldsymbol{R}^l$, $\omega^j \in X^j$, *and $\precsim_j$ is weakly convex, for every $j \in N$, then the associated game V is balanced.*

Proof of (3.3.1). Let $\mathcal{B}$ be a balanced family with the associated balancing coeffiecients $\{\lambda_S \mid S \in \mathcal{B}\}$, and choose any $u \in \bigcap_{S \in \mathcal{B}} V(S)$. Then, for each $S \in \mathcal{B}$, there exists $(x^{i,S})_{i \in S} \in \prod_{i \in S} X^i$ such that $\sum_{i \in S} x^{i,S} \leqslant \sum_{i \in S} \omega^i$ and $u_i \leqslant u^i(x^{i,S})$ for every $i \in S$. Define:

$\bar{x}^j \equiv \sum_{S \in \mathcal{B}: S \ni j} \lambda_S x^{j,S}$, for every $j \in N$. By convexity of X^j, $\bar{x}^j \in X^j$; and by quasi-concavity of u^j, $u_j \leqslant u^j(\bar{x}^j)$. Moreover, $\sum_{j \in N} \bar{x}^j = \sum_{j \in N} \sum_{S \in \mathcal{B}: S \ni j} \lambda_S x^{j,S} =$

$= \sum_{S \in \mathcal{B}} \lambda_S \sum_{j \in S} x^{j,S} \leqslant \sum_{S \in \mathcal{B}} \lambda_S \sum_{j \in S} \omega^j = \sum_{j \in N} \sum_{S \in \mathcal{B}: S \ni j} \lambda_S \omega^j = \sum_{j \in N} \omega^j$. Thus, $u \in V(N)$.

Q.E.D.

Denote by $A(S)$ the set of attainable states for the coalition S: $A(S) \equiv \{(x^i)_{i \in S} \in \prod_{j \in S} X^i \mid \sum_{i \in S} x^i \leqslant \sum_{i \in S} \omega^i\}$. It is clear that the set $A(S)$ is bounded, if for every $i \in S$, X^i is bounded from below, i.e., if there exists $b^i \in \boldsymbol{R}^l$ such that $X^i \subset \{b^i\} + \boldsymbol{R}^l_+$.

Theorem 3.3.2. Let $\mathcal{E} \equiv \{X^j, \precsim_j, \omega^j\}_{j \in N}$ *be a pure exchange economy. If* X^j *is a convex, closed subset of* $\boldsymbol{R}^l$ *and is bounded from below,* $\omega^j \in X^j$, *and* $\precsim_j$ *is complete, transitive, closed, and weakly convex for each* $j \in N$, *then there exists a core allocation of* $\mathcal{E}$.

Proof of (3.3.2). Let $u^j: X^j \to \boldsymbol{R}$ be a continuous utility function that represents $\precsim_j$ (see (1.3.1)). It will be shown that all the four assumptions in (3.2.2) are satisfied for the associated game V. The condition (1) [Comprehensiveness] is a consequence of the definition of $V(S)$. To show the conditions (2) and (3), it suffices to note that $\tilde{V}(S) = \{\tilde{u}^S(A(S))\} - \boldsymbol{R}^S_+$, where the continuous function $\tilde{u}^S: \prod_{j \in S} X^j \to \boldsymbol{R}^S$ is defined by: $\tilde{u}^S_j((x^i)_{i \in S}) \equiv u^j(x^j)$ if $j \in S$; and $\tilde{u}^S_j((x^i)_{i \in S}) \equiv 0$ if $j \notin S$, and that $A(S)$ is compact. The condition (4) [Balancedness] is the result of (3.3.1). Q.E.D.

3.4 Notes

Von Neumann/Morgenstern [1974] introduced the sidepayment game, but their interpretation of the characteristic function v was specific: Consider a zero-sum n-person game. Using the notation of the third paragraph of Section 2.4, it is the game which satisfies $\sum_{j \in N} a^j_{h_1 \ldots h_n} = 0$ for every $(h_1, \ldots, h_n) \in \sum_{j \in N} \{1, \ldots, m_j\}$. Given the coalition S, construct a zero-sum two-person game as follows: The two "players" are S and $N \setminus S$, the strategy set for the "player S" (for the "player $N \setminus S$", resp.) is $\prod_{j \in S} X^j$ ($\prod_{j \in N \setminus S} X^j$, resp.), and the payoff for the "player S" (for the "player $N \setminus S$", resp.) is $\sum_{j \in S} u^j(x, x^j)$ ($\sum_{j \in N \setminus S} u^j(x, x^j)$, resp.). By the Minimax Principle, this zero-sum two-person game has the value (see the first paragraph of Section 2.4). The number v(S) was originally interpreted as this value.

The concept of core of a sidepayment game was discovered by *Gillies* [1959] and Lloyd S. Shapley during their investigation of the von Neumann-Morgenstern solutions in 1952 – 1953. *Bondareva* [1962, 1963] and *Shapley* [1967] independently established (3.1.2). Denote by C(v) the core of the sidepayment game v.

A class of balanced sidepayment games has been extensively studied, because of a close relationship between the core and another cooperative solution concept, the Shapley value, for a game of this class. See *Shapley* [1953] for the definition and a characterization of the Shapley value. Let G_n be the symmetric group on N; i.e., the set of all permutations on N. Given a sidepayment game v and a member σ of G_n, define the *marginal worth vector* $a^\sigma(\mathrm{v}) \in R^n$ by: $a_j^\sigma(\mathrm{v}) \equiv \mathrm{v}(P_j^\sigma \cup \{j\}) - \mathrm{v}(P_j^\sigma)$, where $P_j^\sigma \equiv \{i \in N \mid \sigma(i) < \sigma(j)\}$ is the set of members in N who precedes j with respect to the order σ. The *Shapley value* of v can be defined by: $\varphi(\mathrm{v}) \equiv \sum_{\sigma \in G_n} (1/n!)\, a^\sigma(\mathrm{v})$. *Shapley* [1971] and a supplementary note, *Ichiishi* [1981c], established:

Theorem 3.4.1. Let $\mathrm{v}: \mathcal{N} \to R$ *be a sidepayment game. The following three conditions are equivalent*: 1) *For any* $S, T \in \mathcal{N}$, $\mathrm{v}(S) + \mathrm{v}(T) \leqslant \mathrm{v}(S \cup T) + \mathrm{v}(S \cap T)$. [*Here,* $\mathrm{v}(\phi) \equiv 0$.]; 2) *For any* $S, T \in \mathcal{N}$ *and any* $j \in N$ *for which* $S \subset T \subset N \setminus \{j\}$, *it follows that* $\mathrm{v}(S \cup \{j\}) - \mathrm{v}(S) \leqslant \mathrm{v}(T \cup \{j\}) - \mathrm{v}(T)$; *and* 3) *For any* $\sigma \in G_n$, $a^\sigma(\mathrm{v}) \in C(\mathrm{v})$.

A game satisfying the condition (1) of (3.4.1) is called a *convex game.* The condition (2) of (3.4.1) is the *increasing returns with respect to the coaliton size.* Since the core of a sidepayment game is convex, (3.4.1) implies that $\varphi(\mathrm{v}) \in C(\mathrm{v})$, for every convex game v.

A sidepayment game may be identified with a point in the $(2^n - 1)$-dimensional Euclidean space, $R^{\mathcal{N}}$. The *core correspondence* is a correspondence $C: R^{\mathcal{N}} \to R^n$, $\mathrm{v} \mapsto C(\mathrm{v})$. Since the core is the set of solutions of a linear programming problem (indeed, for a balanced game v, $C(\mathrm{v})$ is the set of optimal solutions of: Minimize $\chi_N \cdot x$, subject to $\chi_S \cdot x \geqslant \mathrm{v}(S)$ for all $S \in \mathcal{N}$), a little modification of the argument in *Walkup/Wets* [1969] establishes:

Theorem 3.4.2. Let $B(n)$ *be the set of all n-person balanced sidepayment games, identified with a subset of the* $(2^n - 1)$-dimensional Euclidean space $R^{\mathcal{N}}$. *Let* $C: B(n) \to R^n$ *be the core correspondence. Then, there are finitely many continuous piecewise linear functions,* $c^i: B(n) \to R^n$, $i \in I$, *such that for each* $\mathrm{v} \in B(n)$, $\{$*the extreme points of* $C(\mathrm{v})\} \subset \{c^i(\mathrm{v}) \mid i \in I\} \subset C(\mathrm{v})$.

In particular, (3.4.2) shows that C is both u.s.c. and l.s.c. in $B(n)$, since $C(\mathrm{v})$ is compact in R^n.

The theory of the core of a sidepayment game with infinitely many players has been well developed. Let A be a set, and $\mathcal{A}$ an algebra of subsets of A: The measurable set $(A, \mathcal{A})$ is fixed throughout the present and next two paragraphs. The set A is interpreted as the player set, and $\mathcal{A}$ as the family of feasible coalitions. Denote by *ba* the space of all bounded additive scalar functions defined on $\mathcal{A}$. For each $S \in \mathcal{A}$, its *characteristic function* is a function $\chi_S: A \to R$, defined by: $\chi_S(a) = 1$ if $a \in S$; and $\chi_S(a) = 0$ if $a \in A \setminus S$. Given a finite subfamily $\mathcal{B}$ of $\mathcal{A}$ and an indexed set $\{\lambda_S \mid S \in \mathcal{B}\}$ of non-negative numbers, one can find the unique finite subfamily $\{T_i\}_{i=1}^m$ of $\mathcal{A}$ and the associated set $\{\gamma_{T_i}\}_{i=1}^m$ of positive numbers such that $T_1 \supsetneq T_2 \supsetneq \ldots \supsetneq T_m$ and that $\sum_{S \in \mathcal{B}} \lambda_S \chi_S = \sum_{i=1}^m \gamma_{T_i} \chi_{T_i}$. The collection $\{\gamma_i, T_i\}_{i=1}^m$ is called the *canonical form of* $\sum_{S \in \mathcal{B}} \lambda_S \chi_S$. A *sidepayment game* is a function $\mathrm{v}: \mathcal{A} \to R_+$ such that $\mathrm{v}(\phi) = 0$. The *core* of the game v is the set $\{\mu \in ba \mid \mu(A) \leqslant \mathrm{v}(A)$, and $\mu(S) \geqslant \mathrm{v}(S)$ for every $S \in \mathcal{A}\}$, and is denoted by $C(\mathrm{v})$. A game v is called *balanced,* if for any finite subfamily $\mathcal{B}$ by $\mathcal{A}$ and any indexed set $\{\lambda_S \mid S \in \mathcal{B}\}$ of non-negative numbers for which $\sum_{S \in \mathcal{B}} \lambda_S \chi_S \leqslant \chi_A$, it follows that $\sum_{S \in \mathcal{B}} \lambda_S \mathrm{v}(S) \leqslant \mathrm{v}(A)$.

A game v is called *exact*, if for any $S \in \mathcal{A}$, there exists $\mu \in C(\mathrm{v})$ such that $\mu(S) = \mathrm{v}(S)$. A game v is called *convex*, if for any $S, T \in \mathcal{A}$, it follows that $\mathrm{v}(S) + \mathrm{v}(T) \leqslant \mathrm{v}(S \cup T) + \mathrm{v}(S \cap T)$.

Theorem 3.4.3. Let $\mathrm{v}: \mathcal{A} \to \boldsymbol{R}_+$ *be a game. The core of* v *is non-empty, if and only if the game* v *is balanced.*

Theorem 3.4.4. Let $\mathrm{v}: \mathcal{A} \to \boldsymbol{R}_+$ *be a game. The game* v *is exact, if and only if for any* $T \in \mathcal{A}$, *it follows that* $\mathrm{v}(T) = \sup\{\sum_{S \in \mathcal{B}} \lambda_S \mathrm{v}(S) - \kappa \mathrm{v}(A) \mid \mathcal{B}$ *is a finite subfamily* of $\mathcal{A}$, $\{\lambda_S \mid S \in \mathcal{B}\} \subset \boldsymbol{R}_+, \kappa \in \boldsymbol{R}_+, \sum_{S \in \mathcal{B}} \lambda_S \chi_S - \kappa \chi_A \leqslant \chi_T\}$.

Theorem 3.4.5. Let $\mathrm{v}: \mathcal{A} \to \boldsymbol{R}_+$ *be a game. The following three conditions are equivalent:* 1) *The game* v *is convex*; 2) *For any finite subfamily* $\mathcal{B}^i$ *of* $\mathcal{A}$ *and any indexed set* $\{\lambda_S^i \mid S \in \mathcal{B}^i\}$ *of non-negative numbers,* $i = 1,2$, *for which* $\sum_{S \in \mathcal{B}^1} \lambda_S^1 \chi_S \leqslant \sum_{S \in \mathcal{B}^2} \lambda_S^2 \chi_S$, *it follows that* $\sum_{S \in \mathcal{B}^1} \lambda_S^1 \mathrm{v}(S) \leqslant \sum_{T \in C} \gamma_T \mathrm{v}(T)$ *where* $\{\gamma_T, T\}_{T \in C}$ *is the canonical form of* $\sum_{S \in \mathcal{B}^2} \lambda_S^2 \chi_S$; 3) If $S_1 \underset{\neq}{\supset} S_2 \underset{\neq}{\supset} \ldots \underset{\neq}{\supset} S_m$, *where* $S_i \in \mathcal{A}$, *then there exists* $\mu \in C(\mathrm{v})$ *such that* $\mu(S_i) = \mathrm{v}(S_i)$ *for all* $i = 1, \ldots, m$.

Schmeidler [1967] established (3.4.3). *Kannai* [1969] pointed out that one can prove (3.4.3) by a direct application of *Fan* [1956, Theorem 13, 126–128] on a system of linear inequalities. Theorem (3.4.4) is due to *Schmeidler* [1972]; but, again, one can prove it by a direct application of *Fan* [1956, Corollary 6, p. 126], as was noted by *Delbean* [1974, (2) ⇒ (3), p. 216]. See a work by *Rosenmüller* [1971] on convex games. *Delbean* [1974] proved (3.4.5). *Kannai* [1969] also provided a necessary and sufficient condition for the core to have a countably additive set function. *Schmeidler* [1972] identified a necessary and sufficient condition for an exact game to have a core whose members are all countably additive. His technique has proven useful for obtaining the Radon-Nikodym derivative of a member of the core.

Denote by $\boldsymbol{B}$ ($\boldsymbol{E}$, $\boldsymbol{C}$, resp.) the set of balanced games (the set of exact games, the set of convex games, resp.). The above theorems imply: $\boldsymbol{C} \subset \boldsymbol{E} \subset \boldsymbol{B}$. Each inclusion is strict. Endow $\boldsymbol{B}$ with the topology induced by the distance d: $d(\mathrm{v}, \mathrm{v}') \equiv \sup_{S \in \mathcal{A}} |\mathrm{v}(S) - \mathrm{v}'(S)|$. The space *ba* has the topology induced by the total variation norm. Based upon his own result (3.4.5), *Delbean* [1974] studied the continuity properties of the core correspondence, $C: \boldsymbol{B} \to ba$. Since the core $C(\mathrm{v})$ may not be compact in *ba*, one has to be careful of the definitions of continuity. Given a correspondence F from a metric space X to another (Y, d), it is *V-u.s.c. in* X (here, "V" stands for "Vietoris"), if for every sequence $\{x^q\}_q$ in X converging to $\bar{x}$ and for every open subset U of Y for which $F(\bar{x}) \subset U$, it follows that $F(x^q) \subset U$ for all q sufficiently large. It is *V-l.s.c. in* X, if for every sequence $\{x^q\}_q$ in X converging to $\bar{x}$ and for every open subset U of Y for which $F(\bar{x}) \cap U \neq \phi$, it follows that $F(x^q) \cap U \neq \phi$ for all q sufficiently large. It is *H-u.s.c. in* X (here, "H" stands for "Hausdorff"), if for every sequence $\{x^q\}_q$ in X converging to $\bar{x}$, $\sup_{y \in F(x^n)} \inf_{\eta \in F(\bar{x})} d(y, \eta)$ converges to 0. It is *H-l.s.c. in* X, if for every sequence $\{x^q\}_q$ in

X converging to $\bar{x}$, $\sup_{\eta \in F(\bar{x})} \inf_{y \in F(x^n)} d(y, \eta)$ converges to 0. V-upper semi-continuity implies H-upper semi-continuity, and H-lower semi-continuity implies V-lower semi-continuity. When F is compact-valued, a V-concept is equivalent to the corresponding H-concept. Now, *Delbaen* [1974] proved that *the core correspondence C is H-u.s.c. and V-l.s.c. in* **C**. He also showed by examples that *V-lower semi-continuity of C on* **B** *does not necessarily hold.* Compare these (non-) continuity results [for the infinite-person games] with the continuity results (3.4.2) [for the n-person games]. Whether C is u.s.c. and l.s.c. in **E**, and whether C is *V-u.s.c.* and H-l.s.c. in **C** are still open questions.

Given a measurable space of players which is isomorphic to the unit interval endowed with the Borel σ-algebra, *Aumann/Shapley* [1974] developed the (Shapley) value theory on several important classes of sidepayment games. For a game in some of these classes, the (Shapley) value is the unique member of the core. See *Aumann* [1975] for a significant application of this field to the theory of pure exchange.

Aumann/Peleg [1960] formulated the non-sidepayment game, and *Aumann* [1961] developed the core concept within this framework.

The first successful theorem (3.2.2) for non-emptiness of the core was established by *Scarf* [1967a]. There, he applied the "path-following" technique of *Lemke/Howson* [1964], and constructed an algorithm for a member of the core. By using the constructive "path-following" technique, one can obtain as deep theorems as, or deeper theorems than one can by using the non-constructive fixed-point method of (A.3) – (A.5); see *Scarf* [1967b]. It is an interesting question whether the fixed-point method (which is very handy!) can generally yield as deep results as the "path-following" technique [apart from the computational merit of the latter]. The works of *Scarf* [1967a, 1967b] opened an important field of research in economics: the computation of economic equilibria; see e.g., *Scarf* [1973]. Also using the "path-following" technique, *Shapley* [1973] established the K-K-M-S Theorem (3.2.1), and then applied (3.2.1) to prove (3.2.2). Shapley's proof of (3.2.2) is reproduced in Section 3.2. Ichiishi [1981a] showed that (3.2.1) can be proved by a simple application of a non-constructive fixed-point theorem. The present proof of (3.2.1) is a variant of the proof of *Ichiishi* [1981a]. *Todd* [1978] (and his private communication) has given an alternative proof of (3.2.1), and also a proof of a modified version of (3.2.1) which only uses an easier non-constructive fixed-point theorem (A.4). In this modified version, the assumption of (3.2.1) is replaced by a stronger condition: For all $S, T \in$ N, $[\Delta^T \cap C_S \neq \phi]$ implies $[S \subset T]$. As is evident from the present proof of (3.2.2), Todd's modified version of (3.2.1) is enough to prove (3.2.2). The modified version is not, however, a generalization of the K-K-M Theorem (A.2).

Billera [1970] assumed convexity of $\tilde{V}(S)$'s, and using the support functions of $\tilde{V}(S)$'s, established a necessary and sufficient condition for non-emptiness of the core of a non-sidepayment game V. He also showed an example of a non-sidepayment game which is not balanced and yet has a non-empty core.

The theory of the core of a non-sidepayment game with infinitely many players is now being developed. *Kannai* [1969] applied (3.2.2) to the case in which there are countably many players, and provided a sufficient condition for non-emptiness of the core. He did not treat an atomless measure speace of players. The following general model was constructed by *Ichiishi/Weber* [1978]: Let $(A,$ A$, \nu)$ be a σ-finite, positive measure space of players. Denote by L^∞ the vector lattice of all (equivalence classes modulo ν-null sets of) ν-essentially bounded $\mathcal{A}$-measurable real-valued functions on A. A member $u \in L^\infty$ is interpreted as a utility allocation as follows: With u understood as a specific function in the equivalence class, the player a enjoys his utility level $u(a)$, ν-a.e. in A. For each $S \in \mathcal{A}$, define $\text{Proj}_S: L^\infty \to L^\infty$ by: $(\text{Proj}_S u)(a) = u(a)$ if $a \in S$; and $(\text{Proj}_S u)(a) = 0$ if $a \in A \setminus S$. Define also: $L^\infty_+ \equiv \{u \in L^\infty \mid u \geqslant O\}$. Since the coalitions with positive measure are relevant for the cooperative theory based upon a measure space of players, define $\mathcal{A}_0 \equiv \{S \in \mathcal{A} \mid \nu(S) > 0\}$. A *non-sidepayment game* is a correspondence $V: \mathcal{A} \to L^\infty$, satiesfying: 1) For all $S, T \in \mathcal{A}$ with $\nu(T) = 0$, $V(S \setminus T) = V(S)$, and 2) For all $S \in \mathcal{A}$ and $u, v \in L^\infty$ with $\text{Proj}_S u = \text{Proj}_S v$, $u \in V(S)$ if and only if $v \in V(S)$. The *core* of a non-sidepayment game V is the set of all $u^* \in L^\infty$, such that 1) $u^* \in V(A)$; and 2) it is not true that there exist $S \in \mathcal{A}_0$ and $u \in V(S)$ for which $u^*(a) < u(a)$, ν-a.e. in S. *Ichiishi/Weber* [1978] establsihed several necessary and sufficient conditions for non-emptiness of the core, 1) by applying *Fan* [1956, Theorem 13, 126–128] repeatedly; or else 2) by generalizing this Fan theorem in the context of vector lattices and then applying the somewhat generalized version. However, no sufficient condition, which is simple enough to be practical, has been found. *Ichiishi/Schäffer* [1979] introduced a weaker core concept: Given an arbitrary topology $\mathcal{T}$ on L^∞, the $\mathcal{T}$-*core* is defined as the set $V(A) \setminus \bigcup_{S \in \mathcal{A}_0} \overset{\circ}{V}(S)$, where $\overset{\circ}{V}(S)$ is the topological interior of $V(S)$ in $(L^\infty, \mathcal{T})$, The following practical theorem is a special case of the main theorem of *Ichiishi/Schäffer* [1979]:

Theorem 3.4.6. Given a probability measure space $(A, \mathcal{A}, \nu)$ of players, let $V: \mathcal{A} \to L^\infty$ be a non-sidepayment game such that $V(S) \cap L^\infty_+ \neq \phi$ for every $S \in \mathcal{A}$. Let $\mathcal{T}$ be a Hausdorff vector-space topology which is either 1) stronger than the norm-topology, or 2) weaker than the norm-topology, but strong enough so that L^∞_+ is *$\mathcal{T}$-closed. The $\mathcal{T}$-core is non-empty, if 1) $V(S) - L^\infty_+ = V(S)$, for every $S \in \mathcal{A}$; 2) For every $S \in \mathcal{A}_0$ there exists a number $M_S \in R$ such that $[u \in V(S) \cap L^\infty_+]$ implies $[u(a) < M_S$, ν-a.e. in $S]$; 3) There exists a $\mathcal{T}$-compact subset K of L^∞_+* such that *$V(A) \cap L^\infty_+ = (K - L^\infty_+) \cap L^\infty_+$; and if 4) V is balanced, i.e., for every balanced finite subfamiliy $\mathcal{B}$ of $\mathcal{A}$, $\bigcap_{S \in \mathcal{B}} V(S) \subset V(A)$.*

When the player set A is finite, so that L^∞ is finite-dimensional, (3.4.6) reduces precisely to (3.2.2). When the topology $\mathcal{T}$ is chosen to be the weak* topology $\sigma(L^\infty, L^1)$, the assumption (3) of (3.4.6) can be replaced by a weaker conditon: $V(A)$ is $\mathcal{T}$-closed. Given any position number $\epsilon > 0$, the ϵ-*core* of a non-sidepayment game V is the set of all $u^* \in L^\infty$, such that 1) $u^* \in V(A)$; and 2) it is not true that there exist $S \in \mathcal{A}_0$ and $u \in V(S)$ for which $u^*(a) + \epsilon < u(a)$, ν-a.e. in S. Under the assumption (1) of (3.4.6), when $\mathcal{T}$ is chosen to be the norm-topology, the $\mathcal{T}$-core is identical to $\bigcap_{\epsilon > 0}$ [the ϵ core]. *Rosenmüller* [1975] considered a model in which A is a Polish space and $\mathcal{A}$ is the σ-algebra of Borel subset of A. In this setup, the space of utility allocations is not L^∞ but rather the space of all Radon measures on A endowed with the weak* topology. His core concept is very close, in spirit, to the above $\mathcal{T}$-core concept, when $\mathcal{T}$ is the weak* topology.

Theorems (3.3.1) and (3.3.2) are due to *Scarf* [1967a]. Note that the assumptions in (3.3.2) are substantially weaker than the assumptions in (2.4.4). In fact, the set of core allocations is larger than the set of competitive allocations. Related to (3.3.1) is the following concept: A non-sidepayment game V: $N \to R^n$ is called *strongly balanced*, if for every balanced subfamily $\mathcal{B}$ of N with the associated balancing coefficients $\{\lambda_S \mid \lambda \in \mathcal{B}\}$, it follows that $\sum_{S \in \mathcal{B}} \lambda_S \tilde{V}(S) \subset V(N)$, where $\tilde{V}(S) \equiv \{u \in V(S) \mid \forall_j \notin S; u_j = 0\}$. A strongly balanced non-sidepayment game is balanced. Now, *let* $E \equiv \{X^j, \precsim_j, \omega^j\}_{j \in N}$ *be a pure exchange economy, such that each* X^j *is a convex subset of* R^l *and each* $\precsim_j$ *is represented by a concave utility function* u^j. *Then, the associated non-sidepayment game* V *(constructed as in the first paragraph of Section 3.3, using these concave functions* u^j*'s) is strongly balanced, and each* $V(S)$ *is convex.*

The concept of core allocation within the framework of the pure exchange economy goes as far back as *Edgeworth* [1881]. There, using a model of pure exchange with two commodities and two types of consumers, he asserted that a competitive allocation is a core allocation, and that the set of core allocations "converges" to the set of competitive allocations as the number of consumers of each type goes to infinity. The Edgeworth proposition has drawn the attention of economists during the past two decades, due to the pioneering work of *Shubik* [1959]. There are two successful theorems in the early stage of their investigations: a limit theorem by *Debreu/Scarf* [1963] on the replica economies, and an equivalence theorem by *Aumann* [1964] on the economy with an atomless measure space of consumers. Further works were done on the Edgeworth proposition, in particular by Karl Vind, Yakar Kannai, Jean-François Mertens, Werner Hildenbrand, Trumann F. Bewley; each of their contributions plays a key role in a treatise, *Hildenbrand* [1974]. See also *Arrow/Hahn* [1971]. More recent works have appeared in the theoretical journals, such as *Econometrica* and the *Journal of Mathematical Economics.*

Some other works related to the core of a game in characteristic function form: 1) *Aubin* [1979] studied the core of a game, sidepayment or non-sidepayment, with fuzzy coalitions. 2) in the first paragraph of Section 3.3, a non-sidepayment game was constructed from a given pure exchange economy. *Billera* [1974], and also some of his other works done jointly with Bixby, asked the converse: Given a non-sidepayment game, can one construct a pure exchange economy whose associated non-sidepayment game is precisely the given one? 3) *Kalai/Schmeidler* [1977] studied a broadly applicable concept, *admissible set.* Given a non-sidepayment game satisfying a mild condition, the admissible set is identical to the core. Given a game in normal form, the admissible set contains the Nash equilibria.

4. Unified Treatment

4.1 Social Coalitional Equilibrium of a Society

The two strands in game theory, surveyed in Sections 2. and 3., are unified here. A more general behavioral pattern is formulated, the relevant solution concept proposed, and its existence theorem provided.

The price-taking behavior of a consumer can be regarded as a particular case of the passive, non-cooperative behavior formulated in Section 2.2 (See the proof of (2.3.2).) It is undeniable that in free societies the market mechanism, which assumes the price-taking behavior of the economic agents, works to a large extent. On the other hand, researchers of the theory of the firm have long emphasized certain non-market mechanisms as essential determinants in the modern capitalistic economy. These non-market meachnisms involve cooperative behavior of the agents. Thus, to build a descriptive model of the modern capitalistic economy, one needs a game-theoretical foundation for a behavioral pattern which contains both non-cooperation and cooperation. It turned out that the theorem established in this general setup ((4.1.1) below) can also supply an answer to a welfare question on a Nash equilibrium of a game in normal form.

Given the set N of players, and hence the set $\mathcal{N}$ of non-empty coalitions of players, an abstract model of a society is now constructed. The model explicitly formulates how the members of a coalition are influenced by the outsiders. For the player j, denote by X^j his strategy set, and define: $X^S \equiv \prod_{j \in S} X^j$ for every $S \in \mathcal{N}$. Put $X \equiv X^N$, for notational convenience. The feasible strategy correspondence of the coalition S is a correspondence $F^S: X \to X^S$. The subset $F^S(x)$ of X^S is interpreted as the set of all feasible strategy bundles for S as a cooperative unit when $x \equiv (x^1, \ldots, x^n) \in X$ has been chosen. It is postulated that the preference relation of the j-th player in S, when the members of S agree to cooperate, is represented by a utility function, u^j_S: Gr $F^S \to \boldsymbol{R}$. Here, the dependence of the utility function on S reflects the possible fact that the members in S enjoy the environment (i.e., non-strategical elements) specific to S. Thus, the players outside a coalition S influence the members of S 1) indirectly by restricting the feasible joint strategies of the members of S to $F^S(x)$; and 2) directly by affecting the utility level u^j_S for all $j \in S$. [Compare with the first paragraph of Section 2.2.] Let $\mathcal{T}$ be the set of admissible coalition structures. A *society* is now defined as a list of specified data, $(\{X^j\}_{j \in N}, \{F^S\}_{S \in \mathcal{N}}, \{u^j_S\}_{j \in S \in \mathcal{N}}, \mathcal{T})$.

A *social coalitional equilibrium* of a society is a pair of a strategy bundle and an admissible coalition structure, $(x^*, \mathcal{T}^*) \in X \times \mathcal{T}$, such that 1) for each $T \in \mathcal{T}^*$, $x^{T*} \equiv (x^{j*})_{j \in T} \in F^T(x^*)$; and 2) it is not true that for some $S \in \mathcal{N}$ there exists $\xi^S \in F^S(x^*)$ for which $u^j_S(x^*, \xi^S) > u^j_{T(j)}(x^*, x^{T(j)*})$ for every $j \in S$, where $T(j)$ is the member of $\mathcal{T}^*$ such that $T(j) \ni j$. The condition (1) signifies the feasibility condition. The term $u^j_S(x^*, \xi^S)$ of the condition (2) is the utility level that the player j would get by participating in the new coalition S and agreeing to take the strategy ξ^S. Here, he passively accepts the strategies currently taken by the players outside S. The term $u^j_{T(j)}(x^*, x^{T(j)*})$ is the utility level he currently enjoys. The condition (2) signifies, therefore, the stability condition.

Theorem 4.1.1. Let $(\{X^j\}_{j \in N}, \{F^S\}_{S \in \mathcal{N}}, \{u^j_S\}_{j \in S \in \mathcal{N}}, \mathcal{T})$ *be a society. There exists a social coalitional equilibrium of the society, if 1)* X^j *is a non-empty, convex, compact subset of a Euclidean space for every* $j \in N$; *2)* F^S *is both u.s.c. and l.s.c. in* X, *and* $F^S(x)$ *is non-empty for any* $x \in X$, *for every* $S \in \mathcal{N}$; *3)* u^j_S *is continuous in* Gr F^S *for every* $S \in \mathcal{N}$ *and every* $j \in S$; *4) given any* $(x, v) \in X \times \boldsymbol{R}^n$, *[there exists a balanced collection* $\mathcal{B}$ *such that for each* $S \in \mathcal{B}$ *there exists* $\xi(S) \in F^S(x)$ *for which* $v_j \leqslant u^j_S(x, \xi(S))$ *for every* $j \in S$] *implies [there exist* $\mathcal{T} \in \mathcal{T}$ *and* $\eta^T \in F^T(x)$ *for every* $T \in \mathcal{T}$ *such that* $v_j \leqslant u^j_T(x, \eta^T)$ *for all* $j \in T \in \mathcal{T}$]; *and if 5) given any* $(x, v) \in X \times \boldsymbol{R}^n$, *the set*

$\bigcup_{T\in\mathcal{T}} \{\xi\in X \mid$ *For every* $T\in\mathcal{T}$, $\xi^T\in F^T(x)$ *and* $v_j \leqslant u_T^j(x,\xi^T)$ *for each* $j\in T\}$ *is convex.*

In order to re-state the assumption (4) of (4.1.1) in somewhat more fimiliar terms, define for a given $x\in X$ a non-sidepayment game $V_x\colon \mathcal{N}\to \boldsymbol{R}^n$ by: $V_x(S)\equiv\{v\in\boldsymbol{R}^n \mid \exists\,\xi^S\in F^S(x)\colon\ \forall j\in S\colon v_j\leqslant u_S^j(x,\xi^S)\}$, for each $S\in\mathcal{N}$. Then, the assumption (4) says that the generalized non-sidepayment game $(V_x, \mathcal{T})$ is balanced (see the second-to-the-last paragraph of Section 3.2) for every $x\in X$. When $\mathcal{T}$ is a singleton $\{T\}$, the assumption (5) of (4.1.1) is reduced to convexity of $\prod_{T\in\mathcal{T}}\{\xi^T\in X^T \mid \xi^T\in F^T(x)$, $v_j\leqslant u_T^j(x,\xi^T)$ for each $j\in T\}$ for every $(x,v)\in X\times\boldsymbol{R}^n$, and under compactness of X^j and continuity of u_T^j, the latter condition is equivalent to [convexity of $F^T(x)$, and quasi-concavity of $u_T^j(x,\cdot)$ of $F^T(x)$, for every $x\in X$ and $j\in T$, given any $T\in\mathcal{T}$]. Thus, the assumption (5) may be regarded as an extension of this last convexity assumption to the case in which $\#\mathcal{T}$ can be greater than 1.

Proof of (4.1.1). Step 1. Define $\widetilde{V}_x(S)\equiv V_x(S)\cap\boldsymbol{R}^S$, $H_x\equiv\bigcup_{\mathcal{T}\in\boldsymbol{T}}\sum_{T\in\mathcal{T}}\widetilde{V}_x(T)$. By the assumptions (1) – (3), and by the finiteness of the cardinality of $\boldsymbol{T}$, it is straightforward to check that the correspondence, $H\colon X\to\boldsymbol{R}^n$, $x\mapsto H_x$, is both u.s.c. and l.s.c. So is the correspondence, $V(S)\colon X\to\boldsymbol{R}^n$, $x\mapsto V_x(S)$, for each $S\in\mathcal{N}$.

Step 2. Define $m(x)\in\boldsymbol{R}^n$ by: $m_j(x)\equiv\operatorname{Max}\{u^j_{\{j\}}(x,\xi^j)\mid \xi^j\in F^{\{j\}}(x)\}$. Then there exists a real number $M>0$ such that for every $x\in X$, for every $S\in\mathcal{N}$ and for every $v\in V_x(S)$, $v_j-m_j(x)<M$ for all $j\in S$. Denote by D^S the set $\operatorname{co}\{-Mne^j \mid j\in S\}$. Put $\chi_S'\equiv -Mn\,\chi_S/(\#S)$; this is a member of D^S. Define a function $\tau\colon X\times D^N\to\boldsymbol{R}$ by: $\tau(x,y)\equiv\operatorname{Max}\{r\in\boldsymbol{R}\mid y+m(x)+r\cdot\chi_N\in\bigcup_{S\in\mathcal{N}}V_x(S)\}$. The function τ is well-defined, and is continuous by Step 1. The function $f\colon X\times D^N\to\boldsymbol{R}^n$, $(x,y)\mapsto y+m(x)+\tau(x,y)\cdot$ $\cdot\,\chi_N$, is also continuous. Define finally, $C_S(x)\equiv\{y\in D^N \mid f(x,y)\in V_x(S)\}$. For each $S\in\mathcal{N}$, the correspondence $C_S\colon X\to D^N$, $x\mapsto C_S(x)$, is u.s.c. Now, by the same argument as in the claim of the proof of (3.2.2), one can show that for every $x\in X$, [$S,T\in\mathcal{N}$, $D^T\cap C_S(x)\neq\phi$] implies [$S\subset T$].

Step 3. Define a correspondence $F\colon X\times D^N\to X\times D^N$ by: $F(x,y)\equiv\operatorname{co}\bigcup_{\mathcal{T}\in\boldsymbol{T}}\{\xi\in X \mid$ $\forall T\in\mathcal{T}\colon \xi^T\in F^T(x)$, and $\forall w\in H_x\colon \|f(x,y)-u(x,\xi)\|\leqslant\|f(x,y)-w\|\}\times\{\chi_N'\}$, where the j-th component of $u(x,\xi)$ is $u^j_{T(j)}(x,\xi^{T(j)})$, with $j\in T(j)\in\mathcal{T}$. Define another correspondence $G\colon X\times D^N\to X\times D^N$ by: $G(x,y)\equiv\{x\}\times\operatorname{co}\{\chi_S'\mid C_S(x)\ni y\}$. Both F and G are u.s.c. in $X\times D^N$, and are non-empty- and convex-valued. Choose any $(x,y)\in X\times D^N$ and any $(p,q)\in\boldsymbol{R}^{\dim X}\times\boldsymbol{R}^n$ such that $(p,q)\cdot(x,y)\leqslant(p,q)\cdot(x',y')$ for every $(x',y')\in X\times D^N$. By the same argument as in the proof of (3.2.1), there exist $(\xi,\chi_N')\in F(x,y)$ and $(x,\chi_S')\in G(x,y)$ such that $(p,q)\cdot(\xi,\chi_N')\geqslant(p,q)\cdot(x,\chi_S')$.

Step 4. By Step 3, all the conditions for Ky Fan's Theorem (A,5) are satisfied: There exist (x^*, y^*), $(\bar{x}, \bar{y}) \in X \times D^N$ such that $(\bar{x}, \bar{y}) \in F(x^*, y^*) \cap G(x^*, y^*)$. This means that (i) $\bar{x} \in \text{co} \bigcup_{T \in \mathcal{T}} \{\xi \in X \mid \forall T \in \mathcal{T}: \xi^T \in F^T(x^*)$, and $\forall w \in H_{x^*}: \| f(x^*, y^*) - u(x^*, \xi) \| \leqslant \| f(x^*, y^*) - w \|\}$; (ii) $\bar{y} = \chi'_N$; (iii) $\bar{x} = x^*$; (iv) $\bar{y} \in \text{co}\{\chi'_S \mid C_S(x^*) \ni y^*\}$. By (ii) and (iv), the collection $\mathcal{B}^* \equiv \{S \in \mathcal{N} \mid C_S(x^*) \ni y^*\}$ is balanced: Thus, $f(x^*, y^*) \in H_{x^*}$, by the assumption (4). Then, $\text{Min}\{\| f(x^*, y^*) - w \| \in \boldsymbol{R} \mid w \in H_{x^*}\} = 0$, and (i) and (iii) become: $x^* \in \text{co} \bigcup_{T \in \boldsymbol{T}} \{\xi \in X \mid \forall T \in \mathcal{T}: \xi^T \in F^T(x^*)$, and $f(x^*, y^*) = u(x^*, \xi)\} \subset \text{co} \bigcup_{T \in \boldsymbol{T}} \{\xi \in X \mid \forall T \in \mathcal{T}: \xi^T \in F^T(x^*)$, and $f(x^*, y^*) \leqslant u(x^*, \xi)\}$. The last set is identical to $\bigcup_{T \in \boldsymbol{T}} \{\xi \in X \mid \forall T \in \mathcal{T}: \xi^T \in F^T(x^*)$, and $f(x^*, y^*) \leqslant u(x^*, \xi)\}$, by the assumption (5), so there exists $\mathcal{T}^* \in \boldsymbol{T}$ such that (v) $x^{*T} \in F^T(x^*)$ for every $T \in \mathcal{T}^*$; and (vi) $f(x^*, y^*) \leqslant u(x^*, x^*)$. The coalitional equilibrium condition (1) is satisfied by (v), and so is (2) by (vi) and the definition of $\tau(x^*, y^*)$. Q.E.D.

The balancedness assumption (4) and the convexity assumption (5) of (4.1.1) are probably too obscure to capture, since each imposes on the model an implicit relation between F^S's and u^j_S's. The following theorem shows that an assumption only on F^S's and another assumption only on u^j_S's jointly imply balancedness and convexity. Denote by $\tilde{F}^S(x)$ the set $\{\xi \mid \xi^S \in F^S(x), \xi^{N \setminus S} = O\}$.

Theorem 4.1.2. Let $(\{X^j\}_{j \in N}, \{F^S\}_{S \in \mathcal{N}}, \{u^j_S\}_{j \in S \in \mathcal{N}}, \boldsymbol{T})$ *be a society. Assume: 6) for any* $x \in X$ *and for any balanced collection* $\mathcal{B}$ *with the associated balancing coefficients* $\{\lambda_S \mid S \in \mathcal{B}\}$, *it follows that* $\sum_{S \in \mathcal{B}} \lambda_S \tilde{F}^S(x) \subset \bigcup_{\mathcal{T} \in \boldsymbol{T}} \sum_{T \in \mathcal{T}} \tilde{F}^T(x)$; *and 7) for each* $j \in N$, *there exists a function* $u^j: X \times X^j \to \boldsymbol{R}$, *such that* $u^j(x, \cdot)$ *is quasi-concave on* X^j *for any* $x \in X$, *and such that for every* $S \in \mathcal{N}$ *containing* j, $u^j_S(x, \xi^S) = u^j(x, \xi^j)$ *for all* $\xi^S \in F^S(x)$. *Then, the society satisfies both balancedness and convexity.*

Proof of (4.1.2). Balancedness. Take any $x \in X$ and any $\mathrm{v} \in \boldsymbol{R}^n$, and suppose there exists a balanced collection $\mathcal{B}$ such that for each $S \in \mathcal{B}$ there exists $\xi(S) \in F^S(x)$ for which $\mathrm{v}_j \leqslant u^j(x, \xi^j(S))$ for every $j \in S$. Let $\{\lambda_S\}_{S \in \mathcal{B}}$ be the associated balancing coefficients, and define $\eta \in X$ by: $\eta^j \equiv \sum_{S \in \mathcal{B}: S \ni j} \lambda_S \xi^j(S) \in X^j$. By the assumption (7), $\mathrm{v}_j \leqslant u^j(x, \eta^j)$ for every $j \in N$; and by the assumption (6), there exists $\mathcal{T} \in \boldsymbol{T}$ such that $\eta^T \in F^T(x)$ for every $T \in \mathcal{T}$.

Convexity. Given $x \in X$ and $\mathrm{v} \in \boldsymbol{R}^n$, take any $\xi, \xi' \in X$ such that $\xi \in \sum_{T \in \mathcal{T}} \tilde{F}^T(x)$, $\xi' \in \sum_{T \in \mathcal{T}'} \tilde{F}^T(x)$, and that $\mathrm{v}_j \leqslant u^j(x, \xi^j)$, $\mathrm{v}_j \leqslant u^j(x, \xi'^j)$. Take also any $\alpha \in [0,1]$. Then,

$\mathcal{B} \equiv \mathcal{T} + \mathcal{T}'$ is a balanced collection, and $\{\lambda_S\}_{S \in \mathcal{B}}$, defined by: $\lambda_S = \alpha$ if $S \in \mathcal{T}$: $\lambda_S = 1 - \alpha$ if $S \in \mathbf{T}$, is a set of associated weights. It is straightforward to check:
$\alpha\xi + (1-\alpha)\xi' \in \bigcup_{\mathcal{T} \in \mathbf{T}} \sum_{T \in \mathcal{T}} \tilde{F}^T(x)$, and $v_j \leqslant u^j(x, \alpha\xi^j + (1-\alpha)\xi'^j)$ for every $j \in N$

Q.E.D.

In order to relate the present discussion to the discussion of Section 2.2, assume that $\mathbf{T}$ consists only of the finest partition $\{\{1\}, \ldots, \{n\}\}$, and that for every $x \in X$ and for every $j \in S \in \mathcal{N}$ with $\#S \geqslant 2$, $u^j_{\{j\}}(x, \xi^j) > u^j_S(x, \eta^S)$ for all $\xi^j \in F^{\{j\}}(x)$ and all $\eta^T \in F^T(x)$. Then, the players do not benefit from cooperation; the present model is reduced to the abstract economy of Section 2.2, and the social coalitional equilibrium is simply the social equilibrium. In this case, the assumption (4) of (4.1.1) is automatically satisfied, and the assumption (5) is equivalent to [convexity of $F^{\{j\}}(x)$, and quasi-concavity of $u^j_{\{j\}}(x, \cdot)$ on $F^{\{j\}}(x)$, for every $x \in X$ and every $j \in N$]. Thus, (4.1.1) is in this case reduced precisely to (2.2.1).

Assume, on the other hand, that $\mathbf{T}$ consists only of the coarsest partition $\{N\}$, and that for each $S \in \mathcal{N}$, F^S is a constant correspondence (i.e., $F^S(x) = F^S(x')$ for all x, x'), and that for every $j \in S \in \mathcal{N}$, u^j_S is independent of its first argument (i.e., $u^j_S(x, \cdot) = u^j_S(x', \cdot)$ for all x, x'). Then, what a coalition can do is not influenced by outsiders; the present model is reduced to the non-sidepayment game of Section 3.2, and the set of social coalitional equilibria gives rise exactly to the core. The assumptions (1) – (3) of (4.1.1) correspond roughly to the assumptions (1) – (3) of (3.2.2). The assumption (4) of (4.1.1) is the balancedness condition, as was noted earlier. Put $\bar{F}^S \equiv F^S(x)$, $\bar{u}^j_S(\xi^S) \equiv u^j_S(x, \xi^S)$. The assumption (5) of (4.1.1) is the convexity assumption: convexity of $\bar{F}^N$ and quasi-concavity of $\bar{u}^j_N$ on $\bar{F}^N$. Thus, in this case (4.1.1) is weaker than (3.2.2); the convexity assumption is not used in (3.2.2).

The present section is based upon *Ichiishi* [1981].

4.2 Equilibrium of a Private Ownership Economy

Recall the definition of a pure exchange economy $\{X^i, \precsim_i, \omega^i\}_{i=1}^m$. A *production economy* is obtained by adding to this list of data, *n production sets* $\{Y^j\}_{j=1}^n$. The precise definition of the set Y^j differs according to the particular economic context, but in all cases it is intended to describe the technology of the j-th production unit. Within the static framework, each Y^j is a subset of the commodity space $\boldsymbol{R}^l$. Here, a vector $y \in \boldsymbol{R}^l$. is interpreted as an *activity*: if $y_h < 0$ ($y_h > 0$, resp.), then $|y_j|$ – units of the h-th commodity are used as *input* (produced as *output*, resp.) in the activity y. An activity y^j is technologically feasible in the j-th production unit, if and only if $y^j \in Y^j$.

The following model, due to *Arrow/Debreu* [1954], has probably been considered *the* standard production economy. Let the production set Y^j be a subset of $\boldsymbol{R}^l$, with the above static interpretation. The consumer i holds the relative share θ_{ij} in the firm j; so given a market price vector $p \in \Delta^L$, he receives the dividend $\theta_{ij} p \cdot y^j$ from the firm j when the firm chooses its activity y^j. Here, $\theta_{ij} \geqslant 0$, and $\sum_{i=1}^{m} \theta_{ij} = 1$. A *private ownership economy* is a list of specified data, $\mathcal{E} \equiv \{\{X^i, \precsim_i, \omega^i\}_{i=1}^m, \{Y^j\}_{j=1}^n, \{\theta_{ij}\}_{i=1}^m{}_{j=1}^n\}$. An *equilibrium* of a private ownership economy $\mathcal{E}$ is an $(m+n+1)$ – tuple $((x^{i*})_{i=1}^m, (y^{j*})_{j=1}^n, p^*)$ of points of $\boldsymbol{R}^l$ such that 1) x^{i*} is a maximal element of $\{x^i \in X^i \mid p^* \cdot x^i \leqslant p^* \cdot \omega^i + \sum_{j=1}^{n} \theta_{ij} p^* \cdot y^{j*}\}$ with respect to $\precsim_i$, for every i; 2) y^{j*} is a maximizer of $p^* \cdot y^j$ subject to $y^j \in Y^j$, for every j; and 3) $\sum_{i=1}^{m} x^{i*} \leqslant \sum_{i=1}^{m} \omega^i + \sum_{j=1}^{n} y^{j*}$.

Some of the characteristic features of this economy: First, every market (including the labor market) is perfectly competitive; i.e., each economic agent, consumer or producer, can immediately identify the market prices of all commodities and behave as a price-taker. Second, each firm is controlled by the owners. As an owner of the firm j, the consumer i wants to receive the maximal dividend $\theta_{ij}\, p \cdot y^j$, and so (since θ_{ij} is a given constant), orders the firm to make the maximal profit $p \cdot y^j$. All the owners of the firm j unanimously order the maximal profit. Third, there exist all the futures markets (see Section 1.3 for the definition).

An equilibrium existence theorem for a private ownership economy can be proved as in Section 2.3: One constructs an abstract economy consisting of $(m+n+1)$ players, and a social equilibrium of this abstract economy turns out to be the required equilibrium. The set of attainable states $\{((x^i)_i, (y^j)_j) \in \prod_{i=1}^{m} X^i \times \prod_{j=1}^{n} Y^j \mid \sum_{i=1}^{m} x^i \leqslant \sum_{i=1}^{m} \omega^i + \sum_{j=1}^{n} y^j\}$ is also shown to be compact, although the proof is not trivial. Therefore the argument for (2.4.4) is applicable. In this way, *Arrow/Debreu* [1954] established:

Theorem 4.2.1. Let $\mathcal{E} \equiv \{\{X^i, \precsim_i, \omega^i\}_{i=1}^m, \{Y^j\}_{j=1}^n, \{\theta_{ij}\}_{i=1}^m{}_{j=1}^n\}$ *be a private ownership economy. Assume: 1) for every i,* X^i *is a non-empty, convex, closed subset of* $\boldsymbol{R}^l$ *which is bounded from below;* $\precsim_i$ *is complete, transitive, closed, and convex; no point* $x^i \in X^i$ *is satiated with respect to* $\precsim_i$*; and* Min $\{p \cdot x^i \mid x^i \in X^i\} < p \cdot \omega^i$ *for each* $p \in \Delta^L$*; and 2) for every j,* Y^j *is a closed convex subset of* $\boldsymbol{R}^l$ *containing* $\boldsymbol{O}$, $(\sum_{j=1}^{n} Y^j) \cap \boldsymbol{R}^l_+ = \{\boldsymbol{O}\}$, *and* $(\sum_{j=1}^{n} Y^j) \cap (-\sum_{j=1}^{n} Y^j) = \{\boldsymbol{O}\}$. *Then, there exists an equilibrium of* $\mathcal{E}$.

Now, while the work of *Arrow/Debreu* [1954] set a standard for logical consistency that any economic model should meet, many economists have criticized the private ownership economy, on the basis that it does not capture the essence of the modern capitalistic economy. Since the 1930's a voluminous literature has developed under the title "theory of the firm," which concerns the raison d'être of the firm, new fact finding about firm activities, etc. It should be pointed out that the private ownership economy has little to do with this theory of the firm. *Coase* [1937], for example, asked why there is an organization called a firm. If the owner of production factors could find any type and any quantity of labor in the market at any moment, there would be no need for him to organize a firm; he could simply purchase all the necessary labor on a free-lance basis. In reality, however, he finds it costly to identify the right labor on the market each time he needs it; i.e., the information on the labor market is incomplete. Instead of relying on the price mechanism, therefore, he organizes a hierarchical system called a firm, in which he can dictate allocation of labor. The object of contracts between the owner and laborers is cooperation, rather than detailed specification of labor. Thus, in Coase's view, a firm is identified with a coalition of laborers (including supervisors), and the labor market mechanism is replaced by a certain cooperative resource allocation mechanism. This nature of the firm is not captured in the private ownership economy, as was mentioned in the third paragraph of this section (the first characteristic feature).

Another strand in the theory of the firm concerns the empirical fact, studied first by *Berle/Means* [1932], that the ownership and control of modern corporations are separated. Any consumer can become an owner of a firm by buying its stock, and yet have only negligible influence on its management. Management is carried out independently by the laborers (especially the executives) who work in the firm, in accordance with their utility maximization. In short (and roughly speaking), laborers hire capital in the modern capitalistic economy, whereas, as was mentioned in the third paragraph of this section (the second characteristic feature), capitalists hire laborers in the private ownership economy.

Many authors have extended the private ownership economy, in an attempt to treat explicitly the time element and uncertainty. But once the futures markets are assumed to be incomplete, a serious difficulty is raised in regard to the objective of a firm: More than one person usually controls a firm, and there are differences in their subjective probabilities on the future events. In the (extended) private ownership economy, each owner orders the firm to choose an activity that maximizes his *subjective* expected profit, but his order may contradicts the order of another owner based upon the latter's subjective expected profit.

4.3 Equilibrium of a Labor-Managed Market Economy

In the previous section, the standard mathematical model of an economy with production was reviewed, and some of its basic difficulties pointed out. The purpose of this section is to present an abridged version of the model of *Ichiishi* [1979b, 1979c], which was constructed to incorporate the economic visions that have prevailed in the theory of the firm. In particular, it involves *a* formulation of *Coase* [1937]'s view on the nature of the firm. Since each economic agent behaves both non-cooperatively (as a consumer) and cooperatively (as a laborer in his firm, i.e., as a member of a coaliton) in this view, the basic game-theoretical foundation here is not (2.2.1) but (4.1.1).

A *labor-managed market economy* is an economy where each firm is managed by the laborers who work for it and where the products of all firms are traded within the competitive market. There are n economic agents. A coalition S is identified with a (potential) firm; when the firm S is actually formed, the agent j works for S as a full-time laborer if and only if $j \in S$. Let $\mathcal{T}$ be the non-empty family of admissible coalition structures on N. Each agent j plays three roles in the economy: that of consumer, that of member of a production unit as a laborer [here, a manager is considered a laborer], and that of an owner of production units. The economy is called *socialistic*, when an agent can be an owner only of the firm he works for. The economy is called *capitalistic*, when each firm is allowed to issue an asset, called a stock, and ownership of the firm is defined as stock-holding.

There are l types of marketed commodities; a commodity bundle is a member of $\boldsymbol{R}^l$. One of the crucial features of the labor-managed market economy is that labor is not marketed. The wages and the labor supplies are determined not through the market mechanism (a typical example of a non-cooperative game), but through the society-wide cooperative game played by the laborers. For each agent j, his strategy space X^j is a subset of $\boldsymbol{R}^l \times \boldsymbol{R}^l \times E^j$, where E^j is a Euclidean space. A generic element x^j of X^j is denoted by (x_1^j, x_2^j, x_3^j), with $x_1^j \in \boldsymbol{R}^l$, $x_2^j \in \boldsymbol{R}^l$, $x_3^j \in E^j$. The commodity bundle x_1^j signifies the excess demand made by j as an individualistic consumer, and some components of the vector (x_2^j, x_3^j) are "signals" (to be specified below) which he is committed to send to the firm he works for.

Formally, the model under construction is static, but it is best interpreted as a model of temporary equilibrium. There are two periods: today and future. All the endogenous variables (x^j's and the price vector) are determined today, based upon the agents' subjective expectations about future events. In particular, it takes a firm one period to produce outputs (random variables). To make the firm work, funds are first raised (from members of the coalition in the socialistic version, or through the stock market in the capitalistic version), and these funds are used to pay wages and buy marketed inputs today. In the future, the revenue (i.e., the value of the outputs) will be distributed to the owners.

Suppose $(\bar{x}, \bar{p}) \equiv ((\bar{x}^j)_{j\in N}, \bar{p}) \in \prod_{j\in N} X^j \times \Delta^L$ is given at the outset. The firm $S \in \mathcal{N}$ is formed, once the members of S agree to cooperate; they jointly assign to themselves (most components of) the strategies $(x_2^j, x_3^j)_{j\in S}$. The vector $\sum_{j\in S} x_2^j$ is interpreted as the (marketed) input bundle. [In reality, the firm determines only the l-dimensional vector $\sum_{j\in S} x_2^j$, rather than the $(\#S)$-tuple of vectors $(x_2^j)_{j\in S}$. The present convention is adopted, however, because it does no harm, and because this way, the present economic model can be regarded as a special case of the abstract model of a society developed in Section 4.1.] The vector x_3^j consists of: the amount of labor the agent j is assigned to supply, the wages he receives, his subjective probability measure on the outputs, – and, in the case of the capitalistic version, his signal q^j for the firm's stock price (so that the firm sets its stock price at $\sum_{j\in S} q^j$), and his portfolio of various stocks. All the components of (x_2^j, x_3^j), except the last (i.e., the portfolio), are chosen jointly by the members of S, say, by consensus. Feasibility of the new strategies $(x^j)_{j\in S}$ is restricted by the prevailing values $(\bar{x}, \bar{p})$, in particular, by the prevailing price system $\bar{p}$; each agent is a price-taker. Denote by $F^S(\bar{x}, \bar{p})$ $(\subset \prod_{j\in S} X^j)$ the set of all feasible strategies, given $(\bar{x}, \bar{p})$. After the joint strategies (i.e., most components of $(x_2^j, x_3^j)_{j \in S}$) are chosen cooperatively, the individual j chooses his individualistic strategy (i.e., x_1^j and his portfolio) subject to $(x^j)_{j \in S} \in F^S(\bar{x}, \bar{p})$.

For each member j of S, his expected-indirect-utility function u_S^j: Gr $F^S \to \boldsymbol{R}$ is given. The intended interpretation of $u_S^j(\bar{x}, \bar{p}, (x^i)_{i \in S})$ is the following: Suppose the firm S is formed when $(\bar{x}, \bar{p})$ prevails, and its members choose the strategies $(x^i)_{i \in S}$. An elementary event in the future is particular values of the market price vector and of the output levels realized by each firm. The agent j now imagines each elementary event of the future, and given the elementary event, his future optimizing behavior. The indirect utility (the optimal level of utility) depends upon the elementary event, and with respect to his subjective probability on the future events, he takes the expectation of the indirect utility level. This expectation is denoted by $u_S^j(\bar{x}, \bar{p}, (x^i)_{i \in S})$. [In order to make the convention on the input bundle harmless, one should assume that u_S^j depends upon $\sum_{i \in S} x_2^i$, rather than upon $(x_2^i)_{i \in S}$.].

When a coalition structure $\mathcal{T} \in \mathbb{T}$ is realized (i.e., when each firm $S \in \mathcal{T}$ is formed) and each firm S chooses new strategies $(x^i)_{i \in S}$, today's total excess demand for the marketed commodities is: $\sum_{j \in N} (x_1^j + x_2^j)$.

Given a finite set of economic agents N, a *labor-managed market economy* is a list of specified data $\mathcal{E} \equiv \{\{X^i\}_{j \in N}, \{F^S\}_{S \in \mathcal{N}}, \{u_S^j\}_{j \in S \in \mathcal{N}}, \mathbb{T}\}$. An *equilibrium* of the economy $\mathcal{E}$ is a triple $(x^*, p^*, \mathcal{T}^*)$ of members of $\prod_{j \in N} X^j$, Δ^L, $\mathbb{T}$, respectively, such that 1) for each $T \in \mathcal{T}^*$, $(x^{i*})_{i \in T} \in F^T(x^*, p^*)$; 2) it is not true that for some $S \in \mathcal{N}$ there exists $\xi \in F^S(x^*, p^*)$ for which $u_S^j(x^*, p^*, \xi) > u_{T(j)}^j(x^*, p^*, (x^{i*})_{i \in T(j)})$ for every $j \in S$, where $j \in T(j) \in \mathcal{T}^*$; and 3) $\sum_{j \in N} (x_1^j + x_2^j) \leqslant \mathbf{0}$.

Given $(\bar{x}, \bar{p})$, the agents play a cooperative game; this changes the strategical components $\bar{x}$ of $(\bar{x}, \bar{p})$ in disequilibrium. At the same time, given $(\bar{x}, \bar{p})$, the market price mechanism works in the (spot) commodity market; this changes the other component $\bar{p}$ of $(\bar{x}, \bar{p})$. An equilibrium (x^*, p^*) is achieved (i.e., the feasibility condition (1)), in which no coalition as a price-taker can bring about by its own effort a higher expected-indirect-utility level to each of its members (and hence no coalition has incentives to change the strategies) (condition (2)), and all the commodity markets are cleared (condition (3)). There is no futures market. Note that the difficulties of a private ownership economy pointed out in the last three paragraphs of Section 4.2 no longer apply here.

For each i: $1 \leqslant i \leqslant 4$, let the assumption ($i'$) be the condition on a labor-managed market economy $\mathcal{E}$ obtained from the assumption (i) of (4.1.1) by replacing, X, x, by $\prod_{j \in N} X^j \times \Delta^L$, (x, p), respectively. The assumption (5′) says: For every $(x, p) \subset \prod_{j \in N} X^j \times \Delta^L$ and for every $v \in \boldsymbol{R}^n$, the set $\bigcup_{\mathcal{T} \in \mathbb{T}} \{\xi \in \prod_{j \in N} X^i \mid$ For every $T \in \mathcal{T}$, $\xi^T \in F^T(x, p)$ and $v_j \leqslant u_T^j(x, p, \xi^T)$ for each $j \in T\}$ is convex. Just as in the proof of

(2.3.2), one can construct a society with $(n + 1)$ players, apply (4.1.1) to prove:

Theorem 4.3.1. Let $\mathcal{E}$ *be a labor-managed market economy. Suppose that* $\mathcal{E}$ *satiesfies the assumptions (1') – (5'), and the Weak Walras Law:*

(WW) *For every* $(x, p) \in \prod_{j \in N} X^j \times \Delta^L$ *and every* $T \in \mathcal{T}$, *if*

$$(x^i)_{i \in T} \in F^T(x, p) \text{ for each } T \in \mathcal{T}, \text{ then } p \cdot \sum_{j \in N} (x_1^j + x_2^j) \leq 0.$$

Then, there exists an equilibrium of $\mathcal{E}$.

4.4 Optimality of Nash Equilibrium: Strong Nash Equilibrium

To close the present survey, the initial model of Section 2.1 will be reconsidered here. It is well known that a competitive equilibrium of a private ownership economy is Pareto optimal, and the converse (in a certain sense) also holds true [see, e.g., *Debreu*, 1959, Chap. 6]. The purpose of the present section is to investigate the same welfare problem within the most basic framework: the game in normal form.

The following example of a bimatrix game (see the last paragraph of Section 2.1 for the definition), given by Albert W. Tucker, serves as an excellent counter-example for this question:

$$\begin{pmatrix} (10, & 10) & (0, & 15) \\ (15, & 0) & (5, & 5) \end{pmatrix}.$$

The scenario for this game is the following: Suppose the two players are prisoners who have been charged with some joint crime. For each player, the first strategy is to plead innocent, and the second strategy is to plead guilty. If both plead guilty, they will be punished. If both plead innocent, there is no solid evidence of their crime, and so they will be punished lightly. If one pleads guilty and the other pleads innocent, the one who confesses will be pardoned for his honesty, and the one who denies wrongdoing will be punished most severly. This game is customarily called the *prisoner's dilemma.* It is easy to check that the unique Nash equilibrium is: (the second row, the second column) $\in$ $\in X^1 \times X^2$, which is not Pareto optimal. Thus, just going by the assumptions of (2.1.1), one cannot hope for the existence of a Pareto optimal Nash equilibrium.

Let $\{X^j, u^j\}_{j \in N}$ be a game in normal form. To highlight the present problem, use the second interpretation of the game (see the first paragraph of Section 2.1), and define $\tilde{u}^j: X \to R$ by: $\tilde{u}^j(x^1, \ldots, x^{j-1}, \xi^j, x^{j+1}, \ldots, x^n) \equiv u^j(x, \xi^j)$. The following convenience will also be adopted by abuse of notation: Given $x, x' \in X$ and $S \in \mathcal{N}$, define $y \in X$ by: $y^i \equiv x^i$ if $i \notin S$; and $y^i \equiv x^{i\prime}$ if $i \in S$. Then, $\tilde{u}^j((x^i)_{i \notin S}, (x^{i\prime})_{i \in S}) \equiv \tilde{u}^j(y)$. An n-tuple of strategies $x^* \in X$ is called a *strong Nash equilibrum,* if it is not true that there exist $S \in \mathcal{N}$ and $(x^i)_{i \in S} \in \prod_{i \in S} X^i$ such that $\tilde{u}^j((x^{i*})_{i \notin S}, (x^i)_{i \in S}) > \tilde{u}^j(x^*)$ for every $j \in S$. In particular, this is a Nash equilibrium which is Pareto Optimal. The concept of strong Nash equilibrium was first introduced by *Aumann* [1959].

Theorem 4.4.1. Let $\{X^j, u^j\}_{j \in N}$ *be a game in normal form, and* $\mathcal{T}$ *a non-empty family of coalition structures. There exists a strong Nash equilibrium, if 1)* X^j *is a non-empty, convex, compact subset of a Euclidean space for every* $j \in N$; *2)* $\tilde{u}^j$ *is continuous in* X *for every* $j \in N$; *3) given any* $(x, v) \in X \times R^n$, *[there exists a balanced collection* $\mathcal{B}$ *such that for each* $S \in \mathcal{B}$ *there exists* $(y^{i,S})_{i \in S} \in \prod_{i \in S} X^i$ *for which* $v_j \leqslant \tilde{u}^j((x^i)_{i \notin S}, (y^{i,S})_{i \in S})$ *for every* $j \in S$*] implies [there exist* $T \in \mathcal{T}$ *and* $z \in X$ *such that* $v_j \leqslant \tilde{u}^j((x^i)_{i \notin T}, (z^i)_{i \in T})$ *for all* $j \in T \in \mathcal{T}$*]: and* if *4) given any* $(x, v) \in X \times R^n$, *the set* $\bigcup_{\mathcal{T} \in \mathcal{T}} \{y \in X \mid v_j \leqslant \tilde{u}^j((x^i)_{i \notin T}, (y^i)_{i \in T})$ *for all* $j \in T \in \mathcal{T}\}$ *is convex.*

Proof of (4.4.1). This is a straightforward consequence of (4.1.1). Given the present game in normal form, construct a society $(\{X^j\}_{j \in N}, \{F^S\}_{S \in \mathcal{N}}, \{u^j_S\}_{j \in S \in \mathcal{N}}, \mathcal{T})$ by $F^S(x) \equiv \prod_{j \in S} X^j$ for all $x \in X$; $u^j_S(x, \xi^S) \equiv \tilde{u}^j((x^i)_{i \notin S}, (\xi^i)_{i \in S})$ for all $(x, \xi^S) \in X \times X^S$.
Then, a social coalitional equilibrium of this society is precisely a strong Nash equilibrium.

Q.E.D.

The convexity assumption (4) of (4.4.1) is seldom satisfied when $\#\mathcal{T} \geqslant 2$. In view of the discussion made between the statement of (4.1.1) and its proof, one can establish a more useful version:

Corollary 4.4.2. Let $\{X^j, u^j\}_{j \in N}$ *be a game in normal form, and* $\mathcal{T}$ *a coalition structure. There exists a strong Nash equilibrium, if the assumptions (1) and (2) of (4.1.1) are satisfied; if 3') given any* $(x, v) \in X \times R^n$, *[there exists a balanced collection* $\mathcal{B}$ *such that for each* $S \in \mathcal{B}$ *there exists* $(y^{i,S})_{i \in S} \in \prod_{i \in S} X^i$ *for which* $v_j \leqslant \tilde{u}^j((x^i)_{i \notin S}, (y^{i,S})_{i \in S})$ *for every* $j \in S$*] implies [there exists* $z \in X$ *such that* $v_j \leqslant \tilde{u}^j((x^i)_{i \notin T}, (z^i)_{i \in T})$ *for all* $j \in T \in \mathcal{T}$*]; and if 4') given any* $x \in X$ *and any* $T \in \mathcal{T}$, *the function* $\tilde{u}^j((x^i)_{i \notin T}, \cdot)$ *is quasi-concave in* $\prod_{i \in T} X^i$, *for every* $j \in T$.

In order to comment on (4.4.2), consider the above example of the prisoner's dilemma. If $\mathcal{T} = \{\{1,2\}\}$, choose $x =$ (the first row, the first column), $v = (15, 15)$, $\mathcal{B} = \{\{1\}, \{2\}\}$, $y =$ (the second row, the second column). Then the hypothesis in the assumption (3′) is satisfied, but the conclusion of (3′) is false. Therefore the assumption (3′) excludes the prisoner's dilemma. If $\mathcal{T} = \{\{1\}, \{2\}\}$, choose $x =$ (the second row, the second column), $v = (10, 10)$, $\mathcal{B} = \{\{1,2\}\}$, $y =$ (the first row, the first column). Then, the hypothesis in (3′) is satisfied, but the conclusion of (3′) is false. Again, the assumption (3′) excludes the prisoner's dilemma.

Appendix

Theorem A.1. Let X, Y *be topological spaces,* Γ *a correspondence from* X *to* Y, *and* φ *a function from* $X \times Y$ *to* R. *Assume that* Y *is* T_3, Γ *is both u.s.c. and l.s.c. in* X, $\Gamma(x)$ *is* *non-empty and compact for every $x \in X$, and φ is continuous in $X \times Y$. Then: 1) the function $M: X \to \boldsymbol{R}$, $x \mapsto \text{Max}\,\{\varphi(x, y) \mid y \in \Gamma(x)\}$ is continuous; and 2) the correspondence $\Phi: X \to Y$, $x \mapsto \{y \in \Gamma(x) \mid \varphi(x, y) = M(x)\}$ is u.s.c.*

Theorem A. 2. Let $\{C_j\}_{j \in N}$ be a family of closed subsets of Δ^N, indexed by the members of N, such that for each $T \in \mathcal{N}$, $\Delta^T \subset \bigcup_{j \in T} C_j$. Then, $\bigcap_{j \in N} C_j \neq \phi$.

Theorem A.3. Let X be a non-empty, convex, compact subset of a Euclidean space, and f a continuous function of X to X. Then, there exists a fixed-point of f; i.e., $x^* \in X$ such that $x^* = f(x^*)$.

Theorem A.4. Let X be a non-empty, convex, compact subset of a Euclidean space and F a correspondence from X to X. Assume that F is u.s.c. in X, and $F(x)$ is non-empty and convex for every $x \in X$. Then, there exists a fixed-point of F; i.e., $x^* \in X$ such that $x^* \in F(x^*)$.

Theorem A. 5. Let X be a non-empty, convex, compact subset of $\boldsymbol{R}^n$. Let F, G be two u.s.c. correspondences from X to X such that for each $x \in X$, $F(x)$ and $G(x)$ are both non-empty and convex. Assume for any $x \in X$ and any $p \in \boldsymbol{R}^n$ for which $p \cdot x \leqslant p \cdot y$ for every $y \in X$, there exist $u \in F(x)$ and $v \in G(x)$ such that $p \cdot u \geqslant p \cdot v$. Then, there exists $x^* \in X$ such that $F(x^*) \cap G(x^*) \neq \phi$.

Theorem (A.1) is cutomarily called the maximum theorem, and one can prove it exactly in the same way as in *Berge* [1959, Chap. VI, Section 3]; the theorem was anticipated by *Nash* [1950, p. 49, lines 13–16], and is the essential contribution of *Debreu* [1952]. The fixed-point theorem (A.3) is due to *Brouwer* [1912]. *Knaster/Kuratowski/Mazurkiewicz* [1929] established (A.2), and then used (A.2) to prove (A.3). Conversely, one can use (A.3) to prove (A.2). The generalization (A.4) of (A.3) is due to *Kakutani* [1941], which reformulates the main lemma of *von Neumann* [1937]. *Fan* [1972] established (A.5) by combining beautifully (A.2) and the separation theorem on convex sets. It should be noted that (A.5) reduces to (A.4) when the correspondence G is given by $G(x) \equiv \{x\}$. Actually, *Fan* [1972] established a more general theorem than (A.5).

References

Arrow, K.J., and *G. Debreu*: Existence of an Equilibrium for a Competitive Economy. Econometrica **22**, 1954, 265–290.

Arrow, K.J., and *F.H. Hahn*: General Competitive Analysis. San Francisco 1971.

Aubin, J.-P.: Mathematical Methods of Game and Economic Theory. Amsterdam–New York–Oxford, 1979.

Aumann, R.J.: Acceptable Points in General Cooperative *n*-Person Games. Contributions to the Theory of Games, Vol. IV. Ed. by A.W. Tucker and R.D. Luce (eds.). Princeton, 1959, 287–324.

–: The Core of a Cooperative Game without Side Payments, Transactions of the American Mathematical Society **98**, 1961, 539–552.

–: Markets with a Continuum of Traders. Econometrica **32**, 1964, 39–50.

–: Existence of Competitive Equilibria in Markets with a Continuum of Traders. Econometrica **34**, 1966, 1–17.

–: Values of Markets with a Coninuum of Traders. Econometrica **43**, 1975, 611–646.

Aumann, R.J., and *B. Peleg*: Von Neumann-Morgenstern Solutions to Cooperative Games without Side Payments. Bulletin of the American Mathematical Society **66**, 1960, 173–179.

Aumann, R.J., and *L.S. Shapley*: Values of Non-Atomic Games. Princeton 1974.

Berge, C.: Espaces Topologiques. Paris 1959. Translated into English as: Topological Spaces, Edinburgh–London 1963.

Berle, Jr., A.A., and *G.C. Means*: The Modern Corporation and Private Property. New York 1932.

Billera, L.J.: Some Theorems on the Core of an *n*-Person Game Without Side-Payments. SIAM Journal of Applied Mathematics **18**, 1970, 567–579.

–: On Games without Side Payments Arising from a General Class of Markets. Journal of Mathematical Economcs **1**, 1974, 129–139.

Bondareva, O.N.: Teoriia iadra v igre n lits. Vestnik Leningrad University **13**, 1962, 141–142.

–: Nekotorye primeneniia metodov linejnogo programmirovaniia k teorii kooperativnykh igr. Problemy Kibernetiki **10**, 1963, 119–139.

Brouwer, L.E.J.: Über Abbildungen von Mannigfaltigkeiten. Mathematische Annalen **71**, 1912, 97–115.

Coase, R.H.: The Nature of the Firm. Economica, **4**, 1937, 386–405. Reprinted in Readings in Price Theory. Ed. by K.E. Boulding and G.J. Stigler (eds.). Chicago 1952, 331–351.

Cournot, A.A.: Recherches sur les principes mathématiques de la théorie des richesses. Paris 1838. Translated into English as: Researches into the Mathematical Principles of the Theory of Wealth. New York 1897.

Debreu, G.: A Social Equilibrium Existence Theorem. Proceedings of the National Academy of Sciences of the U.S.A. **38**, 1952, 886–893.

–: Theory of Value. New York 1959.

Debreu, G., and *H. Scarf*: A Limit Theorem on the Core of an Economy. International Economic Review **4**, 1963, 235–246.

Delbaen, F.: Convex Games and Extreme Points. Journal of Mathematical Analysis and Applications **45**, 1974, 210–233.

Edgeworth, F.Y.: Mathematical Psychics. London 1881.

Fan, K.: On Systems of Linear Inequalities. Linear Inequalities and Related Systems. Ed. by H.W. Kuhn and A.W. Tucker (eds.). Princeton 1956, 99–156.

–: A Minimax Inequality and Applications. Inequalities-III. Ed. by O. Shisha. New York 1972, 103–113.

Gillies, D.B.: Solutions to General Non-Zero-Sum Games. Contributions to the Theory of Games, Vol. IV. Ed. by A.W. Tucker and R.D. Luce (eds.). Princeton 1959, 47–85.

Hildenbrand, W.: Core and Equilibria of a Large Economy. Princeton 1974.

Ichiishi, T.: On the Knaster-Kuratowski-Mazurkiewicz-Shapley Theorem. Journal of Mathematical Analysis and Applications **81**, 1981a, 297–299.

–: A Social Coalitional Equilibrium Existence Lemma. Econometrica **49**, 1981b, 369–377.

–: Super-Modularity: Applications to Convex Games and to the Greedy Algorithm for LP. Journal of Economic Theory **25**, 1981c, 283–286.

–: Management Versus Ownership, I. International Economic Review **23**, 1982.

–: Management Versus Ownership, II. Mimeo, 1979.

Ichiishi, T., and *J.J. Schäffer*: The $\mathcal{T}$-Core of a Game without Side-payments. Working Paper No. 9-79-80, Graduate School of Industrial Administration, Carnegie-Mellon University, 1979.

Ichiishi, T., and *S. Weber*: Some Theorems on the Core of a Non-Sidepayment Game with a Measure Space of Players. International Journal of Game Theory **7**, 1978, 95–112.

Kakutani, S.: A Generalization of Brouwer's Fixed-Point Theorem. Duke Mathematical Journal **8**, 1941, 457–459.

Kalai, E., and *D. Schmeidler*: An Admissible Set Occurring in Various Bargaining Situations. Journal of Economic Theory **14**, 1977, 402–411.

Kannai, Y.: Countably Additive Measures in Cores of Games. Journal of Mathematical Analysis and Applications **27**, 1969, 227–240.

Knaster, B., C. Kuratowski and *S. Mazurkiewicz*: Ein Beweis des Fixpunktsatzes für *n*-dimensionale Simplexe. Fundamenta Mathematicae **14**, 1929, 132–137.

Lemke, C.E., and *J.T. Howson*: Equilibrium Points of Bi-Matrix Games SIAM Journal of Applied Mathematics **12**, 1964, 413–423.

Mas-Colell, A.: An Equilibrium Existence Theorem Without Complete or Transitive Preferences. Journal of Mathematical Economics **1**, 1974, 237–246.

Moulin, H.: Two and Three Person Games: A Local Study. International Journal of Game Theory **8**, 1979, 81–107.

Nash, Jr., J.F.: Equilibrium Points in *n*-Person Game. Proceedings of the National Academy of Sciences of the United States of America **36**, 1950, 48–49.

–: Non-Cooperative Games, Annals of Mathematics **54**, 1951, 286–295.

Nikaidô, H.: Convex Structures and Economic Theory. New York 1968.

Nikaidô, H., and *K. Isoda*: Note on Noncooperative Convex Games. Pacific Journal of Mathematics **5**, 1955, 807–815.

Prakash, P., and *M.R. Sertel*: On the Existence of Noncooperative Equilibria in Social Systems. Discussion Paper No. 92, The Center for Mathematical Studies in Economics and Management Science, Northwestern University, 1974.

Rosenmüller, J.: On Core and Value. Operations Research Verfahren **9**, 1971, 84–101.

–: Large Games without Side Payments. Operations Research Verfahren **20**, 1975, 107–128.

Scarf, H.: The Core of an *N* Person Game. Econometrica **35**, 1967a, 50–69.

–: The Approximation of Fixed Points of a Continuous Mapping. SIAM Journal of Applied Mathematics **15**, 1967b, 1328–1342.

–: The Computation of Economic Equilibria. New Haven 1973.

Schmeidler, D.: On Balanced Games with Infinitely Many Players. Research Program in Game Theory and Mathematical Economics, Research Meorandum No. 28, Department of Mathematics. The Hebrew University of Jerusalem, 1967.

–: Cores of Exact Games, I. Journal of Mathematical Analysis and Applications **40**, 1972, 214–225.

–: Equilibrium Points of Nonatomic Games. Journal of Statistical Physics 7, 1973, 295–300.

–: Walrasian Analysis via Strategic Outcome Functions. Econometrica **48**, 1980, 1585–1593.

Shafer, W., and *H. Sonnenschein*: Equilibrium in Abstract Economies Without Ordered Preferences. Journal of Mathematical Economics **2**, 1975, 345–348.

Shapley, L.S.: A Value for *n*-Person Games. Contributions to the Theory of Games, Vol. II. Ed. by H.W. Kuhn and A.W. Tucker. Princeton 1953, 307–317.

–: On Balanced Sets and Cores. Naval Research Logistics Quarterly **14**, 1967, 453–460.

–: Cores of Convex Games. International Journal of Game Theory **1**, 1971, 11–26.

–: On Balanced Games without Side Payments. Mathematical Programming. Ed. by T.C. Hu and S.M. Robinson (eds.). New York 1973, 261–290.

Shubik, M.: Edgeworth Market Games. Contributions to the Theory of Games, Vol. IV. Ed. by A.W. Tucker and R.D. Luce (eds.). Princeton 1959, 267–278.

Todd, M.: Lecture Note. School of Operations Research and Industrial Engineering, Cornell University, 1978.

Von Neumann, J.: Zur Theorie der Gesellschaftsspiele. Mathematische Annalen **100**, 1928, 295–320. Translated into English as: On the Theory of Games of Strategy. Contributions to the Theory of Games, Vol. IV. Ed. by A.W. Tucker and R.D. Luce (eds.). Princeton 1959, 13–42.

–: Über ein ökonomisches Gleichungssystem und eine Verallgemeinerung des Brouwerschen Fixpunkt-Satzes. Ergebnisse eines Mathematischen Seminars **8**, 1937, 73–83. Translated into English as: A Model of General Economic Equilibrium. Review of Economic Studies **13**, 1945–46, 1–9.

Von Neumann, J., and *O. Morgenstern*: Theory of Games and Economic Behavior. 2nd ed., Princeton 1947.

Walkup, D.W., and *R.J.-B. Wets*: Lifting Projections of Convex Polyhedra. Pacific Journal of Mathematics **28**, 1969, 465–475.

Yamazaki, A.: An Equilibrium Existence Theorem without Convexity Assumptions. Econometrica **46**, 1978, 541–555.

Added in proof: Theorem (3.4.6) was significantly improved in the November 1981 version of *Ichiishi/Schäffer* [1979].

Games, Economic Dynamics, and Time Series Analysis. 1982 ©Physica-Verlag, Wien–Würzburg

Noncooperative Bargaining Models

By *J.C. Harsanyi*, Berkeley[1])[2])

1. Cooperative and Noncooperative Games

Classical game theory makes a fundamental distinction between cooperative and noncooperative games. This distinction was first proposed by *Nash* [1950a, 1951], who defined *cooperative* games as games permitting *both* communication and enforceable agreements between the players, and defined *noncooperative* games as games permitting *neither* communication nor enforceable agreements. Later writers have found these definitions unsatisfactory because any two-way classification based on *two* different criteria at the same time is always logically problematic since it immediately poses the question, What about objects possessing the first property but lacking the second, and what about objects possessing the second property but lacking the first? [cf. *Harsanyi*, 1976, 100–105.]

Thus, it is now commonly agreed that it is preferable to distinguish cooperative games and noncooperative games on the basis of one single criterion. It turns out that enforceability or unenforceability of agreements is a much more important characteristic of a game than presence or absence of communication is. For example, in a Prisoner's Dilemma game, free communication among the players in itself will be insufficient to make the cooperative outcome achievable by rational players: To be sure, if the two players are free to talk to each other, they can always *agree* to use their cooperative strategies. But such an agreement will be worse than useless if it cannot be enforced because the players in general cannot rationally expect each other to *keep* such unenforceable agreements (*loc. cit.*).

Accordingly, it is now customary to define cooperative games as games permitting enforceable agreements (and possibly also permitting other binding commitments, such as irrevocable promises and/or irrevocable threats) and to define noncooperative games as games not permitting them.

From an analytical point of view, the importance of this distinction lies in the fact that the solution of a noncooperative game must always be a *Nash equilibrium point*

[1]) The author wants to thank the National Science Foundation for supporting this research through Grant SOC77-06394 to the Center for Research in Management, University of California, Berkeley. He also wants to state his indebtedness to Professor Reinhard Selten, of the University of Bielefeld, West Germany. Many ideas stated in this paper are the results of our joint research over more than a decade.

[2]) Prof. *J.C. Harsanyi*, School of Business Administration, University of California, Berkeley, CA 94720, U.S.A.

[*Nash,* 1950a, 1951], whereas the solution of a cooperative game can also be a nonequilibrium strategy combination (or even a probability mixture of such strategy combinations). The argument for this conclusion is this: Suppose somebody proposes a solution theory which would make a specific strategy combination $s = (s_1, \ldots, s_n)$ the solution of a given noncooperative game G. Then the very least we must require is that this strategy combination s should *not* be *self-destabilizing,* in the sense that if any particular player i ($i = 1, \ldots, n$) expected the other players to use their solution strategies $s_1, \ldots, s_{i-1}, s_{i+1}, \ldots, s_n$, then this very fact in itself should *not* give him a positive incentive *not* to use his own solution strategy s_i. But this is equivalent to requiring that the solution strategy s_i of every player i should be his *best reply* to the other players' solution strategies $s_1, \ldots, s_{i-1}, s_{i+1}, \ldots, s_n$. That is to say, it is equivalent to requiring that the solution s of any noncooperative game G should be a *Nash equilibrium point.*

On the other hand, the solution of a cooperative game need not be an equilibrium point because such a game will permit the players to reach a binding agreement to use *any* specific strategy combination (or even any desired probability mixture of two or more strategy combinations, i.e., any desired jointly randomized mixed strategy). Once such a binding agreement has been reached in a cooperative game, it will remain binding even if some players' solution strategies are not their best replies to the other players' solution strategies.

2. Difficulties with the Classical Theory of Cooperative Games

Whereas the classical theory of noncooperative games is based on one specific solution concept, that of Nash equilibrium points, the classical theory of cooperative games proposes a sizeable number of alternative solution concepts (such as von Neumann- Morgenstern stable sets, the core, Nash's, Raiffa's and several other authors' solution concepts for two-person bargaining games, the Shapley value, the Aumann-Maschler bargaining sets, the kernel, the nucleolus, and many others – see *Luce/Raiffa* [1957] and *Owen* [1968]. Taken one by one, most of these solution concepts have considerable intuitive appeal. But, taken in conjunction, they do not add up to a convincing theory of cooperative games.

First of all, the various solution concepts have little logical connection with each other; and they obviously cannot be interpreted in any way as special cases of one basic theory. Moreover, the classical theory provides no clear criterion as to *which* particular solution concept should be used in analyzing a given game in any specific case – which makes applications of classical theory to real-life cooperative game situations a rather arbitrary procedure.

Yet, the fact that classical theory offers *several* mutually incompatible solution concepts for some classes of cooperative games is perhaps less objectionable than the fact that it provides *no* useable solution concepts at all for some other classes of cooperative (or half-cooperative) games, including some game classes extremely important for theoretical reasons or for the purposes of empirical application. These include cooperative games with incomplete information [cf. *Harsanyi*, 1967-68, 329–334], cooperative games played in two or more consecutive stages, and games intermediate between fully cooperative and fully noncooperative games (i.e., games in which agreements are fully binding and enforceable under some conditions but not under others).

There is, however, an even more fundamental objection to the classical theory of cooperative games. By the very nature of a cooperative game, its outcome is always decided by *bargaining* among the players (except if the game has only one unique Pareto-optimal outcome). Therefore, any acceptable theory of cooperative games must be based on a systematic analysis of the bargaining process among the players. Yet most of the classical cooperative solution concepts fail to provide such an analysis.

Instead of relying on a systematic study of this bargaining process, most of the classical solution concepts are based on a set of intuitively appealing axioms. The basic difficulty with this approach is that, as experience shows, it is extremely hard to decide whether it is reasonable to assume that the outcome of a given bargaining process will in fact satisfy any particular axiom – without making very specific assumptions about the actual bargaining moves and countermoves available to the players, and without a systematic study of the various players' strategic interests in the game, given the nature of the bargaining moves and countermoves available to them. (For example, whether the continuity and linearity requirements associated with the Shapley value are reasonable requirements or not will crucially depend on the nature of the bargaining process assumed to be used by the players. See *Harsanyi* [1981]).

3. Analysis of cooperative games by means of noncooperative bargaining models

Already in 1951, in one of the two papers introducing the very concepts of cooperative and of noncooperative games, Nash suggested an alternative approach to analyzing cooperative games [*Nash*, 1951, p. 295; cf. also *Nash*, 1953, p. 129]. He pointed out that the bargaining process deciding the outcome of any cooperative game G can be represented by a bargaining game $B(G)$ having the nature of a noncooperative game in extensive form or in normal form and that the solution of this cooperative game G then can be defined in terms of the equilibrium points of that noncooperative bargaining game $B(G)$.

Unfortunately, Nash's suggestion gives rise to a very basic difficulty, which lies in the fact that almost every nontrivial noncooperative game – and certainly almost every noncooperative bargaining game – has several, and quite often infinitely many, essentially different equilibrium points. Thus, we gain very little by the suggestion that the solution of the game will be one of these equilibrium points, unless we are told also *which* one of these is likely to be the actual outcome. For easier reference, I will describe this problem as the equilibrium-point *multiplicity problem.*

Nash himself encountered this problem in his theory of two-person bargaining games. In the second paper that he wrote about this subject [*Nash*, 1953], he proposed an extremely simple noncooperative bargaining model. But in spite of its great simplicity, this bargaining model had infinitely many essentially different equilibrium points. Nash's bargaining solution is fundamentally an attempt to find a suitable mathematical criterion for choosing *one* of these equilibrium points as the actual solution.

To illustrate the nature of the multiplicity problem, I will briefly describe Nash's bargaining model. Two players, 1 and 2, can obtain any payoff vector $u = (u_1, u_2)$

within a given compact and convex feasible set F if they can agree on which payoff vector u they want to choose. If they cannot agree, they will obtain a predetermined conflict-payoff vector $c = (c_1, c_2)$.

To analyze this bargaining problem, Nash proposes the following bargaining model. Both players will simultaneously announce their payoff demands d_1 and d_2. If their demands are mutually compatible, i.e., if the demand vector $d = (d_1, d_2)$ lies within the feasible set F, they will obtain the payoffs $u_1 = d_1$ and $u_2 = d_2$ corresponding to their payoff demands. But if this is not the case, they will obtain only their conflict payoffs with $u_1 = c_1$ and $u_2 = c_2$.

It is easy to verify that in general this game has infinitely many equilibrium points (except in degenerate cases, where the equilibrium set may shrink to a unique point). This is so because all points $d = (d_1, d_2)$ on the upper-right boundary B of F will be equilibrium points as long as they satisfy the individual-rationality requirements $d_1 \geqslant c_1$ and $d_2 \geqslant c_2$.

Nash's axioms (or, equivalently, his stability argument in *op. cit.*, 131–136) are then used to select as the solution that particular equilibrium point which maximizes the Nash product $\pi = (d_1 - c_1)(d_2 - c_2)$.

In my opinion, Nash's method of choosing a solution for two-person bargaining games (and even its extension to n-person bargaining games with fixed conflict payoffs) is very appealing. But what we really need is a *general* solution theory which will always select one specific equilibrium point as the solution for *every* possible n-person noncooperative game. As some people in this audience will know, in recent years Reinhard Selten and I have developed such a solution theory, which in fact is a direct generalization of the two-person (as well as of the n-person) Nash solution. We hope to finish a book manuscript describing our theory in the near future.[3])

Our solution theory enables us to implement Nash's suggestion and to analyze every *cooperative* game G by means of a *noncooperative* bargaining model $B(G)$, defining the solution of G in terms of the solution that our theory assigns to this noncooperative game $B(G)$.

Thus, our theory represents a far-reaching unification of game theory as a whole: Analysis of cooperative games is reduced to analysis of noncooperative bargaining games; and at the same time all noncooperative games, including noncooperative bargaining games, are brought under the same solution theory, which always selects the solution of any given noncooperative game from the set of all its Nash equilibrium points on the basis of the same general mathematical criteria.

4. Bargaining Models: Successive Moves vs. Simultaneous Moves

Virtually all bargaining in the real world involves *successive* offers and counteroffers by the participants, which makes it into a game with *perfect information*. (That is to say, the players typically possess perfect information at least about each other's *personal*

---

[3]) For a preliminary account, see *Harsanyi* [1975, 1977]. A more comprehensive and more up-to-date description will be found in *Harsanyi/Selten* [1980].

moves. If the game involves incomplete information, this latter fact may be modelled by postulating various *chance moves* in the game; and the players may then be assumed to have only imperfect information about some of these chance moves [cf. *Harsanyi*, 1967–68]. But they will still have perfect information about all personal moves made in the game.)

Yet, most game-theoretical bargaining models require the players to present *simultaneous* offers to each other, making these models into games with *imperfect information* also with respect to the players' personal moves. (Many bargaining models assume two or more consecutive rounds of simultaneous offers. But each round typically involves simultaneous offers by the players.)

Why should there be such a fundamental discrepancy between real-life bargaining and its game-theoretical representation? One possible answer is that real-life bargaining processes with consecutive moves are games in *extensive form*, whereas the one-round bargaining models with simultaneous moves used by game theorists are the *normal-form* counterparts of the former. But this answer at best tells us only part of the story: These one-round bargaining models do satisfy the definition of games in normal form. Yet, obviously they are *not* the normal forms of the real-world sequential bargaining games we are talking about.

For, in the normal form of a sequential bargaining game, the strategy of any player must be a mathematical function assigning a specific move to any possible past history of the game over the first k stages ($k = 1, 2, \ldots$), where k is unbounded, giving each player *infinitely many* degrees of freedom in choosing his bargaining strategy. In contrast, in the customary one-round bargaining models, each player's strategy consists in choosing just one real number (usually interpreted as his payoff demand), giving him only *one* degree of freedom.

It has been one of Nash's brilliant insights that, in many bargaining situations, from a game-theoretical point of view the *only relevant aspect of any given player's bargaining strategy is the lowest payoff he is willing to accept* and that all other aspects of his bargaining strategy can be disregarded without any real loss of generality. Thus, when a game theorist moves from a real-life sequential bargaining process to an abstract one-round bargaining model, he really does two things: First, he replaces the empirically given extensive-form game by a bargaining game in normal form; and then he replaces the resulting very complicated normal-form bargaining game, whose strategies involve infinitely many adjustable parameters, by a much simpler normal-form bargaining game whose strategies can be characterized by one single real number.

In my opinion, Nash's discovery of the simultaneous-moves representation for bargaining games has been a major intellectual achievement. It has opened the way for a much deeper understanding of bargaining situations than had been possible before. This is so because many important aspects of the bargaining problem are obscured by using the traditional consecutive-offers perfect-information representation of bargaining games, but become immediately obvious by using the simultaneous-offers imperfect-information representation. For example, under the latter representation, the fundamental *symmetry* between the strategic possibilities available to the players becomes much clearer. Likewise, the basic difference between *ultimatum games* (where one player can present a take-it-or-leave-it offer to the other player, making the bargaining situation fundamentally asymmetric between the two players) and true *bargaining games* (where every offer is potentially subject to further negotiation) becomes much more transparent when we realize that true bargaining games do, while ultimatum games do not, admit representation by a simultaneous-offers model.

At the same time, the use of simultaneous-offers bargaining models does have its disadvantages. It increases the analytic distance between real-life bargaining behavior and its game-theoretical representations, which makes it much harder to judge in many cases *which* particular abstract bargaining model is the best theoretical representation for a given real-life bargaining process. In my opinion, this is a very important area for future game-theoretical research.

Of course, even under Nash's modelling approach, one-round simultaneous-offers bargaining models will be sufficient only in the case of the very simplest bargaining situations. Even Nash himself used a two-stage model for representing a bargaining game with variable threats. But even without variable threats, a two-or-more-stage bargaining model is needed for analyzing many bargaining games involving incomplete information, in order to permit the players to learn something about each other's "types" by observing each other's bargaining moves at earlier stages of the game.

5. Alternative Approaches to Anticonflicts

The problem I am now going to discuss arises both in two-person and in n-person bargaining games. But for convenience, I will discuss mainly the two-person case, though my remarks can be easily extended to the n-person case in an obvious way.

In a Nash-type simultaneous-offers model, there are three classes of possible outcomes:

(1) The players' payoff demands may be mutually *incompatible*, with $d = (d_1, d_2) \notin F$. In this case, the game will end in a *conflict*; and the players will obtain only their conflict payoffs c_1 and c_2.

(2) The players' payoff demands may be just *barely* compatible, with $d \in B$, where B is the upper-right boundary of the feasible set F. In this case, the game will end with an *agreement*; and the players will obtain exactly their payoff demands d_1 and d_2.

(3) The players' payoffs may be *more than* compatible (in the sense that even somewhat higher payoff demands would be compatible) with $d \in F^0$, where $F^0 = F - B$. Nash treats this case in the same way as he treats case (2), assuming that in this case, also, both players will receive payoffs equal to their payoff demands d_1 and d_2.

Probably no game theorist objects to Nash's handling of cases (1) and (2). But his treatment of case (3) is more open to objections. For reasons that will soon become obvious, I propose to describe case (3) as the *"anticonflict"* case, in contrast to the case of a *conflict* proper [case (1)] and that of an *agreement* [case (2)].

Nash's approach to anticonflicts does have the merit of mathematical simplicity (though I will propose a mathematically even simpler approach). But in many cases, it represents an unrealistic and rather artificial assumption. For example, suppose that two players have to divide \$100 and that player 1 demands $d_1 = 40$, while player 2 demands $d_2 = 45$. Then, under Nash's assumptions, both players will actually obtain their payoff demands, which means that the total amount to be distributed between them will be only \$40 + \$45 = \$85, and the amount \$100 – \$85 = \$15 will remain unclaimed. In many cases, it is at least very unlikely (and, indeed, may be contrary to the rules under which the game is played) that any money should be left undistributed – unless the game ends in a full-fledged conflict.

In connection with our work on our solution concept, Reinhard Selten and I have come to the conclusion that – at least in the case of *one-stage* bargaining models – the most natural approach to anticonflicts is to treat them in the same way as conflicts proper are treated and to assume that in the case of an anticonflict, also, the players will obtain only their conflict payoffs c_1 and c_2.

The basic reason is that "agreement" must be defined as an agreement *on a specific outcome* – on a specific joint strategy to be used in the game, or at least on a specific payoff vector to be assigned to the players. Yet, any anticonflict will violate this requirement. For instance, in our example, if player 1 asks for $d_1 = 40$, he is really proposing the payoff vector $(u_1, u_2) = (40, 60)$; whereas if player 2 asks for $d_2 = 45$, he is really proposing the payoff vector $(u_1, u_2) = (55, 45)$. Yet, these are two quite *different* payoff vectors; and if these are the payoff vectors proposed by the players, we cannot really say that they have agreed on the *same* payoff vector.

To be sure, when one envisages bargaining as a process continuing over time, it will be natural to treat anticonflicts differently from conflicts proper because it is reasonable to expect that the former will be much easier to resolve than the latter by subsequent negotiations. (Though it is quite possible for an anticonflict to be transformed into a conflict proper – for example, when player 1 proposes the payoff vector $u^* = (40, 60)$ while player 2 proposes the payoff vector $u^{**} = (55, 45)$, it can easily happen that they will then exchange roles and player 1 will now come to insist on the payoff vector u^{**} originally proposed by player 2, while player 2 will now insist on the payoff vector u^* originally proposed by player 1, giving rise to a conflict in the usual sense of the word.)

Yet, if we represent the bargaining process by a one-stage bargaining model, stage one of the bargaining process will not be followed by any further negotiations that could resolve any as yet unresolved anticonflict between the players, so that an anticonflict must be treated as an unresolved disagreement, i.e., as a conflict.

Note, that by treating anticonflicts on a par with conflicts proper, we make any one-stage bargaining model into a *unanimity game* – defined as a game in which the players can obtain any payoff vector u from a specified set $U = \{u\}$ of admissible payoff vectors as long as all players choose the *same* payoff vector u; but in which they will obtain only a predetermined conflict-payoff vector c if there is the slightest disagreement between the players about which payoff vector to choose. Since unanimity games are the simplest possible class of nontrivial noncooperative games (if we define a nontrivial game as a game having more than one equilibrium point), our approach to one-stage bargaining games not only has the conceptual advantages already mentioned but also has the advantage of much greater mathematical simplicity.

Of course, if we use a two-or-more-stage bargaining model, we can always add an additional round of mutual offers (i.e., an additional stage of the bargaining game) in order to resolve anticonflicts that remain unresolved at (what would otherwise be) the last stage of the game. But this always adds to the mathematical complexity of the bargaining model;

and it is not clear that the additional strategic flexibility that our bargaining model may gain in this way will offset this disadvantage of increased mathematical complexity.

If we do not want to assimilate anticonflicts to conflicts proper, permitting an extra round of bargaining seems to be the only nonarbitrary approach. The only alternative to this is to assume that if players' last payoff demands d_1 and d_2 give rise to an anticonflict, they will receive payoffs u_i ($i = 1, 2$) defined as specified functions $u_i = f_i(d_i, d_j)$ of these payoff demands. For example, Nash himself proposed the functions $u_i = d_i$ ($i = 1, 2$). Another natural proposal would be to choose the functions $u_i = [d_i + g_i(d_j)]/2$, where $g_i(d_j)$ is the highest payoff that player i can receive if player j is to receive the payoff d_j demanded by him. But making the players' final payoffs to be determined by any such function f_i is a somewhat unsatisfactory procedure because it violates the game-theoretical principle that the players' payoffs should be determined by mutual agreement, rather than by some mechanical rule invented by the game theorist.[4])

6. Outcome-Selection and Outcome-Retention Models

Many bargaining models assume that the players start from an initial "neutral" no-agreement situation (often associated with zero payoffs or at least relatively low payoffs) and then try to agree on one specific outcome – typically on an outcome preferred over the initial situation by all players. To reach such an agreement is a nontrivial problem because usually there are many alternative outcomes that the players could select; and the purpose of the bargaining model is to predict *which* particular outcome they will actually choose, given their strategic possibilities and given their strategic interests in the game. Models of this kind may be called *bargaining models proper* or *outcome-selection models.*

Other bargaining models are less ambitious. They do not try to predict what particular outcome the players will choose, starting from a "neutral" position. They only try to characterize stable outcomes, i.e., positions the players will not move away from once they have been placed in these positions – presumably because not enough players will prefer any given alternative position to be able to enforce a move to it.

For example, Nash's bargaining model is clearly meant to be an *outcome-selection* model. On the other hand, even though von Neumann and Morgenstern have not offered a formal bargaining model in support of their concept of stable sets, it is reasonably clear that they had some *outcome-retention* model in mind. They do not try to explain how the players may come to agree on any given imputation x belonging to a specific stable set V. Rather, they claim only that *if* the players ever come to agree on any given imputation x belonging to a particular stable set V and *if* the players' expectations become

[4]) Some readers may object that my detailed discussion of the anticonflict problem is largely irrelevant because the approach we choose to treating anticonflicts will have very little influence, if any, on the set of equilibrium points occurring in any given bargaining game. This is, of course, correct. But under our solution theory, the treatment of anticonflicts nevertheless may have an important influence on the actual solution of the game because it may strongly influence the players' incentives in situation where they are *uncertain* about which particular equilibrium point of the game will be the actual outcome. This, in turn, may have a strong effect on risk-dominance relations between different equilibrium points.

focussed on this stable set *V*, *then* they will not shift from x to any other payoff vector $x' \neq x$. In an earlier paper [*Harsanyi*, 1974], I have tried to reconstruct the actual noncooperative-game outcome-retention model underlying von Neumann and Morgenstern's theory.

In a more recent paper [*Harsanyi*, 1981], I proposed an outcome-selection model (more specifically, a dividend model) for generating the Shapley value and showed that it did yield the Shapley value in the case of decomposable games, but failed to do so in the case of indecomposable games. In the same paper, I also proposed an outcome-retention model based on Myerson's graph interpretation of the Shapley value and showed that this model yielded the Shapley value in the case of *all* superadditive games, both decomposable and indecomposable.[5])

In the case of outcome-selection models, it is virtually essential that they should yield a unique outcome, and this fact makes them fundamentally dependent on an equilibrium-point-selection theory such as our solution theory is. In the case of outcome-retention models, a unique outcome is in many cases not required. (For instance, an outcome-retention model associated with von Neumann-Morgenstern stable sets obviously need not have a unique outcome.) But an outcome-retention model in support of the Shapley value does need a one-point solution theory (though it does not require a solution theory so powerful as ours – it can be based also on Nash's two-person bargaining theory, or even on a much weaker theory using only Nash's efficiency and symmetry axioms).

In any case, it seems to me that the distinction between outcome-selection models and outcome-retention models (stability models) can be very helpful in analyzing cooperative games and also in trying to understand various cooperative solution concepts proposed by classical game theory.

7. Conclusion

I have argued that analysis of cooperative games by means of noncooperative bargaining models is a very powerful analytical tool – at least if we have a suitable solution theory that can help us to resolve the equilibrium-point multiplicity problem. I have also discussed the use of bargaining models assuming simultaneous moves by the players; the problem of how to deal with anticonflict situations; and the distinction between the two main types of bargaining models, viz., outcome-selection models (i.e., bargaining models in a narrower sense) and outcome-retention models (stability models).

[5]) I understand that Reinhard Selten is working on an outcome-selection model for the Shapley value, based also on Myerson's graph approach.

References

Harsanyi, J.C.: Games with Incomplete Information Played by Bayesian Players. Parts I–III. Management Science **14**, 1967–68, 159–182, 320–334, and 486–502.

–: An Equilibrium-point Interpretation of Stable Sets and a Proposed Alternative Definition. Management Science **20**, 1974, 1472–1495.

–: The Tracing Procedure. International Journal of Game Theory **4**, 1975, 61–94.

–: Essays on Ethics, Social Behavior, and Scientific Explanation. Dordrecht 1976.

–: A Solution Concept for *n*-person Noncooperative Games. International Journal of Game Theory **5**, 1977, 211–225.

–: A General Solution Concept for Both Cooperative and Noncooperative Games. Papers of the North Rhine-Westphalian Academy of Sciences, No. 287. Opladen 1979, 7–28.

–: The Shapley Value and the Risk-dominance Solutions of Two Bargaining Models for Characteristic-function Games. Essays in Game Theory and Mathematical Economics in Honor of Oskar Morgenstern. Mannheim 1981, 43–68.

Harsanyi, J.C., and *R. Selten*: A Noncooperative Solution Concept with Cooperative Applications. Book ms. in progress, 1980.

Luce, R.D., and *H. Raiffa*: Games and Decisions. New York 1957.

Nash, J.F.: Equilibrium Points in *n*-person Games. Proc. Nat. Acad. Sciences, U.S.A. **36**, 1950a, 48–49.

–: The Bargaining Problem. Econometrica **18**, 1950b, 155–162.

–: Noncooperative Games. Annals of Mathematics **54**, 1951, 286–295.

–: Two-person Cooperative Games. Econometrica **21**, 1953, 128–140.

Owen, G.: Game Theory. Philadelphia 1968.

Games, Economic Dynamics, and Time Series Analysis. 1982 ©Physica-Verlag, Wien–Würzburg

Economic Analysis via Strategy Outcome Functions: A Survey of Recent Results[1])

By *D. Schmeidler*, Tel Aviv[2])

1. General Remarks

The concept of a strategic outcome function is used for representing the institutions of trade or exchange in the economy. In this description every economic agent has access to a set of messages or *strategies*. Given a *selection of strategies*, one for each agent in the economy, the *strategic outcome function* assigns it an outcome. In the description of economic institutions of exchange an *outcome* is a list of net trades, one for every agent. *Net trade* is represented as a vector in Euclidean space whose dimension is equal to the number of commodities traded in the economy or in the institution described in the model. In order that a list of net trades will be an outcome it also has to satisfy the condition that summation of the net trades over agents yields zero in each coordinate. So, formally, a *strategic outcome function* maps selections of strategies to a subset of lists of net trades, i.e., outcomes.

A concrete example may help at this point. One of the biggest institutions of trade is the New York Stock Exchange. Economic agents are all holders or potential buyers of bonds or shares traded in the NYSE. A set of strategies consists of all conceivable orders that an economic agent can give his broker, the "commodity" in this case being a specific bond or share, or U.S. dollars. The strategie outcome function is the rule that maps the list of daily orders to changes in portfolios. This rule is not completely specified as long as trading is performed by people, not machines. When considered as an example of a strategic outcome function, the stock exchange in its daily trade has several questionable features. Some of them are related in an essential way to the concept of informational decentralization and will be discussed later. The problem of simultaneous selection of strategies is discussed now.

In the NYSE, orders are accepted during the trade period and after information about early trade becomes available. So construction of a detailed descriptive model of the NYSE calls for the extensive form (game) outcome function instead of the strategic form. Of course there is a standard way to pass from the extensive to the strategic form, but it involves a loss of information and quite complicated strategies. Let us follow the problem of a detailed description one step further. Suppose that a strategic outcome function is

---

[1]) Partially supported by NSF grant #77-27403. Thanks for helpful remarks are due to Pradeep Dubey, John Ledyard, Karl Vind and David Wettstein.

[2]) *D. Schmeidler*, Tel-Aviv University, P.O.Box 39286 Ramat-Aviv, Tel-Aviv, Israel.

intended to describe economic decisions in an economy made during, say, one year. In this case, detailed description of all the acts of economic agents does not seem to be a helpful analytical step. Our concept of strategy is therefore an abstract one: It is a rule governing the actual acts of economic agents. It should be simple enough to work with, and sophisticated enough to achieve nontrivial results. Examples of specific strategic outcome functions, particularly the last one, will elaborate on the meaning of abstract strategy sets.

What are the aims of the research surveyed here? And what is its immediate purpose? A point of view offered here is based on the presumption that institutions of trade are a human invention to the same extent as the electric engine and the internal combustion engine are human inventions. However, some of the institutions conceived for trade or for aggregation of preferences find their analogue in the concept of perpetuum mobile. Characterization of the theoretically feasible economic institutions would be a satisfactory conclusion of the first phase of this research. The key words of the last sentence are "theoretically feasible," and a concept which requires further elaboration.

Consider the problem of a planner who is asked to suggest an institution for trade that will result in allocations satisfying certain properties. The planner does not know the characteristics of the economic agents that will use the institution. He only knows that they are of a class having *neoclassical* characteristics. Agent's characteristics consist of his initial *endowments* and *preferences.* Initial endowments are represented by a nonnegative vector in Euclidean space. This vector defines, in turn, the set of *feasible net trades* for the agent; it is the set of all those net trades which, added to the initial endowment yield nonnegative vectors. The preferences are represented by a *transitive* and *total binary relation* defined on the set of feasible net trades. It is further assumed that this relation can be represented by a *quasi-concave continuous real-valued function monotonic increasing in each coordinate,* with the set of feasible net trades as its domain. This binary relation is extended to all net trades so that any feasible net trade is strictly preferred to any nonfeasible net trade.

The planner's ignorance of agents' characteristics is essential and incorrigible. The institutions he is asked to devise will be used repeatedly, and each time agents' characteristics may be different. Returning to our example, the rules of trade on NYSE will not be adjusted daily while agents' preferences and initial endowments will. On the other hand each economic agent knows not only his own characteristics and the rules of exchange, i.e. the strategic outcome function, but may have a "good" prediction as to the strategies of others.

At this point a short digression as to the concepts of descriptive predictive, and prescriptive models (or theories) is necessary. The term "prescriptive" is used here instead of the term "normative" to emphasize the noncategorical and restricted nature of the imperative. An example of a prescriptive statement would be our planner's claim: If you wish Pareto efficient outcomes you should restrict yourself to institutions, i.e. strategic outcome functions, of such and such a type. The advocated institutions are not ultimately self-compelling; the prescription is contingent on the goals stated in terms of properties of the outcomes. The relations between the three kinds of models, as well as the fact that there is no predictive theory without description and no prescription without prediction, are well known [see *Morgenstern*]. Some of the basic problems of prediction in economic or social sciences are nevertheless restated here.

Prediction of astronomic phenomena, or the weather, do not affect the behavior of nature. However, predictions of human action may affect those acts because people make their decisions on the basis of "information" in the most general sense and a prediction becomes part of the information. Hence prediction may be self-defeating. A classical example is that of the prophet Jonah who was forced by God to "predict" the destruction of Ninve in forty days. The peoples' reaction to this prophecy resulted in its nullification. An example of "successful prediction" is Cassandra's prediction of the destruction of Troy. Cassandra had the gift of foresight but was condemned to be completely disbelieved by all people. So when Cassandra told the Trojans that bringing in the horse that the Hellines had left outside the city would lead to the destruction of Troy she was totally ignored and the prophecy came true.

Is there room for correct predictions, except those totally disbelieved and ignored? A prediction which is not self defeating must have the property that given the prediction every person acts accordingly, i.e. as predicted. This is the called Nash property. Formally, a selection of strategies is said to be a *Nash equilibrium* relative to given agents' characteristics if there is no agent who can obtain, by a unilateral switch to another strategy, a net trade he considers preferable to the net trade resulting from the selection under consideration.

The prediction discussed here is made for the users of the economic institution at the time they have to choose their strategies: The prediction is assumed to be public knowledge. Secret predictions do not have to obey the Nash property and situations where differences in the information possessed by agents persist are not discussed here. In economically advanced countries economic predictions are public knowledge: There are laws and regulations whose purpose is to improve the predictions and to make information public, i.e. accessible to everyone.

I want to emphasize that the Nash property is a necessary but not necessarily a sufficient condition of successful (public) prediction. Even if each economic agent alone cannot improve his outcome on his own using a Nash prediction, a group of agents may do so by means of correlated action. So in order that a prediction will not be self-defeating it should have the strong Nash property. A selection of strategies is said to be a *strong* (Nash) *equilibrium* if for any set of economic agents and any strategies that they may select the following implication holds under the assumption that the rest of the agents stick to their original selection: If some agent in the set is better off under the new selection then there is another agent in the set that is worse off under this selection.

Of course, strong equilibrium as a necessary property of successful predictions should be qualified by availability of communication and information possibilities which greatly exceed the communication and information instruments required for Nash equilibria. However, if the strategic outcome function in use has the property that every Nash equilibrium is a strong equilibrium, then no group of agents has an incentive to invest resources in additional information.

Another two conditions necessary to obtain Nash prediction or any meaningful prediction at all are simplicity and continuity of the strategic outcome function. I will explain first the term simplicity. It seems difficult to predict the choice of strategy by each individual agent but it is easier to predict a simple function of these strategies selection, i.e. average strategy. For example, in the commuters game it is next to impossible to predict with a restriction on resources, each person's route, but good predictions of the congestion in main junctions and roads exist. Furthermore, this information suffices for a person to compute his best response, given the prediction. We refer to a function from strategies to a Euclidean space as a signalling function. A *Nash sufficient* signalling function is, by definition, such that for all strategies selections, and for each agent, optimizing his preferences over his strategies set given the strategies selection leads to the same outcome as optimizing given the signal of this strategies selection.

The condition on strategic outcome function, we have in mind, is that it will have a "simple" Nash sufficient signalling function. Here simplicity means that the signalling function is smooth and its values are of dimension of order of the number of commodities and independent of the number of agents.

The other condition necessary for any prediction of strategies to be useful is the continuity of the outcomes as a function of the strategies selected, at least in the relevant part of the domain. Otherwise any small error in the prediction, which is essentially unavoidable, will make the prediction at best irrelevant and generally confusing.

To sum up, I suggest a program of research whose first purpose is to present a menu of economic institutions fitting the different tastes in the allocations achievable via each institution. As a by-product we shall lean which distributive and allocative goals are attainable and which are not. The first phase of this program is confined completely to theory: Construction of strategic outcome functions meeting the different conditions mentioned earlier. Having evolved an idea, a first step would be to test it on a simple and well-known problem.

The allocation rule analyzed the most is no doubt the Walrasian correspondence. The first version of *Schmeidler* [1976] introduced a strategic outcome function whose Nash equilibria are Walrasian for neoclassical agents' characteristics. The second version of that work, described next, satisfies the additional condition that every Nash equilibrium is strong equilibrium. For a survey of previous works the reader is referred to the notes by *Postlewaite/Schmeidler* [1979].

2. Description of the Results

We denote the set of agents by T, the set of strategies by S and the number of commodities by l. Thus a strategic outcome function (SOF for short) $f\colon S^T \to (R^l)^T$ such that $\Sigma_{t \in T} f_t(\underset{\sim}{s}) = 0$ for all $\underset{\sim}{s}$ in S^T.

Agents' characteristics are denoted by $(\succ_t)_{t \in T}$ where $\succ_t$ stands for agent's t neoclassical preferences over R^l. We use the term *strictly neoclassical* when $\succ_t$ is induced by a vector of initial endowments, w_t, positive in each coordinate and a utility function with continuous partial derivatives.

Theorem: [*Schmeidler*, 1978]. Define $S = \{(p, z) \in R^l_{++} \times R^l \mid pz = 0 \text{ and } \sum_{i=1}^{l} p^i = 1\}$, and for all $\underset{\sim}{s} = (p_t, z_t)_{t \in T}$ in S^T and h in T define $Th = \{t \in T \mid p_t = p_h\}$ and $f_h(\underset{\sim}{s}) = z_h - \sum_{t \in Th} z_t \,/\, \#Th$. The SOF f defined here satisfies for every economy with strictly neoclassical agent's characteristics and $\#T \geqslant 3$: a) Every Nash equilibrium is strong equilibrium. b) The set of Nash equilibrium allocations is equal to the set fo Walras equilibrium allocations.

I denote by R^l_{++} the positive vectors in R^l and by R^l_+ the nonnegative vectors in R^l, where the inequalities are assumed to hold coordinatewise. Is also is assumed for *neo-classical* economy $\sum_{t\in T} w_t \in R^l_{++}$ and $\#T > 2$.

The SOF of the theorem above is not continuous. A continuous SOF whose Nash allocations coincide with Walras allocations was first constructed by *Hurwicz* [1979b]. A simplified version is presented below.

Theorem: [*Postlewaite*]. Let S be as in the previous theorem and for every $\underline{s}$ in S^T and h in T define: $a_h = \sum_{t,t' \neq h} |p_t - p_{t'}|$, $a = \sum_{t\in T} a_t$, $b_h = a_h/a$ if $a > 0$ and $b_h = 1$ if $a = 0$, $\bar{p} = \sum_{t\in T} b_t p_t$, $x_h = z_h - \bar{p}\,(\bar{p}z/\bar{p}\bar{p})$. (i.e., x_h is the orthogonal projection of z_h on the hyperplane perpendicular to $\bar{p}$), and $f_h(\underline{s}) = x_h - \sum_{t\in T} x_t/\#T$. Then for every neoclassical economy Nash allocations coincide with Walras allocations.

The term *economy* is used instead agents' characteristics and *Nash allocations* are of course the allocations resulting from Nash equilibrium.

A questionable aspect of these restuls is the individual nonfeasibility of the outcome with respect to certain neoclassical characteristics for some selections of strategies. In other words, it may happen that for some $\underline{s}$ in S^T, some agents' characteristics and some t in T, $f_t(\underline{s}) + w_t \notin R^l_+$. The possibility of individual nonfeasibility is attributed to the total informational decentralization of the model. Any (totally decentralized) SOF $f(.)$ that is balanced and nontrivial, i.e., with an $\underline{s}$ in S^T, an h in T, and $k \leqslant l$, with $f^k_h(\underline{s}) < 0$, is individually nonfeasible for some agents' characteristics where $0 < w^k_h < |f^k_h(\underline{s})|$.

To achieve feasibility for all strategies selections some of the informational decentralization must be given up. So a partially decentralized strategic outcome function, f, maps $S^T \times (R^l_+)^T$ to $(R^l)^T$ such that $f_h(\underline{s}, (w_t)_{t\in T}) + w_h \geqslant 0$ for all h in T. The initial endowments are part of the centrally collected information.

The work of Hurwicz-Maskin-Postlewaite (H-M-P) is devoted to feasible strategic outcome functions. They first observe that if for some given SOF the set of Nash allocations contains the set of Walras allocations for every neoclassical economy, that the set of Nash allocations also contains the set of *constrained Walras allocations* for every neoclassical economy. In the constrained Walras allocation every agent optimizes his preferences, by definition, over the budget set constrained by the aggregate initial endowment. (For h in T, $B_h(p, w) = \{z \in R^l \mid pz = 0 \text{ and } z + w \geqslant 0\}$ where $w = \sum_{t\in T} w_t$ and p is the vector of prices.) Once again a simplified version of a partially decentralized SOF is presented here.

Theorem: [*Postlewaite*]. Let the strategies set be the Cartesian product of the set S of the first theorem and the positive numbers. Given a selection of strategies $\underline{s} = (p_t, z_t, r_t)_{t\in T}$ and a list of initial endowments $\underline{w} = (w_t)_{t\in T}$ define, for all h in T, a_h, a, b_h, $\bar{p}$ as in the previous theorem, and define x_h to be the closest point to z_h in

$B_h(\bar{p}, w_h)$. Finally $f_h(\underline{s}) = r^* r_h x_h + (r^* r_h - 1) w_h$ where $r^* = \max \{r \in R \mid r r_t \leqslant 1, \forall t \in T$ and $\sum_{t \in T} r r_t (x_t + w_t) \leqslant w\}$. Then for every neoclassical economy the Nash allocations coincide with the constrained Walras allocations.

The SOF of the last theorem is continuous whereas the SOF of the corresponding H-M-P Theorem is not continuous. The main results in H-M-P deal with weakening of the partial informational centralization required for feasible outcomes. Instead of assuming that initial endowments are centrally known, every agent is asked to announce his initial endowment as part of his strategy, and the center can verify that the agent does not overstate his endowment for any commodity. Another way to represent this partial informational centralization is to make each agent's strategies dependent on his endowment as follows: $S_h = S \times \{x \in R^l_+ \mid x \leqslant w_h\}$.

Returning to our example of NYSE it seems that precisely this kind of partial decentralization is satisfied there. A broker will not accept every order, but only those consistent with person's initial endowment (credit and portfolio). H-M-P show in their paper that there exists a feasible partially decentralized SOF in the weak sense as above (i.e., its domain is of the form $\times_{t \in T} S_t$, given $\underline{w}$) for which the conclusion of the last theorem holds. They have a more general result, but their SOF is not continuous.

We now turn to the question of achieving redistributive goals without giving up on efficiency. *Hurwicz* [1979a] paper is a most important contribution to this topic. In our language the question can be stated as follows: *Consider a totally decentralized SOF whose Nash allocations are Pareto efficient and individually rational for every neoclassical economy.* (An allocation is said to be *individually rational* if any agent does not prefer the zero net trade to his net trade. Intuitively is means that he is not forced to participate in the trade.) The question then is, to what extent the set of Nash allocations differs from the set of Walras allocations?

Theorem [*Hurwicz*, 1979a]. a) Given a SOF as above, if the correspondence from neoclassical economies to Nash allocations is upper semicontinuous with nonempty values then Walras allocations are contained in Nash allocations for each economy. b) Given a SOF, say f, as above define for each $\underline{s}$ in S^T and h in T, $C_h(\underline{s}) = \{f_h(\underline{s} \mid h, s) \mid s \in S\}$ and $D_h(\underline{s}) = C_h(\underline{s}) - R^l_+$, and suppose that all the $D_h(\underline{s})$'s are convex. Then for any neoclassical economy each interior Nash allocation is Walrasian.

An allocation $(z_t)_{t \in T}$ is said to be *interior* if for all t in T, $z_t + w_t \in R^l_{++}$.

Theorem: [*Schmeidler*, 1980]. Suppose that a SOF is given whose Nash allocations are Pareto efficient for all strictly neoclassical economies and such that the sets $D_h(\underline{s})$, defined in the previous Theorem, are star-shaped around the origin for all $\underline{s}$ and h. Then for any strictly neoclassical economy any interior Nash allocation is Walrasian.

The last Theorem differs from but does not extend Hurwicz's Theorem part b): Although a convex set is star-shaped it does not necessarily contain the origin. However all of the SOF's appearing explicitly in this paper satisfy the star-shaped condition. It is easy to see that the last two Theorems have their analogues for feasible and partially centralized SOF's. It also should be mentioned that the results in Hurwicz's two papers quoted here extend to public goods and Lindahl equilibria.

The view of the results surveyed till now was that prescriptions of design problems for decentralized allocation mechanisms. Shubik however emphasized the descriptive (positive) aspect of the SOF that he and others investigate. The model to the surveyed now is a natural continuation of these works.

If we think to Walras equilibrium as an ill defined SOF it has an aspect totally unrealistic for markets with oldigopolists: When an agent considers his best response he assumes that the price is fixed (zero elasticity) independently of the quantities he is going to buy or sell. The Shapley/Shubik SOF has an equally unrealistic assumption on the quantity side. While considering his best response (at Nash equilibrium) the agent assumes that the quantities committed by others on each market will not be changed independently of the quantities supplied by him. Okuno/Schmeidler make the assumption that the economic agent commit themselves to a linear excess demand function (i.e. linear response)

I will discuss here the numeraire version of the model. Shapley and Shubik choose as agents' strategic variables quantity of commodity offered and quantity of numeraire offered on each market. Okuno/Schmeidler also assign two numbers to each commodity, the coefficients of the linear excess demand function for this commodity (as a function of price in units of the numeraire). An agent considering his best response assumes that others are committed to these linear excess demand functions and not to constant demands and supplies. The difference between Shapley/Shubik and Okuno/Schmeidler rules is the same as approximating a function by a constant function and approximating a function by a linear function.

Formally set $S = R^{l-1}_{++} \times R^{l-1}$ where l is the numeraire commodity. Given $s = (a, b)$, agent's t excess demand for commodity k, $(1 \leqslant k \leqslant l-1)$ is $b^k_t - a^k_t p^k$. Denoting $\bar{a}^k = \sum_{t \in T} a^k_t$ and $\bar{b}^k = \sum_{t \in T} b^k_t$ the price that clears the k-th market is $\bar{b}^k/\bar{a}^k$. So given a selection of strategies $\underline{s} = (a_t, b_t)_{t \in T}$, agent h in T and commodity k, $(1 \leqslant k \leqslant l-1)$;

$$f^k_h(\underline{s}) = b^k_h - a^k_h \bar{b}^k/\bar{a}^k; \; f^l_h(\underline{s}) = -\sum_{k=1}^{l-1} (b^k_h - a^k_h \bar{b}/\bar{a}^k)\, \bar{b}^k/\bar{a}^k.$$

Theorem: [*Okuno/Schmeidler*] a) There exists a Nash equilibrium for any neoclassical economy. Furthermore, for any list $(a_t)_{t \in T}$ in $(R^{l-1}_{++})^T$ and for any neoclassical economy (same T) there exist a list $(b_t)_{t \in T}$ in $(R^{l-1})^T$ such that $\underline{s} = (a_t, b_t)_{t \in T}$ is a Nash equilibrium for that economy. b) Given $(a_t)_{t \in T}$ as above but T also variable and all a^k_t uniformly bounded away from zero, then for "large" T any corresponding Nash allocation is approximately efficient. c) Fix T and make $(a_t)_{t \in T}$ variables. If for each k and t, a^k_t is "large" then the corresponding Nash allocation is approximately Walrasian.

The approximation concepts are those of Postlewaite/Schmeidler. In this model Nash equilibria may not be perfect. Agent facing (or predicting) a random strategy of others is better off to commit himself to a linear excess demand function at equilibrium. This result and other properties of perfect Nash equilibria also appear in Okuno/Schmeidler. Finally I would like to point out that agent's strategies in this model can not be interpreted as his acts but as rules governing his actual acts on the market.

The survey is concluded with a question. Except for the first theorem, the Nash equilibria of all other SOF's are not necessarily strong equilibria. Is it possible to construct a *continuous* SOF whose Nash equilibria are strong and Pareto efficient for all economies?

References

Hurwicz, L.: On Allocations Attainable Through Nash Equilibria. Journal of Economic Theory **21**, 1979a, 140–165.

–: Outcome Functions Yielding Walrasian and Lindahl Allocations at Nash Equilibrium Points. Review of Economic Studies, 1979b, 217–225.

Hurwicz, L., E. Maskin and *A. Postlewaite* (in prepatation): Feasible Implementation of Social Choice Correspondence by Nash Equilibria.

Morgenstern, O.: Descriptive, Predictive and Normative Theory. Kyklos **25**, 1972, 699–714.

Okuno, M., and *D. Schmeidler*: In preparation.

Postlewaite, A.: Private correspondence, 1980.

Postlewaite, A., and *D. Schmeidler*: Notes on Optimality and Feasibility of Informationally Decentralized Mechanisms. Game Theory and Related Topics. Ed. by O. Moeschlin and D. Pallaschke (eds.). Amsterdam 1979, 365–382.

Schmeidler, D.: Walrasian Analysis via Strategic Outcome Functions (It is a revised version of "A Remark on a Game Theoretical Interpretation of Walras Equilibria", mimeo 1976). Econometrica **48**, 1980, 1585–1593.

–: A Condition Guaranteeing that the Nash Allocation is Walrasian, 1980. To appear in Journal of Economic Theory.

Schotter, A., and *G. Schwödiauer*: Economics and Game Theory: A Survey, 1979.

Games, Economic Dynamics, and Time Series Analysis. 1982 ©Physica-Verlag, Wien–Würzburg

The Worth of a Cooperative Enterprise to Each Member

By *M. Maschler*, Jerusalem[1])

1. Introduction

It is well known that game theory – especially cooperative game theory – is rich in "solution concepts"; namely, recommendations to choose particular payoff-vectors as outcomes of games in a given class. This state of affairs makes it necessary to choose a particular solution, whenever one encounters a real-life conflict. Thus, it is highly desirable to know, when and why a certain solution should be preferred to others. Putting it more mildly, it is desirable to know, what aspects does each solution reflect in any given real case. Contributions in these areas increase the applicability of game theory. They also shed light on the nature of the various solutions.

The present paper is a contribution of this type. We address ourselves to the following "real conflict": Consider a cooperative enterprise whose members have decided to sell it out and distribute its worth among themselves. How should they share the revenue? One method, often employed, is to share it in proportion to the investments of the members. Variants of this method appear in the form of shares, which are distributed by many companies. But, there is another method, based on a different principle, which is often employed by an "enterprise" consisting of husband and wife, who want to decide on a divorce settlement. According to this method, wife takes back every item that she brought to the marriage, husband does the same and the rest is divided equally among the couple[2]). Can this procedure be generalized to more than two members?

In Section 2 we describe the various real situations we have in mind. We then construct abstract games to represent them. Section 3 suggests a procedure that generalizes the divorce procedure. *A priori,* this procedure raises some queries and suggests conjectures. In Section 4 we resolve the queries and prove the conjectures. It turns out that our procedure leads to a celebrated solution of the corresponding abstract game[3]). Section 5 is devoted to various comments, concerning, among other things, the insight gained on the nature of the solution concept.

---

[1]) *M. Maschler*, The Hebrew University, Jerusalem, Israel.

[2]) I owe this observation to Heinz Schleicher, who drew my attention to the fact that this procedure is often used. In fact, there are countries in which this is the legal procedure, unless marriage arrangements specify otherwise.

[3]) To keep an element of surprise, we do not disclose at present the identity of the solution. Everyone who wants to miss the fun may turn directly to Section 4.

2. Cooperative Enterprises and their Representation as Games

To generalize a "marriage enterprise", we consider a set $N = \{1,2, \ldots, n\}$ of *members* of the enterprise, whom we allow to *own* assets of the enterprise. As long as the enterprise is functioning, these assets serve its needs and all profits are distributed to the members in a way that need not concern us[4]). However, the assets are still legally owned by the members, who are entitled to claim their worths when the enterprise is sold out.

Of course, if there are debts on such assets, such as mortgages and other loans, the owners are responsible to pay them off.

We also allow for the possibility that certain assets are owned by sets consisting of several members. Thus, if one identifies a member i with the set $\{i\}$, one can associate with each subset S of N, called "coalition", the set $a(S)$ of all the assets owned by S. We can also speak about $b(S)$, which is the set of all assets owned by subsets of S:

$$b(S) = \cup \{a(R): R \subseteq S\}. \tag{2.1}$$

Example 2.1. A cooperative enterprise of three members 1, 2 and 3 operates a garage, a gasoline station, a store and a restaurant. Historically, it developed as follows: 1, who owned the garage, formed a partnership with 2, who owned the gasoline station. They worked together for a while, and since business was prosperous, they both bought and opened the store, hiring someone to serve the customers. Later, their neighbour 3, who owned the restaurant, jointed the partnership and they all hoped that this enlarged enterprise will attract additional customers. Unfortunately, difficulties originating from differences in personalities made it impossible to continue and all agreed to sell everything and terminate the partnership. Of course, 1 still owned the garage, etc. Thus[5])

$$\begin{array}{llll} a(\{1\}) = \{\text{garage}\}, & a(\{2\}) = \{\text{gasoline station}\}, & & \\ a(\{3\}) = \{\text{restaurant}\}, & a(\{1,2\}) = \{\text{store}\}, & & a(\{1,3\}) = \emptyset, \\ a(\{2,3\}) = \emptyset, & a(\{1,2,3\}) = \emptyset, & \text{and} & a(\emptyset) = \emptyset. \end{array}$$

The function $b(\cdot)$ can now be computed, using (2.1).

Our next step will be to represent situations such as the above as characteristic-function games $(N; v)$. To do so, we shall define:

$$v(S) = \textit{the present net worth of the set of assets } b(S). \tag{2.2}$$

The worth is measured in a fixed monetary unit. We base the definition of $v(S)$ on $b(S)$, instead of on $a(S)$, in order to reflect the idea that a coalition S can claim all the benefits when $b(S)$ is sold. It may well be, for example, that $b(S)$ can get a better price if it is sold as one package instead of as separate items. Of course, when $v(S)$ is claimed by S, one still has to decide on its distribution among the members of S. Such distribution should take into account the various claims $v(R)$, $R \subseteq S$.

---

[4]) We do not rule out the possibility that this distribution is also influenced by arguments used in this paper.

[5]) For simplicity we ignore items that were bought, say, for the garage, after the partnership started; these should be included in $a(\{1,2\})$ or in $a(\{1,2,3\})$.

Example 2.1 (cont.). The characteristic function for this example could be:

$$\nu(\{1\}) = 30, \quad \nu(\{2\}) = 12, \quad \nu(\{3\}) = 6,$$
$$\nu(\{1,2\}) = 36, \quad \nu(\{1,3\}) = 36, \quad \nu(\{2,3\}) = 48,$$
$$\nu(\{1,2,3\}) = 81, \quad \nu(\emptyset) = 0,$$

where the worths are measured in a certain monetary unit. There is a high mortgage on the store, which accounts for the fact that $\nu(\{1,2\}) < \nu(\{1\}) + \nu(\{2\})$. The gasoline station and the restaurant can get a higher price if sold as one package instead of as separate items; therefore, $\nu(\{2,3\}) > \nu(\{2\}) + \nu(\{3\})$, etc.

3. Sharing the Worth of the Enterprise

To find a procedure for sharing the worth of the enterprise in a way which resembles the divorce settlement, let us proceed naively, working with the figures in Example 2.1.

Let us assume that $\{3\}$ claims the worth of his restaurant; then 3 gets paid 6 units, and this amount should be deducted from all coalitions containing $\{3\}$. Indeed, their worth is based on a package of items that contains $b(\{3\})$, but they have to return $\nu(\{3\})$ to 3, whenever he claims it. We thus arrive at a new game $(N; \nu^1)$, where

$$\nu^1(\{1\}) = 30, \quad \nu^1(\{2\}) = 12, \quad \nu^1(\{3\}) = 0, \quad \nu^1(\{1,2\}) = 36,$$
$$\nu^1(\{1,3\}) = 30, \quad \nu^1(\{2,3\}) = 42, \quad \nu^1(\{1,2,3\}) = 75, \quad \nu^1(\emptyset) = 0.$$

Suppose now that $\{1,2\}$ claims its worth of 36 units, then 1 and 2 get 18 each, and we arrive at a game $(N; \nu^2)$ by deducting 36 from each coalition containing $\{1,2\}$, leaving the rest unchanged. Later, $\{1\}$ will claim the worth of his assets. He will get paid 30 units and a debt of 30 will be imposed on all coalitions containing 1, including $\{1,2\}$. Similar debts will be imposed when 2 claims his worth. These debts will be shared by $\{1,2\}$ in equal parts, so that in fact, $\{1,2\}$ will be sharing equally only $\nu(\{1,2\}) - \nu(\{1\}) - \nu(\{2\})$. Similar reasonings hold for all coalitions. Table 1 exhibits a possible sequence of events. It leads to a final payoff-vector: (30,27,24).

1	2	3	{1}	{2}	{3}	{1,2}	{1,3}	{2,3}	{1,2,3}	
0	0	0	30	12	6	36	36	48	81	: ν^1
0	0	6	30	12	0	36	30	42	75	: ν^2
18	18	0	30	12	0	0	30	42	39	: ν^3
30	0	0	0	12	0	−30	0	42	9	: ν^4
0	12	0	0	0	0	−42	0	30	−3	: ν^5
0	15	15	0	0	0	−42	0	0	−33	: ν^6
−11	−11	−11	0	0	0	−42	0	0	0	: ν^7
−21	−21	0	0	0	0	0	0	0	42	: ν^8
14	14	14	0	0	0	0	0	0	0	: ν^9
30	27	24								

Tab. 1: A possible sequence for arriving at a share

The above procedure certainly generalizes the divorce settlement, but it raises several doubts: Does every sequence lead to the same payoff-vector? Must it be a finite process? Shall one always obtain a share of $v(N)$? These questions will be answered in Section 4. Here we would like to examine a particular sequence; namely, a shortest sequence obtained when 1-person coalitions claim their worths first, then – 2-person coalitions and finally – the grand coalition. Table 2 exhibits such a sequence.

1	2	3	{1}	{2}	{3}	{1,2}	{1,3}	{2,3}	{1,2,3}	
0	0	0	30	12	6	36	36	48	81	: v^1
30	0	0	0	12	6	6	6	48	51	: v^2
0	12	0	0	0	6	−6	6	36	39	: v^3
0	0	6	0	0	0	−6	0	30	33	: v^4
− 3	− 3	0	0	0	0	0	0	30	39	: v^5
0	15	15	0	0	0	0	0	0	9	: v^6
3	3	3	0	0	0	0	0	0	0	: v^7
30	27	24								

Tab. 2: A shortest sequence for arriving at a share

The fact that we have arrived at the same final payoff-vector suggests that the procedure may have some merits. Let us therefore formulate it precisely:

Procedure 3.1. Starting with the original game $(N; v)$, define a sequence of games $(N; v) \equiv (N; v^0)$, $(N; v^1)$, $(N; v^2)$, . . . and payoff-vectors as follows: At game $(N; v^k)$, a coalition S_k, for which $v^k(S_k) \neq 0$, claims its worth $v^k(S_k)$, which is shared by the members of S_k in equal parts. The game $(N; v^{k+1})$ is given by

$$v^{k+1}(R) = \begin{cases} v^k(R) - v^k(S_k), & \text{whenever} \quad R \supseteq S_k, \\ v^k(R), & \text{otherwise.} \end{cases} \tag{3.1}$$

The process terminates when all coalitions arrive at a zero worth. The final payoff is the amount of money that was accumulated at each step.

4. Justifying the Procedure

The next two theorems will show that Procedure 3.1 is sound.

Theorem 4.1. Procedure 3.1 must always terminate in a finite number of steps.

Proof: When a coalition claims its worth, its new worth becomes zero. It can regain a non-zero worth only after a proper subcoalition has claimed its own worth. Suppose that a process is endless, then at least one coalition claims its worth infinitely often, so that there exists a coalition S of minimal size, that claims its worth infinitely often. This can only occur, if a proper subcoalition claims its own worth infinitely often, contrary to the minimality of the size of S. The contradiction shows that each sequence of Procedure 3.1 must be finite.

Theorem 4.2. Regardless of the sequence chosen for Procedure 3.1, the final share is the Shapley value of the game $(N; v)$.

Proof: By (3.1), $v^k = v^{k+1} + w^k$, where

$$w^k(R) = \begin{cases} v^k(S_k) & \text{whenever } N \supseteq R \supseteq S_k, \\ 0 & \text{otherwise.} \end{cases} \tag{4.1}$$

Here, $(N; v^k)$, $k = 0,1, \ldots, p$, is a particular sequence. Thus, $v = v^1 + w^0 = v^2 + w^1 + + w^0 = \cdots = v^p + w^{p-1} + w^{p-2} + \cdots + w^0$. Now, $v^p = 0$; therefore, $v = w^0 + + w^1 + \cdots + w^{p-1}$. In the game $(N; w^k)$, the players of Sk are symmetric and the others are zero-players; therefore, its Shapley value specifies $v(S_k)/|S_k|$ to each member of S_k and 0 to the others. This is precisely the way $v(S_k)$ was shared in the procedure. The proof concludes by using the additivity property of the Shapley value. See *Shapley* [1953].

Remark 4.3; The shortest sequences obtain if 1-person coalitions claims their worths first, then – two-person coalitions, etc. In such sequences no coalition claims its worth more than once. For a game "in a general position" it takes $2^n - 1$ steps. This short sequence was treated by *Harsanyi* [1959], and he already observed that it leads to the Shapley value. Thus, Theorem 4.2 is a generalization of Harsanyi's result. The proof is new. Harsanyi used the procedure in order to describe a bargaining process that leads participants of an arbitrary cooperative game to the Shapley value. We apply the procedure for the particular case of liquidating a cooperative enterprise, where, we believe, it is particularly attractive; at any rate, it is not a game in the usual sense (see Section 5).

Remark 4.4. [6]) Largest sequences are obtained if a coalition is allowed to claim its non-zero worth only if each coalition containing it properly has a zero worth. Such sequences may be quite long even for small values of n. Let s_n be the number of steps needed by such a sequence for a game "in a general position". It can easily be shown that s_n satisfies the recursion formula:

$$s_n = \binom{n}{0}(s_0 + 1) + \binom{n}{1}(s_1 + 1) + \ldots + \binom{n}{n-1}(s_{n-1} + 1), \quad s_0 = 0. \tag{4.2}$$

This recursive formula can be used to compute s_n for a small n; however, for theoretical purposes it is worthwhile to note that

$$s_n = \sum_{k=1}^{\infty} \frac{k^n}{2^k} - 1. \tag{4.3}$$

[6]) The problems described in this remark were raised and solved by Micha A. Perles. We supply here enough information so that the reader can prove the results for himself, but we omit the details in order not to depart significantly from the main line of this paper.

(The proof is by varifying (4.2).) Using the Stirling numbers of the second kind, $S(n, k)$, we can express s_n as a finite sum:

$$s_n = 1!\, S(n,1) + 2!\, S(n,2) + \ldots + n!\, S(n,n). \tag{4.4}$$

Estimating (4.3) by the integral $\int_0^\infty x^n/2^x\,dx$, we can obtain a rough estimate for s_n; namely,

$$s_n = \frac{n!}{(\ln 2)^{n+1}} \left(1 + O\left(\frac{1}{\sqrt{n}}\right)\right), \tag{4.5}$$

which yields a good idea about the speed of the growth of s_n, as n grows.

5. Afterthought

It is well known that many solution concepts for side-payment cooperative games $(N; v)$ can be employed, even if v is measured in monetary units instead of utilities. No requirement of transferable utility is needed; one merely requires that utility of money is a concave function for each player or, alternatively, that the rules of the game prohibit performing lotteries. Among such solutions one can name the core, the von-Neumann Morgenstern stable sets and the bargaining set. Indeed, one can employ them directly on "money games", because all they need to be justified is the obviously true assumption, that each player prefers to have more money than less.[7]) The Shapley value is an exception: Indeed, if one uses the Shapley value to find the expectation from playing a game, one must measure v in von-Neumann Morgenstern utilities, and one must assume that these utilities are transferable. This paper shows that the Shapley value can also be employed for finite "money games" – although of a certain kind.

If one agrees that Procedure 3.1 is sound, it is natural for him to ask whether the Shapley value could be recommended without the procedure – merely on the merit of the axioms that define it in *Shapley* [1953]. Clearly, one wants to share $v(N)$. The symmetry axiom imposes an obvious fairness requirement. Null players are players without assets – clearly they cannot claim anything, if the property of the enterprise is sold. It remains to check the additivity axiom: Imagine that the same members participate in two enterprises $(N; v)$ and $(N; w)$. Suppose also that there are no complementarity relations between the assets of the two enterprises so that $b^v(S) \cup b^w(S)$ is worth exactly $v(S) +$ $+ w(S)$ for each $S, S \subseteq N$. Under such circumstances it seems only reasonable that $v(N)$ and $w(N)$ be shared separately,[8]) even if one happens to regard both enterprises as a single enterprise $(N; v + w)$.

---

[7]) Thus an objection (a domination relation) is a sound concept for "money games", because it yields each player of a coalition actually more money. (See *Aumann* [1967, section 8], where this issue is dealt more thoroughly and in relation to the theory of cooperative games without side payments.)

[8]) In fact, the method of sharing in proportion to the investments (see Section 1) can be criticized, *because it is not additive.* Try the games: $N = \{1,2\}$, $v(\{1\}) = 20$, $v(\{2\}) = 30$, $v(\{1,2\}) = 100$, $w(\{1\}) = 10$, $w(\{2\}) = 40$, $w(\{1,2\}) = 1000$, $v(\phi) = w(\phi) = 0$.

Mathematically, $(N; v)$ is an abstract game. When applied to real cases, it may have various interpretations. For example, $v(S)$ can be interpreted as the worth of S, *if it is formed.* Under such an interpretation, one may argue that $(N; v + w)$ does not represent "properly" the aggregate of the games $(N; v)$ and $(N; w)$, because S may be "more likely" to form in one of these games and less likely – in the other. No such objection can be raised in the case of the cooperative enterprise. Here, *all coalitions already exist.* They were formed before and while the organization of the enterprise was completed. These coalitions are responsible for their assets (including debts) and they all must liquidate. Under such circumstances, the additivity axiom is particularly attractive. Having observed this, perhaps we should not be surprised to find out that the Shapley value emerged.

References

Aumann, R.J.: A survey of cooperative games without side payments. Essays in Mathematical Economics in Honor of Oskar Morgenstern. Ed. by M. Shubik. Princeton 1967, 3–27.

Harsanyi, J.C.: A bargaining model for the cooperative n-person game. Contributions to the Theory of Games, IV. Ed. by A.W. Tucker and R.D. Luce. Annals of Mathematics Studies 40, Princeton 1959, 325–355.

Shapley, L.S.: A value for n-person games. Contributions to the Theory of Games, II. Ed. by H.W. Kuhn and A.W. Tucker. Annals of Mathematics Studies 28, Princeton 1953, 307–317.

Games, Economic Dynamics, and Time Series Analysis. 1982 ©Physica-Verlag, Wien–Würzburg

On Values, Location Conflicts, and Public Goods

By *J. Rosenmüller*, Bielefeld[1])

1. Introduction

1.1 General Remarks

The purpose of this paper is to define a concept of equilibrium for economies with public goods and production. Generally speaking, this concept represents an attempt to generalize the notion of the Lindahl-equilibrium while simultaneously the idea of the "fair value", as defined within the framework of Game Theory, is introduced into the model. Also we are dealing with the question which kind of possible taxation policies are feasible in order to admit our notion of equilibrium.

As the production mechanism of our economy is just given by an aggregate production set, the taxation mechanism may be viewed just as a method to decentralize the decision as to which bundle of public goods should be produced. In fact, there are two quantities that can be viewed as externally imposed institutional financing mechanism: The value (in the sense of Cooperative Game Theory) and the taxation structure or policy. These notions will interact as follows.

As the consumer pays taxes towards the consumption of the public goods, his budget set, given prices for private goods, is restricted. Hence, if it so happens that for large bundles of public goods the marginal cost of providing these goods for the consumer exceeds his marginal utilities for the private goods, then his preference for public goods eventually will decrease. This idea is discussed e.g. in the paper of *Zeckhauser/Weinstein* [1974]. It will then happen that, given prices for private goods, the consumer will have "satiation points", "bliss points", with respect to the public goods. However, in general these satiation points will vary with different consumers, and hence the question occurs which public bundle actually should be produced.

The Lindahl equilibrium concept can be interpreted as to answer this question as follows: Taxes can be set up linearly and individually for each consumer such that the consumers do have a common bliss point while simultaneously maximizing their utility within their budget constraints. In our context, however, it is suggested that different policies of taxations are considered; for instance taxation might be linear and equal for each consumer. In this case we cannot expect that consumers have a common "bliss point". This is where the game theoretical value enters the picture as has been discussed in several recent papers [*Ostmann*, 1978, 1979; *Richter*, 1979a, b, c; *Rosenmüller*,

[1]) Prof. Dr. *J. Rosenmüller*, Institut für Mathematische Wirtschaftsforschung, Universität Bielefeld, Universitätsstraße, D–4800 Bielefeld 1.

1978, 1979]. Values, as discussed in Game Theory, can be redefined or newly defined in conflict situations that do not feature the usual game theoretical assumption of a "threat point" but rather enjoy the property of having "bliss points". Such situations typically occur in what we would like to call "location conflicts": This is a structure which features utility functions having a bliss point that is usually different for all players involved. The value is then a mapping which assigns fair solutions or "fair locations" to a certain class of bliss point problems or "location problems".

As our analysis of the underlying economy leads to a system where the consumers do have different bliss points with respect to the utility of public goods, it is suggested that a notion of the fair value as developed in *Ostmann* [1979], *Richter* [1979c], *Rosenmüller* [1978] might be applied to the corresponding location problem. This then can be seen as adding the notion of "fairness" to the institutional financing mechanism. Hence the society has the possibility of choosing a certain value concept which is then applied to the location problem resulting from the utilities as defined for public goods. This yields what one could call the "fair bundle of public goods". Prices for private goods and taxes (within the constitutional framework) should then be set in a way such that every consumer maximizes utility within his budget set with respect to the private goods. Moreover, the "fair bundle" is produced and finally the result is feasible in a sense that it can be obtained by the underlying production mechanism. As it turns out in most cases (and in particular in the case of linear but equal taxation as considered here) that production is effective in the sense that it takes place at the boundary of the aggregate production set provided the production structure is of constant returns to scale. However, typically it will happen that the distribution of private goods cannot be identified to be Pareto optimal, that is, the advocated equilibrium concept is a "second best model" or, to use a phrase of *Zeckhauser/Weinstein* [1974], a "mechanism constrained Pareto optimum".

In other words, if the society chooses to have the notion of justice enter via introduction of a "value" and a "fair tax system", then it usually will have to pay for it with a non-Pareto-optimal solution. On the other hand, the Lindahl equilibrium is an example where the taxation policy admits of a Pareto optimal solution – but in the framework of our concept cannot be called a fair taxation policy.

It should be noted that our present model also bears a resemblance to certain set-ups which appear within the framework of "voting equilibria", "voting market equilibria", etc. In this context, we restrain ourselves to citing only a few relevant papers, e.g. *McKelvey/Wendell* [1976], *Slutsky* [1977], and *Denzau/Parks* [1978]. Conceivably, a "voting equilibrium" is a "value" in the sense of Section 3 and thus, our general existence theorem may have implications with respect to the existence problem treated in *Slutsky* [1977], *Denzau/Parks* [1978].

However, the general version of a value (in the sense of Game Theory, or as defined in Section 3) respects the shape of the players' utilities more generally compared to "voting in finitely many directions". Also, we prefer the taxation functions not to be fixed in advance, the relation, say, between the equilibrium treated in *Slutsky* [1977] and the present model is not quite obvious. At this state of affairs we prefer to postpone this question to a possible latter treatment.

In what follows Section 2 gives a short introduction and specifies the conditions to be imposed upon utilities and taxations. Section 3 will recall some basic features of location conflicts as defined in *Richter* [1979a, 1979c]. Finally Section 4 will define the equilibrium concept and give proofs for existence.

1.2 Notations

Vectors $x \in \mathbf{R}^m \times \mathbf{R}$ will be written $x = (\mathring{x}, x_{m+1}) = (\mathring{x}, \xi)$ where $\mathring{x} \in \mathbf{R}^m_+$ and $x_{m+1} = \xi \in \mathbf{R}$. Similarly, if

$$\mathbf{P}^{m+1} := \{p \in \mathbf{R}^{m+1} \mid p \geqslant 0, \sum_{i=1}^{m+1} p_i = 1\}$$

denotes the "price simplex", then $p \in \mathbf{P}^{m+1}$ is written

$$p = (\mathring{p}, p_{m+1}) = (\mathring{p}, \rho).$$

Symbols e^i are reserved for the i-th unit vector while $e = (1, \ldots, 1)$.

$|\ |$ is the Euclidian norm, α^+ denotes max $(\alpha, 0)$ (for $\alpha \in \mathbf{R}$). As for vectors, x^+ is defined coordinate-wise. If $f: T \to \mathbf{R}$ is a function, then $M_{T_0} f$ denotes the maximizers of f with respect to $T_0 \subseteq T$.

$S_r(x)$ denotes the sphere with center x and radius r.

2. Economies

2.1 General Definitions

An *economy* (with public goods and production) is a tupel

$$\mathbf{M} = (\Omega, X \times \mathbf{R}^l_+, U, A, b, Y)$$

where the quantities are specified as follows.

$\Omega = \{1, \ldots, n\}$ represents the set of *players* (traders, agents, consumers) and $X = \mathbf{R}^m_+ \times \mathbf{R}$ is the system of bundles of private goods. Private good $m + 1$ appears in negative quantities and has certain aspects of a booking account; thus players may be willing to accept negative quantities of $m + 1$ in exchange for goods of other types. $\mathbf{R}^l_+$ represents bundles of public goods.

Next, $U = (u^i)_{i \in \Omega}$, where $u^i := X \times \mathbf{R}^l_+ \to \mathbf{R}$ $(i \in \Omega)$ is the family of *utility functions* of the players. Each u^i is assumed to be continuous, strictly monotone, and concave.

$A = (a^i)_{i \in \Omega}, 0 < a^i \in X$ $(i \in \Omega)$ indicates the players' initial *holdings* of *private goods*, while $b \in \mathbf{R}^l_+$ is the economy's *initial endowment* of *public goods*.

Finally, $Y \subseteq \mathbf{R}^{m+1} \times \mathbf{R}^l_+$ is the *aggregate production set*. We assume that Y is closed, convex, and contains 0. Moreover, if $(x, y) \in Y$ and $x' \in \mathbf{R}^{m+1}$, $x' \leqslant x$, then $(x', y) \in Y$ ("free disposal"). Thus, in particular, $(x, 0) \in Y$ for all $x \in \mathbf{R}^{m+1}_-$ is required. In addition,

$$\{(x, y) \in Y \mid x \geqslant x'\}$$

is assumed to be compact for every $x' \in \mathbf{R}^{m+1}_+$.

If $(x, y) \in Y$ is such that $(x', y') \geqslant (x, y)$, $(x', y') \in Y$ implies $x' = x$, $y' = y$, then we shall say that (x, y) is *efficient*.

For technical reasons, it will be necessary to have truncated versions of **M**. Thus, let k be an integer such that

$$\sum_{i \in \Omega} a^i \leqslant ke. \tag{1}$$

Define

$${}^0\mathcal{X}^k := \{x = (\mathring{x}, \xi) \in \mathbf{R}_+^{m+1} \mid x \leqslant ke\} \tag{2}$$

$${}^k\mathcal{X}^k := \{x = (\mathring{x}, \xi) \in \mathbf{R}_+^m \times \mathbf{R} \mid \mathring{x} \leqslant ke, -k \leqslant \xi \leqslant k\} \tag{3}$$

$${}^k\mathcal{Z}^k := \{x = (\mathring{x}, \xi) \in \mathbf{R}^m \times \mathbf{R} \mid -ke \leqslant x \leqslant ke\} \tag{4}$$

$$\mathcal{Y}^k := \{(x, y) \in \mathcal{Y} \mid -x \in {}^0\mathcal{X}^{nk}\} \tag{5}$$

$$\underline{\bar{Y}}^k := \{y \in \mathbf{R}^{l+} \mid \exists\, x \in {}^0\mathcal{X}^{nk}: (-x, y) \in \mathcal{Y}^k\} = \mathrm{Proj}_2\, \mathcal{Y}^k \tag{6}$$

Then

$$\mathbf{M}^k := (\Omega, {}^k\mathcal{X}^k \times \underline{\bar{Y}}^k, U, A, b, \mathcal{Y}) \tag{7}$$

is the *truncated version* of **M**.

Note that, by our requirements, $\mathcal{X}^k$, $\underline{\bar{Y}}^k$, and $\mathcal{Y}^k$ are compact sets. Also, u^i $(i \in \Omega)$ should be restricted to $\mathcal{X}^k \times \underline{\bar{Y}}^k$ in (7), however, we shall not introduce a further symbol.

As has been said, commodity $m + 1$ playes a particular role as it is available in large negative quantities; in fact we are tempted to call it "fiat money". (In particular our results should be applicable in the case of a "transferable utility market" as introduced by *Shapley* [1964] and extensively treated e.g. in *Aumann/Shapley* [1974], *Aumann* [1975], and similar papers.)

However, we want the consumer to be aversive against high debts in terms of "money" compared with positive quantities of the non-monetarian private goods. More exactly, if he pays proportionally to private goods in terms of the monetarian good, then given any proportional constant, the consumer should not be willing to buy arbitrarily large amounts of private non-monetarian goods in return for "money". This is a requirement to the utility functions as expressed by the following definition. In fact, mathematically it is necessary to insure that maximizing within someones budget constraints is a reasonable concept.

Definition 2.1: u^i is said to be *admissible* if, for $y \in \mathbf{R}_+^l$, $t > 0$, there exists $r > 0$ such that

$$u^i(\mathring{x}, -t\,|\mathring{x}|, y) < u^i(0, 0, y) \text{ whenever } |\mathring{x}| \geqslant r. \tag{8}$$

M is *admissible* if u^i is admissible for $i \in \Omega$.

Given prices for private goods, say $p \in \mathbf{P}^{m+1}$ and a bundle $y \in \mathbf{R}_+^l$, consumer i, having some wealth $w \in \mathbf{R}$ available, wants to maximize his utility within his budget constraints. Indeed, we have

Lemma 2.2: If u^i is admissible, then, for $p \in \mathbf{P}^{m+1}$, $y \in \mathbf{R}^l_+$, $w \in \mathbf{R}$

$$\max \{u^i(x, y) \mid x \in X, px \leqslant w\}$$

exists whenever $p > 0$.

The proof is an easy exercise:
If $|x|$ is sufficiently large and w.l.o.g. $\mathring{x} \neq 0$, then

$$px \leqslant w, \mathring{p}\mathring{x} + \rho \xi \leqslant w$$

implies

$$\xi \leqslant \frac{w - \mathring{p}\mathring{x}}{\rho} \leqslant -t \, |\mathring{x}| \quad \text{for a suitable } t > 0.$$

Hence

$$\begin{aligned} u^i(x, y) &= u^i(\mathring{x}, \xi, y) \\ &\leqslant u^i(\mathring{x}, -t\,|\mathring{x}|, y) < u^i(0, 0, y). \end{aligned}$$

For fixed prices of private goods, the players will have utility functions defined on public goods and wealth via

Definition 2.3: Let u^i be admissible.
Then, for $p \in \mathbf{P}^{m+1}$, $p > 0$

$$\mathring{u}^{pi}: \mathbf{R}^l_+ \times \mathbf{R} \to \mathbf{R}$$

is defined by

$$\mathring{u}^{pi}(y, w) := \max \{u^i(x, y) \mid x \in X, px \leqslant w\}. \tag{9}$$

Similarly, for $p \in \mathbf{P}^{m+1}$ and k sufficiently large,

$$\overset{kpi}{u} : \underline{\bar{Y}}^k \times [-p_{m+1}k, \infty) \to \mathbf{R}$$

is defined by

$$\overset{kpi}{u}(y, w) := \max \{u^i(x, y) \mid x \in {}^k X^k, px \leqslant w\}. \tag{10}$$

Of course, the existence of (10) is trivial while Lemma 2.2.2 ensures the existence of (9).

2.2 Taxation

We have so far discussed properties of the underlying economy. Let us now turn to the taxation structure. Generally speaking, taxation is used as a means to decentralize the decision of producing a certain bundle of public goods. Hence the players will be asked to pay a certain fee towards the production of public goods. This in turn will restrict their budget possibilities. We shall assume that taxation function will provide increasing marginal costs for the players.

Definition 2.4: A *taxation function* is a continuous, strictly monotone, and convex mapping

$$c: \mathbf{R}^l_+ \to \mathbf{R}.$$

If c^i is a taxation function ($i \in \Omega$), then $C = (c^1, \ldots, c^n)$ is a *taxation scheme.*
Let $\mathbf{C} := \{C \mid C \text{ is a taxation scheme}\}$, then $\mathbf{C}^0 \subseteq \mathbf{C}$ is called a *taxation policy.*

By introducing the notation of a "taxation policy" as a subset of the possible taxation schemes we imagine that the society has certain notions in advance as to which tax schemes are in some sense "feasible" by customs or institutional restrictions. This is a decision which enters the picture externally. It concerns the type of taxes that are to be applied. Later on we will then discuss the welfare implications of a certain taxation policy. For instance, one might face the institutional restriction that the individual tax burden should be proportional to the output level of public goods without discriminating between individuals. This obviously defines a certain specified taxation policy. Another decision would be that the taxation policy consists of linear functions possibly differing among the players. A taxation policy is based upon reasoning which is not inherent to the economical structure. It is imposed upon the economy in order to find a means for allocation private goods and supplying a certain bundle of public goods.

Example 2.5

$$\mathbf{Q} := \{C = (c^1, \ldots, c^n) \mid \Omega \ni i \; \exists q^i \in \mathbf{R}^l_+, \\ \alpha_i \in \mathbf{R}: c^i(y) = q^i y + \alpha_i\} \subseteq \mathbf{C} \tag{11}$$

is the *affine taxation policy.* If $\mathbf{Q}$ is adopted, then players pay towards public goods proportionally to the size of the various public commodities. However, the proportionality constants might differ among the players. Within the framework of the Lindahl equilibrium [see *Lindahl* or *Milleron* for a survey] the "Lindahl prices" constitute a particular example of an "affine taxation scheme".

Here we have $\alpha_i = 0$ while q^i represents the individual marginal rates of substitution of private for public goods. As it turns out, α_i is of no significance; we shall write "q^i" instead of "c^i" whenever $\mathbf{Q}$ is adopted.

Example 2.6

$$\mathbf{Q}^0 := \{C = (c^1, \ldots, c^n) \mid \exists q \in \mathbf{R}^l_+, \alpha \in \mathbf{R}: \\ c^i(y) = qy + \alpha \; (y \in \mathbf{R}^l_+, i \in \Omega)\} \subseteq \mathbf{C}. \tag{12}$$

We shall write "q" instead of "c^i" whenever $\mathbf{Q}^0$ is adopted.

The next step apparently is common in the literature, see e.g. *Zeckhauser/Weinstein* [1974] or *Slutsky* [1977]. Given a taxation scheme C, the consumer take private goods prices p and the provision of public goods y for granted. He then evaluates his budget constraints to be

$$w = pa^i + c^i(b) - c^i(y).$$

Thereafter he is going to maximize his utility with respect to the private goods only. This maximization procedure allows us to eliminate private goods completely from consideration; thus we are capable of deriving the utility of the public goods bundle y for a fixed taxation scheme C. Hence we have the following definition.

Definition 2.7: Let **M** be an admissible economy and C a taxation system, s.t. $c^i(b) \geqslant 0$ $(i \in \Omega)$. Given $p \in \mathbf{P}^{m+1}$, $p > 0$, the function

$$\hat{u}^i := \hat{u}^{pc^i i} : \mathbf{R}^l_+ \to \mathbf{R}$$

(the "*derived utility function*") is defined by

$$\begin{aligned} \hat{u}^i(y) &= \mathring{u}^{pi}(y, pa^i + c^i(b) - c^i(y)) \\ &= \max\{u^i(x, y) \mid x \in X, px \leqslant pa^i + c^i(b) - c^i(y)\}. \end{aligned} \tag{12}$$

Moreover, let

$$\hat{X}^i(p, c^i, y) := \{x \in X \mid px \leqslant pa^i + c^i(b) - c^i(y), u^i(x, y) = \hat{u}^i(y)\} \tag{13}$$

denote the *maximizing private bundles* given prices p, taxation and a public bundle. Then $\hat{X}(\cdot,\cdot,\cdot)$ is a correspondence, which, given a suitable topology on **C**, might turn out to be u.h.c. at certain arguments p, c^i, y.

Definition 2.8: Let **M** be an economy and C a taxation system. Given $p \in \mathbf{R}^{m+1}$ and k sufficiently large, define

$${}^kB^i := \underline{\bar{Y}}^k \cap \{y \in \mathbf{R}^l_+ \mid c^i(y) \leqslant pa^i + c^i(b) + p_{m+1}k\} \tag{14}$$

and a function

$${}^k\hat{u}^i(y) := {}^k\hat{u}^{pc^i i} : {}^kB^i \to \mathbf{R}$$

by

$$\begin{aligned} {}^k\hat{u}^i(y) &:= \overset{kpi}{u}(y, pa^i + c^i(b) - c^i(y)) \\ &= \max\{u^i(x, y) \mid x \in {}^kX^k, px \leqslant pa^i + c^i(b) - c^i(y)\}. \end{aligned} \tag{15}$$

Moreover let, for $y \in \underline{\bar{Y}}^k$

$${}^k\hat{X}^i(p, c^i, y) := \begin{cases} \{x \in {}^kX^k \mid px \leqslant pa^i + c^i(b) - c^i(y), u^i(x, y) = {}^k\hat{u}^i(y)\} & \text{for } y \in {}^kB^i \\ \{x \in {}^kX^k \mid px \leqslant -kp_{m+1}, u^i(x, y) = \mathring{u}^{pi}(y, -kp_{m+1})\} & \text{otherwise.} \end{cases} \tag{16}$$

It should be noted that, for large bundles y of public goods, $C^i(y)$ might increase as to render the budget set

$$\{x \in {}^kX^k \mid px \leqslant pa^i + c^i(b) - c^i(y)\}$$

to be empty. However, for $y \in {}^kB^i$, clearly the private bundle $(0, k)$ is within this budget constraints.

Once a taxation system has been chosen and prices for private goods are fixed, the consumer values public goods according to how much utility he will gain by maximizing w.r.t. the private goods given his imposed budget constraints; this is expressed by $\hat{u}^i$. Certain properties of u^i are at once carried over to the derived utility functions.

Theorem 2.9: $\hat{u}^{pi}$ is continuous, strictly monotone, and concave. $\hat{u}^{pc^i i}$ is continuous and concave.

The same holds true for the k-truncated version.

The *proof* is an easy exercise. See also *Zeckhauser/Weinstein* [1974], where a proof is indicated for the case of one private and one public good as well as linear taxation. However, arbitrarily many private and public goods and a generally convex taxation are feasible.

As has been observed by *Zeckhauser/Weinstein* [1974] we cannot expect that the derived utility functions $\hat{u}^i$ are in addition monotone. However, the remark in their paper that the tax payers' bliss point is achieved at an internal location where the marginal cost to him of providing more of each public good just equals his valuation of a marginal unit cannot be seen as a statement or theorem.

In fact it is rather a condition concerning the utility functions although it is a very reasonable one. Of course the properties of a bliss point ought to be defined in terms of marginal utilities (partial derivatives of the utility functions), that is, by some version of "Gossen's Law". However, its *existence* is a requirement concerning the *global* behaviour of the utilities "far outside".

Intuitively we are to require that, given prices p and a taxation system, the marginal increase of utility of large public bundles will *eventually* become small compared to marginal costs of the sacrifices that are necessary in order to provide these bundles. As we do not want to introduce differentiability conditions at this stage of affairs, we shall choose a rather different formulation in order to ensure that the players enjoy bliss points with respect to the derived utility functions.

Since commodity $m + 1$ plays a separate role, we shall just ensure that the consumer facing large bundles of public goods for which he has to pay by the taxation system as well as large bundles of non-monetarian private goods for which he has to pay proportionally will eventually have decreasing utility if his debts are to appear in his money coordinate.

More precisely, we have

Definition 2.10: Let **M** be an economy and C a taxation system. (u^i, c^i), $(i \in \Omega)$, is said to be *compatible* if the following condition holds true:

For $w \in \mathbf{R}$, $s > 0$ there is $R > 0$ such that

$$u^i(\mathring{x}, w - c^i(y) - s\,|\mathring{x}|, y) < u^i(0,0,0) \tag{17}$$

whenever $|(\mathring{x}, y)| \geqslant R$.
$\mathbf{M}$ and C are *compatible* if (17) holds true for $i \in \Omega$.

It is not hard to see that, given $p \in \mathbf{P}^{m+1}$, $p > 0$ and u^i admissible, it follows that $\hat{u}^{pc^i_i}$ has maximizers within some compact set and only there. For the purpose of a later existence theorem we shall, however, rephrase our definition for the case of linear taxation and prove somewhat more.

Definition 2.11: An economy $\mathbf{M}$ is said to be *compatible with nearly linear taxation* if, for $i \in \Omega$, $w \in \mathbf{R}$, s, $t > 0$, there is $R \geqslant 0$ such that

$$u^i(\mathring{x}, w - t\,|y| - s\,|\mathring{x}|, y) < u^i(0,0,0) \tag{18}$$

whenever $|(\mathring{x}, y)| \geqslant R$.

Note that (0,0,0) is chosen for convenience, the definition may be reformulated such that the existence of any $(\bar{\mathring{x}}, \bar{\xi}, \bar{y})$ replacing (0,0,0) is required.

Theorem 2.12: Let $\mathbf{M}$ be an admissible economy, compatible with nearly linear taxation, and let $\mathbf{C}^0 \subseteq \mathbf{C}$ be a taxation policy such that there is $\eta_0 > 0$, $r_0 > 0$ satisfying

$$c^i(y) \geqslant \eta_0\,|y|\,(C \in \mathbf{C}^0, |y| \geqslant r_0) \tag{19}$$

$$c^i(b) = 0. \tag{20}$$

Then, for any $\epsilon_0 > 0$, there is $R_0 > 0$ such that, for all $p \in \mathbf{P}^{m+1}$, $p > \epsilon_0 e$ and for all $C \in \mathbf{C}^0$ it follows that

$$\emptyset \neq M_{\mathbf{R}^l_+}\,\hat{u}^{pc^i_i} \subseteq S_{R_0}(0) \quad (i \in \Omega). \tag{21}$$

That is, if prices are bounded away from zero and taxes behave nearly linearly, then maximizers of the derived utility functions exist and are uniformly located within some compact set.

Proof: Choose $\epsilon_0 > 0$. Write $\bar{w} := \sum_{i \in \Omega} ea^i$ and let R_0 be such that

$$|y| > R_0 \quad \text{implies } c^i(y) > \eta_0\,|y| \tag{22}$$

as well as

$$\eta_0\,|y| > \bar{w} \tag{23}$$

$$u^i(\mathring{x}, \bar{w} - \eta_0\,|\bar{y}| - \epsilon_0\,|\mathring{x}|, \bar{y}) < u^i(0,0,0) \tag{24}$$

for $|(\mathring{x}, y)| \geqslant R_0$; this is clearly possible by Definition 2.11. Now, let $|\bar{y}| > R_0$. We are going to show that

$$\hat{u}^{pc^i{}_i}(\bar{y}) < \hat{u}^{pc^i{}_i}(0)$$

for all $p > \epsilon_0 e$ and $C \in \mathbf{C}^0$.

Indeed, if $x = (\mathring{x}, \xi^0)$ is such that

$$px + c^i(\bar{y}) \leqslant pa^i + c^i(b)$$

then, observing (20)

$$\mathring{p}\mathring{x} + \rho\xi + c^i(\bar{y}) \leqslant pa^i \leqslant ea^i \leqslant \bar{w},$$

i.e., using (22)

$$\xi \leqslant \frac{\bar{w} - c^i(\bar{y}) - \mathring{p}\mathring{x}}{\rho}$$

$$\leqslant \frac{\bar{w} - \eta_0 |\bar{y}| - \epsilon_0 |x|}{\rho}.$$

Hence, as the numerator is negative by (23),

$$\xi < \bar{w} - \eta_0 |\bar{y}| - \epsilon_0 |\mathring{x}|$$

and, using (24),

$$u^i(\mathring{x}, \xi, \bar{y}) \leqslant u^i(\mathring{x}, \bar{w} - \eta_0 |y| - \epsilon_0 |x|, \bar{y})$$
$$< u^i(0,0,0) \leqslant \hat{u}^i(0)$$

q.e.d.

Remark 1.13: Let **M** be an admissible economy and let C be a taxation system such that **M** and C are compatible. If $p \in \mathbf{P}^{m+1}$, $p > 0$, then

$$M_{\mathbf{R}^l_+}\ \hat{u}^{pc^i{}_i} \neq \emptyset \quad (i \in \Omega).$$

The proof is trivial.

3. Location Conflicts

3.1 Location Conflicts and Values

We are going to use some topics of the theory of location conflicts and their values as well as of games with "bliss points" as developed in recent papers by *Ostmann* [1978, 1979], *Richter* [1979a, b, c], and *Rosenmüller* [1978, 1979]. However, in order to make our treatment selfcontained, we shall just informally discuss the concept of location conflicts and their fair values, the latter term referring to the "value" as defined within the framework of Game Theory.

Suppose a planning agency has to consider the problem where to locate an attractive object (for instance a park, a swimming pool, a public library) given the location of n individuals (players, communities, cities) within the plain (or n-dimensional space) that are interested in the site of our object and are capable of expressing their interest in terms of a utility function which attaches a utility to each possible location of the object. Such a utility may or may not be proportional to the negative or inverse of the distance to the object. It is not unreasonable to except that each player involved would prefer to have the object located as close as possible to his own location, in other words we expect the utilities to have satiation points (maximizers) which frequently might coincide with the players' locations:

Let us adopt a formalization: a location conflict is a tripel $\Sigma = (\Omega, B, U)$, where the data are defined as follows: $\Omega = \{1, \ldots, n\}$ is the set of players, $B \subset \mathbf{R}^l$ is a convex closed subset of $\mathbf{R}^l$ which is called the planning area, $U = (u^i)_{i \in \Omega}$, $u^i \colon B \to \mathbf{R}$ is a family of continuous concave utility functions for the players such that $M_B u^i \neq \emptyset$.

Given a location conflict as defined, the planning agency faces the problem of finding a "fair location" or "fair value" of Σ. "Classical location theory" when dealing with such problems is frequently adopting a naive solution concept like minimizing the sum of the distances between individual players and the object to be located. However, we would rather consider this a problem which should be tackled by methods of Game Theory as has been done for instance in *Richter* [1979a].

Formally this would mean that we consider cooperative games without sidepayments, that is, tripels $(\Omega, \underline{\underline{P}}, V)$, where again $\Omega = \{1, \ldots, n\}$, while $\underline{\underline{P}} = \mathcal{P}(\Omega)$ is the power set of Ω (meaning the coalitions) and $V \colon \underline{\underline{P}} \to \mathcal{P}(\mathbf{R}^n)$ is a mapping which attaches a set of feasible utility vectors to each coalition.

The mapping V should obey certain regularity conditions. For instance, it should take values which are closed convex and comprehensive subsets of $\mathbf{R}^n$ and it should be superadditive or the like. Now, clearly a location conflict Σ gives rise to a game $(\Omega, \underline{\underline{P}}, V)$ where V is defined for instance by means of the formula:

$$V_\Sigma(S) = \text{comprehensive hull of } \{(u^i(x))_{i \in S} \mid x \in B\}$$
$$\text{(imbedded in } \mathbf{R}^n).$$

However, the game which is induced by the mapping $\Sigma \to V_\Sigma$ will in general *not* enjoy superadditivity. In fact, the usual interpretation of the mapping V_Σ as common in Game Theory cannot be maintained because we cannot assume that coalitions will be able to place the desirable object within the limits (convex null) of their own locations. Rather one should adopt the idea that the planning agency just considers the merits or demerits that coalitions would obtain if planning the object was restricted to the interests of such coalitions. This topic is discussed at length in *Richter* [1979c].

In fact, the mapping $\Sigma \to V_\Sigma$ as defined above is not the only feasible one. Quite naturally, one might restrict the discussion to the case where only the utility vectors of the grand coalition and of the single player coalitions really matter. This means that we consider the set $V_\Sigma(\Omega)$ which gives the utilities of all players obtained by varying the object in the planning area and certain sets $V(\{i\})$ which define the utility of a single player if the object is to be located in his "position", that is, in a satiation point of his utility. Such a cooperative game without sidepayments is usually called a "pure bargaining game". However, it should be noted that there is no threatpoint at hand. Rather, this game exhibits a "bliss point". This is the vector $\underline{x}(V_\Sigma) \in \mathbf{R}^n$ (utility space) which is obtained by computing the utility of each player at his satiation point simultaneously, i.e.,

$$\underline{x}_i(V_\Sigma) = u^i(x) \qquad (x \in M_B(u^i)).$$

In general, the bliss point is not feasible $(\underline{x}(V_\Sigma) \notin V_\Sigma(\Omega))$, and the planning agency considers the problem as to which point of the feasible set of the grand coalition would be a fair value given the bliss point of the game.

There are values for games without sidepayments which may easily be defined for non-superadditive games, that is for games with bliss points. Compare for instance *Shapley* [1964], *Harsanyi* [1959, 1963], *Richter* [1979b] and *Rosenmüller* [1978]. As this is not our present topic it suffices to mention that such values in principle could be carried over as to define values for location conflicts; for instance by a formula like

$$\Psi(\Sigma) := \Psi(V_\Sigma)$$

where Ψ is a value which is defined for games without sidepayments featuring bliss points.

On the other hand it seems sometimes reasonable to discuss values for location conflicts axiomatically. As it turns out one might argue that a value like the Nash bargaining solution [*Nash*] might not be intuitively feasible for location conflicts. An axiomatic definition of values for location conflicts has been given in *Richter* [1979c]. This author adopts the viewpoint that defining fair values for location conflicts is rather a problem of Welfare Theory and not so much of Game Theory. He then gives axioms and definitions of values and introduces a certain class of values which for instance are defined for games in the "pure bargaining" form, that is where only the grand coalition and the bliss point matters. Typically such a value would be obtained by minimizing the distance of the bliss point and some point on the Pareto surface of the feasible set of the grand coalition where the word "distance" has to be interpreted in the sense of a certain p-norm. It is important to note that such a value would enjoy in addition to the axiomatically stated properties also certain continuity properties which are to be used in our later treatment. Such continuity properties will possibly not be attached to values for games with bliss points as defined for instance in *Rosenmüller* [1978]. It is quite possible that they enjoy the property of being upper semicontinuous correspondence given the appropriate topology on location conflicts. At this stage of our analysis we shall not enter the problem of continuity but rather make this a requirement. For the following discussion we shall just assume that values for location conflicts are available and that they enjoy certain properties to be defined in the next section.

3.2 Fair Distribution of Public Goods

Definition 3.1: Let $\mathfrak{T} := \{\Sigma = (\Omega, B, U)\}$ denote the set of location conflicts.
Given $\mathfrak{T}^0 \subseteq \mathfrak{T}$, a *value* (for $\mathfrak{T}^0$) is a correspondence $\Psi: \mathfrak{T}^0 \to P(\mathbf{R}^l)$ enjoying the following properties:

1. $\Psi(\Sigma) \subseteq B$.
2. Ψ *preserves bliss points.*
   (i.e., if $M_\Sigma := \bigcap_{i\in\Omega} M_B u^i \neq \emptyset$, then $\Psi(\Sigma) = M_\Sigma$).
3. Ψ is *finitely determined.*
   (i.e., for any family $\mathfrak{T}' \subset \mathfrak{T}^0$ of location conflicts admitting of a compact set K such that $M_{B'} u^{i'} \subseteq K$ ($\Sigma' \in \mathfrak{T}'$), there is a compact convex set $\bar{K}$ such that $\bar{K} \supseteq K$ and $u^{i'}|_{\bar{K}} = u^{i''}|_{\bar{K}}$ ($i \in \Omega$; $\Sigma', \Sigma'' \in \mathfrak{T}'$) implies $\Psi(\mathfrak{T}') = \Psi(\mathfrak{T}'')$.
4. $\Psi(\Sigma) \subseteq$ convex hull of $\bigcup_{i\in\Omega} M_B u^i$.

The fourth condition is not extremely appealing. Preferably it should be replaced by Pareto optimality. There are clearly situations such that *both* requirements are easily satisfied (e.g., if the location conflict is one-dimensional, i.e. if $l = 1$, or if the utilities of the players enjoy some symmetry, i.e., if they are norms). On the other hand, in the case of two players and two dimensions of the planning area, the intersection of the contract curve and the convex hull might just contain the satiation points of the players. By technical reasons we shall impose the above convexity condition (cf. Theorem 4.8, second step) and leave Pareto optimality for later treatments. Further requirements possible are invariance under permutations of the players, invariance under linear rescaling of the utility functions and the like. However, every value should at least choose Pareto optimal points and, if bliss points are feasible at all, then the value should choose these feasible bliss points.

Let us now recall the results of Section 2. We have seen that given suitable conditions, positive prices and an appropriate taxation system, the resulting derived utility functions are concave and enjoy satiation points. This means that given prices and a taxation systems the market or economy induces a location conflict. Now let us assume that some planning agency, knowing the preference structure of the individuals with respect to the public goods and some "concept of fairness" Ψ, will compute some public good to be produced which might in the ideal case of course be a "bliss point" but usually will be something which is just "fair". The value to be chosen may be opted for by society in advance. What is left to the planning agency is just to compute the fair value given the location conflict that results from the market at present prices and tax structure. (There is of course the serious counter-argument to this procedure that individuals might possibly tend to reveal false preferences in order to influence the choice of the public goods).

Definition 3.2: Let **M** be an economy and C a taxation system s.t. **M** and C are compatible. Given $p \in \mathbf{P}^{m+1}$, $p > 0$,

$$\Sigma^{pC} := (\Omega, \mathbf{R}^l_+, \hat{U}^{pC}) \text{ (where } \hat{U}^{pC} = (\hat{u}^{pc^i i})_{i\in\Omega}) \tag{1}$$

is the *location conflict generated by* **M** (via C at p).

Definition 3.3: Let **M** be an economy and C a taxation system. Define

$${}^kB := \bigcap_{i\in\Omega} {}^kB^i \quad \text{(cf. Def. 2.8).}$$

Then, given $p \in \mathbf{P}^{m+1}$

$$ {}^k\Sigma^{pC} := (\Omega, {}^kB, {}^k\hat{U}^{pC}) \text{ (where } {}^k\hat{U}^{pC} = ({}^k\hat{u}^{pc^i i})_{i\in\Omega}) \tag{2} $$

is the *location conflict generated by* $\mathbf{M}^k$.

Note. If $C \in \mathbf{Q}$ (Example 1.5) is an affine taxation system, then budget restrictions of the type

$$ px \leqslant pa^i + c^i(b) - c^i(y) $$

can be rewritten as

$$ px \leqslant pa^i + q^i(b - y) $$

or

$$ px + q^i y \leqslant pa^i + q^i b $$

provided $c^i(y) = q^i y + \alpha_i$. Hence, $\hat{u}^i = \hat{u}^{pc^i i}$ depends on q^i and not on α_i. We shall use the notations $Q = (q^1, \ldots, q^n)$ (instead of C) as well as

$$ \hat{u}^i = \hat{u}^{pq^i i},\ \hat{U}^{pQ},\ \Sigma^{pQ} $$

and the like. Similary, if $C \in \mathbf{Q}^0$ (Example 1.6), then we shall identify c^i, $c^i(y) = qy + \alpha$, and q, i.e., write

$$ \hat{u}^i = \hat{u}^{pqi},\ \hat{U}^{pq},\ \Sigma^{pq}. $$

4. Equilibrium

4.1 Definitions and the General Affine Taxation Case

Definition 4.1: Let $\mathbf{M}$ be an admissible economy, $\mathbf{C}^0 \subseteq \mathbf{C}$ a taxation policy, and $\Psi: \mathfrak{T}^0 \to P(\mathbf{R}^n)$ a value for location conflicts. Then

$$ (\bar{p}, \bar{C}, \bar{X}, \bar{y}) \in \mathbf{P}^{m+1} \times \mathbf{C}^0 \times (\mathbf{R}_+^m \times \mathbf{R}^n) \times \mathbf{R}_+^l $$

is a Ψ-$\mathbf{C}^0$*-equilibrium for* $\mathbf{M}$ if

0. $\bar{p} > 0$
1. $\mathbf{M}$ and $\bar{C}$ are compatible
2. $\Sigma^{\bar{p}\bar{C}} \in \mathfrak{T}^0$
3. $\bar{y} \in \Psi(\Sigma^{\bar{p}\bar{C}})$
4. $\bar{x}^i \in \hat{X}^i(\bar{p}, \bar{c}^i, \bar{y}) \quad (i \in \Omega)$
5. $(\sum_{i\in\Omega} \bar{x}^i - a^i, \bar{y} - b) \in Y$.

Of course, conditions 1 – 3 are of technical nature, Hence the obvious interpretation of the definition is that, given equilibrium prices and taxes, the public bundle is considered to be "fair" within the location conflict induced. Given this bundle, every player maximizes his utility with respect to the private goods, and finally the result obtained this way is feasible and efficient with respect to the production technology.

Mathematically, it could be considered to be a blunder carrying the taxation policy $\mathbf{C}^0$ in the definition of equilibrium. However, it is our idea that a taxation policy as well as the value are institutional data and selected in advance.

Hence one is looking for a taxation scheme which allows an equilibrium within a certain prescribed family or policy of taxations. Let us also formulate the definition in case of the truncated version.

Definition 4.2: Let $\mathbf{M}$ be an economy and $\mathbf{C}^0 \subseteq \mathbf{C}$ a taxation policy. Let $\Psi: \mathfrak{T}^0 \to P(\mathbf{R}^l)$ be a value for location conflicts. Then

$$(\bar{p}, \bar{C}, \bar{X}, \bar{y}) \in \mathbf{P}^{m+1} \times \mathbf{C}^0 \times ({}^kX^k)^n \times \mathbf{R}^l_+$$

is a Ψ-$\mathbf{C}^0$-*equilibrium for* $\mathbf{M}^k$ if

2'. ${}^k\Sigma^{\bar{p}\bar{C}} \in \mathfrak{T}^0$.

3'. $\bar{y} \in \Psi({}^k\Sigma^{\bar{p}\bar{C}})$.

4'. $\bar{x}^i \in {}^k\hat{X}^i(\bar{p}, \bar{c}^i, \bar{y}) \quad (i \in \Omega)$.

5'. $\sum_{i \in \Omega} (\bar{x}^i - a^i, \bar{y} - b) \in Y$.

A first and obvious result is that, given affine but arbitrary taxation, the Ψ-$\mathbf{Q}$-equilibrium is a generalization of the well-known Lindahl equilibrium. As we do not want to enter the formal definition of Lindahl equilibria the reader is referred to *Lindahl* [1967], *Milleron* [1972].

The definition of a "Lindahl equilibrium" within our framework is rather obvious. Note that, given linear taxation, compatibility of $\mathbf{M}$ and $Q = (q^1, \ldots, q^n)$ is easily verified if Q is positive, say, in the presence of strict concavity or utility functions that are not increasing too fast with respect to the private goods. In fact, such requirement can be imposed upon linear taxation functions in a uniform manner. (Cf. Definition 2.11 and Theorem 2.12).

Theorem 4.3: Let $\mathbf{M}$ be an admissible economy and let $\Psi: \mathfrak{T}^0 \to P(\mathbf{R}^n)$ be a value such that

$$\Sigma \in \mathfrak{T}^0 \text{ whenever } M_\Sigma = \bigcap_{i \in \Omega} M_B u^i \neq \emptyset. \tag{1}$$

Suppose $(\bar{p}, \bar{Q}, \bar{X}, \bar{y}) \in \mathbf{P}^{m+1} \times \mathbf{Q} \times (\mathbf{R}^m_+ \times \mathbf{R})^n \times \mathbf{R}^l_+$ is a Lindahl-equilibrium such that $\mathbf{M}$ and $\bar{Q}$ are compatible. Then $(\bar{p}, \bar{Q}, \bar{X}, \bar{y})$ is a Ψ-$\mathbf{Q}$-equilibrium for $\mathbf{M}$.

Proof. For $i \in \Omega$, $(\bar{x}^i, \bar{y})$ maximizes i's utility within

$$\{(x, y) \mid x \in X, y \in \mathbf{R}^l_+, \bar{p}x + \bar{q}^i y \leqslant \bar{p}a^i + \bar{q}^i b\}. \tag{2}$$

This shows that for x with $\bar{p}x \leqslant \bar{p}a^i + \bar{q}^i b - \bar{q}^i y$ we have

$$u^i(x, \bar{y}) \leqslant u^i(\bar{x}^i, \bar{y})$$

i.e.,

$$\bar{x}^i \in \hat{X}^i(\bar{p}, \bar{q}^i, \bar{y})$$

and 4. of Definition 3.1 is satisfied.

Moreover, (2) implies

$$\begin{aligned}\hat{u}^{\bar{p}\bar{q}^i i}(\bar{y}) &= u^i(\bar{x}^i, \bar{y})\\ &= \max\{u^i(x, y) \mid x \in X, y \in \mathbf{R}^l_+, \bar{p}x + \bar{q}^i y \leqslant \bar{p}a^i + \bar{q}^i b\}\\ &\geqslant \max\{u^i(x, y) \mid x \in X, \bar{p}x + \bar{q}^i y \leqslant \bar{p}a^i + \bar{q}^i b\}\\ &= \hat{u}^{\bar{p}\bar{q}^i i}(y) \qquad \text{for all } y \in \mathbf{R}^l_+.\end{aligned}$$

This means obviously $\bar{y} \in \bigcap_{i \in \Omega} M_{\mathbf{R}^l_+} \hat{u}^{\bar{p}\bar{q}^i i}$.

Hence, $\Sigma^{\bar{p}\bar{Q}} \in \mathfrak{T}^0$ and $\bar{y} \in \Psi(\Sigma^{\bar{p}\bar{Q}})$, be Definition 3.1, hence 2. and 3. of 4.1 are satisfied. Given strict monotony, 0. of 4.1 is clear while 5. is part of the definition of a Lindahl equilibrium. q.e.d.

4.2 Equal Taxation

This section is dealing with an existence proof for equal taxation. This does not mean that equal taxation is a principle advocated generally, but it should rather imply that it is possible to prove the existence of equilibria in the presence of certain restricted taxation policies.

Clearly, we have so far not been dealing with properties of the production set Y. In fact, the conditions we are to impose result from fairly general properties of Y. This is a problem that has already been carried through by *Roberts* [1973]. This author provides a list of the requirements for Y sufficient to prove that our conditions as stated below are satisfied; in particular it is claimed that Y should feature constant returns to scale, that is, Y should be a convex cone. However, we believe that decreasing returns to scale are sufficient, that is, that convexity of Y essentially would be a sufficient condition.

In any case as we do not want to enter this discussion we shall just make the results of *Roberts* [1973] as to be our conditions in order to establish equilibrium. This motivates the following definitions:

Definition 4.4: Y is *smooth*, if

1. $G: \mathbf{P}^{m+1} \times \mathbf{R}^l_+ \to P(-X \times \mathbf{R}^l_+)$

$$(\tilde{p}, \tilde{y}) \to \{(\tilde{x}, \tilde{q}) \mid -\tilde{x} \in X, \tilde{q} \in \mathbf{R}^l_+, (\tilde{x}, \tilde{y}) \in Y,$$

$$\tilde{p}\tilde{x} + \tilde{q}\tilde{y} = \max\{\tilde{p}x + \tilde{q}y \mid (x, y) \in Y\}\}$$

is a nonempty, convex valued, compact valued u.h.c. correspondence.

2. For every k sufficiently large

$$G^k: \mathbf{P}^{m+1} \times \underline{\bar{Y}}^k \to \mathcal{P}(-{}^0\chi^{nk} \times \mathbf{R}^l_+)$$

$$(\tilde{p}, \tilde{y}) \to G(\tilde{p}, \tilde{y}) \cap (-{}^0\chi^{nk} \times \mathbf{R}^l_+)$$

is nonempty (and, of course, as well convex valued, compact valued, u.h.c.).

Theorem 4.5: (Equal taxation, truncated market)
Let $\mathbf{M}$ be an economy with smooth $\mathcal{Y}$ and $b = 0$. Let $\mathbf{Q}^0$ be equal taxation. Furthermore, let $\Psi: \mathfrak{T}^0 \to \mathcal{P}(\mathbf{R}^1)$ be a value such that

$${}^k\Sigma^{pq} \in \mathfrak{T}^0$$

for all $p \in \mathbf{P}^{m+1}$, $q \in \mathbf{Q}^0$ and some $k \in \mathbf{N}$ sufficiently large. If

$$(p, q) \to \Psi({}^k\Sigma^{pq})$$

$$\mathbf{P}^{m+1} \times \mathbf{Q}^0 \to \mathcal{P}(\mathbf{R}^l_+)$$

is a convex valued u.h.c. correspondence, then there exists a Ψ-$\mathbf{Q}^0$-equilibrium for $\mathbf{M}^k$.

Proof. Step 1. Define

$$\overset{\circ}{H}{}^k := \frac{1}{n} \operatorname{Proj}_2 \bigcup_{\substack{p \in \mathbf{P}^{m+1} \\ y \in \underline{\bar{Y}}^k}} G^k(p, y),$$

this is a compact set (since G^k is u.h.c.). Let H^k be its convex hull (as well compact). We are going to define a correspondence

$$F: \Delta^k \to \mathcal{P}(\Delta^k)$$

where

$$\Delta^k := \mathbf{P}^{m+1} \times H^k \times {}^{2nk}Z^{2nk} \times \underline{\bar{Y}}^k$$

as follows:
Given $(p, q, x, y) \in \Delta^k$, *define*

$$p' := \frac{p + x^+}{1 + \sum_j x_j^+} \tag{3}$$

Next, *choose*

$$y' \in \Psi({}^k\Sigma^{pq}). \tag{4}$$

As $\mathcal{Y}$ is smooth, *there is*

$$\tilde{x} \in -{}^0\chi^{nk}, \; q' \in \mathbf{R}^l_+ \tag{5}$$

such that

$$(\tilde{x}, nq') \in G^k (p, y). \tag{6}$$

Next, *choose*

$$\hat{x}^i \in {}^k\hat{X}^i (p, q, y) \tag{7}$$

and *define*

$$x' := \sum_{i \in \Omega} \hat{x}^i - a^i - \tilde{x}. \tag{8}$$

Now, $F(p, q, x, y)$ is defined to be the set of all (p', q', x', y') that are obtained by this procedure. Formally

$$F(p, q, x, y) = \{(p', q', x', y') \mid$$
$$p' = \frac{p + x^+}{1 + \sum_j x_j^+}, y' \in \Psi ({}^k\Sigma^{pq}),$$
$$x' = \sum_{i \in \Omega} \hat{x}^i - a^i - \tilde{x}, (\tilde{x}, nq') \in G^k (p, y)$$

for some $(\hat{x}^i)_{i \in \Omega}$, $\hat{x}^i \in {}^kX^i (p, q, y)$, and some $\tilde{x} \in - {}^0X^{nk}\}$.

It might be useful to visualize F by means of the following diagramm.

Step 2. Let us check that F takes values that are subsets of Δ^k.

Now, $p' \in \mathbf{P}^{m+1}$ is obvious. Next, as $y \in \underline{\tilde{Y}}^k$, $p \in \mathbf{P}^{m+1}$, we have

$$(\tilde{x}, nq') \in G^k (p, y)$$

i.e.

$$nq' \in \text{Proj}_2\, G^k (p, y)$$
$$q' \in \frac{1}{n} \text{Proj}_2\, G^k (p, y) \subseteq H^k.$$

Moreover, as ${}^k\Sigma^{pq} = (\Omega, {}^kB, {}^k\hat{U}^{pq})$, by Property 0, of Definition 2.1,

$$y' \in \Psi ({}^k\Sigma^{pq}) \subseteq {}^kB \subseteq \underline{\tilde{Y}}^k$$

(cf. Definition 2.8, (14)). Therefore, it remains to show that $x' \in {}^{2nk}Z^{2nk}$, i.e.

$$-2nke \leqslant x' \leqslant 2nke.$$

To this end, note that by definition of G^k, $-\tilde{x} \in {}^0X^{nk}$, i.e.

$$0 \leqslant -\tilde{x} \leqslant nke.$$

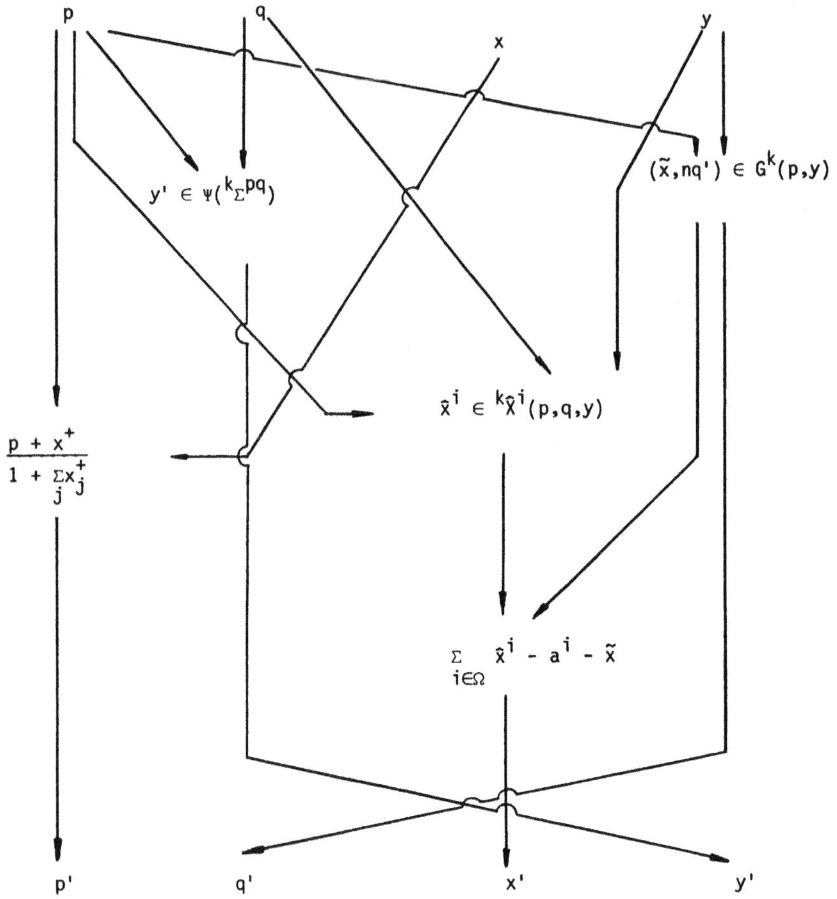

Similarly $\hat{x}^i \in {}^k\chi^k$

$$-k \leqslant \hat{\xi} \leqslant k$$

$$0 \leqslant \hat{\hat{x}}^i \leqslant ke.$$

In view of $a^i \geqslant 0$ $(i \in \Omega)$, it follows that

$$x' = \sum_{i \in \Omega} \hat{x}^i - a^i - \tilde{x} \leqslant nke - \tilde{x}$$

$$\leqslant nke + nke = 2nke$$

and, as $a^i \leqslant ke$,

$$x' \geqslant \sum_{i \in \Omega} \hat{x}^i - a^i \geqslant - nke - nke = -2nke,$$

completing Step 2.

Step 3. By assumption, Ψ and G^k are convex valued and u.h.c. correspondences. It can be verified that ${}^k\hat{X}^i(\cdot,\cdot,\cdot)$ is u.h.c. and convex valued as well. From this it follows at once that

$$F: \Delta^k \to \Delta^k$$

is u.h.c. and convex valued, and hence satisfies the conditions of Kakutani's fixed point theorem.

Let $(\bar{p}, \bar{q}, \bar{x}, \bar{y}) \in \Delta^k$ be a fixed point. I.e., there is $\tilde{x}, (\hat{x}^i)_{i \in \Omega}$ s.t.

$$\bar{p} = \frac{\bar{p} + \bar{x}^+}{1 + \sum_j \bar{x}_j^+} \tag{9}$$

$$\bar{x} = \sum_{i \in \Omega} \hat{x}^i - a^i - \tilde{x} \tag{10}$$

$$(n\bar{q}, \tilde{x}) \in G^k(\bar{p}, \bar{y}) \tag{11}$$

$$\hat{x}^i \in \hat{X}^i(\bar{p}, \bar{q}, \bar{y}) \tag{12}$$

$$\bar{y} \in \Psi({}^k\Sigma^{\bar{p}\bar{q}}) \tag{13}$$

Let us disprove

$$\bar{x}^+ \neq 0. \tag{14}$$

Indeed, if (14) holds true, then from (9):

$$\bar{p} \sum \bar{x}_j^+ = \bar{x}^+$$

and

$$0 < \bar{p}\bar{x}^+ = \bar{p}\bar{x}$$

$$\overset{(10)}{=} \bar{p}\,(\sum_{i \in \Omega} (\bar{x}^i - a^i) - \tilde{x})$$

$$= \sum_{i \in \Omega} (\bar{p}\bar{x}^i - \bar{p}e^i) - \bar{p}\tilde{x} \ldots \tag{15}$$

As $b = 0$ was assumed for convenience, we have for $\hat{x}^i \in \hat{X}^i(\bar{p}, \bar{q}, \bar{y})$

$$\bar{p}\hat{x}^i - \bar{p}a^i \leqslant -\bar{q}\bar{y}$$

i.e., (15) continues

$$\ldots \leqslant -n\bar{q}\bar{y} - \bar{p}\tilde{x} \ldots$$

and since $(0,0) \in X^k$ and $(\tilde{x}, n\bar{q}) \in G^k(\bar{p}, \bar{y})$, it follows that $n\bar{q}\bar{y} + p\tilde{x} \geqslant nq0 + p0 = 0$,

$$\ldots \leqslant 0,$$

a contradiction.

Hence (14) is wrong, i.e.

$$\bar{x}^+ = 0$$

$$\bar{x} \leqslant 0$$

meaning

$$\Sigma \hat{x}^i - a^i \leqslant \tilde{x}. \tag{16}$$

But as $(\tilde{x}, \bar{y}) \in \mathcal{Y}^k$, this implies

$$(\Sigma \hat{x}^i - a^i, \bar{y}) \in \mathcal{Y}. \tag{17}$$

Now, (13), (12) and (17) imply that

$$(\bar{p}, \bar{q}, (\hat{x}^i)_{i \in \Omega}, \bar{y})$$

is a Ψ-$\mathbf{Q}^0$-equilibrium for $\mathbf{M}^k$. q.e.d.

In order to prove the general existence theorem for the non-truncated market a few additional conditions are necessary. First of all it is necessary to have some kind of strictly decreasing marginal utility imposed upon the players. In particular we shall require that the consumer has a very urgent desire to receive at least some quantity of every private good. His desire for acquiring private goods when having none should be very high compared with his desire to hold cash. This is not all together unreasonable. On the other hand we shall ask that his marginal utility with respect to the public goods is bounded. Again one could imagine that consumers in a situation where they have almost no private good would certainly prefer some private goods to public goods with great urgency.

The fact that we are going to formulate these questions in terms of partial derivatives does not mean that the theorem hinges on the existence of continuous partial derivatives as required. In fact, the experienced reader will see at once that appropriate formulations could replace the differentiability requirements in an obvious manner.

There will also be an additional requirement with respect to $\mathcal{Y}$. In fact we want that taxes are bounded away from 0. This means essentially that the q-coordinates of tangents to the production set $\mathcal{Y}$ can be chosen as to be bounded away from 0, and this as is easily seen is only a requirement which concerns the boundary of $\mathcal{Y}$. Similarly we want that taxes are ranging within some set bounded from above.

Definition 4.6: Let $\mathbf{M}$ be an economy. Suppose each utility function u^i $(i \in \Omega)$ admits of continuous partial derivatives $(\partial u^i)/(\partial x_j)$ $(x_j > 0)$, $(\partial u^i)/(\partial \xi)$ $(\xi \in \mathbf{R})$, $(\partial u^i)/(\partial y_j)$ $(y_j > 0)$, such that

$$\frac{\partial u^i}{\partial y_i} \text{ is bounded,} \tag{18}$$

$$\frac{\partial u^i}{\partial \xi} (\mathring{x}, 0, y) \geqslant \eta \quad \text{for some } \eta > 0 \tag{19}$$

and

$$x_j \frac{\partial u^i}{\partial x_i}(x_1, \ldots, x_j, \ldots, x_m, \xi, y) \uparrow \infty \, (x_j \downarrow 0). \tag{20}$$

(Think of $e^{-1/x}$, locally!)

Let $\mathcal{Y}$ have a closed efficiency set. In addition, assume that $\mathcal{Y}$ is smooth and there is some $\Delta, \delta > 0$ such that for $p \in \mathbf{P}^{m+1}$, $y \in \mathbf{R}^l_+$, there is $(x, q) \in G^k(p, y)$ with $\Delta e \geqslant q \geqslant \delta e$ for k sufficiently large.

Then **M** will be called *smooth.*

We are now in a position to formulate a general existence theorem for linear and equal taxation. Of course this is running via a limit theorem of the truncated versions. It should be noted however that the general procedure applied to such limit theorems is to be changed with respect to several details. The main obstacle is that the bundel of private and public goods that the single consumer receives in the equilibrium will in general not maximize his total utility. Instead his total utility is maximized by the maximizer of the derived utility function $\hat{u}$. This causes some problems when arguing that prices in the long run will be positive.

Theorem 4.7: (Equal taxation, general version)

Let **M** be an economy which is smooth, admissible, and compatible with nearly linear taxation. Assume that $b = 0$. Let $\mathbf{Q}^0$ be the equal taxation policy. Furthermore, let $\Psi: \mathfrak{T}^0 \to \mathcal{P}(\mathbf{R}^l)$ be a value such that

$$^k\Sigma^{pq} \in \mathfrak{T}^0 \tag{21}$$

for all $p \in \mathbf{P}^{m+1}$, $q \in \mathbf{Q}^0$ and sufficiently large $k \in \mathbf{N}$,

$$\Sigma^{pq} \in \mathfrak{T}^0 \tag{22}$$

for all $p > 0, q > 0$.

Assume, in addition, that for all $k \in \mathbf{N}$ sufficiently large

$$(p, q) \to \Psi(^k\Sigma^{pq}) \tag{23}$$

is a convex valued u.h.c. correspondence. Also,

$$(p, q) \to \Psi(\Sigma^{pq}) \tag{24}$$

is a convex valued u.h.c. correspondence for $p, q > 0$.

Then there is a Ψ-$\mathbf{Q}^0$-equilibrium for **M**. If $\mathcal{Y}$ has constant returns to scale, then production is efficient.

Proof. Step 1. Within the proof of Theorem 4.5, we may replace the correspondence G^k, by $G^{k,\delta,\Delta}$ where

$$G^{k,\delta,\Delta}(\tilde{p}, \tilde{y}) = G^k(\tilde{p}, \tilde{y}) \cap \{(x, q) \mid \Delta e \geqslant q \geqslant \delta e\}.$$

Hence we may assume that equilibrium taxes range within some compact set and are bounded away from zero *independently of* $k \in \mathbf{N}$.

Now, for $k \in \mathbf{N}$ sufficiently large, Theorem 4.5 guarentees the existence of a Ψ-$\mathbf{Q}^0$-equilibrium for $\mathbf{M}^k$, say

$$(p^k, q^k, X^k, y^k).$$

We may assume that

$$p^k \underset{k}{\rightarrow} \bar{p} \in \mathbf{P}^{m+1}, q^k \rightarrow \bar{q} \in \mathbf{R}^l_+, \bar{q} > 0. \tag{25}$$

Also, since

$$(\sum_{i \in \Omega} x^{ki} - a^i, y^k) \in Y \tag{26}$$

we have

$$0 \leqslant \sum_{i \in \Omega} \mathring{x}^{ki} \leqslant \sum_{i \in \Omega} \mathring{a}^i \tag{27}$$

and hence, w.l.o.g.

$$\mathring{x}^{ki} \underset{k}{\rightarrow} \mathring{x}^i \tag{28}$$

where $\mathring{x}^i \in \mathbf{R}^m_+$ and $\sum_{i \in \Omega} \mathring{x}^i \leqslant \sum_{i \in \Omega} a^i$.

Step 2. Let us verify that

$$\bar{p} = \bar{p}_{m+1} > 0. \tag{29}$$

To this end, assume first of all that

$$p^k a^i - q^k y^k \leqslant 0 \tag{30}$$

for all $i \in \Omega$ and all $k \in \mathbf{N}$ sufficiently large. By property 4. of Definition 3.1, there is $y^{ki} \in M_{k_B} \hat{u}^{p^k q^k i}$; s.t. y^k is a convex combination of the y^{ki} ($i \in \Omega$). From (30) it follows that

$$p^k a^i - q^k y^{ki} \leqslant 0 \tag{31}$$

for *some* $i \in \Omega$. Let $\overset{*}{x}^{ki} \in \hat{X}(p^k, q^k, y^{ki})$, that is

$$\hat{u}^{p^k q^k i}(y^{ki}) = u^i(\overset{*}{x}^{ki}, y^{ki}) \tag{32}$$

and

$$p^k \overset{*}{x}^{ki} \leqslant p^k a^i - q^k y^{ki} \leqslant 0. \tag{33}$$

Since $a^i > 0$ ($i \in \Omega$), there is j such that y_j^{ki} is bounded away from zero. On the other hand, (33) implies that $\overset{*}{\xi}^{ki} \leqslant 0$. Therefore, given small $\epsilon > 0$, the bundle

$$(\tilde{x}^k, \tilde{y}^k) := \left(\overset{\circ}{\overset{*}{x}}{}^{ki}, \overset{*}{\xi}{}^{ki} + \epsilon, y^{ki} - \epsilon \frac{\rho^k}{q_j^k} e^j \right) \tag{34}$$

(where $\rho^k := p_{m+1}^k$) is in ${}^k\chi^k$. Obviously

$$p^k \tilde{x}^k = p^k \overset{*}{x}{}^{ki} + \rho^k \epsilon \leqslant p^k a^i - q^k y^{ki} + \rho^k \epsilon = p^k a^i - q^k \tilde{y}^k,$$

and hence

$$\hat{u}^{p^k q^k i} (\tilde{y}^k) \geqslant u^i (\tilde{x}^k, \tilde{y}^k)$$

$$= u^i (\overset{*}{x}{}^{ki}, y^{ki}) + \epsilon \left(\frac{\partial u^i}{\partial \xi} - \frac{\rho^k}{q_j^k} \frac{\partial u^i}{\partial y_j} \right) (\overset{*}{x}{}^{ki}, y^{ki}) + o^k(\epsilon) \tag{35}$$

where $\frac{o^k(\epsilon)}{\epsilon} \to 0 \ (\epsilon \to 0)$.

As $\overset{*}{\xi}{}^{ki} \leqslant 0$ and u^i concave, the term $(\partial u^i)/(\partial \xi)\ (\cdot, \cdot)$ in (35) is larger than η (by (19)). The term $(\partial u^i)/(\partial y_j)$ is bounded. If $\rho^k \to 0\ (k \to \infty)$, the coefficient of ϵ will, therefore, become positive. We may then choose ϵ small enough (for fixed but large k) such that (35) implies

$$\hat{u}^{p^k q^k i} (\tilde{y}^k) > u^i (\overset{*}{x}{}^{ki}, y^{ki}) = \hat{u}^{p^k q^k i} (y^{ki}),$$

contradicting the maximizer property of y^{ki}. This takes care of (30); for the rest of this step assume now

$$p^k a^i - q^k y^k > 0 \tag{36}$$

for *some* $i \in \Omega$ and (by choosing a subsequence) for all k sufficiently large.

For this player i, 0 is a feasible private bundle, i.e.,

$$p^k 0 \leqslant p^k a^i - q^k y^k.$$

Hence, $\xi^{ki} \to -\infty$ *cannot* happen. For, boundedness of $(y^k)_{k \in \mathbb{N}}$ (by (36)) and of $\overset{\circ}{x}{}^{ki}$ (by (27), (28)) would imply

$$u^i (x^{ki}, y^k) = u^i (\overset{\circ}{x}{}^{ki}, \xi^{ki}, y^k) \to -\infty$$

(u^i is concave and strictly monotone), i.e.

$$u^i (x^{ki}, y^k) < u^i (0, y^k) \quad (k \text{ large}),$$

contradicting $x^{ki} \in \hat{X} (p^k, q^k, y^k)$.

Thus, ξ^{ki} is now bounded (by $\sum_{i \in \Omega} a^i_{m+1}$ from above). Now, if $p^k a^i - q^k y^k \geqslant \delta > 0$ for some δ, then $x^\delta = (0, \delta/\rho^k)$ would be feasible in players i's budget set. Clearly, $u^i (0, \delta/\rho^k), y^k) \to \infty$ if $\rho^k \to 0$, contradicting the fact that $u^i (x^{ki}, y^k)$ is bounded and x^{ki} is i's maximizer.

It remains to treat the case that

$$p^k a^i - q^k y^k := \delta^k \to 0.$$

Now, as $(0, \delta^k/\rho^k)$ is feasible for i, we conclude that δ^k/ρ^k is bounded (otherwise, like above, $u^i(0, \delta^k/\rho^k, y^k) \to \infty$), say

$$\frac{\delta^k}{\rho^k} < C_0. \tag{37}$$

Assuming $\rho^k \to 0$, there is j such that p_j^k is bounded away from zero; consider the bundle

$$\tilde{x}^{ki} := x^{ki} - e^{m+1} + \frac{\rho^k}{p_j^k} e^j$$

which is in i's budget set. We have by concavity

$$u^i(\tilde{x}^{ki}, y^k) \geqslant u^i(\tilde{x}^{ki}, y^k) + \left(\frac{\rho^k}{p_j^k}\frac{\partial u^i}{\partial x_j} - \frac{\partial u^i}{\partial \xi}\right)(\tilde{x}^{ki}, y^k) \tag{38}$$

The term $(\partial u^i)/(\partial \xi)$ is bounded. The j-th argument in $(\partial u^i)/(\partial x_j)$ is $\tilde{x}_j^{ki} = x_j^{ki} + \rho^k/p_j^k$.

Because of

$$p^k x^{ki} \leqslant \delta^k$$

we have in view of (37)

$$x_j^{ki} \leqslant \frac{\delta^k}{p_j^k} \leqslant \frac{C'\rho^k}{p_j^k} \text{ (with } C' \geqslant C_0 \text{, since } \xi^{ki} \text{ is bounded)}$$

and hence $\tilde{x}_j^{ki} \leqslant C_1\rho^k$; $C_1 \geqslant (C'+1)/p_j^k \quad (k \in \mathbf{N})$.

$$\frac{\rho^k}{p_j^k}\frac{\partial u^i}{\partial x_j}(\tilde{x}^{ki}, y^k) \geqslant \frac{\rho^k}{p_j^k}\frac{\partial u^i}{\partial x_j}(\ldots, \underset{\substack{\uparrow \\ j}}{C_1\rho^k}, \ldots, y^k) \uparrow \infty$$

by (20). This again contradicts the maximality of x^{ki} via (38).

We have thus completed step 2. and proved (29).

Step 3. As $\bar{\rho} > 0$ it follows clearly that $\bar{p} > 0$. For, if $\bar{p}_j = 0$, then

$$\tilde{x}^{ki} := x^{ki} + \epsilon e^j - \epsilon \frac{p_j^k}{\rho^k} e^{m+1}$$

would be a feasible bundle for i with higher utility than $\tilde{x}^{ki}$, if k is large (using $(\partial u^i)/(\partial x_j) > 0$).

Step 4. We are now going to invoke Theorem 2.12.

Because of $\bar{p} > 0$, there is $\epsilon_0 > 0$ such that

$$p^k > \epsilon_0 e \tag{39}$$

for large $k \in \mathbf{N}$. By Theorem 2.12., the maximizers of $\hat{u}^{p^k q^k i}$ are uniformly located within some compact set. Clearly, $\hat{u}^{p^k q^k i} \geqslant {}^k\hat{u}^{p^k p^k i}$; also it is not hard to see (inspect 2.12) that, for large k, the maximizing values of $\hat{u}^{p^k q^k i}$ will be attained by ${}^k\hat{u}^{p^k q^k i}$ as well; meaning that both functions have equal maximizers for large k. Hence, the maximizers of ${}^k\hat{u}^{p^k q^k i}$ will be uniformly located within some compact set. By Definition 3.1., Property 4., it follows that y^k is a bounded sequence. Hence, there is $\bar{y} \in \mathbf{R}^l_+$ s.t. $y^k \underset{k}{\to} \bar{y}$ w.l.o.g. We have established that

$$(p^k, q^k, X^k, y^k) \underset{k \in \mathbf{N}}{\to} (\bar{p}, \bar{q}, \bar{X}, \bar{y})$$

w.l.o.g., because

$$p^k x^{ki} \leqslant p^k a^i - q^k y^k$$

and boundedness of y^k together with $\bar{p}_{m+1} > 0$ will prevent ξ^{ki} from tending to $-\infty$, as this would contradict the budget maximizing properties of x^{ki} eventually.

Step 5. It remains to show that

$(\bar{p}, \bar{q}, \bar{X}, \bar{y})$ is a Ψ-$\mathbf{Q}^0$-equilibrium.

Conditions 0., 1., and 2. of Definition 4.1 are obviously satisfied, 5. follows from closedness of Y. As to 4., it is not hard to verify that $\hat{X}^i$ is u.h.c. at $\bar{p} > 0, \bar{q} > 0$ and $\bar{y}$.

Concerning condition 3., observe that ${}^k\hat{u}^{p^k q^k i}$ and $\hat{u}^{p^k q^k i}$ will coincide on increasingly large stets. By Definition 3.1, as Ψ is finitely determined, this means $\Psi({}^k\Sigma^{p^k q^k}) = \Psi(\Sigma^{p^k q^k})$ for large k. Because Ψ is u.h.c. as $\bar{p}, \bar{q} > 0$ we conclude that $\bar{y} = \Psi \Sigma^{\bar{p}\bar{q}}$).

Suppose now that Y has.constant returns to scale. Then (0,0) is efficient, and returning to the proof (and notation) of Theorem 3.5., we find that (16) implies

$$0 = \bar{p}0 + n\bar{q}0 = \bar{p}\tilde{x} + n\bar{q}\bar{y} \geqslant \bar{p} \sum_{i \in \Omega} (\bar{x}^i - a^i) + n\bar{q}\bar{y}.$$

This holds within the framework of $\mathbf{M}^k$. However, turning to the limit, we find

$$0 \geqslant \bar{p} \sum_{i \in \Omega} (\bar{x}^i - a^i) + n\bar{q}\bar{y} \tag{40}$$

holds true also w.r. the equilibrium established for **M**. But ">" in (39) would establish

$$\bar{p}(\bar{x}^i - a^i) + \bar{q}\bar{y} < 0$$

for at least one $i \in \Omega$ – a contradiction to the fact that u^i is strictly monotone.

q.e.d.

References

Albers, W.: Grundzüge einiger Lösungskonzepte, die auf Forderungsniveaus der Spieler basieren. OR-Verfahren/Methods of Operations Research, 1974, 1–8.

–: Bloc forming tendencies as characteristics of bargaining behaviour in different versions of Apex games. Coalition Forming Behaviour. Tübingen 1978, 172–203.

Aumann, R.J.: Values of markets with a continuum of traders. Econometrica **43**, 1975, 611–646.

Aumann, R.J., and *L.S. Shapley*: Values of non-atomic games. Princeton, N.Y., 1974.

Denzau, A.T., and *R.P. Parks*: Existence of voting market equilibria. C.O.R.E. Diskussion paper 7831, 1978.

Harsanyi, J.C.: A bargaining model for the cooperative *n*-person game. Ann. Math. Stud. **40**, 1959, 325–356.

–: A simplified bargaining model for the *n*-person cooperative game. Int. Ec.-Review **4** (2), 1963, 194–220.

Lindahl, E.: Just taxation: a positive solution. Classics in the theory of public finance. Ed. by R.A. Musgrave and A.T. Peacock. London 1967.

McKelvey, R.D., and *R.E. Wendell*: Voting equilibria in multidimensional choice spaces. Mathematics of Operations Research **1** (2), 1976, 144–158.

Milleron, J.-C.: Theory of value with public goods. A survey article. Journal of Economic Theory **5**, 1972, 419–477.

Nash, J.F.: The bargaining problem. Econometrica **18**, 1954, 152–162.

Ostmann, A.: Fair play und Standortparadigma. Thesis, Institute of Statistics and Mathematical Economics, University of Karlsruhe, 1978.

–: On location conflicts and their fair solution concepts. Working papers, Institute of Mathematical Economics, University of Bielefeld, Nr. 77, 1979.

Richter, W.F.: A game-theoretic approach to location-allocation conflicts. Habilitation thesis, Faculty of Economics, University of Karlsruhe, 1979a.

–: Shapley's value and fair solutions of location conflicts. Institute of Statistics and Mathematical Economics, University of Karlsruhe, 1979b, to appear.

–: Social choice for bliss-point problems. Institute of Statistics and Mathematical Economics, University of Karlsruhe, 1979c, to appear.

Roberts, D.J.: Existence of Lindahl equilibrium with a measure space of consumers. Journal of Economic Theory **6**, 1973, 355–381.

Rosenmüller, J.: Selection of values for non-sidepayment games. Working papers, Institute of Mathematical Economics, University of Bielefeld, Nr. 75, 1978.

–: Einstimmigkeitsspiele 2. Art, Standortspiele und Fortsetzungsmöglichkeiten des NASH-Wertes. Mathematical Systems in Economics **45**, 1979, 40–56.

Shapley, L.S.: A general exchange economy with money. The RAND Corporation, RM-4248-PR, 1964.

–: Utility comparism and the theory of games. Paris 1969.

Slutsky, S.: A voting model for the allocation of public goods, existence of an equilibrium. Journal of Economic Theory **14** (2), 1977, 299–325.

Zeckhauser, R.J., and *M.C. Weinstein*: The topology of Pareto-optimal regions with public goods. Econometrica **42**, 1974, 643–666.

Games, Economic Dynamics, and Time Series Analysis. 1982 ©Physica-Verlag, Wien–Würzburg

Equilibrium Point Selection in a Class of Market Entry Games

By *R. Selten*, Bielefeld[1]) and *W. Güth*, Köln[2])

1. Introduction

It is the purpose of this paper to investigate a class of games, where each player has to decide whether to enter a market or not. A player's payoff is the difference of two components, market profits and entry costs. The game is symmetric with respect to market profits, but entry costs are different for each player. Since only the entry decisions are modelled explicitly each player has two pure strategies.

It is assumed that the incentive to enter is a non-increasing function of the number of players who enter the market. It will be shown that under this assumption the game always has equilibrium points in pure strategies, moreover, the number m of players in the market is the same for all pure strategy equilibrium points. With the help of the solution concept developed by Harsanyi and Selten one of these equilibrium points will be selected as the solution of the game. Harsanyi and Selten recently agreed to change their solution concept in several aspects. Our treatment will be based on the new version and not on that outlined in earlier publications [*Harsanyi*, 1975, 1977; *Güth*]. The solution of the game is that equilibrium point where the firms with the lowest entry costs enter the market.

Finally, examples of oligopoly situations will be discussed which are special cases of the class under consideration.

2. The Game Structure

The game we want to investigate is an n-person game in normal form where each player i has two pure strategies 0 and 1; here 0 stands for the decision not to enter and 1 indicates the decision to enter the market.

Each player i has entry costs C_i. The entry costs are different for different players. The players are numbered in such a way that we have:

$$C_1 < C_2 < \ldots < C_n . \tag{1}$$

Let m be the number of players who enter the market. Those who enter the market re-

[1]) *R. Selten*, IMW, Universität Bielefeld, Universitätsstr., D–4800 Bielefeld.
[2]) *W. Güth*, Universität zu Köln, D–5000 Köln.

ceive R_m and those who do not enter the market receive S_m as market profits. Let $\pi = (\pi_1, \ldots, \pi_n)$ be a combination of pure strategies where π_i is one of both pure strategies of player i and let $m(\pi)$ be the number of players with $\pi_i = 1$. Then the payoff function H_i of player i is as follows:

$$H_i(\pi) = \begin{cases} R_{m(\pi)} - C_i & \text{for } \pi_i = 1 \\ S_{m(\pi)} & \text{for } \pi_i = 0. \end{cases} \tag{2}$$

The expression

$$A_m = R_m - S_{m-1} \tag{3}$$

will be called *incentive to enter*. We shall assume that A_m is a non-increasing function of m:

$$A_1 \geqslant A_2 \geqslant \ldots \geqslant A_n. \tag{4}$$

Assumption (4) will be referred to as incentive monotonicity. In order to exclude border cases, which would complicate the analysis without adding much to the economic significance of the results, we require non-degeneracy in the following sense:

$$C_i \neq A_m \qquad \text{for } i, m = 1, \ldots, n \tag{5}$$

$$C_i + C_j \neq C_k + C_l \qquad \text{for } i, j, k, l = 1, \ldots, n \text{ pairwise different} \tag{6}$$

For the same reason equality has been excluded in (1).

Obviously, the game is fully specified by $3n$ real numbers, namely $C_1, \ldots, C_n$, $R_1, \ldots, R_n$, $S_0, \ldots, S_{n-1}$, satisfying (1), (4), (5) and (6). In the following a game of this kind will be called a *market entry game.*

Note that we do not assume anything on the sign of C_i, R_m and S_m. Even if for the application, which we have in mind, the C_i generally will be positive numbers.

3. Pure Strategy Equilibrium Points

Let $\bar{m}$ be that integer which satisfies

$$C_{\bar{m}} < A_{\bar{m}} \quad \text{or } \bar{m} = 0 \tag{7}$$

and

$$C_{\bar{m}+1} > A_{\bar{m}+1} \quad \text{or } \bar{m} = n. \tag{8}$$

Since C_m is monotonically increasing and A_m is monotonically non-increasing in m and since equalities are excluded by (5), it is clear that exactly one $\bar{m}$ exists which satisfies (7) and (8). As we shall see, $\bar{m}$ is the equilibrium number of players who enter the market.

Let $\pi = (\pi_1, \ldots, \pi_n)$ be a pure strategy combination and let π_1' be a strategy of player

i, then π/π_i' denotes that strategy combination which results from π by substituting π_i' for π_i and leaving all other components of π unchanged:

$$\pi/\pi_i' = (\pi_1, \ldots, \pi_{i-1}, \pi_i', \pi_{i+1}, \ldots, \pi_n). \tag{9}$$

With the help of this notation an equilibrium point in pure strategies can be defined as a pure strategy combination $\pi^* = (\pi_1^*, \ldots, \pi_n^*)$ with

$$H_i(\pi^*) = \max_{\pi_i \in \Pi_i} H_i(\pi^*/\pi_i) \tag{10}$$

for $i = 1, \ldots, n$ where Π_i is player i's set of pure strategies, in our case the set $\{0,1\}$.

Theorem 1: Let $\bar{\pi} = (\bar{\pi}_1, \ldots, \bar{\pi}_n)$ be the following pure strategy combination

$$\bar{\pi}_i = \begin{cases} 1 & \text{for } i = 1, \ldots, \bar{m} \\ 0 & \text{for } i = \bar{m}+1, \ldots, n \end{cases} \tag{11}$$

where $\bar{m}$ is defined by (7) and (8). The strategy combination $\bar{\pi}$ is an equilibrium point in pure strategies.

Proof: Obviously, the payoffs for $\bar{\pi}$ are as follows:

$$H_i(\bar{\pi}) = \begin{cases} R_{\bar{m}} - C_i & \text{for } i = 1, \ldots, \bar{m} \\ S_{\bar{m}} & \text{for } i = \bar{m}+1, \ldots, n. \end{cases} \tag{12}$$

Consider a player i with $i = 1, \ldots, \bar{m}$. If he deviates to $\pi_i = 0$ he receives

$$H_i(\bar{\pi}/\pi_i) = S_{\bar{m}-1}. \tag{13}$$

In view of (3) and (7) this is smaller than $H_i(\bar{\pi})$. Now, consider a player $i = \bar{m}+1, \ldots, n$. If he deviates to $\pi_i = 1$ he receives

$$H_i(\bar{\pi}/\pi_i) = R_{\bar{m}+1} - C_i. \tag{14}$$

In view of (3) and (8) this is smaller than $H_i(\bar{\pi})$.

Theorem 2: The pure strategy combination $\pi^* = (\pi_1^*, \ldots, \pi_n^*)$ is an equilibrium point if and only if the following conditions are satisfied:

$$m(\pi^*) = \bar{m} \tag{15}$$

$$C_i < A_{\bar{m}} \quad \text{for every } i \text{ with } \pi_i^* = 1 \tag{16}$$

$$C_i > A_{\bar{m}+1} \quad \text{for every } i \text{ with } \pi_i^* = 0. \tag{17}$$

Proof: In the same way as in the proof of theorem 1 it can be seen immediately that each player looses by deviating from a strategy combination π^* satisfying (15), (16), and (17). This proves the if-part of the theorem.

Now suppose that π^* is an equilibrium point. We must show that (15), (16), and (17) are satisfied. Define $m^* = m(\pi^*)$. Inequalities (16) and (17) must be satisfied with m^* instead of $\bar{m}$, since otherwise in view of (3) a deviation would be profitable for at least on one player.

It remains to show $m^* = \bar{m}$. Suppose that $m^* < \bar{m}$. Then at least one of the players $i = 1, \ldots, \bar{m}$ employs the strategy $\pi_i^* = 0$. For this player i we have $C_i < A_{m^*+1}$ since $A_{m^*+1} \geqslant A_{\bar{m}}$. This player i could gain by deviating to $\pi_i = 1$.

Suppose that $m^* > \bar{m}$. Then at least one of the players $i = \bar{m} + 1, \ldots, n$ employs the strategy $\pi_i^* = 1$. For this player i we have $C_i > A_{m^*}$, since $A_{\bar{m}} \geqslant A_{m^*}$. This player i could gain by deviating to $\pi_i = 0$.

This shows that π^* cannot be an equilibrium point unless we have (15).

Remark: The proof of theorem 2 shows that all the pure strategy equilibrium points are strong in the sense that every player looses by deviating to another strategy.

4. Elimination of Dominated Strategies

It can be seen easily that a player i has a dominated strategy if and only if either

$$C_i > A_1 \tag{18}$$

or

$$C_i < A_n \tag{19}$$

holds. In case (18) the strategy $\pi_i = 1$ and in the case (19) the strategy $\pi_i = 0$ is dominated. In both cases we have strict dominance, weak dominance is excluded by (5).

It is intuitively clear that the game situation remains essentially unchanged if the players with dominated strategies are fixed at their undominated strategies. In this way, the original game can be mapped into another game where the set of players is reduced by the elimination of those who have dominated strategies in the original game. It can be seen without difficulties that after an appropriate renumbering of the remaining players the new game is in the general class of games considered here. Therefore, we do not suffer a real loss of generality if we restrict our attention to games where no player has a dominated strategy. Accordingly, we shall assume

$$C_i < A_1 \quad \text{for } i = 1, \ldots, n \tag{20}$$

$$C_i > A_n \quad \text{for } i = 1, \ldots, n. \tag{21}$$

It may, of course, happen that new dominated strategies occur after we have gone through the process of eliminating strategies once, but after a finite number of repetitions we shall receive a game without dominated strategies.

The solution concept developed by Harsanyi and Selten specifies a reduction procedure which among other things eliminates dominated strategies [*Harsanyi,* 1975, 1977; *Güth*]. It could be formally shown that the application of the solution concept leads to the result that in our case instead of a game with dominated strategies that game must be solved which is received by iterated elimination of dominated strategies. In order to avoid lengthy details we shall not do this here. We shall restrict our attention to games satisfying (20) and (21). Such games will be called *regular market entry games.*

5. Formations

The solution concept requires us to look at certain substructures of the game called formations. Consider a game which results from the original one by restricting the pure strategy sets of the players to nonempty subsets of the original pure strategy sets; the new payoff function is the old one restricted to the new set of strategy combinations. Games which arise in this way are called formations if for every player i the following is true for every joint mixture of pure strategy combinations of the other players in the new game: Player i's best replies to this joint mixture are the same in the original and the new game.

A primitive formation is a formation which has no proper subformation. Consider a pure strategy equilibrium point $\pi = (\pi_1, \ldots, \pi_n)$ which is strong in the sense that for $i = 1, \ldots, n$ player i's equilibrium strategy π_i is the only best reply to π. Clearly, we receive a primitive formation if we restrict every player i's pure strategy set to the single strategy π_i. It may happen that a game has primitive formations which do not arise from strong pure strategy equilibrium points. As we shall see, this is not the case in the games considered here.

In the solution concept developed by Harsanyi and Selten the primitive formations are of special significance. In a game which cannot be further decomposed or reduced the solutions of the primitive formations are considered to be natural solution candidates which must be compared with each other in order to eliminate all but one if this is possible.

Theorem 3: In a market entry game the primitive formations are exactly those substructures which arise from a pure strategy equilibrium point $\pi = (\pi_1, \ldots, \pi_n)$ by restricting every player i's strategy set to his equilibrium strategy π_i.

Proof: As we have seen at the end of section 3, all pure strategy equilibrium points are strong. This shows that they yield primitive formations. It remains to show that no primitive formation can have more than one strategy for any player. Let C be the set of players which have two strategies in their restricted pure strategy set. Since the other players are fixed at their formation strategies the players in C find themselves in a situation which after an appropriate renumbering of the players is equivalent to a game in our class. Therefore, by theorem 1 the formation has a strong pure strategy equilibrium point. It follows by the definition of a formation that this equilibrium point is a strong equilibrium point of the whole game, too. This shows that the formation is not primitive.

6. Payoff Dominance

As we have explained before, the solutions of primitive formations are regarded as natural candidates for the solution of the game. They are called initial candidates. The set of all initial candidates is referred to as the first candidate set since in the process of finding the solution a sequence of a finite number of candidate sets may have to be considered.

In our case the initial candidate set is the set of all strong equilibrium points.

We say that an equilibrium point φ payoff dominates an equilibrium point ψ if we have

$$H_i(\varphi) > H_i(\Psi) \quad \text{for } i = 1, \ldots, n. \tag{22}$$

The next step after the determination of the first candidate set consists in the elimination of all initial candidates which are payoff dominated by other initial candidates. In this way one receives the second candidate set.

In order to see how in our case the second candidate set differs from the first one we investigate the circumstances under which one strong equilibrium point $\varphi = (\varphi_1, \ldots, \varphi_n)$ payoff dominates another strong equilibrium point $\Psi = (\Psi_1, \ldots, \Psi_n)$.

We first observe that the following equations hold for players who use the same strategy in φ and Ψ:

$$H_i(\varphi) = H_i(\Psi) = S_{\bar{m}} \quad \text{for } \varphi_i = \Psi_i = 0 \tag{23}$$

$$H_i(\varphi) = H_i(\Psi) = R_{\bar{m}} - C_i \quad \text{for } \varphi_i = \Psi_i = 1. \tag{24}$$

Since payoff dominance is defined by strong inequality we must have

$$\varphi_i \neq \Psi_i \quad \text{for } i = 1, \ldots, n \tag{25}$$

if φ payoff dominates Ψ. Therefore a payoff dominance relationship requires

$$n = 2\bar{m} \tag{26}$$

since those players who are in the market in one equilibrium point must be outside the market in the other. If φ payoff dominates Ψ, thus the following conditions must be satisfied:

$$R_{\bar{m}} - C_i > S_{\bar{m}} \quad \text{for } i \text{ with } \varphi_i = 1 \tag{27}$$

$$S_{\bar{m}} > R_{\bar{m}} - C_i \quad \text{for } i \text{ with } \varphi_i = 0. \tag{28}$$

On the left hand side of the inequalities (27) and (28) we find the payoffs in φ and on the right hand side those in Ψ. This shows that the players i with $\varphi_i = 1$ and $\Psi_i = 0$ must be the players $1, \ldots, \bar{m}$. Consequently, φ cannot payoff dominate Ψ unless we have

$$\varphi = (1, \ldots, 1, 0, \ldots, 0) \tag{29}$$

$$\Psi = (0, \ldots, 0, 1, \ldots, 1). \tag{30}$$

This shows that the second candidate set either agrees with the first one or has exactly one candidate less, namely $(0, \ldots, 0, 1, \ldots, 1)$.

7. Risk Dominance

In order to narrow down the second candidate set a notion of risk dominance is employed. For any two equilibrium points it can be determined whether one risk dominates the other. It may also happen that there is no risk dominance relationship between two equilibrium points. The definition of risk dominance is based on the idea that for the purpose of comparing two equilibrium points φ and Ψ one has to look at a hypothetical situation where one player i is convinced that either φ or Ψ is the solution and that all other players know which one of both equilibrium points is the solution.

It may happen that $\varphi_i = \Psi_i$. In this case player i does not have to know whether φ or Ψ is the solution. He just can play $\varphi_i = \Psi_i$.

Consider a player i with $\varphi_i \neq \Psi_i$; he must have a subjective probability z for φ being the solution. With this probability z his expected payoff for playing a pure strategy π_i is equal to

$$E_i(\pi_i, z) = zH_i(\varphi/\pi_i) + (1-z)H_i(\Psi/\pi_i). \tag{31}$$

We say that π_i is a best reply to z if π_i is a pure strategy which maximizes $E_i(\pi_i, z)$. Let r_i^z be that mixed strategy of player i which assigns equal positive probability to all best replies to z and zero probability to all other pure strategies. It is reasonable to suppose that player i will use the strategy r_i^z if his payoff expectation is given by (31). He has no reason to prefer one of the pure best replies to z.

For each of the players i with $\varphi_i \neq \Psi_i$ we define a strategy p_i which can be thought of as a preliminary theory on his behavior. Since this strategy plays a similar role as a prior probability distribution it is called player i's prior strategy. Assume that z is a random variable uniformly distributed over the interval [0,1]. If this is the case the probability, with which any pure strategy π_i is used by player i, is given by the following integral:

$$p_i(\pi_i) = \int_0^1 r_i^z(\pi_i)\,dz. \tag{32}$$

Equation (32) defines player i's prior strategy.

We shall first define risk dominance for the case that we have $\varphi_i \neq \Psi_i$ for $i = 1, \ldots, n$. The definition is based on the application of the tracing procedure to the prior strategy combination $p = (p_1, \ldots, p_n)$. The tracing procedure which will not be described here in detail [see *Harsanyi* 1975, 1977] can be thought of as a mathematical model of a reasoning process which starts with a prior strategy combination and ends with an equilibrium point. The initial non-equilibrium strategy combination is gradually changed into an equilibrium point.

In the case $\varphi_i \neq \Psi_i$ for $i = 1, \ldots, n$ we say that φ risk dominates Ψ if φ is the equilibrium point which results if the tracing procedure is applied to p.

If for some players i we have $\varphi_i = \Psi_i$ the definition of risk dominance requires that the tracing procedure is not performed in the original game but in a restricted game; the restricted game is derived from the smallest formation which contains both φ and Ψ by fixing the players i with $\varphi_i = \Psi_i$ at these strategies. Obviously, in our case this formation contains both strategies for all players i with $\varphi_i \neq \Psi_i$. The restricted game differs from the original one by the fact that it has fewer players, namely those with $\varphi_i \neq \Psi_i$. The payoffs in the restricted game are derived from the original ones by fixing the players with $\varphi_i = \Psi_i$ at these strategies.

φ risk dominates Ψ if the application of the tracing procedure to the prior strategy combination in the restricted game yields φ as the final equilibrium point.

Since it may happen that neither φ nor Ψ results from the application of the tracing procedure it is not excluded that neither one of both equilibrium points risk dominates the other.

In the analysis of the market entry games investigated here it will not be necessary to apply the tracing procedure. It is known that the result of the tracing procedure is the best reply to the prior combination if this best reply is a strong equilibrium point. This is the situation which we find in the risk dominance computations arising in the analysis of our model.

8. Strategic Distance and Maximal Stability

Not all risk dominance comparisons between elements of the second candidate set are regarded as equally important. Comparison between equilibrium points, which are in a certain sense near to each other, are given priority.

Ideally, one would want to select an equilibrium point which risk dominates each other equilibrium point in the second candidate set. Unfortunately, this is not always possible. In view of this fact it seems to be reasonable to look for equilibrium points which are undominated by other equilibrium points within a large neighbourhood. One would like to make this neighbourhood as large as possible.

In order to make these ideas more precise it is necessary to introduce a measure of strategic distance. The measure adopted in the theory of Harsanyi and Selten is closely connected to the way in which the prior strategies are computed. For the sake of simplicity we shall explain the distance measure for the case $\varphi_i \neq \Psi_i$ for $i = 1, \ldots, n$. If we have $\varphi_i = \Psi_i$ for some players the same definitions apply to the restricted game.

Let r^z be the following strategy combination

$$r^z = (r_1^z, \ldots, r_n^z) \tag{33}$$

where the r_i^z are defined as in section 7. We call r^z the average best reply to z. The interval $0 \leqslant z \leqslant 1$ is divided into a finite number of subintervals where different strategy combinations are average best replies to z. Some of these subintervals are single points. Those strategy combinations, which are average best replies on a subinterval of positive length, are called essential for the comparison between φ and Ψ.

The strategic distance $e(\varphi, \Psi)$ is defined as the number of average best replies which are essential for the comparison between φ and Ψ.

If two strong equilibrium points φ and Ψ are compared the distance $e(\varphi, \Psi)$ is at least 2 since φ and Ψ are always essential average best replies.

The distance measure $e(\varphi, \Psi)$ has the following interpretation: It counts the number of critical subjective probabilities z where at least one player shifts from one best reply to another. The greater this number of critical probabilities is the greater is the confusion which arises in the risk dominance comparison between φ and Ψ. In this sense $e(\varphi, \Psi)$ measures the intensity of confusion. We may say that a preference for more clear cut comparisons is involved in giving priority to comparisons at small strategic distances.

The diameter $\bar{e}$ of the second candidate set is defined as the greatest distance $e(\varphi, \Psi)$ between two equilibrium points φ and Ψ in the second candidate set. For a given equilibrium point φ in the second candidate set let $\sigma(\varphi)$ be the greatest number k among the integers $1, \ldots, \bar{e}$ such that the second candidate set contains no Ψ with $e(\varphi, \Psi) \leqslant k$ which risk dominates φ. This number $\sigma(\varphi)$ is called the stability radius of φ. Let $\bar{\sigma}$ be the maximal stability radius of equilibrium points in the second candidate set. The elements φ of the second candidate set with $\sigma(\varphi) = \bar{\sigma}$ are called maximally stable.

If the second candidate set contains only one maximally stable element then this equilibrium point is the solution of the game. The determination of the solution is more complicated if there are several maximally stable equilibrium points. Fortunately, this more difficult case need not concern us here since the analysis of our model will exhibit a unique maximally stable equilibrium point.

9. Strategic Distances in Market Entry Games

If a regular market entry game has only one pure strategy equilibrium point then this must be the equilibrium point $\bar{\pi}$ described in theorem 1. Obviously, $\bar{\pi}$ is the solution if the game has no other equilibrium point. We can restrict our attention to the case that there are at least two strong equilibrium points.

Consider two different strong equilibrium points $\varphi = (\varphi_1, \ldots, \varphi_n)$ and $\Psi = (\Psi_1, \ldots, \Psi_n)$. Let M be the set of all players i with $\varphi_i \neq \Psi_i$. The set M is the player set of the restricted game for the risk dominance comparison between φ and Ψ. A player i in M must have an incentive not to enter if there are $\bar{m}$ other players in the market and he must have an incentive to enter if there are $\bar{m} - 1$ other players inside the market. Otherwise he could not have different strategies in both equilibrium points. Hence

$$A_{\bar{m}+1} < C_i < A_{\bar{m}} \qquad \text{for all } i \in M. \tag{34}$$

In order to compute the prior strategies p_i and the strategic distance $e(\varphi, \Psi)$ we must determine the best replies to z. Consider a player i with $\varphi_i = 1$ and $\Psi_i = 0$. For $\pi_i = 1$ and $\pi_i = 0$ equation (31) assumes the following form:

$$E_i(1, z) = z(R_{\bar{m}} - C_i) + (1 - z)(R_{\bar{m}+1} - C_i) \tag{35}$$

$$E_i(0, z) = z\, S_{\bar{m}-1} + (1 - z)\, S_{\bar{m}}. \tag{36}$$

Let $Z(\varphi_i)$ and $Z(\Psi_i)$, respectively, be the subintervals of $0 \leqslant z \leqslant 1$ where φ_i and Ψ_i are best replies to z. It follows by (35) and (36) that we have

$$Z(\varphi_i) = \left[\frac{C_i - A_{\bar{m}+1}}{A_{\bar{m}} - A_{\bar{m}+1}}, 1\right] \qquad \text{for } \varphi_i = 1 \tag{37}$$

$$Z(\Psi_i) = \left[\, 0, \frac{C_i - A_{\bar{m}+1}}{A_{\bar{m}} - A_{\bar{m}+1}} \right] \qquad \text{for } \varphi_i = 1. \tag{38}$$

Now consider a player $i \in M$ with $\varphi_i = 0$ and $\Psi_i = 1$. Here we have

$$E_i(1, z) = z(R_{\bar{m}+1} - C_i) + (1 - z)(R_{\bar{m}} - C_i) \tag{39}$$

$$E_i(0, z) = z\, S_{\bar{m}} + (1 - z)\, S_{\bar{m}-1}. \tag{40}$$

This yields

$$Z(\varphi_i) = \left[\frac{A_{\bar{m}} - C_i}{A_{\bar{m}} - A_{\bar{m}+1}}, 1 \right] \qquad \text{for } \varphi_i = 0 \tag{41}$$

$$Z(\Psi_i) = \left[\, 0, \frac{A_{\bar{m}} - C_i}{A_{\bar{m}} - A_{\bar{m}+1}} \right] \qquad \text{for } \varphi_i = 0. \tag{42}$$

Equations (37), (38), (41) and (42) show that player i shifts from his best reply Ψ_i to his best reply φ_i at the following critical probability z_i:

$$z_i = \frac{C_i - A_{\bar{m}+1}}{A_{\bar{m}} - A_{\bar{m}+1}} \qquad \text{for } \varphi_i = 1 \tag{43}$$

$$z_i = \frac{A_{\bar{m}} - C_i}{A_{\bar{m}} - A_{\bar{m}+1}} \qquad \text{for } \varphi_i = 0. \tag{44}$$

In view of (34) it is clear that $0 < z_i < 1$ holds for $i = 1, \ldots, n$. Suppose that any two z_i are different from each other. It can be seen immediately that in this case there are $|M| + 1$ different essential average best replies r^z where $|M|$ is the number of players in M; the $|M|$ critical probabilities z_i subdivide the interval $0 \leqslant z \leqslant 1$ into $|M| + 1$ subintervals. This yields $e(\varphi, \Psi) = |M| + 1$.

The distance may be smaller than $|M| + 1$ if several of the z_i are equal to each other. In view of (1) two z_i of the form (43) for different players cannot be equal to each other; the same is true for two z_i of the form (44). Therefore for $i \neq j$ we cannot have $z_i = z_j$ unless both players use different strategies in φ. Suppose that for $\varphi_i = 0$ and $\varphi_j = 1$ the critical probabilities z_i and z_j are equal.

Then it follows by (43) and (44) that we must have

$$C_i + C_j = A_{\bar{m}} + A_{\bar{m}+1}. \tag{45}$$

In the case $\varphi_i = 1$ and $\varphi_j = 0$ the same condition must be satisfied. In view of the non-degeneracy assumption (6) there can be only one pair i, j with $i \neq j$ such that (45) holds. Suppose that i, j is a pair of this kind and that both players are in M. Then $e(\varphi, \Psi)$ is equal to $|M|$.

Since the number of players in the market is $\bar{m}$ in both equilibrium points, $|M|$ must be an even number. For $|M| = 2$ the distance is either $e(\varphi, \Psi) = 2$ or $e(\varphi, \Psi) = 3$. For $|M| = 4$ the distance $e(\varphi, \Psi)$ is either 4 or 5. Obviously for $|M| > 2$ the distance $e(\varphi, \Psi)$ is always greater than for $|M| = 2$.

As we shall see, a regular market entry game has one and only one equilibrium point, namely $\bar{\pi}$ as defined by (11) which is not risk dominated by any other equilibrium point at a distance of at most 3. From what we have said, it is clear that nothing more has to be shown in order to prove that $\bar{\pi}$ is the solution.

10. Risk Dominance in Market Entry Games

For the reasons mentioned above it will be sufficient to look at risk dominance comparisons between equilibrium points φ and Ψ with only two players using different strategies in φ and Ψ or, in other words, with $|M| = 2$. Let i and j be the two players in M and assume

$$\varphi_i = 1 \text{ and } \varphi_j = 0. \tag{46}$$

It follows by the definition of p_i in (32) and by (37), (38), (41) and (42) that we have

$$p_i(\varphi_i) = \frac{A_{\bar{m}} - C_i}{A_{\bar{m}} - A_{\bar{m}+1}} \tag{47}$$

$$p_i(\Psi_i) = \frac{C_i - A_{\bar{m}+1}}{A_{\bar{m}} - A_{\bar{m}+1}} \tag{48}$$

$$p_j(\varphi_j) = \frac{C_j - A_{\bar{m}+1}}{A_{\bar{m}} - A_{\bar{m}+1}} \tag{49}$$

$$p_j(\Psi_j) = \frac{A_{\bar{m}} - C_j}{A_{\bar{m}} - A_{\bar{m}+1}}. \tag{50}$$

Player i's strategy $\pi_i = 1$ is his only best reply to p_j in the restricted game if

$$\begin{aligned} &p_j(\varphi_j)(R_{\bar{m}} - C_i) + p_j(\Psi_j)(R_{\bar{m}+1} - C_i) \\ &> p_j(\varphi_j) S_{\bar{m}-1} + p_j(\Psi_j) S_{\bar{m}}. \end{aligned} \tag{51}$$

This inequality compares player i's expected payoff for his strategy $\pi_i = 1$ with the expected payoff for $\pi_i = 0$. (51) can be written as follows:

$$p_j(\varphi_j)(A_{\bar{m}} - C_i) + p_j(\Psi_j)(A_{\bar{m}+1} - C_i) > 0. \tag{52}$$

With the help of (49) and (50) it can be seen that this is equivalent to the following condition:

$$(C_j - A_{\bar{m}+1})(A_{\bar{m}} - C_i) > (A_{\bar{m}} - C_j)(C_i - A_{\bar{m}+1}). \tag{53}$$

Here we have used the fact that in view of (34) we have $A_{\bar{m}} > A_{\bar{m}+1}$. The case $A_{\bar{m}} = A_{\bar{m}+1}$ is not excluded by the model but by the assumption that there are at least two different strong equilibrium points. Suppose that we hace $C_i < C_j$. It can be seen with the help of (34) that all factors in (53) are positive. The first factor of the left-hand side of (53) is greater than the second factor on the right-hand side, and the second factor on the left-hand side is greater than the first one on the right hand side. In this way we can see that (53) holds if and only if C_i is smaller than C_j, i.e. for $i < j$.

Player j's strategy $\pi_j = 0$ is his only best reply to p_i in the restricted game if

$$\begin{aligned} &p_i(\varphi_i) S_{\bar{m}} + p_i(\Psi_i) S_{\bar{m}-1} \\ &> p_i(\varphi_i)(R_{\bar{m}+1} - C_j) + p_i(\Psi_i)(R_{\bar{m}} - C_j). \end{aligned} \tag{54}$$

With the help of (47) and (48) it can be seen in the same way as above that (54) is equivalent to (53). Consequently, player j's best reply to p_i is φ_j if and only if $C_i < C_j$ holds.

It is now clear that both φ_i and φ_j are the only best replies to the prior strategies in the restricted game if and only if we have $C_i < C_j$. (Note that the limiting case $C_i = C_j$ is excluded by (1).) If the tracing procedure is applied in the restricted game for the comparison of φ and Ψ the final result will be φ in the case $C_i < C_j$ and Ψ in the case $C_j < C_i$. If (46) holds for a comparison with $|M| = 2$ then φ risk dominates Ψ if and only if $C_i < C_j$ holds.

11. The Solution of Regular Market Entry Games

It now can be shown without much difficulty that $\bar{\pi}$ as given by (11) is the solution. For this purpose we shall prove two assertions a) and b):

a): Let Ψ be a strong equilibrium point with $e(\bar{\pi}, \Psi) \leqslant 3$ and $\Psi \neq \bar{\pi}$. Then $\bar{\pi}$ risk dominates Ψ.

b): Let Ψ be a strong equilibrium point with $\Psi \neq \bar{\pi}$. Then there exists a strong equilibrium point φ with $e(\varphi, \Psi) \leqslant 3$ such that φ risk dominates Ψ.

It is clear that a) and b) have the consequence that $\bar{\pi}$ is the only maximally stable strong equilibrium point in the second candidate set. (We have shown in section 5 that $\bar{\pi}$ is not payoff dominated). It follows by a) that the stability radius of $\bar{\pi}$ is at least 3 and it follows by b) that the stability radius of any other strong equilibrium point is smaller than 3.

We now proceed to show a). Let i and j be the two players who use different strategies in $\bar{\pi}$ and Ψ and assume $\bar{\pi}_i = 1$ and $\bar{\pi}_j = 0$. It follows by definition (11) of $\bar{\pi}$ that we must have $C_i < C_j$. In view of the result of section 10 this shows that a) is true.

It remains to show b). The equilibrium point Ψ prescribes $\Psi_i = 0$ to at least one of the players $1, \ldots, \bar{m}$ and $\Psi_j = 1$ to at least one of the players $\bar{m} + 1, \ldots, n$. Let i and j be two such players. Define $\varphi = (\varphi_1, \ldots, \varphi_n)$ as follows:
$\varphi_i = 1, \varphi_j = 0$ and $\varphi_k = \Psi_k$ for every k different from i and j. Since in view of (1) we have $C_i < C_j$ it follows by the result of section 10 that φ risk dominates Ψ.

As the result of our analysis we can state the following theorem:

Theorem 4: The solution of a regular market entry game is the equilibrium point $\bar{\pi}$ described in theorem 1.

12. The Linear Cournot-Market Entry Game

The most obvious example is based on the linear Cournot-model. The model is embedded in a two stage-game which can be described as follows:

Stage 1 (entry stage): n potential suppliers $1, \ldots, n$ simultaneously choose $\pi_i = 0$ (no entry) or $\pi_i = 1$ (entry). The choices are made without knowing the decisions of the others. At the end of Stage 1 the vector $\pi = (\pi_1, \ldots, \pi_n)$ is made known to all players $1, \ldots, n$.

Stage 2 (supply stage): All players with $\pi_i = 1$ simultaneously choose a supply $x_i \geqslant 0$. The choices are made without knowing the decisions of the others. For $\pi_i = 0$ we define $x_i = 0$.

Payoffs: The payoff functions H_i are defined as follows:

$$H_i = \begin{cases} x_i p - kx_i - C_i & \text{for } \pi_i = 1 \\ 0 & \text{for } \pi_i = 0 \end{cases} \tag{55}$$

where the price p is given by

$$p = \min\,[b - ax, 0] \tag{56}$$

and x is total supply:

$$x = x_1 + \ldots + x_n \tag{57}$$

a, b and k are positive constants with $b > k$. The entry costs $C_1, \ldots, C_n$ are positive and satsify inequality (1).

The two stage-game model is a game in extensive form. Each situation, which can arise at the beginning of stage 2, corresponds to a subgame. We call these subgames supply decision subgames. For every vector $\pi = (\pi_1, \ldots, \pi_n)$ with $\pi \neq (0, \ldots, 0)$ the game has one supply decision subgame Γ_π. There are no other proper subgames.

A natural solution concept which can be applied to the extensive game is that of subgame perfect equilibrium point. An equilibrium point is called subgame perfect if it induces an equilibrium point on every subgame [*Selten*, 1973, 1975]. In order to find the subgame perfect equilibrium points of the two stage-model we have to look at the equilibrium points of the supply decision subgames.

As we shall see each of the Γ_π has a uniquely determined equilibrium point which can be found as follows: For $\pi_i = 1$ we have

$$H_i = x_i (b - k - ax) - C_i. \tag{58}$$

It follows that for $x_i > 0$ the condition

$$\frac{\partial H_i}{\partial x_i} = b - k - ax - ax_i = 0 \tag{59}$$

must be satisfied at the equilibrium point. Let m be the number of players with $x_i > 0$ at the equilibrium point. Summing the necessary conditions (59) for all i with $x_i > 0$ yields

$$x = \frac{m}{m+1} \frac{b-k}{a}. \tag{60}$$

This together with (59) leads to the following conclusions:

$$x_i = \frac{1}{m+1} \frac{b-k}{a} \quad \text{if } x_i > 0 \tag{61}$$

$$p = k + \frac{b-k}{m+1}. \tag{62}$$

Since p is greater than k a player i with $\pi_i = 1$ cannot have the equilibrium supply $x_i = 0$; a sufficiently small $x_i > 0$ would still yield a price greater than k and thereby raise player i's payoff above $-C_i$. Consequently, m is nothing else than the number of players with $\pi_i = 1$ and (61) holds for all these players. It can be seen immediately that the marginal conditions are not only necessary but also sufficient for equilibrium. Consequently, we have found an equilibrium point which is uniquely determined.

The equilibrium profits for Γ_π are functions of π; player i's equilibrium payoff will be denoted by $H_i(\pi)$. Equation (55), (61) and (62) yield

$$H_i(\pi) = \begin{cases} \frac{1}{a}\left(\frac{b-k}{m(\pi)+1}\right)^2 - C_i & \text{for } \pi_i = 1 \\ 0 & \text{for } \pi_i = 0 \end{cases} \tag{63}$$

where $m(\pi)$ is the number of players with $\pi_i = 1$ in π.

The subgame perfect equilibrium points of the two stage-model can be found with the help of the truncated game which results from the original extensive form if every subgame Γ_π is replaced by the corresponding payoff vector $H(\pi) = (H_1(\pi), \ldots, H_n(\pi))$. This truncated game will be denoted by $\bar{\Gamma}$.

As we shall see, the truncated game $\bar{\Gamma}$ is a market entry game if the non-degeneracy conditions (5) and (6) are satisfied. The theory of Harsanyi and Selten can be used in order to select one of the equilibrium points of $\bar{\Gamma}$. For this purpose we can make use of the results obtained above. Together with the uniquely determined subgame equilibria the solution of $\bar{\Gamma}$ determines a subgame perfect equilibrium point for the two stage-model. It is natural to think of this equilibrium point as the solution of the two-stage model even if the theory of Harsanyi and Selten has been developed for finite games only and, therefore, cannot be applied directly to a game with infinitely many pure strategies.

In order to see that $\bar{\Gamma}$ is a market entry game if the non-degeneracy conditions (5) and (6) are given it remains to show that (4) is satisfied.

In our case we have

$$R_m = \frac{1}{a}\left(\frac{b-k}{m+1}\right)^2 \tag{64}$$

$$S_m = 0. \tag{65}$$

This yields

$$A_m = \frac{1}{a}\left(\frac{b-k}{m+1}\right)^2. \tag{66}$$

Equation (66) shows that A_m is a decreasing function of m. Assumption (4) is satisfied. If, in addition to this, (5) and (6) are satisfied the solution of $\bar{\Gamma}$ is given by theorem 4. Those $\bar{m}$ players who have the lowest entry costs enter the market while the other players stay outside. This is the result one would intuitively expect. Nevertheless, it is important to see that it can be obtained by a general theory without making use of ad hoc-arguments related to specific features of market entry games.

13. Further Possible Applications of Market Entry Games

In the following we do not want to describe examples of market entry games in detail. Instead of this we shall give verbal descriptions of economic situations which could be modelled as market entry games under appropriate assumptions of functional form and parameters.

In the last section, we have opened up the linear Cournot-oligopoly model by adding a market entry stage which precedes the supply decisions. The same embedding procedure can be applied to many other oligopoly models, e.g. to models with differentiated products where prices, advertising expenditures or quality parameters are the decision variables.

It is also possible to look at two stage-models where the first stage is not an entry stage but an innovation stage. Suppose that each of n suppliers can adopt a method of production which saves labour but requires investment costs which are different for different firms in view of variation of technical experience. The second stage subgame equilibria will depend on the number m of suppliers who have adopted the new production method at the innovation stage.

In a paper by *Güth/Meyer* [1980] a multi-stage-oligopoly model is investigated which describes a situation where a successful production method already used by one oligopolist can be imitated by his competitors. One may think of a patent whose time of protection is running out. It has been shown in the paper that the analysis of this model leads to a market entry game.

Schelling [1973] discusses several examples of game situations where each player i has just two pure strategies $\pi_i = 0$ and $\pi_i = 1$. Some of these games typically will satisfy all structural relationships of market entry games. Applying our results, which are based on the equilibrium selection theory of Harsanyi and Selten, these games now can be more thoroughly investigated.

There are many examples in the area of public choice which, in principle, permit a description in terms of market entry games even if the application of a game theoretical theory of equilibrium point selection does not seem to be really adequate. Suppose, for example, that vaccination against an infectious disease, say polio, is available on a voluntary basis. Since the danger of infection is a decreasing function of the number of people vaccinated the incentive to obtain vaccination also decreases with this number. Those who obtain vaccination receive a utility R derived from security against disease and from which an individually different cost component C_i must be subtracted which stands for the inconvenience of vaccination (it is assumed that utilities are additive in these components; the assumption that R is equal to everybody can be secured by an appropriate scaling of utility units). Whereas $R_m = R$ is constant the utility S_m obtained by the vaccination of m other individuals increases with m. Therefore A_m is a decreasing function of m. Clearly, theorems 1 and 2 can be applied to this model but it is debatable whether it makes sense to apply the selection theory of Harsanyi and Selten. The game model assumes that every player knows the costs C_i of every other player. If information is incomplete in this respect a different and more difficult game is played.

References

Güth, W.: Zur Theorie kollektiver Lohnverhandlungen. Baden-Baden 1978.

Güth, W., and *U. Meyer*: Innovationsentscheidungen in oligopolistischen Märkten. Zeitschrift für die gesamte Staatswissenschaft, March 1980.

Harsanyi, J.C.: The tracing procedure: A Bayesian approach to defining a solution for n-person noncooperative games. International Journal of Game Theory, 1975, 61–94.

–: A solution concept for n-person noncooperative games. International Journal of Game Theory. 1977, 211–225.

Schelling, T.C.: Hockey helmets, concealed weapons, and daylight saving – A study of binary choices with externalities. Journal of Conflict Resolution, 1973, 381–428.

Selten, R.: A simple model of imperfect competition, where 4 are few and 6 are many. International Journal of Game Theory, 1973, 141–201.

–: Reexamination of the perfectness concept for equilibrium points in extensive games. International Journal of Game Theory, 1975, 25–55.

Games, Economic Dynamics, and Time Series Analysis. 1982 ©Physica-Verlag, Wien–Würzburg

Insuring and Auditing the Auditor

By *K. Borch*, Bergen[1])

1. Introduction

1.1 Auditing of accounts is often based on sampling inspection, simply because it seems unnecessarily costly to check every voucher and every entry in the books. The possibility that any transaction may be checked in full detail is believed to have a detering effect likely to prevent irregularities. A theoretical analysis of problems in this field naturally leads to a search for suitable sampling methods, and there exist handbooks of sampling techniques for the use of auditors. A short outline of these methods has been given by *Kaplan* [1973], who also gives references to relevant literature.

1.2 The sampling approach implies that the auditor believes he plays a game against nature, and that he finds it optimal to use a mixed strategy. It is not unreasonable to assume that in the real world the game is played against an intelligent opponent, who does his best to get away with fraud, or to steal without being discovered. This assumption leads to a non-zero-sum game of a type, which first seems to have been studied by *Maschler* [1966] and [1967]. He called it the inspector's game, and in the following we shall discuss some varieties of this game.

In the next section we shall show that the sampling approach may be inappropriate, and in the following sections we shall indicate how the situation can be analysed as a two- and three-person game.

2. The Sampling Approach – A Simple Model

2.1 We shall begin by studying a simple model of the type discussed by *Kaplan* [1973]. Let the stochastic variable x_t represent the profits of the firm on day t. The profit becomes first known to an accountant, who can embezzle a non-negative amount c_t, and report a profit $y_t = x_t - c_t$ to the owner of the firm. If the owner finds the sequence $\{y_1, \ldots, y_t, \ldots, y_n\}$ suspicious, he may carry out an extra audit. The owner's problem is to determine when he should carry out the audit, i.e. for each n he must determine a critical region for the vector $\{y_1, \ldots, y_n\}$.

It is difficult to analyse this problem without assuming that the stochastic process generating the profits is completely known. The simplest assumption of this kind would be that the $x_1, \ldots, x_t, \ldots$ are stochastically independent and identically distributed.

[1]) *K. Borch*, Norwegian School of Business, Helleveien 30, N–5000 Bergen.

2.2 The problem formulated above is too general to admit simple analysis. To simplify it we shall assume that n is given, for instance equal to the number of days in the month. If the owner finds the sequence $\{y_1, \ldots, y_n\}$ suspicious, he will audit the accounts for every day in the month. We shall assume that this will cost him an amount q.

We have

$$E\{y_t\} = E\{x_t\} - E\{c_t\}.$$

If the accountant chooses c_t independently of x_t, we will have

$$\text{Var}\{y_t\} = \text{var}\{x_t\}.$$

It is however evident that the accountant can choose the sequence $\{c_1, \ldots, c_n\}$ so that var $\{y_t\} \lessgtr$ var $\{x_t\}$.

Kaplan suggests that the owner should choose a number r, and consider the y-sequence as suspicious if

$$y < E\{x\} - r\sqrt{\text{var}\{x\}} = E\{x\} - r\sigma.$$

Here

$$x = \sum_{t=1}^{n} x_t \text{ and } y = \sum_{t=1}^{n} y_t.$$

Presumably the owner will choose r considerably lower than by the usual significance tests. If there is a probability of say 0.1 that an observed sequence has arisen when there is no embezzlement, a complete audit may be called for.

The test indicated is obviously crude, since it is based only on monthly profits, i.e. on the average of reported daily profits. To a statistician it may be tempting to design a more refined test to decide whether a reported sequence $\{y_1, \ldots, y_n\}$ differs in any suspicious way from the expected outcome.

2.3 Clearly an intelligent accountant will embezzle only if this can be done without resulting in a suspicious y-sequence. Such sequences can however arise naturally with a probability α. The owner will then audit the accounts for the corresponding months, without discovering any fraud. The average monthly cost of this auditing will be αq. To illustrate let the distribution of x be $F(x)$, and $E\{x\} = \bar{x}$, so that

$$\alpha = Pr(x < \bar{x} - r\sigma) = F(\bar{x} - r\sigma) = F(z).$$

The expected amount which the accountant can steal each month will then be

$$\int_{z}^{\infty} (x - z)\, dF(x).$$

This is clearly less than the total amount $\bar{x}$, which he could embezzle in the absence of any auditing, but the amount may still be substantial.

If $Pr(x_t = 0) = Pr(x_t = 1) = 1/2$ and $n = 25$, we have

$$E\{x\} = 12.5 \quad \text{and} \quad \text{var}\{x\} = 2.5$$

and approximately

$$Pr(x \leqslant 9) = 0.1.$$

If the owner audits only the months showing a profit less than 10, an intelligent accountant can steal a day's profit in more than half the months, without being discovered, and possibly even without being suspected of dishonesty.

The owner might dismiss his statistical consultant, and decide to audit the accounts of arbitrary months selected at random with a probability α. This will give the same average auditing cost, and it will also give him a possibility of discovering fraud. If the accountant is unaware of the element of surprise introduced in the auditing, he may continue to steal at a fraction $1-\alpha$ of the months. The probability that he shall not be caught is $1-\alpha(1-\alpha) = 1-\alpha+\alpha^2 \geqslant 0.75$.

2.4 The assumption that the stochastic process is completely known is obviously unrealistic, and it is tempting to formulate the problem in a Bayesian manner. This will however place the owner in an even more disadvantageous position. The accountant can clearly manipulate his embezzlements so that the owner is led to believe that $E\{x\}$ is smaller and var$\{x\}$ greater than in reality. Theoretically the embezzlements could continue until the Bayesian owner is convinced that his firm is unprofitable, and decides to close it.

We shall not discuss these long-term aspects of the situation. It is clear that a number of elements have been assumed away in order to formulate the situation as a simple two-person game. These elements are discussed in some detail in the papers by Maschler referred to. The problem of the accountant is obviously to gain the confidence of the owner, and then exploit it to his own advantage.

The application which Maschler has in mind is a nuclear test ban, with rights to inspect when certain seismic events are observed. These events can be due either to an earthquake, or to a nuclear test. Obviously an inspection will be carried out only if an event has occurred. If the two causes lead to more or less different seismic events, some statistical problems can occur. One would then carry out an inspection only if the pattern of the seismic event indicated a fairly high probability that the cause was a nuclear test.

The conclusion of these considerations should be familiar from many applications of game theory. The solution to a difficult decision problem may be to draw lots or toss a coin.

3. A Two-person Game

3.1 To formulate the problem as a game, we shall consider an Accountant (player A) who works for a Businessman (player B). It is possible for the accountant to falsify the books and steal some money. The businessman is aware of this possibility, and has engaged an auditor to check the books. As a complete audit is expensive, the businessman has decided that some spot checks made at random will be sufficient. The accountant may try to outguess his employer, and conclude that if he steals on just some occassions, picked at random, he will have a fair chance of not being caught with his hand in the till.

To give a formal description of this situation, we shall introduce three symbols:

G = the gain player A will make if he uses every opportunity of embezzlement, and is not discovered. We shall assume that the gain of A is the loss of B.

C = the cost to player B of a complete audit, i.e. of checking every opportunity of fraud open to A.

P = the penalty to be paid by player A if he is caught in fraud. If the penalty includes a jail sentence, we must think of P as the monetary equivalent of the punishment. The penalty does not constitute any gain for player B.

We can then summarize the options open to the two players in Table 1.

		Player B	
		Trust	Audit
Player A	Be honest	$0, \quad 0$	$0, \quad -C$
	Steal	$G, \quad -G$	$-P, \quad -C$

Tab. 1

Each cell gives the gains of respectively player A and player B, corresponding to a pair of options, i.e. to a pair of pure strategies.

As indicated above, the players may find it advantageous to use mixed strategies. This will mean that:

Player A cheats on a fraction x of the opportunities.
Player B, or his auditor, checks a fraction y of the opportunities.

If both players make their choices independently, and in a random manner, there will be a probability xy that A shall be caught cheating. In this case player A will have to pay the penalty P, and player B will have the auditing cost C.

Similarly there will be a probability $x(1-y)$ that a theft is not discovered, and a probability $(1-x)y$ that an audit is made without discovering any irregularity.

3.2 If the two players use mixed strategies represented by the pair (x, y) the expected payoffs will be

Player A:

$$v_A(x, y) = x(1-y)G - xyP = x(G-(G+P)y)$$

Player B:

$$v_B(x, y) = -(1-x)yC - x(1-y)G - xyC) = -xG - y(C - xG).$$

From the former of these expressions we see that if

$$y \geqslant \frac{G}{G+P} \quad \text{we have} \quad v_A\,(x, y) \leqslant 0.$$

Hence by doing spot checking with sufficiently high frequency, the auditor can ensure that crime is not expected to pay.

A pair of mixed strategies $(\bar{x}, \bar{y})$ is an equilibrium point in the game if

$$v_A\,(x, \bar{y}) \leqslant v_A\,(\bar{x}, \bar{y}) \quad \text{for all } x \in (0,1)$$

$$v_B\,(\bar{x}, y) \leqslant v_B\,(\bar{x}, \bar{y}) \quad \text{for all } y \in (0,1).$$

It is easy to show that

$$\bar{x} = \frac{C}{G} \quad \text{and} \quad \bar{y} = \frac{G}{P+G}$$

satisfy the equilibrium conditions, and that the game has no other equilibrium points. For the equilibrium point we find:

$$v_A\,(\bar{x}, \bar{y}) = 0 \quad \text{and} \quad v_B\,(\bar{x}, \bar{y}) = -C.$$

3.3 The equilibrium strategies give the same payoffs as the pure strategies of the point (0,1), corresponding to: "Complete audit" and "Complete honesty", as we have $v_A\,(0,1) = 0$ and $v_B\,(0,1) = -C$.

The point (0,1) is however not an equilibrium point. We have $v_A\,(x, 1) = -xP$, so that the Accountant can not expect to gain by cheating, but we also have $v_A\,(0, y) = -yC$, so that the Businessman can gain by spending less on auditing.

In the equilibrium point, the Businessman will spend $(GC)/(P+G) < C$ on auditing, but he will suffer an expected loss of $G\,(1 - G/(P+G))\,C/G = (PC)/(P+G)$, so that savings on auditing are just balanced by an increase in losses caused by embezzlement. Similarly the Accountant can expect to gain $(PC)/(G+P)$ from undiscovered embezzlement, but this is just offset by the expected penalty he must pay if he is caught.

3.4 If the problem we have discussed is analysed as a cooperative game, it is trivial. The cooperative solution is obviously "No audit" and "Complete honesty". There is no real element of "threat" in the situation, since an accountant who threatens to steal presumably will be dismissed immediately. The possibility of embezzlement is however present, and this is clearly to the businessman's disadvantage. In real life the possibility seems to be used as an argument for higher renumeration of the accountant. Higher renumeration should have the same effect as an increase in the penalty P, since a part of the penalty may be the loss of a well paid job.

4. A Three-person Game

4.1 The Businessman can usually buy insurance to cover losses caused by the dishonesty of his employees. In the simple model we have studied there should be no need for insurance, because the Businessman could prevent such losses by strict auditing. This conclusion rests however on the assumption that the Accountant behaves rationally, and does not try to steal if it cannot be expected to be profitable. The assumption may be unrealistic, so we shall assume that the Businessman buys fidelity guarantee insurance, and brings in a player C, the insurance company.

Further we shall assume that the insurance contract obliges the Businessman to carry out a complete audit of his books, and we shall introduce the symbols:

D = the cost to player C of checking that player B meets his obligations under the insurance contract.

Q = the penalty which player B must pay to player C, if it is discovered that his auditing procedures are less strict than assumed in the contract.

There is of course a premium to be paid for the insurance, and this premium may depend on the auditing system of player B. We shall ignore this element for the time being. In practice the penalty, Q, may be that the insurance contract becomes null and void, or that B must pay the higher premium corresponding to a less satisfactory auditing system.

4.2 The Company may find it expensive to check the auditing system of all its clients. We shall assume that it settles for some random spot checking, so that there is a probability z that a check will be made of B. This assumption leads to a situation similar to the one considered in the preceding section, and it can be described by Table 2.

		Player B	
		Trust A	Audit A
Player C	Trust B	$0, \quad -xG$	$-xG, \quad -C$
	Check B	$Q-D, \quad -Q-xG$	$-D-xG, \quad -C$

Tab. 2

Behind the table there is an assumption that only an audit can reveal an embezzlement. Hence if C checks, and finds that B's auditing is not in accordance with the insurance contract, B must pay the penalty Q, but a possible embezzlement will remain undiscovered.

4.3 If the three players in this game use mixed strategies represented by the triple (x, y, z), their payoffs will be:

Player A:

$$v_A(x, y, z) = x(G-(G+P)y)$$

Player B:

$$v_B(x, y, z) = y(xG + zQ - C) - (xG + zQ)$$

Player C:

$$\nu_C(x, y, z) = z(Q - D - yQ) - xyG.$$

We see as before that for $y > G/(G+P)$ player A can only expect to lose by cheating. Further we see that for $y > (Q-D)/Q$, player C can only expect to lose by checking. It is easy to show that the game has a unique equilibrium point

$$\left(0, \frac{Q-D}{Q}, \frac{C}{Q}\right) \quad \text{if} \quad \frac{Q-D}{Q} \geqslant \frac{G}{G+P}.$$

This gives the following expected gains for the three players:

$$\nu_A = 0, \ \nu_B = -C \ \text{and} \ \nu_C = 0.$$

This case corresponds to high penalties, and the interpretation may be as follows: The risk of substantial penalties leads the Businessman to strict auditing, and this forces the Accountant to complete honesty. The Company spends some money on checking, but expects to collect an equal amount in penalty from the Businessman.

The game also has a unique equilibrium point

$$\left(\frac{C}{G}, \frac{G}{G+P}, 0\right) \quad \text{if} \quad \frac{Q-D}{Q} < \frac{G}{G+P}.$$

The corresponding gains are

$$\nu_A = 0, \ \nu_B = -C \ \text{and} \ \nu_C = \frac{-CG}{G+P}.$$

The interpretation of this result is that low penalties lead the Accountant fo fraud. He does not profit from this, but the fraud causes some losses to the insurance company. The company cannot recover these losses by checking on the Businessman's auditing system.

4.4 It is natural to assume that C, D and G are given, technical parameters.

The penalty for fraud, P represents a decision by society, and may be beyond the control of the three players.

The penalty for breaking the insurance contract, Q is essentially fixed by the insurance company, although it must of course be acceptable to the businessman, and within the law. It is in the interest of the Company to set Q so that

$$\frac{Q-D}{Q} > \frac{G}{G+P}.$$

This leads to the first of the two cases considered in the preceding paragraph, and hence the Company is not expected to lose. It should induce a rational Accountant to be honest. An element of moral hazard may be present, since the Businessman may be tempted to be more lax in his auditing than assumed in the insurance contract. The penalty Q does however prevent him from gaining, and the Company from losing by such violations of the contract.

In a very permissive society P may be close to Zero, so that it is impossible to set Q

high enough to satisfy the inequality above. This leads to the second of the two cases. The auditing will be so strict that crime does not pay, and the company will not find it necessary to check that the audits actually are carried out. Still the company will lose money. An insurance company will not usually make contracts which are expected to be unprofitable, so we must assume that the expected loss $CG(G+P)^{-1}$ is added to the premium paid by the Businessman. Hence we arrive at the fairly obvious conclusion that lower penalties for fraud lead to higher insurance premiums. The possibly surprising, remedy may be as indicated in para 3.4, to pay accountants really well.

4.5 Large risks are often reinsured. In such cases the reinsurers pay parts of the claims, but usually the direct insurer settles the claims. The reinsurers have the right to check that the claim settlements are in accordance with the insurance contract, so the situations we have considered may really be *n*-person games. In the insurance world it is always stressed that reinsurance arrangements are made in the "utmost good faith" (uberrimae fidei), and in the gentlemen's game which reinsurance is (or was), it is simply not done to check the books of a direct insurer. It may however be tempting for an insurer to make a generous settlement with a good client, knowing that reinsurers will cover a substantial part of the cost, and this possibility may be considered when reinsurance premiums are agreed upon.

5. Other Applications of the Model

5.1 In the example we have discussed it was assumed that a theft could be discovered only by the auditor. There are situations where an assumption of this kind does not hold, and a simple example can be found in traveller's baggage insurance.

An airline is responsible for lost baggage, and usually it will take insurance to cover this liability. The airline can make certain that no baggage is stolen in the claim area by checking the tag on every suitcase against the ticket stub, but this may be a costly procedure.

The insurance company may do some checking of its own, to satisfy itself that the airline has reasonable control of who pick up whose suitcases. This leads to a situation which can be described by the following table:

Airline (Player B)

Insurer (Player C)		No check	Check
	No Check	$-G$, 0	0, $-C$
	Check	$Q-D-G$, $-Q$	$-D$, $-C$

Tab. 3

The notation here is the same as in Table 2, except that x, the probability of theft is not brought in explicitly. Hence G must be interpreted as expected loss due to theft, in the absense of any checking by the airline. The checking done by the insurer is assumed to have no effect on the expected loss. If the two players B and C check at an arbitrary arrival with probabilities y and z respectively, expected payments will be

$$v_B(y, z) = -zQ - y(C - zQ)$$

$$v_C(y, z) = -(1 - y)G + z(Q - D - yQ).$$

The equilibrium strategies are found to be

$$\bar{y} = \frac{Q-D}{Q} \quad \text{and} \quad \bar{z} = \frac{C}{Q}.$$

The corresponding payments are

$$v_B(\bar{y}, \bar{z}) = -C \quad \text{and} \; v_C(\bar{y}, \bar{z}) = -\frac{DG}{Q}.$$

5.2 The result above leads to two observations:

(i) The airline cannot make any savings by relaxing the checking. If the insurance company double-checks in an optimal manner, the airline must expect to pay an amount equal to the cost of complete checking.

(ii) The insurance company will not make a contract that is expected to lead to a loss. Hence the amount $(DG)/Q$ will be added to the premium, so that the airline will have to pay both the cost of a 100 percent checking, and the cost of the double checking of the insurance company. This situation, which is discussed in more detail in another paper [*Borch*, 1980], illustrates how the mere existence of moral hazard will lead to costs, even to those who have no intention of cheating. Actually $(DG)/Q$ is the expected cost of claim payments, if the airline cheats in an optimal manner.

5.3 The methods from game theory used in the preceding examples seem to have many potential applications in insurance. In any situation where the insured has undertaken to take special measures to prevent accidents and reduce losses, there is a risk – usually called moral hazard – that he may neglect his obligations. This may lead to more and larger claims against the insurance company, and usually the company reserves the right to inspect that the insured really carries out the safety measures foreseen in the insurance contract. This inspection costs money, and the insured must pay for it in the form of an addition to the premium.

It is not easy to estimate the increase in claim payments which will be the result of relaxed safety measures. A promising field for further studies may be product liability insurance. Often the quality of industrial products is controlled by sampling inspection, and the statistical methods used for this purpose give the probability that a defective product shall be delivered to the customer. This probability is obviously of interest for the setting of premiums for insurance of product liability. The insurance contract is usually written under the assumption that a specific control plan is followed. It may be tempting to the producer to cut costs by relaxing the control, and this will induce the insurer to do his own checking. This will cost money, and the costs must be paid by the producer. The question has been discussed in some earlier papers [*Borch*, 1978, 1979] in a preliminary manner.

5.4 Sampling inspection in industry can naturally be considered as a game against nature. The purpose is to check that the production process is under control. Machines are not usually credited with intelligence or a vicious desire to deliver faulty products. The sampling approach discussed in Section 2 may therefore be more appropriate in industrial production than in financial auditing. It is however interesting to note that many inspection plans are based on minimax considerations of the same kind as those used in game theory. This may be unfair to the machines, but insurance people will tend to see this as a confirmation of Murphy's law: If something can go wrong, it will.

References

Borch, K.: Product Liability, Quality Control and Insurance. Rivista di matematica per le scienze economiche e sociali, 1978, 89–98.

–: Insurance and Loss Prevention: Producer's Liability. Greek Economic Review, 1979, 56–69.

–: The Price of Moral Hazard. Scandinavian Actuarial Journal, 1980.

Kaplan, R.S.: A Stochastic Model for Auditing. Journal of Accounting Research, 1973, 38–46.

Maschler, M.: A Price Leadership Method for solving the Inspector's Non-Constant-Sum Game. Naval Research Logistics Quarterly, 1966, 11–33.

–: The Inspector's Non-Constant-Sum Game: Its Dependence on a System of Detectors. Naval Research Logistics Quarterly, 1967, 275–290.

Games, Economic Dynamics, and Time Series Analysis. 1982 ©Physica-Verlag, Wien–Würzburg

When is the Incentive Problem Real?

By *S.M. Berman*[1]) and *A. Schotter*[2])[3])

Section 1: Introduction

The incentive problem or "free rider" problem has been with us for quite some time. Finding its roots in the work of *Wicksell* [1896] and *Lindahl* [1964], its modern formulation dates back to *Samuelson*'s [1954] classic article "The Pure Theory of Public Expenditure." In that article, Samuelson first derives the Pareto-optimal conditions determining the societally optimal level of public good provision but then despairs over ever being able to achieve such a social state through market institutions. He states:

> ***However no decentralized policy system can serve to determine optimally these levels of collective consumption.*** Other kinds of "voting" or "signalling" would have to be tried. But, and this is the point sensed by Wicksell but perhaps not fully appreciated by Lindahl, now it is in the selfish interest of each person to give ***false*** signals, to pretend to have less interest in a given collective consumption activity than he really has, etc...
>
> One could imagine every person in the community being indoctrinated to behave like a "parametric decentralized bureaucrat" who ***reveals*** his preferences by signalling in response to price parameters or Lagrangean multipliers, to questionnaires, or to other devices. But there is still this fundamental technical difference going to the heart of the whole problem of ***social*** economy: by departing from his indoctrinated rules, any one person can hope to snatch some selfish benefit in a way not possible. under the self-policing competitive pricing of private goods; and the "external economies" or "jointness of demand" intrinsic to the very concept of collective goods and governmental activities makes it impossible for the grand ensemble of optimizing equations to have that special pattern of zeros which makes ***laissez-faire*** competition even ***theoretically*** possible as an analogue computer. [*Samuelson*, 1954, 388–389].

Recently, *Groves* [1973], *Clarke* [1971], *Groves/Ledyard* [1977] and others have attempted solutions to Samuelson's problem and have, by and large, met with a fair amount of success. Their approach was to devise allocating schemes or mechanisms which in turn define *n*-person non-cooperative games whose appropriately defined equilibria are characterized by the fact that all agents reveal their true preference for the public good under consideration. However interesting the above literature is, there still exists the empirical problem of how important is the free rider problem to begin with. In other

[1]) *S.M. Berman*, Courant Institute of Mathematical Sciences, New York University, 10003 New York U.S.A.

[2]) *A. Schotter*, Department of Economics, New York University, 15-19 W 4-th Street, 10003 New York, U.S.A.

[3]) Professors Schotter's participation was made possible by Contract No. N00014-78-C-0598, given to him by the Office of Naval Research. Their support is gratefully appreciated. Professor Berman's work was done under National Science Foundation Grant NSF MCS 79-02020.

words, is it true that economic agents always lie and try to become free riders every time the opportunity arises or do they sometimes refrain from such asocial behavior and reveal their true preferences even though they know they could lie and get away with it? More importantly, what factors determine whether or not they lie?

In this paper we present a model which tries to come to grips with these very questions. It is our belief that whether a society of economic agents decides to all reveal their preferences honestly or not in any particular recurrent public goods provision situation is solely a function of the convention of behavior (social ethic) they develop which is created to guide their behavior in such situations. Such conventions (or social institutions as they are called in *Schotter* [1981]) will be represented by us as the non-cooperative Nash equilibrium of the super-game defined by the infinite iteration of the same simple public goods provision game we will define. Hence, in the model presented below there will exist two non-cooperative equilibria or conventions to the public goods provision supergame we define. One will consist of a convention of behavior in which all agents tell the truth and voluntarily reveal how much they would be willing to contribute to construct a public good, while in the other they lie. These results are not new [see *Friedman; Telser*]. Our aim is to present a model which can be used to define the probabilities with which we can expect either one of these conventions to emerge as the game is iterated over time. As we will see, the model we define depicts the process of convention building (or convention evolution) as a Markov chain which is defined in what we call the state space of societal norms. The absorbing states of this chain are then shown to be identified with the non-cooperative equilibria (social conventions) of the public goods supergame and, by calculating the absorption probabilities at these points, we can give an answer to the question phrased above: How likely is the free rider problem to be a real problem?

From a social welfare point of view our analysis raises questions for the role of the state in the economic lives of its agents. For if, in a given public goods provision situation, it is determined that the probability is quite low that the agents will, by their own voluntary action, create a truth telling convention of behavior, then the state would be forced to enter the economy and institute a Groves-Ledyard type scheme to help out the agents. It would be only if voluntary action failed, however, that such a mechanism need be used; if its use could be avoided by voluntary action, society would obviously benefit since there is a real economic cost involved in using one of these schemes. Another argument for state intervention can arise even if the probability of a truthful revelation convention emerging is high as long as the number of periods expected to occur before the convention is established is also high. In terms of our model this expected number of periods is characterized as the first passage time to the absorbing state identified with the truth telling convention. If this first passage time is great then the discounted present value of the benefits achieved by using a state-run incentive compatible mechanism and achieving Pareto-optimal outcomes today as opposed to voluntarily achieving them in the future may very well outweigh the costs of instituting the mechanism.

In this paper we will proceed as follows: In Section 2 we present a simple public goods provision prisoners' dilemma supergame which serves as the basic public goods provision situation to be studied by us. Section 3 presents and abstract description of the play of an iterated game. We shall demonstrate that the process described defines a Markov chain. This process is applied in Section 4 to the Prisoners' dilemma public goods provision problem described in Section 2. Our purpose is to demonstrate that the equilibrium convention established by the players can be looked at as an absorbing state of the Markov chain described in Section 3. Finally, in Section 5 we offer some conclusions.

Section II: The Public Goods Provision Problem: Free Ridership and Prisoners' Dilemma

The free rider problem is an exceedingly easy problem to understand. Assume that a non-excludable public good (a pure Samuelson public good) is proposed to a society of agents. The Samuelson-Lindahl solution to the financing of this public good is to have the quantity of the public good determined by a first order condition stating that the optimal quantity of the public good to provide is that quantity at which the sum of the marginal willingnesses to pay for the public good (the sum of the marginal rates of substitution between private and public goods) just equals the marginal cost of providing that quantity. According to the benefit theory of taxation [see *Lindahl*], each agent is to be taxed an amount exactly equal to his willingness to pay – i.e., a personalized tax for each member of society. The problem is, of course, that a priori there is no way in which society can estimate an agent's marginal willingness to pay except by direct examination, but in that case the agent would obviously lie and report a lower value for his willingness to pay. The question for each player, then, is: When asked to contribute should he tell the truth and reveal how much he is willing to pay of the public good or should he lie and, if so, what is the optimal lie? Abstracting from the final part of this question leaves the agent two alternatives – to lie or not to lie. In order to most easily illustrate our approach we will assume that there are only two agents in the society we are investigating and a social planner who asks them to transmit a message to him defining their true willingness to pay (demand function) for the public good. Consequently, let the message space for agent 1, M_1, be the set of all monotonically decreasing functions which define the demand for the public good as a function of its price for agent 1, and let M_2 be the same message space for agents 2. Given any pair of messages $m = (m_1, m_2)$, $m_1 \in M_1$, $m_2 \in M_2$, the planner then sets that quantity of the public good such that $MRS_1 + MRS_2 = MRT$, where MRS_1 and MRS_2 are the marginal rates of substitution of private (composite) goods for public goods for agents 1 and 2, and MRT is the marginal rate of transformation. In other words the social planner sets the Samuelson optimal level of the public good, given the messages he receives, and taxes each agent his marginal willingness to pay at that level. Hence the planner's behavior can be modeled as a function (outcome function) $\Phi: M_1 \times M_2 \to R^1 \times R^1 \times R^1$, i.e., mapping each pair of messages into a triple (q, τ_1, τ_2) where q is the amount of public good he constructs, and τ_1 and τ_2 are the taxes he levies on the agents. To simplify our analysis we assume that player i has only two possible messages, $m_i(L)$ and $m_i(T)$, representing a lying message and a truthful message respectively, $i = 1, 2$. Hence, if we let $O(m_1(L), m_2(T)) = [q^{L,T}, \tau_1(L, T), \tau_2(L, T)]$ be the outcome that results when player 1 tells a lie and player 2 tells the truth, then four outcomes can result:

$$O(m_1(L), m_2(T)), O(m_1(L), m_2(L)), O(m_1(T), m_2(L)), O(m_1(T), m_2(T)).$$

We can consequently represent this mechanism as a game-form [see *Gibbard*]. If we assume that the agents have Von Neumann-Morgenstern utility functions we can represent the game-form as a 2-person game in normal form. Pursuing this even further, if we want we can restrict our utility function such that the game defined is in fact a 2-person prisoners' dilemma game Γ defined below by assuming that for player 1 his preferences are such that

$$O(m_1(L), m_2(T)) > O(m_1(T), m_2(T)) > O(m_1(L), m_2(L)) > O(m_1(T), m_2(L))$$

while for player 2 his preferences are such that

$$O(m_1(T), m_2(L)) > O(m_1(T), m_2(T)) > O(m_1(L), m_2(L)) > O(m_1(L), m_2(T))$$

Γ =

	Truth $m_2(T)$	Lie $m_2(L)$
Truth $m_1(T)$	$o_1^{TT},\ o_2^{TT}$	$o_1^{TL},\ o_2^{TL}$
Lie $m_1(L)$	$o_1^{LT},\ o_2^{LT}$	$o_1^{LL},\ o_2^{LL}$

matrix 2.1.

All public goods provision problems need not be isomorphic to prisoners' dilemma games, of course, but typically the problem is presented in that form. Now in this paper we are interested in the game that results when this simple public goods provision game is iterated an infinite number of times and where the final payoffs for each player are the discounted present values of the utility stream that results from the play of the supergame. Hence, if $P_i^t(m_i, m_j)$ is the payoff that player i receives in period t when he sends message m_i and player j sends message m_j, then his final supergame payoff would simply be

$$\pi_i = \sum_{t=1}^{\infty} \left[\frac{1}{(1+r_i)}\right]^{t-1} P_i^t(m_i, m_j)$$

where r_i is the dicount rate for player i. Each player obviously wants to make π_i as large as possible. The fact that we limit ourselves to only two messages might be considered a severe restriction on our model but from our point of view it is not that grave since our purpose is simply trying to decide whether agents will lie or not when asked about their preferences in constructing public goods, not what the magnitude of their lie is. Our emphasis is strictly on the convention of behavior established by the agents which in our case is merely a truth-telling or lying convention. Hence we consider no other strategies.

2.1 Supergame Strategies

As we indicated before, we are interested in the outcome of the supergame which is defined by the infinite iteration of the public goods provision game defined by Γ in matrix 2.1. Although supergame strategies can be quite complex, we will limit ourselves to one very simple kind of supergame strategy called a strategy of the (*)-type by

Berman/Schotter [1979] but used previously by *Telser* [1972] and *Friedman* [1977]. Calling the lie message strategy L and the truth message strategy T, one example of a supergame strategy of the (*)-type can be represented as follows:

$$\sigma^i(T \mid T) = \begin{cases} m_{i_1} = m_i^T & \\ m_{i_t} = m_i^T & \text{if } m_{j_\tau} = m_i^T \quad \text{for } \tau = 2, \ldots, t-1 \\ m_{i_t} = m_i^L & \text{otherwise} \end{cases}$$

where m_{i_t} is the message sent by agent i in period t.

This strategy describes a complete plan of action for player i for every iteration of the game Γ from period one to infinity. It describes a "mode of behavior" for player i in which he plans to send a truthful message in period one and then proceed to tell the truth in every period t as long as player j has told the truth in every period up until that time. If agent j ever deviates and sends a non-truthful message, he will lie from that point on. If we realize that each player will resort to lying if he ever catches the other player not playing the way he wants him to (i.e., the lying strategy is the punishing strategy in the game), it becomes obvious that there are four supergame strategies for each player which define two strategy sets Σ^1 and Σ^2 for the players in the supergame defined by the infinite iteration of Γ (when these strategies are restricted to be of the (*)-type). They can be represented as

$$\Sigma^1 = [\sigma^1(T \mid T), \sigma^1(T \mid L), \sigma^1(L \mid T), \sigma^1(L \mid L)]$$

and

$$\Sigma^2 = [\sigma^2(T \mid T), \sigma^2(L \mid T), \sigma^2(T \mid L), \sigma^2(L \mid L)].$$

The strategies in this strategy set have identical explanations as the strategy described above, although some define somewhat peculiar modes of behavior. For instance, consider the strategy

$$\sigma^i(T \mid L) = \begin{cases} m_{i_1} = m_i^T & \\ m_{i_t} = m_i^T & \text{if } m_{j_\tau} = m_j^L \qquad \text{for } \tau = 2, \ldots, t-1 \\ m_{i_t} = m_i^L & \text{otherwise.} \end{cases}$$

This supergame strategy for player i or mode of behaviour prescribes behavior in which player i intends to send a truthful message in period 1 and then continue to tell the truth as a long as player j lies. If agent j in any period t ever deviates and tells the truth, he will punish him by lying from that period on. Clearly, such behavior is masochistic since player i is demanding that player j punish him in every period. While we do not expect player i to ever employ such a strategy it is still a logical possibility and must be included in the strategy sets. These strategy sets then define a game $\mathfrak{s}$ in normal form where $\mathfrak{s} = (\{I: i = 1,2\}; \Sigma^i, \pi_1; \pi_2)$ where

I is the set of players in the game;
Σ^i is the strategy set for agent i whose components are now supergame strategies; and
π_i is a payoff function mapping $\Sigma^1 \times \Sigma^2 \to R$; i.e., defining the supergame payoff resulting from any pair of strategies $\sigma^1 \in \Sigma^1, \sigma^2 \in \Sigma^2$.

Since the strategy sets in Γ are finite so must the sets Σ^1 and Σ^2 be finite (in our case they are four dimensional) and hence the game $\mathcal{S}$ is a finite game in normal form which in our particular model can be represented as follows:

$$\mathcal{S} = \begin{array}{c} \\ \sigma^1(T \mid T) \\ \sigma^1(T \mid L) \\ \sigma^1(L \mid T) \\ \sigma^1(L \mid L) \end{array} \begin{array}{c} \sigma^2(T \mid T) \quad \sigma^2(L \mid T) \quad \sigma^2(T \mid L) \quad \sigma^2(L \mid L) \\ \left[\begin{array}{c} \cdot \\ \cdots\cdots\cdots\cdots\cdots\cdots \\ \cdot \\ \cdot \end{array}\right] \end{array} \quad \text{matrix 2.2.}$$

The entries in the cells of this matrix define the supergame payoffs that result when one agent behaves according to one mode of behavior and the other behaves according to another. For instance, the payoff associated with the pair of choices $\sigma[(T \mid T), (T \mid T)] = [\sigma^1(T \mid T), \sigma^2(T \mid T)]$ defines the payoffs that would occur when both agents tell the truth in all periods of the supergame. Such a pair, $\sigma\ [(T \mid T, (T \mid T)] = [\sigma^1(T \mid T), \sigma^2(T \mid T)]$ represents what we shall call a "convention of behavior" (or social institution; see *Schotter* [1981]) since it is a behavioral rule which prescribes behavior for each of our agents at each iteration of the underlying game. In this particular case it instructs them to tell the truth. As can be seen from matrix 2.2 there are 16 possible conventions of behavior that can be defined. Our program here is to locate which of those conventions are equilibrium conventions and, given that, to define what the probability is that any one of these possible conventions will emerge as *the* convention of behavior for the society. If the convention $\sigma\ [(L \mid L), (L \mid L)]$ (the lying convention in which all agents lie on each iteration of Γ) is a stable convention of behavior and if the probability that the society establishes this convention of behavior is great, then we consider the incentive problem to be a *real* problem for those agents and one for which some type of incentive compatible mechanism would be required. If not, we can rely on the agents' own selfish motives to establish a truth-telling convention and adhere to it if it turns out to be an equilibrium.

As we will see in Section 4 our model relies on the players playing the game in matrix 2.2 repeatedly and not the game defined by matrix 2.1. Hence, we depict the iterated play of a game whose strategies are supergame strategies or a "supergame of a supergame." This will be seen to have a natural interpretation when we get to Section 4.

Having thus motivated our problem and set out its structure, let us proceed to a quick description of a process describing the repeated play of an abstract game and then apply that process in Section 4 to answer the question phrased above: How likely is any stable non-cooperative supergame equilibria (social convention) to emerge from a given finite game S with multiple equilibria?

Section 3

In this section we demonstrate that a particular dynamic process of iterated play of an abstract game defines a Markov chain in what we call the state space of norms. To do this, let us start by characterizing a Markov chain in the conventional way. Let (S, β) be a measurable space, where S is an arbitrary set of elements s and β is a sigma-field of subsets B. We assume there is a family of probability measures $P(s, B)$ $B \in \beta$, defined for each $s \in S$; $P(s, B)$ is the transition probability measure and represents the probability of passage in one step from the current state s into the set B. The Markov property is that the conditional probability of passage into a set B given that the current state is s, and given other information about the history of the process before the current time, is independent of the latter information and is, in fact, equal simply to $P(s, B)$.

Now consider an arbitrary game played by a set of n players. Assume, for simplicity, that the players have identical finite strategy sets S. In other words, $S_i = S$ for all players i, where S_i is the strategy set of players i. Let ρ be the family of probability measures on S and let ρ_0 be the sub-family consisting of probability measures which assign probability 1 to individual members of S. Hence, ρ is the family of mixed strategies definable on S and ρ_0 is the family of pure strategies.

Play starts in time period 0 when each player chooses an element of ρ (a mixed strategy) and then selects an element of S at random according to the dictates of the mixed strategy chosen. The n selections are done independently. Let $\underset{\sim}{X}_{0,i}$ be the element of S selected by player i in the initial (period 0) play $i = 1, \ldots, n$ and put $\underset{\sim}{X}_0 =$ $= (X_{0,1}, \ldots, X_{0,n})$.

As a result of this play, whose outcome is defined by the vector of action $\underset{\sim}{X}_0$, the players receive payoffs $\pi_1(\underset{\sim}{X}_0), \ldots, \pi_n(\underset{\sim}{X}_0)$, and we denote the latter as $\pi(\underset{\sim}{X}_0)$.

When the payoff vector is observed by all of the players[4]) each of them forms a subjective opinion of the randomized strategy to be used on the next play by each of the other $n - 1$ players. Using these subjective opinions, the players will choose their strategies in the next play of the game. Put

$g_{ij}(\underset{\sim}{X}_0)$ = the element of ρ that player i believes will be used by player j in period 1 when $\underset{\sim}{\pi}(\underset{\sim}{X}_0)$ is observed in period 0, $i \neq j$.

$g_{ii}(\underset{\sim}{X}_0)$ = the element of ρ that player i intends to use on the next (period 1) play given his belief distributions g_{ij}, $i \neq j$.

The players, in period 1, select strategies $(X_{11}, \ldots, X_{1n}) = \underset{\sim}{X}_1$ according to the probability measures $g_{ii}(\underset{\sim}{X}_0)$, $i = 1, \ldots, n$ and independently of each other. The procedure above is repeated for the vector $\underset{\sim}{X}_1$ in place of $\underset{\sim}{X}_0$: $\Pi(\underset{\sim}{X}_1)$ and $(g_{ij}(\underset{\sim}{X}_1))$ are computed, and then $\underset{\sim}{X}_2 = (X_{21}, \ldots, X_{2n})$ is selected according to the probability

[4]) Actually the entire payoff vector is not observed by any player but merely his own payoff and the outcome of the game. He must then try to infer the payoff to other players as we will see in Section 4.

measures $g_{ii}(\underset{\sim}{X}_1)$. In general for $t \geqslant 1$, after $\underset{\sim}{X}_t$ has been observed and the matrix $(g_{ij}(\underset{\sim}{X}_t))$ has been computed, the vector $\underset{\sim}{X}_{t+1}$ is selected according to the vector probability measure $(g_{ii}(\underset{\sim}{X}_t))$.

The array $(g_{ij}(\underset{\sim}{X}_t))$ is an $n \times n$ matrix whose entries are elements of ρ. Since S (the common strategy set) is finite, each element of ρ may be represented as a vector with non-negative real components of sum 1, and whose dimension is equal to the number of elements of S. Let K be the latter number; then each element of ρ may be represented as a K-dimensional row vector. Thus the matrix $(g_{ij}(\underset{\sim}{X}_t))$ may be viewed as an $n \times nK$ matrix with real entries. We shall call it a "norm matrix" since it represents the set of beliefs expressing the subjective feelings that each player has about the intended actions of the other.

If we assume, as does *Harsanyi* [1975], that g_{ij} is identical for all $i \neq j$, so that $g_{ij} = g_i$, then at each point in time there is a vector $\underset{\sim}{g} = (g_1, \ldots, g_i, \ldots, g_n)$ consisting of K-dimensional probability distributions expressing the commonly held beliefs of all players about the intended actions of each other.

The process we have just described can be easily proved to be a Markov chain in the state space of "norm matrices" as Proposition 3.1 demonstrates.

Proposition 3.1: The sequence of random matrices $(g_{ij}(X_t))$, $t = 0, 1, \ldots$, is a Markov chain whose state space is a subset of the set of $n \times nK$ real matrices.

Proof: This follows from the conventional definition of the Markov chain given above, and from our description of the rules of the game. Indeed, for any $t \geqslant 0$ the conditional distribution of $\underset{\sim}{X}_{t+1}$, given the state $(g_{ij}(\underset{\sim}{X}_t))$ and any other information about the state at previous times, depends only on the probability measures $(g_{ij}(\underset{\sim}{X}_t))$ and not on the latter information. Therefore, as a function of $\underset{\sim}{X}_{t+1}$, the matrix $(g_{ij}(\underset{\sim}{X}_{t+1}))$ has a distribution determined by that of the former, and so $(g_{ij}(\underset{\sim}{X}_{t+1})$ also has a conditional distribution, given $(g_{ij}(\underset{\sim}{X}_t))$, which is independent of the past. ■

We note that if the rules of the game specify that there is a finite subset of ρ such that $(g_{ij}(\underset{\sim}{X}_t))$ belongs to the latter subset for all $t \geqslant 0$, then $(g_{ij}(\underset{\sim}{X}_t))$ $t \geqslant 0$, forms a finite Markov chain. If the states of the chain are labeled $i, j, \ldots$, then the transition probability measures are described be means of a stochastic matrix (p_{ij}) where p_{ij} is the probability of passage in one step from state (norm matrix) i to state j. A state is called *persistent* if, starting from i the probability of eventual return to i is 1; otherwise it is called *transient*. A state is called absorbing if $p_{ii} = 1$; such a state is obviously persistent.

We now consider a Markov chain with the following property:

There is a set C of absorbing states such that, in starting from any state, there is a positive probability of eventually being absorbed in some state in C.

Under this hypothesis, the states outside C are necessarily transient; this follows from the basic renewal property of successive visits to a given state. We denote the complement of the set of states C as the set of states T. It is well known that a Markov chain satisfying the condition of this hypothesis has a convenient *convergence property*: the probability of ultimate passage from any state in T to some state in C is 1; furthermore, the expected time of first passage is finite. [See *Feller*, chapt. 15 and 16].

Finally, since we are ultimately interested in calculating the absorption probabilities and expected first passage times to absorbing states (what we will see are equilibrium conventions), the following classical propositions will be of use.

Proposition 3.2: Let i be a transient state and j an absorbing state; and let f_{ij} be the probability of absorption in j given the starting state i. Then f_{ij} is the unique solution of the system

$$f_{ij} = \sum_{k \text{ transient}} p_{ik} f_{kj} + p_{ij} \tag{3.1}$$

Proof: See *Feller* [1968].

Proposition 3.3: If m_i is the expected first passage time from state i into the set C, then m_i is the unique solution of

$$m_i = 1 + \sum_{k \text{ transient}} p_{ik} m_k.$$

Proof: See *Feller* [1968].

Section 4

Our task in this section is to apply the process described in Section 3 to our analysis of the public goods provision problem and interpret the creation and evolution of social conventions as a Markov process (more specifically, as a Markov chain).

Before we start, however, it is important to note that although one can contemplate a game existing for an infinite length of time, it is unrealistic to think that the players in it could themselves be immortal. Hence games, and the societal problems they are metaphors for, are *the* permanent features of societies and the players in them merely transient fiduciary agents playing a role for a specific period of time. What the players actually do, however, is create conventions of behavior and then pass these conventions on to future generations of players who use them to guide their behavior. The passage of these regularities of behavior (conventions) from one generation of players to another is a process of institutionalization and socialization described by *Schotter* [1981, Chap. 4].

Hence, let us envision the players who play the game described in matrix 2.2 as sequences or teams of non-overlapping fiduciary agents each of which plays the role of player 1 or player 2 for a finite period of time, say L periods. After his time is up, he is replaced by the next agent on his team. Hence define player 1 or Team 1 as $T_1 = a_{10}, a_{1L}, a_{12L}, \ldots$, and player 2 or Team 2 as $T_2 = a_{20}, a_{2L}, a_{22L}, \ldots$; where, a_{it} is the agent on team i active in time period t. The model we describe then depicts the iterated play, by a sequence of non-overlapping agents, of a supergame. It is a supergame of a supergame.

Time starts in period 0 when agents a_{10} and a_{20} are active. They are supposed to choose one of their 4 available supergame strategies from Σ^1 and Σ^2 (see Section 2).

(Notice that although we depict them as having finite lives, we still allow them to act as if they will live forever by allowing them to choose supergame strategies which are plans of action of infinite duration. This fiction is common practice in economics where managers of firms behave as if they were maximizing the discounted present value of an infinite stream of profits even though they know their own connection with the firm has a finite duration). Now, at time period 0 let us assume that agents a_{10} and a_{20} have no previous knowledge of the other agents and hence have no basis upon which to estimate how they are likely to behave. Hence, let $\underset{\sim}{g}^0_{12} = (1/4, 1/4, 1/4, 1/4)$ be the agent on team 1's estimate of the likelihood with which the agent on team 2 will use any one of his four supergame strategies in Σ^2, and define $\underset{\sim}{g}^0_{21} = (1/4, 1/4, 1/4, 1/4)$ likewise. $\underset{\sim}{g}^0 = (\underset{\sim}{g}^0_{12}, \underset{\sim}{g}^0_{21})$ then defines the period 0 or initial period norm.

Based on $\underset{\sim}{g}^0_{12}$ and the payoff matrix 2.2 we assume that agent a_{10} chooses a mixed strategy $\underset{\sim}{g}^0_{11}$ which dictates the probability with which he will actually choose one of his four supergame strategies, and then chooses one of his strategies with the probabilities dictated by this strategy. Agent a_{20} is also assumed to choose a mixed strategy $\underset{\sim}{g}_{22}$ based upon $\underset{\sim}{g}_{21}$ and matrix 2.2 and act likewise.

The way these strategies are chosen needs some discussion. What we do is to assume that there exists some relevant theory M which defines behavior for the players in the game. Mathematically, M can be considered to be a function mapping the t-th period norm g^t and the game $\mathcal{S}$ into a pair of mixed strategies $\underset{\sim}{g}_{11}$ and $\underset{\sim}{g}_{22}$, where $\underset{\sim}{g}_{11}, \underset{\sim}{g}_{22} \in \rho$. More specifically,

$$M: ((\underset{\sim}{g}^t = (\underset{\sim}{g}^t_{12}, \underset{\sim}{g}^t_{21})); \mathcal{S}) \rightarrow \rho \times \rho.$$

There are several possible candidates for this theory. One obvious one is the "tracing procedure" of *Harsanyi* [1975] which is a function mapping $(\underset{\sim}{g}^t, S)$ into one of the equilibria of $\mathcal{S}$. Another may be what is called by *Harsanyi* [1975] the "naive Bayesian" theory which instructs each player to choose that $g_{ii} \in \rho$ that maximizes $\pi_i\,(g_{ii}, g^t_{ij})$, where g^t_{ij} is agent i's estimate of the intended actions of agent a_{jt} in period t. It instructs agent a_{it} to use his best response to his subjective belief g^t_{ij}. A point that needs to be stressed, however, is that we place no rationality in requirements whatsoever on the theory that agents use. Our model, to that extent, is more descriptive than prescriptive. Their actions can be highly rational or highly irrational. What we want to demonstrate is that *no matter how they behave,* if the theory they use satisfies two simple assumptions, the process defined will be identical to the one described in Section 3 and we will be allowed to employ Propositions 3.2 and 3.3 to answer the questions posed in the introduction (once we demonstrate the equivalence between the absorbing states of our Markov chain and the equilibira in Matrix 2.2). If these two assumptions are not satisfied, the process defined is still tractable and of interest, but merely not readily applicable to our present analysis. In general, however, the particular theory used in our model may be arbitrary.

The two assumptions we presently require of our theory M are described in more detail in *Berman/Schotter* [1979] and can be stated as:

Assumption 1: Best Responce Satisfactoryness:

If $\sigma = (\sigma^1\ (l \mid k), \sigma^2\ (k \mid l))$ is an equilibrium convention of behavior, or a Nash equilibrium to the game in Matrix 2.2, and if the norm existing at time period t leads player 1 to expect player 2 will use $\sigma^2(k \mid l)$ with probability 1 and all other strategies with probability 0, and simultaneously leads player 2 to believe that player 1 will use $\sigma^1(k \mid l)$ with probability 1 and all other strategies with probability 0, then M must dictate the choices $g_{11}, g_{22} \in \rho_0$ in which player 1's mixed strategy is a degenerate pure strategy dictating that he actually use $\sigma^1(l \mid k)$ with probability 1 and player 2's mixed strategy is also a degenerate pure strategy dictating the use of $\sigma^2(k \mid l)$ with probability 1.

The assumption requires that the theory M be rational *at least at the equilibrium* in that it requires that if the agents totally believe that the other agents they will face will behave according to an equilibrium convention, they must play their best response to that belief and also adhere to the convention. Out of equilibrium, we allow for any type of behavior as long as it satisfies the following assumption.

Assumption 2: Non-Equilibrium Positiveness

If the norm existing at time t does not lead player i to believe that the other will play his part in an equilibrium convention of behavior with probability 1, then g_{ii}^t is completely mixed.

This assumption requires merely that the theory M be such that if the norm existing at a given time t does not lead the agents to expect the others to adhere to an equilibrum convention of behavior for certain, then there is a finite probability, no matter how small, that the player will use any one of his four supergame strategies. Some of these probability weights, however, may be arbitrarily small and merely represent mistake probabilities depicting the fact that out of equilibrium, before each player knows precisely what to expect from the others, there is always the possibility of making a strategic mistake, no matter how small that probability is.

The game now proceeds in a fashion identical to the one described in Section 3. Agents a_{10} and a_{20} employ their theory M on g^0 and $\mathcal{S}$ and choose g_{11}^0 and g^0. They then perform the mixed strategy experiments dictated by these strategies and follow the dictates of the pure strategy chosen during their lifetimes. If their lifetimes are L periods, they will receive an L period sequence of payoffs $P_{a_{i0}}^1(\cdot), P_{a_{i0}}^2(\cdot), \ldots, P_{a_{i0}}^L(\cdot)$, $i = 1,2$.

In period L agents a_{1L} and a_{2L} are alive and can observe the outcome of the game up until their arrival. Using some interpreting rule R, they infer what strategy must have been used by agents a_{10} and a_{20} (i.e., they infer $\underset{\sim}{X}_0$, in the notation of Section 3), and given this L period history (which is common knowledge to the players in the sense of *Aumann* [1976] they update the period 0 norm $g^0 = (g_{12}^0, g_{21}^0)$ using some reasonable rule, yielding $g^1 = (g_{12}^1, g_{21}^1)$. One rule, used by *Berman/Schotter* [1979] would be the following. If the payoff sequence $P_{a_{i0}}^1(\cdot), \ldots, P_{a_{i0}}^L(\cdot)$ to agent a_{0i} indicates that agent a_{j0} was adhering to supergame strategy $\sigma^{a_{j0}}(T \mid T)$ (i.e., the truthful strategy) over his L period existence, then agent a_{iL} will increase the probability that agent a_{jL} will choose the same supergame strategy during his lifetime by ϵ (arbitrarily small), and decrease the probability that he will use any one of his other three supergame strategies by $\epsilon/3$. This is a simple rule which is based on the assumption that the agents think that if something happened in the past it is likely to happen again in the future. This process of strategy choice, outcome observation, outcome interpretation, probability updating, and then choice goes on generation after generation and defines the dynamics of the game's play, and the stochastic evolution of the norms existing among the players over time.

What we must now demonstrate is that this stochastic evolution of norms:

1) Is Markovian,
2) defines states which are either transient or absorbing and finally,
3) has absorbing states which define behavior consistent with the non-cooperative equilibria of the supergame $\mathcal{S}$ defined by matrix 2.2.

This is easily done, however, given our two assumptions and the updating rule we have briefly sketched.

Proposition 4.1: The sequence of random norm vectors $g^t = (g_{12}^t, g_{21}^t)$, $t = 0, L, 2L, \ldots$, is a Markov chain.

Proof: The proof that the evolution of norms is Markovian is easily accomplished and follows the proof of Proposition 3.1. Since the theory M is time invariant and depends only on the norm g^t and the game $\mathcal{S}$ ($\mathcal{S}$ is constant throughout the analysis), and since the interpretation rule R and the norm updating rules are state and time invariant, the conditional distribution of $\underset{\sim}{X}_{t+L}$, given the norm $g^t = (g_{12}^t, g_{21}^t)$ and any other information about the history of the game, depends only on g^t and not on the latter information. Therefore, as a function of $\underset{\sim}{X}_{t+L}$, the updated norm vector g^{t+L} $(\underset{\sim}{X}_{t+L})$ has a distribution determined by that of the former and so g^{t+L} $(\underset{\sim}{X}_{t+L})$ also has a conditional distribution, given g^t $(\underset{\sim}{X}_t)$, which is independent of the past.

To prove that the states of our chain are either transient or absorbing we need only refer to our two assumptions. The following proposition then follows:

Proposition 4.2: The states of the Markov chain defined in Section 4 are either transient or absorbing.

Proof: Divide the norm space into two sets, those consisting of degenerate norms indicating that each player expects the others to adhere to a particular equilibrium convention with probability 1, and adhere to any other strategy with probability 0, and all other norms. (In the game defined by matrix 2.2 there are only two such equilibrium norms.) Call the first set C and the latter T. It should be obvious that the set C consists of absorbing points since from Assumption 1, if either a_{it}, $i = 1, 2$ expects the other to play his part in an equilibrium convention with probability 1, then he must play his part in that convention as well. Hence we will observe an L period sequence of payoffs indicating adherence to that equilibrium convention. When agents $a_{i_{t+L}}$, $i = 1, 2$, enter the game they will want to update $\underset{\sim}{g}^t = (\underset{\sim}{g}_{12}^t, \underset{\sim}{g}_{21}^t)$ to $\underset{\sim}{g}^{t+L} = (\underset{\sim}{g}_{12}^{t+L}, \underset{\sim}{g}_{21}^{t+L})$ using the updating rule. However, the updating rule specified dictates that they add ϵ to the elements of $\underset{\sim}{g}_{12}^t$ and $\underset{\sim}{g}_{21}^t$ that are already equal to 1, and subtract $\epsilon/3$ from those elements already 0. However, since the sum of $\underset{\sim}{g}_{12}^t$ and $\underset{\sim}{g}_{21}^t$ must be 1 and each element must be non-negative, our updating rule must leave the norm unaltered. Hence $\underset{\sim}{g}^t = \underset{\sim}{g}^{t+L}$. But, by Assumption 1 again, the agents in period $t + L$ must adhere to the same equilibrium convention and by a similar argument we can demonstrate that $\underset{\sim}{g}^{t+2L} = \underset{\sim}{g}^{t+L}$. Therefore, once the norm indicates that each player expects the other to adhere to the same equilibrium convention with probability 1, the norm, from that period on, will never change. Such norms, by definition, are absorbing states. For any other norms, Assumption 2 indicates that there is a positive probability of observing behavior that will cause the players to update their norms such that $g^t \neq g^{t+L}$. Hence, from the general facts about Markov chains stated in Section 3, these states are all transient.

Finally, it should be obvious that the absorbing states of our Markov chain define behavior which is consistent with the non-cooperative equilibria of matrix 2.2, since if the norm is ever in an absorbing state, by Assumption 1 we know we will always observe behavior consistent with some non-cooperative equilibria in the same Δ. Hence,

Proposition 4.3: The behavior consistent with the absorbing states of our Markov chain is also consistent with the non-cooperative equilibria of matrix 2.2.

Our task is now complete, since if we want to answer the question of when is the incentive problem real, all we must do is to rely on Propositions 3.2 and 3.3 to answer the questions:

1) What is the probability of being absorbed in a norm supporting a non-cooperative (lying) convention of behavior given that we have started out initially in any norm g^0?, and
2) What is the expected first passage times to such norms?

If the absorption probabilities or expected first passage time are great, then the incentive problem will be a real one and would dictate state intervention. If the opposite is true, the state should not spend its limited resources on the problem, but can rather use its time and resources elsewhere.

Finally, since our states are either transient or absorbing, questions about convergence have a clear answer since probability of absorption is equal to 1 and the expected absorption time is finite. [See *Feller*, Chapt. 15 and 16.]

Section 5: Conclusion

This paper has tried to demonstrate that the judgement of whether or not a particular social problem (i.e., the incentive problem) is a real one for a society of agents depends upon the conventions of behavior established by the agents in that society. These conventions are built upon a foundation of societal norms which are informational devices which support the various conventions much like prices are informational devices which support competitive allocations in Walrasian economies. Our main point has been to describe the evolution of conventions of behavior in society as a random process governed by the mathematical laws of a Markov chain. Hence the social mores that a society of agents develop are as much a function of their commonly observed behavior as their basic human nature; furthermore a wide variety of different social behaviors may emerge from one set of social agents.

It is also interesting to point out that our equilibrium has all of the properties of a fully rational expectations equilibrium since it depicts a state in which each player expects with probability 1 that the other will adhere to a particular convention of behavior and given these expectations, that is exactly what they indeed do. Hence, at the equilibrium all expectations are self-fulfilled while out of equilibrium anything is possible. It is important, we feel, to point out the difference in behavior that is allowable before and after a convention is established. It is precisely the function of conventions to unambigiously prescribe behavior for agents to follow and it is precisely the function of norms to furnish the information necessary for agents to have the faith that the other agents in society will actually adhere to those conventions. The existence of such norms and conventions has been regrettably ignored by most game theoretical analyses up until now and it is our purpose to call attention to their potential importance.

References

Aumann, R.: Agreeing to disagree. Annals of Statistics **4**, 1976, 1236–1239.

Berman, S., and *A. Schotter*: Supergames and Diffusion Processes: A Theory of Norm and Institution Assisted Supergames. Discussion Paper No. 79-01, C.V. Starr Center for Applied Economics, New York University, April, 1979.

Clarke, E.: Multi-Part Pricing of Public Goods. Public Choice **11**, 1971, 17–44.

Feller: An Introduction to Probability Theory and Its Applications. Vol. 1, Third Edition, 1968.

Friedman, J.: Oligopoly and the Theory of Games, 1977.

Gibbard, A.: Manipulation of Voting Schemes: A General Result. Econometrica **41** (4), 1973, 581–601.

Groves, T.: Incentives in Teams. Econometrica **41** (4), 1973, 617–631.

Groves, T., and *J. Ledyard*: Optimal Allocation of Public Goods: A Solution to the 'Free Rider Problem'. Econometrica **45**, 1977.

Harsanyi, J.: The Tracing Procedure: A Bayesian Approach to Defining a Solution for *n*-Person Non-Cooperative Games. International Journal of Game Theory **4** (1), 1975, 61–95.

Lindahl, E.; Just Taxation: A Positive Solution. Classics in the Theory of Public Finance. Ed. by R.A. Musgrave and A.T. Peacock. London 1964, (First published 1896).

Samuelson, P.: The Pure Theory of Public Expenditures. Review of Economics and Statistics **36**, 1954, 387–389.

Schotter, A.: The Economic Theory of Social Institutions. Cambridge 1981.

Telser, L.: Compotition, Collusion, and Game Theory. London 1972.

Wicksell, K.: A New Principle of Just Taxation. Classics in the Theory of Public Finanace. Ed. by R.A. Musgrave and A.T. Peacock. London 1964, (First published 1896).

Part II

Expanding and Contracting Economies

Games, Economic Dynamics, and Time Series Analysis. 1982 ©Physica-Verlag, Wien–Würzburg

Part II: Expanding and Contracting Economies

Introduction

By G. Schwödiauer

In 1936 John v. Neumann presented a paper in Karl Menger's famous Mathematical Colloquium on the relationship between a system of economic equations and Brouwer's fixed-point theorem which became later known as the v. Neumann model of an expanding economy. Again, Oskar Morgenstern, who because of travelling abroad had not been able to meet v. Neumann then, was probably the first economist to recognize the significance of v. Neumann's model for the theory of capital and growth. Morgenstern was at that time deeply interested in the role of time in value theory and had just published a rather critical article on the concept of production period which was central to the Austrian capital theory. In 1941 he wrote an extensive and not too friendly review of Hicks's Value and Capital for the Journal of Political Economy in which he emphatically referred to v. Neumann's model. Its breakthrough in economics came with Morgenstern's, Kemeny's and Thompson's 1956 generalization in which some assumptions were relaxed, the existence proof was considerably simplified by showing the equivalence of the problem with that of solving a matrix game, and the interesting concept of subeconomies (giving rise to a non-uniqueness of growth and profit rates) was introduced. Later, Oskar Morgenstern and Gerald L. Thompson further extended the model by introducing consumption and saving activities and considering the interaction of several open expanding economies. In 1976 Morgenstern and Thompson wrote an expository introduction to their theory of expanding and contracting economies for the Scientific American which for some reason, however, never appeared there. The editors of the conference proceedings have theorefore with pleasure followed Gerald Thompson's suggestion to publish it in this volume. In his paper presented in the symposium *Gerald Thompson* analyzes a one-good open economy model which is a continuous-time analogue of the Morgenstern-Thompson discrete open model, and *Diethard Pallaschke* provides a mathematical generalization of the closed v. Neumann model, and in particular the closed Leontief model, to the case with infinitely many commodities and productive processes.

The v. Neumann model of an expanding or contracting economy is in a certain sense both a very general and a rather special model of economic growth. On the one hand it contains the Leontief model or the Sraffa model as special cases and is so general in its formulation that to some extent it even tends to obscure the peculiar role of time in the production process emphasized by the Austrian theory of capital, on the other hand it can itself be regarded as a very special case of an intertemporal Walrasian equilibrium. As is well known, time can be introduced into a static Walrasian equlibrium by dating commodities and prices and by giving a time structure both to consumer preferences (via some notion of impatience) and to production possibility sets which can be thought of as being made up of the elementary technologies linking feasible inputs at the beginning of each period to feasible outputs at the end of each period. Such a time structure is, e.g., explicitly described for a very special case in *Dieter Reetz's* paper. A Walrasian „full equilibrium over time" or "perfect foresight path" may, however, display changing relative prices and a multitude of own-rates of interest, while a v. Neumann equilibrium is semi-stationary. Moreover, the constant-returns-to-scale technology of the v. Neumann model makes the demand side irrelevant for the determination of equilibria.

The so-called "von Neumann method" of modelling the time structure of production processes implies, of course, the extension of the list of different types of goods by all the intermediate products and capital goods. A durable capital good appears as a stock-input in some production process and as a stock-output of another type of capital good (viz., one period older) in the same process; if used also in some other process it will emerge at the end of the period as still another type of capital good (because it is used more or less intensively in the second process than in the first). The shorter we choose the elementary period the more commodities we will in general have to include, a feature which may lend some plausibility to the case of infinitely many goods. Moreover, Walrasian logic implies that each commodity has a price, which means that we have to assume the existence of markets for all intermediate commodities and used capital goods. It is mainly in this aspect that the so-called neo-Austrian approach to capital theory – represented in this volume by the papers by *Winfried Reiss* and *Malte Faber*, and by *Alois Wenig* – differs from the v. Neumann model. In concentrating on the vertical structure of production processes the neo-Austrian theory typically works just with an input function describing the time profile of primary inputs and an output function giving the time shape of the flow of consumption goods. Usually neo-Austrian theories are also steady-state models assuming the economy always to be on the efficiency frontier. *Wenig's* paper is a novelty in so far as he drops this assumption and allows the real wage to fluctuate in accordance with the rate of unemployment. If under this condition the real rate of interest is fixed exogenously the economy produces cyclical fluctuations in all the important endogenous variables.

In the contribution by *Werner Böge, Malte Faber* and *Werner Güth* the impact of the number and strategic interdependence of producers on the equilibrium of a simple one-good economy with a temporal production structure is investigated. For this purpose a non-cooperative dynamic game is analyzed both for the case of a finite number of investment periods and for an infinite horizon by means of a closed-loop approach. A strategy for a producer is an investment policy that determines an investment decision at each discrete point of time contingent on the history of the economy up to that period. It is shown that the game possesses a unique subgame-perfect equilibrium point whose behavior under a variation of the number of producers between one (monopoly) and infinity (perfect competition) is studied by means of numerical methods.

Games, Economic Dynamics, and Time Series Analysis. 1982 ©Physica-Verlag, Wien–Würzburg

Continuous Expanding and Contracting Economies[1])

By *G.L. Thompson*, Pittsburgh[2])

1. Introduction

In *Morgenstern/Thompson* [1976] a fairly complete account was given of the work done on the von Neumann expanding economy model from its inception in 1932 to the mid seventies. Over the years we, and others, had worked to generalize the original model and to remove some of its imperfections. Morgenstern and I always had the goal of making the model economically more realistic, with the eventual aim of creating a model sufficiently close to reality that it could be applied by economic planners to the analysis of real economies. Of course, we did not completely succeed in reaching the goal in that book, but we were able in Chapter 9, to talk about long run planning models for a single economy, and in Chapter 11 to talk about the interactions of several economic models included in a single world model.

In the present paper I want to use the idea of mathematical control theory such as is exposited by *Arrow/Kurz* [1971] and *Sethi/Thompson* [1981] to study the optimal control over time of an economy which must support a growing population. These models are similar to the original capital accumulation model of *Ramsey* [1928], but are extended here to include exports and imports, foreign aid, discretionary consumption, etc. In another paper I intend to extend these models further to multiple goods and many country models, by using the theory of differential games.

In essence, the models studied here are continuous versions of the discrete von Neumann type models presented in *Morgenstern/Thompson* [1976]. The use of the ideas of mathematical control theory permit conclusions to be drawn about characteristics of long run solutions which cannot easily be obtained from the multi-stage linear programming models of Chapter 9 of *Morgenstern/Thompson* [1976]. It is hoped that the results of this paper will help in the economic understanding of the control of economies over time.

---

[1]) This report was prepared as part of the activities of the Management Sciences Research Group, Carnegie-Mellon University, under Contract N00014-75-C-0621 NR 047-048 with the U.S. Office of Naval Research. Reproduction in whole or in part is permitted for any purpose of the U.S. Government.

[2]) *G.L. Thompson*, Graduate School of Industrial Administration, Carnegie-Mellon University, Pittsburgh, PA 15213, U.S.A.

2. One Good Deterministic Model

The first model we consider is a simple deterministic differential equation economic model having a single consumption good, and which does not have control variables. It should be regarded as merely an introductory exerice, and will be extended in the models of later sections.

We use the following notation

T = the horizon planning time; $0 < T$.
$x(t)$ = the stock of the (single) good of the model at time T
x_0 = the initial stock of the good at $t = 0$.
α = the expansion factor of the economy, i.e., the multiplicative factor by which the stock can be changed due to operating the economic production process; we require $\alpha > 0$; if $\alpha > 1$ the economy expands, if $\alpha = 1$ it is stationary, and if $0 < \alpha < 1$ it contracts. It is assumed that α is the expansion factor net of the amount of production needed to renew production facilities.
$c(t)$ = specified consumption rate at time t
$U(c)$ = utility of consuming at rate c; U is assumed to be concave and differentiable; we frequently assume that $U(c) = \ln c$ to to obtain explicit solutions.
ρ = discount rate; assume $\rho < \alpha$.
r = population growth rate; we assume $\alpha > r$ for otherwise the economy makes an insignificant contribution.
c_1 = subsistence consumption rate for the population in existence at time 0; hence $c_1 e^{rt}$ is the subsistence consumption rate for the population at time t.

Given this notation we can write the state equation for the stock of the good at time t as

$$\dot{x} = \alpha x - c,\ x(0) = x_0. \tag{1}$$

The discounted utility of the consumption stream $c(t)$ is

$$J = \int_0^T e^{-\rho t} U[c(t)]\, dt. \tag{2}$$

Given a specified consumption rule $c(t)$ it is easy to solve (1) as

$$x(t) = x_0 e^{\alpha t} - e^{\alpha t} [\int_0^t c(\tau) e^{-\alpha \tau} d\tau]. \tag{3}$$

This expression gives the growth (or decay) path the economy over time. We consider two special cases.

Case 1. Constant consumption; $c(t) = c_1$. It is easy to see from (3) that

$$x'(t) = \left(x_0 - \frac{c_1}{\alpha} \right) e^{\alpha t} + \frac{c_1}{\alpha}. \tag{4}$$

From this it follows that if $c_1 < \alpha x_0$ the economy grows in size, if $c_1 = \alpha x_0$ the economy is stationary; and if $c_1 > \alpha x_0$ the economy contracts.

Case 2. Subsistence consumption for a growing population; $c(t) = c_1 e^{rt}$. Here the solution to (3) gives

$$x(t) = \left(x_0 - \frac{c_1}{\alpha - r}\right)e^{\alpha t} + \left(\frac{c_1}{\alpha - r}\right)e^{rt}. \tag{5}$$

It is easy to see that the economy will expand faster than the population if $x_0(\alpha - r) > > c_1$; it will expand at the same rate if $x_0(\alpha - r) = c_1$; and it will expand more slowly if $x_0(\alpha - r) < c_1$. Note that we can obtain Case 1 from Case 2 by setting $r = 0$.

As pointed out earlier the model developed here is merely a differential equations model with no objective function and no control variables. The model of the next section adds these two features.

3. One Good Closed Model with Discretionary Consumption

Our next model is an extension of the second model of the previous section in which there is discretionary consumption as well as subsistence consumption. An objective function, that of maximizing the discounted utility of the discretionary consumption stream, is added. Finally, an ending constraint is added so that the economy will try to reach the economic take-off size before the terminal time is reached.

The model is stated as the following problem:

$$\text{Maximize } \{J = \int_0^T e^{-\rho t}\, U[c(t)]\, dt\} \tag{6}$$

Subject to

$$\dot{x} = \alpha x - c_1 e^{rt} - c,\ x(0) = x_0 \tag{7}$$

$$x(T) \geqslant x_1 e^{rT}. \tag{8}$$

The model in (6) – (8) is called a mathematical control theory model. It is a linearized version of Ramsey's capital accumulation model [*Ramsey*]. In the control theory terminology, x is the state variable and c is the control variable; constraint (7) is the state equation, and (8) is an end point condition.

We solve the model by using the Pontryagin maximum principle, see *Arrow/Kurtz* [1971] and *Sethi/Thompson* [1981]. The current value Hamiltonian function, stated in terms of the adjoint variable λ, is

$$H = U(c) + \lambda[\alpha x - c_1 e^{rt} - c]. \tag{9}$$

The Hamiltonian maximizing condition is obtained by setting the derivative H_c to zero which gives

$$U'(c) = \lambda. \tag{10}$$

When $U(c) = \ln c$, equation (1) becomes

$$c = \frac{1}{\lambda} \tag{11}$$

which is the optimal discretionary consumption rule for the logarithmic utility function. For this rule to make sense we must (and will) show that $\lambda(t) > 0$, provided T is large enough.

The adjoint differential equation is

$$\dot{\lambda} = \rho\lambda - \frac{\partial H}{\partial x} = (\rho - \alpha)\,\lambda. \tag{12}$$

The transversality conditions needed to ensure the end point condition (8) are

$$\lambda(T) \geqslant 0 \text{ and } \lambda(T)\,[x(T) - c_1\, e^{rt}] = 0. \tag{13}$$

Note that (13) is a kind of complementary slackness condition which says that either $\lambda(T) = 0$ or $\lambda(T) > 0$ and (8) is satisfied as an equality. It is easy to solve (12) as

$$\lambda = Be^{(\rho\text{-}\alpha)t} \tag{14}$$

where B is a parameter to be determined so that (13) holds.

We now substitute (14) and (11) into (3) and carry out the integration. We evaluate $x(T)$ and substitute into (8) to obtain the condition

$$B[x_0\, e^{\alpha T} - c_1\, e^{rt}] \geqslant e^{\alpha T}\left(\frac{1 - e^{-\rho T}}{\rho}\right). \tag{15}$$

Note first that the term

$$K = \frac{1 - e^{-\rho T}}{\rho} \tag{16}$$

is the actuarial value of \$1 invested in a source that pays interest at rate ρ and continuously compounded from 0 to T. Second, note that (15) can be solved for a positive B if and only if T is sufficiently large that

$$x_0\, e\alpha^T > c_1\, e^{rT} \tag{17}$$

that is, T is long enough so that the economy, working at its growth rate α can overtake and pass the subsistance level demands of the population. On the assumption that T is large enough so that (17) is true, we can solve (15) for the smallest positive B as

$$B = \frac{Ke^{\alpha T}}{(x_0\, e^{\alpha T} - c_1\, e^{rT})}. \tag{18}$$

This value of B insures that (13) and hence (8) are true. The smallest value of B also insures through (11) that the maximum of (6) is obtained.

In Figure 1 the graphs of $c_1 e^{rT}$, $x(t)$, $c(t)$ and $\lambda(t)$ are plotted for a typical example where B is chosen as in (18). Note that the discretionary consumption $c(t)$ is chosen so that the economy size $x(t)$ just equals the goal $c_1 e^{rt}$ when $t = T$. Consumption in this case need not always be actual physical consumption. It can also be not using the productive facilities of the economy to the fullest extent; i.e., the economy does not have to produce all the steel, automobiles, etc. that potentially could be physically produced.

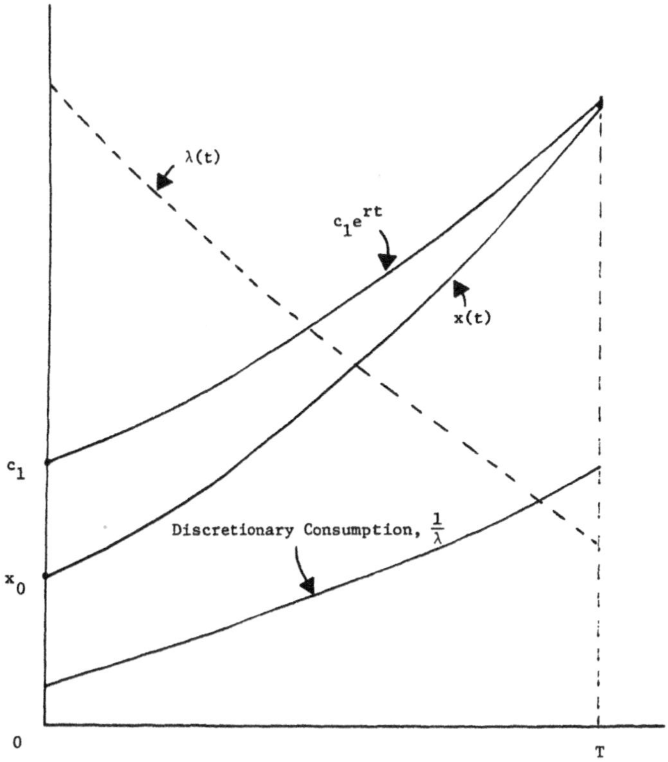

Fig. 1: Graphs of the optimal solutions to the closed model

4. One Good Open Model with Discretionary Consumption

To obtain an open model from the closed model of the previous section, we add the possibility of exporting and importing the single good. Because there is only one good available in the economy we cannot require a continuous balance of payments condition so we instead permit the economy to adjust its exports and imports so that, over the planning period T, the total value of imports equals the total value of exports. We begin by introducing some additional notation:

$w^i(t)$ = the rate of importing of the good; we assume $0 \leqslant w^i(t) \leqslant W^i$, where W^i is the maximum import rate.

$w^e(t)$ = the rate of exporting of the good; we assume that $0 \leqslant w^e(t) \leqslant W^e$, where W^e is the maximum export rate.

$p^i(t)$ = price of import goods at time t

$p^e(t)$ = price of export goods at time t; we assume that

$$p^e(t) < p^i(t) \qquad \text{for } 0 \leqslant t \leqslant T \tag{19}$$

to account for transportation costs.

The open model can be stated with the same objective function as (6), and the following state and terminal constraints:

$$\dot{x} = \alpha x - c_1 e^{rt} - c + w^i - w^e, x(0) = x_0 \tag{20}$$

$$\int_0^T e^{-\rho t}(p^e w^e - p^i w^i)\,dt \geqslant 0 \tag{21}$$

$$x(T) \geqslant c_1 e^{rT}. \tag{22}$$

Note that (19) corresponds to (6), (20) to (7) and (22) to (8). Condition (21) is the discounted balance of payments condition. Since it is stated in integral form it is clumsy to handle. We recast it in differential form by adding the variable y, defined by

$$\dot{y} = e^{-\rho t}(p^e w^e - p^i w^i), y(0) = 0 \tag{23}$$

and note that since

$$y(t) = \int_0^t e^{-\rho\tau}(p^e w^e - p^i w^i)\,d\tau \tag{24}$$

we can impose (21) by adding the terminal constraint $y(T) \geqslant 0$. The open model can now be stated as:

$$\text{Maximize } J = \int_0^T e^{-\rho t}\, U[c(t)]\,dt \tag{25}$$

Subject to

$$\dot{x} = \alpha x - c_1 e^{rt} - c + w^i - w^e, x(0) = x_0 \tag{26}$$

$$\dot{y} = e^{-\rho t}(p^e w^e - p^i w^i),\ y(0) = 0 \tag{27}$$

$$x(T) \geqslant c_1 e^{rT}, y(T) \geqslant 0. \tag{28}$$

In the new model we have three control variables, c, w^e, and w^i, and we have two end point conditions given in (28).

The solution of the new model is obtained in the same manner as was the precious one. Letting λ_1 and λ_2 be adjoint variables for equations (26) and (27), respectively, the current value Hamiltonian is

$$H = U[c(t)] + \lambda_1 (\alpha x - c_1 e^{rt} - c + w^i - w^i) + \lambda_2 [e^{-\rho t} (p^e w^e - p^i w^i)]. \tag{29}$$

The optimal consumption rule when $U[c] = \ln c$ is the same as in (11), namely

$$c = \frac{1}{\lambda_1}. \tag{30}$$

The import and export variables appear linearly in the Hamiltonian (29) so that their optimal values are bang-bang as follows:

$$w^i = \begin{cases} W^i & \text{if } \lambda_1(t) > p^i \lambda_2(t) e^{-\rho t} \\ \text{undetermined} & \text{if } \lambda_1(t) = p^i \lambda_2(t) e^{-\rho t} \\ 0 & \text{if } \lambda_1(t) < p^i \lambda_2(t) e^{-\rho t} \end{cases} \tag{31}$$

$$w^e = \begin{cases} 0 & \text{if } \lambda_1(t) > p^e \lambda_2(t) e^{-\rho t} \\ \text{undetermined} & \text{if } \lambda_1(t) = p^e \lambda_2(t) e^{-\rho t} \\ W^e & \text{if } \lambda_1(t) < p^e \lambda_2(t) e^{-\rho t}. \end{cases} \tag{32}$$

The equalities in the rules of (31) and (32) which fail to determine w^i and w^e correspond to singular control. However, such equalities occur only at single instants of time and hence do not make any essential difference in the optimal strategies.

The adjoint differential equation for λ_1 is like (12) and its solution is

$$\lambda_1 = B_1 e^{(\rho-\alpha)t}. \tag{33}$$

The adjoint differential equation for λ_2 is

$$\dot{\lambda}_2 = \rho\lambda_2 - \frac{\partial H}{\partial y} = \rho\lambda_2$$

so that its solution is

$$\lambda_2 = B_2 e^{\rho t}. \tag{34}$$

We now outline the solution of the problem. From (33) and $\alpha > \rho$ it follows that there is exactly one value of t, call it t_1, for which the equality in (31) holds. Substituting (33) and (34) and solving gives

$$t_1 = \frac{1}{\alpha - \rho}\left[\ln \frac{B_1}{B_2} - \ln p^i\right]. \tag{35}$$

Because $\lambda_1(t)$ is monotone decreasing we see that for $t \in [0, t_1]$ the optimal policy is to import at maximum rate W^i. Similarly, putting (33) and (34) into the equality rule of (32) and solving gives a time t_2 with

$$t_2 = \frac{1}{\alpha - \rho}\left[\ln \frac{B_1}{B_2} - \ln p^e\right]. \tag{36}$$

Because $p^e < p^i$ we see that $t_1 < t_2$. Also, because λ_1 is monotone decreasing, the optimal policy is to export at maximum rate W^e in the time interval $t \in (t_2, T]$. Note that the optimal policy in the interval (t_1, t_2) is to do nothing. The optimal policy at times t_1 and t_2 is not determined because they correspond to singular control. Since it doesn't matter we assume that no exports or imports are made at these two times.

To go further requires that we know either W^e or W^i. We shall assume $W^e = 1$. Using the optimal policy enunciated in the previous paragraph, (35), (36), and (21) it is easy to show that

$$W^i \leqslant \frac{p^e}{p^i}\left(\frac{e^{-\rho(T-t_2)} - 1}{e^{-\rho t_1} - 1}\right)e^{-\rho t_2}. \tag{37}$$

Let us assume that W^i is chosen to be the largest value corresponding to the equality in (37). If we let

$$\gamma = B_1/B_2 \tag{38}$$

we see from (35), (36), and (37) that t_1, t_2, and W^i all depend on γ. We show how to determine γ.

Because of the form of the optimal policy we can give the state equations for the three different time intervals.

$$\dot{x} = \alpha x - \frac{1}{B_1}e^{(\rho-\alpha)t} + W^i,\ x(0) = x_0, \quad \text{for } t \in [0, t_1] \tag{39}$$

$$\dot{x} = \alpha x - \frac{1}{B_1}e^{(\rho-\alpha)t},\ x(t_1) \text{ given by (39)}, \quad \text{for } t \in [t_1, t_2] \tag{40}$$

$$\dot{x} = \alpha x - \frac{1}{B_1}e^{(\rho-\alpha)t} - W^e,\ x(t_2) \text{ given by (40)}, \quad \text{for } t \in [t_2, T]. \tag{41}$$

These equations are elementary but lengthy to integrate, so that we do not show the answer here. From (41) we can calculate $x(T)$ and substitute into $x(T) \geqslant c_1 e^{rT}$ to determine γ. The formula will be similar to (18) and requires the assumption that T is sufficiently long.

Having determined γ, we have to make one more choice to completely specify the problem. If we select B_1 we note from (30) and (33) that this determines the rate of discretionary consumption. A large B_1 means small consumption and vice versa. Once B_1 is chosen, B_2 is determined by (38) and the explicit forms of x, are calculated from (39) – (41).

Figure 2 shows a typical solution. Note that the optimal policy is to import at maximum rate from 0 to t_1, and during this time the size of x increases very rapidly. From t_1 to t_2, we neither import not export, and x grows at rate α. Finally from t_2 to T, we export at maximum rate, which makes x grow more slowly. It still manages to reach the target level at T. Also shown are the trajectories of the adjoint variable λ and the optimal discretionary consumption. The value to the country of being able to import and export according to this optimal policy can be determined by starting at x_0 in Figure 2 and drawing a curve parallel to the curve shown in the figure between t_1 and t_2, which corresponds to the no-export, no-import situation. Clearly, the stock of goods at time T with this policy will be considerably less than the optimal stock of goods actually achieved.

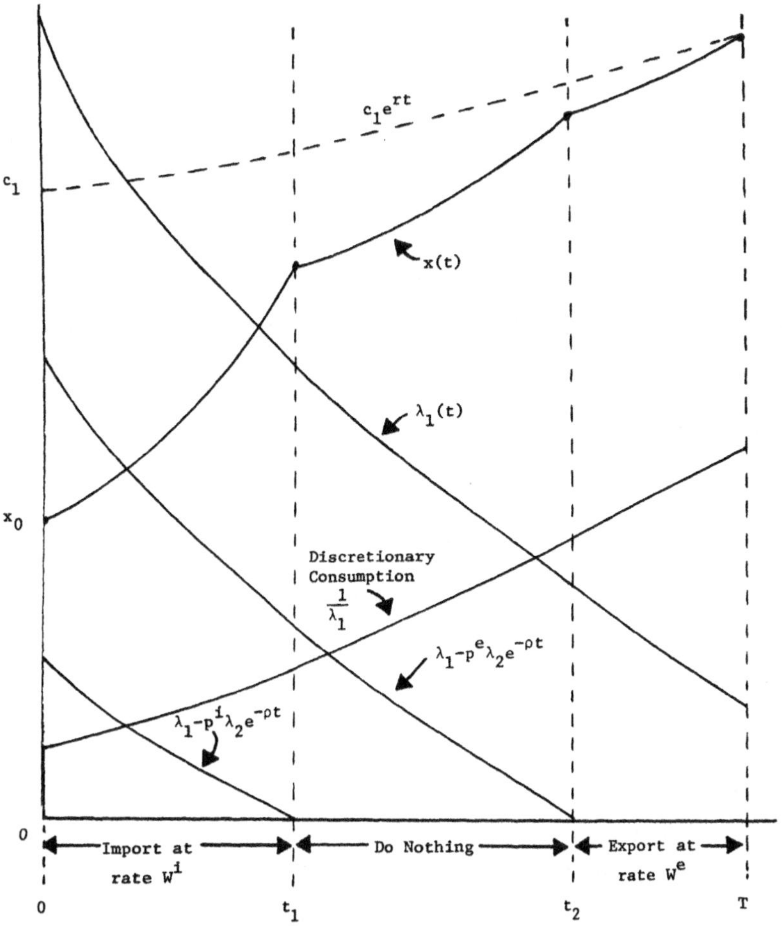

Fig. 2: Graphs of the optimal solutions to the open model

References

Arrow, K.J., and *M. Kurtz*: Public Investment. The Rate of Return, and Optimal Fiscal Policy. Baltimore, Maryland 1971.

Morgenstern, O., and *G.L. Thompson*: Mathematical Theory of Expanding and Contracting Economies. Lexington, Mass., 1976.

Ramsey, F.: A Mathematical Theory of Saving. Economic Journal **38**, 1928, 543–559.

Sethi, S.P., and *G.L. Thompson*: Optimal Control Theory: Management Science Applications. Boston, Mass. 1981.

Games, Economic Dynamics, and Time Series Analysis. 1982 ©Physica-Verlag, Wien–Würzburg

Some Examples of von Neumann Models in Banach Spaces

By *D. Pallaschke*, Bonn[1])

In this lecture we will give a generalization of the closed Leontief model which can be considered as a linear model for an expanding economy with infinitely many commodities and productive processes.

The generalization of the Leontief model, which we present here is purely formal. It is done by substituting for the euclidean n-space $\mathbf{R}^n$ a partially ordered real Banach space and for the input matrix a positive compact operator.

We have already shown [*Pallaschke*] that the classical result on the existence of an equilibrium remains also valid for this generalized model.

We use the standard notion and denote for a real Banach space $(E, \| \ \|)$ by

$$E' := \{p: E \longrightarrow \mathbf{R} \mid p \text{ is continuous and linear}\}$$

the topological dual space of E. By

$$B(x, r) := \{y \in E \mid \|y - x\| \leqslant r\}$$

we denote the closed ball in E with center x and radius $r \geqslant 0$. Furthermore, a linear mapping

$$A: E \longrightarrow E$$

is said to be *"compact"* if there exists a compact subset $K \subseteq E$ with

$$A(B(0,1)) \subseteq K.$$

In the terminology of *Burmeister/Dobel* [1970] we will now give the definition of a generalized von Neumann Model.

Let $(E, \| \ \|)$ be a partially ordered real Banach space such that the positive cone $E^+ \subseteq E$ is closed convex and non trivial. Then the partial order on E is given by:

$$x \leqslant y \text{ if and only if } y - x \in E^+.$$

We denote by

$$\operatorname{End}(E) := \{A: E \longrightarrow E \mid A \text{ is continuous and linear}\}$$

the Banach algebra of all continuous linear operators from E into itself.

[1]) *D. Pallaschke*, Institut für Angewandte Mathematik, Universität Bonn, Wegelerstr. 6, D–5300 Bonn.

For any two positive operatos

$$A, B \in \mathrm{End}_+(E) := \{A \in \mathrm{End}(E) \mid A(E^+) \subseteq E^+\}$$

the cone

$$T_{A,B} := \{(x, y) \in E^+ \times E^+ \mid \text{there exists a } z \in E^+ \text{ such that } x \geqslant Az \text{ and } y \leqslant Bz\}$$

of $E^+ \times E^+$ is called a *"generalized von Neuman model"* in E with input operator A and output operator B. If $B := \mathrm{Id}_E$, then it is called a *"generalized Leontief model"* and is denoted by T_A.

A tupel

$$(z, \lambda) \in E^+ \times (\mathbf{R}^+ \setminus \{0\})$$

is said to be an *"equilibrium"* of $T_{A,B}$ if the following conditions are satisfied:

i) $\lambda Az \leqslant Bz$

ii) there exists a positive linear functional

$$p^* \in (E^+)' := \{p \in E' \mid p(E^+) \subseteq \mathbf{R}^+\}$$

such that

$$p^*B \leqslant \lambda p^*A, \text{ i.e.:}$$

for all $x \in E^+$

$$p^*(Bx) \leqslant \lambda p^*(Ax).$$

iii) $p^*Bz > 0$.

The positive number $\lambda > 0$ is called the *"level of equilibrium"* and $z \in E^+$ the *"equilibrium point"*.

In *Pallaschke* [1977] we have proved the following result:

Theorem: Let $(E, \| \ \|)$ be a partially ordered real Banach space such that the positive cone E^+ satisfies:

$$E^+ \cap \{-E^+\} = \{0\}.$$

Furthermore, let us suppose, that for any two elements $x, y \in E^+$ with $x \leqslant y$ we have

$$\| x \| \leqslant \| y \|,$$

and let

$$A \in \mathrm{End}_+(E)$$

be compact.

Then the tupel

$$(z, \lambda) \in E^+ \times (\mathbf{R}^+ \setminus \{0\})$$

is an equilibrium of T_A if and only if

i) λ^{-1} is an eigenvalue of A

which is

ii) associated with an eigenvector

$$\check{x} \in E^+ \setminus \overline{((\mathrm{Id}_E - \lambda A)(E^+) - E^+)}$$

with

$$z \geqslant \check{x}.$$

Let us remark, that from the second condition follows, that the inequality

$$\check{x} \leqslant (\mathrm{Id}_E - \lambda A) w, \; w \in E^+$$

has no solution in E^+.

As a first example, we start with the neoclassical model of economic growth [see *Krelle/Gabisch*].

For this model, the existence of a differentiable production function

$$Y_t = f(L_t, K_t, \tau_t)$$

is postulated, which links the output Y to the inputs labour L, capital K and technological knowledge τ. The subindex t denotes the dependence of time.

The production function is supposed to be positively homogeneous in L and K, i.e.

$$\lambda Y_t = f(\lambda L_t, \lambda K_t, \tau_t), \qquad \lambda > 0$$

and to satisfy the first order differential equation:

$$w_{Y,t} = \epsilon_{L,t}\, w_{L,t} + \epsilon_{K,t}\, w_{K,t} + w_{\tau,t} \tag{*}$$

with

$$\epsilon_{X,t} := \left.\frac{\partial f}{\partial X}\right|_t \cdot \frac{X_t}{Y_t}$$

and

$$w_{X,t} := \frac{1}{X_t}\left[\left.\frac{d}{dt}\right|_t X_t\right]$$

for $X \in \{Y, L, K, \tau\}$.

Now we have for the elasticities the identity:

$$\epsilon_{L,t} + \epsilon_{K,t} = 1.$$

If we assume that the rate of growth of output Y and capital K coincide and assume that the rate of growth of labour L is constant, i.e.:

$$w_{Y,t} = w_{K,t}$$
$$w_{L,t} = w_L = \text{const} > 0$$

for $t \in [0,1]$, then the basic equation (*) turns into:

$$\frac{d}{dt}(Y_t) - N(t)\, Y_t = w_L\, Y_t,$$

where

$$N(t) := \frac{w_{\tau,t}}{\epsilon_{L,t}}.$$

Now take

$$E := C_0[0,1] := \{x : [0, 1] \to \mathbf{R} \mid x \text{ is continuous}\}$$
$$E^+ := \{x \in E \mid x(t) \geqslant 0, \qquad \text{for all } t \in [0,1]\}$$

and

$$A: C_0\,[0,1] \longrightarrow C_0\,[0,1]$$

with

$$Ax\,|_t = \frac{x(0)}{L}\, e^{\int_0^t N(\rho)d\rho} \int_0^t (e^{\int_\sigma^t N(\rho)d\rho}\, x(\sigma))\, d\sigma.$$

Let us remark, that A is the right inverse of the differential operator

$$Lx := \frac{dx}{dt} - N \cdot x.$$

Then $(w_L)^{-1}$ is a simple eigenvalue of A, associated to the eigenvector

$$x: [0,1] \longrightarrow \mathbf{R}$$

given by

$$x(t) := x_0 e^{(w_L t + \int_0^t N(\rho)d\rho)}$$

Hence

$$(x, w_L)$$

is an equilibrium.

Now assume that a cyclic growth model is described by a linear second order differential equation

$$p_0(t)x''(t)+p_1(t)x'(t)+p_2(t)x(t)=f(t),$$

where $p_0 \neq 0$, x denotes the output, f is an autonomous factor and $t \in [0,1]$.

If we assume that

$$x(0)=x(1)=0$$

then the inverse of the differential operator

$$Lx=p_0x''+p_1x'+p_2x$$

is given by

$$Av\,|_t := \int_0^1 g(t,\tau)\,v(\tau)\,d\tau$$

with:

$$g(t,\tau) := \begin{cases} \dfrac{u_1(t)\,u_2(\tau)}{p_0(\tau)\,[u_2(\tau)\,u_1'(\tau)-u_1(\tau)\,u_2'(\tau)]} & 0 \leqslant t \leqslant \tau \leqslant 1 \\[2ex] \dfrac{u_2(t)\,u_1(\tau)}{p_0(\tau)[u_2(\tau)u_1'(\tau)-u_1(\tau)\,u_2(\tau)]} & 0 \leqslant \tau \leqslant t \leqslant 1. \end{cases}$$

Here u_1, u_2 are fundamental solutions of L.

We will now discuss the case for which autonomous factor f, we will have:

$$Lx = \lambda x = f,$$

with $\lambda > 0$.

Now let us remark that A is a compact operator on the Hilbert space

$$L^2[0,1] := \{x\colon [0,1] \longrightarrow \mathbf{R} \mid \int_0^1 |x(t)|^2 d\mu < \infty \text{ and the function } x \text{ is measurable}\}$$

endowed with the norm

$$\|x\| := (\int_0^1 |x(t)|^2 dt)^{1/2}.$$

In the case where $p_1 = p_0'$, the compact operator

$$A\colon L^2[0,1] \longrightarrow L^2[0,1]$$

has countably infinitely many non zero real eigenvalues $(\lambda_n)_n \in \mathbf{N}$. If $e_n \in L^2[0,1]$ is a normalized eigenvector to λ_n, then $(e_n)_{n\in\mathbf{N}}$ is an orthonormal basis of $L^2[0,1]$ and A can be represented in the form:

$$A\colon L^2[0,1] \longrightarrow L^2[0,1]$$

with

$$Au := \sum_{n=0}^{\infty} \lambda_n < u, e_n > e_n.$$

Here we denote for $x, y \in L^2[0,1]$ by

$$\langle x, y \rangle := \int_0^1 x(t)\, y(t)\, dt$$

the inner product.

Let us now take

$$E := L^2[0,1]$$

and

$$E^+ := \{x \in E \mid \langle x, e_n \rangle \geqslant 0, \text{ for all } n \in \mathbf{N} \cup \{0\}\}.$$

Then our theorem is applicable to the Leontief model T_A in $L^2[0,1]$ and we get countably infinitely many equilibrium points

$$(e_n, \lambda_n^{-1}),\ n \in \mathbf{N} \cup \{0\}.$$

References

Burmeister, E., and *A.R. Dobel*: Mathematical Theory of Economic Growth. London 1970.

Krelle, W., and *G. Gabisch*: Wachstumstheorie. Lecture Notes in Economics and Math. Systems Nr. 62. Berlin–Heidelberg–New York 1972.

Pallaschke, D.: Infinite dimensional von Neumann models. Math. Econ. and Game Theory. Lect. Notes in Economics and Math. Systems Nr. 141. Berlin–Heidelberg–New York 1973, 312–321.

Games, Economic Dynamics, and Time Series Analysis. 1982 ©Physica-Verlag, Wien–Würzburg

Rational Planning in Exponentially Growing Input – Output Systems Using Labor Values

By *D. Reetz*, Berlin[1])

1. Introduction

In this paper the problem of an optimal choice of the technology is investigated within the framework of a multiperiod exponentially growing input-output substitution system. Let $t = 0, 1, 2, \ldots, T$ denote the discrete period index, representing for example a day, a month or a year. The letter T indicates the length of the production process measured in periods. We consider a closed economic system decomposed into n sectors, each producing one commodity within a period using homogeneous labor and commodities produced in the previous period as inputs. Each sector j $(1 \leqslant j \leqslant n)$ has available a finite set K_j of *methods of production.* In order to produce one unit of commodity j (in sector j) using the method $k \in K_j$ in period t $(1 \leqslant t \leqslant T)$ a direct labor input of $a_{0j}(k)/(1+\alpha)^{t-1}$ units of time say in hours as well as $a_{ij}(k)$ units of commodities i $(1 \leqslant i \leqslant n)$ are required. The constant $\alpha > -1$ represents the rate of (labor augmenting) technical progress. So as to simplify our mathematics we shall assume that $a_{0j}(k) > 0$ for all j and k.

In each period t every sector j selects a method of production k_j^t. The n-dimensional vector $(k_j^t)_{1 \leqslant j \leqslant n} = f^t$ is called the *technology* of period t. It determines a vector of direct labor inputs $a_0(f^t)/(1+\alpha)^{t-1} = [a_{0j}(k_j^t)/(1+\alpha)^{t-1}]_{1 \leqslant j \leqslant n}$ and an input-output matrix $A(f^t) = [a_{ij}(k_j^t)]_{1 \leqslant i, j \leqslant n}$. Let F denote the finite set of all technologies. A (finite) sequence of technologies is called a (finite) *plan* and is represented by $\bar{f}^T = \{f^1, \ldots, f^t, \ldots, f^T\} = \{f^t \mid 1 \leqslant t \leqslant T\}$. According to this plan the technology to be selected in period t $(1 \leqslant t \leqslant T)$ is given by $f^t = (k_j^t)$. A plan specifying the technologies for the periods $\tau \leqslant t \leqslant T$ is denoted by $\bar{f}_\tau^T = \{f^t \mid \tau \leqslant t \leqslant T\}$. Let $\bar{F}^T$ be the finite set of all T-period plans. An infinite period plan is defined as an infinite sequence of technologies. For such plans we use the symbols $\bar{f}^\infty = \{f^t \mid 1 \leqslant t\}$ and $\bar{f}_\tau^\infty = \{f^t \mid \tau \leqslant t\}$. The set of all infinite period plans is denoted by $\bar{F}^\infty$. A finite or infinite period plan is called *stationary*, if all of the component technologies are equal, $f^1 = f^2 = f^3 = \ldots$ We use the symbol $\tilde{}$ to designate such plans. Thus, for example, $\tilde{f}^T = \{f \mid 1 \leqslant t \leqslant T\} = \{f, f, \ldots, f\}$ and $\tilde{f}_\tau^\infty = \{f \mid \tau \leqslant t\} = \{f, f, f, \ldots\}$. The finite set of all $\tilde{f}^T$, denoted by

[1]) *D. Reetz*, Freie Universität Berlin, FB Wirtschaftswissenschaft, Corrensplatz 2, D–1000 Berlin 33.

$\tilde{F}^T$, is a subset of $\bar{F}^T$. The set $\tilde{F}^\infty$ of all infinite period stationary plans is isomorphic to F and is a subset of $\bar{F}^\infty$.

In our investigation we shall take an Austrian approach to the production process. The concept of a plan, as a representation of the temporal structure of the process, is therefore of great importance. As a first step we shall look at quantity systems for arbitrary finite T-period plans in Section 2. For stationary plans we subsequently derive the classical steady-state quantity system by letting $T \to \infty$ in the case of exponentially growing consumption. Section 3 is concerned with labor values. We establish a dual representation of the *total* labor time for a T-period production process with the help of labor values. Such a representation is used to determine a plan minimizing the total labor time. It also plays a role in proving a nonsubstitution theorem for a finite period process, allowing for nonstationary plans. This is followed by an investigation of asymptotic rational value systems as $T \to \infty$ (Theorems 2 and 3, Corollary 1). Subsequently we present a brief critique of synchronized values as an instrument of rational planning. We close Section 3 by developing some dual representations of asymptotic normalized total labor times in the case of stationary plans. In Section 4 price systems with exponentially growing nominal wage rates are studied. It is shown that competitive prices minimize the total discounted labor costs, if the growth rate of nominal wages and the rate of profit are given. Properties of such price systems are derived for the asymptotic case $T \to \infty$. Several dual representations of asymptotic normalized labor costs are stated. The final part of Section 4 concerns the relation of the growth rate of nominal wages and the rate of profit with the average real wage rate. For given average real wage rates we obtain nominal wage-profit indifference curves in the case of finite and infinite period processes. Simultaneously, prices of production and an associated technology are shown to be generated by some nonlinear systems (Theorem 5 and 6). The final Section 5 establishes a link between the value system and the price systems. An average and an asymptotic rate of exploitation are defined and conditions are given, under which these exploitation rates are positive. This result may be interpreted as a generalized Fundamental Marxian Theorem for exponentially growing input-output substitution systems.

2. Quantity Systems

Let us consider the quantity system of a production process lasting T periods, using a given plan $\bar{f}^T$. To abbreviate our notation we write $A(t) = A(f^t)$ and $a_0(t) = a_0(f^t)$. The *gross product* of period t $(1 \leqslant t \leqslant T)$ is represented by the vector $x(t) = [x_i(t)]_{1 \leqslant i \leqslant n}$. *Consumption goods* produced in period t are denoted by the vector $y(t) = [y_i(t)]_{1 \leqslant i \leqslant n} \geqslant 0$. The vector of goods produced in period t $(1 \leqslant t \leqslant T-1)$ and used as *input* in period $t+1$ is written as $z(t) = [z_i(t)]_{1 \leqslant i \leqslant n}$. Let $z(0) = [z_i(0)]$ be the vector of *initial capital goods* and $z(T) = [z_i(T)]_{1 \leqslant i \leqslant n}$ the vector of *final capital goods.* In each period the gross product $x(t)$ may be split into a consumption vector $y(t)$ and into an input vector $z(t)$, i.e. $x(t) = y(t) + z(t)$. The vector $z(t)$ in turn may be determined by $z(t) = A(t+1)\,x(t+1)$ if $x(t+1)$ is given. This leads us to the quantity recursion

$$x(t) = y(t) + z(t) = y(t) + A(t+1)\,x(t+1) \tag{1}$$

which we have schematically represented in Figure 1.

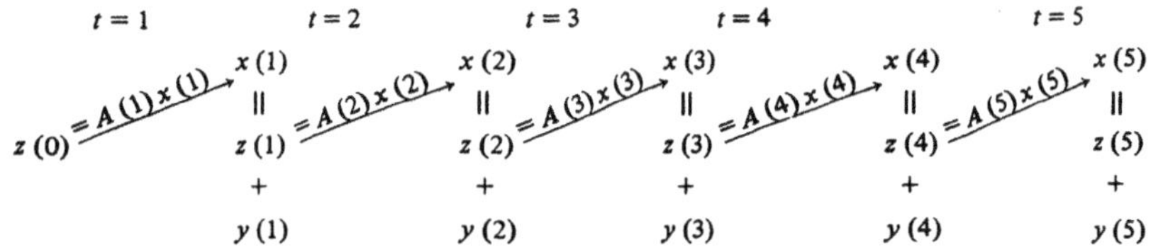

$$L^T(\tilde{f}^T) = w^0\, z(0) + a_0(1)\,x(1) + \frac{a_0(2)}{1+\alpha}x(2) + \frac{a_0(3)}{(1+\alpha)^2}x(3) + \frac{a_0(4)}{(1+\alpha)^3}x(4) + \frac{a_0(5)}{(1+\alpha)^4}x(5)$$

$$L^T(\tilde{f}^T) = w^1 y(1) + w^2 y(2) + w^3 y(3) + w^4 y(4) + w^5\,[y(5) + z(5)]$$

Fig. 1

If the desired final capital goods $z(T)$ and the consumption vectors $y(t)$ $(1 \leqslant t \leqslant T)$ are given, we may calculate $x(t)$ $(1 \leqslant t \leqslant T)$ and $z(1)$ using (1). The explicit expressions are given in (2) and (3).

$$x(t) = \sum_{s=t}^{T} \prod_{\tau=t+1}^{s} A(\tau)\,y(s) + \prod_{\tau=t+1}^{T} A(\tau)\,z(T) \quad (1 \leqslant t \leqslant T) \tag{2}$$

$$z(0) = \sum_{s=1}^{T} \prod_{\tau=1}^{s} A(\tau)\,y(s) + \prod_{\tau=1}^{T} A(\tau)\,z(T). \tag{3}$$

By convention, a matrix product over the empty set is equal to the identity matrix I, so that for example $\prod_{\tau=T+1}^{T} A(\tau) = I$. For the most part we shall assume exponential growth of consumption, i.e.

$$y_i(t) = (1+\eta)^{t-1} y_i \qquad (1 \leqslant i \leqslant n,\ 1 \leqslant t \leqslant T). \tag{4}$$

Here $\eta > -1$ is a (possibly negative) growth rate of consumption and $y = [y_i]$ some specified initial consumption vector. For a stationary plan $\tilde{f}^T$ the gross products $x(t)$ in case of consumption (4) are given by

$$x(t) = (1+\eta)^{t-1} \sum_{s=0}^{T-t} (1+\eta)^s A^s(f)\,y + A^{T-t}(f)\,z(t). \tag{5}$$

Letting $A^0(f) = I$ we define the *growth rate* $\gamma(f)$ of a technology f by

$$\gamma(f) := \sup\{\gamma \mid \sum_{m=0}^{\infty} (1+\gamma)^m (f) < \infty\}\ A^m(f) < \infty\} \tag{6}$$

and call f a productive technology if $\gamma(f) > 0$. Alternatively the technology f is productive if and only if a positive gross production vector x exists allowing for a positive net output $x - A(f)x$. The (maximal) *growth rate of the substitution system* is given by $\gamma = \max_{f \in F} \gamma(f)$. The substitution system is called productive if $\gamma > 0$, that is, if at least one productive technology exists.

In case $\eta < \gamma(f)$, the series (5) converges as $T \to \infty$ to

$$x(t) = (1+\eta)^{t-1} \sum_{s=0}^{\infty} (1+\eta)^s A^s(f) y = (1+\eta)^{t-1} \bar{x}(f) \tag{7}$$

with $\bar{x}(f)$ being the unique solution of the normalized (steady state) quantity equation for the given technology f

$$\bar{x}_i(f) = y_i + (1+\eta) \sum_{j=1}^{n} a_{ij}(f) \bar{x}_j(f) \quad (1 \leqslant i \leqslant n). \tag{8}$$

3. Value Systems

Having calculated the gross products for a given plan, we seek as a next step to determine the required labor time. The labor time expended in period t $(1 \leqslant t \leqslant T)$ depends on the present and future technologies $f^t, f^{t+1}, \ldots, f^T$ and is given by

$$\begin{aligned} L^T(t; \bar{f}^T) = L^T(t; \bar{f}_t^T) &= \frac{a_0(t)}{(1+\alpha)^{t-1}} x(t) \\ &= \frac{a_0(t)}{(1+\alpha)^{t-1}} \left[\sum_{s=t}^{T} \prod_{\tau=t+1}^{s} A(\tau) y(s) + \prod_{\tau=t+1}^{T} A(\tau) z(T) \right]. \end{aligned} \tag{9}$$

A sufficient supply of labor is assumed to exist, so that we have no restrictions on $L^T(t; \bar{f}^T)$. Let $w^0 = (w_j^0) \geqslant 0$ be a given *initial value vector.* (Superscript 0 is an index, not an exponent.) Its purpose is to measure the *value* of the initial input of capital goods as follows.

$$\begin{aligned} L^T(0; \bar{f}^T) &= w^0 z(0) \\ &= w^0 \left[\sum_{s=1}^{T} \prod_{\tau=1}^{s} A(\tau) y(s) + \prod_{\tau=1}^{T} A(\tau) z(T) \right]. \end{aligned} \tag{10}$$

The total labor time of a T-period process is obtained by adding the expressions (9) over all t $(1 \leqslant t \leqslant T)$. The reader is referred to *von Weizsäcker* [1974] for a discussion of metaphysical problems surrounding such a definition. We wish to modify the definition of total labor time by including in it the given value of the initial capital goods (which may be zero). Thus the expression (11) is called the *total labor time* for a given plan $\bar{f}^T$

$s=6$	$w^0 \prod_{\tau=1}^{5} A(\tau) z(5)$	$a_0(1) \prod_{\tau=2}^{5} A(\tau) z(5)$	$\frac{a_0(2)}{1+\alpha} \prod_{\tau=3}^{5} A(\tau) z(5)$	$\frac{a_0(3)}{(1+\alpha)^2} \prod_{\tau=4}^{5} A(\tau) z(5)$	$\frac{a_0(4)}{(1+\alpha)^3} A(5) z(5)$	$= \frac{a_0(5)}{(1+\alpha)}$
$s=5$	$w^0 \prod_{\tau=1}^{5} A(\tau) y(5)$	$a_0(1) \prod_{\tau=2}^{5} A(\tau) y(5)$	$\frac{a_0(2)}{1+\alpha} \prod_{\tau=3}^{5} A(\tau) y(5)$	$\frac{a_0(3)}{(1+\alpha)^2} \prod_{\tau=4}^{5} A(\tau) y(5)$	$\frac{a_0(4)}{(1+\alpha)^3} A(5) y(5)$	$\frac{a_0(5)}{(1+\alpha)^4} y(5)$
$s=4$	$w^0 \prod_{\tau=1}^{4} A(\tau) y(4)$	$a_0(1) \prod_{\tau=2}^{4} A(\tau) y(4)$	$\frac{a_0(2)}{1+\alpha} \prod_{\tau=3}^{4} A(\tau) y(4)$	$\frac{a_0(3)}{(1+\alpha)^2} A(4)\ y(4)$	$\frac{a_0(4)}{(1+\alpha)^3}\ y(4)$	
$s=3$	$w^0 \prod_{\tau=1}^{3} A(\tau) y(3)$	$a_0(1) \prod_{\tau=2}^{3} A(\tau) y(3)$	$\frac{a_0(2)}{1+\alpha}\ A(3)\ y(3)$	$\frac{a_0(3)}{(1+\alpha)^2}\ y(3)$		
$s=2$	$w^0 \prod_{\tau=1}^{2} A(\tau) y(2)$	$a_0(1) A(2) y(2)$	$\frac{a_0(2)}{1+\alpha}\ y(2)$			
$s=1$	$w^0 A(1)\ y(1)$	$a_0(1)\ y(1)$				
	$t=0$	$t=1$	$t=2$	$t=3$	$t=4$	$t=5$

Fig. 2

$$L^T(\bar{f}^T) := \sum_{t=0}^{T} L^T(t; \bar{f}^T)$$

$$= w^0 \left[\sum_{s=1}^{T} \prod_{\tau=1}^{s} A(\tau) y(s) + \prod_{\tau=1}^{T} A(\tau) z(T) \right]$$

$$+ \sum_{t=1}^{T} \frac{a_0(t)}{(1+\alpha)^{t-1}} \left[\sum_{s=t}^{T} \prod_{\tau=t+1}^{s} A(\tau) y(s) + \prod_{\tau=t+1}^{T} A(\tau) z(T) \right]. \tag{11}$$

We have represented the total labor time (11) by the second lowest row in Figure 1. The term of the series (11) may also be depicted in a two-dimensional diagram (Figure 2). This is a restricted finite version ($T = 5 < \infty$) of an infinite matrix in *von Weizsäcker* [1971, p. 24]. A column t of the diagram lists the labor time expended in period t ($1 \leqslant t \leqslant T$). Entry s ($t \leqslant s \leqslant T$) of column t ($1 \leqslant t \leqslant T$) gives the labor time in period t needed for the production of consumption goods at time s. The top element of a column t ($1 \leqslant t \leqslant T$) represents the time in period t going into the production of the final capital good $z(T)$. Element s ($1 \leqslant s \leqslant T$) of the first column ($t = 0$) lists the value of the initial capital goods embodied in goods produced in period s. The top element of the first column represents the value of the initial capital goods incorporated in the final capital stock.

In (11) we have successively summed the columns $t = 0, 1, \ldots, T$. In order to obtain a *dual representation* of (11) we go about adding up rows. Then we obtain

$$L^T(\bar{f}^T) = \sum_{s=1}^{T} \left[w^0 \prod_{\tau=1}^{s} A(\tau) + \sum_{t=1}^{s} \frac{a_0(t)}{(1+\alpha)^{t-1}} \prod_{\tau=t+1}^{s} A(\tau) \right] y(s)$$

$$+ \left[w^0 \prod_{\tau=1}^{T} A(\tau) + \sum_{t=1}^{T} \frac{a_0(t)}{(1+\alpha)^{t-1}} \prod_{\tau=t+1}^{T} A(\tau) \right] z(T). \tag{12}$$

For a given initial value vector w^0 and a given plan $\bar{f}^T$ we generate the following *value vectors* $w^t(\bar{f}^t)$

$$w^t(\bar{f}^t) = \frac{a_0(t)}{(1+\alpha)^{t-1}} + w^{t-1}(\bar{f}^{t-1}) A(t) \quad (1 \leqslant t \leqslant T). \tag{13}$$

Note that $w^t(\bar{f}^t)$ depends on $f^1, \ldots, f^t$ but not on $f^{t+1}, \ldots, f^T$. An iterative reduction of (13) yields

$$w^t(\bar{f}^t) = w^0 \prod_{\tau=1}^{t} A(\tau) + \sum_{s=1}^{t} \frac{a_0(s)}{(1+\alpha)^{s-1}} \prod_{\tau=s+1}^{t} A(\tau). \tag{14}$$

Substitution of (14) into (12) now gives us the following *dual representation of the total labor time*

$$L^T(\bar{f}^T) = w^0 z(0) + \sum_{t=1}^{T} \frac{a_0(t)}{(1+\alpha)^{t-1}} x(t)$$

$$= \sum_{t=1}^{T} w^t (\bar{f}^t) y(t) + w^T (\bar{f}^T) z(T). \tag{15}$$

We refer the reader to Figure 1.

The dual representation (15) is useful for the calculation of a plan minimizing $L^T(\bar{f}^T)$. We shall show that the following recursion generates such an optimal plan. Letting $w^0 = (w_j^0)$ be the initial value vector we define *rational values* $w^t = (w_j^t)$ $(1 \leq t \leq T)$ and *rational technolgies* $f_*^t = (k_{j*}^t)$ $(1 \leq t \leq T)$ compromising a *rational plan* $\bar{f}_*^T = \{f_*^t \mid 1 \leq t \leq T\}$ by

$$\begin{array}{l} f_*^t = (k_{j*}^t) \\ \uparrow \\ w_j^t = \min\limits_{k \in K_j} \left\{ \dfrac{a_{0j}(k)}{(1+\alpha)^{t-1}} + \sum\limits_{i=1}^{n} w_i^{t-1} a_{ij}(k) \right\} \quad (1 \leq j \leq n, 1 \leq t \leq T). \end{array} \tag{16}$$

The above recursion may easily be interpreted. The rational value w_j^t of one unit of commodity j in period t is equal to the minimum of the sum of the direct labor inputs $a_{0j}(k)/(1+\alpha)^{t-1}$ and the previous value of the required means of production $\sum_{i=1}^{n} w_i^{t-1} a_{ij}(k)$. Note that minimization takes place decentralized, with respect both to sectors and to time, generating *rational methods of production* k_{j*}^t $(1 \leq j \leq n, 1 \leq t \leq T)$. We observe that rational technologies f_*^t and the rational plan $\bar{f}_*^T$ need not be unique. The rational values on the other hand are obviously unique. It may easily be shown by induction on t, that rational values are minimal in the sense that

$$w_j^t = w_j^t(\bar{f}_*^t) \leq w_j^t(\bar{f}^t) \qquad (1 \leq j \leq n, 1 \leq t \leq T) \tag{17}$$

for *all* $\bar{f}^t$. This property allows us to obtain the following lower bound for the *minimal* total labor time L^T

$$\begin{aligned} L^T := \min_{\bar{f}^T} L^T(\bar{f}^T) &\geq \sum_{t=1}^{T} \sum_{j=1}^{n} \min_{\bar{f}^t} w_j^t(\bar{f}^t) y_j(t) \\ &\quad + \sum_{j=1}^{n} \min_{\bar{f}^T} w_j^T(\bar{f}^T) z_j(T) \\ &= \sum_{t=1}^{T} w^t y(t) + w^T z(T) \\ &= \sum_{t=1}^{T} w^t (\bar{f}_*^t) y(t) + w^T (\bar{f}_*^T) z(T). \end{aligned} \tag{18}$$

A reversed inequality may also be shown:

$$L^T = \min_{\bar{f}^T} L^T(\bar{f}^T) \leqslant \sum_{t=1}^{T} \sum_{j=1}^{n} w_j^t(\bar{f}_*^t) y_j(t) + \sum_{j=1}^{n} w_j^T(\bar{f}_*^T) z_j(T) = \sum_{t=1}^{T} w^t y(t) + w^T z(T). \tag{19}$$

The inequalities (18) and (19) yield

$$L^T = \min_{\bar{f}^T} L^T(\bar{f}^T) = \sum_{t=1}^{T} w^t(\bar{f}_*^t) y(t) + w^T(\bar{f}_*^T) z(T) = \sum_{t=1}^{T} w^t y(t) + w^T z(T). \tag{20}$$

Our results may now be summarized in the following theorem.

Theorem 1: Nonsubstitution and rational values.
A plan minimizing the total labor time of a T-period process does not depend on the composition of the consumption vectors $y(t)$ nor on the final capital goods vector $z(T)$. Such a plan is rational and is generated by the functional recursion (16). The minimal value of the total labor time is a linear function (20) of the rational values.

According to Theorem 1 the problem of determining a plan minimizing the total labor time can be solved without first determining the intensities of production. In particular, the minimal plan is independent of the growth rate η, if $y(t)$ is given by (4). On the other hand, the intensities of production do depend on the selected plan. A look at (2) shows this.

The reader will have observed that the initial value vector w^0 plays a role in determining the rational values, the rational technology and the minimal total labor time.

As our next task we shall be looking for conditions under which the influence of w^0 disappears as $T \to \infty$. As a first step we *normalize* our values. Let $\bar{w}^t(\bar{f}^t) :=$ $:= w^t(\bar{f}^t)\ (1+\alpha)^{t-1}$ be the normalized values of (13) or (14). Furthermore let $\bar{w}^t := w^t(1+\alpha)^{t-1}$ be the normalized rational values. The vectors $\bar{w}^t$ are generated by an operator Θ: $\mathbf{R}^n \to \mathbf{R}^n$ which is independent of the period: $\bar{w}^t = \Theta\, \bar{w}^{t-1}$,

$$f_*^t = (k_{j*}^t)$$

$$\uparrow$$

$$\bar{w}_j^t = \min_{k \in K_j} \{a_{0j}(k) + \sum_{i=1}^{n} \bar{w}_i^{t-1}(1+\alpha)\, a_{ij}(k)\} \quad (1 \leqslant j \leqslant n, 1 \leqslant t \leqslant T). \tag{21}$$

Note that Θ is an isotonic operator: $u \geqslant v \Rightarrow \Theta u > \Theta v$; $u, v \in \mathbf{R}^n$. If $\alpha < \min_{f \in F} \gamma(f)$ then Θ is also a contracting operator. In such a case we could appeal to the classical fixed point theorem for contracting operators to show that $\bar{w}^t$ of (21) converges to the unique fixed point $\bar{w}$ of Θ. If, however, $\min_{f \in F} \gamma(f) \leqslant \alpha < \max_{f \in F} \gamma(f) = \gamma$, then Θ is no longer a contraction mapping. The following theorem shows that even in this situation $\bar{w}^t$ converges to the unique positive fixed point $\bar{w}$ of Θ.

Theorem 2: Asymptotic rational values.
If the rate of technical progress α is less than the maximal growth rate of the substitution system, γ, then the normalized rational values (21) converge to the unique positive solution of the functional equation

$$\bar{w}_j = \overset{f_* = (k_{j*})}{\overset{\uparrow}{\min_{k \in K_j}}} \{a_{0j}(k) + \sum_{i=1}^{n} \bar{w}_i (1+\alpha) a_{ij}(k)\} \quad (1 \leqslant j \leqslant n). \tag{22}$$

Proof: The existence and uniqueness of $\bar{w} > 0$ satisfying (22) is shown in *Reetz* [1977, 160–162]. Since $a_{0j}(k) > 0$, equation (22) yields

$$\bar{w}_j - \sum_{i=1}^{n} \bar{w}_i (1+\alpha) a_{ij}(k_{j*}) > 0. \tag{23}$$

Consequently the quantity c defined in (24) is strictly positive

$$c := \max_{1 \leqslant j \leqslant n} \left\{ \frac{a_{0j}(k_{j*})}{\bar{w}_j - \sum_{i=1}^{n} \bar{w}_i (1+\alpha) a_{ij}(k_{j*})} \right\} > 0. \tag{24}$$

Denote d by

$$d := \max \left\{ c, \max_{1 \leqslant j \leqslant n} \left\{ \frac{\bar{w}_j^0}{\bar{w}_j} \right\} \right\} \tag{25}$$

with $\bar{w}^0$ being the initial vector in recursion (21). If the $u_j^0 = d\,\bar{w}_j > 0\ (1 \leqslant j \leqslant n)$ are selected as the initial values in recursion (21), then according to (25) and (24) we obtain

$$\begin{aligned} u_j^1 - u_j^0 &= \min_{k \in K_j} \{a_{0j}(k) + \sum_{i=1}^{n} d\,\bar{w}_i (1+\alpha) a_{ij}(k)\} - d\,\bar{w}_j \\ &\leqslant a_{0j}(k_{j*}) - d\,[\bar{w}_j - \sum_{i=1}^{n} \bar{w}_i (1+\alpha) a_{ij}(k_{j*})] \\ &\leqslant a_{0j}(k_{j*}) + c\,[\bar{w}_j - \sum_{i=1}^{n} \bar{w}_i (1+\alpha) a_{ij}(k_{j*})] \leqslant 0. \end{aligned} \tag{26}$$

Thus we have $u^0 \geqslant u^1$. On the other hand, if initial values v_j^0 are set equal to 0, then $v^1 = \Theta v^0 \geqslant v^0 = 0$ because $a_{0j}(k) > 0$. All in all, we have $0 = v^0 \leqslant u^0$, $0 = v^0 \leqslant v^1$, and $u^1 \leqslant u^0$. Since Θ is an isotone operator we may now appeal to a theorem in *Collatz*

[1964, p. 278] and claim the validity of

$$0 = v^0 \leqslant v^1 \leqslant \ldots \leqslant v^{t-1} \leqslant v^t \leqslant \ldots < u^t \leqslant u^{t-1} \leqslant \ldots \leqslant u^1 \leqslant u^0. \tag{27}$$

Since v^t is a monotonically increasing sequence of vectors bounded above, $v := \lim v^t$ exists. The uniqueness of the fixed point $\bar{w} > 0$ of Θ guarantees that $v = \bar{w}$. Likewise $u := \lim u^t = \bar{w}$. Thus, $v^t \nearrow \bar{w} \swarrow u^t$. In order to prove convergence of $\bar{w}^t \to \bar{w}$, it suffices to show that the inequalities $v^t \leqslant \bar{w}^t \leqslant u^t$ are satisfied for all $t \geqslant 0$. If $t = 0$ then, in view of (25), we have the inequalities (28) for all $1 \leqslant j \leqslant n$.

$$u_j^0 = d\,\bar{w}_j \geqslant \left[\max_{1 \leqslant j \leqslant n} \frac{\bar{w}_j^0}{\bar{w}_j}\right] \bar{w}_j \geqslant \frac{\bar{w}_j^0}{\bar{w}_j}\,\bar{w}_j = w_j^0. \tag{28}$$

Since Θ is isotone, an induction argument yields $u^t \geqslant \bar{w}^t$ for all t. In an analogous manner it may be shown that $v^t \leqslant \bar{w}^t$. □

The above Theorem 2 presents a sufficient condition: $\alpha < \gamma$ for the convergence of the normalized rational values $\bar{w}^t$ to the *asymptotic* (normalized) *rational value vector* $\bar{w}$. In order to prove the convergence of rational technologies we need an additional condition, namely the uniqueness of the technology f_* in (22), as the next Corollary 1 shows.

Corollary 1: Turnpike property
Let $\alpha < \gamma$. If the technology $f_* = (k_{j*})$ determined in (22) is unique, then the technologies $f_*^t = (k_{j*}^t)$ generated by (21) converge to f_*.

Proof: According to Theorem 2 the functions

$$W_j^{t-1}(k) := a_{0j}(k) + \sum_{i=1}^{n} \bar{w}_i^{t-1} (1+\alpha)\, a_{ij}(k) \tag{29}$$

converge to

$$W_j(k) := a_{0j}(k) + \sum_{i=1}^{n} \bar{w}_i (1+\alpha)\, a_{ij}(k). \tag{30}$$

Since f_* is unique, we have

$$\delta := \min_{\substack{k \in K_j \\ k \neq k_{j*}}} W_j(k) - W_j(k) - W_j(k_{j*}) > 0. \tag{31}$$

Convergence of (29) implies that there exists an index t^* such that for all $t \geqslant t^*$

$$W_j(k) - \frac{\delta}{2} \leqslant W_j^{t-1}(k) \leqslant W_j(k) + \frac{\delta}{2} \quad (1 \leqslant j \leqslant n,\ k \in K_j). \tag{32}$$

Using (32), (31) and again (32) we obtain

$$W_j^{t-1}(k_{j*}) \leqslant W_j(k_{j*}) + \frac{\delta}{2} = \min_{k \neq k_{j*}} W_j(k) - \frac{\delta}{2}$$

$$\leqslant \min_{k \neq k_{j*}} W_j^{t-1}(k). \tag{33}$$

This shows that for all $t \geqslant t^*$

$$\min_{k \in K_j} W_j^{t-1}(k) = \min \{W_j^{t-1}(k_{j*}), \min_{k \neq k_{j*}} W_j^{t-1}(k)\}$$

$$= W_j^{t-1}(k_{j*}). \tag{34}$$

For sufficiently large T the rational plan generated by (21) has the structure $\bar{f}^T = \{f^1, \ldots, f^{t^*-1}, f^{t^*}, f^{t^*}, \ldots, f^{t^*}\}$. Only the initial technologies f^t $(1 \leqslant t \leqslant t^* - 1)$ depend an w^0. □

Using Theorem 2 it is possible to obtain asymptotic expressions for the minimal total labor time (18) as $T \to \infty$ in the case of exponential consumption (4) and $z(T) = 0$. If the growth rate of consumption is less than the rate of technical progress, then the minimal total labor time approaches a finite limit (35). As can be seen, the initial value vector w^0 plays an essential role here, whereas the rational values in later periods do not greatly influence $L^\infty := \lim_{T \to \infty} L^T$. A different qualitative behavior arises if $\eta \geqslant \alpha$. In such a case the rational values towards the end of the process influence L^T more so than the initial values. For large T, Theorem 3 shows that L^T may be approximated by $T\bar{w}y$ if $\eta = \alpha$ and by $[(1+\eta)^T/(\eta-\alpha)^{T-1}]\,\bar{w}y$ if $\eta > \alpha$.

Theorem 3: Asymptotic minimal total labor time.
Let $y(t)$ be given by (4) and $z(T) = 0$. Suppose $\alpha < \gamma$. Then

$$\lim_{T \to \infty} L^T = \sum_{t=1}^{\infty} \frac{(1+\eta)^{t-1}}{(1+\alpha)^{t-1}} \bar{w}^t y \qquad \text{if } \eta < \alpha \tag{35}$$

$$\lim_{T \to \infty} \frac{L^T}{T} = \bar{w}\,y = \bar{w}\,(f^*)\,y \qquad \text{if } \eta = \alpha \tag{36}$$

$$\lim_{T \to \infty} \frac{(1+\alpha)^{T-1}}{(1+\eta)^{T-1}} L^T = \frac{1+\eta}{\eta - \alpha} \bar{w}\,y = \frac{1+\eta}{\eta-\alpha} \bar{w}\,(f^*)\,y \qquad \text{if } \eta > \alpha \tag{37}$$

Proof: Since $\alpha < \gamma$, $\bar{w}^t$ converges to $\bar{w}$ according to Theorem 2. In the case $\eta < \alpha$ the series (35) can be shown to converge using the ratio test. Convergence of (36) follows by a theorem of Cauchy [*Knopp*, p. 74]: If $\bar{w}^t y \to \bar{w}\,y$, then the arithmetic means $\sum_{t=1}^{T-1} \bar{w}^t y/T$ also converge to $\bar{w}\,y$. In order to prove (37) we appeal to a theorem of Toeplitz [*Knopp*, p. 75], obtaining

$$\frac{(1+\alpha)^{T-1}}{(1+\eta)^{T-1}} L^T = \sum_{t=1}^{T} \frac{(1+\eta)^{t-T}}{(1+\alpha)^{t-T}} \bar{w}^t y = \sum_{s=0}^{T-1} \left[\frac{1+\alpha}{1+\eta}\right]^s \bar{w}^{(T-s)} y$$

$$\xrightarrow[(T\to\infty)]{} \sum_{s=0}^{\infty} \left[\frac{1+\alpha}{1+\eta}\right]^s \bar{w}y = \frac{1+\eta}{\eta-\alpha} \bar{w}y. \qquad (38)$$

□

Our investigation up to this point has shown that plans, minimizing the *total* labor time of a multi-period production process, are independent of the growth rate of consumption η. The dual variables associated with such plans are our rational values (16) or (22). These variables are of a different nature than the synchronized values of [*v. Weizsäcker/Samuelson*], which do depend on η. In the following we shall uncover properties of synchronized values *within the substitution system,* which make these dual variables unsuitable in our eyes as instruments of (socialist) planning. This position differs from that of Samuelson, v. Weizsäcker, Wolfstetter, Nutzinger and Baisch. Consider a production process with $y(t)$ given by (4) and $z(T) = 0$. Let $T \to \infty$, so that our Figure 2 agrees with the diagram in *v. Weizsäcker* [1971, p. 24]. If $\eta < \gamma$, then there exists at least one infinite plan $\bar{f}_t^\infty = \{f^\tau \mid t \leqslant \tau\}$ such that the labor time in period t, as given in (39), is finite

$$L^\infty(t; \bar{f}_t^\infty) = \lim_{T\to\infty} L^T(t; \bar{f}_t^T)$$

$$= \frac{(1+\eta)^{t-1}}{(1+\alpha)^{t-1}} a_0(f^t) \sum_{s=t}^{\infty} \prod_{\tau=t+1}^{s} A(f^\tau)(1+\eta)^{s-t} y < \infty. \qquad (39)$$

Suppose a planner wishes to minimize the labor time $L^\infty(t; \bar{f}_t^\infty)$ in *each* period $t = 1, 2, \ldots$ For each t we should then perform the following minimizations (40). (We are assuming that all minima exist.)

$$\min_{\bar{f}_t^\infty \in \bar{F}^\infty} L^\infty(t; \bar{f}_t^\infty) = \frac{(1+\eta)^{t-1}}{(1+\alpha)^{t-1}} \min_{f^t \in F} a_0(f^t) \; .$$

$$\min_{\bar{f}_{t+1}^\infty \in \bar{F}^\infty} \sum_{s=t}^{\infty} \prod_{\tau=t+1}^{s} A(f^\tau)(1+\eta)^{s-t} y \qquad (t = 1, 2, \ldots). (40)$$

According to (40) the first component of a plan minimizing $L^\infty(t; \bar{f}_t^\infty)$ is a technology $f_{**}^t = (k_{j**})$ minimizing the direct labor input $a_{0j}(k_{j**}^t) = \min_{k \in K_j} a_{0j}(k)$. We call such a technology *myopic.* The remaining components of a plan minimizing $L^\infty(t; \bar{f}_t^\infty)$ will generally *not* be myopic, a look at the last minimization in (40) shows this. Should the planner perform a minimization in the next period $t + 1$ he will find a myopic technology f^{t+1} which is not a solution of the previous (namely the last) minimization in (40). We state our result: In the class of *all* infinite plans $\bar{F}^\infty$, there does *not* in general exist a plan, which minimizes the labor time of *each* period. In other words, there is no solution (plan) to the vector minimization problem (40). If the planner is satisfied with less than the best, he may restrict himself to *stationary* plans. In this case the vector minimization problem (40) does in fact have a solution. It is given in the next theorem.

Theorem 4: Synchronized values.
If $\eta < \gamma$, then there exists a unique positive solution $\nu = (\nu_j)$ of the functional equation

$$f_{\prime} = (k_{j'})$$
$$\uparrow$$
$$\nu_j = \min_{k \in K_j} \{a_{0j}(k) + \sum_{i=1}^{n} \nu_i (1+\eta) a_{ij}(k)\} \quad (1 \leqslant j \leqslant n). \tag{41}$$

We call ν_j the *synchronized values* of the substitution system. A *synchronized technology* $f_{\prime}$ generated in (41) determines a stationary plan $\tilde{f}_{\prime}^{\infty}$, which minimizes within the class of stationary plans $\tilde{F}^{\infty}$ the labor time of *each* period:

$$L^{\infty}(t; \tilde{f}_{\prime}^{\infty}) = \min_{\tilde{f}_t^{\infty} \in \tilde{F}^{\infty}} L^{\infty}(t; \tilde{f}_t^{\infty}) \qquad (t = 1, 2, 3, \ldots). \tag{42}$$

Proof: The first assertion has been proved by [*Reetz*, 1977, p. 160–162]. Since $\eta < \gamma$ there exists at least one stationary plan $\tilde{f}_t^{\infty} = \{f, f, \ldots\}$ such that $L^{\infty}(t; \tilde{f}_t^{\infty}) < \infty$. Furthermore the variables $\nu_j(f)$ defined by

$$0 < \nu_j(f) := \sum_{t=0}^{\infty} a_0(f)(1+\eta)^t A^t(f) \tag{43}$$

are finite for such a plan. As demonstrated in *v. Weizsäcker/Samuelson* [1971], the labor time of period t may be represented by (44) using the dual variables (43).

$$L^{\infty}(t; \tilde{f}_t^{\infty}) = \frac{(1+\eta)^{t-1}}{(1+\alpha)^{t-1}} \nu(f) y. \tag{44}$$

A straightforward application of the nonsubstitution theorem [cf. *Reetz*, p. 163] yields

$$\min_{\tilde{f}_t^{\infty} \in \tilde{F}^{\infty}} L^{\infty}(t; \tilde{f}_t^{\infty}) = \frac{(1+\eta)^{t-1}}{(1+\alpha)^{t-1}} \min_{\{f | \nu(f) < \infty\}} \nu(f) y$$
$$= \frac{(1+\eta)^{t-1}}{(1+\alpha)^{t-1}} \nu y = \frac{(1+\eta)^{t-1}}{(1+\alpha)^{t-1}} \nu(f_{\prime}). \tag{45}$$

□

It is important to observe that the selection of a technology in (41) and the simultaneous determination of synchronized values ν are independent of the rate of technical progress α. This property distinguishes our synchronized values (41) from those of *v. Weizsäcker/Samuelson*. Only in the case $\alpha = 0$ do the v. Weizsäcker/Samuelson synchronized values posses the properties of Theorem 4. So called *modified synchronized values* have been introducted by *v. Weizsäcker/Samuelson* [1971] implicitly and by *Wolfstetter* [1973] explicitly for the case $\alpha \neq 0$. Within the substitution system these values may be defined as the unique positive solution of

$$f_{\shortparallel} = (k_j^{\shortparallel})$$
$$\uparrow$$
$$\bar{u}_j = \min_{k \in K_j} \{a_{0j}(k) + \sum_{i=1}^{n} \bar{u}_i (1+\alpha)(1+\eta) a_{ij}(k)\} \quad (1 \leqslant j \leqslant n). \tag{46}$$

For the existence of $\bar{u} > 0$ if suffices to assume that $(1+\alpha)(1+\eta) < (1+\gamma)$. The reader may wish to compare (46) in the case that all sets K_j contain one element, with the equations (5.6) in *Wolfstetter* [1973]. The functional equation (46) does not coincide with the previous functional equations (22) and (41). As we have done so for (22) and (41), we shall determine the (asymptotic) labor time which is minimized by a technology $f_{\shortparallel}$ of (46). Let $w^0 = 0$, $z(T) = 0$ and $y(t)$ be given by (4). If $\eta > 0$, we define a lower bound for $L^T(\bar{f}^T)$ as follows

$$L^T(\bar{f}^T) = \sum_{s=1}^{T} \sum_{t=1}^{s} \frac{a_0(f^t)}{(1+\alpha)^{t-1}} \prod_{\tau=t+1}^{s} A(f^\tau)(1+\eta)^{s-t}(1+\eta)^{t-1} y$$

$$= \sum_{s=1}^{T} \sum_{t=1}^{s} \frac{a_0(f^t)}{(1+\alpha)^{t-1}} \prod_{\tau=t+1}^{s} [(1+\eta) A(f^\tau)](1+\eta)^{t-1} y$$

$$> \sum_{s=1}^{T} \sum_{t=1}^{s} \frac{a_0(f^t)}{(1+\alpha)^{t-1}} \prod_{\tau=t+1}^{s} [(1+\eta) A(f^\tau)] y$$

$$=: G^T(\bar{f}^T). \tag{47}$$

The inequality in (47) is reversed if $\eta < 0$. We call $G^T(\bar{f}^T)$ a *modified total labor time.* It is *not* a synchronized labor time, since it includes labor expended over different periods. Note that $G^T(\bar{f}^T)$ is obtained, if we replace A by $(1+\eta)A$ and $y(t)$ by y in the formula for $L^T(\bar{f}^T)$. We may thus obtain a dual representation of $G^T(\bar{f}^T)$ using our previous results. Let $\bar{u}^0 = 0$ be the initial vector in the recursion

$$\bar{u}^t(\bar{f}^t) = a_0(f^t) + \bar{u}^{t-1}(\bar{f}^{t-1})(1+\alpha)(1+\eta) A(f^t). \tag{48}$$

The vectors of (48) allow us to express $G^T(\bar{f}^T)$ as follows

$$G^T(\bar{f}^T) = \sum_{t=1}^{T} \frac{1}{(1+\alpha)^{t-1}} \bar{u}^t(\bar{f}^t) y. \tag{49}$$

The minimal modified total labor time is given by

$$G^T := \min_{\bar{f}^T} G^T(\bar{f}^T) = \sum_{t=1}^{T} \frac{1}{(1+\alpha)^{t-1}} \bar{u}^t y = \sum_{t=1}^{T} \frac{1}{(1+\alpha)^{t-1}} \bar{u}^t(\bar{f}^t_{\shortparallel}) y. \tag{50}$$

Here $\bar{u}^t$ and $\bar{f}^t_{\shortparallel}$ and $\bar{f}^t_{\shortparallel}$ are generated by

$$f^t_{\shortparallel} = (k^t_{j\shortparallel})$$
$$\uparrow$$
$$\bar{u}^t_j = \min_{k \in K_j} \{a_{0j}(k) + \sum_{i=1}^{n} \bar{u}^{t-1}_i (1+\alpha)(1+\eta) a_{ij}(k)\} \quad (1 \leqslant j \leqslant n, 1 \leqslant t \leqslant T). \tag{51}$$

The role of (46) as the asymptotic form of (51) now becomes apparent. The technology $f_{,,}$ (if it is unique) is the limiting technology $\lim f_{,,}^{t}$ in a sufficiently long plan minimizing the modified total labor time. The $\bar{u}_j$ are the associated dual variables. If $-1 < \alpha < 0$, then the limit of the normalized minimal modified total labor time $(1+\alpha)^{T-1} G^T$ is a function of $\bar{u}$, namely $\bar{u}\, y/(-\alpha)$. If $\alpha = 0$, then $\lim G^T/T = \bar{u}\, y = v\, y$. Using the dual variables (51) or (46) therefore makes sense, if and only if we accept the modified total labor time as a labor criterion. We are not able to give a rationale for such an arbitrary criterion. In any case, it may *not* be claimed, that the dual variables (46) or (51) are synchronized.

The reader should observe that two different approaches to infinity have been employed in the above models. The first approach considers finite T-period production processes, for which technologies are determined minimizing total labor times. Subsequently we have let T go to infinity. In the second approach the minima and the limits are interchanged. Thus in Theorem 4 the labor time of each period in an infinitely long process was calculated first, and then minimized. Although we consider the first approach more realistic, we shall apply the second procedure in the remaining part of this section, using the criteria of (normalized) total labor times. It becomes necessary to restrict ourselves to *stationary* plans $\tilde{f}^{\infty}$. If $z(T) = 0$ and $y(t)$ is given by (4), then the dual representation of the total labor time in a finite-period process is given by

$$L^T(\tilde{f}^T) = w^0 A(f)\,\bar{x}^T + a_0(f) \sum_{t=1}^{T} \left[\frac{1+\eta}{1+\alpha}\right]^{t-1} \bar{x}^{T-t}(f)$$

$$= \sum_{t=1}^{T} \left[\frac{1+\eta}{1+\alpha}\right]^{t-1} \bar{w}^t(\tilde{f}^T)\,y. \tag{52}$$

Cf. (11) – (12). The terms $\bar{x}^t(f)$ appearing in (52) are defined by

$$\bar{x}^t(f) = \sum_{s=0}^{t-1} (1+\eta)^s A^s(f)\,y. \tag{53}$$

They will converge to the steady-state quantities $\bar{x}(f)$ of (8) if $\eta < \gamma(f)$. A look at Theorem 3 tells us, that we should normalize the total labor times (52) in the following manner

$$\bar{L}^T(\tilde{f}^T) := \begin{cases} L^T(\tilde{f}^T) & \text{if } \eta < \alpha \\ \frac{1}{T} L^T(\tilde{f}^T) & \text{if } \eta = \alpha \\ \left[\frac{1+\alpha}{1+\eta}\right]^{T-1} L^T(\tilde{f}^T) & \text{if } \eta > \alpha \end{cases}. \tag{54}$$

If $\alpha < \gamma(f)$, then finite *asymptotic normalized total labor times*

$$\bar{L}(\tilde{f}^{\infty}) := \lim_{T\to\infty} \bar{L}^T(\tilde{f}^T) \tag{55}$$

exist for each of the three cases specified in (54). Using the Theorems of Cauchy and

Toeplitz we shall determine $\bar{L}(\tilde{f}^{\infty})$ separately for the three cases.

In *case 1*: $\eta < \alpha < \gamma(f)$ we substitute the *first* expression (52) into (55), giving us

$$\bar{L}(\tilde{f}^{\infty}) = \left[w^0 A(f) + a_0(f)\left(\frac{1+\alpha}{\alpha-\eta}\right)\right] \bar{x}(f). \tag{56}$$

Let $a_0'(f)$ denote the expression in the brackets of (56). A dual representation of (56) is then given by

$$\bar{L}(\tilde{f}^{\infty}) = a_0'(f)\bar{x}(f) = \tilde{v}(f)y \tag{57}$$

where $\tilde{v}(f)$ are the *transformed synchronized values* determined by

$$\tilde{v}(f) = a_0'(f) + \tilde{v}(f)(1+\eta)A(f). \tag{58}$$

Observe that the criterion $\bar{L}(\tilde{f}^{\infty})$ links the steady-state quantity system (8) with the system of tranformed synchronized values (58). If we are interested in minimizing $\bar{L}(\tilde{f}^{\infty})$ in the class of *stationary* plans, then use should be made of the transformed synchronized values. Specifically, if $w^0 = 0$, then the functional equation (41) will yield a plan $\tilde{f}_r^{\infty}$ such that $\bar{L}(\tilde{f}_r^{\infty}) \leqslant \bar{L}(\tilde{f}^{\infty})$ for all $\tilde{f}^{\infty}$. Furthermore $\tilde{v}(f_r) = (1+\alpha)v/(\alpha-\eta)$.

In *case 2*: $\eta = \alpha < \gamma(f)$ we may substitute either of the expressions (52) into (55). An appeal to the theorem of Cauchy results in

$$\bar{L}(\tilde{f}^{\infty}) = a_0(f)\bar{x}(f) = \bar{w}(f)y. \tag{59}$$

Thus the dual of the steady state quantity system (8) is given by the following value system

$$\bar{w}(f) = a_0(f) + \bar{w}(f)(1+\alpha)A(f). \tag{60}$$

A plan minimizing $\bar{L}(\tilde{f}^{\infty})$ within the class of stationary plans is obviously rational: $\bar{L}(\tilde{f}_*^{\infty}) \leqslant \bar{L}(\tilde{f}^{\infty})$ for all $\tilde{f}^{\infty}$. Cf. (22).

In *case 3*: $\eta > \alpha < \gamma(f)$ we substitute the *second* expression (52) into (55). The theorem of Teoplitz then gives us

$$\bar{L}(\tilde{f}^{\infty}) = \bar{w}(f)\left[\frac{1+\eta}{\eta-\alpha}y\right] = a_0(f)x'(f) \tag{61}$$

where $x'(f)$ is the unique solution of

$$x'(f) = \left[\frac{1+\eta}{\eta-\alpha}\right]y + (1+\alpha)A(f)x'(f). \tag{62}$$

Here we may say that the value system (60) and the quantity system (62) are dual. Within the class of stationary plans, the rational plan $\tilde{f}_*^{\infty}$ of (22) minimizes the asymptotic normalized total labor times $\bar{L}(\tilde{f}^{\infty})$.

4. Price System

The fundamental assumption underlying the value systems of Section 3 is the equivalence of labor expended in *different* periods. This assumption does not hold for the price systems investigated in the present section. Just as an hour's work today is equal to an hour's work tomorrow, so surely a dollar today is not equal to a dollar tomorrow. We shall in fact assume that a dollar in period t is equal to $(1 + \rho)$ dollars in period $t + 1$, or equivalently, $1/(1 + \rho)$ dollars in period t are equal to 1 dollar in period $t + 1$. The factor $\rho > -1$ is called the *rate of profit* and $1/(1 + \rho)$ represents the *discount factor*. Furthermore we make the symmetrical assumption that the *nominal wage rate* in period t is given by $p_0(t) = (1 + \beta)^{t-1} p_0$ $(1 \leqslant t \leqslant T)$. The quantity $\beta > -1$ represents the (possibly negative) *growth rate of nominal wages* and p_0 the nominal wage rate in the first period. In the first part of this section we shall take ρ and β to be exogenously given. We shall then demonstrate how these rates are determined if *real* wage rates are specified (Theorem 5 and 6). For a given plan $\bar{f}^T$ the *discounted labor costs of period t* are given by

$$H^T(t;\bar{f}^T) = \frac{(1+\beta)^{t-1} p_0 a_0(t)}{(1+\rho)^{t-1}(1+\alpha)^{t-1}} x(t)$$

$$= \frac{(1+\beta)^{t-1} p_0 a_0(t)}{(1+\rho)^{t-1}(1+\alpha)^{t-1}} [\sum_{s=t}^{T} \prod_{\tau=t+1}^{s} A(\tau) y(s) + \prod_{\tau=t+1}^{T} A(\tau) z(T)]. \tag{63}$$

The cost of the initial capital stock is equal to

$$H^T(0;\bar{f}^T) = p^0 z(0)$$

$$= p^0 [\sum_{s=1}^{T} \prod_{\tau=1}^{s} A(\tau) y(s) + \prod_{\tau=1}^{T} A(\tau) z(T)]. \tag{64}$$

The vector $p^0 = (p_j^0)$ represents an initial price vector and is assumed to be given. The *total discounted (labor) costs* for the plan $\bar{f}^T$ are obtained by aggregating (63) and (64):

$$H^T(\bar{f}^T) = \sum_{t=0}^{T} H(t;\bar{f}^T)$$

$$= \sum_{s=1}^{T} \left[p^0 \prod_{\tau=1}^{s} A(\tau) + \sum_{t=1}^{s} \frac{(1+\beta)^{t-1} p_0 a_0(t)}{(1+\rho)^{t-1}(1+\alpha)^{t-1}} \prod_{\tau=t+1}^{s} A(\tau) \right] y(s)$$

$$+ \left[p^0 \prod_{\tau=1}^{T} A(\tau) + \sum_{t=1}^{s} \frac{(1+\beta)^{t-1} p_0 a_0(t)}{(1+\rho)^{t-1}(1+\alpha)^{t-1}} \prod_{\tau=t+1}^{T} A(\tau) \right] z(T). \tag{65}$$

The function (65) has the same structure as (11). In order to obtain a dual representation of (65) we define price vectors $p^t(\bar{f}^t)$ by the recursion

$$p^t(\bar{f}^t) = (1+\rho) \left[\frac{(1+\beta)^{t-1} p_0 a_0(t)}{(1+\alpha)^{t-1}} + p^{t-1}(\bar{f}^{t-1}) A(t) \right]. \tag{66}$$

Reducing (66) iteratively gives us

$$p^t(\bar{f}^t) = p^0 (1+\rho)^t \prod_{\tau=1}^{t} A(\tau)$$

$$+ \sum_{s=1}^{t} \frac{(1+\beta)^{s-1} p_0 a_0(s)}{(1+\rho)^{s-t-1}(1+\alpha)^{s-1}} \prod_{\tau=s+1}^{t} A(\tau). \tag{67}$$

As can be seen, each $p^t(\bar{f}^t)$ is continuous in (ρ, β), monotonically strictly increasing in ρ and strictly decreasing in β. Substituting of (67) into (65) yields the desired dual representaion of the total discounted costs

$$H^T(\bar{f}^T) = \sum_{t=1}^{T} \frac{1}{(1+\rho)^t} p^t(\bar{f}^t)\, y(t) + \frac{1}{(1+\rho)^T} p^T(\bar{f}^T)\, z(T). \tag{68}$$

In a decentralized competitive capitalistic system each sector j will select a method of production in period t, minimizing the unit cost of commodity j. Such a procedure also generates *competitive prices* according to

$$p_j^t = (1+\rho) \underset{k \in K_j}{\overset{f_{\cdot}^t = (k_{j\cdot}^t)}{\overset{\uparrow}{\min}}} \left\{ \frac{(1+\beta)^{t-1} p_0 a_{0j}(k)}{(1+\alpha)^{t-1}} + \sum_{i=1}^{n} p_i^{t-1} a_{ij}(k) \right\}$$

$$(1 \leqslant j \leqslant n,\ 1 \leqslant t \leqslant T). \tag{69}$$

The terms in braces represent the costs of producing one unit of commodity j in period t for the various methods $k \in K_j$. Each such term is composed of expenditure for labor $(1+\beta)^{t-1} p_0 a_{0j}(k)/(1+\alpha)^{t-1}$ and the costs of the means of production $\sum_{i=1}^{n} p_i^{t-1} a_{ij}(k)$.

The minimal unit cost is calculated and multiplied by $(1+\rho)$ to give the competive price p_j^t. The technologies $f_{\cdot}^t$ determined in this manner are called *competitive* and the sequence $\bar{f}^t = \{f_{\cdot}^t \mid 1 \leqslant t \leqslant T\}$ a *competitive plan*. By induction an t it can be shown that competitive prices are also minimal prices:

$$p_j^t = \min_{\bar{f}^t} p_j^t(\bar{f}^t) \qquad (1 \leqslant j \leqslant n,\ 1 \leqslant t \leqslant T). \tag{70}$$

As a result, we see that competitive prices, being the lower envelopes of (67), posses the same continuity and monotonicity properties as (67). A look at the proof of Theorem 1 shows that a competive plan minimizes the total discounted costs irrespective of $y(t)$ $(1 \leqslant t \leqslant T)$ and $z(T)$ (nonsubstitution property):

$$H^T := \min_{\bar{f}^T} H^T(\bar{f}^T) = \sum_{t=1}^{T} \frac{1}{(1+\rho)^t} p^t(\bar{f}_{\cdot}^t)\, y(t) + \frac{1}{(1+\rho)^T} p^T(\bar{f}_{\cdot}^T)\, z(T)$$

$$= \sum_{t=1}^{T} \frac{1}{(1+\rho)^t} p^t\, y(t) + \frac{1}{(1+\rho)^T} p^T z(T). \tag{71}$$

For the study of the asymptotic case $T \to \infty$ we need to normalize the prices (66) – (67), (69). Let $\bar{p}^t(\tilde{f}^t) := (1+\alpha)^{t-1} p^t(\tilde{f}^t)/(1+\rho)(1+\beta)^{t-1} p_0$ and $\bar{p}^t :=$ $:= (1+\alpha)^{t-1} p^t / (1+\rho)(1+\beta)^{t-1} p_0$. The normalized competitive prices along with competive technologies are generated according to

$$f_{.}^{t} = (k_{j.}^{t})$$
$$\uparrow$$
$$\bar{p}_j^t = \min_{k \in K_j} \left\{ a_{0j}(k) + \sum_{i=1}^{n} \bar{p}_i^{t-1} \frac{(1+\rho)(1+\alpha)}{1+\beta} a_{ij}(k) \right\} (1 \leqslant j \leqslant n, 1 \leqslant t \leqslant T). \tag{72}$$

If $(1+\rho)(1+\alpha) < (1+\beta)(1+\gamma)$ then the normalized competive prices (72) converge to the unique positive solution $\bar{p}$ of

$$f_{.} = (k_{j.})$$
$$\uparrow$$
$$\bar{p}_j = \min_{k \in K_j} \left\{ a_{0j}(k) + \sum_{i=1}^{n} \bar{p}_i \frac{(1+\rho)(1+\alpha)}{1+\beta} a_{ij}(k) \right\} \quad (1 \leqslant j \leqslant n, 1 \leqslant t \leqslant T). \tag{73}$$

See the proof of Theorem 2. We call $\bar{p}_j$ *asymptotic* (normalized) *competitive prices.* If in addition $f_{.}$ is unique, then the technologies $f_{.}^{t}$ converge to $f_{.}$ (Corollary 1). In analogy to Theorem 3 we obtain the following asymptotic minimal labor costs if $z(T) = 0$ and $y(t)$ is given by (4)

$$\lim_{T \to \infty} H^T = \sum_{t=1}^{T} \left[\frac{(1+\eta)(1+\beta)}{(1+\alpha)(1+\rho)} \right]^{t-1} p_0 \bar{p}^t y \quad \text{if } (1+\eta)(1+\beta) < (1+\alpha)(1+\rho) \tag{74}$$

$$\lim_{T \to \infty} \frac{1}{T} H^T = p_0 \bar{p} y \qquad \text{if } (1+\eta)(1+\beta) = (1+\alpha)(1+\rho) \tag{75}$$

$$\lim_{T \to \infty} \left[\frac{(1+\alpha)(1+\rho)}{(1+\eta)(1+\beta)} \right]^{T-1} H^T = p_0 \bar{p} \left[\frac{(1+\eta)(1+\beta)}{(1+\eta)(1+\beta) - (1+\alpha)(1+\rho)} y \right] \quad \text{if } (1+\eta)(1+\beta) > (1+\alpha)(1+\rho). \tag{76}$$

The results in the final part of Section 2 can easily be extended to the total labor cost criterion. If $z(T) = 0$ and $y(t)$ is given by (4), then for an arbitrary *stationary* plan $\tilde{f}^\infty$ the T-period costs are given by

$$H^T(\tilde{f}^T) = p^0 A(f) \bar{x}^T + p_0 a_0(f) \sum_{t=1}^{T} \left[\frac{(1+\eta)(1+\beta)}{(1+\alpha)(1+\rho)} \right]^{t-1} \bar{x}^{T-t}(f)$$

$$= \sum_{t=1}^{T} \left[\frac{(1+\eta)(1+\beta)}{(1+\alpha)(1+\rho)} \right]^{t-1} p_0 \bar{p}^t(\tilde{f}^T) y. \tag{77}$$

We normalize the costs in the following manner

$$\bar{H}^T(\tilde{f}^T) = \begin{cases} H^T(\tilde{f}^T) & \text{if } (1+\eta)(1+\beta) < (1+\alpha)(1+\rho) \\ \frac{1}{T} H^T(\tilde{f}^T) & \text{if } (1+\eta)(1+\beta) = (1+\alpha)(1+\rho) \\ \left[\frac{(1+\alpha)(1+\rho)}{(1+\eta)(1+\beta)}\right]^{T-1} H^T(\tilde{f}^T) & \text{if } (1+\eta)(1+\beta) > (1+\alpha)(1+\rho). \end{cases} \quad (78)$$

If $(1+\alpha)(1+\rho) < (1+\beta)(1+\gamma(f))$ then $\bar{p}^t(f) \to \bar{p}(f)$ and the following *asymptotic normalized total discounted labor costs* are finite

$$\bar{H}(\tilde{f}^\infty) := \lim_{T\to\infty} \bar{H}^T(\tilde{f}^T) < \infty. \quad (79)$$

As we have done in Section 2 we need to consider the three normalization cases in (78) separately.

In *case 1*: $(1+\eta)(1+\beta) < (1+\alpha)(1+\rho) < (1+\beta)(1+\gamma\ (f))$ we substitute the first expression (77) into (79), so as to be able to use the theorem of Toeplitz. Therefore

$$\bar{H}(\tilde{f}^\infty) = \left[p^0 A(f) + p_0 a_0(f) \left[\frac{(1+\alpha)(1+\rho)}{(1+\alpha)(1+\rho) - (1+\eta)(1+\beta)}\right]\right] \bar{x}(f). \quad (80)$$

Letting $a_0''(f)$ denote the expression in the brackets of (80) we obtain the dual representation (81) of $\bar{H}(\tilde{f}^\infty)$

$$\bar{H}(\tilde{f}^\infty) = a_0''(f)\,\bar{x}(f) = v''(f)\,y \quad (81)$$

where $v''(f)$ are specialized synchronized values

$$v''(f) = a_0''(f) + v''(f)(1+\eta)A(f). \quad (82)$$

It is advisable to use them, if $\bar{H}(\tilde{f}^\infty)$ is to be minimized over the class of stationary plans. If $p^0 = 0$, then $v''(f) = v(f)p_0(1+\alpha)(1+\rho)\,/\,[(1+\alpha)(1+\rho) - (1+\eta)(1+\beta)]$. Therefore the functional equation (41) will yield a stationary plan $\tilde{f}^\infty$, such that $\bar{H}(\tilde{f}_,^\infty) \leqslant \bar{H}(\tilde{f}^\infty)$ for all $\tilde{f}^\infty$.

In *case 2*: $(1+\eta)(1+\beta) = (1+\alpha)(1+\rho) < (1+\beta)(1+\gamma(f))$ we obtain the following dual representation of $\bar{H}(\tilde{f}^\infty)$

$$\bar{H}(\tilde{f}^\infty) = p_0\, a_0(f)\,\bar{x}(f) = p_0\,\bar{p}(f)\,y. \quad (83)$$

Here $\bar{p}(f)$ is the unique solution of

$$\bar{p}(f) = a_0(f) + \bar{p}(f)\frac{(1+\alpha)(1+\rho)}{1+\beta}A. \quad (84)$$

The competitive plan $\tilde{f}_\cdot^\infty$ of (73) minimizes $\bar{H}(\tilde{f}^\infty)$ within the class of stationary plans.

In *case 3*: $(1+\eta)(1+\beta) > (1+\alpha)(1+\rho) < (1+\beta)(1+\gamma(f))$, the theorem of Toeplitz in conjunction with the second equation (77) yields

$$\bar{H}(\tilde{f}^\infty) = p_0\,\bar{p}(f)\left[\frac{(1+\eta)(1+\beta)}{(1+\eta)(1+\beta) - (1+\alpha)(1+\rho)}y\right]. \quad (85)$$

Let y'' be defined by the expression in the brackets of (85) and let $x''(f)$ be the unique solution of

$$x''(f) = y'' + \frac{(1+\rho)(1+\alpha)}{1+\beta} A(f)\, x''(f). \tag{86}$$

Then we may write

$$\bar{H}(f^\infty) = p_0\, \bar{p}(f)\, y'' = p_0\, a_0(f)\, x''(f). \tag{87}$$

We see that the competitive plan $\tilde{f}^\infty$ minimizes $\bar{H}(\tilde{f}^\infty)$ within the class of stationary plans.

As we have been, the compeitive prices and technologies can be determined according to (69), (72) or (73), if ρ and β are given. In the following we shall show, how these rates depend on the real wages. Let $b = (b_j)$ be a specified semi-positive *standard consumption bundle* which the workers receive in the *first* period. The remaining bundle $c = (c_j) = y - b$ is consumed by capitalists. In succeeding periods the workers receive $(1+\eta)^{t-1}$ standard bundels b. We assume that workers do not save, so that the whole of their (nominal) wages are spent immediately in buying standard bundles. For a given plan $\bar{f}^T$ let $l(t; \bar{f}^T)$ be the *real wage rate in period t*, measured in the number of standard bundles received for one hour's work in period t. The price of a standard bundle in period t is equal to $\bar{p}(\bar{f}^t)\, b$. The savings assumption thus gives us the following equations

$$l(t; \bar{f}^T)\, p^t(\bar{f}^t)\, b = p_0(t) \qquad (1 \leqslant t \leqslant T). \tag{88}$$

Using normalized prices we may rewrite (88) as

$$l(t; \bar{f}^T) = \frac{(1+\alpha)^{t-1}}{(1+\rho)\, \bar{p}^t(\bar{f}^t)\, b} \qquad (1 \leqslant t \leqslant T). \tag{89}$$

Since the real wage rates will in general differ over the individual periods, it is desirable to define an *average* of these real wage rates in order to explain the size of the uniform rates ρ and β. We choose to define an *average real wage rate* $l^T(\bar{f}^T)$ as the total number of standard bundles b received by workers in T periods, namely $\sum_{t=1}^{T} (1+\eta)^{t-1}$, divided by the total number of hours, which have to be worked so that these bundles may be consumed in a capitalistic system. The total number of hours worked in T periods is variable in the present model and may be determined as follows. Let $L(t; \bar{f}^T)$ be the number of hours worked in period t. For all $1 \leqslant t \leqslant T$ we then have

$$l(t; \bar{f}^T)\, L(t; \bar{f}^T) = (1+\eta)^{t-1}. \tag{90}$$

Note that we have set $z(T) = 0$. Solving (90) for $L(t; \bar{f}^T)$ and summing over all t gives us the total labor time

$$\sum_{t=1}^{T} L(t; \bar{f}^T) = \sum_{t=1}^{T} \frac{(1+\eta)^{t-1}}{l(t; \bar{f}^T)} = (1+\rho) \sum_{t=1}^{T} \frac{(1+\eta)^{t-1}}{(1+\alpha)^{t-1}}\, \bar{p}^t(\bar{f}^t)\, b. \tag{91}$$

The *average real wage rate* for T periods may now be determined as a weighted average of the individual real wage rates:

$$l^T(\bar{f}^T) = \frac{\sum_{t=1}^{T}(1+\eta)^{t-1}}{\sum_{t=1}^{T}((1+\eta)^{t-1})/(l(t;\bar{f}^T))}$$

$$= \frac{\sum_{t=1}^{T}(1+\eta)^{t-1}}{(1+\rho)\sum_{t=1}^{T}((1+\eta)^{t-1}/(1+\alpha)^{t-1})\,\bar{p}^t(\bar{f}^t)\,b} =: R^T(\rho,\beta;\bar{f}^T). \qquad (92)$$

Note that $R^T(\rho,\beta;\bar{f}^T)$ defined in (92) is a function in ρ and β since $\bar{p}^t(\bar{f}^t)$ is a function in ρ and β. In the following we shall use the notation $\bar{p}^t(\rho,\beta;\bar{f}^t)$ or $\bar{p}^t(\rho,\beta)$ (for (72)) to stress this fact. If β is held fixed, then $R^T(\tau,\beta;\bar{f}^T)$ is continuous and monotonically strictly decreasing in ρ. We have $\lim_{\rho\searrow -1} R^T(\rho,\beta;\bar{f}^T) = +\infty$ and $\lim_{\rho\to\infty} R^T(\rho,\beta;\bar{f}^T) = 0$. For a fixed ρ, the function $R^T(\rho,\beta;\bar{f}^T)$ is continuous and monotonically strictly increasing in β with $\lim_{\beta\searrow -1} R^T(\rho,\beta;\bar{f}^T) = 0$ and $\lim_{\beta\to\infty} R^T(\rho,\beta;\bar{f}^T) < \infty$. The upper envelope of all $R^T(\rho,\beta;\bar{f}^T)$ is denoted by

$$R^T(\rho,\beta) = \max_{\bar{f}^T} R^T(\rho,\beta;\bar{f}^T) = \frac{\sum_{t=1}^{T}(1+\eta)^{t-1}}{(1+\rho)\sum_{i=1}^{T}((1+\eta)^{t-1}/(1+\alpha)^{t-1})\,\bar{p}^t(\rho,\beta)\,b}. \qquad (93)$$

The above stated continuity, monotonicity and limiting properties of $R^T(\rho,\beta;\bar{f}^T)$ are inherited by $R^T(\rho,\beta)$. For a fixed β, $R^T(\rho,\beta)$ is called the *average wage-profit curve* of the substitution system. If ρ is held fixed then (93) relates the growth rate of nominal wages to the average real wage rate.

Although $R^T(\rho,\beta)$ of (93) can become arbitrary large, the average real wage rate l^T cannot. In our system, the maximal average real wage rate l^T_* is reached if $y = b$ (No consumption for capitalists!) and the total labor time, denoted by L^T, which is needed to produce the workers' consumption stream $(1+\eta)^{t-1}b$ $(1 \leqslant t \leqslant T)$ is minimized. Note that we have excluded the time required to procedure $z(T)$, but have included the labor time embodied in the initial capital stock. Thus l^T_* is given by

$$l^T_* = \frac{\sum_{t=1}^{T}(1+\eta)^{t-1}}{L^T_b} = \frac{\sum_{t=1}^{T}(1+\eta)^{t-1}}{\sum_{t=1}^{T}((1+\eta)^{t-1}/(1+\alpha)^{t-1})\,\bar{w}^t\,b}. \qquad (94)$$

Let a *feasible* average real wage rate l^T $(0 < l^T \leqslant l^T_*)$ be given. We are interested in finding all (growth) rates of profit ρ and growth rates of nominal wages β, which may be realized in a system minimizing production costs as in (72). To solve this problem we set $R^T(\rho,\beta) = l^T$. We assume that initial values are equal to initial prices: $w^0 = p^0 > 0$.

(This condition will turn out to be inessential in the asymptotic case $T \to \infty$, if $\alpha \leqslant \eta$.)

Let $\Phi^T(l^T)$ be the *nominal wage-profit indifference curve* for a given feasible average real wage rate l^T:

$$\Phi^T(l^T) = \{(\rho, \beta) \mid R^T(\rho, \beta)) = l^T; \rho > -1, \beta > -1\}. \tag{95}$$

It contains all points (ρ, β) which have the same average real wage rate. Letting $P_b^T(\rho, \beta)$ denote

$$P_b^T(\rho, \beta) = \sum_{t=1}^{T} \frac{(1+\eta)^{t-1}}{(1+\alpha)^{t-1}} \bar{p}^t(\rho, \beta)\, b \tag{96}$$

we may rewrite (95) as

$$\Phi^T(l^T) = \left\{ (\rho, \beta) \mid \frac{\sum_{i=1}^{T} (1+\eta)^{t-1}}{(1+\rho) P_b^T(\rho, \beta)} = l^T \right\}. \tag{97}$$

The function $P_b^T(\rho, \beta)$ is continuous in $\rho > -1$ and $\beta > -1$. For fixed β it is monotonically strictly increasing in ρ approaching $+\infty$ as $\rho \nearrow \infty$. For fixed ρ, the function $P_b^T(\rho, \beta)$ is monotonically strictly decreasing in β, approaching the limit (98) which is independent of ρ.

$$P_b^T(\rho, \infty) := \lim_{\beta \nearrow \infty} P_b^T(\rho, \beta) = \sum_{t=1}^{T} \frac{(1+\eta)^{t-1}}{(1+\alpha)^{t-1}} \underline{a}_0\, b. \tag{98}$$

The expression $\underline{a}_0$ in (93) is equal to $\min_f a_0(f) = a_0(f_{**}), f_{**}$ being a myopic technology. The above properties of $P_b^T(\rho, \beta)$ imply that $\Phi^T(l^T)$ may be represented by the *nominal wage-profit indifference function* φ^T: $\beta = \varphi^T(\rho; l^T)$. This function is continuous in ρ and monotonically strictly increasing. Let $\tilde{\rho}(l^T)$ be defined by

$$\tilde{\rho}(l^T) = \frac{\sum_{t=1}^{T-1} (1+\eta)^{t-1}}{l^T \sum_{t=1}^{T-1} ((1+\eta)^{t-1}/(1+\alpha)^{t-1})\, \underline{a}_0\, b} - 1. \tag{99}$$

As ρ approaches $\tilde{\rho}(l^T)$ from the left, $\beta = \varphi^T(\rho; l^T)$ diverges to $+\infty$. This has interesting consequences. If the growth rate of nominal wages β is high, then a large increase in β need only be compensated by a small increase in the rate of profit if the average real wage rate is to remain constant. Finally we note that $\lim_{\rho \searrow -1} \varphi^T(\rho; l^T) = -1$.

In the construction of the indifference curve (95) we have used the function (93) which is based on cost minimization. The influence of such minimization on ρ and β is easily seen. For an arbitrary plan let $\Phi^T(l^T, \bar{f}^T)$ be the indifference curve obtained, if we replace $R^T(\rho, \beta)$ in (70) by $R^T(\rho, \beta; \bar{f}^T)$. The associated indifference function $\beta = \varphi^T(\rho; l^T, \bar{f}^T)$ lies above or on the indifference function $\varphi^T(\rho; l^T)$, i.e. $\varphi^T(\rho; l^T) \leqslant \varphi^T(\rho; l^T, \bar{f}^T)$ for all $\bar{f}^T$. Therefore, if β is held fixed, cost minimization will lead to a plan with maximal rate of profit. On the other hand, if ρ is held fixed, then cost minimization will generate a plan with minimal growth rate of nominal wages. In both cases, the average real wage rate l^T is assumed to be constant. In our Figure 3 the three cross hatched curves represent the lower envelopes $\varphi^T(\rho; l^T) = \min_{\bar{f}^T} \varphi^T(\rho; l^T, \bar{f}^T)$ for three different average real wage rates $l_*^T > l_{\prime}^T > l_{\prime\prime}^T$. A look at the construction of the indifference curve (95) shows that a decrease in l^T will lead to a decreased indifference function: $\varphi^T(\rho; l_{\prime}^T) > \varphi^T(\rho; l_{\prime\prime}^T)$ $(-1 < \rho < \tilde{\rho}(l_{\prime}^T) \Leftrightarrow l_{\prime}^T > l_{\prime\prime}^T$. Thus the largest indifference function is obtained if l^T is maximal. Because of its importance we investigate this case in the following.

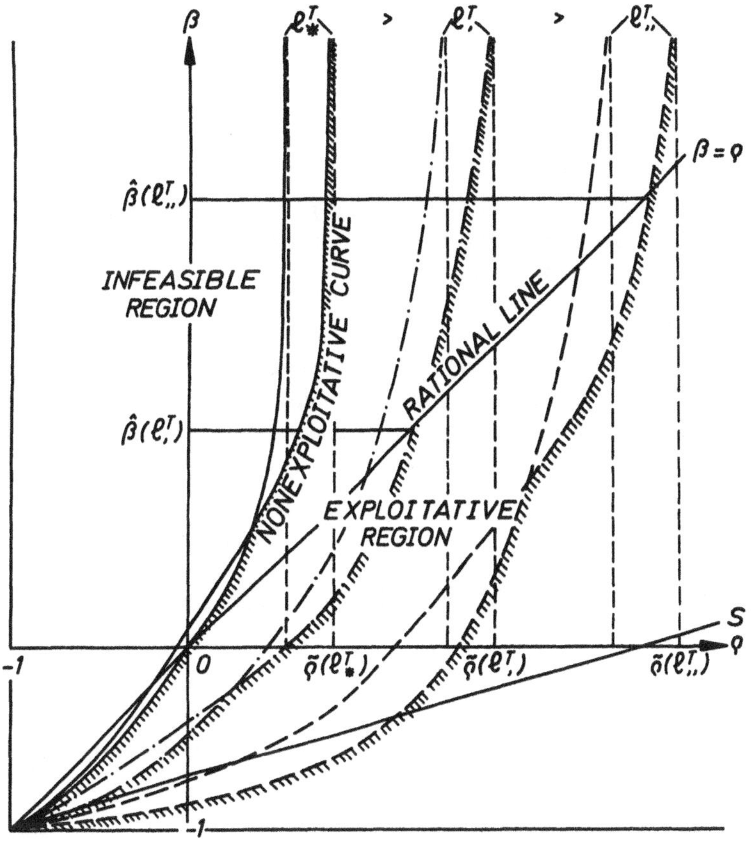

Fig. 3: Nominal wage-profit indifference curves
Rate of profit ρ
Growth rate of nominal wages β
Average real wage rates l^T

For reasons which will become apparent, we choose to call the nominal wage-profit indifference curve in the case of a maximal average real wage rate the *nonexploitative curve*. It is given by

$$\Phi_*^T := \Phi^T(l_*^T) = \{(\rho, \beta) \mid (1+\rho) P_b^T(\rho, \beta) = L_b^T; \rho > -1, \beta > -1\}. \qquad (100)$$

The associated function $\beta = \varphi^T(\rho; l_*^T) = \varphi_*^T(\rho)$ is called the *nonexploitative function.* If $w^0 = p^0$, then $\bar{p}^t(\rho, \rho) = \bar{w}^t$. Consequently $P_b^T(\rho, \rho) = L_b^T$. The nonexploitative curve thus goes through the point $(\rho, \beta) = (0, 0)$, lying below the *rational* line $\beta = \rho$ if $-1 < \rho < 0$, and above if $\rho > 0$. All points (ρ, β) such that $\rho = \beta > -1$ are called *rational*. For these points the normalized competitive prices are equal to (normalized) values and the plan generated by cost minimization is rational. The indifference curves for all feasible average real wage rates lie on or below the nonexploitative curve. Consequently each indifference curve $\Phi^T(l^T)$ possesses a non-negative rational point

$$\hat{\rho}(l^T) = \hat{\beta}(l^T) = \frac{\sum_{t=1}^{T} (1+\eta)^{t-1}}{l^T L_b^T} - 1. \qquad (101)$$

We have seen that a given average real wage rate determines a whole set of rates of profit and growth rates of nominal wages. In this set *one* point, namely (101), may be singled out as being rational in our definition. We have restated some of the above results in the following Theorem 5.

Theorem 5: Prices of production, rates of profit, and growth rates of nominal wages.

Let the initial prices and values be equal: $p^0 = w^0 > 0$, and suppose l^T to be a given feasible average real wage rate. There exists a unique nominal wage-profit indifference function $\beta = \varphi^T(\rho; l^T)$ which is equal to the lower envelope

$$\beta = \varphi^T(\rho; l^T) = \min_{\bar{f}^T} \varphi^T(\rho; l^T, \bar{f}^T) = \varphi^T(\rho; l, \bar{f}_\cdot^T). \qquad (102)$$

The indifference function can be obtained by solving the recursive system

$$\bar{p}_j^t = \min_{k \in K_j}\overset{\overset{f_\cdot^t}{\uparrow}}{} \left\{ a_{0j}(k) + \sum_{i=1}^{n} \bar{p}_i^{t-1} \frac{(1+\rho)(1+\alpha)}{1+\beta} a_{ij}(k) \right\} \quad (1 \leq j \leq n, 1 \leq t \leq T). \qquad (103)$$

$$l^T = \frac{\sum_{t=1}^{T} (1+\eta)^{t-1}}{(1+\rho) \sum_{t=1}^{T} ((1+\eta)^{t-1}/(1+\alpha)^{t-1}) \bar{p}^t b} \qquad (104)$$

for all ρ in the interval $0 < \rho < \tilde{\rho}(l^T)$. The indifference function $\beta = \varphi^T(\rho; l^T)$ is continuous and monotonically strictly increasing in ρ, diverging to $+\infty$ as $\rho \nearrow \tilde{\rho}(l^T)$. There exists a unique nonnegative rational point $\hat{\rho}(l^T) = \hat{\beta}(l^T)$ on the indifference curve. If this point is selected, then the (normalized) *prices of production* of (103) – (104) are equal to the normalized rational values (21). In a rational point (and in a neighborhood of it) a plan generated by (103) – (104) is rational: $\bar{f}^T = \bar{f}^T_*$. Given a fixed l^T cost minimization in the system (103) – (104) will lead to the maximal rational point.

The reader should carefully distinguish between the systems (72) and (103) – (104). The calculation of competitive prices and technologies according to (72) presupposes knowledge of ρ and β, whereas the growth rate η of the quantity system need not be known. In order to solve the system (103) – (104) the average real wage rate must be given. This determines a nominal wage-profit indifference curve and with each point on this curve price vectors $\bar{p}^t$ $(1 \leqslant t \leqslant T)$. These price vectors along with the associated pairs (ρ, β), however, do depend on η as (104) shows. If we hold β fixed, then average real-profit curves are obtained from Theorem 5. Three cases may occur, namely $\beta > 0, \beta = 1$ and $-1 < \beta < 0$. We state some properties of these curves in the following Corollary 2.

Corollary 2: Average wage-profit curves
Let $p^0 = w^0 > 0$.
Case a: If $\beta > 0$ is given, then the average wage-profit curve $l^T = R^T(\rho) = R^T(\rho, \beta)$ is a continuous and monotonically strictly decreasing function in $\rho \geqslant \rho^T_*$ approaching zero as $\rho \to \infty$. The point ρ^T_* is the unique solution of $R^T(\rho^T_*) = l^T_*$. $R^T(\rho)$ is the upper envelope of all $R^T(\rho, \beta; \bar{f}^T)$.Cf. cross hatched curve in Figure 4a.
Case b: If $\beta = 0$, then the average wage-profit curve is defined for all $\rho > 0$ and possesses the above properties. Cf. Figure 4b and *Morishima* [1973, p. 55.]
Case c: If $-1 < \beta < 0$ is given, then the average wage-profit curve is defined for all $\rho \geqslant \rho^T_* < 0$ and possesses the above stated properties.

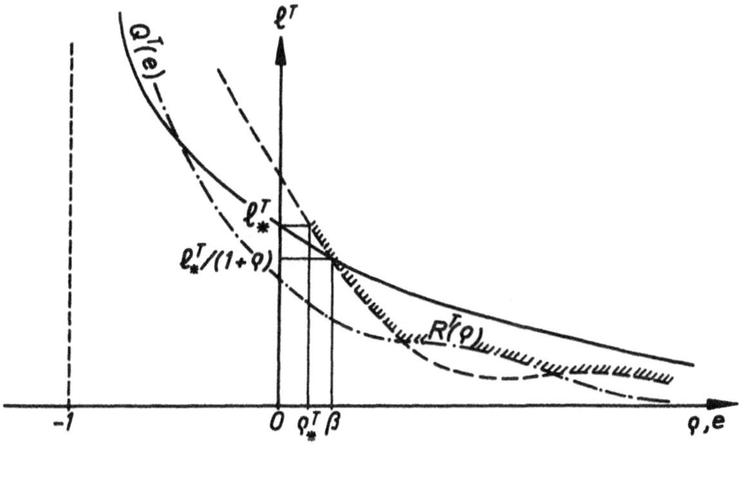

Fig. 4a: $\beta > 0$

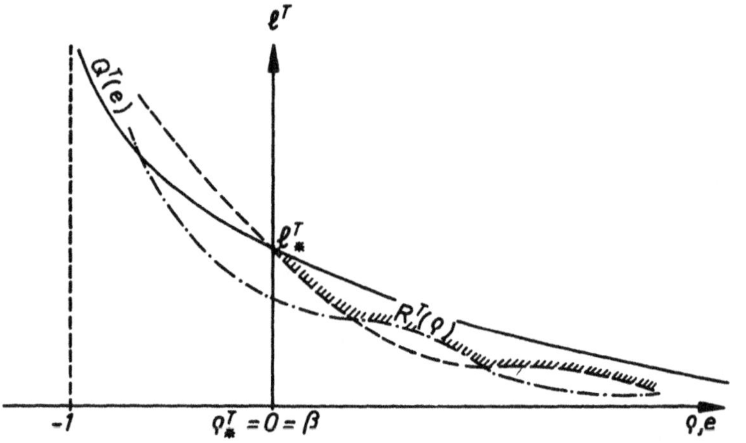

Fig. 4b: $\beta = 0$

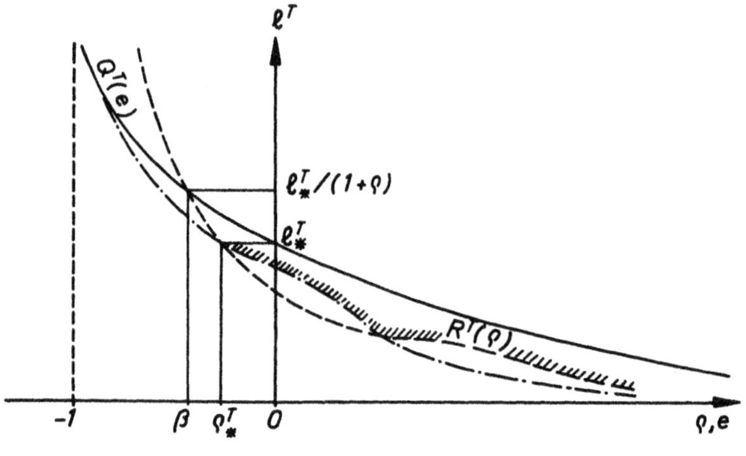

Fig. 4c: $\beta < 0$

Fig. 4: Average real wage profit curves and exploitation rate curves

In Theorem 5 we investigated a finite period system for prices of production, rates of profit and growth rates of nominal wages. In the final part of this section we are concerned with the asymptotic behavior of this system as $T \to \infty$. We wish to derive a system in which the period index disappears. Such a system can be obtained, if we assume $\alpha \leqslant \eta$ and $\alpha < \gamma$. Whereas l^T in Theorem 5 was exogeneously given, we shall now assume a time (period) path[2]) for l^T, namely

$$l^T = g^T(\alpha, \eta)\, l \qquad (T = 1, 2, \ldots). \tag{105}$$

[2]) As an alternative to (105) it is possible to assume that the real wage rates in all periods are given by $l(t) = g^t(\alpha, \eta)\, l/h(\alpha, \eta)$. Cf. table (106) for a definition of $h(\alpha, \eta)$.

For six possible constellations of α and η the functions $g^T(\alpha, \eta)$ are specified in the following table (106)

		$g^T(\alpha, \eta)$	$h(\alpha, \eta)$
1	$-1<\alpha<\eta>0$	$(1+\alpha)^{T-1}$	$(\eta-\alpha)/\eta$
2	$-1<\alpha<\eta=0$	$(1+\alpha)^{T-1}\,T$	$-\alpha$
3	$-1<\alpha<\eta<0$	$(1+\alpha)^{T-1}/(1+\eta)^{T-1}$	$(\eta-\alpha)/-\eta(1+\eta)$
4	$\alpha=\eta>0$	$(1+\eta)^{T-1}/T$	$(1+\eta)/\eta$
5	$\alpha=\eta=0$	1	1
6	$-1<\alpha=\eta<0$	$1/T$	$1/T$

(106)

Thus, in case 1: $-1<\alpha<\eta>0$, the average real wage rate of a T-period process is given by $l^T=(1+\alpha)^{T-1}\,l$. Case 5 represents the traditional, so-called *stationary model* with no technical progress ($\alpha=0$) and no expansion of the quantity system ($\eta=0$). According to (106) and (105) l^T is constant over all T for such a model. The factor l in (105) is equal to a *normalized average real wage rate* $\bar{l}^T := l^T/g^T(\alpha, \eta) = l$. The *normalized asymptotic real wage rate*, defined by $\bar{l} := \lim_{T\to\infty} \bar{l}^T$, is also equal to l. Let $\bar{l}_*^T$ be the upper bound for $\bar{l}^T$, determined by $\bar{l}_*^T = l_*^T/g^T(\alpha, \eta)$. (Cf. (94), (105), (106)). We call $\bar{l}_*^T$ the *normalized maximal average real wage* rate. The next Lemma investigates the convergence of $\bar{l}_*^T$.

Lemma
If $\alpha<\gamma$, then the *normalized maximal asymptotic real wage* rate $\bar{l}_* := \lim l_*^T$ exists and is given by

$$\bar{l}_* = \frac{h(\alpha, \eta)}{\bar{w}\,b}. \tag{107}$$

The function $h(\alpha, \eta)$ is specified in the last column of Table (106).

Proof: We demonstrate (107) for case 1: $-1<\alpha<\eta>0$ only, since the proofs of the other cases proceeds along the same lines. After some manipulation on $\bar{l}_*^T$ we may apply the theorem of Toeplitz (as in the proof of Theorem 3). This gives us

$$\bar{l}_*^T = \frac{\sum_{t=1}^{T}(1+\eta)^{t-1}}{(1+\alpha)^{T-1}\sum_{t=1}^{T}\left((1+\eta)^{t-1}/(1+\alpha)^{t-1}\right)\bar{w}^t\,b}$$

$$= \frac{\sum_{t=1}^{T}(1+\eta)^{t-1}/(1+\eta)^{T-1}}{\sum_{t=1}^{T}\left((1+\eta)^{t-1}/(1+\eta)^{T-1}\right)\left((1+\alpha)^{T-1}/(1+\alpha)^{t-1}\right)\bar{w}^t\,b}$$

$$= \frac{\sum_{s=0}^{T-1} [1/(1+\eta)]^s}{\sum_{s=0}^{T-1} [(1+\alpha)/(1+\eta)]^s \, \bar{w}^{T-s} \, b}$$

$$\xrightarrow[T\to\infty]{} \frac{\sum_{s=0}^{\infty} [1/(1+\eta)]^s}{\sum_{s=0}^{\infty} [(1+\alpha)/(1+\eta)]^s \, \bar{w} \, b} = \frac{h(\alpha,\eta)}{\bar{w}\, b}. \tag{108}$$

For l^T as specified in (105) – (106), the nominal wage-profit indifference curve $\Phi^T(l^T) = \Phi^T(l)$ depends on l and is given by

$$\Phi^T(l) = \left\{ (\rho, \beta) \mid l = \frac{\sum_{t=1}^{T} (1+\eta)^{t-1}}{g^T(\alpha,\eta)(1+\rho) P_b^T(\rho,\beta)} ; \rho, \beta > -1 \right\}. \tag{109}$$

We wish to investigate the limiting behavior of (109) as $T \to \infty$. Let S be the straight line

$$\beta = \left[\frac{1+\alpha}{1+\gamma}\right] \rho + \frac{\alpha - \gamma}{1+\gamma}. \tag{110}$$

This line goes through the point $(-1, -1)$ in the (ρ, β)-plane and has a positive slope less than 1 since $\alpha < \gamma$. Hence S lies below the rational line $\beta = \rho$ in our Figure 3. For all (ρ, β) lying above S, $\bar{p}^t(\rho,\beta) \to \bar{p}(\rho,\beta)$ so that an appeal to the theorems of Cauchy and Toeplitz yields

$$\lim_{T\to\infty} \frac{\sum_{t=1}^{T} (1+\eta)^{t-1}}{g^T(\alpha,\eta)(1+\rho) P_b^T(\rho,\beta)} = \frac{h(\alpha,\eta)}{(1+\rho)\bar{p}(\rho,\beta)\, b}. \tag{111}$$

For all (ρ, β) lying on or below S, the limit in (111) converges to zero. Hence the indifference curves (109) will lie above S for all sufficiently large T and they will converge to the *asymptotic nominal wage-profit indifference curve*

$$\Phi(l) = \left\{ (\rho, \beta) \mid l = \frac{h(\alpha,\eta)}{(1+\rho)\bar{p}(\rho,\beta)\, b} ; \rho, \beta > -1 \right\}. \tag{112}$$

Associated with (112) is the asymptotic nominal wage-profit indifference function $\beta = \varphi(\rho; l)$, a continuous and monotonically strictly increasing function in ρ. Substituting (105) into (99) we see that $\beta = \varphi(\rho; l)$ will diverge to $+\infty$ as $\rho \nearrow \tilde{\rho}(l) := h(\alpha,\eta)/l\, \underline{a}_0\, b - 1$.

If we let l be equal to the normalized maximal asymptotic real wage rate $\bar{l}_*$ of (82), then the indifference curve (112) can be written as

$$\Phi_* = \Phi(\bar{l}_*) = \{(\rho,\beta) \mid \bar{w}\, b = (1+\rho)\bar{p}(\rho,\beta)\, b ; \rho, \beta > -1\}. \tag{113}$$

We call Φ_* the *asymptotic nonexploitative curve* and $\beta = \varphi_* (\rho)$ the associated *asymptotic nonexploitative function.* The function $\beta = \varphi_* (\rho)$ is an upper bound for all asymptotic nominal wage-profit indifference functions: $\varphi_* (\rho) \geqslant \varphi (\rho; l), (0 < l \leqslant \bar{l}_*)$. If $\rho = 0$ then $\beta = \varphi_* (0) = 0$. As $\rho \nearrow \tilde{\rho}_* := \bar{w}\, b/\underline{a}_0\, b - 1$, we see $\beta = \varphi_* (\rho)$ diverging to $+\infty$. Since $\varphi_* (\rho) \geqslant \varphi (\rho; l), \varphi_* (0) = 0$ and $\varphi (\rho; l) \to +\infty$ as $\rho \nearrow \tilde{\rho} (l)$, there exists a unique nonnegative rational point $\hat{\rho} (l) = \hat{\beta} (l) = h (\alpha, \eta)/l\, \bar{w}\, b - 1$ on the asymptotic indifference curve. We collect our results in Theorem 6.

Theorem 6: Asymptotic prices of production, rates of profit, and growth rates of nominal wages.

Let $-1 < \alpha < \gamma$ and $\alpha \leqslant \eta$. Suppose that the average real wage rates are given by

$$l^T = g^T (\alpha, \eta)\, l \qquad (T = 1, 2, \ldots). \tag{114}$$

Let l^T be less than or equal to the normalized maximal asymptotic real wage rate (107). Then there exists a unique asymptotic nominal wage-profit indifference function $\beta = \varphi (\rho, l) = \lim_{T \to \infty} \varphi^T (\rho, l^T)$, which is equal to the limit of lower envelopes

$$\beta = \varphi (\rho, l) = \lim_{T \to \infty} \min_{\bar{f}^T} \varphi^T (\rho; l^T, \bar{f}^T) = \lim_{T \to \infty} \varphi^T (\rho; l^T, f.^T). \tag{115}$$

It can be obtained by solving the system

$$\begin{array}{c} f. = (k_j.) \\ \uparrow \end{array}$$
$$\bar{p}_j = \min_{k \in K_j} \left\{ a_{0j} (k) + \sum_{i=1}^{n} \bar{p}_i \frac{(1 + \rho)(1 + \alpha)}{1 + \beta} a_{ij} (k) \right\} \quad \begin{pmatrix} 1 \leqslant j \leqslant n, \\ 1 \leqslant t \leqslant T \end{pmatrix} \tag{116}$$

$$l = \frac{h (\alpha, \eta)}{(1 + \rho)\, \bar{p}\, b} \tag{117}$$

for all ρ in the interval $0 < \rho < \tilde{\rho} (l) = h (\alpha, \eta)/l\, \underline{a}_0\, b - 1$. The asymptotic indifference function is continuous and monotonically strictly increasing in ρ, diverging to $+\infty$ as $\rho \nearrow \tilde{\rho} (l)$. It is bounded below by $[(1 + \alpha)/(1 + \gamma)]\, \rho + (\alpha - \gamma)/(1 + \gamma)$ and above by the asymptotic nonexploitative function $\varphi_* (\rho)$. There exists a unique nonnegative rational point $\hat{\rho} (l) = \hat{\beta} (l) = h (\alpha, \eta)/l\, \bar{w}\, b - 1$ on the asymptotic indifference curve. If this point is selected, then the (normalized) *asymptotic prices of production* of (116) – (117) are equal to the (normalized) asymptotic rational values (22) and the technology generated by (116) – (117) is rational: $f. = f_*$.

It should be observed that the expansion rate of the quantity system η influences the asymptotic prices of production, the rates of profit and the growth rates of nominal wages by way of equation (117). However, there are important cases in which the system (116) – (117) is independent of η. For example, if $\alpha = 0$ then $h (0, \eta) = 1$ for all $\eta \geqslant 0$, according to cases 1 and 5 in table (106), so that (116) – (117) is then independent of η. The same holds true for all $-1 < \alpha = \eta < 0$ (Case 6 in (106).) If $\alpha = \eta$ approach infinity then the influence of η on the system (116) – (117) disappears since $h (\eta, \eta) \to 1$ (Case

4 in (106).) In the stationary case: $\alpha = \eta = \beta = 0$ the system (116) – (117) coincides with one investigated by *Reetz* [1977]. If, in addition, all K_j contain exactly one element, then (116) – (117) is equivalent to the systems of *Okishio* [1963] and *Morishima* [1973].

As a result of Theorem 6 we obtain normalized asymptotic wage-profit curves. They possess the same structure as the average wage-profit curves of Corollary 2, with the expectation that they cross the abscissa at a finite point.

Corollary 3: Normalized asymptotic wage-profit curves
Let $-1 < \alpha < \gamma$ and $\alpha \leqslant \eta$. Then there exists a continuous monotonically strictly decreasing normalized asymptotic wage profit curve

$$l = \bar{R}(\rho, \beta) = \lim_{T \to \infty} \frac{R^T(\rho, \beta)}{g^T(\alpha, \eta)} = \frac{h(\alpha, \eta)}{(1 + \rho) p(\rho, \beta) b}. \tag{118}$$

In *case a*: $\beta > 0$, the curve is defined for all ρ in the interval $\rho_* \leqslant \rho \leqslant \rho' :=$ $= (1 + \gamma)(1 + \beta)/(1 + \alpha) - 1$. The point ρ_* is defined by $\bar{w}\, b = (1 + \rho_*) \bar{p}(\rho_*, \beta) b$ and is less than β (cf. (113)). As $\rho \to \rho'$, $\bar{R}(\rho, \beta)$ approaches zero. $\bar{R}(\beta, \beta) = \bar{l}_*/(1 + \rho)$ and $\bar{R}(\rho_*, \beta) = \bar{l}_*$.

In *case b*: $\beta = 0$, the point ρ_* is equal to $\beta = 0$. $\bar{R}(0, 0) = \bar{l}_*$. (The curve $\bar{R}(\rho, 0)$ corresponds to a curve in *Morishima* [1973, p. 55].)

In *case c*: $-1 < \beta < 0$, the point ρ_* lies in the interval $\beta < \rho_* < 0$. $\bar{R}(\beta, \beta) = \bar{l}_*/(1 + \rho)$ and $\bar{R}(\rho_*, \beta) = \bar{l}_*$.

5. Rate of Exploitation, Rates of Profit and Growth rates of Nominal Wages

In this section we wish to demonstrate an extension of the so-called "Fundamental Marxian Theorem" of *Okishio* [1963] and *Morishima* [1973] to the two-dimensional (ρ, β)-space. The theorem links the (normalized) rational value systems (21) and (22) with the (normalized) production price systems (103) – (104) and (116) – (117). Consider at first a finite T-period production process with a plan $\bar{f}^T$ selected by capitalists according to (103) – (104). Under such a plan the total labor time for the production of exponential consumption (4) is given by $L_y^T(\bar{f}^T)$. (We have set $z(T) = 0$.) $L_y^T(\bar{f}^T)$ may be decomposed into the *paid total labor time* $L_b^T(\bar{f}^T)$ and an *unpaid total labor time* $L_c^T(\bar{f}^T)$. These quantitites may be calculated according to (15), replacing y by b or c, respectively. The paid total labor time in turn may be decomposed into a rational part, namely the necessary (minimum) labor time $L_b^T(\bar{f}_*^T)$ using a rational plan $\bar{f}_*^T$ according to (20) and into a nonrational (inefficient) part $L_b^T(\bar{f}^T) - L^T(\bar{f}_*^T)$. The nonrational part of paid total labor time is hidden. It stems from the fact, that a rational plan will not in general be generated within the price system (116) – (117), unless $\beta = \rho$. The total *surplus* labor time is defined as the sum of unpaid total labor time $L_c^T(\bar{f}^T)$ and the nonrational part of paid total labor time $[L_b^T(\bar{f}^T) - L_b^T(\bar{f}_*^T)]$. Thus total surplus labor time is equal to $L_y^T(\bar{f}^T) - L_b^T(\bar{f}_*^T)$. As a quantitative index of exploitation for the T-period production process we define an *average rate of exploitation* e^T as the ratio of total surplus labor time divided by the necessary (minimum) total labor time:

$$e^T = \frac{L_y^T(\bar{f}^T) - L_b^T(\bar{f}_*^T)}{L_b^T(\bar{f}_*^T)} = \frac{1 - L_b^T(\bar{f}_*^T)/L_y^T(\bar{f}^T)}{L_b^T(\bar{f}_*)/L_y^T(\bar{f}^T)}. \tag{119}$$

According to (119), $L_y^T(\bar{f}^T) = (1 + e^T) L_b^T(\bar{f}_*^T)$. Hence we may obtain the following expression for the average real wage rate (total number of standard bundless $\sum_{t=1}^{T}(1+\eta)^{t-1}$ divided by total labor time $L_y^T(\bar{f}^T)$) in terms of rational values

$$l^T = \frac{\sum_{t=1}^{T}(1+\eta)^{t-1}}{L_y^T(\bar{f}^T)} = \frac{\sum_{t=1}^{T}(1+\eta)^{t-1}}{(1+e^T)L_b^T(\bar{f}_*^T)}$$

$$= \frac{\sum_{t=1}^{T}(1+\eta)^{t-1}}{(1+e^T)\sum_{t=1}^{T}((1+\eta)^{t-1}/(1+\alpha)^{t-1})\,\bar{w}^t b} =: Q^T(e^T). \tag{120}$$

The last line in (120) defines the *exploitation-rate curve* $Q^T(e^T)$ which we have plotted in Figure 4. Using (92) we may rewrite (120) as

$$e^T = \frac{(1+\rho)P_b^T(\rho,\beta) - L_b^T}{L_b^T}. \tag{121}$$

It may now be observed that $e^T = 0$ on the nonexploitative curve (100); hence its name. Furthermore, e^T is positive if $(1+\rho)P_b^T(\rho,\beta) > L_b^T$, and negative if $(1+\rho)P_b^T(\rho,\beta) < L_b^T$. Thus $e^T > 0$ for all points (ρ,β) lying below the nonexploitative curve, and $e^T < 0$ for all (infeasible) points (ρ,β) lying above the nonexploitative curve. We refer the readers to Figure 3.

As a next step we compare e^T with ρ. If $w^0 = p^0$, then $\bar{p}^t(\rho,\beta) < \bar{w}^t$ if $\beta > \rho$, $\bar{p}^t(\rho,\beta) = \bar{w}^t$ if $\beta = \rho$, and $\bar{p}^t(\rho,\beta) > \bar{w}^t$ if $\beta < \rho$ $(1 \leq t \leq T)$. Consequently, $P_b^T(\rho,\beta)$ is less than, equal to, or greater than L_b^T depending on which of the conditions $\beta > \rho$, $\beta = \rho$, and $\beta < \rho$ holds. Substituted into (121) these three cases yield

$$e^T \lesseqgtr \rho \Leftrightarrow \beta \gtreqless \rho. \tag{122}$$

Our results are summarized in the following theorem.

Theorem 7: Average rate of exploitation.
Let the initial prices and values be equal: $p^0 = w^0 > 0$. The average rate of exploitation e^T is equal to zero on the nonexploitative curve (100), and positive in the *exploitative region*

$$E^T = \{(\rho,\beta) \mid (1+\rho)P_b^T(\rho,\beta) > L_b^T;\ \rho,\beta > -1\}. \tag{123}$$

In the *infeasible region* $(l_*^T < l^T)$, consisting of all points $(\rho,\beta) > (-1,-1)$ such that $(1+\rho)P_b^T(\rho,\beta) < L_b^T$, the average rate of exploitation is negative. If the growth rate of nominal wages is equal to the (growth) rate of profit, then both rates are equal to the rate of exploitation. If the growth rate of nominal wages lies below the rate of profit, then the rate of exploitation is greater than the rate of profit. Otherwise, the rate of exploitation is less than the rate of profit, but will still be positive in the exploitative region (123).

The results of Theorem 7 can easily be applied to the average real wage-profit curves $R^T(\rho)$ and the exploitation-rate curves of Figures 4. Suppose $\beta > 0$ (Figure 4a). If l^T lies in the interval $l_*^T/(1+\rho) < l^T \leqslant l_*^T$, then $Q^T(e)$ lies below $R^T(e)$, so that the rate of exploitation will be positive but less than the rate of profit. If $l^T = l_*^T(1+\rho)$, then the rate of exploitation is equal to the rate of profit and both are equal to β. If $0 < l^T < l_*^T/(1+\rho)$, then the rate of exploitation is greater than the rate of profit (which is greater than β) Since $Q^T(e)$ lies above $R^T(\rho)$. If $\beta = 0$ (Figure 4b) then $Q^T(e)$ lies above $R^T(\rho)$ for all feasible l^T. A positive rate of exploitation is then a necessary and sufficient condition for a positive rate of profit. Furthermore, the rate of exploitation is an upper bound for the rate of profit. If $\beta < 0$ (Figure 4c) then the exploitation-rate curve lies above the wage-profit curve for all feasible l^T. The rate of exploitation will be non-negative and greater than the rate of profit (which may be negative).

Next we investigate the asymptotic case $T \to \infty$. If the assumptions of Theorem 6, namely $-1 < \alpha < \gamma$, $\alpha \leqslant \eta$ and (114) are satisfied, then all asymptotic indifference functions will lie above S and we have convergence of $\bar{p}^t(\rho, \beta) \to \bar{p}(\rho, \beta)$. If $f_.$ of (116) – (117) is unique, an appeal to Corollary 1 and the theorems of Cauchy and Teoplitz yields the existence of the following limit of (119)

$$e = \lim_{T\to\infty} e^T = \frac{1 - \bar{w}\,b\,/\,\bar{w}\,(f_.)\,y}{\bar{w}\,b\,/\,\bar{w}\,(f_.)\,y}\,. \tag{124}$$

Alternatively, we can take the limit of (121) so as to obtain

$$e = \lim_{T\to\infty} e^T = \frac{(1+\rho)\,\bar{p}\,b - \bar{w}\,b}{\bar{w}\,b}\,. \tag{125}$$

We call e of (124) or (125) the *asymptotic rate of exploitation.* A look at (125) shows that $e \gtreqless 0 \Leftrightarrow (1+\rho)\,\bar{p}\,b - \bar{w}\,b \gtreqless 0$. Thus $e = 0$ on the asymptotic nonexploitative curve (113). Below this curve, in the *asymptotic exploitative region*

$$E = \left\{ (\rho, \beta) \;\middle|\; \begin{array}{l} (1+\rho)\,\bar{p}\,(\rho,\beta)\,b > \bar{w}\,b;\ \rho, \beta > -1 \\ \beta > [(1+\alpha)/(1+\gamma)]\,\rho + (\alpha-\gamma)/(1+\gamma) \end{array} \right\} \tag{126}$$

the asymptotic rate of exploitation is positive. Note that points below S cannot occur in the asymptotic case under investigation. The points $(\rho, \beta) > (-1, -1)$ lying above the asymptotic nonexploitative curve (113) are infeasible ($l > \bar{l}_*$).

In defining the asymptotic exploitative region (126) use was made of the normalized forms of prices and values. If nonnormalized prices and values are employed, then the first inequality in (126) may be replaced by the following condition: There exists a finite t^* such that for all $t \geqslant t^*$

$$\frac{p^t b}{p_0(t)} > w^t b. \tag{127}$$

Thus we find ourselves in the asymptotic exploitative region if the number of hours worked for one standard bundle in all periods $t \geqslant t^*$ is greater than the labor embodied in it. Exploitation may thus be related to individual bundles.

As in Theorem 7 we may compare the rate of exploitation with the rate of profit. We have $\bar{p}(\rho, \beta) \lesseqgtr \bar{w} \Leftrightarrow \beta \gtreqless \rho$. Substituting these inequalities into (125) we obtain

$$e \lesseqgtr \rho \Longleftrightarrow \beta \gtreqless \rho. \tag{128}$$

Theorem 8: Asymptotic rate of exploitation

Let the assumption $-1 < \alpha < \gamma, \alpha \leqslant \eta$ and (114) of Theorem 6 be satisfied. The asymptotic rate of exploitation is zero on the nonexploitative curve (113), positive in the asymptotic exploitative region (126) and negative in the infeasible region. If $\beta = \rho$ then the rate of profit or the growth rate of nominal wages functions as an exact rate of exploitation: $e = \rho = \beta$. If $\beta > \rho$, then the rate of exploitation is less than the rate of profit: $e < \rho$. On the other hand, if $\beta < \rho$, then the rate of exploitation is greater than the rate of profit: $e > \rho$.

Finally we note that a *normalized asymptotic exploitation rate curve* can be defined by

$$\bar{Q}(e) := \lim_{T \to \infty} \frac{Q^T(e)}{g^T(\alpha, \eta)} = \frac{h(\alpha, \eta)}{(1+e)\,\bar{w}\,b}. \tag{129}$$

Cf. (120). It possesses similar properties as $Q^T(e)$ sketched in our Figures 4.

References

Baisch, H.: A Critique of Labour Values for Planning. World Development 7, 1979.

Collatz, L.: Funktionalanalysis und numerische Mathematik. Berlin 1964.

Knopp, K.: Theorie und Anwendung der unendlichen Reihen. Berlin 1964.

Morishima, M.: Marx's Economics. Cambridge 1973.

Nutzinger, H.G.: Value Theory and Social Relations of Production: The Fundamental Theorm Reconsiderd, Discussion Paper, Kassel, March, 1980.

Nutzinger, H.G., and *E. Wolfstetter* (Ed.): Die Marxsche Theorie und ihre Kritik II. Frankfurt–New York 1974.

Okishio, N.: A Mathematical Note on Marxian Theorems. Weltwirtschaftliches Archiv 91, 1963, 287–299. (German version in: Die Marxsche Theorie und ihre Kritik II. Ed. by H.G. Nutzinger and E. Wolfstetter. Frankfurt–New York 1974.)

Reetz, D.: Prices of Production and Labour Values in Input-Output Substitution Systems. Operations Research Verfahren XXIV, 1977, 155–175.

v. Weizsäcker, C.C.: Steady State Capital Theory. Berlin 1971.

–: Notizen zur Marxschen Werttheorie. Die Marxsche Theorie und ihre Kritik II. Ed. by H.G. Nutzinger and E. Wolfstetter. Frankfurt–New York 1974, 94–107.

v. Weizsäcker, C.C., and *P.A. Samuelson*: A New Labor Theory of Value for Rational Planning through Use of the Bourgeois Profit Rate. Proc. Nat. Acad. Sci. USA 68, 1971, 1192–1194. (German version in: Die Marxsche Theorie und ihre Kritik II. Ed. by H.G. Nutzinger and E. Wolfstetter, Frankfurt–New York 1974.)

Wolfstetter, E.: Surplus Labor, Synchronized Labor Costs and Marx's Labour Theory of Value. The Economic Journal 83, 1973, 787–809. (German version in: Die Marxsche Theorie und ihre Kritik II. Ed. by H.G. Nutzinger and E. Wolfstetter. Frankfurt–New York 1974.)

Games, Economic Dynamics, and Time Series Analysis. 1982 ©Physica-Verlag, Wien–Würzburg

Own Rates of Interest in a General Multisector Model of Capital[1])

By *W. Reiss*, Hamburg and *M. Faber*, Heidelberg[2])

1. Introduction

Oskar Morgenstern contributed with his paper „Zur Theorie der Produktionsperiode" (On the Theory of the Production Period) [1935] to the great controversy in the theory of capital in the thirties. In this article he perhaps made the most convincing criticism of this central concept of Austrian capital theory. He thus was partly responsible for the Austrian capital theory's fall into oblivion for about thirty years at the end of the thirties.

But *Morgenstern* also indirectly contributed to its revival with his work on activity analysis [*Morgenstern*, 1954] and the *von Neumann*-model [*Kemeny/Morgenstern/Thompson*], since the activity approach of the *von Neumann* model offered a suitable frame for incorporating the temporal aspect of production [*Burmeister*], on which the Austrian had focussed.[3]) In contrast to Walras they did not use a temporally horizontal, but a vertical approach to the production process. The transformation of the primary factors into intermediate goods and final products was stressed in this way. This temporal aspect of production has mostly been neglected by neoclassical growth and capital theory [*Hicks*, 1976]. In our opinion, this neglect led to a renaissance of Austrian capital theory in the seventies. The debate concerning the reswitching phenomenon has probably accelerated it. One of the main results of the discussion was that reswitching can only occur if heterogeneous goods are used [*Bruno/Burmeister/Sheshinski*]. The heterogeneity of the goods implies that the time structure of production becomes so intricate that some of the conventional relations such as the inverse relationship between the interest rate and the capital intensity are not generally valid.

During the last decade *Bernholz* and the present authors – among others – have tried to revive Austrian capital theory. Our main aim has been to analyze under what conditions the rate of interest is positive in market economies as well as in planning economies. Like *Hicks* [1973] we have studied the substitution of techniques, which implies non-steady-state behavior, since we are interested in structural change, which is, in our opinion, one

[1]) We are grateful to Peter Bernholz, Friedrich Breyer, Ailsa Gruber, Johann Irsigler, Gerhard Maier, Manfred Nermuth, Gerhard Orosel and Gunter Stephan for critical comments (while remaining responsible for any remaining error) and to the Deutsche Forschungsgemeinschaft for financial support.

[2]) *W. Reiss*, Fachbereich Wirtschaftswissenschaften, Universität Hamburg and *M. Faber*, Alfred-Weber-Institut, Universität Heidelberg, Grabengasse 14, D–6900 Heidelberg.

[3]) The temporal aspect in the theory of value was already the theme in *Morgenstern* [1934].

of the main characteristics of industrial economies. Our approach combines ideas of von *Böhm-Bawerk* and of *Schumpeter.* We have reformulated the former's law of superiority of roundabout methods of production. Roughly spoken, we examine the change from one technique to a superior one. This change corresponds to an innovation [*Faber,* 140–142], which we consider to be "roundabout", if it is connected with a reduction of current consumption.

Our analysis began with a two-period-two-sector model [*Bernholz*], which was gradually extended in several directions [see *Reiss*, 1979a]. We intend to generalize our multisector model [*Bernholz/Faber/Reiss*] further in the three following respects:

1. We want to extend the economic horizon from two to T periods;
2. instead of using a linear technology we shall employ a convex technology; we explicitly allow for resources and for pollution in the form of emissions;
3. up to now we have employed in our papers characteristics of the transformation surface to demonstrate that the rate of interest is positive. These characteristics, however, are difficult to determine in general models. We therefore shall show that instead it suffices to use characteristics of feasible consumption sets, which are much easier to handle. This approach will allow us to formulate and prove more general results concerning the structure of the rates of interest for nonbalanced growth.

In Section 2 the assumptions of our model are stated and in Section 3 some theorems concerning separating hyperplanes are recapitulated. Our propositions regarding the sign of the rate of interest rate derived in Section 4. In Section 5 we show the relationships of our approach to *Fisher's.*

Finally we want to note that this paper is based on Chapter 5 of *Reiss* [1979b] and extends it.

2. The Model

We employ the following assumptions:

Assumption 2.1 (Time Horizon, Number of Goods)
The time horizon has T periods, indexed by superscript t $(0 \leqslant t \leqslant T)$. There are M goods, indexed by subscript m, $1 \leqslant m \leqslant M$.

Assumption 2.2 (Production)
Production takes place by means of activities. An activity A^t consists of a nonnegative M-input-vector a^t in period t and of a nonnegative M-output-vector b^{t+1} in $t + 1$. The set of all feasible activities A^t, called the technology E^t, is assumed to be convex and constant over time.

This assumption implies a temporal production structure, i.e. goods produced in period t are not available before $t + 1$.

Assumption 2.3 (Primary Factors)
In each period t an M-dimensional bounded bundle of goods s^t ($s^t \geqslant 0$, $s_m^t < \infty$ for all

$1 \leqslant m \leqslant M$ and all t) enters the model from outside. This bundle contains such primary factors as labour, resources and services of land. We define the vector s by $s =$ $= (s^1, \ldots, s^T)$.

We note that joint production is included in our approach. Before proceeding we want to describe the composition of inputs and outputs. Since resources and pollution in form of emissions have gained so much importance during the last decades we incorporate them in our model (see Figure 2.1).

Resources available at period 0 are denoted by the M-vector s^0. Let the M-vector k^0 contain the amounts of intermediate goods which are given historically at the beginning of period 0. These intermediate goods are produced goods, i.e. capital goods. To produce intermediate goods one normally needs intermediate goods as inputs. Yet at some moment in the history of men, intermediate goods had been produced without intermediate goods – just with labour and natural resources. Following this line of argument, each produced set of inputs can be reduced to labour and natural resources if only the starting point is fixed early enough in time. For a developed economy, however, this is not really important. We, therefore, assume that there exist certain stocks of capital goods, with which we can produce. We do not need to presuppose that the activities are such that all goods can be produced by a chain of production processes starting solely from resources. The reason for this procedure is that we are interested only in those developments, which start after a fixed point in time, and not in the development of capital stocks in the whole human history.

The inputs of period 0, a^0, which are formed by the sum of k^0 and s^0, produce the outputs b^1, available in period 1. b^1 is split into a residual M-vector r^1, which contains consumption c^1 and garbage (emissions) g^1, and into k^1. Again k^1 and s^1 form the inputs a^1 of period 1.

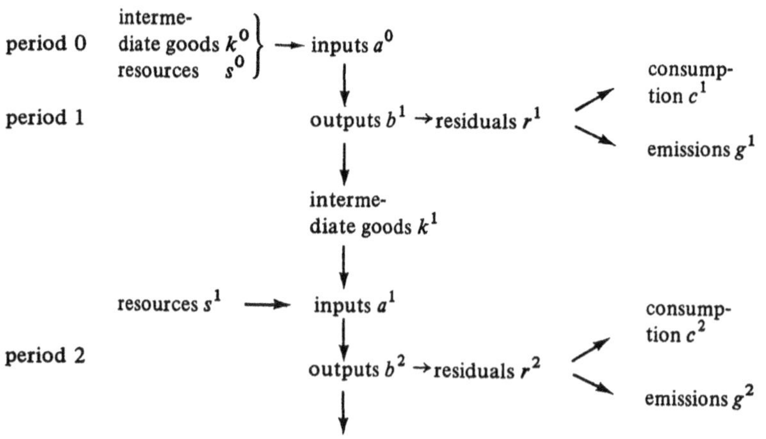

Production Process: Structure of Inputs and Outputs

Fig. 2.1

Definition 2.4 (Production Program, Feasible Production Program)
A $2T \cdot M$-dimensional vector $x = (A^0, \ldots, A^{T-1}) = (a^0, b^1; a^1, b^2; \ldots; a^{T-1}, b^T)$ is called production program if $A^t \in E^t$ for each $0 \leqslant t \leqslant T-1$.

A production program x is called feasible if

$$s^t + b^t - a^t \geqslant 0 \qquad 0 \leqslant t \leqslant T \tag{2.1}$$

(with $b^0 := k^0$ and $a^T := 0$).

The set of all feasible production programs for given s and given k^0 is denoted by $\Pi(s, k^0)$.

Lemma 5
For given s, k^0 the set of feasible production programs $\Pi(s, k^0)$ is convex and bounded.

Proof: The convexity can be proved straightforwardly. The boundedness can easily be shown by induction.

Assumption 2.6 (Consumption Goods)
The residual vector r^t is given by $r^t := s^t + b^t - a^t$.

Out of the M goods of the economy N are consumption goods ($N \leqslant M$). We get the bundle of the consumption goods by the projection

$$\psi : R^{M \cdot T} \rightarrow R^{N \cdot T}, c = \psi(r),$$

where each element of $r = (r^1, \ldots, r^T)$ is eliminated, if it is not apt for consumption.

For the sake of simplicity we do not in this paper consider the effects of emissions g^t on the welfare of individuals.[4])

Definition 2.7 (Feasible Consumption Bundle)
A nonnegative NT-vector $c = (c^1, c^2, \ldots, c^T)$ is called a consumption bundle, if there is a feasible production program

$$x = (A^0, \ldots, A^{T-1}), A^t = (a^t, b^{t+1}), r^t = s^t + b^t - a^t, c = \psi(r).$$

Lemma 2.8
The set $C(s, k^0)$ of all feasible consumption bundles is convex and bounded.

Proof: Immediate.

Definition 2.9 (Efficient Consumption Bundle)
A feasible consumption bundle $\bar{c}$ is efficient, if there is no feasible $\bar{\bar{c}}$ such that $\bar{\bar{c}} \geqslant \bar{c}$.

We note that Lemma 2.8 implies existence and concavity of the intertemporal transformation curve, which we have explicitly derived in some of our previous papers [e.g. *Bernholz/Faber/Reiss* and *Reiss*, 1979a]. The reason for employing Lemma 2.8 instead

---

[4]) These environmental problems are extensively analyzed in *Niemes* [1981, Chap. 3].

of the explicit transformation function is that it considerably simplifies our task to determine the signs of the rates of interest.

To incorporate demand considerations into our analysis we introduce:

Assumption 2.10 (Welfare Function)
A continuous[5]), quasi-concave, strictly increasing intertemporal welfare function $W(c)$ exists.

Instead of using a welfare function, which comprehends all relevant information concerning the preferences of the consumers – and, in particular, their time preference, in which we are interested – we could have used individual preference functions and derived demand functions from them. This approach, however, would enlarge and complicate our analysis. Because of Lemma 2.8 and A2.10 our model is much more simply structured than general intertemporal equilibrium models.

3. Separating Hyperplanes

Almost all of our conclusions will be derived by means of separating hyperplanes. It is therefore expedient to recapitulate first some of their characteristics.

Definition 3.1 (Hyperplanes)
Let $\bar{p} \neq 0$ be an NT-vector and $\bar{\beta}$ a scalar. The set of all NT-vector c which satisfy $\bar{p}c = \bar{\beta}$ is called hyperplane. $\bar{p}$ is called normal to the hyperplane or vector of present prices of the hyperplane.

Definition 3.2 (Separating Hyperplanes)
Let X and Y be two sets in R^N. If for all $x \in X$, $y \in Y$ either

$$\bar{p}x \leqslant \bar{\beta} \leqslant \bar{p}y$$

or

$$\bar{p}x \geqslant \bar{\beta} \geqslant \bar{p}y,$$

then we say that the hyperplane $\bar{p}c = \bar{\beta}$ separates the sets X and Y.

Theorem 3.3
Let X and Y be convex sets in R^N. Let the interior of X, X^0, be unequal to the empty set $\emptyset$ and let $X^0 \cap Y = \emptyset$. Then there exists a hyperplane separating X and Y. (A proof of this well-known theorem is given e.g. in *Roberts/Varberg* [1973, p. 83].)

Definition 3.4 (Preference Set)
Given a welfare function, the preference set of $\bar{c}$ is the set of consumption bundles indifferent or preferred to consumption bundle $\bar{c}$.

---

[5]) A concave function is continuous in the interior of its domain; a quasi-concave, however, is only almost continuous [e.g. *Roberts/Varberg*, p. 332]. The assumption of continuity therefore is an additional restriction.

Because of A2.10 these preference sets are convex and their interiors are nonempty. Due to Lemma 2.8 the set of all feasible consumption bundles is convex, too. Since we know that for an optimal consumption bundle $\bar{c}$ the intersection of the interior of the preference set and of the set of feasible consumption bundles is empty, we conclude from Theorem 3.3 that a hyperplane $\bar{p} \cdot c = \bar{\beta}$ exists, which separates the preference set of $\bar{c}$ from the set of all feasible consumption bundles.

Theorem 3.5
The price vector $\bar{p}$ of the separating hyperplane $\bar{p}c = \bar{\beta}$ is strictly positive and the scalar $\bar{\beta}$ is nonnegative. For all feasible consumption bundles $\tilde{c}$ we have $\bar{p}\tilde{c} \leqslant \bar{\beta}$. For all consumption bundles, $\approx{c}$, which are at least as preferred as the optimal consumption bundle $\bar{c}$ we have $\bar{p}\approx{c} \geqslant \bar{\beta}$.

Similar theorems are well-known in mathematical economics. The proof of the particular formulation of Theorem 3.5 is given in *Reiss* [1979b, 173–174].

4. Positivity of Interest Rates

The central problem in the theory of interest is generally considered to be the question why interest rates are positive in all real economic systems, [e.g. *Malinvaud*, p. 256; *Gale/Rockwell*, p. 347]. In particular the latter two authors believe that the Malinvaud-Starrett Theory of Interest gives a complete answer to this problem: every efficient steady state with growth rate γ in a multisector model is characterized by $\rho \geqslant \gamma$, where ρ denotes the interest rate; the equality sign is valid for a golden rule steady state.

We consider their important result only a partial answer, since it is restricted to a relatively small subset of all efficient programs, viz. the class of proportional programs. To cite [*Solow*, 1970a, p. 7]: "My general conclusion is that the steady state is not a bad place for the theory of growth to start, but may be a dangerous place for it to end." Although" . . . steady states may be a fair first approximation", we know that "Real economies are not in steady states" [*Solow*, 1970b, p. VII–VIII]. In addition, the study of models of heterogeneous capital goods, which we want to investigate in this paper, has shown that there is considerable doubt as to whether the solutions converge to steady states [*Hahn*, and e.g. *Kuga*].

For all these reasons we have directed our analysis at the class of all efficient programs. Our results presented below show that the answer is by no means so clear-cut as in the case of proportional programs: even if there is superiority, roundaboutness and impatience to consume, the rates of interest – except for one own interest rate in one period – need not be positive!

First we prove a similar result as the Malinvaud-Starrett Theory of Interest. In contrast to it we do not assume proportional growth, we do, however, employ impatience to consume or neutrality (Proposition 4.2). In Proportions 4.4 and 4.6 we do not even employ the assumptions of growth or stationarity. First we have to introduce the following concepts: interest rate, interest factor, discount rate, and discount factor.

If $\hat{t} < \hat{\hat{t}}$ the term $p_\nu^{\hat{t}}/p_\nu^{\hat{\hat{t}}}$ is called $(\hat{t}, \hat{\hat{t}})$-period own interest factor of good ν ($\nu = 1, \ldots, N$); the inverse $p_\nu^{\hat{\hat{t}}}/p_\nu^{\hat{t}}$ is called $(\hat{t}, \hat{\hat{t}})$-period own discount factor of good ν.

The term $p_\nu^{\hat{t}}/p_\nu^{\hat{\hat{t}}} - 1 = \rho_\nu^{\hat{t},\hat{\hat{t}}}$, is called $(\hat{t}, \hat{\hat{t}})$-period own interest rate for good ν or $(\hat{t}, \hat{\hat{t}})$-period own discount rate for good ν respectively. From

$$\frac{p_\nu^{\hat{t}}}{p_\nu^{\hat{\hat{t}}}} = \frac{p_\nu^{\hat{t}}}{p_\nu^{\hat{t}+1}} \frac{p_\nu^{\hat{t}+1}}{p_\nu^{\hat{t}+1}} \cdots \frac{p_\nu^{\hat{\hat{t}}-2}}{p_\nu^{\hat{\hat{t}}-1}} \frac{p_\nu^{\hat{\hat{t}}-1}}{p_\nu^{\hat{\hat{t}}}}, \hat{t} < \hat{\hat{t}}, \tag{4.1}$$

it follows that the $(\hat{t}, \hat{\hat{t}})$-period own interest factor is the product of the intermediate one period own interest factors. In the following we will simply speak of interest rates whenever it is clear from the context that we mean an own interest rate of a particular good.

Next we define impatience to consume, which we will say to prevail for good ν if shifting an amount of good ν to an earlier period increases the welfare.

Definition 4.1 (Impatience to Consume)
"Impatience to consume good ν" prevails for a given consumption bundle $\hat{c}$ between τ and $\tau + 1$ if

a) in case $\hat{c}_\nu^\tau \neq \hat{c}_\nu^{\tau+1}$ we have

$$\begin{aligned} &W(\hat{c}) < W(\hat{\hat{c}}) \text{ if } \hat{c}_\nu^\tau < \hat{c}_\nu^{\tau+1} \\ &W(\hat{c}) > W(\hat{\hat{c}}) \text{ if } \hat{c}_\nu^\tau > \hat{c}_\nu^{\tau+1} \end{aligned} \tag{4.2}$$

with [6] $\hat{\hat{c}} := \hat{c} + e_{(\tau-1)N+\nu} (\hat{c}_\nu^{\tau+1} - \hat{c}_\nu^\tau) + e_{\tau N+\nu} (\hat{c}_\nu^\tau - \hat{c}_\nu^{\tau+1})$,

b) in case $\hat{c}_\nu^\tau = \hat{c}_\nu^{\tau+1}$ there exists an $\epsilon > 0$ so that

$$W(\hat{c}) < W(\hat{\hat{c}})$$

with $\hat{\hat{c}} := \hat{c} + e_{(\tau-1)N+\nu}\,\epsilon - e_{\tau N+\nu}\,\epsilon$.

Proposition 4.2
Assume that impatience to consume good ν for $\hat{c}$ between τ and $\tau + 1$ exists. Let $\hat{c}$ be the optimal bundle with

$$\hat{c}_\nu^{\tau+1} \geqslant \hat{c}_\nu^\tau, \tag{4.3}$$

i.e. consumption of good ν does not decrease between τ and $\tau + 1$. In this case, the own interest rate of good ν between τ and $\tau + 1$ is positive.

[6] e_n is the n-th unit vector of dimension NT.

Proof
Let $\hat{p}$ be the normal of the hyperplane to $\hat{c}$.
Assume, contrary to the proposition

$$\hat{p}_\nu^\tau \leqslant \hat{p}_\nu^{\tau+1}. \tag{4.4}$$

a) Assume $\hat{c}_\nu^{\tau+1} > \hat{c}_\nu^\tau$.
Consider $\hat{\hat{c}}$ which is equal to $\hat{c}$ except that the components of good ν in period τ and $\tau + 1$ are interchanged, then we obtain

$$\hat{p} \cdot \hat{\hat{c}} = \hat{p} \cdot \hat{c} - \hat{p}_\nu^\tau \hat{c}_\nu^\tau + \hat{p}_\nu^\tau \hat{c}_\nu^{\tau+1} + \hat{p}_\nu^{\tau+1} \hat{c}_\nu^\tau - \hat{p}_\nu^{\tau+1} \hat{c}_\nu^{\tau+1}$$

$$= \hat{p}\hat{c} + (\hat{p}_\nu^\tau - \hat{p}_\nu^{\tau+1})(\hat{c}_\nu^{\tau+1} - \hat{c}_\nu^\tau). \tag{4.5}$$

The first bracket is nonpositive because of (4.4) and the second nonnegative because of (4.3). Hence

$$\hat{p}\hat{\hat{c}} \leqslant \hat{p}\hat{c} = \hat{\beta}.$$

$\hat{\hat{c}}$ therefore does not lie above the hyperplane $\hat{p}c - \hat{\beta} = 0$. On the other hand from the definition of impatience we get

$$W(\hat{\hat{c}}) > W(\hat{c}),$$

which implies that $\hat{\hat{c}}$ lies above the hyperplane, so that $\hat{c}$ cannot be optimal.
The proof for the case $\hat{c}_\nu^{\tau+1} < \hat{c}_\nu^\tau$ is analogous.

b) Assume $\hat{c}_\nu^\tau = \hat{c}_\nu^{\tau+1}$

$$\hat{\hat{c}} := \hat{c} + \epsilon(e_{(\tau-1)N+\nu} - e_{\tau N+\nu})$$

$$\hat{p}\hat{\hat{c}} = \hat{p}\hat{c} + \epsilon(\hat{p}_\nu^\tau - \hat{p}_\nu^{\tau+1}) \leqslant \hat{p}\hat{c} = \beta.$$

On the other hand we have

$$W(\hat{\hat{c}}) > W(\hat{c}),$$

which again gives a contradiction.

We note that we have used only growth or stationarity concerning good ν and impatience to consume good ν in Proposition 4.2. However, it can be shown for a special kind of a two period multisector model that superiority and roundaboutness must be present in the circumstances of Proposition 4.2 [see *Bernholz/Faber/Reiss*, Proposition 3.4, p. 46].

In the next two propositions we will investigate the interrelation between roundaboutness, superiority and the positivity of own interest rates. First we state

Definition 4.3 (Short-Term-Superiority and -Roundaboutness)
Assume that bundle $\bar{c}$ of program $\bar{x}$ differs from bundle $\bar{\bar{c}}$ of program $\bar{\bar{x}}$ only in the

components of good ν, i.e.

$$\bar{c}_j^t = \bar{\bar{c}}_j^t \quad \text{for all} \quad \begin{array}{l} 1 \leqslant j \leqslant N \\ 1 \leqslant t \leqslant T \\ j \neq \nu . \end{array} \tag{4.6}$$

$\bar{\bar{x}}$ is called "short-term-superior to $\bar{x}$ in period τ regarding good ν" if

$$\bar{\bar{c}}_\nu^{\tau+1} + \bar{\bar{c}}_\nu^\tau > \bar{c}_\nu^{\tau+1} + \bar{c}_\nu^\tau \tag{4.7}$$

and

$$\bar{\bar{c}}_\nu^t \geqslant \bar{c}_\nu^t \quad t \neq \tau, \tau+1. \tag{4.8}$$

It is called "short-term-roundabout to $\bar{x}$ in period τ regarding good ν" if

$$\begin{array}{l} \bar{\bar{c}}_\nu^\tau < \bar{c}_\nu^\tau \\ \bar{\bar{c}}_\nu^t \leqslant \bar{c}_\nu^t \quad 1 \leqslant t < \tau . \end{array} \tag{4.9}$$

To motivate our definition we observe: If in an arbitrary period τ we switch from one program $\bar{x}$ to another one $\bar{\bar{x}}$, we change nothing in the bygone periods, this follows from (4.8) and (4.9). Let us assume that switching to $\bar{\bar{x}}$ in period τ is combined with "saving", which means abstaining from the respective consumption good in τ. If this sacrifice is more than compensated after one period without sacrifices in later periods (and without sacrifices in other consumption goods), we call program $\bar{\bar{x}}$ short-term-superior and short-time-roundabout to $\bar{\bar{x}}$.

Proposition 4.4
Let $\bar{x}$ be the optimal program. If there exists a program $\bar{\bar{x}}$ which is short-term-roundabout and short-term-superior to $\bar{x}$ in period τ regarding good ν then the one period interest rate is positive in τ.

Proof
Let $\bar{c}$ be the consumption bundle of the optimal program and $pc = \bar{\beta}$ the separating hyperplane through $\bar{c}$.

Assume the one period interest rate is nonpositive, i.e.

$$p_\nu^\tau \leqslant p_\nu^{\tau+1}. \tag{4.10}$$

From (4.7) and Theorem 3.5 we get

$$p_\nu^\tau \sum_{t=\tau}^{\tau+1} (\bar{\bar{c}}_\nu^t - \bar{c}_\nu^t) > 0 \tag{4.11}$$

and from (4.11), (4.7), (4.9) and (4.10)

$$0 < p_\nu^\tau (\bar{\bar{c}}_\nu^\tau - \bar{c}_\nu^\tau) + p_\nu^\tau (\bar{\bar{c}}_\nu^{\tau+1} - \bar{c}_\nu^{\tau+1}) \leqslant p_\nu^\tau (\bar{\bar{c}}_\nu^\tau - \bar{c}_\nu^\tau) + p_\nu^{\tau+1} (\bar{\bar{c}}_\nu^{\tau+1} - \bar{c}_\nu^{\tau+1}) =$$

$$= \sum_{t=\tau}^{\tau+1} p_\nu^t (\bar{\bar{c}}_\nu^t - \bar{c}_\nu^t) \tag{4.12}$$

and from (4.8) and (4.9) $\bar{\bar{c}}_\nu^t = \bar{c}_\nu^t$, $1 \leqslant t < \tau$. Hence we obtain

$$0 < \sum_{t=1}^{\tau+1} p_\nu^t (\bar{\bar{c}}_\nu^t - \bar{c}_\nu^t). \tag{4.13}$$

Applying (4.8) we obtain from (4.13)

$$0 < \sum_{t=1}^{T} p_\nu^t (\bar{\bar{c}}_\nu^t - \bar{c}_\nu^t). \tag{4.14}$$

Since $\bar{c}$ is optimal, we know that $p\bar{\bar{c}} \leqslant \bar{\beta}$, hence because of Theorem 3.5 p cannot be a price vector to $\bar{c}$, which proves our Proposition 4.4.

Next we introduce:

Definition 4.5 (Long-Term-Superiority and -Roundaboutness)
A program $\bar{\bar{x}}$ with consumption bundle $\bar{\bar{c}}$ is called "long-term-superior to $\bar{x}$ regarding good ν" if

$$\bar{c}_j^t = \bar{\bar{c}}_j^t \quad \text{for all} \quad \begin{array}{l} 1 \leqslant j \leqslant N \\ 1 \leqslant t \leqslant T \\ j \neq \nu \end{array} \tag{4.15}$$

and

$$\sum_{t=1}^{T} \bar{\bar{c}}_\nu^t > \sum_{t=1}^{T} \bar{c}_\nu^t. \tag{4.16}$$

It is called "long-term-roundabout to $\bar{x}$ regarding good ν" if (4.15) holds and if there exists a τ with

$$\bar{\bar{c}}_\nu^\tau < \bar{c}_\nu^\tau \tag{4.17}$$

$$\bar{\bar{c}}_\nu^t \leqslant \bar{c}_\nu^t \qquad t < \tau \tag{4.18}$$

$$\bar{\bar{c}}_\nu^t \geqslant \bar{c}_\nu^t \qquad t > \tau. \tag{4.19}$$

Proposition 4.6
The interest rate of good ν is positive in at least one period if there exists a long-term-superior and long-term-roundabout program $\bar{\bar{x}}$ to the optimal program $\bar{x}$.

Proof
Let $\bar{c}$ be the consumption bundle of the optimal program and $\bar{\bar{c}}$ that of $\bar{\bar{x}}$. Let us assume that all interest rates are non-positive, i.e.

$$p_\nu^1 \leqslant p_\nu^2 \leqslant \cdots \leqslant p_\nu^T. \tag{4.20}$$

Then we get from (4.17), (4.18) and (4.20)

$$p_\nu^t(\bar{\bar{c}}_\nu^t - \bar{c}_\nu^t) \geqslant p_\nu^\tau(\bar{\bar{c}}_\nu^t - \bar{c}_\nu^t) \qquad t \leqslant \tau \tag{4.21}$$

and from (4.19) and (4.20)

$$p_\nu^t(\bar{\bar{c}}_\nu^t - \bar{c}_\nu^t) \geqslant p_\nu^\tau(\bar{\bar{c}}_\nu^t - \bar{c}_\nu^t) \qquad t > \tau. \tag{4.22}$$

We therefore conclude from (4.21) and (4.22)

$$p_\nu^t(\bar{\bar{c}}_\nu^t - \bar{c}_\nu^t) \geqslant p_\nu^\tau(\bar{\bar{c}}_\nu^t - \bar{c}_\nu^t) \qquad \text{for all} \quad 1 \leqslant t \leqslant T \tag{4.23}$$

and from (4.23) and (4.16)

$$\sum_{t=1}^{T} p_\nu^t(\bar{\bar{c}}_\nu^t - \bar{c}_\nu^t) \geqslant p_\nu^\tau \sum_{t=1}^{T} (\bar{\bar{c}}_\nu^t - \bar{c}_\nu^t) > 0. \tag{4.24}$$

Using Theorem 3.5 we thus obtain that p is not a price vector of $\bar{c}$, which is contrary to our assumption. Hence we conclude that at least one interest rate is positive. If this is a short-term rate of interest, we have proved our Proposition 4.6. Let us now assume it is a long-term rate of interest. We know that the long-term interest factor is equal to the product of the corresponding short-term interest factors. To make this product bigger than one, again at least one short term rate of interest has to be positive. Q.e.d.

From the existence of long-term-superior and long-term-roundabout programs alone we can get only relatively weak conclusions. Only one interest rate has to be positive. If one wants to obtain stronger conclusions, one has to use stronger assumptions; such stronger assumptions are e.g. used in Propositions 4.2 and 4.4. We call the reader's attention to the fact that we have employed only the quasi-concavity of the welfare function but not the form of the time preference for Proposition 4.6. Thus one might surmise that the inclusion of this characteristic leads to stronger results. This, however, is not the case as Remark 4.7 shows.

Remark 4.7
Quasiconcavity, impatience, long-term superiority and long-term-roundaboutness do not imply a positive rate of interest for each period.

We will discuss below the economic implications of this remark, which we demonstrate by the following

Example
We set $N = 1$ and use a time horizon of $T = 4$ periods and assume that the welfare function is given by

$$W(c^1, c^2, c^3, c^4) = (c^1 + \alpha^1)(c^2 + \alpha^2)(c^3 + \alpha^3)(c^4 + \alpha^4) \tag{4.25}$$

with

$\alpha^1 = 0.005637$ $\qquad \alpha^2 = 0.015637$
$\alpha^3 = 0.024546$ $\qquad \alpha^4 = 0.036$

Given this quasiconcave welfare function, there is impatience to consume in each period.[7] Let the set of feasible bundles be given by

$$C = \{c: c \geqslant 0, \bar{a}c \leqslant 3.742\overline{36}, \bar{a} = (1.0, 1.0, 0.8, 1.\overline{09})\}. \tag{4.26}$$

We examine bundle $\bar{c}$ given by

$$\bar{c} = (0.95, 0.94, 1.17, 0.84).$$

This bundle is feasible as

$$\bar{a} \cdot \bar{c} = 3.742\overline{36};$$

it is optimal because the derivations of W in point $\bar{c}$, viz. $\partial W/\partial c^t = \prod_{\substack{\tau=1 \\ \tau \neq t}}^{4} (c^\tau + \alpha^\tau)$ have the values

$$(\partial W/\partial c^1, \partial W/\partial c^2, \partial W/\partial c^3, \partial W/\partial c^4) = (1.0, 1.0, 0.8, 1.\overline{09}) = \bar{a}.$$

Thus in $\bar{c}$ the indifference surface is tangent to the boundary plane of the feasible set.

The prices in $\bar{c}$ are given by

$$\bar{p} = \bar{a} = (1.0, 1.0, 0.8, 1.\overline{09}).$$

Hence we get the following interest rates

$$\rho^{12} = 0\%, \rho^{23} = 20\%, \rho^{34} = -26.\overline{6}\%$$

$$\rho^{13} = 25\% \;\; \rho^{24} = -8.3\%$$

$$\rho^{14} = -8.3\%.$$

Usually the average interest rate is defined by

$$\bar{\rho} = \left(\sqrt[3]{\frac{p^1}{p^4}} - 1\right) 100\,\% = -2.3\%.$$

It therefore follows that the average interest rate between periods 1 and 4 is negative, too.

Finally we have to show that a long-term-superior and long-term-roundabout program $\tilde{x}$ to the optimal program $\bar{x}$ exists. Such a program is e.g. that with the bundle

$$\tilde{c} = (0.94, 0.93, 1.18, 0.851).$$

This program is feasible because

$$\bar{a}\tilde{c} = 3.742\overline{36}.$$

---

[7]) These special values of α^t are introduced only to get smooth results for $\bar{c}$ and $\bar{p}$. It can be easily shown that impatience holds if $\alpha^t < \alpha^{t+1}$.

It is long-term-roundabout and long-term-superior compared with $\bar{x}$ as

$$\tilde{c}^1 < \bar{c}^1, \tilde{c}^2 < \bar{c}^2, \tilde{c}^3 > \bar{c}^3, \tilde{c}^4 > \bar{c}^4$$

and

$$\tilde{c}^1 + \tilde{c}^2 + \tilde{c}^3 + \tilde{c}^4 = 3.901 > 3.900 = \bar{c}^1 + \bar{c}^2 + \bar{c}^3 + \bar{c}^4.$$

We want to comment on this example and demonstrate how our Propositions 4.2, 4.4 and 4.6 apply. First $\bar{x}$ is characterized by decreasing consumption supplies between periods one and two and between three and four; otherwise – according to Proposition 4.2 – interest rates ρ^{12} and ρ^{34} would have been positive. Second, there is one positive rate of interest; this meets Proposition 4.6. Although all assumptions of Remark 4.7 are fulfilled, the short-term interest rate ρ^{34} and above all the average rate of interest $\bar{\rho}$ are negative.

In order to show that we have used all of *Böhm/Bawerk*'s [1921, 328–362] three reasons in our example, we still have to demonstrate that the welfare function (4.25) implies his first reason. For this purpose we quote that passage which seems to us most pertinent: "If a person in the present has a lack of certain goods, or goods in general, and while he can hope to be better provided for a future period, he will value a given amount of immediately available goods more highly than the same amount of future goods" [p. 328] (our translation).

There are, of course, several possibilities to formalize this first reason [e.g. *Frisch*, p. 421; see also *Arvidson*]. We will employ the following one: We say that the first reason holds[8]) if for all consumption bundles c with $c_\nu^{\hat{t}} < c_\nu^{\hat{\hat{t}}}$ $(\hat{t} < \hat{\hat{t}})$ we get $W(c + \epsilon e_{(\hat{t}-1)N+\nu}) > W(c + \epsilon e_{(\hat{\hat{t}}-1)N+\nu})$. We have to show that the welfare function of our example (with $N = 1$ and $\nu = 1$) has this property:

$$W(c + \epsilon e_{\hat{t}}) = W(c) + \epsilon \prod_{\substack{t=1 \\ t \neq \hat{t}}}^{4} (c^t + \alpha^t)$$

$$W(c + \epsilon e_{\hat{\hat{t}}}) = W(c) + \epsilon \prod_{\substack{t=1 \\ t \neq \hat{\hat{t}}}}^{4} (c^t + \alpha^t).$$

As $c^{\hat{t}} < c^{\hat{\hat{t}}}$ and $\alpha^{\hat{t}} < \alpha^{\hat{\hat{t}}}$ we get

$$\epsilon \prod_{\substack{t=1 \\ t \neq \hat{t}}}^{4} (c^t + \alpha^t) > \epsilon \prod_{\substack{t=1 \\ t \neq \hat{\hat{t}}}}^{4} (c^t + \alpha^t),$$

---

[8]) For those readers who have the impression that our formalization of the first reason is already implied by our impatience definition we point out that it is possible to construct examples of welfare functions with impatience but where the first reason (as formalized by us) does not hold. These examples, however, are not quasiconcave.

hence $W(c + \epsilon e_{\hat{t}}) > W(c + \epsilon e_{\hat{\hat{t}}})$.

Obviously, the reason for our relatively weak result concerning the signs of the rates of interest in Proposition 4.6 in comparison to Proposition 4.4 is that we have employed in the former the long-term-superiority (Definition 4.5) and in the latter the short-term-superiortiy (Definition 4.3). Which form prevails in reality depends partly on the choice of the length of the periods. If they are long enough, then we believe that short-term-superiority prevails in most sectors of an economy.

A long period, however, would imply a high level of aggregation in the technology of our model. To avoid this, we prefer to choose a short unit for the time period, which means that we have to apply the weak form of superiority and thus obtain Proposition 4.6. We want to stress that Proposition 4.6 does not say that the rates of interest have to be nonpositive in some periods, but only that this is not excluded.

Examples for which the presuppositions of Remark 4.7 are valid and for which we find negative rates of interest are easily found in reality, viz. in the agricultural sector: the present real prices of fruits or vegetables during the summer are considerably lower than those during the winter. Proposition 4.6 allows for these kinds of phenomena.

5. Relationship to Fisher's 'The Theory of Interest'

Finally, we want to comment on the relationship between Fisher's and our approach. We will proceed in two steps:

1. We show the influence of Böhm-Bawerk's work on Fisher's theory of interest and the difference between the two approaches.
2. The same questions will be answered for Fisher's and our approach.

To 1)

To indicate the extent of this influence, it is useful to remember that *Fisher* dedicated his book "To the memory of John Rae and of Eugen von Böhm-Bawerk who laid the foundations upon which I have endeavoured to build". While he accepted the first two of Böhm-Bawerk's reasons he maintained: "It is the third circumstance – the so-called superiority of present over future goods – which, as I shall try to show, contains fundamental errors. My criticism . . . does not . . . consist in denying the *existence* or *importance* of the 'technical' element in interest but in denying the soundness of the way in which Böhm-Bawerk applies it," [*Fisher*, p. 474/5]. *Fisher* sees the main fault in the fact" . . . that technical superiority actually depends for its force on the presence of these other two circumstances and is *not* independent." [*Fisher*, p. 483]. We agree not only on this point[9]) and on his assessment that the "concept of an average production period is . . . far too arbitrary and indefinite to form a basis for the reasoning that Böhm-Bawerk attempts to base upon it" [*Fisher*, p. 465], but also that: "Perhaps the most interesting point about Böhm–Bawerk's failure correctly to formulate the 'technical' feature which he thus vainly sought is that it is really much simpler than he imagined." [*Fisher*, p. 484]. *Fisher's* solution to this problem was the introduction of his investment opportunity principles [*Fisher*, chap. VII, VIII, XI and XIII]. It is interesting to note that he justifies

[9]) See also ***Kuenne*** [1962] for an elaborate discussion.

it in the following way: "I have generally avoided the term productivity of capital . . . because it suggests that capital produces income value instead of the reverse . . . The concept of investment opportunity rests on that of an 'option'. An option is any possible income stream open to an individual by utilizing his resources, capital, labor, land money, to produce or secure said income stream." [*Fisher*, pp. 151/2]. Thus he concentrates on the income stream and disentangles the theory of interest from the complications of the production side: ". . . it does not seem to me that the theory of interest is called upon to launch itself upon a lengthy discussion of the production process, division of labor, utilization of land, capital, and scientific management. The problem is confined to discover how production is related to the rate of interest." [*Fisher*, p. 473]. This procedure enabled him to realize his main aim to reduce the theory of interest to its simplest terms [*Fisher*, p. 485].

To 2)
The conciseness and elegance of Fischer's approach has led us to employ a similar one in this paper. While he used income, we have disaggregated to a consumption set, whose boundaries correspond to his investment opportunity curve. But there is one great difference, which the reader of this paper, who is not familiar with our previous ones, may perhaps be not so much aware of. In contrast to Fisher we have not reduced the production side of the economy to its bones but have at least retained its time structure (see Figure 2.1). In particular, this time element shows up in our formulation of the law of superiority of roundabout methods (see Definitions 4.3 and 4.5), which we have used to characterize the consumption sets in this paper. In *Bernholz/Faber/Reiss* [1978] and *Reiss* [1979a] we even explicitly derived the respective intertemporal transformation curves.

Why do we stress this difference so much, although one could simply determine the signs of the rate of interest in a Fisherian model by making assumptions regarding the slope of the boundaries of the consumption set? We would not be so concerned if we were just interested in a modern restatement of his theory of interest in a general multiperiod multisector model. But this paper is, as we have mentioned in our introduction, only one link in a series of papers to develop a modern formulation of Austrian capital theory for which in our opinion the consideration of the time structure of production is of fundamental importance.

Fisher's justified neglect of it for the sake of simplicity has led neoclassical writers to use malleable capital and implicity the assumption of a balanced stock of capital goods, which ". . . abstracts from problems association in a growing and changing world with the building up and running down of productive operations, which obviously make the static 'production function' relation between inputs, including capital, and outputs inapplicable without considerable modification in the direction of attaching a time-profile to the process." [*Johnson*, p. 129]. We believe it is this neglect of the time aspect of production, which is the reason, why *Schumpeter* [1954, p. 872] wrote: "Fisher did not fully realize the extent of Böhm-Bawerk's achievement and was unduely influenced by the surface defects of the latter's exposition."

References

Arvidson: On the Reasons for a Rate of Interest. International Economic Papers **6**, 1956, 23–33. (Originally published in Swedish in Ekonomisk Tidskrift, March 1953.)

Bernholz, P.: Superiority of Roundabout Processes and Positive Rate of Interest. A Simple Model of Capital and Growth. Kyklos **24**, 1971, 687–721.

Bernholz, P., M. Faber and *W. Reiss*: A Neo-Austrian Two Period Multisector Model of Capital. Journal of Economic Theory **17**, 1978, 38–50.

Böhm-Bawerk, E.v.: Kapital und Kapitalzins. 2. Abteilung, Positive Theorie des Kapitales. 1st and 2nd Volume, 4th edition, Jena 1921. English Translation: Positive Theory of Capital. London 1891.

Bruno, M., E. Burmeister and *E. Sheshinski*: The Nature and Implications of the Reswitching of Techniques. Quarterly Journal of Economics **80**, 1966, 526–553.

Burmeister, E.: Synthesizing the Neo-Austrian and Alternative Approaches to Capital Theory: A Survey. Journal of Economic Literature **12**, 1974, 413–456.

Faber, M.: Introduction to Modern Austrian Capital Theory, Lecture Notes in Economics and Mathematical Systems 167. Heidelberg 1979.

Fisher, I.: The Theory of Interest. New York 1930.

Frisch, R.: Dynamic Utility. Econometrica **32**, 1964, 418–424.

Gale, D., and *R. Rockwell*: On the Interest Rate Theorems of Malinvaud and Starrett. Econometrica **43**, 1975, 347–359.

Hahn, F.H.: Equilibrium Dynamics with Heterogeneous Capital Goods. Quarterly Journal of Economics **80**, 1966, 633–646.

Hicks, J.R.: Capital and Time: A Neo-Austrian Theory. Oxford 1973.

–: Some Questions of Time in Economics. Evolution, Welfare, Time in Economics. Ed. by A.M. Tang, F.M. Westfield and J.S. Worley. Lexington, Mass. Toronto 1976, 135–151.

Johnson, H.G.: The Theory of Income Distribution. London 1973.

Kemeny, J.G., O. Morgenstern and *G.L. Thompson*: A Generalization of the von Neumann Model of an Expanding Economy. Econometrica **24**, 1956, 115–135.

Kuenne, R.E.: The Stationary State and the Technological Superiority of Present Goods. Quarterly Journal of Economics **76**, 1962, 648–652.

Kuga, K.: General Saddlepoint property of the Steady-State of a Growth Model with Heterogeneous Capital Goods. International Economic Review **18**, 1977, 29–58.

Malinvaud, E.: Capital Accumulation and Efficient Allocation of Resources. Econometrica **21**, 1953, 233–268.

Morgenstern, O.: Das Zeitmoment in der Wertlehre. Zeitschrift für Nationalökonomie **5**, 1934, 433–458.

–: Zur Theorie der Produktionsperiode (On the Theory of the Production Period). Zeitschrift für Nationalökonomie **6**, 1935, 196–208.

– (Ed.): Economic Activity Analysis. New York 1954.

Niemes, H.: Die Umwelt als Schadstoffempfänger. Wasergütewirtschaft als Beispiel. Tübingen 1981.

Reiss, W.: Substitution in a Neo-Austrian Model of Capital. Zeitschrift für Nationalökonomie **39**, 1979a, 33–52.

–: Umwegproduktion und Positivität des Zinses. Eine neo-österreichische Analyse. Habilitationsschrift, Heidelberg 1979b.

Roberts, A.W., and *D.E. Varberg*: Convex Functions. New York–London 1973.

Schumpeter, J.A.: History of Economic Analysis. London 1954.

Solow, R.M.: Growth Theory. Oxford 1970a.

–: Foreword of Mathematical Theories of Economic Growth by E. Burmeister and A.R. Dobell. London 1970b.

Games, Economic Dynamics, and Time Series Analysis. 1982 ©Physica-Verlag, Wien–Würzburg

The Time Structure of Inputs and Outputs and the Formation of Employment Cycles

By *A. Wenig*, Bielefeld[1])

1. Introduction and Summary

After *Hicks* [1973] published his book "Capital and Time" in 1973 economists have paid growing attention to the so-called "Neo-Austrian" economic theory. The bulk of issues hitherto discussed in this field belongs to capital and growth theory. In particular research has been concentrated upon the analysis of steady states and the traverse between two steady states with different technologies [see e.g. *Burmeister; Bernholz/Faber/ Reiss; Weizsäcker*].

Characteristic of Neo-Austrian theories is the way in which they describe a production process. In these models it is assumed that an input today does not only help to produce the current output but that it contributes to the production of the output of a sequence of future periods. On the other hand the output today must be considered as the result of a series of inputs in the past. Accordingly, a Neo-Austrian production process is formally given by two function $a(\theta)$ and $b(\theta)$ which represent respectively the inputs and the outputs at operational time θ (the time elapsed after the start of the process). But while in conventional production models the notion of "input" comprises all types of intermediate products (tools, machines, semi-finished products, etc.) inputs in the Neo-Austrian models are only the "original" factors of production, namely labour services and natural resources. These "commodities of the highest order" are step by step transformed into commodities of lower order (capital goods). The final result on the last stage of production is a flow of consumption commodities which are the commodities of the first order. This flow is given by the function $b(\theta)$. The intermediate products do not explicitely appear in the formal representation of a Neo-Austrian production process.

In general, $a(\theta)$ and $b(\theta)$ must be supposed to be vectors of different commodities. We simplify, however, drastically by assuming that homogenous labour is the only original factor of production. The output is composed of various consumption commodities. But they are assumed to be produced in fixed proportion so that output can be measured in "standard baskets" of consumption commodities. Therefore, both $a(\theta)$ and $b(\theta)$ are scalars. Operational time θ and, subsequently, calendar time t are continuous variables.

Given the real wage rate and the rate of interest on the credit market an investor can calculate the real yield (capital value in terms of "standard baskets" of consumption com-

[1]) Prof. Dr. *A. Wenig*, Universität Bielefeld, Fakultät für Wirtschaftswissenschaften, Universitätsstr., D–4800 Bielefeld 1.

modities) by discounting the real net profits of future periods. If the capital value is positive then there is an extra profit as compared to an investment in a financial asset. A negative capital value indicates a rate of return on investment in a production process which is lower than the rate of interest on the credit market. In Neo-Austrian theories it is usually assumed that neither of these two cases can occur. The interaction of demand and supply on both the credit and the labour market are assumed to establish a rate of interest and a real wage at which there is no difference in the yield of an investment in a production process or in a financial asset. In other words in Neo-Austrian theories the economy is always assumed to be on the factor price frontier (the "efficiency curve" in Hicks' terminology).

In our model we shall drop this assumption. We shall let the real wage gradually go up or down according to the rate of unemployment on the labour market. The real rate of interest, on the other hand, will be considered as an exogenous variable. We assume that the monetary authorities manipulate the credit market such that the difference between the money rate of interest and the rate of inflation remains constant. Then the real rate of interest does not change over time. Under these conditions we shall show that our model economy produces a permanent cyclical impulse. All important variables such as employment, output, investment, real wage, income distribution etc. will turn out to continuously fluctuate. This result is obtained under various assumptions on the way in which investors decide upon the number of processes started in each period.

2. The Model

We assume that there is one elementary production process that lasts a period of length T. This process is described by two functions $a(\theta)$ and $b(\theta)$, $0 \leqslant \theta \leqslant T$, which give the time profiles of, respectively, inputs and outputs. In particular, we assume that $a(\theta)$ and $b(\theta)$ are the following two step functions:

$$a(\theta) = \begin{cases} a_k & \text{for } \theta \in [t_{k-1}, t_k),\ k = 1, \ldots, m' - 1, \\ a_{m'} & \text{for } \theta \in [t_{m'-1}, t_{m'}] \end{cases}$$

$$b(\theta) = \begin{cases} b_k & \text{for } \theta \in [s_{k-1}, s_k),\ k = 1, \ldots, m'' - 1, \\ b_{m''} & \text{for } \theta \in [s_{m''-1}, s_{m''}] \end{cases}$$

where the a_k's, b_k's, $a_{m'}$, $b_{m''}$ are constants and where $t_0 = s_0 = 0$, and $t_{m'} = s_{m''} = T$. "[" and "(" mean closed and open interval ends respectively. $a(\theta)$ denotes the flow of labour inputs at time θ and $b(\theta)$ is the flow of final outputs measured in standard baskets of consumption commodities.

As we do not require $a_k \neq a_{k+1}$ or $b_k \neq b_{k+1}$ we may allow for $m' = m''$ and $t_k = s_k$ for $k = 1, \ldots, m'$. Furthermore, let the interval ends $t_1, t_2, \ldots$ be rational numbers (which is not a restriction under an economic point of view). Then there is a largest rational number Ω such that $t_1, t_2, \ldots$ are integer multiples of Ω. We can, therefore, assume that all intervals $[0, t_1), [t_1, t_2), \ldots, [t_{m'-1}, t_{m'}]$ have the same length and our two profile functions are thus described by

$$a(\theta) = \begin{cases} a_k & \text{for } \theta \in [(k-1)\,\Omega, k\Omega),\ k = 1, \ldots, m-1 \\ a_m & \text{for } \theta \in [(m-1)\,\Omega, m\Omega] \end{cases} \tag{1}$$

$$b(\theta) = \begin{cases} b_k & \text{for } \theta \in [(k-1)\,\Omega, k\Omega),\ k = 1, \ldots, m-1 \\ b_m & \text{for } \theta \in [(m-1)\,\Omega, m\Omega]. \end{cases} \tag{2}$$

Obviously, $a_1, \ldots, a_m$ and $b_1, \ldots, b_m$ must all be non-negative. In addition we have $a_1 > 0$ since the process should really begin at time 0.

Firms are assumed to be able to operate the process on any non-negative scale. Let t stand for (continuous) calendar time and let $x(t)$ denote the scale ("number") of processes started at time t. Processes that began more than $m\Omega$ time units ago are dead. If $\tau \in [(k-1)\,\Omega, k\Omega)$ with $k = 1, \ldots, m-1$ or $\tau \in [(m-1)\,\Omega, m\Omega]$ then total labour input at time t of processes startet at time $t-\tau$ is, respectively, $a_k x(t-\tau)$ or $a_m x(t-\tau)$. Total labour input $N(t)$ of all processes still operating at time t is

$$N(t) = \sum_{k=1}^{m} a_k \int_{(k-1)\Omega}^{k\Omega} x(t-\tau)\, d\tau. \tag{3}$$

Analogously, total output $C(t)$ of consumption commodities at time t can be derived as

$$C(t) = \sum_{k=1}^{m} b_k \int_{(k-1)\Omega}^{k\Omega} x(t-\tau)\, d\tau. \tag{4}$$

A crucial issue in Neo-Austrian models is the determination of the activity level. How many processes will be started at time t? There are several ways of answering this question. In steady state analysis the time path of $x(t)$ can be derived from the full employment condition. In a Hicks-type fix wage model a constant "take out" (consumption out of profits) determines how much firms can and will invest into new processes. Close to this assumption would be the following "Keynes-type" hypotheses: Suppose $x(t)$ is changed in proportion with the excess of consumption demand $C^d(t)$ over actual output $C(t)$ of consumption commodities, i.e.

$$\dot{x}(t) = \gamma\,[C^d(t) - C(t)] \tag{5}$$

where γ is some positive constant. Furthermore, assume a constant consumption C_0 out of profits and a constant marginal propensity to consume for labour income. Let w denote the real wage. Then $C^d(t) = C_0 + cwN(t)$ and (5) can be written as

$$\dot{x}(t) = \gamma\,[C_0 + \sum_{k=1}^{m} (cwa_k - b_k) \int_{(k-1)\Omega}^{k\Omega} x(t-\tau)\, d\tau]. \tag{6}$$

This equation will, however, not be analysed in detail. We shall come back to it in the last section where we show that it can formally be treated like the model we deal with first. Here, we assume that the rate of starts $x(t)$ is proportional with the profit $K(t)$ a process is expected to yield. In particular we write

$$x(t) = \begin{cases} \mu K(t) & \text{of } K(t) > 0 \\ 0 & \text{otherwise} \end{cases} \tag{7}$$

because it should be obvious that no new processes will be started if they are not profitable. μ is a positive constant. In a world without uncertainty the type of investment behaviour described by (7) would not be rational. Since we have constant returns to scale a positive expected profit out of one process would induce investors to start an infinite number of processes in order to maximise their total profit. We assume, however, that investment is risky because profit expectations may (and will) turn out to be wrong in the future. A high indicator $K(t)$ of expected profits is interpreted only as a good chance for a high return on investment while the risk of a loss firms reckon with is considered as low. A small $K(t)$ indicates just the opposite.

What expected profits are depends on how firms forecast future prices because we assume that the input output coefficients of the process are known to the investors. The price of a unit of output (one standard basket of consumption commodities) is taken as a numéraire. The real rate of interest r is exogenously given and constant over time. We assume the banking system to borrow and to lend money at a money rate of interest which is the sum of r and the rate of inflation. At time t let investors expect that the real wage at time $\theta \geqslant t$ will be $v(\theta, t)$. Then future profits of a process discounted at time t (i.e. the capital value of the process) are given by

$$K(t) = \sum_{k=1}^{m} e^{-r(k-1)\Omega} \int_{(k-1)\Omega}^{k\Omega} (b_k - v(\theta, t)\, a_k)\, e^{-r\theta}\, d\theta. \tag{8}$$

In the first part of the paper we assume investors to be myopic, i.e. they expect that the current real wage $w(t)$ continues to prevail in the future:

$$v(\theta, t) = w(t). \tag{9}$$

In the last section we shall, however, also briefly discuss alternative hypotheses concerning the formation of wage expectations. (8) and (9) together imply

$$K(t) = B - w(t)A \tag{10}$$

with the two positive constants

$$A = \sum_{k=1}^{m} a_k e^{-r(k-1)\Omega} \cdot \frac{1}{r} (e^{-r(k-1)\Omega} - e^{-rk\Omega})$$

$$B = \sum_{k=1}^{m} b_k e^{-r(k-1)\Omega} \cdot \frac{1}{r} (e^{-r(k-1)\Omega} - e^{-rk\Omega}).$$

In contrast to the investor's expectations the real wage will, in general, not remain on its current level. We assume that at a high rate of employment the nominal wage increase exceeds the rate of inflation while high unemployment makes the growth of nominal wages fall short of the price mark up.

Taking the supply of labour as exogenously given and measuring the rate of employment by the total input of labour $N(t)$ we express our hypotheses in its simplest mathematical form as

$$\dot{w}(t) = -g + h\,N(t) \tag{11}$$

in which g and h are positive constants. In other words, we assume that, up to an additive constant $-g$, the real wage $w(t)$ changes in proportion with the rate of employment.

Inserting (3) into (11) and (10) into (7) we finally obtain

$$\dot{w}(t) = -g + h \sum_{k=1}^{m} a_k \int_{(k-1)\Omega}^{k\Omega} x(t-\tau)\,d\tau \tag{12}$$

and

$$x(t) = \begin{cases} \mu(B - Aw(t)) & \text{if } w(t) < \dfrac{B}{A} \\ 0 & \text{otherwise.} \end{cases} \tag{13}$$

which are the two simultaneous equations we have to analyse.

3. Existence and Properties of a Solution Path

(12) and (13) can more compactly be written as

$$\dot{w}(t) = -g + h \sum_{k=1}^{m} a_k \int_{(k-1)\Omega}^{k\Omega} f(w(t-\tau))\,d\tau \tag{14}$$

where f is a continuous function defined by

$$f(w) = \begin{cases} \mu(B - uA) & \text{if } u < \dfrac{B}{A} \\ 0 & \text{otherwise} \end{cases}$$

f, too, possesses continuous derivatives everywhere except at $w = B/A$. At this point, however, both the left-hand and the right-hand derivative exist.

(14) is a retarded functional differential equation (in particular, an integro-differential equation) for an unknown function $w(t)$. In order to define the concept of a solution of equation (14) we introduce the following notation:

Let $C([a,b], R)$ denote the Banach space of continuous functions with domain $[a,b]$ and range $R = (-\infty, +\infty)$. Define the norm of an element $\phi \in C([a,b], R)$ by

$\| \phi \| = \max_{a \leqslant s \leqslant b} | \phi(s) |$. If $d \geqslant 0, t \in R, w \in C([t_0 - m\Omega, t_0 + d], R)$ then for any $t \in [t_0, t_0 + d]$ let $w_t \in C([-m\Omega, 0], R)$ be defined by $w_t(\phi) = w(t + \phi)$, $-m\Omega \leqslant \phi \leqslant 0$. In other words the graph of w_t is the graph of w on $[t - m\Omega, t]$ shifted to the interval $[-m\Omega, 0]$. Let M denote the set of mappings of $C([-m\Omega, R)$ into R. Elements of M will be called functionals. A system of the form $\dot{w} = V(w_t)$ with some functional V is an (autonomous) functional differential equation.

Definition. Let $\phi \in C([-m\Omega, 0], R)$ be some given function (the "initial function"). Then w_ϕ is called a solution of $\dot{w}(t) = V(t, w_t)$ on $[-m\Omega, d)$ with respect to the initial function ϕ if there is a number $d > 0$ such that

(I) $w_\phi \in C([-m\Omega, d], R)$
(II) $w_\phi(t) = \phi(t)$ for $t \in [-m\Omega, 0]$
(III) For $t \in [0, d)$ the derivative $\dot{w}_\phi(t)$ exists (half sided at $t = 0$) and satisfies the equation $\dot{w}(t) = V(w_t)$.

Obviously, if ϕ is differentiable on $[-m\Omega, 0]$ we do not require the half sided derivatives of w_ϕ at $t = 0$ to be equal. If this holds true, however, then w_ϕ is differentiable on $(-m\Omega, d)$. In order to avoid subscripts we shall subsequently write $w(t, \phi)$ instead of $w_\phi(t)$.

Since the right hand side of (14) integrates backwards from t to $t - m\Omega$ we can express this equation in the form

$$\dot{w}(t) = -g + h \sum_{k=-1}^{-m} a_{-k} \int_{k\Omega}^{(k+1)\Omega} f(w_t(\theta))\, d\theta \tag{14}$$

or, more compactly,

$$\dot{w}(t) = W(w_t) \tag{14'}$$

where $W \in M$, i.e. (14) is an autonomous functional differential equation.

As our main concern in this paper is to describe how the economic variables develop over time we shall be as brief as possible concerning the problem of existence and uniqueness of solutions of (14). It is a well known proposition in the theory of functional differential equations [see e.g. *Hale*, p. 41] that (14′) possesses a solution if the functional W is continuous in $C([-m\Omega, 0], R)$. In addition, if there is a Lipschitz constant L such that for any two solution $w_1(t, \phi) = y(t)$ and $w_2(t, \psi) = z(t)$ the inequality

$$| W(y_t) - W(z_t) | \leqslant L \| y_t - z_t \|$$

holds true for all t for which $y(t)$ and $z(t)$ are defined then the solution with respect to a given initial function is unique. Both conditions are met by equation (14). In what follows we shall, in addition, assume that the solutions $w(t, \phi)$ we consider are defined for $t \in [-m\Omega, \infty)$ [for a proof of this assumption see e.g. *Lakshmikanthan/Leela*, p. 8]. Finally, we suppose $w(t, \phi)$ to be continuously differentiable for $t \in [0, \infty)$ except may be at a countable number of points t (in particular "corner points" $t = n\Omega$, $n = 1,2, \ldots$) at which discontinuities of $\dot{w}(t, \phi)$ are allowed for.

As soon as we know how the real wage w develops over time the path of all other variables is given, too. In particular, (13) shows how many processes are started at the respective real wage. Inserting (13) into (3) provides the time path of employment. By (4) we geht the path of consumption.

At first we prove that equation (14) has a unique equilibrium solution, i.e. a solution that is constant over time. Such an equilibrium path w^* is defined by the equation

$$0=-g+h\sum_{k=1}^{m} a_k \int_{(k-1)\Omega}^{k\Omega} f(w^*)\,d\tau.$$

Suppose $w^* \geqslant B/A$. Then $f(w^*)=0$ and $0=-g$ which is a contradiction because $g>0$ by assumption. If $w^* < B/A$ then $f(w^*)=\mu(B-w^*A)$ and, therefore,

$$0=-g+h\mu(B-w^*A)\sum_{k=1}^{m} a_k \int_{(k-1)\Omega}^{k\Omega} d\tau.$$

From this equation we can immediately derive

Theorem 1: Equation (14) possesses a unique equilibrium path w^* for which

$$w^*=\frac{B}{A}-\frac{g}{h\mu\Omega A\sum_{k=1}^{m} a_k}<\frac{B}{A} \tag{15}$$

holds true.

The following lemma shows that any solution path is directed towards the equilibrium path w^* if it was over or under w^* for a period of length $m\Omega$ or longer.

Lemma. If $w(t,\phi)>w^*$ for $t\in[t_0-m\Omega, t_0]$ with $t_0\geqslant 0$ then $\dot{w}(t_0,\phi)<0$. Analogously, $w(t,\phi)<w^*$ for $t\in[t_0-m\Omega, t_0]$, $t_0\geqslant 0$, implies $\dot{w}(t_0,\phi)>0$. (Again, $\dot{w}(0,\phi)$ denotes the right-hand derivative).

The proof of this lemma is simple and can be omitted. In particular it follows from the lemma that neither $\lim_{t\to\infty} w(t,\phi)=\infty$ nor $\lim_{t\to\infty} w(t,\phi)=-\infty$ can occur. Furthermore, the lemma shows that there are really cases in which $w(t,\phi)$ is not differentiable at $t=0$. Assume $\phi(t)>w^*$ on the initial interval $[-m\Omega, 0]$ and suppose the left-hand derivative $\dot{\phi}(0)$ to be positive. By the lemma the right-hand derivative $\dot{w}(0,\phi)$ must be negative and hence $\dot{w}(0,\phi)\neq\dot{\phi}(0)$.

Now consider a solution $w(t,\phi)$ with $\phi(t)\geqslant B/A$ for $t\in[-m\Omega, 0]$, i.e. a solution for which on the initial interval the real wage is not below the "profitability barrier" B/A. This means that no processes are started on the initial interval so that employment is at zero level for $t=0$. In this case equation (14) reduces to $\dot{w}=-g$ in a certain neighbourhood of $t=0$. In particular, we have the solution

$$w(t,\phi)=\phi(0)-gt \qquad \text{for } 0\leqslant t\leqslant t_0$$

with

$$t_0=\frac{\phi(0)-B/A}{g}.$$

But also on the interval $[t_0, t_0 + \epsilon]$ with some $\epsilon > 0$ the solution $w(t, \phi)$ must continue to decline. This follows from our lemma because of $w(t, \phi) > w^*$ for $t \in [t_0 - m\Omega, t_0]$.

Hence, $w(t, \phi)$ really enters the area below the horizontal axis

$w = \frac{B}{A}$ (see fig. 1).

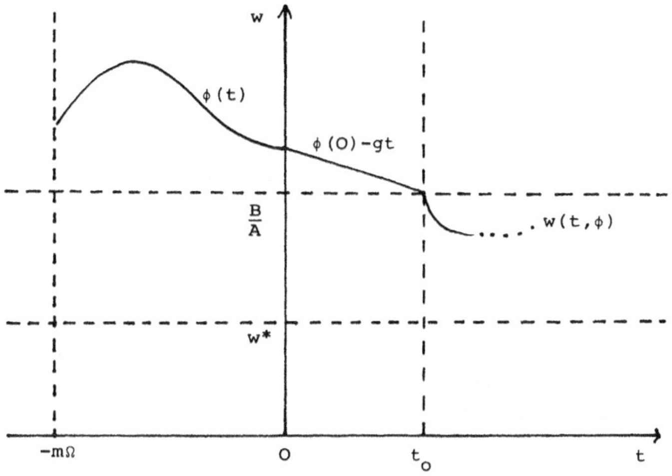

Fig. 1

The same argument applies to the case $w(t, \phi) \geqslant B/A$ for a solution path on an interval $[t_1, t_1 + m\Omega]$ with an arbitrary $t_1 > -m\Omega$. Here we have $w(t, \phi) = w(t_1 + m\Omega, \phi) - g(t_1 - (t_1 + m\Omega))$ for

$$t \in [t_1 + m\Omega, t_2]$$

with

$$t_2 = \frac{1}{g}[w(t_1 + m\Omega, \phi) - \frac{B}{A} + g(t_1 + m\Omega)].$$

Furthermore, $w(t, \phi) < B/A$ for $t \in [t_2, t_2 + \delta]$ with some $\delta > 0$. Hence, a solution path that comes from the area below the B/A-line must return into this area within finite time.

Now let us analyse the behaviour of a solution below the B/A-line. If $w(t, \phi) < B/A$ for $t \geqslant -m\Omega$ then equation (14) takes the form

$$\dot{w}(t) = -g + h \sum_{k=1}^{m} a_k \int_{(k-1)\Omega}^{k\Omega} \mu(B - Aw(t-\tau))\, d\tau \tag{16}$$

which can be written as

$$\dot{w}(t) = \alpha_0 - \sum_{k=1}^{m} \alpha_k \int_{(k-1)\Omega}^{k\Omega} w(t-\tau)\, d\tau \tag{17}$$

with

$$\alpha_0 = -g + h\mu B\Omega \sum_{k=1}^{m} a_k \text{ and } \alpha_k = h\mu A a_k > 0,\ k = 1, \ldots, m.$$

(17) is a linear integro-differential equation. If the initial function ϕ possesses a continuous derivative of at least second order everywhere on the initial interval the same holds true for the solutions $w(t, \phi)$ of (17) on the positive half axis $(0, \infty)$ except maybe at the corner points $n\Omega$, $n = 0, 1, 2, \ldots$ Differentiating (17) with respect to time yields

$$\ddot{w}(t) = -\sum_{k=1}^{m} \alpha_k \int_{(k-1)\Omega}^{k\Omega} \dot{w}(t-\tau)d\tau .$$

By integration this can be transformed into

$$\ddot{w}(t) + \alpha_1 w(t) = \alpha_m w(t - m\Omega) + \sum_{k=1}^{m-1} (\alpha_k - \alpha_{k+1}) w(t - k\Omega) \tag{18}$$

which is an ordinary second order differential equation with m delayed arguments.

Denote the right hand side of (18) by $F(t)$. If $w(t, \phi)$ is given on some interval $[(n-m)\Omega, n\Omega]$ with an arbitrary fixed $n \in \{0, 1, 2, \ldots\}$ then $F(t)$ is defined for $t \in [n\Omega, (n+1)\Omega]$. On this interval the function F can be represented by a Fourier series because $w(t, \phi)$ is differentiable for $t \in [(n-m)\Omega, n\Omega]$.

For our next proposition we introduce the following

Definition. Let F_n denote the set of functions with domain $[n\Omega, (n+1)\Omega]$ and range $(-\infty, \infty)$ which can be represented by a Fourier series. Suppose $F \in F_n$, i.e.

$$F(t) \equiv \sum_{\nu=-\infty}^{\infty} S_\nu e^{2i\pi\nu t/\Omega}$$

with the coefficients

$$S_\nu = \frac{1}{\Omega} \int_{n\Omega}^{(n+1)\Omega} F(\xi)\, e^{-2i\pi\nu\xi/\Omega} d\xi .$$

Then we define the function $\rho(F) \in F_n$ by

$$\rho(F)(t) = \sum_{\nu=-\infty}^{\infty} S'_\nu e^{2i\pi\nu t/\Omega}$$

with the coefficients

$$S'_\nu = \frac{\Omega^2}{4\pi^2} \frac{S_\nu}{(\alpha_1 \Omega/2\pi)^2 - \nu^2}$$

Remark. We assume $\alpha_1 \Omega/2\pi \neq \nu$ for all $\nu = 0, \pm 1, \pm 2, \ldots, \pm \infty$. Then the operator ρ which maps F_n into itself is well defined because the series $\sum_{\nu=-\infty}^{\infty} S'_\nu e^{2i\pi\nu t/\Omega}$ converges uniformly [for a proof see e.g. *Ostrowski*, p. 434].

Theorem 2. Let $w(t, \phi)$ be a solution of (18) which possesses continuous derivatives of at least second order for $t > -m\Omega$ except maybe at $t = 0$ and at corner points $t = n\Omega$, $n = 1,2, \ldots$ Suppose $w(t, \phi)$ to be known on some interval $[(n-m)\Omega, n\Omega]$ with a given $n = 1,2, \ldots$ Then for $t \in [n\Omega, (n+1)\Omega]$ the solution $w(t, \phi)$ has the form

$$w(t, \phi) = G(t) + C_1 \sin\sqrt{\alpha_1}\,t + C_2 \cos\sqrt{\alpha_1}\,t \tag{19}$$

where $G = \rho(F)$ and where the constants C_1 and C_2 are given by the boundary conditions

$$C_1 = \frac{1}{\sqrt{\alpha_1}}\left[(\dot{w}(n\Omega, \phi) - \dot{G}(n\Omega))\,C + (w(n\Omega, \phi) - G(n\Omega))\sqrt{\alpha_1}\,S\right]$$

$$C_2 = \frac{1}{\sqrt{\alpha_1}}\left[(\dot{w}(n\Omega, \phi) - \dot{G}(n\Omega))\,S - (w(n\Omega, \phi) - G(n\Omega))\sqrt{\alpha_1}\,C\right]$$

with $S = \sin\sqrt{\alpha_1}\,n\Omega$ and $C = \cos\sqrt{\alpha_1}\,n\Omega$.

Proof. Denote the right hand side of equation (18) by $F(t)$. Since $w(t, \phi)$ is supposed to be known on the interval $[(n-m)\Omega, n\Omega]$ the function $F(t)$ is given on the interval $[n\Omega, (n+1)\Omega]$. Furthermore, $F(t)$ possesses continuous derivatives of at least second order on the interval $[n\Omega, (n+1)\Omega]$ (half sided at corners) because $w(t, \phi)$ is twice continuously differentiable except maybe at the corner points $k\Omega$, $k = (n-m)\Omega, \ldots,$ $, \ldots, (n-1)\Omega, n\Omega$. On the interval $[n\Omega, (n+1)\Omega]$ the function $F(t)$ can be represented by a Fourier series. Equation (18) then becomes

$$\ddot{w}(t) + \alpha_1 w(t) = \sum_{\nu=-\infty}^{\infty} S_\nu\, e^{2i\pi\nu t/\Omega} \tag{18'}$$

with the coefficients

$$S_\nu = \frac{1}{\Omega}\int_{n\Omega}^{(n+1)\Omega} F(\xi)\, e^{-2i\pi\nu\xi/\Omega}\, d\xi.$$

(18′) is a second order linear differential equation defined for $t \in [n\Omega, (n+1)\Omega]$. It is well known from physics as a mathematical description of the linear oscillator with forced oscillations. The homogeneous part $\ddot{w} + \alpha_1 w = 0$ has the solution $C_1 \sin\sqrt{\alpha_1}\,t +$ $+ C_2 \cos\sqrt{\alpha_1}\,t$ with two arbitrary constants C_1 and C_2. The complete solution of (18′) on the interval $[n\Omega, (n+1)\Omega]$ is given by

$$G(t) + C_1 \sin\sqrt{\alpha_1}\,t + C_2 \cos\sqrt{\alpha_1}\,t$$

where the function G can be represented by the (convergent) Fourier expansion [see *Ostrowski*, 432–437].

$$G(t) = \frac{\Omega^2}{4\pi^2}\sum_{\nu=-\infty}^{\infty} S_\nu \frac{e^{2i\pi\nu t/\Omega}}{(\alpha_1\Omega/2\pi)^2 - \nu^2}. \tag{20}$$

For $t = n\Omega$ the two initial conditions are

$$w(n\Omega, \phi) = G(n\Omega) + C_1 \sin\sqrt{\alpha_1}\,n\Omega + C_2 \cos\sqrt{\alpha_1}\,n\Omega$$

and

$$\dot{w}(n\Omega, \phi) = \dot{G}(n\Omega) + C_1 \sqrt{\alpha_1} \cos \sqrt{\alpha_1} n\Omega - C_2 \sqrt{\alpha_1} \sin \sqrt{\alpha_1} n\Omega$$

from which C_1 and C_2 are uniquely determined because the determinant

$$(\sin \sqrt{\alpha_1} n\Omega) (-\sqrt{\alpha_1} \sin \sqrt{\alpha_1} n\Omega) - (\cos \sqrt{\alpha_1} n\Omega) (\sqrt{\alpha_1} \cos \sqrt{\alpha_1} n) = -\sqrt{\alpha_1}$$

does not vanish. Q.E.D.

Remark. This proposition can also be used to prove the existence of a solution of (18) on the whole half axis $[0, \infty)$ because the proof of the theorem shows how the solution can be constructed stepwise for the intervals $[0, \Omega]$, $[\Omega, 2\Omega]$, etc.

Equation (9) of Theorem 2 demonstrates that the model economy we are analysing produces endogenous cyclical impulses. This cyclical component occurs always when the real wage was low enough to guarantee profitable production for a period of length $m\Omega$ (or longer). In other words, if new processes were started for a sufficiently long time then the economic variables will begin to fluctuate.

It should be noted that the phase of the endogenous cyclical impulse is a function of $\alpha_1 = h\mu A a_1$ and is thus independent of the coefficients $g, b_1, \ldots, b_m$. Since the two trigonometric terms in (19) are superimposed by the function $G(t)$ the fluctuations of $w(t, \phi)$ will in general, however, be quite irregular. The function $G(t)$ carries the heritage of past periods into the future. It is determined by the path of $w(t, \phi)$ on the interval $[(n-m)\Omega, n\Omega]$ and by the coefficients $\alpha_1, \ldots, \alpha_m$. If $F(t)$ – i.e. the right hand side of (18) – is known explicitely then $G(t)$ can, in general, also be derived explicitely.

Examples

$F(t)$	$G(t)$
C	$\frac{C}{\alpha_1}$
e^{rt}	$\frac{e^{rt}}{r^2 + \alpha_1}$
$\cos t$	$(\alpha_1 - 1) \cos t$
$p_0 + p_1 t + p_2 t^2 + \ldots + p_s t^s$	$q_0 + q_1 t + q_2 t^2 + \ldots + q_s t^s$ with $q_s = \frac{p_s}{\alpha_1}$, $q_{s-1} = \frac{p_{s-1}}{\alpha_1}$, and $q_\nu = \frac{1}{\alpha_1} [p_\nu - (\nu+1)(\nu+2) q_{\nu+1}]$ for $\nu = s-2, s-3, \ldots, 2,1,0.$

Theorem 2 gives the solution of (18) on an interval $[n\Omega, (n+1)\Omega]$ for some given

$n = 0,1,2, \ldots$ Next we describe the structure of the solution of (18) on the whole half axis $[0, \infty)$ under the assumption that the initial function is a polynomial of degree $s \geqslant 1$. For convenience we shall now measure time in such units that the length of subperiod Ω of the production process is $\Omega = 2\pi/\sqrt{\alpha_1}$. Finally, we assume that the first two input coefficients a_1 and a_2 are not equal (which implies $\alpha_1 \neq \alpha_2$).

Theorem 3. Let $\Omega = 2\pi/\sqrt{\alpha_1}$, $a_1 \neq a_2$, and suppose the initial function ϕ to be a polynomial of degree $s \geqslant 1$, i.e.

$$\phi(t) = \phi_0 + \phi_1 t + \phi_2 t^2 + \ldots + \phi_s t^s \text{ with } \phi_s \neq 0.$$

Then on any interval $[n\Omega, (n+1)\Omega]$, $n = 0,1,2, \ldots$, the solution of (18) has the form

$$w(t, \phi) = P_n(t) + Q_n(t) \sin \sqrt{\alpha_1}\, t + R_n(t) \cos \sqrt{\alpha_1}\, t$$

where

$$P_n(t) = p_{n0} + p_{n1} t + p_{n2} t^2 + \ldots + p_{ns} t^s$$

is a polynomial of degree s (i.e. $p_{ns} \neq 0$) and ($Q_n(t)$ and $R_n(t)$ are polynomials of degree n. Furthermore, $p_{ns} = p_{n-1,s}$ for $n = 1,2, \ldots$

Proof. For abbreviation, we define the intervals $I_n = [n\Omega, (n+1)\Omega]$ and the functions $\psi_n(t) = w(t, \phi)$ for $t \in I_n$. In addition, let

$$P_n(t) = p_{n0} + p_{n1} t + \ldots + p_{ns} t^s$$

$$Q_n(t) = q_{n0} + q_{n1} t + \ldots + q_{nn} t^n$$

$$R_n(t) = r_{n0} + r_{n1} t + \ldots + r_{nn} t^n.$$

We prove the theorem by induction. Suppose $\psi_{n-m}(t), \ldots, \psi_{n-1}(t)$ are given such that for $\nu = n-m, \ldots, n-1$

$$\psi_\nu(t) = P_\nu(t) + Q_\nu(t) \sin \sqrt{\alpha_1}\, t + R_\nu(t) \cos \sqrt{\alpha_1}\, t$$

with

$$p_{\nu s} = p_{\nu-1,s} \neq 0, q_{\nu\nu} \neq 0, \text{ and } r_{\nu\nu} \neq 0.$$

Then, for $\psi_n(t)$ try

$$\psi_n(t) = P_n(t) + Q_n(t) \sin \sqrt{\alpha_1}\, t + R_n(t) \cos \sqrt{\alpha_1}\, t.$$

In order to obtain that $\psi_n(t)$ is indeed identical with $w(t, \phi)$ on the interval I_n we must prove the equation

$$\ddot{\psi}_n(t) + \alpha_1 \psi_n(t) = \alpha_m \psi_{n-m}(t) + \sum_{k=1}^{m-1} (\alpha_k - \alpha_{k+1}) \psi_{n-k}(t) \tag{21}$$

to hold for $t \in I_n$. Furthermore, it is required that $p_{ns} \neq 0, q_{nn} \neq 0, r_{nn} \neq 0$, and $p_{n-1,s} = p_{ns}$.

Since $\sin\sqrt{\alpha_1}\,(t-\nu\Omega) = \sin\sqrt{\alpha_1}\,t - 2\pi\nu = \sin\sqrt{\alpha_1}\,t$ and $\cos\sqrt{\alpha_1}\,(t-\nu\Omega) = \cos\sqrt{\alpha_1}\,t - 2\pi\nu = \cos\sqrt{\alpha_1}\,t$ for $\nu = 0,1,2,\ldots$ the right hand side of (21) can be written as

$$\alpha_m P_{n\text{-}m}(t-m\Omega) + \sum_{k=1}^{m\text{-}1}(\alpha_k - \alpha_{k+1}) P_{n\text{-}k}(t-k\Omega) +$$

$$+ [\alpha_m Q_{n\text{-}m}(t-m\Omega) + \sum_{k=1}^{m\text{-}1}(\alpha_k - \alpha_{k+1}) Q_{n\text{-}k}(t-k\Omega)] \sin\sqrt{\alpha_1}\,t +$$

$$+ [\alpha_m R_{n\text{-}m}(t-m\Omega) + \sum_{k=1}^{m\text{-}1}(\alpha_k - \alpha_{k+1}) R_{n\text{-}k}(t-k\Omega)] \cos\sqrt{\alpha_1}\,t.$$

Differentiation of $\psi_n(t)$ yields

$$\dot\psi_n(t) = \dot P_n(t) + [\dot R_n(t) + \sqrt{\alpha_1}\,Q_n(t)] \cos\sqrt{\alpha_1}\,t + [\dot Q_n(t) - \sqrt{\alpha_1}\,R_n(t)] \sin\sqrt{\alpha_1}\,t$$

and

$$\ddot\psi_n(t) = \ddot P_n(t) - \alpha_1\,[Q_n(t)\sin\sqrt{\alpha_1}\,t + R_n(t)\cos\sqrt{\alpha_a}\,t] +$$
$$+ [\ddot R_n(t) + 2\sqrt{\alpha_1}\,\dot Q_n(t)] \cos\sqrt{\alpha_1}\,t +$$
$$+ [\ddot Q_n(t) - 2\sqrt{\alpha_1}\,\dot R_n(t)] \sin\sqrt{\alpha_1}\,t$$

so that

$$\ddot\psi_n(t) + \alpha_1\psi_n(t) = \ddot P_n(t) + \alpha_1 P_n(t) +$$
$$+ [\ddot Q_n(t) - 2\sqrt{\alpha_1}\,\dot R_n(t)] \sin\sqrt{\alpha_1}\,t +$$
$$+ [\ddot R_n(t) + 2\sqrt{\alpha_1}\,\dot Q_n(t)] \cos\sqrt{\alpha_1}\,t$$

which is the left hand side of (21). Since both sides must be identical for $t \in I_n$ we finally conclude that on this interval

$$\ddot P_n(t) + \alpha_1 P_n(t) \equiv \alpha_m P_{n\text{-}m}(t-m\Omega) + \sum_{k=1}^{m\text{-}1}(\alpha_k - \alpha_{k+1}) P_{n\text{-}k}(t-k\Omega) \qquad (22)$$

$$\ddot Q_n(t) - 2\sqrt{\alpha_1}\,\dot R_n(t) \equiv \alpha_m Q_{n\text{-}m}(t-m\Omega) + \sum_{k=1}^{m\text{-}1}(\alpha_k - \alpha_{k+1}) Q_{n\text{-}k}(t-k\Omega) \quad (23)$$

$$\ddot R_n(t) + 2\sqrt{\alpha_1}\,\dot Q_n(t) \equiv \alpha_m R_{n\text{-}m}(t-m\Omega) + \sum_{k=1}^{m\text{-}1}(\alpha_k - \alpha_{k+1}) R_{n\text{-}k}(t-k\Omega). \quad (24)$$

The right hand side of (22) is a weighted sum of polynomials of degree s. Collecting the coefficients of the terms t^s we obtain

$$(\alpha_m p_{n\text{-}m,s} + \sum_{k=1}^{m\text{-}1}(\alpha_k - \alpha_{k+1}) p_{n\text{-}k,s}) t^s = \alpha_1 p_{n\text{-}1,s} t^s.$$

On the left hand side of (22) the term t^s appears only in $P_n(t)$ so that we have $\alpha_1 p_{ns} t^s = \alpha_1 p_{n-1,s} t^s$.

Hence, $P_n(t)$ is a polynomial of degree s with $p_{ns} = p_{n-1,s} \neq 0$. The right hand sides of (23) and (24) are also weighted sums of polynomials the highest degreee of which is $n-1$. Thus, $\ddot{Q}_n(t) - 2\sqrt{\alpha_1}\dot{R}_n(t)$ and $\ddot{R}_n(t) + 2\sqrt{\alpha_1}\dot{Q}_n(t)$ are also polynomials of degree $n-1$. From this it follows that $R_n(t)$ and $Q_n(t)$ are polynomials of degree n provided that $r_{nn} \neq 0$ and $q_{nn} \neq 0$.

Collecting the terms in which t^{n-1} appears we get for all $t \in I_n$

$$-2\sqrt{\alpha_1}\, n r_{nn} t^{n-1} = (\alpha_1 - \alpha_2) q_{n-1,n-1} t^{n-1}$$

$$2\sqrt{\alpha_1}\, n q_{nn} t^{n-1} = (\alpha_1 - \alpha_2) r_{n-1,n-1} t^{n-1}$$

so that

$$r_{nn} = -\frac{\alpha_1 - \alpha_2}{2n\sqrt{\alpha_1}} q_{n-1,n-1} \neq 0$$

because $\alpha_1 \neq \alpha_2$, $r_{n-1,n-1} \neq 0$, and $q_{n-1,n-1} \neq 0$.

In the same way it can also be shown that

$$\psi_\nu(t) = P_\nu(t) + Q_\nu(t)\sin\sqrt{\alpha_1}\,t + R_\nu(t)\cos\sqrt{\alpha_1}\,t \quad \text{for } \nu = 0,1,\ldots,m-1.$$

By induction it therefore follows that the assertion holds true for all $n = 0,1,2,\ldots$

Q.E.D.

Remark. Since $P_n(t)$ is a polynomial of degree s and $Q_n(t)$ and $R_n(t)$ are polynomials of degree n there are $(s+1) + 2(n+1)$ unknown coefficients $p_{n0}, p_{n1}, \ldots, p_{ns}, q_{n0}, q_{n1}, \ldots, q_{nn}, r_{n0}, r_{n1}, \ldots, r_{nn}$. In (22), (23), and (24) a comparison of the coefficients belonging to the respective exponents t^j ($j = 0,1,2,\ldots$) on both the left hand and the right hand side yields $(s+1) + 2n$ equations. The "missing" two equations are given by $\psi_{n-1}(n\Omega) = \psi_n(n\Omega)$ and $\dot{\psi}_{n-1}(n\Omega) = \dot{\psi}_n(n\Omega)$. Because of $\sin\sqrt{\alpha_1}\,n\Omega =$ $= \sin\sqrt{\alpha_1}(n-1)\Omega = \sin 2n\pi = \sin(n-1)\pi = 0$ and $\cos\sqrt{\alpha_1}\,n\Omega = \cos\sqrt{\alpha_1}(n-1)\Omega =$ $= \cos 2n\pi = \cos 2(n-1)\pi = 1$ these two equations can also be written as

$$P_{n-1}(n\Omega) + R_{n-1}(n\Omega) = P_n(n\Omega) + R_n(n\Omega) \tag{25}$$

$$\dot{P}_{n-1}(n\Omega) + \dot{R}_{n-1}(n\Omega) + \sqrt{\alpha_1}\,\dot{Q}_n(n\Omega) = \dot{P}_n(n\Omega) + \dot{R}_n(n\Omega) + \sqrt{\alpha_1}\,\dot{Q}_n(n\Omega). \tag{26}$$

We are now able to describe how the path $w(t, \phi)$ of the real wage develops over time in our model. If the wage is below the "profitablility barrier" B/A for a sufficiently long period of time then $w(t, \phi)$ begins to oscillate. From the Lemma together with Theorem 2 it follows that the path cannot always lie over or under the equilibrium w^* so that the function $w(t, \phi)$ will repeatedly cross w^* and the real wage will thus alternately be smaller and larger than its equilibrium level. The oscillations of the wage may become so strong that $w(t, \phi)$ pushes through the B/A-line. Then no new processes will be started and employment must eventually decrease. This induces a fall in the real wage which will not end before the wage enters again the profitability area below the B/A-line (see fig. 2).

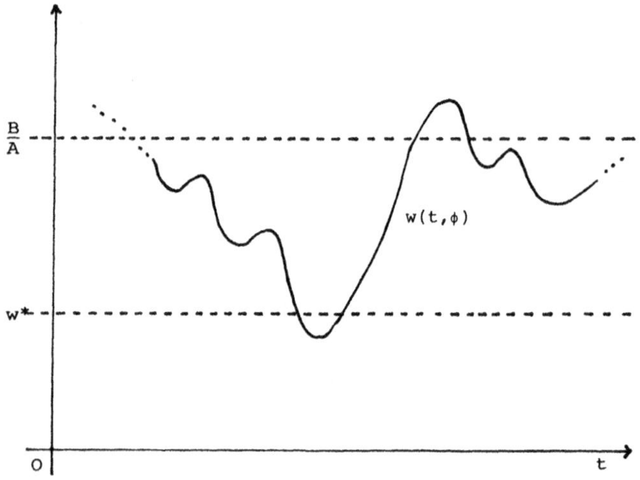

Fig. 2

4. Alternative Assumptions

Suppose now that the investors in new processes forecast the future average real wage $v(\phi, t)$ as a weighted sum of the wage at selected points of time $t, t-Z_1, t-Z_2, \ldots, t-Z_s$ in the past. Then, instead of equation (9), we have

$$v(\theta, t) = \frac{1}{\xi} \sum_{\sigma=0}^{s} \xi_\sigma w(t-Z_\sigma) \tag{27}$$

with $\xi = (\sum_{\sigma=0}^{s} \xi_\sigma)^{-1}$ and $\xi_\sigma > 0$ for $\sigma = 0,1,\ldots,s$, $Z_\sigma >$ for $\sigma = 1, \ldots, s$, and $Z_0 = 0$. In this case equation (14) is replaced by

$$\dot{w}(t) = -g + h \sum_{k=1}^{m} a_k \int_{(k-1)\Omega}^{k\Omega} f\left(\frac{1}{\xi} \sum_{\sigma=0}^{s} \xi_\sigma w(t-Z_\sigma-\tau)\right) d\tau \tag{28}$$

where the function f is again defined as

$$f(u) = \begin{cases} \mu(B-uA) & \text{if } u < \dfrac{B}{A} \\ 0 & \text{otherwise.} \end{cases}$$

The results that can be derived for the integro-differential equation (28) are very similar to those obtained in the foregoing section. Theorem 1 holds true word for word. In the Lemma the interval $[t_0 - m\Omega, t_0]$ must be replaced by the interval $[t_0 - M, t_0]$ with $M = m\Omega + \max\{Z_1, \ldots, Z_s\}$ and the initial interval is $[-M, 0]$ now. If the solution path of (28) remains below the profitability barrier B/A then (28) can be transformed into

$$\ddot{w}(t) = -\frac{\mu h}{\xi} \sum_{k=1}^{m} a_k \int_{(k-1)\Omega}^{k\Omega} \sum_{\sigma=0}^{s} \xi_\sigma \dot{w}(t-\tau-Z_\sigma)\, d\tau. \tag{29}$$

By integration we finally get

$$\ddot{w}(t) + \eta w(t) =$$

$$= \eta w(t - \Omega) + \sum_{\sigma=1}^{s} \frac{h\mu a_1 \xi_\sigma}{\xi} [w(t - \Omega - Z_\sigma) - w(t - Z_\sigma)]$$

$$+ \sum_{k=2}^{m} \sum_{\sigma=0}^{s} \frac{h\mu a_k \xi_\sigma}{\xi} [w(t - k\Omega - Z_\sigma) - w(t - (k-1)\Omega - Z_\sigma)] \tag{30}$$

where $\eta = (h\mu a_1 \xi_0)/\xi > 0$. The formal structure of equation (30) is almost identical with that of equation (18). The largest delay in the arguments of the right hand side of (30) is M. Thus if $w(t, \phi)$ is given on some interval $[t_0 - M, t_0]$ then (30) defines an ordinary second order inhomogeneous linear differential equation on the interval $[t_0, d]$ where $d = \min(\Omega, Z_1, \ldots, Z_s)$. In analogy to Theorem 2 one can prove that for $t \in [t_0, d]$ the solution path has the form

$$w(t, \phi) = G(t) + C_1 \sin\sqrt{\mu}\, t + C_2 \cos\sqrt{\mu}\, t$$

where the function G is again determined by the path of $w(t, \phi)$ in the interval $[t_0 - M, t_0]$. Hence, we observe the same cyclical impulse as described in section 3.

A further generalisation of our model is obtained by dropping the assumption that investors expect the real wage to be constant in the future. Instead of equations (9) or (27) suppose that $v(\theta, t)$ is piecewise constant on the intervals $[t, t + \theta_1)$, $[t + \theta_1, t + \theta_2), \ldots, [t + \theta_{N-1}, t + \theta_N]$ where $\theta_N = m\Omega$ (the length of the production process).

Finally assume that for $\theta \in [t + \theta_\nu, t + \theta_{\nu+1})$ the expected future real wage $v(\theta, t)$ is derived from the past as a weighted sum of the wages observed at time t, $t - Z_{\nu 1}, \ldots, t - Z_{\nu s_\nu}$, i.e.

$$v(\theta, t) = \frac{1}{\delta_\nu} \sum_{\sigma=0}^{s_\nu} \delta_{\nu\sigma}\, w(t - Z_{\nu\sigma}) \quad \text{for } \nu = 1, \ldots, N \tag{31}$$

with the coefficients $\delta_{\nu\sigma}$, and $Z_{\nu\sigma}$ defined in analogy to those in equation (27).

With equation (31) it is tedius to write our model down explicitely. But again its formal structure is not changed essentially. The capital value of a production process remains a linear function of the real wage. Theorem 1 applies directly. Furthermore, a proposition similar to Theorem 2 can be proved so that we have again endogenous cyclical impulses.

Let us, finally, come back to the case of equation

$$\dot{x}(t) = \gamma\, [C_0 + \sum_{k=1}^{m} (cwa_k - b_k) \int_{(k-1)\Omega}^{k\Omega} x(t - \tau)\, d\tau \tag{6}$$

which we briefly dicussed in section 2. Here, the rate of starts of new processes changes in proportion with the excess of final demand over final output. Defining $\beta_0 = \gamma C_0$ and $\beta_k = b_k - cwa_k$, $k = 1, \ldots, m$, equation (6) becomes

$$\dot{x}(t) = \beta_0 - \sum_{k=1}^{m} \beta_k \int_{(k-1)\Omega}^{k\Omega} x(t-\tau)\, d\tau. \tag{32}$$

This is formally identical with equation (17) of the foregoing section. The Lemma applies analogously. The unique equilibrium path is given by $x^* = \beta_0 / (\Omega \sum_{k=1}^{m} \beta_k)$ and Theorems 2 and 3 hold true provided that $\beta_1 > 0$. If $\beta_1 < 0$ and if the solution $x(t, \phi)$ of (32) with respect to some initial function ϕ is known on the interval $[(n-m)\,\Omega,\ n\Omega]$ then

$$x(t, \phi) = G(t) + C_1 e^{\sqrt{-\beta_1}\, t} + C_2 e^{-\sqrt{-\beta_1}\, t} \tag{33}$$

for $t \in [n\Omega, (n+1)\,\Omega]$. In (33) $G(t)$ is again a function determined by the path of $x(t, \phi)$ for $t \in [(n-m)\,\Omega, n\Omega]$. C_1 and C_2 are constants derived from initial conditions at $t = n\Omega$.

Acknowledgement

I am grateful to Professor Joachim Rosenmüller for helpful comments and suggestions.

References

Bernholz, P., M. Faber and *W. Reiss*: A Neo-Austrian Two-Period Multisector Model of Capital. Journal of Economic Theory 17 (1), 1978, 38–50.

Burmeister, E.: Neo-Austrian and Alternative Approaches to Capital Theory. Journal of Economic Literature **VII** (2), 1974, 413–456.

Hale, J.: Theory of Functional Differential Equations. New York–Heidelberg–Berlin 1977.

Hicks, J.: Capital and Time, A Neo-Austrian Theory. Oxford 1973.

Lakshmikanthan, V., and *S. Leela*: Differential and Integral Inequalities, Theory and Application. New York–London 1969.

Ostrowski, A.: Vorlesungen über Differential- und Integralrechnung. Volume III. Basel–Stuttgart 1962.

v. Weizsäcker, C.C.: Steady State Capital Theory. Berlin–Heidelberg–New York 1971.

Games, Economic Dynamics, and Time Series Analysis. 1982 ©Physica-Verlag, Wien–Würzburg

A Dynamic Game with Macroeconomic Investment Decisions under Alternative Market Structures [1])

By *W. Böge*, Heidelberg[2]), *M. Faber*, Heidelberg[3]) and *W. Güth*, Köln[4])

1. Introduction

During the last decade several authors have analyzed the question: Under what conditions does the law of greater productivity of roundabout methods bring about a positive rate of interest[5]) using elements of Böhm-Bawerk's Theory of Interest, and of Schumpeter's Theory of Innovation? All their models, however, assume either that there is one decision unit, namely a central planning agency, or that perfect competition exists. These simplifying assumptions eliminate all the phenomena which are connected with the strategic influence of other agents on the profitability of a specific production method. For this profitablity of a specific production method may well depend on the number of producers who have chosen this method. Here we want to give up these simplifying assumptions and include – what is often called – the oligopolistic or strategic interdependence of the producers[6]). The level of abstraction of our approach will be rather high, mainly for two reasons:

1. We do not want to fix the numbers of producers to particular ones, since we want to analyse how the results are influenced by the market structure which is given by the number n of symmetric producers. This will enable us to cover the monopolistic case or the case of a centrally planned economy ($n = 1$) as well as the oligopolistic case with $1 < n < \infty$, and by approaching infinity we can examine the competitive market, too.
2. More and more economists complain that in macroeconomics the individual behaviour often is regarded as given, i.e. macroeconomic models do not allow for strategic considerations of individual agents. In our model the macroeconomic variables like total investment and total production are determined by the independent and strategic decisions of the n producers, each of them trying to maximize his individual payoff.

[1]) We are grateful to Gunter Stephan for many very helpful and valuable comments and Winfried Reiss for computational assistance.

[2]) *W. Böge*, Institut für Angewandte Mathematik, Universität Heidelberg, Im Neuenh. Feld 294, D–6900 Heidelberg.

[3]) *M. Faber*, Alfred-Weber-Institut, Universität Heidelberg, Grabengasse 14, D–6900 Heidelberg.

[4]) *W. Güth*, Staatswissenschaftliches Seminar, Universität Köln, Albertus-Magnus-Platz, D–5000 Köln 41.

[5]) For a survey of the literature see *Faber* [1979] and *Reiss* [1979, Chapter 4].

[6]) Nelson/Winter have examined this interdependency under Schumpeterian conditions. For this purpose they developed simulation models with four and sixteen firms of one sector of an economy.

Therefore one can say that our model contributes to the development of, what can be called, a "more microeconomic analysis of macroeconomic models" (for another approach in this direction see Nelsen/Winter/Schuette and Selten/Güth).

Since we assume that the actual production possibilities of a specific producer is determined by his previous investment decisions and that the payoff of a producer is given by the expected value of all his future incomes, the analysis of the investment decisions of the n producers will require us to solve a noncooperative dynamic game with the n producers as players. It is dynamic, because the decision situation in period $t + 1$ depends on what has been done in and before period t and because according to the definition of the payoff functions the players will have to take future effects into account. As we exclude binding agreements within the group of producers, the game is noncooperative. Thus our model can be considered as an example how the theory of dynamic games can be applied to the social sciences [for other examples see *Selten*, 1965; *Kydland*].

Many dynamic game models in the literature employ an open loop approach, i.e. all decisions depend only on the initial state in the first period. In contrast to this procedure we use a closed loop model, i.e. the decisions in period $t + 1$ may depend not only on the inital state but on all previous investment decisions. For one producer ($n = 1$) the closed loop and the open loop model give the same result, but for $n > 1$ this does not hold any more. Of course, the closed loop approach is more realistic, it is, however, mathematically much more difficult to study. The latter reason is responsible for the fact that this paper is only a starting point.

We will consider the case of a finite number of investment periods (Section 3) as well as the game with infinite length (Section 4). Finally in Section 5 we discuss the dependence of the interest rate, total investment and total income on the market structure. In a later paper we intend to discuss some crucial assumptions of our model, in particular the border cases for an economic horizon of one and two periods and present a limited rationality approach for the case of developing economies. In addition we will give a continuous version of our model which will allow us in a simple way to study cases with non-circulating capital goods.

2. The Economic Assumptions, Game Structure and Solution Concept

Consider a production economy where agents are households and producers. For the sake of simplicity we assume that the saving behaviour and thus the consumption behaviour of the households can be described by a simple saving function. In every period the n ($n \geqslant 1$) producers independently determine their individual investment amounts and via their production functions their (maximal) production levels in the next period.

Another restrictive assumption is that all producers have the same linear production function. Furthermore in our discrete time version we assume for the sake of simplicity that the time from one investment decision to the next one (which we use as time unit) is at least as large as the time from the investment of a capital good until it is used up by the production process (i.e. for example 1 year).

We use an economy with only one commodity, which may be used either as a consumption or as a capital good. The total amount of this good available at time

$t(t = 1, 2, \ldots, T)$ is $Y(t)$. Thereof the amount $x_i(t) \geqslant 0$ $(i = 1, \ldots, n)$ is reinvested by producer i. Hence we obtain for all firms

$$X(t) = \sum_{i=1}^{n} x_i(t) \leqslant Y(t) \qquad (1 \leqslant t \leqslant T), \tag{2.1}$$

so that $Y(t) - X(t)$ remains for consumption.

Every producer i $(i = 1, \ldots, n)$ has to choose independently his individual investment amount $x_i(t)$. Thus one has to make sure that (2.1) is fulfilled. For the time being we therefore assume

$$0 \leqslant x_i(t) \leqslant \frac{1}{n} Y(t) \qquad (1 \leqslant t \leqslant T) \qquad (i = 1, \ldots, n). \tag{2.2}$$

By imposing restriction (2.2) on the choice sets in every period t we avoid special rules for the event that the total investment demand $X(t)$ exceeds total income $Y(t)$. Herefore one would have to specify a rationing scheme and the costs of being involved in a rationing process. If these costs are high enough, rational producers will never induce the event $X(t) > Y(t)$. Instead of introducing complicated rules of this form, we simply avoid the event by imposing (2.2).

We shall demand below certain assumptions concerning some coefficients of our model such that (2.2) will be fulfilled for the solution anyway, even if conditions (2.1), (2.2) are not imposed.

The fact that the time unit mentioned above is chosen so large that the reinvested amount $x_i(t)$ is used up by the production process during the period from t to $t + 1$ may be formally expressed by stating that the minimum level of productive capital in the next period, $x_i(t + 1)$, is equal to zero regardless of how much capital is available in t. Of course, this implies that we have a model of a circulating capital good. The investement level $x_i(t)$ of producer i $(i = 1, \ldots, n)$ in period t determines the maximal production $y_i(t + 1)$ via the production function

$$y_i(t + 1) = K \cdot x_i(t) + L, \quad \text{with } K > 1 \text{ and } L \geqslant 0, 1 \leqslant t \leqslant T. \tag{2.3}$$

Thus we assume a constant marginal productivity K since because of mathematical reasons we have to restrict ourselves to a linear production function. One could argue that the coefficients K and L could be chosen in such a way that we have a good linear approximation of a more complicated production function.

We note in passing that this production function complies with the neo-Austrian approach. Since production takes one period, the time structure of production is explicitly considered. If investment takes place, i.e. $X(t) > 0$, then production is roundabout and since $K > 1$ there exists superiority [see *Faber*, 70–73].

The total available amount of production at time $t + 1$ is

$$Y(t + 1) = \sum_{i=1}^{n} y_i(t + 1), \tag{2.4}$$

which is determined according to

$$Y(t+1) = K \cdot X(t) + n \cdot L \qquad (t \geq 1). \tag{2.5}$$

$Y(1)$ is given in advance, whereas $Y(2), Y(3), \ldots, Y(T+1)$ are given by (2.5).

To complete our assumptions we have still to explain our concept of a strategy for producer i and have to define his payoff function H_i that he tries to maximize. We start with the latter. We assume that H_i is the sum of all discounted future profits:

$$H_i = \sum_{\tau=1}^{T} \delta^{\tau-1} [y_i(\tau+1) - r(\tau) x_i(\tau)] \quad \text{with } 0 \leq \delta \leq 1. \tag{2.6}$$

δ is the discount factor indicating the constant time preferences, which are the same for all producers. $r(t)$ denotes the interest factor (repayment rate) between period t to $t+1$, for which we assume

$$r(t) = A + B \cdot X(t) - C \cdot Y(t) \quad \text{with } B > 0, C \geq 0, K > A > 0 \tag{2.7}$$

and

$$0 \leq KC < B. \tag{2.7a}$$

Relation (2.7) can be justified as follows:
Assume that the total income in every period τ, indicated by total production $Y(\tau)$, will completely be distributed among the households. Thus the producers have to ask for credits, if they want to invest. Now a familar assumption is that the same interest rate and thus the same repayment rate will prevail for all loans and for all agents. Equation (2.7) then is just a linear from of the hypothesis that via saving behaviour of the households and/or via the behaviour of the banking system credits will become cheaper with increasing total income and with decreasing demand for credits. By simply using a macro-approch [see (2.7)] we do not specify the decision behaviour of households. The main reason for this procedure is to concentrate on the analysis of the strategic choice of the entrepreneurs. Our model can therefore be described as partially macroeconomic and partially microeconomic. We note that our approach is in the tradition of oligopoly theory where the behaviour of the households usually is summarized in a macroeconomic demand function. Of course, one could try to develop other models which would regard the households as players as well. On the one side this would allow to include more structural relationships, on the other side one would have to solve a much more complicated game.

According to (2.7a) coefficient B cannot be too small, i.e. we impose a minimum reactivity of the rate of interest to changes in total investment. With $B > CK$ we require that for an increase in total investment the (positive) effect on the interest rate in the same period is absolutely greater than its (negative) effect on the interest rate in the following period, which is determind by CK. Loosely speaking one could describe assumption $B > CK$ by the requirement that the net effect of an increase in total investment on the rate of interest has to be positive.

It should be mentioned that the linear form of equation (2.3) and equation (2.7) is essential. For our analysis this has the effect that the periodic payoff in period τ to producer i, $y_i(\tau+1) - r(\tau) x_i(\tau)$, is a quadratic function of $x_i(\tau)$ and that the total production $Y(\tau + 1)$ of the economy in period $\tau + 1$ is a linear function of the total investment $X(\tau)$.

Next we have to explain the concept of a strategy. At every time t all players (producers) $(1, \ldots, n)$ know all previous facts and decisions of all players. By $x(t) = [x_1(t), \ldots, x_n(t)]$ we denote the vector of investment decisions in time t. Then the vector $B(t) = [Y(1), x(1), \ldots, x(t-1)]$ [7]) contains all information up to time t, because the $y_i(\tau)$, $y(\tau)$ can be calculated by (2.3) and (2.5) for $\tau = 2, \ldots, t$. These relations are assumed to be known to all producers.

A strategy s_i of player $i (= 1, \ldots, n)$ is a mapping which associates an investment decision $s_i[B(t)] = x_i(t)$ to every possible vector $B(t)$ for all $t = 1, \ldots, T$.

For a given strategy vector $s = (s_1, \ldots, s_n)$, consisting of strategies s_i for every player i and for a given starting amount $Y(1)$ of the good of the economy, the development of the economy is uniquely determined if the players behave according to s. Thus also their payoffs are uniquely determined by (2.6). Indicating this dependence on $Y(1)$ and s we write $H_i[B(1), s]$ where $B(1) = [Y(1)]$. By s^i we denote the vector $(s_1, \ldots, s_{i-1}, s_{i+1}, \ldots, s_n)$ and by $(\bar{s}^i, s_i)$ the vector $(\bar{s}_1, \ldots, \bar{s}_{i-1}, s_i, \bar{s}_{i+1}, \ldots, \bar{s}_n)$.

A strategy vector $\bar{s} = (\bar{s}_1, \ldots, \bar{s}_n)$ is called an equilibrium point of the game starting at $Y(1)$ if

$$H_i[B(1), \bar{s}] \geqslant H_i[B(1), (\bar{s}^i, s_i)] \text{ for all strategies } s_i \text{ and for all } i = 1, \ldots, n. \tag{2.8}$$

Thus an equilibrium point can be characterized as a vector of mutually best reply-strategies. Rational behaviour must be based on an equilibrium point, since only equilibrium points yield self-stabilizing expectations in the sense that no single player can gain by deviating from the expected behaviour.

Since every producer i must independently choose his investment $x_i(t)$, every history $B(t)$ determines a subgame of the dynamic game (for the definition of a subgame see *Selten* [1975]) starting at t. Let s_i be a strategy of producer i in the dynamic game under consideration and let $B(t)$ be a history of period t. By s_i' we denote the restriction of s_i to all history vectors $B(\tau)$, $\tau = t, \ldots, T$, which can still result when $B(t)$ is taken as given. We say that s_i' is the strategy of producer i in the subgame starting in t after $B(t)$ which is induced by s_i. In the same way $s' = (s_1', \ldots, s_n')$ is called the strategy vector in the subgame starting in t after $B(t)$ which is induced by the strategy vector $s = (s_1, \ldots, s_n)$ of the original game.

The payoff of player i in the subgame starting in t after $B(t)$ is given by

$$H_i'[B(t), s'] = \sum_{\tau=t}^{T} \delta^{\tau-t}[y_i(\tau+1) - r(\tau)x_i(\tau)], \tag{2.9}$$

i.e. in every period t player i is interested in the discounted sum of his future profits. (2.9) is used to define equilibrium points of subgames analogously to (2.8).

A strategy vector $\bar{s} = (\bar{s}_1, \ldots, \bar{s}_n)$ is called a subgame perfect equilibrium point, if it induces for all periods $t = 1, \ldots, T$ and all possible histories $B(t)$ of period t a strategy

[7]) It will turn out that we may use instead of $B(t) = [Y(1), x(1), \ldots, x(t-1)]$ also $B(t) = [Y(1), X(1), \ldots, X(t-1)]$, which demands much less information.

vector s' which is an equilibrium point of the subgame starting in t after the history $B(t)$.

Once one has accepted that rational players will always choose equilibrium points, it is obvious that the decision behaviour of rational players must satisfy the condition of a subgame perfect equilibrium point as well. If a player considers only equilibrium points as solution candidates, he will do so in every subgame situation as well. Thus he will accept only subgame perfect equilibrium points as candidates for the solution of the game. It is essential to apply this more selective solution concept because there are lots of non subgame perfect equilibrium points in general (also in our case if $T \geqslant 2$).

It seems worthwhile to mention that in many applications[8]) one can find the equilibrium point as the solution concept for dynamic games. Instead of the definition of a strategy given above, which often is referred to as the concept of closed loop-strategies, in those applications, however, one uses the concept of an open loop-strategy. In our example an open-loop strategy requires a player to determine a specific choice $x_i(t)$ for every period $t = 1, \ldots, T$ already at the beginning of the game. Thus according to the concept of open loop-strategies a player cannot react to what he observes in the course of a dynamic game. This should make it clear how the concept of open loop-strategies eliminates the truly dynamic aspect of strategic interaction of players engaged in a non-cooperative dynamic game.

3. Analysis of the Pseudogame in the Finite Case

The game, which results when condition (2.2) is omitted, is called the pseudogame of the dynamic game. The following results are only valid for the pseudogame[9]). Let us first try to obtain an intuitive idea of the optimal behaviour in our game. Since the profit of period t according to (2.9) and (2.3) is given by

$$y_i(t+1) - r(t)\, x_i(t) = [K - r(t)]\, x_i(t) + L,$$

it follows – given a constant interest factor smaller K – that the profit is the higher the higher the amount of investment. However, r increases according to (2.7) with total investment and therefore also with individual investment $x_i(t)$. To determine the investment amount in period t one has also to consider the future profits which depend mainly on the future interest factors. According to (2.7) the future interest factors are the lower the higher the present investment and therefore the higher the future total incomes. This intertemporal interdependence will cause producer i to invest more in the present period

[8]) See for instance *Hoel* [1978] and *Dasgupta/Stiglitz* [1979].

[9]) We note that the necessity of imposing (2.2) arose because of the special structure of our model, which corresponds to that of the Ramsey model. If we would additionally admit e.g., the possibility to produce the consumption good alone with labor, then the total income of the economy would be composed of that income produced by labor, Y_L, and that by capital Y: $Y' = Y + Y_L$.

Thus the right-hand side of (2.2) $X \leqslant Y$ would be replaced by the weaker inequality $X \leqslant Y + Y_L$. If, in addition, we allow that the capitalists borrow from the workers, then their investment may exceed Y, since their consumption $C = Y - X$ needs only to satisfy $C \geqslant -Y_L$ and not as in our original model $C \geqslant 0$. Thus the left-hand side of (2.2) does not need to hold. With this background in mind, solving our pseudo-game might be more meaningful from an economical point of view, too.

than he would do if he had to consider only the present period. Of course, in a finite game the strength of this influence declines towards the end of the time horizon. Altogether we can therefore expect a development as indicated by figure 3.1 (the upper curve in figure 3.1 represents the limit of the curves if T goes to infinity).

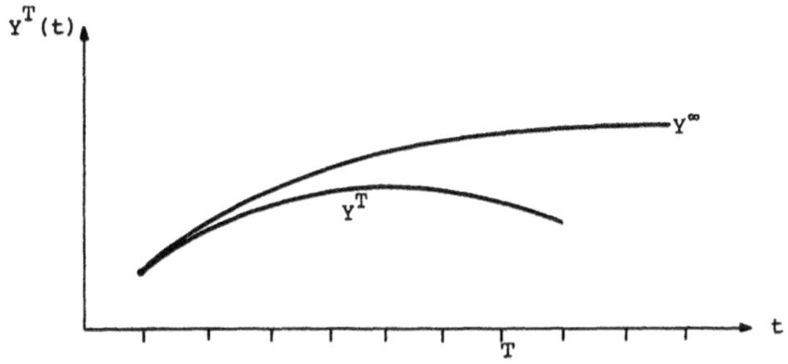

Fig. 3.1: Development of Total Income in a Finite Game

It will turn out that this game has exactly one subgame perfect equilibrium point $\bar{s}$. Moreover we shall prove by induction

$$H_i' [B(t+1), \bar{s}'] = V_{T-t} [Y(t+1)] \tag{3.1}$$

where

$$V_{T-t} [Y(t+1)] = C_{T-t} Y(t+1)^2 + D_{T-t} Y(t+1) + E_{T-t}, \quad (0 \leq t < T) \tag{3.1a}$$

is a quadratic polynomial depending only on the total amount $Y(t+1)$ available at time $t+1$. $Y(t+1)$ can be calculated from $B(t+1)$ by (2.3) and (2.5).

First it can be shown from (2.9) that (3.1) and (3.1a) are true for $t = T$ with

$$C_0 = D_0 = E_0 = 0,$$

since then

$$V_0 \equiv 0.$$

Now let us assume that (3.1) and (3.1a) are true for a given $t \leq T$. We start our game at t instead of $t+1$. Than means $B(t)$ and therefore $Y(t)$ are given. Using (3.1) we get

$$H_i' [B(t), s'] = [y_i(t+1) - r(t) x_i(t)] + \delta V_{T-t} [Y(t+1)]$$

where $x_i(t)$ is determined by s_i' which we assume to coincide with $\bar{s}_i'$ for later time points. For s' being a subgame perfect equilibrium point it is necessary that for every i this expression becomes maximal with respect to $x_i(t)$, especially

$$0 = \frac{\partial}{\partial x_i(t)} H_i' [B(t), s']. \tag{3.2}$$

Hence we obtain in view of (2.5), (2.7) and (3.1a)

$$K - A + CY(t) - B[X(t) + x_i(t)] + 2\delta C_{T-t} [KX(t) + nL] K + \delta D_{T-t} K = 0.$$

A simultaneous solution of these equations for $i = 1, \ldots, n$, say $x_1^*(t), \ldots, x_n^*(t)$, obviously fulfills $x_1^*(t) = x_2^*(t) = \ldots = x_n^*(t)$ since all expressions, except the fourth, do not depend on i and since we known that because of (2.7) we have $B \neq 0$.

We get

$$0 = K - A + CY(t) + 2\delta C_{T\text{-}t}\, nL \cdot K + \delta D_{T\text{-}k} K + [-B(n+1) + 2\delta C_{T\text{-}t} K^2 n]\, x_i^*(t) \tag{3.3}$$

$$x_i^*(t) = \frac{CY(t) + 2\delta C_{T\text{-}t} nLK + \delta D_{T\text{-}t} K + K - A}{(n+1)B - 2\delta n C_{T\text{-}t} K^2}, \tag{3.4a}$$

$$x_i^*(t) = A_{T\text{-}t} + B_{T\text{-}t}\, Y(t), \tag{3.4}$$

with

$$A_j = \frac{2\delta n C_j LK + \delta D_j K + K - A}{(n+1)B - 2\delta n C_j K^2} \tag{3.5}$$

$$B_j = \frac{C}{(n+1)B - 2\delta n C_j K^2}. \tag{3.6}$$

We will also prove in a Lemma (see below) by induction that

$$C_j' = \frac{\delta K^2}{B} C_j < 1/2n < 1 \qquad j = (1, 2, \ldots). \tag{3.7}$$

Thus the coefficient of $x_i^*(t)$ in (3.3) and the denominator in (3.4a) is $\neq 0$, and because of (3.2) and (3.7)

$$\frac{\partial^2}{\partial x_i(t)^2} H_i' [B(t), s'] = -2B + 2\delta C_{T\text{-}t} K^2 = -2B(1 - C_{T\text{-}t}') < 0.$$

Therefore $x_i^*(t)$ is optimal. Thus we get from (3.4) and (2.5)

$$X(t) = nA_{T\text{-}t} + nB_{T\text{-}t} Y(t)$$

$$Y(t+1) = KnA_{T\text{-}t} + KnB_{T\text{-}t} Y(t) + nL. \tag{3.8a}$$

Hence we obtain from (3.1) and by induction hypothesis

$$\begin{aligned} V_{T\text{-}t+1}[Y(t)] &= \delta V_{T\text{-}t}[Y(t+1)] + [K - r(t)]\, x_i^*(t) + L \\ &= \delta C_{T\text{-}t} [KnA_{T\text{-}t} + nL + KnB_{T\text{-}t} Y(t)]^2 \\ &\quad + \delta D_{T\text{-}t} [KnA_{T\text{-}t} + nL + KnB_{T\text{-}t} Y(t)] + \delta E_{T\text{-}t} \\ &\quad + [K - A - nB(A_{T\text{-}t} + B_{T\text{-}t} Y(t)) + CY(t)]\, [A_{T\text{-}t} + B_{T\text{-}t} Y(t)] + L \\ &= C_{T\text{-}t+1} Y(t)^2 + D_{T\text{-}t+1} Y(t) + E_{T\text{-}t+1}. \end{aligned}$$

For $j = T - t$ the coefficients C_{T-t+1}, D_{T-t+1} and E_{T-t+1} are thus given by

$$C_{j+1} = \delta C_j (KnB_j)^2 - nB\, B_j^2 + CB_j \tag{3.8}$$

$$D_{j+1} = 2\delta C_j n^2 KB_j (KA_j + L) + \delta D_j KnB_j + (C - 2nBB_j) A_j + (K - A) B_j \tag{3.9}$$

$$E_{j+1} = \delta C_j n^2 (KA_j + L)^2 + \delta D_j n (KA_j + L) + \delta E_j + (K - A - nBA_j) A_j + L. \tag{3.10}$$

Thus we have proved (3.1a) and therefore that V_{T-t} is a quadratic polynominal depending only on $Y(t + 1)$. Our proof also shows the uniqueness of the subgame perfect equilibrium point $\bar{s}$. It is given by (3.4).

We want to analyze how our coefficients depend on the time difference index $j = T - t$. For this purpose we first turn our attention to (3.7). For a proof of (3.7) for the case $j + 1$ we observe that in (3.8) B_j may be expressed by C_j by (3.6), giving a recursive relation for the $C_0, C_1, C_2, \ldots$ only in terms of the latter. Expressing this relation using the C_j' we get

$$C_{j+1}' = \delta' g_n (C_j'), \text{ where } g_n(x) = \frac{u_n + v_n x}{(w_n - x)^2} \quad \text{for } 0 \leqslant x < w_n \tag{3.11}$$

with

$$u_n = \frac{1}{4n^2}, \; v_n = \frac{n-2}{4n}, \; w_n = \frac{n+1}{2n} \; (n \geqslant 1) \text{ and } \delta' = \delta K^2 C^2 / B^2.$$

Instead of (3.7) we state the following sharper lemma, because for later discussions we need more properties of the sequence C_j', especially its monotonicity and its limiting behaviour.

Lemma

1a) For every natural $n \geqslant 1$ and every real $\delta' \in [0,1]$ the function $\delta' g_n$ has a fix point x' [that means $x' = \delta' g_n(x')$] with $0 \leqslant x' \leqslant 1/2n < w_n$ and $x' = 1/2n$, if $\delta' = 1$. [10])
 b) For $\delta' > 1$, there exists no fixpoint $x' \geqslant 0$.
2) Moreover,
 a) for $\delta' \in [0,1]$ the sequence C_j' ($j = 0, 1, \ldots$) is well defined by (3.11). It fulfils $0 = C_0' \leqslant C_1' \leqslant \ldots$ and has the fixpoint x' as a limit C_∞'.
 b) If $\delta' > 1$, there exists a smallest $j > 0$ such that $C_j' \geqslant w_n$.

The proof is given in the Appendix.

If $\bar{s}$ is applied, we get from (2.5) and (3.4)

$$Y(t+1) = \sum_i [Kx_i(t) + L] = n(KA_{T-t} + L) + nKB_{T-t} Y(t)$$

$$= a_{T-t} + b_{T-t} \cdot Y(t), \tag{3.12}$$

[10]) At the end of Section 4 we have proved (in accordance with our computations in Section 5) that $x' = C_\infty'$ converges to zero faster than $1/2n$ for n to infinity, namely like $\delta'/(1 - \delta') \cdot n^2$.

where

$$a_j = n\,(KA_j + L) \tag{3.13}$$

and

$$b_j = nKB_j \tag{3.14}$$

or in view of (3.6), (3.7) and (3.11)

$$b_j = \frac{KC/2B}{w_n - C'_j}. \tag{3.14a}$$

Since $0 \leqslant \delta \leqslant 1$, $C'_0 = 0$ the Lemma and (2.7a) imply

$$0 \leqslant b_0 = \frac{KC/B}{(n+1)/n} \leqslant b_1 \leqslant b_2 \leqslant \ldots \leqslant b_\infty = \frac{KC/B}{2\,(w_n - C'_\infty)} \leqslant KC/B < 1. \tag{3.15}$$

Substituting the expressions (3.5) and (3.6) for A_j, B_j into the formula (3.9) for D_{j+1} and using

$$\rho_j = 1 - \frac{1}{n}\left(1 + \frac{n-1}{2\,(w_n - C'_j}\right) \tag{3.16}$$

which fulfills because of our Lemma

$$\frac{1}{n} > \frac{n-1}{n\,(n+1)} = \rho_0 \geqslant \rho_1 \geqslant \rho_2 \geqslant \ldots \geqslant \rho_\infty \geqslant 0, \tag{3.17}$$

we get from (3.5), (3.6), (3.7), (3.9) and (3.14a)

$$D_{j+1} = (1-\rho_j)\,\delta b_j D_j + \frac{C}{W_n - C'_j}\left[\frac{L}{K}C'_j\,(n-\rho_j)\right.$$

$$\left. + \frac{K-A}{2B}\left(\frac{1}{n} - \rho_j\right)\right]. \tag{3.18}$$

Because of (2.7) and (3.15) we know that $b_j \cdot \delta \leqslant \delta\,((KC)/B) < 1$. Hence the convergence of b_j implies the convergence of the sequence D_j [11]), A_j, E_j, and, of course, of B_j, a_j.

We also have

$$0 = D_0 \leqslant D_1 \leqslant D_2 \leqslant \ldots \leqslant D_\infty =$$

$$= [1 - (1-\rho_\infty)\,b_\infty\,\delta]^{-1}\,\frac{C}{w_n - C'_\infty}\left[(n-\rho_\infty)\frac{L}{K}C'_\infty + \left(\frac{1}{n} - \rho_\infty\right)\frac{K-A}{2B}\right]. \tag{3.19}$$

This implies because of (3.5) and since C_j and D_j are increasing sequences

[11]) The convergence of D_j follows according to a theorem of Toeplitz on iterations with a converging sequence of linear operators. We are grateful to Dieter Reetz for this hint.

$$0 < A_0 = \frac{K-A}{(n+1)B} \leqslant A_1 \leqslant A_2 \leqslant \ldots \leqslant A_\infty = \frac{1}{n}\frac{1}{w_n - C'_\infty}\left(C'_\infty \frac{nL}{K} + \frac{\delta D_\infty K + K - A}{2B}\right). \tag{3.20}$$

Using (3.14) we can derive from (3.15)

$$0 \leqslant B_0 \leqslant B_1 \leqslant \ldots \leqslant B_\infty = \frac{C/B}{2n\,(w_n - C'_\infty)} \tag{3.20a}$$

and

$$0 \leqslant a_0 = n\left(K\frac{K-A}{(n+1)B} + L\right) \leqslant a_1 \leqslant a_2 \leqslant \ldots \leqslant a_\infty. \tag{3.21}$$

If we start our game with $Y(1) \geqslant 0$, we get

$$Y(t) \geqslant 0 \quad \text{for} \quad 0 < t \leqslant T+1.$$

Thus

$$a_0 + b_0 Y(t) \leqslant Y(t+1) \leqslant a_\infty + b_\infty Y(t). \tag{3.22}$$

Applying (3.22) recursively we obtain

$$\frac{a_0}{1-b_0} + b_0^t\left(Y(1) - \frac{a_0}{1-b_0}\right) \leqslant Y(t+1) \leqslant \frac{a_\infty}{1-b_\infty} + b_\infty^t\left(Y(1) - \frac{a_\infty}{a-b_\infty}\right), \tag{3.23}$$

since $b_0 < 1$ and $b_\infty < 1$ in view of (2.7a) and (3.15). This implies

$$\min\left[Y(1), \frac{a_0}{1-b_0}\right] \leqslant Y(t+1) \leqslant \max\left[Y(1), \frac{a_\infty}{1-b_\infty}\right] \quad (0 \leqslant t \leqslant T). \tag{3.24}$$

Now we have to check $0 \leqslant X(t) \leqslant Y(t)$, i.e. whether restriction (2.2) is fulfilled. Since $A_j \geqslant 0, B_j \geqslant 0$, also $X(t) \geqslant 0$.

In order to show that investment cannot exceed total income we assume

$$(1 - nB_\infty)\left[\min\left(Y(1), \frac{a_0}{1-b_0}\right)\right] - nA_\infty \geqslant 0 \tag{3.25}$$

or via (3.20a)

$$\left(1 - \frac{C/B}{2\,(w_n - C'_\infty)}\right)\left[\min\left(Y(1), \frac{a_0}{1-b_0}\right]\right. - nA_\infty \geqslant 0. \tag{3.25a}$$

Because of (3.20) this implies $C < B2\,(w_n - C'_\infty)$.

Thus from (3.8a), (3.20) and (3.20a) follows:

$$Y(t) - X(t) = Y(t) - nA_{T-t} - nB_{T-t}\,Y(t) \geqslant Y(t) - nA_\infty - nB_\infty\,Y(t)$$

$$= \left[1 - \frac{C/B}{2\,(w_n - C_\infty)}\right] Y(t) - nA_\infty$$

$$\geqslant \left(1 - \frac{C/B}{2(w_n - C'_\infty)}\right) \min \left(Y(1), \frac{a_0}{1-b_0}\right) - nA_\infty \geqslant 0$$

by assumption (3.25a).

Thus we have proved:

Theorem 1. The pseudogame of every dynamic game satisfying the assumptions in Section 2 has a unique subgame perfect equilibrium point which is recursively defined by (3.4), (3.5), (3.6), (3.8) and (3.9).

Theorem 2. If

$$\left(1 - \frac{C/B}{2(w_n - C'_\infty)}\right) \frac{a_0}{1-b_0} - nA_\infty \geqslant 0 \tag{3.26}$$

is fulfilled, we get $0 \leqslant X(t) \leqslant Y(t)$ $(1 \leqslant t \leqslant T+1)$ for all starting points

$$Y(1) \geqslant (1 - nB_\infty)^{-1} nA_\infty = \left(1 - \frac{C/B}{2(w_n - C'_\infty)}\right)^{-1} nA_\infty . \tag{3.27}$$

Let the present time period be $t = 1$ and assume that the number T of future time periods is large enough so that condition (3.27) is a good approximation of the condition which ensures $0 \leqslant X(t) \leqslant Y(t)$ for all $t = 1, \ldots, T$. Now a developing economy could be described as a country where it pays to keep the present consumption level as low as possible since investment yields more profitable prospects. Only if production possibilities are large enough to allow for more than a minimum level of consumption, one would accordingly speak of a developed economy. Given this classification of developing and developed economies condition (3.27) of Theorem 2 gives an exact definition to characterize the production economies, analyzed in this paper as developing or developed: If condition (3.27) is satisfied by the present state variable $Y(1)$, the economy is considered as developed; if not, we speak of a developing economy. To investigate how the parameters determining the structural relationships of the economy influence the state of being developing or developed, one then only has to analyze the way in which condition (3.27) is influenced by changes of these parameter values.

To get some ideas how the coefficients C'_j, B_j, k_j, ρ_j, D_j, A_j, a_j and E_j depend on $j = T - t$ we give the following numerical examples:

$K = 1{,}3$; $A = 0{,}8$; $B = 0{,}4$; $C = 0{,}1$;

$L = 0$; $\delta = 0{,}98$; $n = 3$.

Then $KC/B = 0.325$ and

$$\delta' = \delta \frac{C^2 K^2}{B^2} \doteq 0.98 \frac{0 \cdot 1^2 \cdot 1.69}{0.16} = 0.1035125;$$

$$u_n = \frac{1}{36}, v_n = 1/12, w_n = \frac{2}{3}.$$

The computation gives the following results (see Table 3.1)

j	C_j	B_j	b_j	$1-\rho_j$	D_j	A_j	a_j	E_j
0	0.00000000	0.06250	0.2437	0.1666	0.00000	0.3125	1.219	0.00000
1	0.00646953	0.06311	0.2461	0.1618	0.01690	0.3292	1.284	0.05835
2	0.00672498	0.06314	0.2462	0.1616	0.01693	0.3293	1.284	0.1156
3	0.00673525	0.06314	0.2462	0.1616	0.01693	0.3293	1.284	0.1718
4	0.00673566	0.06314	0.2462	0.1616	0.01693	0.3293	1.284	0.2268
5	0.00673568	0.06314	0.2462	0.1616	0.01693	0.3293	1.284	0.2807
∞	0.00673568	0.06314	0.2462	0.1616	0.01693	0.3293	1.284	0.3336

$X(\infty) = 1.311$, $Y(\infty) = 1.704$, $r(\infty) = 1.15387440$.

Tab. 3.1

To check whether condition (3.26) of our Theorem 2 is fulfilled we carry out the following calculations:

$$\frac{a_0}{1-b_0} = \frac{1.2187}{0.7562} = 1.61157;$$

$$\frac{C/B}{2\,(w_n - C'_\infty)} = \frac{0.75}{4-6C'_\infty} = \frac{0.75}{3.9595848} = 0.1894137.$$

Hence we obtain

$$\left[1 - \frac{C/B}{2\,(w_n - C'_\infty)}\right] \frac{a_0}{1-b_0} = 0.8105863 \cdot 1.61157 = 1.306316 \geqslant nA_\infty = 0.9879.$$

Thus (3.26) is satisfied and therefore our Theorem 2 applies to all starting points with

$$Y(1) \geqslant 0.9879/0.8105863 = 1.2187569. \qquad (3.28)$$

As Theorem 2 and the numerical example show, the solution of the pseudogame is feasible in the original dynamic game if the initial income level $Y(1)$ is high enough. In cases where this is not true the solution of the pseudogame implies $X(t) \geqslant Y(t)$ for at last one period t and thus implies a nonpositive consumption level in t.

Table 3.2 shows the development of income $Y^T(t)$, which depends on the length of the time horizon T and on the period t (for our example with $n = 3$).

Using (3.12), (3.28) and the coefficients of Table 3.1 we have calculated the values of Table 3.1 we have calculated the values of Table 3.2. They are shown in Figure 3.2 [12]).

[12])We note (as one can also see from our Table 3.2) that in general $\lim_{T\to\infty} Y^T(T+1)$ does exist but it is different from $Y^\infty(\infty)$ since in general $\lim_{t\to\infty} \lim_{T\to\infty} Y^T(t) = \lim_{t\to\infty} Y^\infty(t) = Y^\infty(\infty) \neq$ $\neq \lim_{T\to\infty} Y^T(T+1)$ (see Figure 3.2).

T \ t	1	2	3	4	5	6
1	1.218757	1.5158203				
2	1.218757	1.5839360	1.6048344			
3	1.218757	1.5840579	1.6738366	1.6267476		
4	1.218757	1.5840579	1.6739950	1.6959311	1.6321332	
5	1.218757	1.5840579	1.6739950	1.6961375	1.7013686	1.633458
∞	1.218757	1.5840579	1.6739950	1.6961375	1.7015890	1.703369

Tab. 3.2: Development of Income $Y^T(t)$ in Dependence of Time Horizon T and Period t

We note that the analysis of the game with infinite length will be given in Section 4 and its economic discussion in Section 5.

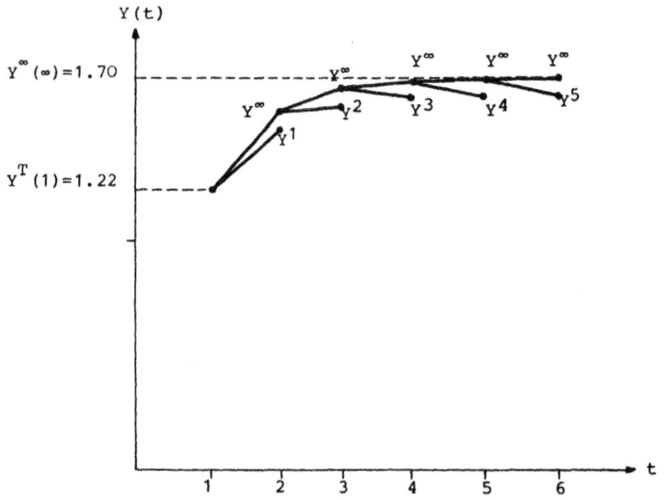

Fig. 3.2: Income $Y^T(t)$ in Dependence on Time Horizon T and Period t for $1 \leqslant t \leqslant T + 1$

We believe that a nonlinear relationship for the return rate, tending to infinity, when consumption tends to zero, is more realistic so that restriction (2.2) would be automatically satisfied by the solution of the game.

For the time being we therefore omit the detailed analysis of the game restricted by (2.2). After this section we will turn over the pseudogame of infinite length in Sectinn 4.

We need the game of infinite length, because a stationary situation, which, of course, is useful for any economic discussion and comparison with other theories, will appear only in the game of infinite length. For the stationary situation we will then discuss also the limit case ($n \to \infty$) of perfect competition.

In the Appendix (Section 6.2) we discuss the restrictions on the parameters δ, K, C, B and T of the game.

4. The Pseudogame with Infinite Length

The solution of the game, not restricted by (2.2) and with $0 < \delta < 1$, [13]) becomes more simple and therefore easier to discuss, if we consider the version of infinite length. That means, we have to replace T in the definition of the payoff function H_i by ∞.

The definition of subgame perfect equilibrium points remains the same[14]). In this section we will show that the unique subgame perfect equilibrium point $\bar{s}^T$ of the corresponding game of length T will converge for $T \to \infty$ to a subgame perfect equilibrium point $\bar{s}$ of the game with infinite length. We believe that this subgame perfect equilibrium point which is the limit of those for finite T is the only one of interest.

Equation (3.4)

$$x_i(t) = A_{T-t} + B_{T-t} Y(t) \qquad (1 \leqslant t \leqslant T)$$

defines the unique subgame perfect equilibrium points $\bar{s}^T$ of the game of length T. Now we have to fix t and let T tend to infinity. Then also $T-t$ tends to infinity and therefore A_{T-t} and B_{T-t} tend to A_∞ and B_∞ respectively, as proved in section 3.1. Therefore $\bar{s}^T$ tends to $\bar{s}$, defined by

$$x_i(t) = A_\infty + B_\infty Y(t) \qquad (1 \leqslant t < +\infty). \tag{4.1}$$

We have to check whether $\bar{s}$ is a subgame perfect equilibrium point of the game with infinite length. This means, that for every history $B(t+1)$ and any strategy s_i we have to prove

$$H_i[B(t+1), \bar{s}] = H_i[B(t+1), (\bar{s}^i, \bar{s}_i)] \geqslant H_i[B(t+1), (\bar{s}^i, s_i)]. \tag{4.2}$$

The payoff for the game of length T shall now be denoted by H_i^T. Of course, it is possible to use the strategies of the infinite game, by applying them only to time points $1, 2, \ldots, T$. For such strategies we have by definition

$$H_i[B(t+1), s] = \lim_{T \to \infty} H_i^T[B(t+1), s]. \tag{4.3}$$

Furthermore we know

$$H_i^T[B(t+1), (\bar{s}^{T,i}, \bar{s}_i^T)] \geqslant H_i^T[B(t+1), (\bar{s}^{T,i}, s_i')] \tag{4.4}$$

for any strategy s_i' of the game of infinite length. Especially we take for s_i' the open loop strategy[15]), which gives the same investment amounts $x_i(\tau)$ $(\tau > t)$ as s_i, when this is applied together with $\bar{s}^i$ starting at $B(t+1)$.

Therefore

$$H_i[B(t+1), (\bar{s}^i, s_i)] = H_i[B(t+1), (\bar{s}^i, s_i')]. \tag{4.5}$$

---

[13]) $\delta = 0$ can be treated as $T = 1$.

[14]) For subgames we use the payoff (2.6) of the total game instead of (2.9). They are equivalent, if $\delta > 0$.

[15]) It should be obvious how the set of open loop-strategies can be embedded into the larger set of closed loop-strategies.

(4.2) is proved, if we show that the left hand side of (4.4) tends to that of (4.2) and that the right hand side of (4.4) tends to that of (4.2) or of (4.5), as T tends to infinity[16]).

We prove (4.2) directly without using (4.4) by employing the potential method which works as follows. First one has to guess a more explicit function for the left hand side of (4.2). Of course, this will be

$$\sum_{\tau=1}^{t} [K - r(\tau)]\, x_i(\tau)\, \delta^{\tau-1} + \delta^t V_\infty [Y(t+1)], \tag{4.6}$$

where

$$V_\infty(Y) = C_\infty Y^2 + D_\infty Y + E_\infty, \tag{4.7}$$

because the left hand side of (4.4) is equal to (4.6) with V_{T-t} instead of V_∞ which converges to (4.6) for $T \to \infty$. We guess that this limit is the left hand side of (4.2).

For the first sum of (4.6) we introduce a new variable w and define the potential by

$$W[w, t+1, Y] = w + \delta^t V_\infty(Y) \tag{4.8}$$

for all real w and Y and all integers $t \geqslant 0$. Our new state space shall consist of all these triples $(w, t+1, Y)$.

Since the strategy vector $\bar{s}^i$ of the other players is considered as given, we can restrate the optimization problem for player i as follows; It is sufficient to compare $\bar{s}_i$ to open loop strategies s_i' consisting merely of a sequence $(x_i(1), x_i(2), \ldots)$. Starting at some state $(w, t+1, Y)$ we get a sequence $(w(\tau), \tau, Y(\tau))$ with $\tau = t+1, t+2, \ldots$, where $w(t+1) = w$, $Y(t+1) = Y$ and

$$\begin{aligned} &Y(\tau+1) = K \cdot X(\tau) + nL \\ &w(\tau+1) = w(\tau) + \delta^\tau [K - A - BX(\tau) + CY(\tau)]\, x_i(\tau). \end{aligned} \tag{4.9}$$

Using (4.1) for all players except player i we obtain for $X(\tau)$ in (4.9)

$$X(\tau) = (n-1)(A_\infty + B_\infty Y(\tau)) + x_i(\tau). \tag{4.9a}$$

Instead of $H_i[B(t+1), \bar{s}^i, s_i']$ we write now $H_i(w, t+1, Y, s_i')$ and define this [instead of (4.3)] as

$$H_i(w, t+1, Y, s_i') = \lim_{\tau \to \infty} \sup w(\tau), \tag{4.10}$$

so that we include also those cases, where the limit does not exist.

Now we state the crucial properties of W which we need for our proof.

$$W[w(\tau+1), \tau+1, Y(\tau+1)] \leqslant W[w(\tau), \tau, Y(\tau)] \quad \text{for every } s_i' \tag{4.11}$$

and

$$W[w(\tau+1), \tau+1, Y(\tau+1)] = W[w(\tau), \tau, Y(\tau)], \tag{4.12}$$

if s_i' is the result of $\bar{s}_i$.

[16]) Both statements are true by Fatou's lemma, if there is a majorizing function g, that means with $\Sigma g(\tau) < +\infty$ and $\delta^\tau \mid (K - r(\tau))\, x_i(\tau) \mid \leqslant g(\tau)$ for all strategies involved. Actually weaker statements suffice provable by the one sided Fatou's Lemma. But in any case this is a cumbersome way.

Of course, one may check (4.11), (4.12) directly. But the most convenient way is to define first W^T instead of W by (4.8) with V_{T-t} instead of V_∞ as potential for the finite game and for $t \leqslant T$. In (4.9a) we have to replace A_∞ and B_∞ by $A_{T-\tau}$ and $B_{T-\tau}$ respectively. Then (4.11) and (4.12) are true for W^T instead of W and $\bar{s}_i^T$ instead of $\bar{s}_i$; because $\bar{s}_i^T$ determines the investment amount $x_i(\tau)$ in such a way as to make W^T $[w(\tau+1), \tau+1, Y(\tau+1)]$ a maximum starting at $(w(\tau), \tau, Y(\tau))$, and $V_{T-\tau+1}$ is defined so that (4.12) holds. With $T \to \infty$ we get (4.11) and (4.12) for W by continuity.

Now, since V_∞ is bounded from below and $\delta^\tau \to 0$ for $\tau \to \infty$, we get by (4.11)

$$\begin{aligned} H_i(w, t+1, Y, s_i') &\leqslant \lim_{\tau \to \infty} \sup \,[w(\tau) + \delta^{\tau-1} V_\infty(Y(\tau))] \\ &= \lim_{\tau \to \infty} \sup W[w(\tau), \tau, Y(\tau)]. \\ &\leqslant W[w, t+1, Y]. \end{aligned} \tag{4.13}$$

This result is also true, if we replace lim sup by lim inf in (4.10) and in the proof.

If s_i' is the result of $\bar{s}_i$, then by (4.12) $\lim\limits_{\tau \to \infty} W(w(\tau), \tau, Y(\tau)) = W(w, t+1, Y)$. If we can prove that

$$\lim_{\tau \to \infty} \delta^{\tau-1} V_\infty (Y(\tau)) = 0 \tag{4.14}$$

is true, then we get

$$\begin{aligned} H_i(w, t+1, Y, s_i') &= \lim_{\tau \to \infty} w(\tau) = \lim_{\tau \to \infty} W(w(\tau)\, \tau, Y(\tau)) \\ &= W(w, t+1, Y). \end{aligned} \tag{4.15}$$

From (4.13) and (4.15) follows the optimality of $\bar{s}_i$ and therefore (4.2). In addition it follows, that $H_i(B(t+1), \bar{s})$ is equal to (4.6).

To prove (4.14) we use

$$Y(\tau+1) = a_\infty + b_\infty Y(\tau). \tag{4.16}$$

As $b_\infty < 1$, $Y(\tau)$ $(\tau = t+1, \ldots)$ remains bounded, because it tends to the stationary value $a_\infty/(1-b_\infty)$, and (4.14) follows. Thus we have proved that $\bar{s}$ is a subgame perfect equilibrium point of the game of infinite length.

Now we will summarize our results.

Theorem 3. There is a subgame perfect equilibrium point $\bar{s}$ of the pseudogame of infinite length. $\bar{s}$ is the limit of the unique subgame perfect equilibrium points of the corresponding games of finite length. $\bar{s}$ is defined by (4.1). It is stationary which means that the coefficients do not depend on t. The payoff for player i, when $\bar{s}$ is applied starting at the history $B(t+1)$, is given by (4.6) with V_∞ from (4.7). Especially, if $\bar{s}$ is applied from the starting point $Y(1)$, the payoff is

$$H_i(Y(1), \bar{s}) = V_\infty(Y(1)). \tag{4.17}$$

For all variables, for example $X(t)$, $Y(t)$, $r(t)$, the limits for $t \to \infty$ do exist independently of the starting point $Y(1)$ for example $X(\infty)$, $Y(\infty)$, $r(\infty)$.

We merely have to prove the last statement.

The development of the total income $Y(t)$ is given by (4.16). As b_∞, given by (3.15), is < 1, we have

$$Y(t) = \frac{a_\infty}{1 - b_\infty} + b_\infty^{t-1} \left(Y(1) - \frac{a_\infty}{1 - b_\infty} \right), \tag{4.18}$$

which shows that $Y(t)$ tends to the stationary value

$$Y(\infty) = a_\infty / (1 - b_\infty) = n(KA_\infty + L) / (1 - b_\infty), \tag{4.19}$$

independently of the starting value $Y(1)$.

Using (2.5), (2.7), (4.1) and (4.19) we see that $X(t)$ tends to $X(\infty) = A_\infty + B_\infty Y(\infty) = (1/K)(Y(\infty) - nL)$ and $r(t)$ tends to $r(\infty) = A + nBA_\infty - (C - nBB_\infty) a_\infty / (1 - b_\infty)$.

From (2.7) and (2.5) we obtain

$$r(t) = A + B \frac{Y(t+1) - nL}{K} - CY(t)$$

and therefore also

$$\begin{aligned} r(\infty) &= A + \frac{1}{K} (B - CK) Y(\infty) - BnL \\ &= A + \frac{1}{1 - b_\infty} (B - CK) nA_\infty - n \frac{BL}{K} \left(\frac{CK}{B} - b_\infty \right). \end{aligned} \tag{4.20}$$

Thus for $L = 0$ we have because of (2.7a)

$$r(\infty) = A + \frac{B - CK}{K} Y(\infty)$$

or

$$r(\infty) = A + \frac{B - CK}{1 - b_\infty} nA_\infty > A. \tag{4.21}$$

In our numerical example of Section 3 we got

$$r(\infty) = 1.15387440.$$

Theorem 4. If we define

$$\bar{Y} = \frac{KnA_\infty}{K - b_\infty} \doteq \frac{a_\infty - nL}{K - b_\infty} < Y(\infty) \tag{4.22}$$
[17])

[17]) $\bar{Y}$ is equal to the right hand side of (3.27).

then for all periods, in which $Y(t) \geqslant \bar{Y}$, (2.2) is fulfilled.

Proof. Because of (4.16)

$$Y(T) - X(t) = Y(t) - (Y(t+1) - nL)/K$$

$$= Y(t) - (a_\infty + b_\infty Y(t) - nL)/K = \frac{1}{K}[(K - b_\infty)Y(t) - (a_\infty - nL)] \geqslant 0.$$

Now let us discuss under the assumption (2.7a) the limit case for $n \to \infty$. Since $C'_\infty < 1/2n$, one knows that $2(w_n - C'_\infty) \to 1$, $b_\infty \to KC/B < 1$, $\rho_\infty \to 0$, $D_\infty \to 0$. The last statement is true, because $n \cdot C'_\infty \to 0$. This can be seen from

$$C'_\infty = \delta' \frac{u_n + v_n C'_\infty}{(w_n - C'_\infty)^2}$$

or

$$nC'_\infty = \delta' \frac{(1/4n) + ((n-2)/4n)\, nC'_\infty}{(1/2 + 1/2n - C'_\infty)^2}$$

or

$$nC'_\infty = \frac{\delta'}{n} \cdot \left[\left(1 + \frac{1}{n} - 2C'_\infty\right)^2 - \delta' \frac{n-2}{n}\right]^{-1}$$

Since $C'_\infty \to 0$, the bracket on the right-hand side tends to $1 - \delta'$. Therefore nC'_∞ tends to 0 like $\delta'/(n \cdot (1 - \delta'))$.

Furthermore $n \cdot A_\infty \to (K - A)/B$ and

$$n \cdot \left(\frac{CK}{B} - b_\infty\right) = \frac{CK}{B} n \cdot \frac{2(w_n - C'_\infty) - 1}{2(w_n - C'_\infty)} = \frac{CK}{B} n \frac{1/n - 2C'_\infty}{2(w_n - C'_\infty)}$$

$$= \frac{CK}{B} \frac{1 - 2nC'_\infty}{2(w_n - C'_\infty)} \to \frac{CK}{B}.$$

Hence we obtain

$$r(\infty) \to A + \frac{1}{(1 - CK)/B}(B - CK)\frac{K - A}{B} - \frac{BL}{K} \cdot \frac{CK}{B} =$$

$$= A + K - A - CL = K - CL. \tag{4.23}$$

Thus in case $L = 0$ and in the limit $n \to \infty$, i.e. in case of perfect competition, we get the usual result

$$r(\infty) \to K.$$

Furthermore for $L = 0$ the stationary income $Y(\infty) = K((nA_\infty)/(1 - b_\infty))$ tends to $K \cdot ((K - A)/(B - KC))$.

But for $L > 0$, $Y(\infty)$ grows for $n \to \infty$ like $K((K - A)/(B - KC)) + n \cdot (L/(1 - KC/B))$.

5. The Dependence of the Interest Rate, of Investment and of Income on the Market Structure

We will conclude our paper with a discussion on how the economic development of X, Y and r depends on the market structure. The relevant formula for $r(\infty)$ for the stationary case has been derived in (4.22). Since A_∞ and b_∞ depend in a nontrivial way on n, which characterizes the market structure, it is difficult to study the influence of n on $r(\infty)$ analytically. We therefore have computed $r(\infty)$ dependent on n for 13 sets of parameters (see Table 5.1).

Run	K	A	B	C	L	δ
1	1.1	0.6	0.5	0.1	0	0.8
2–5	1.1; 1.2; 1.3; 1.8	0.6	0.5	0.1	0	0.98
6–9	1.1; 1.2; 1.3; 1.8	0.8	0.5	0.1	0	0.98
10–13	1.1; 1.2; 1.3; 1.8	0.8	0.4	0.1	0	0.98

Tab. 5.1

Since the development for all the runs is very similar, it suffices to describe one of them. To do this, we employ the situation with $(K = 1.3; A = 8; B = .5; C = 1; L = 0, \delta = .98)$. Besides the interest factor $r(\infty)$ we have also calculated total investment, $X(\infty)$, and total income $Y(\infty)$ for the stationary solution $(j = \infty)$ (see Table 5.2).

n	Investment $X(\infty)$	Income $Y(\infty)$	Interestrate $r(\infty) - 1$	$K - 1 - 1/n$
1	0.6620	0.8606	0.04494095	−0.700
2	0.8649	1.124	0.11999893	−0.200
3	0.9708	1.262	0.15919018	$-0.03\bar{3}$
4	1.038	1.349	0.18395329	0.050
5	1.108	1.410	0.20117569	0.100
6	1.119	1.454	0.21389389	$0.13\bar{3}$
7	1.145	1.489	0.22368813	0.157
8	1.166	1.516	0.23146915	0.175
9	1.183	1.538	0.23780441	$0.18\bar{8}$
10	1.197	1.557	0.24306202	0.200
20	1.268	1.648	0.26912212	0.250
30	1.294	1.682	0.27880955	$0.26\bar{6}$
40	1.308	1.700	0.2838974	0.275
50	1.316	1.711	0.28697872	0.280
60	1.322	1.718	0.28908157	0.285
70	1.326	1.724	0.29060078	0.286
80	1.329	1.728	0.29174805	0.288
90	1.331	1.731	0.29264641	0.289

n	Investment $X(\infty)$	Income $Y(\infty)$	Interestrate $r(\infty)-1$	$K-1-1/n$
100	1.333	1.733	0.29336834	0.290
200	1.342	1.745	0.29665279	0.295
300	1.345	1.749	0.29776192	0.297
700	1.349	1.753	0.29903698	0.2985
1000	1.350	1.754	0.29932499	0.299
5000	1.351	1.756	0.29986477	0.2998
10000	1.351	1.757	0.29993248	0.2999

Tab. 5.2: Stationary Solution ($j = \infty$) for Different Market Structures, Expressed by the Number of of Players, n.
(Run 8: $A = .8, B = .5, C = .1, K = 1.3, L = 0, \delta = .98$)

All three economic variables increase montonously with n. Since the investment/income ratio is constant for all n (this follows from (2.5) and $L = 0$, total consumption, $Y - X$, increases with n, as well. The convergences of X and Y are faster than that of the interest rate, $r - 1$ (see Table 5.3).

Percentage of Value for $n = \infty$	n	$X(\infty)$	$X(\infty)$	n	$r(\infty)-1$
90 %	13	1.219	1.581	21	0.27
95 %	28	1.287	1.672	44	0.285
99 %	190	1.341	1.739	230	0.297
100 %	∞	1.355	1.757	∞	0.30

Tab. 5.3: Comparison between the Convergences of X, Y and $r - 1$
(Run with the same Values as in Table 5.2)

From Table 5.2 we see that the rate of interest $[r(\infty) - 1]$ approximately converges like $K - 1 - 1/n$ for $n \to \infty$. [18]) Our analysis shows that the more competitors we have on the production side the higher is the rate of interest and vice versa, i.e. the more oligopolistic the market structure the lower is the reate of interest. In evaluating this result one should keep in mind that the behaviour of the households as summarized in (2.7) – is based on the assumption that no individual consumer can influence the interest rate. We believe that this characterization comes nearly true in reality. On the other hand, the production sector has a far more oligopolistic structure than the sector of households. In this connexion a remark of *Malinvaud* [1953, p. 256] is worth to be mentioned:
"Interest theory, if not capital theory, has often been thought of as dealing only with one question: why does competition not bring the rate of interest down to zero?" Given the assumption of our model, in particular that K is constant, our answer to this question is: compeition even raises it!

[18]) Precisely (for $L = 0$) it can be shown that $r(\infty) = K - (K - A)/(1 - CK/B) \cdot (1/n)$ + higher powers of $1/n$.

6. Appendix

6.1 Proof of the Lemma

Proof: Our proof proceeds in three steps

1. $$g_n(x) = \frac{u_n + v_n x}{(w_n - x)^2} = \frac{u_n + v_n w_n}{(w_n - x)^2} - \frac{v_n}{w_n - x}.$$

The first respresentation of $g_n(x)$ shows for $v_n \geqslant 0$ that

$$\frac{d^k}{dx^k} g_n(x) = (u_n + v_n x) \frac{d^k}{dx^k} \frac{1}{(w_n - x)^2} + k v_n \frac{d^{k-1}}{dx^{k-1}} \frac{1}{(w_n - x)^2}$$

$$= (u_n + v_n x)\, 2 \cdot 3 \ldots (k+1)/(w_n - x)^{k+2} + k v_n\, 2 \cdot 3 \ldots k/(w_n - x)^{k+1} >$$

$$> 0 \qquad \text{for } 0 \leqslant x < w_n,\ k \geqslant 0.$$

The second representation shows in case $v_n < 0$, that

$$\frac{d^k}{dx^k} g_n(x) = (u_n + v_n w_n) \frac{d^k}{dx^k} \frac{1}{(w_n - x)^2} - v_n \frac{d^k}{dx^k} \frac{1}{w_n - x} > 0$$

for $0 \leqslant x < w_n$, $k \geqslant 0$, since $u_n + v_n w_n \geqslant 0$.

2. We have

$$g_n\left(\frac{1}{2n}\right) = \left(\frac{1}{4n^2} + \frac{n-2}{4n} \frac{1}{2n}\right) / \left(\frac{n+1}{2n} - \frac{1}{2n}\right)^2 = \frac{1}{8n} / \left(\frac{1}{2}\right)^2 = \frac{1}{2n}.$$

Hence if $\delta' = 1$ it follows that $x' = 1/2n$ is a fix point.
Since

$$g_n'\left(\frac{1}{2n}\right) = \left(\frac{1}{4n^2} + \frac{n-2}{4n} \frac{1}{2n}\right) 2 / \left(\frac{n+1}{2} - \frac{1}{2n}\right)^3 + \frac{n-2}{4n} / \left(\frac{n+1}{2n} - \frac{1}{2n}\right)^2$$

$$= \frac{1}{8n} 2 / \left(\frac{1}{2}\right)^3 + \frac{n-2}{4n} / \left(\frac{1}{2}\right)^2 = \frac{2}{n} + \frac{n-2}{n} = 1$$

and $g_n'' > 0$ it follows that $1/2n$ is the only fix point in $[0, w_n]$ (see Figure 6.1).

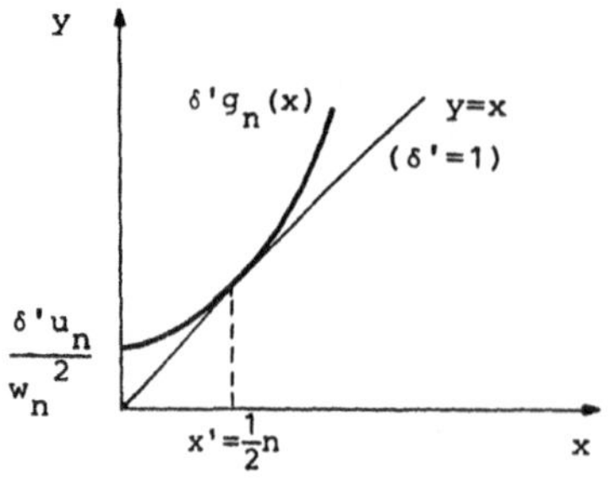

Fig. 6.1

If $0 \leqslant \delta' < 1$ then $[\delta' g(x) - x]$ is $\geqslant 0$ at $x = 0$ and is negative at $x = 1/2n$. The smallest fix point $x' \geqslant 0$ fulfills $x' < 1/2n$ (see Figure 6.2).

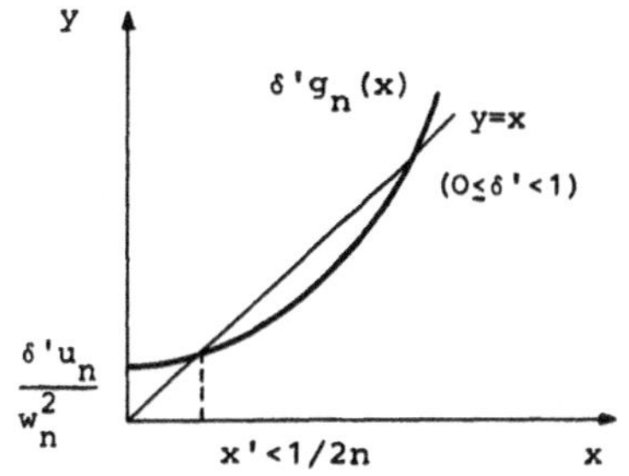

Fig. 6.2

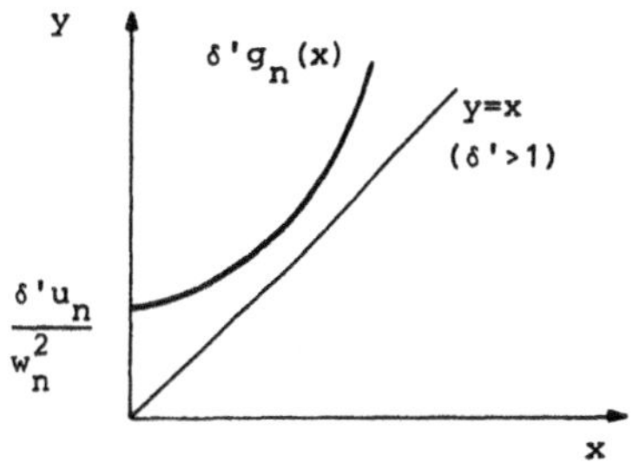

Fig. 6.3

If $\delta' > 1$ we have

$$\delta' g_n(x) - x = (\delta' - 1) g_n(x) + g_n(x) - x \geqslant (\delta' - 1) g_n(x) > 0$$

for all x with $0 \leqslant x < w_n$. Therefore there does not exist a fix point (see Figure 6.3).

3. First we are interested in the case, when there is a fix point x' $(0 \leqslant x' < w_n)$ of $\delta' g_n$, that means $0 \leqslant \delta' \leqslant 1$. Let x' be the smallest one. Then $\delta' g(x) - x \neq 0$ for all x, $0 \leqslant x < x'$.
Since $[\delta' g_n(x) - x] \geqslant 0$ at $x = 0$ and it is continuous, it follows $\delta' g_n(x) - x \geqslant 0$ for all x with $0 \leqslant x \leqslant x'$. By induction we prove $0 \leqslant C_j' \leqslant x'$ and therefore $C_{j+1}' - C_j' = \delta' g_n(C_j') - C_j' \geqslant 0$: Because of the monotony of $\delta' g_n$ it follows $C_{j+1}' = \delta' g_n(C_j') \leqslant \delta' g_n(x') = x'$. Therefore $0 = C_0' \leqslant C_1' \leqslant C_2' \leqslant \ldots \leqslant x'$ and the limit $C_\infty' = \lim_{j \to \infty} C_j' \leqslant x'$ does exist. Because of the continuity of $\delta' g_n$

$$\delta' g_n(C_\infty') = \delta' g_n(\lim_j C_j') = \lim_j \delta' g_n(C_j') = \lim_j C_{j+1}' = C_\infty'$$

C_∞' is a fixed point of $\delta' g_n$ and $\leqslant x'$. Therefore $C_\infty' = x'$.
Now we consider the case $\delta' > 1$, when there is no fixed point of $\delta' g_n$ in $[0, w_n]$. Then $\delta' g_n(x) - x > 0$ for all x, $0 \leqslant x < w_n$.
Therefore $C_{j+1}' > C_j'$, for all j with $0 \leqslant C_j' < w_n$. If $0 \leqslant C_j' < w_n$ for all $j = 0, 1, \ldots,$ then $C_\infty' = \lim C_j' \leqslant w_n$ would exist. If $C_\infty' < w_n$, C_∞' would be again a fix point of $\delta' g_n$, contradicting our assumption. – If $C_\infty' = w_n$, we get again a contradiction from

$$w_n = \lim_j C_j' = \lim_j C_{j+1}' = \lim_j \delta' g_n(C_j') = +\infty.$$

Therefore for one $j > 0$ we get $0 \leqslant C_{j-1}' < w_n$ and $C_j' = \delta' g_n(C_{j-1}') \geqslant w_n$. Thus we have proved our Lemma.

6.2 Discussion of Our Conditions on the Parameters

Now we want to discuss what happens when some of our conditions on the parameters of our game are not fulfilled. First we assume $\delta' > 1$. In this case (see our Lemma) for every $n \geqslant 1$ $\delta' g_n$ has no fixpoint x with $0 \leqslant x < w_n$ and there is a first j depending on n with $C'_j \geqslant w_n$.

If $C'_j = w_n$, then for any length $T \geqslant j + 1$, the equation (3.3) for the determination of $x_i(t)$ for $t = T - j \geqslant 1$ has no solution. That means that there is no subgame perfect equilibrium point, if $T \geqslant j + 1$, but there is one, if $T \leqslant j$.

If $C'_j > w_n$, then the equation for the determination of $x_i(t)$ has a solution, though < 0. If $w_n < C'_j \leqslant 1$, this solution defines again the unique subgame perfect equilibrium point of the game with $T = j + 1$. Of course, one may determine C'_{j+1}, $C_{j+1}, \ldots$ by the same formulae as long as these coefficients remain $\neq w_n$ and $\leqslant 1$. We have not checked, whether this is possible. If $C'_{j+1}, \ldots, C'_{k-1}$ fulfill these conditions, our formula give the unique subgame perfect equilibrium point, if $T \leqslant k$. But for starting points $Y(1) \geqslant 0$ if violates the condition $x_i(t) \geqslant 0$ for $t = T - j$. If then $C'_k = w_n$ or > 1 (for some $k \geqslant j$), the game with a length $T \geqslant k + 1$ has no subgame perfect equilibrium point; in the latter case, because the payoff has a positive second derivative with respect to $x_i(t)$ for $t = T - k$.

References

Dasgupta, P., and *J. Stiglitz*: Market Structure and Resource Depletion. Paper presented at the Arbeitstagung der Gesellschaft für Wirtschafts- und Sozialwissenschaften – Verein für Socialpolitik – Mannheim, 24.–26.9.1979.

Faber, M.: Introduction to Modern Austrian Capital Theory. Lectures Notes in Economics and Mathematical Systems No. 167. Berlin–Heidelberg–New York 1979.

Hoel, M.: Resource Extraction under some Alternative Market Structures. Meisenheim am Glan 1978.

Kydland, F.: Noncooperative and Dominant Player Solutions in Discrete Dynamic Games. International Economic Review **16**, 1975, 321–335.

Malinvaud, E.: Capital Accumulation and Efficient Allocation of Resources. Econometrica **21**, 1953. 233–268.

Nelson, R.R., and *S.G. Winter*: Forces Generating and Limiting Concentration under Schumpeterian Competition. The Bell Journal **9**, 1978, 524–548.

Nelson, R.R., S.G. Winter and *H.I. Schuette*: Technical Change in an Evolutionary Model. Quarterly Journal of Economics **90**, 1976, 90–111.

Reiss, W.: Umwegproduktion und Positivität des Zinses. Eine neo-österreichische Analyse. Habilitationsschrift, Universität Heidelberg, 1979.

Selten, R.: Spieltheoretische Behandlung eines Oligopolmodelles mit Nachfrageträgheit. Zeitschrift für die gesamte Staatswissenschaft **121**, 1965, 301–324.

–: Reexamination of the Perfectness Concept for Equilibrium Points in Extensive Games. International Journal of Game Theory **4**, 1975, 25–33.

Selten, R., and *W. Güth*: Collective Wage Bargaining in a Simple Business Cycle Model. Mimeographed, Institut für Mathematische Wirtschaftsforschung an der Universität Bielefeld, 1978.

Games, Economic Dynamics, and Time Series Analysis. 1982 ©Physica-Verlag, Wien–Würzburg

Expanding and Contracting Economies

By *O. Morgenstern* and *G.L. Thompson*, Pittsburgh[1])

Note. This expository paper was completed in 1976 and was accepted for publication by *Scientific American*. Their delay in publishing it (which apparently is not untypical of that magazine) has made it desirable to issue it in another form.

G.L. Thompson
February, 1980

Expansion of economic activity in most countries has been observed for a long time. But economists have so far been mainly concerned with trying to understand how a static economic system works: a task difficult enough, given the enormous complexity of any economy. The first attempt to establish a rigorous and mathematical theory was that of Leon Walras in 1872 and it took more than 60 years before a proof of the existence of a solution of his system was given by Abraham Wald in 1935.

However, economists could not close their eyes to development and descriptive, historical, verbal explanations were offered, for example by J. Schumpeter who emphasized the role of the entrepreneur mainly in introducing new technology. A Swedish economist, G. Cassel, considered an economy growing at a constant rate; but he had no mathematical theory which produced new theorems about the economy.

Then suddenly, in 1932, the young but already eminent mathematician John von Neumann presented, in a talk a Princeton, a complete model of an expanding closed economy for which he proved the equality of the interest and expansion factors. In this paper (published in 1937 in Vienna) it is assumed that goods are produced from each other, that processes that are unprofitable will be abandoned and that goods produced in excess will have zero price. It was also assumed that every good entered in some amount, no matter how small, into the production of every other good, in order to prevent the economy from breaking apart into disconnected pieces. We discuss his model with examples later.

The proof of the possibility of such a system was of great mathematical depth: it gave rise to a generalization of L.E.J. Brower's fixed-point theorem, already used by von Neumann in his original 1928 paper on game theory. These works have ushered in an entire new epoch of modern economics. Indeed, the two fields belong closely together and thus, in our generalizations of the von Neumann model, game theory appears as a device for calculation as well as a model of economic behavior, for example when the interaction

[1]) *G.L. Thompson*, Carnegie-Mellon University, 5000 Forbes Avenue, 15213 Pittsburgh, PA, U.S.A.

of several expanding economies is investigated (see below) in a world model. Game theory is, of course, also one of the sources of the theory of linear programming now in wide use in business and government. In the present context, where necessary, linear programming is "raised" if this term be permitted, to being a tool that deals with entire economies. Coupled with the developments in computer capabilities, the progress of software and greatly increased algorithmic power, we can say that a new branch of economics now exists which might properly be called *Mathematical Programming Economics*. This involves an entirely new approach to the troublesome distinction between "micro" and "macro" economics and will do away with many, essentially artificial problems which arise mostly from the inability so far to go into sufficient detail, especially in policy decisions. Macroeconomics is obtained from simple addition (aggregation) of smaller economic units – a seemingly harmless operation. But in doing this not only ordinary detail of no importance is eliminated, but far more serious fundamental structural properties of the component parts may be obliterated and falsify the resultant. For example the same increase in the quantity of money circulating will have quite different meaning depending on whether the recipients of the new money were consumers or producers of raw materials, etc. Different flows of incomes will be the consequence. All this is lost information with current aggregation techniques, but not in the present model.

Current and classical economic theory still deals almost exclusively with physical outputs, although in all economies, but certainly in the advanced ones, services play an ever increasing role. Concepts such as "marginal productivity" have an intuitive appeal when applied to physical products. But they lose all meaning when applied to services rendered by judges, lawyers, doctors, policemen, priests, musicians, artists,hairdressers, salesmen, etc., etc., all of which have economic functions of one sort or another and are part of the economic mechanism.

Here we stop: Is the term and concept of a "mechanism" appropriate when describing the interplay of decisions made by individuals, firms, governments, decisions involving consumption, savings, production, sales, etc.?

The great physicist W. Nernst gave a long time ago a clear illustration of the difference between physical mechanisms and social processes by the following device:

Assume a body to be in the position A upon which two physical forces (1) and (2) work as shown:

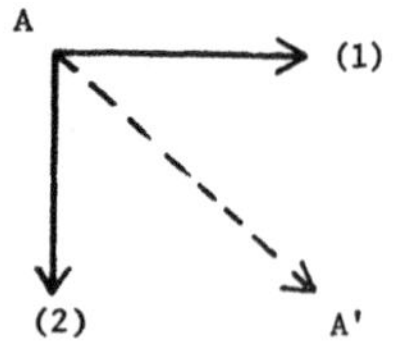

Then the body will obviously, according to the laws of classical mechanics, move along the dotted line to A'. But, Nernst said, suppose the "body" is a dog and in (1) and (2) are sausages, each exerting an influence on A. Clearly, the dog will not walk from A to A' between (1) and (2)!

The lesson from this example is obvious: the social sciences have a domain and structure different from those of the physical sciences: there are decisions to be made by the economic agents, there are alternatives, there are physical bounds, time has to elapse, etc. Psychological "forces", "tastes", "needs", etc. do not behave in the same way as physical forces. Thus the mathematics needed to analyze social science problems is necessarily quite different from that needed for the physical sciences. We will illustrate the difference here.

The mere observation that nothing is produced out of nothing, in other words, that outputs require inputs of something – be it energy, knowledge, materials, services or goods already produced – is, of course, trivial. The question is how much of various inputs a given product needs – what the technical coefficients are – what alternative combinations of inputs are possible, how prices of both inputs and outputs determine the choice of the best combination.

The further observation is that economies expand, some faster than others. Some do that with the given technology constant, some with new technology frequently injected.

There is a close connection between the von Neumann expanding economy model and the well-known input-output economic model proposed by Wassily Leontief. Both models make use of a table (matrix) of input coefficients, although the way these coefficients are gathered differs. However, the output tables in the two models differ considerably and there are numerous other differences. Among these differences are the facts that the Leontief model has neither prices nor expansion and interest coefficients.

An input-output system describes interactions of great complexities among industries, producers and consumers. There are many different economies in the world: some primitive, some technologically advanced, some under close central control, others less so. But all must have some common irreducible traits and it is these, and only these, with which we are going to deal. Thus the theory must have universal applicability. It will describe interrelations that cannot willfully be violated by whatever political system that may prevail or be thought of, short of a collapse of the economy.

In what follows the basic features of the economy will be illustrated by very homely illustrations: farmers, chickens, eggs and wheat. We could just as well have taken steel, oil, automobiles and other more advanced products. But we take those because of their familiarity and they do, indeed, occur anywhere in the world. Sophistication lies in the theory, not in the example!

The theory rests on axioms. There is no firmer way of stating a theory. In some sense the ability to proceed axiomatically is a sign of the maturity of the thoughts presented. The axioms are simply empirical statements and could as such be challenged; they are interdependent and must be free of inner contradictions (i.e., within the system). Further, there are precise statements about the variables and parameters, some obvious, e.g., that the prices to be derived must be greater than or equal to zero but not negative; others are perhaps intelligible only after the first theorems have been proved.

In order to describe expanding economies we shall briefly review the idea of compound interest. If \$100 is invested in a savings account at an *interest rate* of 6 percent per year then it is easy to calculate the value of the savings account in each subsequent year by multiplying by the *interest factor* 1.06 as follows:

Value at End of first year = $100.00 \times 1.06 = \$1.06.00$
Value at End of second year = $(106.00) \times 1.06 = \$112.36$

Value at End of third year = (112.36) × 1.06 = \$119.10
Value at End of fourth year = (119.10) × 1.06 = \$126.25
Etc.

In general if an investment is made at interest rate b percent per year the corresponding interest factor is $\beta = 1 + b/100$.

The same reasoning can be applied to economic growth. If the total economy, consisisting of farms, factories, buildings, roads, etc., increases by an *expansion rate* of a percent per year, then the corresponding *expansion factor* is $\alpha = 1 + a/100$. The size of the economy in subsequent years can be calculated in the same way the size of the bank account was calculated above.

Note that if $b = 0$ or $a = 0$ then $\beta = 1$ or $\alpha = 1$. These correspond to *stationary* bank accounts (0 interest rate) or *stationary economies* (0 expansion rate). We can even think of negative interest rates $b < 0$ ($\beta < 1$) or negative expansion rates $a < 0$ ($\alpha < 1$) which correspond to *contracting bank accounts* or *contracting economies.*

In order to describe expanding and contracting economic models we shall make use of elementary matrix algebra. Only the simplest matrix operations will be used, and each of these will be briefly described so that the reader can understand the elementary examples we wish to discuss later.

A *matrix* is simply a rectangular array or table of numbers. Figure 1 shows two such matrices, A called the *input* and B called the *output* matrix. We have labelled these matrices to correspond to the input and output coefficients of a hypothetical chicken farm, which we use in several different versions to illustrate the economic models. It is to be emphasized that these examples are deliberately kept simple for purposes of this article, and much larger examples, having input and output matrices with hundreds or thousands of rows and columns can be developed and the corresponding models solved in the same way that we solve here the simple examples.

Notice that we have labelled the (horizontal) rows of the input and output matrices with the two production activities Laying and Hatching of the chicken farm. Also we have labelled the (vertical) columns of these matrices with the two goods, Chickens and

$$\text{Activities}\begin{cases}\text{Laying}\\ \text{Hatching}\end{cases} \quad A = \overbrace{\begin{matrix}\text{Chickens} & \text{Eggs}\end{matrix}}^{\text{Goods}} \begin{pmatrix}1 & 0\\ 1 & 4\end{pmatrix} \quad \text{Input Matrix}$$

$$\text{Activities}\begin{cases}\text{Laying}\\ \text{Hatching}\end{cases} \quad B = \overbrace{\begin{matrix}\text{Chickens} & \text{Eggs}\end{matrix}}^{\text{Goods}} \begin{pmatrix}1 & 12\\ 5 & 0\end{pmatrix} \quad \text{Output Matrix}$$

Fig. 1

Eggs, which are produced by the chicken farm. In order to interpret the meaning of these matrices we concentrate on the first row-corresponding to the laying activity – of each matrix. We see that laying requires as inputs 1 chicken and 0 eggs (see the first row of A) and produces after a suitable elapse of time (say one month) two outputs 1 (the original) chicken and 12 eggs (see the first row of B). In the same way, if we look at the second row of each matrix, which give the input and output coefficients for the hatching activity, two inputs 1 chicken and 4 eggs are required which produce at the end of the month 5 chickens (the original one plus 4 new ones) and no eggs.

We have deliberately simplified the whole production process by omitting such biological details as sexual reproduction, the time required for a chicken to grow to maturity, the possibility of using incubators for hatchings eggs, the possibilities of death and disease, etc. We also have used as an illustration a very simple, homely example, of a chicken farm. But our model is applicable to realistic economies whose economic activities are factories that make steel, aluminum, glass, paint, automobiles, etc., and the goods are these quantities themselves. We shall later give the input and output tables of such larger more realistic example.

We must next describe two vectors, the *activity vector* x and the *price vector* y. A vector is a special kind of matrix that has only a single row (a row vector) or a single column (a column vector). Examples are shown in Figure 2. In that figure we see that

Activity Vector (Laying, Hatching):

$$x = (1 \quad , \quad 1)$$

Price Vector:

$$y = \begin{pmatrix} 6 \\ 1 \end{pmatrix} \quad \begin{matrix} \text{Relative price of chickens} \\ \text{Relative price of eggs} \end{matrix}$$

Fig. 2

the entries of the activity vector x, written as a row vector, indicate that we run the laying and hatching industries with equal intensities: that is, if we have 2 chickens we assign one to laying and one to hatching; if we have 4 chickens we assign 2 to each activity. Similarly, the entries of the price vector y, written as a column vector, give the relative prices of chickens and eggs: if we value an egg at \$1 we value a chicken at \$6; if we value an egg at \$2 we value a chicken at \$12, etc.

Now we must multiply the vector x by the input and output matrices as shown in Figure 3.

laying hatching; Chickens Eggs; chickens egs

$$xA = (1 \quad , \quad 1) \begin{matrix} \text{laying} \\ \text{hatching} \end{matrix} \begin{pmatrix} 1 & 0 \\ 1 & 4 \end{pmatrix} = (2 \quad , \quad 4)$$

= inputs needed

laying hatching; Chickens Eggs; chickens eggs

$$xB = (1 \quad , \quad 1) \begin{matrix} \text{laying} \\ \text{hatching} \end{matrix} \begin{pmatrix} 1 & 12 \\ 5 & 0 \end{pmatrix} = (6 \quad , \quad 12)$$

= outputs produced

Fig. 3

Notice that the multiplication xA is performed in two parts and gives a two component row vector as a result. To get the first component we use the entries in x and the entries in the first column of A; we see that if we run the laying and hatching activities each at intensity 1 we will need a total of two chickens (1 for laying, 1 for hatching). To get the second component we use the entries in x and the entries in the second column of A; if we run each of the activities at intensity 1 we need a total of 4 eggs (0 for laying, 4 for hatching).

The entries of xB are obtained in a similar manner and indicate that at the end of one cycle of production there will be 6 chickens (the 2 original ones plus 4 newly hatched ones) and 12 eggs (produced by the laying process).

Notice that by comparing corresponding components of xA and xB in Figure 3 we see that each component in xB is exactly 3 times as large as the corresponding component of xA. We can express this as

$$(6,12) = 3\,(2,4) \tag{1}$$

which can be written symbolically as

$$xB = 3xA. \tag{2}$$

We will see later that these equations mean that $\alpha = 3$ is the expansion factor for the chicken farm.

We next do the corresponding multiplication of the matrices A and B times the price vector y, as shown in Figure 4. Here we indicate the multiplication with the column vector y on the ***right*** of the matrices, and the result in each case is a two-component column

$$Ay = \begin{matrix} \text{Laying} \\ \text{Hatching} \end{matrix} \overset{\text{Chickens Eggs}}{\begin{pmatrix} 1 & 0 \\ 1 & 4 \end{pmatrix}} \begin{pmatrix} 6 \\ 1 \end{pmatrix} \begin{matrix} \text{\$/chicken} \\ \text{\$/egg} \end{matrix} = \begin{pmatrix} 6 \\ 10 \end{pmatrix} \begin{matrix} \text{\$/laying} \\ \text{\$/hatching} \end{matrix}$$

$$By = \begin{matrix} \text{Laying} \\ \text{Hatching} \end{matrix} \overset{\text{Chickens Eggs}}{\begin{pmatrix} 1 & 12 \\ 5 & 0 \end{pmatrix}} \begin{pmatrix} 6 \\ 1 \end{pmatrix} \begin{matrix} \text{\$/chicken} \\ \text{\$/egg} \end{matrix} = \begin{pmatrix} 18 \\ 30 \end{pmatrix} \begin{matrix} \text{\$/laying} \\ \text{\$/hatching} \end{matrix}$$

Fig. 4

vector. The first component of Ay is obtained from the first row of A and y and indicates the total value of the inputs to the laying industry to be \$6 (1 chicken with value \$6). The second component of Ay is obtained from the second row of A and indicates the total value of inputs to the hatching industry to be \$10 (1 chicken worth \$6 plus 4 eggs worth \$1 each).

The entries of the product By are obtained by similar multiplication of the entries in each row of B by the corresponding entries of the vector y. They indicate that after one production cycle the value of the outputs of the laying activity is 18 (1 chicken worth

\$6 plus 12 eggs worth \$1 each) and the value of the outputs of the hatching activity is 30 (5 chickens worth \$6 each).

We note again that by comparing corresponding components of Ay and By, each component of By is exactly 3 times as large as the corresponding component of Ay. We can express this as

$$\begin{pmatrix} 18 \\ 30 \end{pmatrix} = 3 \begin{pmatrix} 6 \\ 10 \end{pmatrix} \tag{3}$$

which can be written symbolically as

$$By = 3Ay. \tag{4}$$

We will see later that these equations mean that $\beta = 3$ is the interest factor for the chicken farm.

We summarizes in Figure 5 all the vector and matrix quantities needed to state the axioms of the closed expanding model together with their dimensions, that is the numbers of rows and columns of each, and the verbal interpretation of each. As indicated m is the number of production activities and n is the number of goods produced. In the chicken farm example m and n were each equal to 2. Notice that some quantities, such as m, n, α, and β, are said to be 1×1 matrices. All that this means is that they are ordinary numerical quantities.

Dimension	Quantity	Interpretation
1×1	m	number of activities
1×1	n	number of goods
1×1	α	expansion factor
1×1	β	interest factor
$1 \times m$	x	activity vector
$n \times 1$	y	price vector
$m \times n$	A	input matrix
$m \times n$	B	output matrix

Fig. 5: Basic Quantities Needed to Define the Models

Dimension	Quantity	Interpretation
$1 \times n$	xA	Input vector
$1 \times n$	xB	Output vector
$m \times 1$	Ay	Input value vector
$m \times 1$	By	Output value vector
1×1	xAy	Total input value
1×1	xBy	Total output value

Fig. 6: Matrix Products Needed to State Axioms

Figure 6 shows the matrix products that will be used to state the axioms of the model together with their interpretations. We have already calculated the first four quantities xA, xB, Ay, and By for the chicken farm example; let us calculate the last two quantities next. For xAy we have by using the matrix product xA from Figure 3

$$xAy = (1,1)\begin{pmatrix}1 & 0\\ 1 & 4\end{pmatrix}\begin{pmatrix}6\\ 1\end{pmatrix}$$

$$= (2,4)\begin{pmatrix}6\\ 1\end{pmatrix}$$

$$= \$16 = \text{total value of all inputs}$$

because $xA = (2,4)$ means we have as 2 chickens and 4 eggs as inputs; the value of these chickens is $2 \times \$6 = 12$ and the value of these eggs are $4 \times \$1 = \$4$; adding we get the total value of \$16.

The latter number can also be calculated by using the matrix product Ay from Figure 4 as

$$xAy = (1,1)\begin{pmatrix}1 & 0\\ 1 & 4\end{pmatrix}\begin{pmatrix}6\\ 1\end{pmatrix}$$

$$= (1,1)\begin{pmatrix}6\\ 10\end{pmatrix}$$

$$= \$16 = \text{total value of all inputs.}$$

The quality of the result for these two ways of calculating $xAy = (xA)y = x(Ay)$ is an illustration of the *associative law* which can be proved to be always valid for multiplication of matrices.

By similar calculations we compute xBy as

$$xBy = (1.1)\begin{pmatrix}1 & 12\\ 5 & 0\end{pmatrix}\begin{pmatrix}6\\ 1\end{pmatrix}$$

$$= (6,12)\begin{pmatrix}6\\ 1\end{pmatrix}$$

$$= \$\,48 = \text{total value of outputs.}$$

Or, by use of the associative law.

$$xBy = (1,1)\begin{pmatrix}1 & 12\\ 5 & 0\end{pmatrix}\begin{pmatrix}6\\ 1\end{pmatrix}$$

$$= (1,1)\begin{pmatrix}18\\ 30\end{pmatrix}$$

$$= \$48 = \text{total value of outputs.}$$

We also note that

$$48 = xBy = 3xAy = 3 \times 16 \tag{5}$$

that is, the total value of outputs is 3 times the total value of the inputs. But something even more important should be noted; from (1) we see that, beginning with 2 chickens and 4 eggs as inputs we have after one month's production 6 chickens and 12 eggs as outputs, and the ratio of the latter is exactly such that we can triple the intensity of production and *repeat the process* for another production period. Without calculating it, explicitly we will have 18 chickens and 36 eggs, which again are in the proper proportion to repeat production once more, etc. Figure 7 shows the inputs and outputs and intensity vectors for 3 repetitions of this expansion process. In Figure 8 the expansion process is shown graphically. Notice that each time we triple the intensity vector, the inputs and the

	Period 1		Period 2		Period 3	
	Inputs	Outputs	Inputs	Outputs	Inputs	Outputs
Chickens	2	6	6	18	18	54
Eggs	4	12	12	36	36	108
	$x = (1,1)$		$x = (3,3)$		$x = (9,9)$	

Fig. 7

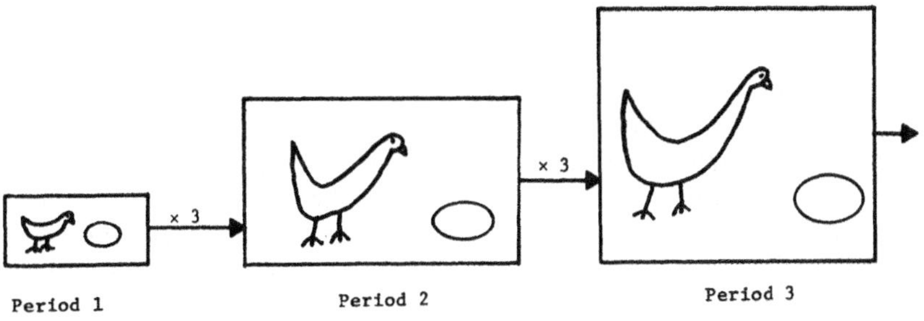

Fig. 8

outputs. But they are all so proportioned that this kind of *balanced expansion* can continue indefinitely. (We are temporarily ignoring the problem of feeding an ever larger number of chickens, and, most important, the reason for raising chickens for the role purpose of producing an ever increasing number of other chickens. We shall return later to answer the latter questions.)

We can now use the quantities given in Figures 5 and 6 to state the axioms for the closed expanding economy model. The five axioms (C1) – (C5) are given, together with their verbal interpretations in Figure 9. In order to be able to read these axioms we must first define what $u \geqslant v$ means when u and v are two vectors of the same dimension, say

Axiom	Interpretation
(C1) $xB \geqslant \alpha xA$	Output of previous period sufficient to supply the expanded inputs of the subsequent period.
(C2) $By \leqslant \beta Ay$	Value of inputs are greater than or equal to the discounted value of the outputs.
(C3) $xBy = \alpha xAy$	Over produced goods have zero price.
(C4) $xBy = \beta xAy$	Inefficient processes are not used.
(C5) $xBy > 0$	Something of value is produced.

Fig. 9

they have n components. By definition the inequality

$$u = (u_1, \ldots, u_n) \geqslant (v_1, \ldots, v_n) = v$$

means simply $u_1 \geqslant v_1, \ldots, u_n \geqslant v_n$. In other words a vector inequality relation is said to hold between two vectors if the same relation holds for each pair of corresponding components of the two vectors.

Let us discuss each of the axioms. From Figure 6 we know that xB is the vector of outputs when the intensity vector x is used; if the economy is to expand so that the intensity vector αx is to be used in the subsequent time period, then the vector of inputs needed for the later time period is αxA; axiom (C1) simply says that outputs xB during the current time period must be sufficient to cover the expanded inputs αxA needed for the next time period. (We here assume that the model is *closed*, that is, it is not possible to import any unfilled needs or to export excess production; later we extend the model to become open and permit both imports and exports.)

Axiom (C2) is an accounting condition sometimes called the "profitless economy" condition. It is easier to interpret by first dividing through by β to obtain $Ay \geqslant (1/\beta)By$, since we can then interpret $1/\beta$ as a "discount factor." The axiom in its new form states that the input value vector is greater than or equal to the discounted output value vector. In other words, the interest rate should be set so that production is not more profitable than investment. (This axiom may also seem to be too strong and unrealistic, but it will be relaxed later in the open model.)

Axiom (C3) should be read in conjunction with Axiom (C1). What these two axioms together state is that if a component, say the j-th component, of the vector xB is greater than the corresponding component of αxA then the price $y_j = 0$. In other words, goods that are produced in excess over requirements must be given 0 price. It may be summarized as: *over produced goods are free*. (The reader may ask, why not export overproduced goods? That is not possible in our present, closed, model, but will become possible later in the open model.)

In the same way, Axiom (C4) must be interpreted together with Axiom (C2). As noted above it is easier to interpret them after dividing through by β. These two axioms state that is a component, say the i-th component, of the discounted output value vector $(1/\beta)By$ is strictly less than the corresponding component of the input value vector Ay, then the i-th process must not be used. This axiom is sometimes referred to as the inefficient processes axiom. (This axiom will also be relaxed in the open model given later.)

The last axiom, (C5), is easy to interpret, for from the interpretation given in Figure 6, we see that it simply means that the total value of all goods produced must be positive.

The reader may check that $\alpha = \beta = 3$ and the quantities A, B, x, and y defined in Figures 1 – 4 for the chicken farm examples satisfy all the axioms given in Figure 8. Such a solution is called an *equilbrium solution.*

The question now arises as to conditions the matrices A and B must satisfy in order that the resulting model will have an equilibrium solution. This is not an idle question because it is easy to construct very simple examples of input and output matrices A and B for which there are no equilibrium solutions.

Two such sets of conditions which if satisfied guarantee solutions are stated in Figure 19. As indicated the first condition was stated as part of the original model stated by von Neumann.

Assumption	Interpretation
$A + E > 0$ von Neumann (1932)	Every activity either uses or produces some quantity (no matter how small) of every good.
a) A has no zero rows b) B has no zero columns, Kemeny, Morgenstern, Thompson (1956)	Every activity requires some inputs Every good can be produced.

Fig. 10

When the von Neumann condition holds it can be shown that the resulting solution has a unique expansion factor. However, the condition is highly restrictive as can be seen from its interpretation given in Figure 10. That is, it seems very unreasonable that every good should be required to appear as either an input or an output of every process.

In order to remove this restrictive assumption we developed in 1956 together with John G. Kemeny, now president of Dartmouth College, a generalization of von Neumann's model that replaced the restrictive assumption $A + B > 0$ by the much weaker pair of assumptions given in Figure 10. The weaker asumptions had an added difficulty however; in the generalized model the expansion and interest factors were no longer necessarily unique. However, we proved that there was at least one, and at most a finite number of such expansion factors having corresponding equilibrium solutions. We give an example later of such a model that has two solutions.

One immediate observation can be made by looking at Axioms (C3), (C4) and (C5). That is, if all three axioms hold, then

$$\alpha = \beta = \frac{xBy}{xAy}. \tag{6}$$

This observation permits us to reduce the problem of finding a solution to that of solving a parametric linear programming problems. The latter can be solved by solving about

20–30 ordinary linear programming problems and hence is well within the capability of modern computers.

The application of the theory of concrete economic problems will involve large scale computations dealing with thousands of variables and thousands of constraints. There now exists a great deal of experience how to approach such tasks without running afoul of round-off errors which would produce meaningless figures. Many parts of the necessary calculations are sequential in nature, another complicating factor. Absolute precision is unattainable except perhaps at exhorbitant costs. Nor is it wanted since the data entering the computations necessarily have error components also, reducible only at a high price. Finally, we must not forget that when even a "perfect" economic policy decision could be made, it is ultimately made also in the light of political acceptability, the given international situation and the like.

Let us return now to the chicken and eggs example whose solution is given in Figures 7 and 8. As noted earlier this model exists merely to expand at the maximum possible rate. No consumption is provided for the hapless farmers who do the work of taking care of the rapidly increasing chicken population.

Our 1956 paper with Kemeny gave a way out of this difficulty by providing a demand matrix D that is added to the input matrix A. An example suppose we have the demand matrix D shown in Figure 11. Note that the entries indicate that the laying and hatching industries each provide consumption in the ratio of 1 chicken to 2 eggs during each time

$$\begin{array}{l} \text{Laying} \\ \text{Hatching} \end{array} \quad D = \overset{\begin{array}{cc}\text{Chickens} & \text{Eggs}\end{array}}{\begin{pmatrix} 1 & 2 \\ 1 & 2 \end{pmatrix}}$$

Fig. 11

period. The new model and its equilibrium solution are shown in Figures 12, 13 and 14.

$$\begin{array}{l} \text{Laying} \\ \text{Hatching} \end{array} \quad B = \overset{\begin{array}{cc}\text{Chicken} & \text{Eggs}\end{array}}{\begin{pmatrix} 1 & 12 \\ 5 & 0 \end{pmatrix}} \qquad A + D = \overset{\begin{array}{cc}\text{Chickens} & \text{Eggs}\end{array}}{\begin{pmatrix} 2 & 2 \\ 2 & 6 \end{pmatrix}}$$

$$x = (1,1), \quad y = \begin{pmatrix} 9 \\ 2 \end{pmatrix}, \qquad \alpha = \beta = \frac{3}{2}$$

Fig. 12

Notice in Figure 12 that the expansion and interest factors are half what they were before, the laying and hatching industries are run with equal intensities as before; however the ratio of the price of chickens to the price of eggs has decreased from \$6 to \$1 down to \$4.50 to \$1. In Figure 13 the numerical quantities of chickens and eggs used for laying and hatching are shown and in Figure 14 a graphical picture of the growth similar to that in Figure 8, but including some "thin" farmers, is shown. The meaning of the thin farmers is that we assume that 1 chicken and 2 eggs per time period represents a bare subsistence diet.

	Period 1		Period 2		Period 3		
	Inputs	Outputs	Inouts	Outputs	Inputs	Outputs	
Chickens	2	6	3	9	4.5	13.5	
Eggs	4	12	6	18	9	27	. . .
Chickens consumed	2		3		4.5		
Eggs consumed	4		6		9		
	$x = (1,1)$		$x = (3/2,3/2)$		$x = (9/4,9/4)$		

Fig. 13

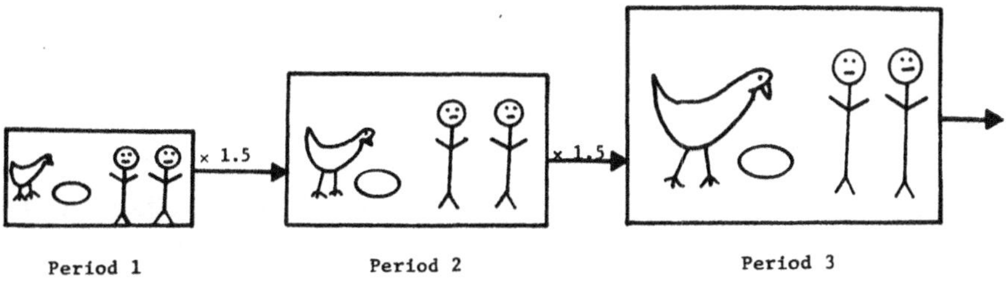

Fig. 14: Subsistence Consumption – Thin Farmers

Suppose the thin farmers of Figure 14 object to their low consumption level and demand that it be doubled. The demand matrix is shown in Figure 15.

$$\begin{array}{l} \text{Laying} \\ \\ \text{Hatching} \end{array} \quad D = \begin{array}{c} \text{Chickens} \;\; \text{Eggs} \\ \begin{pmatrix} 2 & 4 \\ 2 & 4 \end{pmatrix} \end{array}$$

Fig. 15

The new solution is shown in Figures 16, 17 and 18.

$$\begin{array}{l} \text{Laying} \\ \\ \text{Hatching} \end{array} \quad B = \begin{array}{c} \text{Chickens} \;\; \text{Eggs} \\ \begin{pmatrix} 1 & 12 \\ 5 & 0 \end{pmatrix} \end{array} \qquad A + D = \begin{array}{c} \text{Chickens} \;\; \text{Eggs} \\ \begin{pmatrix} 3 & 4 \\ 3 & 8 \end{pmatrix} \end{array}$$

$$x = (1,1), \; y = \begin{pmatrix} 4 \\ 1 \end{pmatrix}, \; \alpha = \beta = 1$$

Fig. 16

	Period 1		Period 2		Period 3		
	Inputs	Outputs	Inputs	Outputs	Inputs	Outputs	
Chickens	2	6	2	6	2	6	. . .
Eggs	4	12	4	12	4	12	
Chickens Consumed	4		4		4		. . .
Eggs Consumed	8		8		8		
	$x = (1,1)$		$x = (1,1)$		$x = (1,1)$		

Fig. 17: Stationary Economy

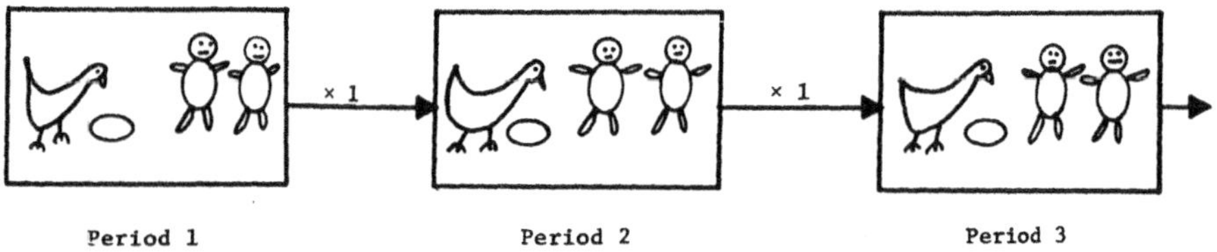

Fig. 18: Luxury Consumption – Fat Farmers

The new consumption – which we call luxury consumption – has two differences, fat farmers, and an expansion factor of 1. In other words, the high consumption demand has made the economy *stationary* – it neither increases nor decreases. A corollary of the stationary of the economy is that the (farm) population must also stay constant. For if it increases the per capita consumption must go down. Actually in our models we assume, as do all other economic theories, that the population change will exactly match the growth or decay of the economy. This assumption seems to be observed in real economics. For instance, the large growth of population in England in the first half of the nineteenth century coincided with the equally large industrial growth in England during the same period.

Note also that the stationary economic model depicted in Figures 16, 17, and 18 represents a "knife edge" balance; if consumption is decreased over its present levels the expansion factor will become grater than 1 and the economy will expand. But if the consumption level is increased – by any small amount – the expansion rate dips below 1 and the economy will contract. The latter case represents "capital consumption" and, if continued very long, will lead to collapse of the economy. Such a collapse, of course, occurs when the last chickens and eggs are consumed and so the laying and hatching industries have to close down completely.

Though the world has largely been fascinated by the phenomenon of growth and all countries seem to want more and more of it, stagnation and contraction may in fact be in store for many. A satisfactory theory must account for contraction and even go further and describe the procedure for deliberate compression of economic activities to essential ones in order to keep a country going. The contraction process here referred to is not the ordinary frequently experienced decline in business activity with unemployment, possibly of a cyclical nature, just as expansion is something more than a cyclical increase in business activity. The causes for contraction might be exhaustion of natural resources or their monopolistic control, more rapid increase in population than supportable by the economy, or shifts to alternate technology. Enormous social programs and other increases in supported activities may force the growth rate down, even below stationarity, until because of the "lumpiness' of economic units, a total collapse occurs.

When the public and government become aware of the nature and role of the growth rate and understand the various forces that influence it, the growth rate will become an important economic variable around which the struggle of contending parties will center. This is a typical game situation and bears out what was said earlier about game theory appearing in its proper, indeed vital role. What the present theory contributes to this struggle is to provide information, so far unavailable, as to where costs and benefits of choosing one rather than another growth rate will fall. Of course, this requires good data of the kind mentioned earlier. And the growth rate is certainly not measured by the rate of change of a highly aggregated index such as GNP.

Deliberate *compression* goes even farther. It means the suppression of some supported activities, the cutting out of "inessential" goods, perhaps in order to transfer resources to expand or maintain activities making up the kernel of the economy, i.e., those without which there would be a complete collapse. Of course, compression can also be used to increase the output of a supported activity, for example, weapons production in war time.

We note in passing that we have also considered generalizations of these models in which the farmers can consume only part of their allotted demand, given by matrix D, and invest the rest back in the chicken farm economy. More on such models will be found in the references.

We can make the chicken farm economy more realistic by adding a wheat field to the farm, so that the wheat grown can be fed to the chickens. The input and output matrices for the model are shown in Figure 19. Note that if we plant one bushel of wheat we get 9 bushels back, also observe that both the laying and hatching activities require 1 bushel

$$\begin{array}{ll} & \quad\ \ \text{Wheat} \quad \text{Chickens} \quad \text{Eggs} \\ \begin{array}{l}\text{Wheat}\\ \text{Laying}\\ \text{Hatching}\end{array} & A = \begin{pmatrix} 1 & 0 & 0 \\ 1 & 1 & 0 \\ 1 & 1 & 4 \end{pmatrix} \\ \begin{array}{l}\text{Wheat}\\ \text{Laying}\\ \text{Hatching}\end{array} & B = \begin{pmatrix} 9 & 0 & 0 \\ 0 & 1 & 12 \\ 0 & 5 & 0 \end{pmatrix} \end{array}$$

Fig. 19

of wheat each time period to feed the chickens in each activity.

This is the first example that does not satisfy the first (von Neumann) assumption given in Figure 10. The reader can easily check that it does satisfy the second (KMT) assumption in that figure, so that we know it has a finite number of solutions. In fact there are two and only two solutions for the model whose data are given in Figure 19.

The first solution involves raising only wheat and is shown in Figure 20. Notice that the expansion and interest factors are 9 and that only wheat is raised and only wheat has positive price. The second solution involves the production of all three goods and appears in Figure 21.

$$x = (1,0,0), \quad y = \begin{pmatrix} 1 \\ 0 \\ 0 \end{pmatrix}, \quad \alpha = \beta = 9$$

Input	Period 1 Input	Period 1 Output	Period 2 Input	Period 2 Output	Period 3 Input	Period 3 Output	
Wheat	1	9	9	81	81	729	
Chickens	0	0	0	0	0	0	. . .
Eggs	0	0	0	0	0	0	
	$x = (1,0,0)$		$x = (9,0,0)$		$x = (81,0,0)$		

Fig. 20: First solution to problem in Figure 19

$$x = (1,1,1), \quad y = \begin{pmatrix} 0 \\ 6 \\ 1 \end{pmatrix}, \quad \alpha = \beta = 3$$

	Period 1 Input	Period 1 Output	Period 2 Input	Period 2 Output	Period 3 Input	Period 3 Output	
Wheat	3	9	9	27	27	81	
Chickens	2	6	6	18	18	54	. . .
Eggs	4	12	12	36	36	108	
	$x = (1,1,1)$		$x = (3,3,3)$		$x = (9,9,9)$		

Fig. 21: Second solution to problem in Figure 19

In the second solution the price of wheat is zero! That is because the wheat industry, considered as a sub-economy by itself, can expand at the much higher rate of 9 (as shown in Figure 20) so that wheat is (potentially) over produced. Axiom 3 in Figure 9 then forces the price of wheat to be zero.

The example in Figure 19 is an economy having two sub-economies:

a) the first sub-economy consists only of the activity wheat growing and the good wheat as shown in the solution in Figure 20;
b) the second sub-economy consists of all three activities and goods and corresponds to the solution shown in Figure 21.

The possibility of sub-economies existing within our model is important since it is well known that they exist in real economies.

Example 19 does not have people (farmers) in it and so is subject to the same criticisms as our first chicken farm example. We could add consumption at various levels to Example 19, but would find results similar to those obtained before, and so do not give the details here.

The closed expanding economy model as we have described and illustrated it above captures many features of real economies, but it also has many deficiencies, some of which are pointed out above. Other possible criticisms of the closed model are:

a) It is isolated, it can neither export nor import; it cannot interact with other economies.
b) Goods produced in excess get zero price; inefficient industries cannot be run, even if they produce goods otherwise desired. To be more explicit, once the expansion rate is chosen, the economy has no choice as to the mixture of goods produced by the economy.
c) There are no "services" in the economy; it is totally production oriented.
d) In order to operate a given sub-economy, exact settings of activity levels and prices are required. Such exact settings are clearly not needed for real economies.

These objections led us to develop, in 1969, an open expanding economy model which does not suffer from the above objections and permits the inclusion of much more of the variability and richness observed in real economies. But it also preserves the ideas of balanced equilibrium expansion, consumption, sub-economies, that were found for the closed model.

In order to state the axioms of the new model we will need all of the vector and matrix quantities given in Figures 5, and 6, together with the new quantities given with their interpretations in Figure 22. The names of the new vector suggest, and we will see that it is true, that the open model will permit exporting and importing goods and running activities (such as services) that show losses (negative profits) as well as operating activities having (positive) profits.

Dimension	Name	Interpretation
$1 \times n$	w^e	Export goods vector
$1 \times n$	w^i	Import goods vector
$n \times 1$	p^e	Export price vector
$n \times 1$	p^i	Import price vector
$m \times 1$	z^p	Positive profits vector
$m \times 1$	z^n	Negative profits vector
$1 \times m$	t^p	Activity upper bound vector
$1 \times m$	t^n	Activity lower bound vector

Fig. 22

The axioms for the open model are given, together with their interpretations in Figure 23.

Axiom	Interpretation
(01) $xB + w^i = w^e + \alpha xA$	Outputs plus imports equal exports plus expanded inputs for next period.
(02) $By + z^n = z^p + \beta Ay$	Value of outputs plus losses equal profits plus future value of inputs for next period.
(03) $w^e p^e = w^i p^i$	External balance of payments requirement.
(04) $t^p z^p = t^n z^n$	Internal balance of profits condition.
(05) $xBy > 0$	Something of value is produced.
(06) $t^n \leqslant x \leqslant t^p$	Activities are within desired bounds.
(07) $p^e \leqslant y \leqslant p^i$	Internal prices are between export and import prices

Fig. 23: Axioms for the Open Model

Axiom (01) should be compared with the corresponding Axiom (C1); note that the import vector w^i is added on the left and the export vector w^e is added on the right. Also the $\geqslant$ sign in (C1) is changed to an $=$ sign in (01). We see that Axiom (C1) thus defines w^e and w^i; any goods needed for inputs are either produced or imported; while goods produced are either exported or used as inputs for the next time period.

Axiom (02), when compared with Axiom (C2) simply gives the definitions of positive profits z^p (added on the right) and negative profits z^n (added on the left). Also the $\leqslant$ sign in (02) is changed to an $=$ sign in (02).

The terms profitable and unprofitable are here meant in the input-output sense only; a profitable activity has the value of its outputs greater than the value of its outputs. For an unprofitable activity the value of its outputs is less than the value of its inputs. We do not wish to attach any derogatory connotation to unprofitable activities since many of them, such as education, research, medical care, personal serivces, etc., are of vital importance to modern economies.

Axiom (03) is the external balance of payments, more commonly known as balance of trade, condition. This condition merely requires that the total value of all exports equal the total value of all imports. This is a well known requirement.

However the internal balance of profits condition, Axiom (04), is not a common economic requirement. What it says is that the total profits of all profitable activities should equal the total losses of all unprofitable activities. Because of this condition we shall also call profitable activities, supporting activities and unprofitable activities, supported activities. What Axiom (04) does is to ensure that the total support given by supporting activities equals the total support demanded by the supported activities.

Axiom (05) is identical with Axiom (C5) and needs no further discussion.

Axiom (06) shows how the control variables t^n and t^p are used to constrain the activity levels of the components of x. If x_i, the i-th component of x, is set equal to t_i^n in the optimum solution then the i-th activity is unprofitable or supported. But if x_i is set equal to t_i^p in the optimum solution then the i-th activity is profitable or supporting. (If x_i is strictly in between t_i^n and t_i^p then the i-th activity is profitless.)

The manner in which the lower and upper bounds are set differes from economy to economy. In a centrally directed economy these control variables are set by government directive – perhaps as a result of a five year plan. In a mixed economy the control variables are set by laws, custom, consumer demand, political decisions, etc.

The last axiom, Axiom (07), requires that the internal prices for goods should lie between their export prices and their import prices. The latter prices are determined by the outside world, and we shall not discuss their determination further here.

It can be shown that the closed model is a special case of the open model, so everything that could happen before can still happen. However, there are many new kinds of things that can happen. For instance, if we can't produce, or don't want to produce, a given good we can import it. Or if we produce too much of a given good we can export it which will help our balance of payments. If a given heavy industry produces excess pollution, we can limit its output by reducing its upper bound. If we want to have a strong national defense we can increase the lower bound on that activity.

Supporting Activities	Restricted Activities	Supported Activities
Agriculture	Heavy Industry	Government
Fishing	Public Land Development	Defense
Mining	Hunting	Education
Light Industry	Blood Sports	Public Transportation
Oil Production	Drug Production	Medical Services
Essential Consumer Goods	Poison Production	Research
Industrial Transportation	Food Additives	Welfare
Food Processing	Weapons Manufacture	Music and Theater
Energy Production		Recreation
Essential Communications		Retirement Benefits

Fig. 24

To get a better idea of the kinds of controls that might be put on activities we have listed some typical examples in Figure 23. In the first column we list supporting activties that (usually) are profitable and are not subject to (strong) upper bounds. In the middle column we list restricted activities that are subject to partial or complete controls that limit their activity. Finally, in the last column we list supported activities that operate only because they are supported by taxes, grants, endowments, gits, etc. In other words, the lower bounds in Axiom (06) are effective for them.

It is necessary to have a clear understanding of what *control variables* mean and do not mean. Control variables have an *indirect* effect on growth. They set upper or lower bounds on activities. Just as production processes have to obey physical laws – e.g., for making one unit of commodity A you need at least $x, y, z, \ldots$ units of certain materials – the controls will tell the producers, e.g., that not more than a certain quantity of smoke and effluent is permitted. Such controls thereby have an indirect influence on growth or expansion. There is no order to produce any given commodity at all, nor, if produced, in what quantities. Controls differ vastly from one country to another and within the same society they are changed from time to time. Some drugs, DDT for example, may at first be freely produced only to become subject to regulation later. This decreases their market and hampers their expansion as well as that of the economy. The point is that limits are being set and that it is important to know – i.e., to be able to calculate from the theory – what influence these limits and their changes have upon the growth of the economy. So far economic theory has not taken this into consideration nor would it have been able to do so without a model such as the one here discussed.

The use of the theory – for evaluating existing or newly planned control variables or for any other purpose – depends not only on the above mentioned power of computation, but on the existence of high quality data. Here the point is that for the major part they are lacking. Yet one can specify exactly what they should be like and how they can be obtained. This is merely a matter of the effort to collect them, mostly a question of financing. For current input-output tables great masses of data have been assembled, a proof that the task of finding technological coefficients would not be an impossible one. Current input-output data cannot be used in the present models because those coefficients are obtained from price sums divided by other price sums; they are thus subject to the monetary price structure with all the various influences working upon prices.

To see how the open model differs from the previous closed one let us treat the chicken farm as an independent country that can export and import chickens and/or eggs from an outside world at stated prices. Figure 25 shows the same example as in Figure 16–18, but with export and import prices on goods and control variables on activities. The solution is also shown and indicates that the country has closed down its

$$\begin{array}{l} \text{Laying} \\ \\ \text{Hatching} \end{array} \quad B = \overset{\text{Chickens}\ \ \text{Eggs}}{\begin{pmatrix} 1 & 12 \\ & \\ 5 & 0 \end{pmatrix}}, \quad A = \overset{\text{Chickens}\ \ \text{Eggs}}{\begin{pmatrix} 1 & 0 \\ & \\ 1 & 4 \end{pmatrix}} \quad D = \overset{\text{Chicken}\ \ \text{Eggs}}{\begin{pmatrix} 2 & 4 \\ & \\ 2 & 4 \end{pmatrix}}$$

Production Constraints

$$2 \leqslant x_1 \leqslant 3$$
$$0 \leqslant x_2 \leqslant 1$$

Price Constraints

$$5 \leqslant y_1 \leqslant 6$$
$$1 \leqslant y_2 \leqslant 2$$

Solution

$$x = (3,0), \quad y = \begin{pmatrix} 6 \\ \cdot \\ 2 \end{pmatrix}, \quad \alpha = \beta = 1.15$$

$$w^e = (0,7.38), \qquad w^i = (2.46,0)$$

Fig. 25

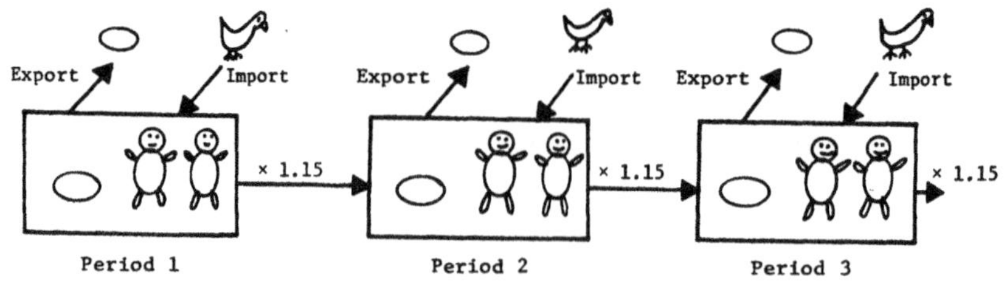

Fig. 25 (continued)

hatching industry completely and produces only eggs. It imports all the chickens that it needs and pays for them by exporting eggs. Although consumption remains at the same high rate as before (2 chickens and 4 eggs per activity per period) the economy is now able to expand at 15% per year.

This is an illustration of our generalization of Ricardo's famous theory of *comparative advantage* – which is the cornerstone of all theories of international trade. The example shows that for the given expansion factor the country can produce only its most efficient product eggs, and import its total requirement for chickens. This strategy enables the country to have both *high consumption* and a *high growth rate*. Ricardo's theory omitted the possibility of a larger expansion rate coming into the question of when a country has a comparative advantage or being a reason for promoting foreign trade. But that comes out clearly in our model and helps to explain why similar nations (i.e., Germany and France) tend to trade much more than dissimilar nations. Similar nations can achieve large expansion rates by trading and quickly achieve economic dominance.

However, the solution shown in Figure 25 makes the country very dependent on the outside world for its supply of chickens. To promote its own economic security suppose the country decides to keep its own hatching industry running. To do this it increases the lower bound on hatching to 1 which forces $x_2 = 1$. The new solution is shown in Figure 26. Notice that in the new solution the country produces some chickens with its protected (subsidized) hatching industry and imports the rest. Input-Output data and price constraints are the same as those given in Figure 25.

Production Constraints

$2 \leqslant x_1 \leqslant 3$ Solution $x = (3,1)$, $y = \begin{pmatrix} 6 \\ 2 \end{pmatrix}$, $\alpha = \beta = 1.07$

$1 \leqslant x_2 \leqslant 1$ $w^e = (0,14.57)$ $w^i = (4.86,0)$

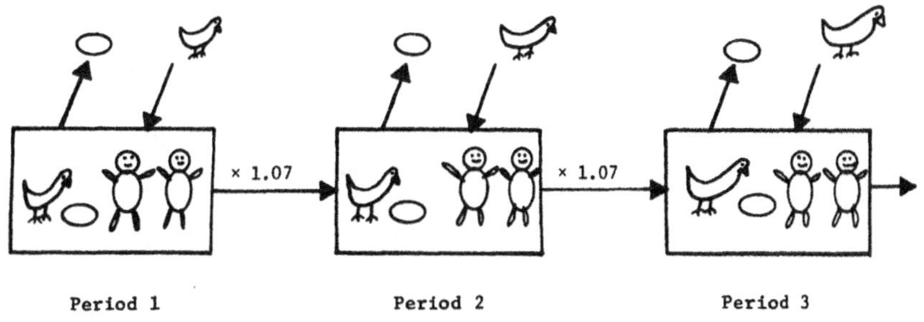

Fig. 26

However the virtue of the solution in Figure 26 over that in Figure 25 is that it satisfies both the consumers with high production and the protectionists with home production of chickens. Only the growth rate suffers, but it still an acceptable 7% per year. If the protectionists demand still further increases in chicken production, they may drive the economy back to its former stationary level, or even to a contracting state.

These examples illustrate how it is possible in the open model to make available by proper settings of control variables some of the outputs of the supporting activities in order to keep the supported activities going. In this way one can think of "spending" the profits of the supporting industries for added consumption, improved "quality of life", national defense, protection of home industries, etc. The "cost" of these decisions is in decreased expansion rate.

Our model considers the conscious control of the expansion rate as one of the important decision variables; which becomes a new objective of the nation. The economic growth rate should be matched to the population growth rate which, in turn, is also becoming an important decision variable for modern economies.

If one wishes to distinguish between mere linear expansion and "growth" where parts of the economy grow at different rates – e.g. agriculture less than electronics – such phenomena can be accounted for in the new model by making gradual changes in control variables. This is due to the model's ability to absorb new technology (the principal reason for such differences) by which it further distinguishes itself from current theory. The application of control variables also makes it possible that some industries expand at rates different from those of others (e.g., pollution control impedes growth of oil refineries but none is imposed on electronics). Thus there are subeconomies of the whole economy and their interrelation becomes an important subject of the investigation.

The consideration of a single open economy that can export to and import from an otherwise unspecified outside world, immediately raises several questions. Suppose we had several such open economies interacting by exporting and importing goods; could we fix our attention on one economy and lump the rest together as an outside world? How do we determine export and import prices in this case? What new results can be proved in the many country case? We discuss these questions next.

The study of such "world economies" has only begun, and much is yet to be learned. However, we have shown that one straight forward way of determining world export and import prices is by putting all the activities from all countries into a single large closed model; the solution to the latter model then gives a feasible set of world prices which can then be applied to each individual country.

A solution found in this way for a three-country three-good problem appears in Figure 27. Notice that there is complete specialization of production with Country 1 producing only wheat, Country 2 producing only eggs and Country 3 producing only chickens. The exports and imports to and from each country are shown by arrows. Although the numerical details are not shown, the countries had individual expansion factors that were below or only slightly above 1 before trading. However, after trade was set up, as shown in Figure 27, the expansion factor for all three countries was 1.257. Here the advantages of specialization and increased expansion are obvious.

One thing that is clear in the world model is that in order for countries to continue trading at substantial levels over a long period of time, it is necessary that they have the same expanstion rate, as do for instance the three countries in Figure 27. This leads us to predict the existence of "trading blocks" of groups of similar countries having the same or similar expansion rates engaging in large amounts of international trade. Countries that do not have an activity that possesses a comparative advantage at that expansion rate, must join a trading block having a lesser rate of expansion, or else stay isolated without trading.

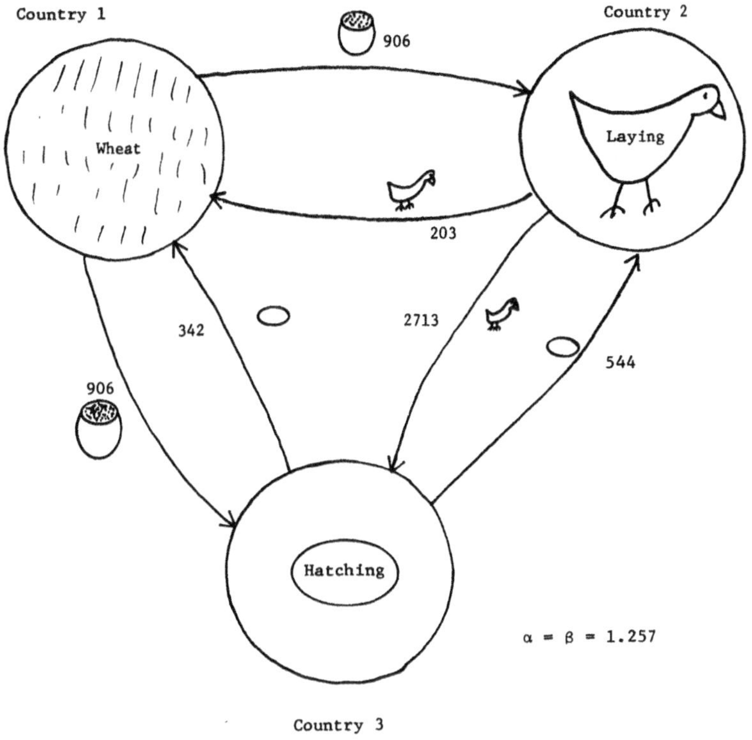

Fig. 27

We can even envision a country that has a single good (e.g., oil, gold, uranium) which it has a comparative advantage in producing, joining for a time a trading block having a large expansion rate. However, if it exhausts its source of supply of that good, thus losing its comparative advantage, it could later be forced out of the trading block.

Much more can be done with the open model. For instance, we have shown elsewhere how to use the open model for long-term planning, how to put several open models together into a world model, how to introduce savings as well as consumption into the open model, etc. Once the necessary data has been collected (no mean task!) we are confident that it can be used to help make policy decisions. But there are also many problems – both empirical and theoretical – still to be solved for the model.

Although von Neumann's ideas have been slow in penetrating into economic science, partly because of their novelty and mathematical sophistication, world-wide interest in them is rapidly increasing in both western and eastern countries. An indication is the fact that two international conferences devoted entirely to von Neumann growth models were held recently, one in Vienna, Austria, in 1970, and the other in Warsaw, Poland in 1972. We expect work on these models to be an important and rapidly growing branch of economics in the future.

References

Bruckmann, G., and *W. Weber*: Contributions to the von Neumann Growth Model. Zeitschrift für Nationalökonomie, Supplementum 1, 1971.

Los, J., and *M.W. Los*: Mathematical Models in Economics. Amsterdam 1974.

Morgenstern, O., and *G.L. Thompson*: Mathematical Theory of Expanding and Contracting Economics. Lexington, Mass., 1976.

von Neumann, J.: A Model of General Economic Equilibrium. Review of Economic Studies **12**, 1945–46, 1–9.

Part III

Economic Time Series Analysis

Games, Economic Dynamics, and Time Series Analysis. 1982 ©Physica-Verlag, Wien–Würzburg

Part III: Economic Time Series Analysis

Introduction

By M. Deistler

Time series analysis is concerned with the extraction of information from data which are ordered in time. Its most important problems are to describe the evolution in time and the dependence between the observations at different points in time and to use this information for analysis, forecasting and control. Clearly, time series analysis is closely related to the statistical analysis of dynamic systems.

Since evolution in time, dependence between observations, and dynamics are common phenomena in economics it is clear that there is a long tradition of both applying time series methods to economic data and of developing time series methods adequate to the genuine problems of empirical economics. Thus a good part of econometrics is time series analysis. However, in econometrics this word has been used in a rather narrow sense for time series methods which do not impose strong economic a-priori restrictions in contrast to the structural case of econometrics.

In the eighteenth and nineteenth century time series methods, mainly for astronomy and meteorology, have been developed to detect or to eliminate unobserved components like secular trends, periodicities or noise from given time series observations.

In the twenties of this century, Yule introduced autoregressive and moving average models as parametric models of time series and especially to allow for models generating "not perfectly" periodic components. The theory of stationary processes developed since the thirties and forties provided useful basic theoretical foundations for time series analysis. About the same time the members of the Cowles commission reached the well known results on identifiability and estimation for simultaneous linear systems.

In 1961 Oskar Morgenstern started a time series project at the Econometric Research Program of Princeton University to investigate the use of advanced time series methods, especially of spectral and crosspectral analysis, in the analysis of economic data and to develop a genuinely economic time series methodology. The project was advised by J. Tukey, the other members of this research program were C.W.J. Granger, M. Godfrey, M. Hatanaka, H. Karreman, M. Suzuki and T. Wonnacott.

Spectral analysis, both as a method of nonparametric estimation of autospectra, crossspectra, transfer functions and coherences, and as a tool of understanding processes and linear systems in terms of frequency decompositions, is now an important part of economic time series analysis. One of the reasons is that often the frequency domain interpretation in terms of business cycles or seasonal patterns is more natural for certain economic questions. Nevertheless the recent developments of time series analysis in general and of economic time series analysis in particular are in favour of parametric time domain models, especially of the ARMA and ARMAX models (or the equivalent state space models). These ARMAX models are a generalization of the classical Cowles commission models to errors which are correlated in time. ARMA processes are just the processes having rational spectral density. The advantage of ARMA (or ARMAX) models is that only a finite number of parameters have to be estimated and that they are flexible enough to approximate every regular stationary process (every finite dimensional time invariant linear system) with arbitrary accuracy.

There has been considerable progress in time series analysis in the last decade. We have now a better understanding of the problems of estimation and specification and the problems associated with causality and exogeneity. The above sketch of problems and research efforts is however far from being complete.

Time series analysis, even only the part relevant for economics, is too large a field to be covered by a symposium of this kind. For this reason, the organizers are particularly glad having been able to bring together a group of researchers who in their papers and their contributions to the discussion managed to present some important branches of and latest developments in econometric time series analysis in accordance with the state of the art in this field.

Games, Economic Dynamics, and Time Series Analysis. 1982 ©Physica-Verlag, Wien–Würzburg

Estimation and Optimal Control of Models of Dynamic Games

By *G.C. Chow*, Princeton[1])

1. Introduction

An outstanding problem in the optimal control literature is the statistical estimation of the parameters of the objective function. Given a linear model

$$y_t = Ay_{t-1} + Cx_t + b + u_t \tag{1}$$

where y_t is a vector of state variables, x_t is a vector of control variables, and u_t is a vector of random disturbances, and given a quadratic objective function

$$-\sum_{t=1}^{T} (y_t - a_t)' K_t (y_t - a_t) \tag{2}$$

having K_t and a_t as parameters, the optimal control problem is to maximize the expectation of (2), resulting in a set of optimal feedback control rules

$$x_t = G_t y_{t-1} + g_t. \tag{3}$$

As in *Chow* [1975, p. 153], (1) may represent a higher-order system including the lagged variables $y_{t-2}, y_{t-3}, \ldots, x_{t-1}, x_{t-2}$, etc., but has been converted to state-space form with the vector y_t incorporating x_t as a subvector by definition. The present paper is concerned with an inverse problem: Having observed the evolution of y_t as generated by the model (1), and the optimal behavior of the decision makers as described by (3), estimate the parameters of (1) and (2).

This problem has important applications in economics. For example, (1) may represent a macroeconometric model of a national economy and (2) the preference function of the government authorities which control x_t. (3) is then the optimal decision rule for the government. Having observed the macroeconomy and the optimal behavior of the government, the econometrician's problem is to estimate the parameters of the econometric model and of the government's preference function. Alternatively, (1) may represent the economic environment facing some economic decision makers in the private sectors (business firms or consumers) and (2) their objective function. (3) would be the optimal investment function, demand function for inputs or consumption function.

The model can be generalized to represent two groups of decision makers who control x_{1t} and x_{2t} respectively, these being the subvectors of x_t in equation (1). Each group of

[1]) *G.C. Chow*, Princeton University, 206 Dickinson Hall, Princeton, New Jersey, 08544, U.S.A.

decision makers will have its own objective function (2) and its optimal decision rule (3). The first group may represent the economic agents in the private sector and the second may represent government authorities. The two groups may represent two private firms as in a duopoly. They may also represent two parts of the government, such as the Board of Governors of the Federal Reserve System and the Executive Branch in the United States. We will have a model of dynamic game, and the problem is to estimate the parameters of the model (1) and of the objective functions of both players.

This paper will be concerned only with a special case of the quadratic objective function (2) in which $K_t = \beta^t K$, β being a discount factor, and $a_t = a$ (constant targets). Furthermore, it will assume that the optimal feedback control equations (3) are time invariant, with $G_t = G$ and $g_t = g$. It is well known, cf. *Chow* [1975, 178–179], that the coefficients G_t and g_t in (3) are obtained by solving the following pairs of equations backward in time

$$(C'H_tC)G_t + C'H_tA = 0 \tag{4}$$

$$H_t - K_t - (A + CG_{t+1})'H_{t+1}\,(A + CG_{t+1}) = 0; \tag{5}$$

$$(C'H_tC)g_t + C'(H_tb - h_t) = 0 \tag{6}$$

$$h_t - K_ta_t + (A + CG_{t+1})'(H_{t+1}\,b - h_{t+1}) = 0 \tag{7}$$

with initial conditions $H_T = K_T$ and $h_T = K_Ta_T$. Under our assumptions $K_t = \beta K$ and $a_t = a$, the steady-state G and g from (4) – (7) are found by solving the following pairs of algebraic equations

$$(C'HC)G - C'HA = 0 \tag{8}$$

$$H - K - \beta(A + CG)'H(A + CG) = 0; \tag{9}$$

$$(C'HC)g + C'(Hb - h) = 0 \tag{10}$$

$$[I - \beta(A + CG)']h - Ka + \beta(A + CG)'Hb = 0. \tag{11}$$

In Section 2, the method of maximum likelihood is applied to estimate the parameters of (1) and (2), the latter including K, β, and a, under the assumption that u_t and a residual introduced in (3) are both normal and uncorrelated. In Section 3, a method of two stage least squares is introduced to provide consistent estimates of these parameters. Section 4 treats the government as the second player who controls x_{2t} and studies the effect of the government decision rule on the behavior of the private economic agents who control x_{1t}. Section 5 derives the optimal feedback rule for the government which anticipates the effects of its own policy on the policy of the private sector. Section 6 considers the estimation of the parameter in a dynamic game model under the assumption that it is in a dominant-player (Stackelberg) equilibrium or a Nash (Cournot) equilibrium.

2. Maximum Likelihood Estimation of the Objective Function

Assume that u_t in (1) is independent and normal, having a covariance matrix Σ, that, due to errors in the execution of the optimal policy, a residual exists in (3) which is also independent and normal, having a covariance matrix V, and that the residuals in (1) and (3) are uncorrelated. The last assumption can easily be relaxed without affecting the major steps used to obtain the maximum likelihood estimates to be stated below. We also assume that the discount factor β is given, as the maximization of the likelihood function with respect to this scalar should present no great difficulty once the remaining parameters can be estimated. Our problem is the estimation of the parameters A, C, b, and Σ or (1), K and a of (2), and G, g, and V of (3), subject to the constraints (8), (9), (10) and (11).

We form a Lagrangian expression which combines the log-likelihood with these constraints

$$
\begin{aligned}
L = \text{constant} &- \frac{n}{2}\log|\Sigma| - \frac{n}{2}\log|V| \\
&- \frac{1}{2}\operatorname{tr}[\Sigma^{-1}(Y' - AY'_{-1} - CX' - bz')(Y - Y_{-1}A' - XC' - zb')] \\
&- \frac{1}{2}\operatorname{tr}[V^{-1}(X' - GY'_{-1} - gz')(X - Y_{-1}G' - zg')] - \operatorname{tr}[\Omega(8)] \\
&- \frac{1}{2}\operatorname{tr}[\Phi(9)] - \omega'[(10)] - \phi'[(11)]
\end{aligned}
$$

where Y is an $n \times p$ matrix of observations on the endogenous variables; Y_{-1} is an $n \times p$ matrix of observations on the lagged endogenous variables; X is an $n \times q$ matrix of observations on the control variables; z represents a dummy variable being a vector consisting of n ones; Ω $(p \times q)$ and $\Phi = \Phi'$ $(p \times p)$ are matrices of Lagrangian multipliers; ω $(q \times 1)$ and ϕ $(p \times 1)$ are vectors of Lagrangian multipliers; the numbers 8–11 in parentheses denote the corresponding constraints. The unknowns in this problem consist of Σ, V, A, C, b, G, H, g, h, K, and a.

Using the differentiation rules $\partial \log|A|/\partial A = A^{-1'}$ and $\partial \operatorname{tr}(AB)/\partial A = B'$, we differentiate L to obtain

$$\frac{\partial L}{\partial \Sigma^{-1}} = n\Sigma - (Y' - AY'_{-1} - CX' - bz')(Y - Y_{-1}A' - XC' - zb') = 0 \tag{12}$$

$$\frac{\partial L}{\partial V^{-1}} = nV - (X' - GY'_{-1} - gz')(X - Y_{-1}G' - zg') = 0 \tag{13}$$

$$
\begin{aligned}
\frac{\partial L}{\partial A'} &= Y'_{-1}(Y - Y_{-1}A' - XC' - zb')\Sigma^{-1} - \Omega C'H + \beta\Phi(A + CG)'H \\
&\quad - \beta\phi(Hb - h)' = 0
\end{aligned} \tag{14}
$$

$$\frac{\partial L}{\partial C'} = X'(Y - Y_{-1}A' - XC' - zb')\Sigma^{-1} - \Omega'(A + CG)'H$$
$$- G\Omega C'H + \beta G\Phi(A + CG)'H$$
$$- g\omega' C'H - \omega g' C'H - \omega(Hb - h)' - \beta G\phi(Hb - h)' = 0 \quad (15)$$

$$\frac{\partial L}{\partial b'} = z'(Y - Y_{-1}A' - XC' - zb')\Sigma^{-1} - \omega' C'H + \beta\phi'(A + CG)'H = 0 \quad (16)$$

$$\frac{\partial L}{\partial G'} = Y'_{-1}(X - Y_{-1}G' - zg')V^{-1} - \Omega C'HC + \beta\Phi(A + CG)'HC$$
$$- \beta\phi(Hb - h)'C = 0 \quad (17)$$

$$\frac{\partial L}{\partial H} = -(A + CG)\Omega C' - C\Omega'(A + CG)' - \Phi + \beta(A + CG)\Phi(A + CG)' - Cg\omega' C'$$
$$- C\omega g' C' - b\omega' C' - C\omega b' - \beta b\phi'(A + CG)' - \beta(A + CG)\phi b' = 0 \quad (18)$$

$$\frac{\partial L}{\partial K} \overset{*}{=} \Phi + a\phi' + \phi a' \overset{*}{=} 0 \quad (19)$$

$$\frac{\partial L}{\partial g'} = z'(X - Y_{-1}G' - zg')V^{-1} - \omega' C'HC = 0 \quad (20)$$

$$\frac{\partial L}{\partial h} = C\omega - [I - \beta(A + CG)]\phi = 0 \quad (21)$$

$$\frac{\partial L}{\partial a} \overset{*}{=} K\phi \overset{*}{=} 0. \quad (22)$$

Although K is a symmetric $p \times p$ matrix and a is a column vector of p elements, many of the elements in K and a are known to be zero. If there are r target variables, only an $r \times r$ submatrix of K and r elements in a are nonzero. The symbol $\overset{*}{=}$ in equations (19) and (22) indicates that only the derivatives of L with respect to the unknown elements of K and a are set equal to zero. Equations (8) – (22) will be solved for the unknown parameters.

First, consider equations (21) and (22). They are $p + r$ linear equations in the $p + q$ unknowns in ϕ and ω. It the number r of target variables equals or exceeds the number q of instruments (as we will so assume to make equation (3) a unique solution of the economic agent's optimization problem), both Lagrangian multipliers ϕ and ω will be zero provided that the $(p + r) \times (p + q)$ matrix, with K^* composed of the r rows of K corresponding to the nonzero elements of a,

$$\begin{bmatrix} C & -[I - \beta(A + CG)] \\ 0 & K^* \end{bmatrix}$$

is of rank $p + q$. The solution $\phi = 0$ and $\omega = 0$ from (21) and (22) simplifies many of the remaining equations.

Secondly, observe that as usual consistent estimates of the covariance matrices Σ and V can be obtained from (12) and (13) respectively, where the coefficients $(A\ C\ b)$ and

$(G\ g)$ are replaced by the least squares estimates. We therefore will treat Σ and V as given for the solution of the remaining equations. A firm believer in the method of maximum likelihood could always revise these estimates of Σ and V after the remaining equations are solved, and iterate until convergence.

Third, given any estimates of $(A\ C\ b)$, $(C\ g)$ and K, we will revise them for the next iteration by solving the following equations. (The initial estimates of $(A\ C\ b)$ and $(G\ g)$ are obtained by least squares; the initial K may be a diagonal matrix with r nonzero elements.) Equations (8) and (9) are used to solve for G and H. On account of (8) and $\phi = 0$, the last two terms of (17) vanish, and (17) can be used to solve for Ω. (18) is used to obtain Φ by iteration.

$$\Phi = \beta(A + CG)\,\Phi\,(A + CG)' - (A + CG)\,\Omega C' - C\Omega'(A + CG)'.$$

Equations (14) and (15) are solved for A and C; they are modified "normal equations" for these coefficients. (16) and (20) then give respectively

$$b = n^{-1}\,(Y' - AY'_{-1} - CX')\,z$$

$$g = n^{-1}\,(X' - GY'_{-1})\,z.$$

Thus, given K, the above equations can be iterated to find $(A\ C\ b)$ and $(G\ g)$. To find K, we use (19) or $\Phi \overset{*}{=} 0$ for the elements of Φ which correspond to the unknown elements on K. These elements are the partials of L with respect to the unknowns in K; they can be used in a gradient algorithm to maximize L with respect to K.

Fourth, there are only two remaining equations (10) and (11) to be solved for h and a. Solving (11) for h and substituting the result in (10), we obtain, denoting $A + CG$ by R,

$$C'[I - \beta R']\,Ka = C'HCg + C'[I - \beta(I - \beta R')^{-1}R']\,Hb. \tag{23}$$

Since C' is $q \times p$, this is a system of q linear equations for the r unknowns in a. If the number r of target variables equals the number q of control variables, the solution for a is unique. If $r > q$, the solution for a is not unique. This result is reasonable because the observable behavior of the economic agents which is relevant for the estimation of a consists of a $q \times 1$ vector g in the optimal feedback control equation. If a has more elements than g, it cannot be estimated uniquely. We have thus provided a solution to the maximum-likelihood estimation of the parameters of (1) and (2) under the assumption that $K_t = \beta^t K$ and $a_t = a$. For alternative approaches to the estimation problem in some special cases, the reader is referred to Sargent [1979], *Hanson/Sargent* [1980], and *Chow* [1980].

3. Method of Two-Stage Least Squares for Estimating the Objective Function

Besides maximum likelihood, we propose a family of consistent estimators for estimating the parameters of (2). It is based on the observations that the least-squares estimator $\hat{G}$ of the coefficients G in the regression of x_t on y_{t-1} (which includes x_{t-1} as a subvector) is consistent, and that, if G is the solution to the optimal control problem, it should satisfy equations (8) and (9). The situation is analogous to the estimation of structural parameters $(B\ \Gamma)$ in a system of linear simultaneous equations

$$By_t + \Gamma x_t = \epsilon_t$$

by the use of the least-squares estimate $\hat{\Pi}$ of the matrix of reduced-form coefficients $\Pi = -B^{-1}\Gamma$. $\hat{\Pi}$ is a consistent estimate of Π, and, if the model is correct, Π satisfies $B\Pi = -\Gamma$ which corresponds to (8) and (9) in the present problem. Therefore, if we solve (8) and (9) for H, K and β (the structural parameters) using the least-squares estimate $\hat{G}$ for G and consistent estimates $\hat{A}$ and $\hat{C}$ for A and C, we will obtain consistent estimates of the former, as we will obtain consistent estimates of B and Γ by solving $B\hat{\Pi} = -\Gamma$.

As the first step of this method, we obtain least-squares estimates $\hat{G}$ of the coefficients in the multivariate regression of x_t on y_{t-1}. Having obtained $\hat{G}$, we will find H, K and β to satisfy equations (8) and (9), but as in the case of overidentified structural equations, there may be more equations than unknowns. Defining $R = (r_{ij}) = \hat{A} + \hat{C}\hat{G}$, we write these equations as

$$C'HR = 0 \tag{24}$$

$$K = H - \beta R'HR. \tag{25}$$

Let H be a symmetric $p \times p$ matrix with elements h_{ij}, and let C be a $p \times q$ matrix with elements c_{ij}. These two equations imply respectively

$$\sum_{i,j}^{p} c_{im}\, r_{jl}\, h_{ij} = 0 \qquad (m = 1, \ldots, q;\ l = 1, \ldots, p) \tag{26}$$

$$h_{ml} - \beta \sum_{i,j}^{p} r_{im}\, r_{jl}\, h_{ij} = 0 \qquad \text{if } k_{ml} = 0 \tag{27}$$

(26) and (27) are linear equations in $h_{ij} = h_{ji}$. Let h be the column vector consisting of the $p(p+1)/2$ elements h_{ij} $(i = 1, \ldots, p;\ j \geqslant i)$. Write (26) and (27) as a system of linear equations in h,

$$Qh = 0. \tag{28}$$

Exact, over- or underidentification occurs according to whether the rank of Q is equal to, larger, or smaller than $p(p+1)/2$ minus one. In the overidentified case, there will be more equations than unknowns in (28); the elements on its right-hand side cannot all vanish. Corresponding to the method of indirect least squares for simultaneous equations, one cân suggest discarding extra equations in (28) and solving the remaining $p(p+1)/2$ homogeneous linear equations which are made non-homogeneous by a normalization $h_{pp} = 1$. This method is still consistent but it discards useful information. Corresponding to the method of two-stage least squares, according to the interpretation of *Chow* [1964], we normalize by setting $h_{pp} = 1$ (or any $h_{ii} = 1$), partition Q and h' respectively as $(Q_1 q_2)$ and $(h_1' 1)$ to write (28) as

$$Q_1 h_1 + q_2 = 0 \tag{29}$$

and estimate h_1 by $\hat{h}_1 = -(Q_1' Q_1)^{-1} Q_1' q_2$ using the method of least squares in the second stage.

Corresponding to the method of limited-information maximum likelihood, according to the interpretation of *Chow* [1964], we normalize symmetrically by setting $h'h =$ constant and find h to minimize $h'Q'Qh$ subject to this normalization constraint. The minimizing h is the characteristic vector associated with the smallest characteristic root of $Q'Q$. Unlike the method of two-stage least squares, this method yields a vector estimate of h which is invariant with respect to the choice of the variable for normalization. However, if the order of Q is very large, the symmetric normalization is not recommended as it is computationally expensive. If β is unknown, one has to find a scalar to minimize the appropriate sum of squares, be it $h_1' Q_1' Q_1 h_1$ or $h'Q'Qh$, but this is an easy problem. Having obtained h and β, we use the remaining equations of (25), other than (27), to compute the nonzero elements of K. Given H, $\hat{A}$ and $\hat{C}$, we can obtain a new estimate $G_{(2)}$ of G by using (8). Having estimated G, g, A, C, b and H consistently, we can use (23) to estimate a.

If the estimates of H, K, β and a by the method of this section are not accepted as final, they can serve as initial estimates to be used in the (more expensive) maximization of the likelihood function by the method of Section 2. The consistent estimates of this section can be recommended if the method of Section 2 is considered too expensive. For an extension of the methods of this section to the case when the model (1) is nonlinear, the reader is referred to *Chow* [1980].

4. Effect of Government Decision Rule on the Behavior of Private Economic Agents

Let there be two sets of decision makers (players) whose control variables are x_{1t} and x_{2t} respectively. The model (1) becomes

$$y_t = Ay_{t-1} + C_1 x_{1t} + C_2 x_{2t} + b + u_t. \tag{30}$$

Let the objective function of the i-th player be, with time invariant K_i and a_i,

$$E_0 \sum_{t=1}^{T} (y_t - a_i)' K_i (y_t - a_i) \qquad (i = 1,2). \tag{31}$$

Further, let their decision rules (however arrived at) be written as

$$x_{it} = G_i y_{t-1} + g_i \qquad (i = 1,2). \tag{32}$$

If Player 2 represents the government which follows a fixed decision rule for x_{2t}, the environment facing the private economic agents (Player 1) will be

$$\begin{aligned} y_t &= (A + C_2 G_2) y_{t-1} + C_1 x_{1t} + (b + C_2 g_2) + u_t \\ &\equiv A_1 y_{t-1} + C_1 x_{2t} + b_1 + u_t. \end{aligned} \tag{33}$$

Assuming that the private economic agents facing the environment (33) solve their optimal control problem to obtain their behavioral equation $x_{1t} = G_1 y_{t-1} + g_1$, one concludes that their behavioral equation will change as the government's decision rule changes. Therefore, an econometrician cannot rely on stable behavioral equations for the private sector to evaluate the consequences of changing government policies, as *Lucas* [1976] has stressed. On the other hand, if the econometrician has estimated the parameters of (1) or (8) and (2) for the private agents, he can infer their behavior (3) once the government's decision rule is known, by solving the optimal control problem with a new environment (33).

Specifically, let the government adhere to a feedback control policy $x_{2t} = G_2 y_{t-1} + g_2$. Player 1 will face (33) as its environment and adopt the optimal equilbrium strategy $x_{1t} = G_1 y_{t-1} + g_1$ where, on account of (8) – (11)

$$C_1' H_1 C_1 G_1 + C_1' H_1 (A + C_2 G_2) = 0 \tag{34}$$

$$H_1 - K_1 - (A + C_2 G_2 + C_1 G_1)' H_1 (A + C_2 G_2 + C_1 G_1) = 0 \tag{35}$$

$$C_1' H_1 C_1 g_1 + C_1' [H_1 (b + C_2 g_2) - h_1] = 0 \tag{36}$$

$$[I - (A + C_2 G_2 + C_1 G_1)'] h_1 - K_1 a_1 - (A + C_2 G_2 + C_1 G_1)' H_1 (b + C_2 g_2) = 0. \tag{37}$$

Given G_2, equations (34) and (35) can be solved to obtain G_1 and H_1. Given g_2 in addition, equations (36) and (37) can be solved to obtain g_1 and h_1. Equations (34) – (37) show exactly how the behavior (G_1, g_1) of the private sector will change as the government policy rule (G_2, g_2) changes.

5. Optimal Control Rule for the Government

Once the government can predict how its decision rule would affect the behavior of the private economic agents, it can choose a rule to maximize its objective function, assuming all parameters of (30) and (31) to be known. An algorithm for the government is given in *Chow* [1981]. The problem is to find the optimal strategy of the dominant player in a two-person dynamic game. We will derive a pair of optimal steady-state strategies (G_1, g_1) and (G_2, g_2) for the two players when the system is in a covariance-stationary equilibrium, assuming that a_{1t}, K_{1t}, a_{2t} and K_{2t} are all time invariant.

Given any government policy (G_2, g_2) and the associated strategy of the private sector as given by equations (34) – (37), the behavior of the system (30) is determined. In a covariance-stationary equilibrium, the system will have a mean vector $\bar{y}$ and a covariance matrix $\Gamma = E(y_t - \bar{y})(y_t - \bar{y})'$ which satisfy [see *Chow*, 1975, 51–52]:

$$(I - A - C_1 G_1 - C_2 G_2)\bar{y} - b - C_1 g_1 - C_2 g_2 = 0 \tag{38}$$

$$\Gamma - (A + C_1 G_1 + C_2 G_2) \Gamma (A + C_1 G_1 + C_2 G_2)' - E u_t u_t' = 0. \tag{39}$$

The problem of the government, here treated as the dominant player, is to minimize its loss function

$$\frac{1}{2}E(y_t - a_2)'K_2(y_t - a_2) = \frac{1}{2}\,\mathrm{tr}\,(K_2\Gamma) + \frac{1}{2}(\bar{y} - a_2)'K_2(\bar{y} - a_2)$$

with respect to G_2 and g_2 in its feedback control equation, subject to the constraints (34) – (39). This problem can be solved by forming the Lagrangian expression

$$L = \frac{1}{2}\,\mathrm{tr}\,(K_2\Gamma) + \frac{1}{2}(\bar{y} - a_2)'K_2(\bar{y} - a_2) - \omega'(36) - \phi'(37) - \lambda'(38)$$

$$- \,\mathrm{tr}\,\{\Omega(34)\} - \frac{1}{2}\,\mathrm{tr}\,\{\Phi(35)\} - \frac{1}{2}\,\mathrm{tr}\,\{\Psi(39)\}$$

where ω, ϕ, λ, Ω, $\Phi = \Phi'$ and $\Psi = \Psi'$ are vectors and matrices of Lagrangian multipliers and, for brevity, the equation number in parantheses denotes the corresponding constraint.

Using the differentiation rule $\partial\,\mathrm{tr}\,(AB)/\partial A = B'$, we obtain the following equations, with R denoting $A + C_1G_1 + C_2G_2$,

$$\frac{\partial L}{\partial g_1} = -C_1'H_1C_1\omega + C_1'\lambda = 0 \tag{40}$$

$$\frac{\partial L}{\partial h_1} = C_1\omega - (I - R)\phi = 0 \tag{41}$$

$$\frac{\partial L}{\partial g_2} = -C_2'H_1C_1\omega + C_2'H_1R\phi + C_2'\lambda = 0 \tag{42}$$

$$\frac{\partial L}{\partial \bar{y}} = K_2(\bar{y} - a_2) - (I - R')\lambda = 0 \tag{43}$$

$$\frac{\partial L}{\partial G_1} = C_1'[H_1C_1\Omega' + H_1R\Phi + \Psi R\Gamma + h_1\phi' + H_1(b + C_2g_2)\phi' + \lambda\bar{y}'] = 0 \tag{44}$$

$$\frac{\partial L}{\partial G_2} = C_2'[H_1C_1\Omega' + H_1R\Phi + \Psi R\Gamma + h_1\phi' + H_1(b + C_2g_2)\phi' + \lambda\bar{y}'] = 0 \tag{45}$$

$$\frac{\partial L}{\partial H_1} = -\Phi + R\Phi R' - C_1g_1\omega'C_1' - C_1\omega g_1'C_1' - (b + C_2g_2)\omega'C_1'$$
$$- C_1\omega(b + C_2g_2)' + (b + C_2g_2)\phi'R + R'\phi(b + C_2g_2)' = 0 \tag{46}$$

$$\frac{\partial L}{\partial \Gamma} = K_2 - \Psi + R'\Psi R = 0. \tag{47}$$

To solve these equations, we start with some tentative solution for G_2, G_1 and H_1. Equations (40), (41), (42) and (43) imply respectively, with $P_1 = C_1(C_1'H_1C_1)^{-1}C_1'$,

$$\omega = (C_1'H_1C_1)^{-1}C_1'\lambda \tag{40a}$$

$$\phi = (I - R)^{-1} P_1 \lambda \tag{41a}$$

$$C_2' \{I - H_1 [I - R (I - R)^{-1}] P_1\} \lambda = 0 \tag{42a}$$

$$\lambda = (I - R')^{-1} K_2 (\bar{y} - a_2). \tag{43a}$$

Equations (43a) and (38) give

$$\lambda = (I - R')^{-1} K_2 [(I - R)^{-1} (b + C_1 g_1 + C_2 g_2) - a_2]. \tag{48}$$

Combining (48) with (42a), we get

$$C_2' \{I - H_1 [I - R (I - R)^{-1}] P_1\} (I - R')^{-1} K_2 [(I - R)^{-1} (b + C_1 g_1 + C_2 g_2) - a_2] = 0. \tag{49}$$

With G_2, G_1 and H_1 given, equations (49), (36) and (37) can be solved for g_2, g_1 and h_1. Equation (48), (40a) and (41a) are then used to find λ, ω, and ϕ, while equation (38) is used to compute $\bar{y}$.

We now solve equations (44) – (47). Equation (46) is used to solve for Φ iteratively, that is $\Phi^{(i+1)} = R\Phi^{(i)}R' +$ known matrix. Equations (44) and (45) imply

$$\Omega' = -(C_1' H_1 C_1)^{-1} C_1' [H_1 R \Phi + \Psi R \Gamma + \ldots] \tag{44a}$$

$$C_2' [I - H_1 P_1] [H_1 R \Phi + \Psi R \Gamma + h_1 \phi' + H_1 (b + C_2 g_2) \phi' + \lambda \bar{y}'] = 0. \tag{45a}$$

Since (39) and (47) can be used to compute Γ and Ψ respectively, (45a) after being post-multiplied by Γ^{-1} can be solved for G_2 iteratively, that is

$$C_2' [I - H_1 P_1] \Psi C_2 G_2 = C_2' [I - H_1 P_1] [H_1 R \Phi \Gamma^{-1} + \Psi (A + C_1 G_1) + \ldots]$$

where we have recalled $R = (A + C_1 G_1 + C_2 G_2)$. Having thus obtained a new matrix G_2, we can continue with the iterative process by returning to the beginning of the preceding paragraph.

Mathematically, the solution to the two-person dynamic game formulated above under a Nash (or Cournot) equilibrium is simpler, for each player would treat the other's strategy as given, without being affected by his own strategy. Given (G_2, g_2), Player 1 would find (G_1, g_1) by equations (34) – (37) as before. Symmetrically, given (G_1, g_1), Player 2 would find (G_2, g_2) by solving an identical set of equations with subscripts 1 and 2 interchanged. A Nash equilibrium is found by solving these two sets of equations.

6. Estimating Models of Dynamic Game

When x_{2t} in (30) represents the policy instruments of the government and the government is treated as the dominant player, we will study the estimation problem in two stages. First, assuming that the government adheres to a policy rule $x_{2t} = G_2 y_{t-1} + g_2$, which is decided upon by whatever means, we will consider the estimation of the parameters of (30) and (31) for $i = 1$ under the assumption that the private sector behaves optimally. Second, from the above framework we take the next step by assuming that the government is also trying to maximize (31) for $i = 2$ and consider the estimation of the parameters of its objective function as well.

For the first problem, the stochastic environment facing the private sector is given by (33). The methods of Sections 2 and 3 can be applied to estimate the parameters of (33) and (31) for $i = 1$. In order to solve the second and more difficult problem of estimating K_{2t} and a_{2t}, we assume $K_{2t} = \beta K_2$ and $a_{2t} = a_2$. Given K_1, a_1, K_2, a_2 and the parameters of (30) we can apply the method of Section 5 to find the optimal pair of strategies (G_1, g_1) and (G_2, g_2); thus the likelihood function can be evaluated. A gradient method can in principle be applied to maximize the likelihood with respect to these parameters, but this numerical maximization problem requires further investigation.

To estimate a dynamic game model under a Nash (or Cournot) equilibrium, the methods of maximum likelihood and two-stage least squares are applicable. Since these methods are fairly straightforward extensions of the methods given in Sections 2 and 3 respectively, we need only sketch them here. For the former, we maximize the likelihood function subject to two sets of constraints. One set of constraints consists of the four equations (34) – (37), and the second set is identical except with the subscripts 1 and 2 interchanged. A Lagrangian expression is formed which is to be maximized. Given the parameters of the objective function and the optimal decision rule for Player 1, the method of Section 2 can be used to find the remaining parameters of the model. Given the estimates of the parameters pertaining to Player 2 so obtained, one can maximize the likelihood function with respect to the parameters for Player 1, and the process proceeds iteratively until convergence.

To apply the method of two-stage least squares, we observe that if the parameters of (30) are consistently estimated, and G_2 and g_2 are consistently estimated, the parameters A_1, C_1 and b_1 of the model (33) are also consistently estimated. These estimates, together with consistent estimates of G_1 and g_1 by regression of x_{1t} on y_{t-1}, can be utilized to form two-stage least-squares estimates of the parameters K_1 and a_1 of the objective function of Player 1 as described by the method of Section 3. These estimates of K_1 and a_1, together with consistent estimates of the parameters of (33) will imply a new set of estimates of G_1 and g_1 through Player 1's solution of his optimal control problem. Similarly, consistent estimates of the parameters of the model facing Player 2 [analogous to (33) for Player 1], and of G_2 and g_2 obtained by regression of x_{2t} on y_{t-1}, can be utilized to form two-stage least-squares estimates of K_2 and a_2. Again, these estimates of K_2 and a_2 can be used to revise our estimate of G_2 and g_2 through Player 2's optimization. The revised estimates of (G_1, g_1) and (G_2, g_2) correspond to the estimates of the reduced-form coefficients in linear simultaneous equations obtained by solving the structural equations which are estimted by the method of two-stage least squares. Here the solution of the simultaneous structural equations becomes the solution of an optimal control problem for the derivation of (G_1, g_1) or (G_2, g_2) using (K_1, a_1) or (K_2, a_2) as parameters.

References

Chow, G.C.: Comparison of Alternative Estimators for Simultaneous Equations. Econometrica **32**, 1964, 532–553.

–: Analysis and Control of Dynamic Economic Systems. New York 1975.

–: Estimation of Rational Expectations Models. Journal of Economic Dynamics and Control **2**, 1980.

–: Estimation and Optimal Control of Dynamic Game Models under Rational Expectations. Econometric Analysis by Control Methods, Chapter 17. Ed by G.C. Chow. New York 1981.

Hansen, L.P., and *T.J. Sargent*: Formulating and Estimating Dynamic Linear Rational Expectations Models. Journal of Economic Dynamics and Control **2**, 1980, 7–46.

Lucas, R.E., Jr.: Econometric Policy Evaluation: A Critique. Carnegie-Rochester Conferences on Public Policy (a supplementary series to the Journal of Monetary Economics), Vol. **1**, 1976, 19–46.

Sargent, T.J.: Macroeconomic Theory. New York 1979.

Games, Economic Dynamics, and Time Series Analysis. 1982 ©Physica-Verlag, Wien–Würzburg

A Time Series Model with Qualitative Variables[1])

By *D.M. Grether*, Pasadena[2]) and *G.S. Maddala*

1. Introduction

The literature on time-series analysis has been largely confined to the analysis of time-series data where:

(i) The number of observations is large, and
(ii) the variables are all observed as continuous variables.

There are a large number of problems of practical interest that depend on time-series analysis of a different type of data sets. These data sets, which are being made available through numerous longitudinal surveys, have the following characteristics:

(1) The number of cross-section units is large and the number of time periods is small. We thus have a large number of short time series.
(2) Very often the dependent variable is either a categorical variable or a censored variable.

In the present paper we consider the estimation of a distributed lag model based on panel data where the time series on the dependent variable is observed as a categorical variable. In Section 2 we provide examples of some situations where this type of model is applicable. In later sections we present the estimation method and some empirical results.

Earlier discussions of similar problems can be found in *Chamberlain* [1980] and *Heckman* [1979]. The model considered here is different from the models discussed by these authors. Briefly stated, the main differences are as follows: Chamberlain considers the model

$$y_{it}^* = \eta_i + \sum_{j=0}^{k} \beta_j x_{i,t-j} + u_{it} \qquad \begin{array}{l} i = 1,2,\ldots,N \\ t = 1,2,\ldots,T \end{array} \tag{1.1}$$

where y_{it}^* is the "index" variable that is observed only as a qualitative variable. A major emphasis in his paper is on how to handle the "incidental" parameters η_i. He suggests

[1]) Financial support from the National Science Foundation is gratefully acknowledged. We would like to thank R.P.H. Fishe for the computations done in Section 5; and D.R. Kiewiet and M.P. Fiorina for their many helpful comments. Also we gratefully acknowledge the Sherman Fairchild Distinguished Scholars Program and the Program for the Study of Enterprise and Public Policy.

[2]) *D.M. Grether*, California Institute of Technology, 91125 Pasadena, California, U.S.A.

some conditional maximum likelihood methods for this model (consider the likelihood function conditional on sufficient statistics for the incidental parameters).

The model that Heckman considers is of the form:

$$y^*_{it} = \alpha y_{i,t-1} + \beta x_{it} + u_{it} \tag{1.2}$$

where

$$\begin{aligned} y_{it} &= 1 \qquad \text{if } y^*_{it} > 0 \\ &= 0 \qquad \text{otherwise}. \end{aligned} \tag{1.3}$$

Thus, it is the realized values of the "index" variable in the previous periods that affect the current value of the index variable. In the case where y^*_{it} determines the probability of a person finding employment in period t, the model says that this depends on whether the person was employed or not in the previous period (what Heckman calls "state dependence"). Heckman's model contains more lags than one and there are other complications in the formulations adopted by Heckman, but the essence of his models is that it is the lagged values of the dichotomous realizations that occur as explanatory variables.

The model we consider can be termed a "lagged index" model, as contrasted to a "lagged dummy" model that Heckman considers. It is

$$y^*_{it} = \alpha y^*_{i,t-1} + \beta x_{it} + u_{it} \tag{1.4}$$

where we do not observe y^*_{it} but observe the variable y_{it} as defined in (1.3) (or alternatively a polychotomous variable). In the case where y^*_{it} determines the probability of finding employment in period t, model (1.4) says that this depends on the corresponding index in period $t-1$. The model (1.2), on the other hand, captures previous employment experience through the variables $y_{i,t-j}$. Thus, in the labor supply case the model (1.2) is more reasonable than (1.4), though one can make a case for (1.4) as well (or perhaps a combination of (1.2) and (1.4)).

In the following section we will give some examples of cases where the "lagged index" model makes more sense.

2. Some Examples of the Lagged Index Model

Consider the following model

$$\begin{aligned} y^*_{it} &= \alpha y^*_{i,t-1} + \beta x_{it} + u_{it} \qquad i = 1, \ldots, N \\ &\qquad\qquad\qquad\qquad\qquad\qquad t = 1, \ldots, T \\ y_{it} &= 1 \qquad \text{if } y^*_{it} > 0 \\ &= 0 \qquad y^*_{it} \leqslant 0. \end{aligned} \tag{2.1}$$

Thus, this is a standard distributed lag model with the dependent variable observed qualitatively. For example, y^*_{it} might be the posterior log-odds in favor of some hypothesis, $y^*_{i,t-1}$ the prior log-odds, and x_{it} the log likelihood ratio. Suppose that individuals on the basis of certain observed data state which of a pair of hypotheses they believe is correct, and suppose further that they receive a valuable prize if their guess is correct, Then their choice of hypotheses is equivalent to the statement that y_{it}^* is positive or negative. If individuals' decisions follow Bayes' rule, then $\alpha = \beta = 1$. Alternatively, if people use the representativeness heuristic of *Kahneman/Tversky* [1972], they tend to ignore their priors, so according to this theory α is less than β. Of course, if instead people use the anchoring and adjustment heuristic [*Tversky/Kahneman*], one might expect α to be greater than β. The same prediction would follow from the theories of *Howell* [1967, 1971]. Thus, there are a number of alternative theories that bear on this setup. For an example of an experimental design that could be used to generate this type of data see *Grether* [1980].

The study of party affiliation by political scientists provides another example for the application of this model. There is a substantial empirical literature for both the United States and the United Kingdom on the concept of party identification. Party identification has been defined as "the individual's effective orientation to an important group-object in his environment" [*Campbell* et. al.] . One feature of party identification that has been subject to considerable debate is its stability. Based upon a survey Campbell et. al estimated that only 20 percent of the population had (as of the survey) ever changed party identification. According to the traditional approach, people have a long-term orientation towards a political party which is much less volatile than voting intentions. This orientation is more stable than positions on issues [*Converse; Converse/Markus*].

Recently some have questioned the importance of the concept and have challenged its stability as well [*Brody; Dreyer; Fiorina*]. In the United States party identification is a measure of degreee of affiliation with either the Democratic or Republican party. This sense of identification is according to the traditional interpretation supposed to change slowly in response to the performance of the party, performance of the president, general economic conditions, domestic turmoil, personal experience, and so forth. These considerations suggest that a partial adjustment model may be appropriate. Let $\tilde{y}_{it}^* = \beta' x_{it}$ be the desired or long-term equilibrium party identification of voter i at time t. If there were no social or psychological costs in changing political affiliations, then we would have

$$y_{it}^* = \tilde{y}_{it}^* + u_{it}$$

where y_{it}^* is the actual party identification. Since there are possibly some social and psychological costs, we have

$$y_{it}^* - y_{i,t-1}^* = \alpha(\tilde{y}_{it}^* - y_{i,t-1}^*) + u_{it}$$

so that

$$y_{it}^* = (1-\alpha) y_{i,t-1}^* + \alpha \tilde{y}_{it}^* + u_{it}$$

$$= (1-\alpha) y_{i,t-1}^* + \alpha\beta' x_{it} + u_{it}.$$

We further assume that

$$E(u_{it}) = 0$$

$$E(u_{it}^2) = \sigma_u^2 .$$

In practice, of course, y^*_{it} is not observed as a continuous variable; party identification being measured as a polychotomy on a five or a seven point scale [e.g. strong Democratic, independent, to strong Republican).

3. Estimation of the Lagged Index Model

Rewrite the model (2.1) as

$$y^*_{it} = \beta x^*_{it}(\alpha) + \alpha^t \eta_{i0} + w_{it} \tag{3.1}$$

where

$$x^*_{it}(\alpha) = \sum_{j=0}^{t-1} \alpha^j x_{i,t-j}$$

$$w_{it} = \frac{u_{it}}{1 - \alpha L}$$

$$\eta_{i0} = \beta \sum_{j=0}^{\infty} \alpha^i x_{i,-j} = E_i(y^*_{i0}).$$

If y^*_{it} were observed, then one could obtain consistent estimates of the parameters of the model using the method suggested by *Klein* [1958]. For the case at hand the same method works using a logit or probit estimation. The proof of consistency is basically that given by *Lee* [1980] who considers the Tobit estimator and parallels that given by *Amemiya* [1973] for the case of serially independent disturbances. For a proof of the strong consistency and a derivation of the limiting distribution of the Tobit estimator with serial correlation see *Robinson* [1980]. In general, w_{it} are going to be autocorrelated so these estimates will not be efficient. Of course, efficient estimates can be obtained by the method of maximum likelihood. While in principle this is the appropriate estimation method, in practice it is not of much use. The reason is that with serial correlation the evaluation of the likelihood function involves the calculation of the T-fold integrals of the multivariate distributions. This leads to excessive computational problems if T is greater than two. The only other problem would be that if N is large relative to T, then there is an incidental parameter problem. If there is only one observation per individual on the dependent variable (i.e. $T = 1$), then one can treat the initial conditions as being random across individuals which simply adds another component to the disturbance term. The contribution of the component is not identified, but the estimation is otherwise straightforward; (3.1) is estimated using a standard probit program searching over admissible values of α. Those estimates corresponding to the maximum value of the likelihood function are chosen. As there is only one observation over time, there cannot be any serial correlation present so these estimates are efficient and consistent as N goes to infinity provided the x's satisfy appropriate regularity conditions.

Now consider the more common situation in which one has many observations (over time) on the y_{it}'s and on the x_{it}'s. Notice that one cannot use the preceding procedure with all the data and obtain consistent estimates. The reason is that the disturbances in the model

$$w_{it} = \alpha^t \eta_{i0} + \frac{u_{it}}{1 - \alpha L} \tag{3.2}$$

are heteroscedastic due to the variation in α^t, and in logit or probit type models heteroscedasticity causes estimates to be inconsistent. One could assume $\eta_{i0} = \eta_0$, but for the application at hand this is equivalent to assuming that, prior to the sample, all voters had identical views of business conditions, of their own financial conditions, of the president's performance, etc. which is surely false. This problem does not arise if one were studying the effect of the state of the economy on party identification, as in this case the x_{it}'s would (for each t) be the same for all individuals. In this case one could simply include α^t as an explanatory variable in the logit or probit estimation. This is not a feasible alternative when studying party identification as the data sources are large but infrequent surveys. Thus, having party ID a function of aggregate measures only would lead to a substantial degrees-of-freedom problem.

Chamberlain [1980] considers the conditional likelihood approach to a similar problem. The model he deals with may be written as

$$y^*_{it} = \beta x_{it} + \eta_i + u_{it}. \tag{3.3}$$

Unfortunately the procedure he uses does not work with dynamic models. To see this, consider the model (3.3) for the case where the observed variable, y_{it}, is a dichotomous variable. For $T = 2$ the conditional likelihood function for individual i for whom the $y^*_{i1} > 0, y^*_{i2} \leq 0$ is

$$\frac{\dfrac{e^{\beta x_{1i}+\eta_i}}{1+e^{\beta x_{1i}+\eta_i}} \; \dfrac{1}{1+e^{\beta x_{2i}+\alpha\eta_i}}}{\dfrac{e^{\beta x_{1i}+\eta_i}}{1+e^{\beta x_{1i}+\eta_i}} \; \dfrac{1}{1+e^{\beta x_{2i}+\alpha\eta_i}} + \dfrac{e^{\beta x_{2i}+\alpha\eta_i}}{1+e^{\beta x_{2i}+\alpha\eta_i}} \; \dfrac{1}{1+e^{\beta x_{1i}+\eta_i}}}$$

$$= \frac{e^{\beta x_{1i}+\eta_i}}{e^{\beta x_{1i}+\eta_i} + e^{\beta x_{2i}+\alpha\eta_i}} = \frac{1}{1+e^{\beta(x_{2i}-x_{1i})-(1-\alpha)\eta_i}}$$

Thus the η_i do not drop out and this form of the conditional likelihood approach does not provide the necessary simplification.

The following procedure, on the other hand, should produce consistent estimates of all the parameters (provided $N \to \infty$). First, estimate

$$y^*_{it} = \beta x^*_{it}(\alpha) + w_{it}$$

using a standard logit or probit program using data on the dependent variable for time t

only. Then reestimate the model using data for some other time period. These estimations provide estimates of α and of

$$\frac{\beta}{(\alpha^{2t}\sigma_\eta^2 + \sigma_u^2)^{1/2}}$$

for two different values of t. This allows one to obtain an estimate of σ_η^2/σ_u^2; call it r. Finally, using all the data we can estimate

$$y_{it} = \beta\tilde{x}_{it}^*(\alpha) + \alpha^t\tilde{\eta}_{it} + u_{it}$$

$$= \frac{\beta x_{it}^*(\alpha)}{(\alpha^{2t}r+1)^{1/2}} + \frac{\alpha^t\bar{\eta}}{(\alpha^{2t}r+1)^{1/2}} + w_{it}$$

where w_{it} is serially correlated but has equal variances for each observation. Obviously there are a variety of ways that one can pool the estimates from separate cross sections to obtain a final set of estimated parameters.

An obvious alternative procedure would be to try to estimate all the parameters by a two step procedure analogous to two stage least squares. First, one would estimate the reduced form equation to obtain $\hat{y}_{i,t-1}^*$ and then estimate the model (1.4) directly by probit or logit using $\hat{y}_{i,t-1}^*$ as an explanatory variable. The trouble with this procedure is that while it produces consistent estimates of the β's (up to a common scale factor) α is not identified. The reason is that the disturbances in the reduced form and structural equations have different (and unidentified) variances.

If N equals one so that the data are for a single time series y_t^*, then things are much simpler. In this case one simply performs a grid search for α using the maximum likelihood probit method applied directly to

$$y_t^* = \beta x_t^*(\alpha) + \eta z_t^*(\alpha) + w_t \qquad (3.1)'$$

where

$$z_t^*(\alpha) = \alpha^t.$$

The parameter estimates chosen are those corresponding to the $\hat{\alpha}$ which produces the maximum value of the likelihood function.

4. An Empirical Illustration

The data are from the 1972, 1974, 1976 election panel study administered by the Center for Political Studies at the University of Michigan. The panel consisted of 1320 individuals who were interviewed both before and after the 1972 election and either before or after the 1974 and 1976 elections. The questions used for this example concerned: party identification, civil rights, the performance of the president, the government's economic performance, future expectations concerning the economy, and personal financial conditions. The party ID variable was measured as a seven point scale (strong

Republican, weak Republican, Independent-Republican, Independent-Independent, Independent-Democrat, weak Democrat, strong Democrat), and the presidential performance was dichotomous (approve, disapprove). All other variables were either three point scales or were collapsed to three point scales which we coded as binary variables with the center category as the control. For example, regarding civil rights, the respondents were asked whether they thought that civil rights leaders were pushing too fast, about right, or too slowly. For this question two binary variables (one for too fast and one for too slow) were created.

Table 1 shows the results of estimating the equation for party identification for 1976. Note that over half the sample was lost due to missing data and split-form questionnaires – not all respondents were asked every question for each election. Note also that since only one year's data on the dependent variable are used, the serial correlation problem does not matter so that the standard errors, etc. are consistently estimated (conditionally upon the value of α). It is clear that presidential performance is highly significant, while chi-square tests indicate that the other variables are not statistically significant at conventional levels. The evaluation of the government's economic performance and the pace of

Variable		Coefficient	t-ratio [1])
Constant		.05	.3
Presidential performance		.97	10.7
Financial condition – good		.03	.4
– Poor		.02	.3
Government' economic performance	–good	.16	1.4
	– poor	–.04	.4
Economic expectation	– good	–.06	.7
	– poor	–.03	.2
Civil rights – too fast		.03	.4
– too slow		–.19	1.3

α = .4

n = 622

$\ln L$ = –1097.95

$\hat{R}^2$ = .23

Estimated Cutoffs	Standard Errors
0.0	n.a.
.8	.06
1.1	.07
1.4	.07
1.8	.08
2.4	.09

Tab. 1: Probit Estimates Party ID 1976[2])

[1]) Calculated conditional upon $\alpha = .4$.

[2]) Data for independent variables taken from 1976, 1974 and 1972 surveys.

Variable	Coefficient	t-ratio [1]
Constant	.04	.3
Presidential performance	.91	10.8
Government's economic performace – good	.15	1.4
– poor	–.02	.2
Civil rights – too fast	.03	.4
– too slow	–.17	1.2

α = .4
n = 622
$\ln L$ = –1098.2
$\hat{R}^2$ = .23

Estimated Cutoffs	Standard Errors
0.0	n.a.
.8	.06
1.1	.07
1.4	.07
1.8	.08
2.4	.09

Tab. 2: Probit Estimate Party ID 1976 [2]

[1]) Calculated conditional upon α = .4.
[2]) Data for independent variables taken from 1976, 1974 and 1972 surveys.

civil rights actions are the only variables that are close to being significant. These results are generally consistent with those of *Fiorina* [1979] who found that presidential performance and a Nixon pardon variable were highly significant in 1976, but that other variables were marginal. Table 2 shows the results when the personal financial condition and economic expectations variables are dropped. Both sets of results are quite similar. In both cases the maximum likelihood estimate of α is .4, which supports the more recent or revisionist arguments and runs counter to the traditional view that party identification changes only very slowly. Hypothesis tests that $\alpha = .8$ or $\alpha = .9$ are rejected ($\chi^2(1) = 10$–14 respectively). From the likelihood ratio statistics one can calculate approximate confidence intervals and estimate the standard deviation of $\hat{\alpha}$. In this case it appears that the standard error of $\hat{\alpha}$ is approximately .14. Notice that in addition to the coefficient estimates being stable the estimated cutoffs are nearly the same, and both sets suggest that the thresholds for the different points on the seven point scale are not evenly spaced (especially towards the ends of the scales). This is of interest as political scientists occasionally code these ordinal variables as interval levels (0, 1, 2, 3, 4, 5, 6) and use the them in regressions, which can have unfortunate consequences [*Grether* 1974, 1976].

The grid search using the 1974 data on party identification (and 1974 and 1972 data on the explanatory variables) did not converge to $\hat{\alpha}$ equal to .4, but produced the boundary solution $\hat{\alpha}$ equal 1.0. As the data for 1976 are richer (three years as opposed to two for the independent variables) we take .4 as the preliminary estimate of α. Table 3

Variable	Coefficient	t-ratio[1])
Constant	.37	2.4
Presidential performance	.55	6.3
Government's economic performance – good	–.22	1.6
– poor	–.08	1.0
Civil rights – too fast	.06	.9
– too slow	–.29	1.9

α = .4
n = 622
ln L = –1157.64
$\hat{R}^2$ = .10

Estimated Cutoffs	Standard Errors
0.00	n.a.
.57	.05
.89	.06
1.16	.06
1.49	.07
2.06	.08

Tab. 3: Probit Estimates Party ID 1974[2])

[1]) Calculated conditional upon $\alpha = .4$.

[2]) Data for independent variables taken from 1974, and 1972 surveys.

shows the estimates obtained for the equation eliminating the financial and expectational variables. The correction factor for the heteroscedasticity was obtained from the ratio of the 1976 and 1974 coefficients for presidential performance, and the model reestimated using all 1244 observations. The results are shown in Tables 4 and 5. Note that estimates of α using both data sets is .5. The presidential performance variable is the only substantive variable that is highly significant, though the civil rights variable is nearly so. It is unreasonable to assume that the average initial condition (presample) was zero and the shift variable is included for this reason. The overall constants in 1974 and 1976 respectively are $a + \alpha^t\bar{\eta}$ and $a + \alpha^{t+1}\bar{\eta}$. Thus the constant terms in Table 4 and Table 5 are estimates of $a + \alpha^t\bar{\eta}$ and the coefficients of the shift variables are estimates of $(\alpha^{t+1} - \alpha^t)\,\bar{\eta}$ and are negative and statistically significant. This suggests that prior to sample period individuals on average were inclined toward the Republican end of the scale. As before $\hat{\alpha}$ is significantly different from the extreme values, e.g. .8 or .2 ($\chi^2(1) = 4.18$ and 5.44 respectively). Thus, to the extent that the traditional view can be fairly represented as arguing that α is close to one, then that position is not supported.

Note that though ignoring serial correlation in the residuals and using the usual probit ML method gives us consistent estimates of the regression parameters, there still remains the problem of getting consistent estimates of the standard errors.

Denote by L^* the (pseudo) likelihood function, i.e. the likelihood function one would have by assuming serially independent residuals. Let θ be the set of parameters to be estimated. Then the appropriate covariance matrix for $\hat{\theta}$ obtained by maximizing the

Variable	Coefficient	t-ratio [1])
Constant	.43	3.5
Presidential performance	.82	11.8
Financial condition – good	.01	.2
– poor	.03	.3
Government's economic performance – good	.02	.2
– poor	–.03	.5
Economic expectation – good	–.04	.5
– poor	–.13	1.1
Civil rights – too fast	.04	.8
– too slow	–.21	1.9
Dummy (1976 = 1)	–.42	4.9

$\alpha = .5$
$n = 1244$
$\ln L = -2265.88$
$\hat{R}^2 = .16$

Estimated Cutoffs	Standard Errors
0.0	n.a.
.7	.04
1.0	.04
1.3	.05
1.6	.05
2.2	.06

Tab. 4: Probit Estimates 1974 and 1976 Pooled[2]

[1]) Calculated conditional upon $\alpha = .5$.
[2]) Data for independent variables taken from 1976, 1974, and 1972 surveys.

pseudo likelihood function is given by:

$$\text{Plim}\left(-\frac{\partial^2 \text{Log}\, L^*}{\partial\theta\partial\theta'}\right)^{-1}\left(\frac{\partial \text{Log}\, L^*}{\partial\theta}\frac{\partial \text{Log}\, L^*}{\partial\theta'}\right)\left(-\frac{\partial^2 \text{Log}\, L^*}{\partial\theta\partial\theta'}\right)^{-1}.$$

Though this expression can, in principle, be computed, it is very cumbersome to do so. In the computation of the standard errors we have reported, we have just used the expression

$$\left(-\frac{\partial^2 \text{Log}\, L^*}{\partial\theta\partial\theta'}\right)^{-1}.$$

As noted earlier, this expression is correct in the case of a single cross-section and thus the standard errors in Table 1 are consistently estimated. Since the main qualitative conclusions following from Tables 1 and 4 are the same, it would seem that not much would be gained from the extra computation of the correct expression in the case of the results of the pooled sample presented in Table 4.

Variable	Coefficient	t-ratio[2])
Constant	.34	4.8
Presidential performance	.84	13.2
Civil rights – too fast	.04	.7
– too slow	–.22	2.0
Dummy (1976 = 1)	–.43	6.0

α = .5
n = 622
ln L = –2266.83
$\hat{R}^2$ = .15

Estimated Cutoffs	Standard Errors
0.0	n.a.
.7	.04
1.0	.04
1.3	.05
1.6	.05
2.2	.06

Tab. 5: Probit Estimates 1974 and 1976 Pooled[2])

[1]) Calculated conditional upon α = .5.
[2]) Data for independent variables taken from 1976, 1974, and 1972 surveys.

After Transition

Before Transition	Party ID	0	1	2	3	4	5	6	Total
	0	147	51	9	5	3	3	0	218
	1	57	149	33	11	14	6	0	270
	2	23	32	54	20	9	6	0	144
	3	6	8	23	55	19	9	2	122
	4	3	12	10	21	64	37	13	160
	5	6	6	3	8	31	85	26	165
	6	2	1	2	3	9	43	105	165
	Total	244	259	134	123	149	189	146	1244

Tab. 6: Party ID Transition 1972–1974 and 1974–1976

An alternative model for political affiliation would be that some people hold strong political opinions and others do not. These transitions are always small for one group while the other will occasionally jump from one extreme to the other. The data in Table 6 suggest that the model is not adequate to describe our data. Note that nearly all transitions are to neighboring cells and there are almost no transitions from one extreme to the other.

5. Some Monte Carlo Evidence

To check the practical usefulness of the estimation procedure we used, we conducted two series of sampling experiments. In each case we generated 100 samples of size 100 each.

In experiment 1, we considered the model:

$$y_t^* = \frac{\beta(1-\alpha)}{1-\alpha L} x_t + u_t \tag{5.1}$$

where L is the lag operator defined as $Lx_t = x_{t-i}$. We set $\beta = 1$ and generated x_t as IN(0,1), and u_t as IN(0, σ_u^2). The variance of u_t was changed for different values of α so that the variance of the systematic part in (5.1) which in this case is $((1-\alpha)/(1+\alpha))$ is four times σ_u^2. The implied theoretical R^2 for equation (5.1) is thus 0.8 in all cases.

The model given in (5.1) was estimated for two cases:

(i) y_i^*observed as a continuous variable

and

(ii) y_t^* observed as a dichotomous variable defined as:

$$\begin{aligned} y_t &= 1 \quad \text{if } y_t^* > 0 \\ &= 0 \quad \text{otherwise.} \end{aligned}$$

For estimation purposes we write (5.1) as:

$$y_t^* = \beta x_t^*(\alpha) + \alpha^t \eta + u_t \tag{5.2}$$

where $x_t^*(\alpha) = [\sum_{i=0}^{t-1} \alpha^i x_{t-i}](1-\alpha)$ and $\eta = E(y_0^*)$ is another parameter to be estimated.

In the case where y_t^* is observed as a continuous variable, we estimate (5.2) by searching over α, i.e. estimating (5.2) by OLS for each value of α and choosing the value of α for which the residual sum of squares is minium. In the case y_t^* is observed as a dichotomous variable, we use the same procedure except that equation (5.2) is estimated by the probit ML method. We choose the value of α for which the likelihood is maximum. Note that β is estimable only up to a scale factor. The search was conducted at intervals of .025 over different values of α.

The summary results are presented in Table 7. We used three values of α in the experiments.

In experiment 2, we considered the model:

$$y_t^* = \alpha y_{t-1}^* + \beta x_t + u_t. \tag{5.3}$$

Again we used the same parameter values as in experiment 1 for β and variance of x_t. The only difference is that the variance of u_t was not varied with α. If we rewrite the model in (5.3) as

$$y_t^* = \left(\frac{\beta}{1-\alpha L}\right)x_t + \left(\frac{1}{1-\alpha L}\right)u_t \tag{5.4}$$

the ratio of the variances of the systematic part and the error, with the specifications we made, is constant for different values of α.

For the case where y_t^* is observed as a continuous variable, we estimate equation (5.3) by OLS, since u_t are serially independent. In the case where y_t^* is observed as a dichotomous variable, we estimate equation (5.4) by the probit ML for different values of α, as in the case of experiment 1 but ignoring the serial correlation in the residuals.

The results of these experiments are also presented in Table 7.

The results of experiment 1 shed light on how much information is lost in the fact that y_t^* is observed only as a dichotomous variable rather than a continuous variable. The bias terms are of comparable magnitude and the variances of α when y_t^* is observed as a dicho-

Experiment 1:

Model: $y_t^* = \frac{\beta(1-\alpha)}{1-\alpha L}x_t + u_t$

α	y_t^* Continuous			y_t^* Observed as Discrete		
	Mean	Bias	Variance	Mean	Bias	Variance
.5	.498	–.002	.001526	.502	+.002	.004153
.6	.598	–.002	.001409	.598	–.002	.003727
.7	.698	–.002	.001205	.699	–.001	.003508

Experiment 2:

Model: $y_t^* = \alpha y_{t-1}^* + \beta x_t + u_t$

α	y_t^* Continuous			y_t^* Observed as Discrete		
	Mean	Bias	Variance	Mean	Bias	Variance
.5	.499	–.001	.00146	.502	+.002	.004805
.6	.601	+.001	.00121	.603	+.003	.004458
.7	.699	–.001	.00099	.704	+.004	.003392

Tab. 7: Results of Sampling Experiments

tomous variable are about 2.5–3.0 times the corresponding variances where y_t^* is observed as a continuous variable.

The results of experiment 2 shed light on the consequences of two factors:

(i) y_t^* is observed as a dichotomous variable rather than as a continuous variable.
(ii) The serial correlation in the residuals in (5.4) is ignored in the probit ML estimation of (5.4).

Again, the bias terms are not large. The variances in the case y_t^* is observed as a dichotomous variable are about 2.5–4 times the corresponding variances when y_{it}^* is continuous.

These results suggest that the estimation procedure we used in our empirical work is expected to perform well for the sample sizes we had.

6. Summary and Conclusions

In this paper we have discussed a number of dynamic models with qualitative variables. For one of these models, the lagged index model, we have proposed a method of obtaining consistent estimates of all the parameters. The method was applied to some United States panel data relevant to the issue of the stability of preferences for political parties. The evidence supports the current view that party identification is subject to short-term fluctuations. Monte Carlo calculations suggest that the method should work reasonably well in practice.

References

Amemiya, T.: Regression Analysis When the Dependent Variable Is Truncated Normal. Econometrica **41**, 1973, 997–1016.

Brody, R.: Stability and Change in Party Identification: Presidential to Off-Years. Paper presented at 1977 annual meeting of the American Political Science Association. Momeographed, 1977.

Campbell, A. et al.: The American Voter. New York 1960.

Chamberlain, G.: Analysis of Covariance with Qualitative Data. Review of Economic Studies **47**, 1980, 225–238.

Converse, P.E.: The Nature of Belief Systems in Mass Publics. Ideology and Discontent. Ed. by D.E. Apter. Glenco, Illinois, 1964.

Converse, P.E., and *G.B. Markus*: Plus ça change . . .: The New CPS Election Study Panel. American Political Science Review 73, 1979, 32–49.

Dreyer, E.: Change and Stability in Party Identification. Journal of Politics **25**, 1973, 712–722.

Fiorina, M.P.: Retrospective Voting in American National Elections. Mimeographed. Pasadena 1979.

Grether, D.M.: Correlations with Ordinal Data. Journal of Econometrics **2**, 1974, 241–246.

–: On the Use of Ordinal Data in Correlation Analysis. American Sociological Review **41**, 1976, 908–912.

–: Bayes Rule as a Descriptive Model: The Representativeness Heuristic. Quarterly Journal of Economics **95**, 1980, 537–557.

Heckman, J.: Statistical Models for Discrete Panel Data. Center for Mathematical Studies in Businiess and Economics Report No. 7902, University of Chicago, 1979.

Howell, W.C.: An Evaluation of Subjective Probability in a Visual Discrimination Task. Journal of Experimental Psychology **75**, 1967, 979–986.
–: Uncertainty from Internal and External Sources: A Clear Case of Overconfidence. Journal of Experimental Psychology **89**, 1971, 240–243.
Kahneman, D., and *A. Tversky*: Subjective Probability: A Judgment of Representativeness. Cognitive Psychology **3**, 1972, 430–454.
Klein, L.R.: The Estimation of Distrubted Lags. Econometrica **26**, 1958, 553–565.
Lee, L.-F.: Strong Consistency of the Tobit Estimator in the Presence of Serially Correlated Disturbance. Minneapolis 1980.
Robinson, P.M.: On the Asymptotic Properties of Estimators of Models Containing Limited Dependent Variables. Mimeographed. Vancouver 1980.
Tversky, A., and *D. Kahneman*: Judgment under Uncertainty: Heuristics and Biases. Science **185**, 1974, 1124–1131.

Games, Economic Dynamics, and Time Series Analysis. 1982 ©Physica-Verlag, Wien–Würzburg

The Estimation of Regression Models with Time-Varying Parameters

By *A.C. Harvey*, London[1]) and *G.D.A. Phillips*

1. Introduction

In analysing time series data, the assumption that the coefficients in a regression model are constant over time may not always be reasonable. One way of handling this problem is to allow the parameters to vary over time according to a particular stochastic process. The parameters in models of this type are said to be *dynamic*, and they represent a generalization of models in which the parameters are *random*, in that they are independent of each other in different time periods; see, for example, *Theil* [1971, 622–627].

There are basically two classes of dynamic parameter models. In the first class, the parameters are generated by stochastic processes which are nonstationary. An important example of this kind of behaviour is when the parameters follow random walks. *Cooley/Prescott* [1976] have studied this type of model, and they cite a number of cases in which it has been applied. An alternative class of models consists of parameters which are generated by *stationary* stochastic processes about a fixed, but unknown, mean. It is the estimation of this type of time-varying parameter model that forms the subject matter of this paper.

The simplest way to model stationary time-varying parameters is to assume that they are generated by a first-order autoregressive process. This was first suggested by Rosenberg. *Schaefer et al.* [1976] have investigated this type of parameter variation in connection with measuring a share's market risk, and found a good deal of support for it. Because the regression coefficients move around fixed means they use the term 'return to normality' to describe the model.

This article deals primarily with the estimation of models with the above type of parameter variation. However, the methods described may be extended to handle the estimation of models where the parameters are generated by any stationary multivariate autoregressive-moving average (ARMA) process. This is discussed in Section 8.

A full maximum likelihood (ML) method and a two-step estimation procedure are described. Both of these methods are based on a technique known as the 'Kalman filter.' This is a recursive method of estimation, originated by *Kalman* [1960], which is widely used in control engineering. The description of the technique in Section 3, however, is specifically geared towards econometrics. In the present context it permits estimation of the various models without the need for the repeated inversion of covariance matrices of

[1]) *A.C. Harvey*, The London School of Economics and Political Science, Houghton Street, Aldwych, London WC2A 2AE, Great Britain.

large dimensions. The use of the technique offers two further, theoretical, advantages. These arise in connection with the derivation of the forecasts and their conditional mean square errors, and the residuals obtained as a by-product of the estimation procedure. For the models considered, these residuals are normally and independently distributed with mean zero and constant variance, *conditional* on certain of the parameters. Hence they may be used for diagnostic checking in the sense in which the term is used by *Box/Jenkins* [1970].

The regression parameters in the model contain a component – the mean – which is fixed. As a result some theoretical problems arise in applying certain of the standard Kalman filter results to this model. These problems may be overcome, however, by linking the Kalman filter with the results on 'recursive residuals' in ordinary least squares (OLS) regression as set out by *Brown/Durbin/Evans* [1975] and *Phillips/Harvey* [1974]. The basis of the estimation procedures proposed here may be regarded as a generalization of the recursion in the classical linear regression model. This method is different to the one considered by *Rosenberg* [1973], where *two* passes of the data are needed in order to estimate the means of the regression parameters, conditional on the other parameters in the model.

The plan of the paper is as follows. The model is formally set out in Section 2, and in the following section the Kalman filter is described. The Kalman filter is then applied to the model, and in Section 5 a method for computing the ML estimator is given. The computionally simpler two-step estimator is then introduced in Section 6, and shown to have the same asymptotic distribution as the ML estimator. In Section 7 the small sample properties of the two estimators are compared on the basis of Monte Carlo experiments. The model is generalized in Section 8, and it is shown that the technique developed may be used to handle a number of important special cases, such as the estimation of regression models with ARMA errors; c.f. *Harvey/Philllips* [1979]. Finally, the conclusions are presented in Section 9.

2. The Return to Normality Model

2.1 Model and Definitions

The regression model with parameters generated by a first-order vector autoregressive process may be written

$$y_t = x_t' \beta_t, \qquad t = 1, \ldots, n, \tag{2.1}$$

$$\beta_t - \bar{\beta} = \Phi (\beta_{t-1} - \bar{\beta}) + \epsilon_t, \tag{2.2}$$

where y_t is the observation on the dependent variable, x_t is a $k \times 1$ vector of non-stochastic observations, and β_t is a $k \times 1$ vector of stochastic parameters, which includes a fixed component, $\bar{\beta}$. The $k \times k$ matrix of parameters, Φ, has characteristic roots less than one in absolute value. The $k \times 1$ vector of disturbances, ϵ_t, is assumed to follow a multivariate normal distribution with mean vector zero and covariance matrix, $E(\epsilon_t \epsilon_t') = \sigma^2 Q$. The introduction of the scalar σ^2 enables the top left-hand element in Q to be standarized by setting it equal to unity. It is further assumed that $E(\epsilon_t \epsilon_s') = 0$ for $t \neq s$. A disturbance vector having all these properties will be written $\epsilon_t \sim \text{NID}(0, \sigma^2 Q)$.

In writing (2.1) it has been assumed that the first element in x_t is unity for all t. Thus the disturbance term usually found in a regression model is incorporated in (2.2). In fact the classical linear regression model emerges as a special case if Q has unity in the top left-hand corner and zeros elsewhere and $\Phi = 0$. The variance of the disturbance term is then σ^2. Similarly a non-zero element in the top left-hand corner of Φ yields a regression model with first-order autoregressive disturbances. Treating the disturbance term in this way shows that the model may, in some sense, be regarded as a natural generalization of the standard regression model with first-order autoregressive disturbances.

Not all of the elements in the coefficient vector β_t need be time-varying. Some of the coefficients may be fixed, in which case they simply drop out of expression (2.2). Other coefficients may be random rather than dynamic. In fact the random coefficient model emerges as a special case of (2.1), (2.2) if $\Phi = 0$.

2.2 Generalized Least Squares

The model (2.1), (2.2) may be written in the form

$$y_t = x_t' \bar{\beta} + \zeta_t, \qquad t = 1, \ldots, n, \tag{2.3}$$

where

$$\zeta_t = x_t' (\beta_t - \bar{\beta}). \tag{2.4}$$

This is a linear regression model with fixed coefficients and serially correlated and heteroscedastic disturbances, ζ_t. The expectation of ζ_t is zero for all t, while the elements in the covariance matrix, $\sigma^2 V$, are given by

$$E(\zeta_t \zeta_s') = \sigma^2 x_t' \Gamma_\tau x_s, \qquad t, s = 1, \ldots, n, \tag{2.5}$$

where $\tau = t - s$, and $\sigma^2 \Gamma_\tau$ is the autocovariance matrix of $(\beta_t - \bar{\beta})$ at lag τ.

The log-likelihood of the model may be written as

$$\log L(y; \Phi, \bar{\beta}, \sigma^2, Q) = \frac{1}{2} n \log 2\pi - \frac{1}{2} n \log \sigma^2 - \frac{1}{2} \log |V|$$
$$- \frac{1}{2} \sigma^{-2} (y - X\bar{\beta})' V^{-1} (y - X\bar{\beta}), \tag{2.6}$$

where y is an $n \times 1$ vector and X is an $n \times k$ matrix whose definitions follow from writing (2.3) in matrix form as

$$y = X\bar{\beta} + \zeta. \tag{2.3$'$}$$

Maximum likelihood estimates of $\bar{\beta}$ and σ^2 could, in theory, be computed conditionally on the parameters in Φ and Q by constructing the matrix V and applying the usual generalized least squares (GLS) formulae. However, this would involve the inversion of the $n \times n$ matrix V. Since full maximum likelihood estimation entails maximizing the concentrated likelihood with respect to the elements in Φ and Q by a numerical optimization procedure, V would have to be inverted a large number of times. This would be very time consuming. The Kalman filter method described here appears to offer important computational advantages in this respect. Furthermore, it enables optimal forecasts of future values of y_t to be constructed very easily.

2.3 Restrictions on the Model

Even with an efficient method of computing the GLS estimates of $\bar{\beta}$, the difficulties involved in maximizing the concentrated likelihood by numerical optimization are likely to be considerable. This is because unless restrictions are placed on the model, Φ and Q will between them contain $(1/2)(3k^2 + k) - 1$ unknown parameters when all the parameters are dynamic. However, it is desirable to place restrictions on Φ and Q not only for computational considerations, but also from the point of view of identification. In a recent paper, *Cooley/Wall* [1976] have shown that the parameters in Φ will always be identified if these matrices are constrained to be diagonal. If Q is also diagonal the number of unknown parameters in Φ and Q is reduced to $2k - 1$, which makes the problem far more manageable. In many situations some of the coefficients in (2.1) will be taken to be random or fixed which reduces the number of unknowns even further.

3. The Kalman Filter

Consider a single 'measurement' equation

$$y_t = z_t' \alpha_t + \omega_t, \qquad t = 1, \ldots, n, \tag{3.1}$$

where y_t is an observed value, z_t is an $m \times 1$ vector of fixed, and known, values and α_t is an $m \times 1$ vector which is usually referred to as the 'state' of the system in the engineering literature. The disturbance terms, ω_t, are assumed to be normally and independently distributed with zero means and variances, $\sigma^2 h_t$.

The 'transition equation' associated with the vector α_t may be written

$$\alpha_t = T_t \alpha_{t-1} + R_t \eta_t, \qquad t = 1, \ldots, n, \tag{3.2}$$

where T_t is an $m \times m$ matrix of fixed coefficients, R_t is an $m \times g$ vector of fixed coefficients and η_t is a $g \times 1$ vector of disturbances following a multivariate normal distribution with zero expectation and covariance matrix, $\sigma^2 Q_t$. It is further assumed that $E(\eta_t \eta_s) =$ $= 0$ for $t \neq s$, $E(\eta_t \omega_s) = 0$ for all t and s, and $E(\alpha_0 \eta_t) = 0$ for $t = 1, \ldots, n$.

The above representation of a linear dynamic system is known as the 'state space form'. The matrices T_t, R_t and Q_t, and the scalar, h_t, are assumed to be known for all t. In the models considered here, however, T_t, R_t and Q_t are all independent of time.

Let a_{t-1} denote the minimum mean square estimator (MMSE) of α_{t-1}, given all the information up to, and including, time $t - 1$, i.e. given $y_{t-1}, y_{t-2}, \ldots$ The estimator is unbiased in the sense that the expectation of the estimation error, $a_{t-1} - \alpha_{t-1}$, is zero. The stochastic nature of α_t also motivates us to follow *Duncan/Horn* [1972] in referring to a_{t-1} as a MMSE, rather than a minimum variance unbiased estimator. If $\sigma^2 P_{t-1}$ denotes the covariance matrix of the estimation error and P_{t-1} is known, then $a_{t/t-1}$, the MMSE of α_t, is obtained from the prediction equations

$$a_{t/t-1} = T_t a_{t-1} \tag{3.3}$$

and

$$P_{t/t-1} = T_t P_{t-1} T_t' + R_t Q_t R_t'. \tag{3.4}$$

Once the observation y_t becomes available the MMSE of α_t is given by the updating equations

$$a_t = a_{t/t-1} + P_{t/t-1} z_t (y_t - z_t' a_{t/t-1})/f_t \tag{3.5}$$

and

$$P_t = P_{t/t-1} - P_{t/t-1} z_t z_t' P_{t/t-1}/f_t \tag{3.6}$$

where

$$f_t = h_t + z_t' P_{t/t-1} z_t. \tag{3.7}$$

The proof of the updating equations given by *Duncan/Horn* [1972] is essentially based on the principle of generalized least squares (GLS), extended to allow for the possibility that α_t may be stochastic. The new information incorporated in y_t is used to amend the predictor, $a_{t/t-1}$, by applying GLS to the model

$$\begin{pmatrix} a_{t/t-1} \\ y_t \end{pmatrix} = \begin{pmatrix} I \\ z_t' \end{pmatrix} \alpha_t + \begin{pmatrix} a_{t/t-1} - \alpha_t \\ \omega_t \end{pmatrix}, \tag{3.8}$$

where the covariance matrix of the 'disturbance term' is given by

$$E\left[\begin{pmatrix} a_{t/t-1} - \alpha_t \\ \omega_t \end{pmatrix} (\alpha_{t/t-1} - \alpha_t, \; \omega_t)\right] = \sigma^2 \begin{bmatrix} P_{t/t-1} & 0 \\ 0 & h_t \end{bmatrix}; \tag{3.9}$$

c.f. *Theil* [1971, 347–351]. The equations (3.5) and (3.6) are then obtained by applying two standard lemmas on matrix inversion.

The proof as presented by Duncan/Horn implicitly assumes that $h_t > 0$, though the recursions are still valid if $h_t = 0$. The justification for such an extension of Duncan/Horn's line of argument may be found in *Theil* [1971, 282–287], and we specifically mention this result as it is important for the model considered here. Note that the above proof does not require all the elements in α_t to be stochastic.

4. Generalized Least Squares

4.1 State-Space Form of the Model

The model (2.1), (2.2) may be cast in state space form by defining the state vector $\alpha_t = (\bar{\beta}_t' \; \delta_t')'$, where $\bar{\beta}_t = \bar{\beta}$ for all t, and $\delta_t = \beta_t - \bar{\beta}$. The transition equation is then

$$\begin{pmatrix} \bar{\beta}_t \\ \delta_t \end{pmatrix} = \begin{pmatrix} I_k & 0 \\ 0 & \Phi \end{pmatrix} \begin{pmatrix} \bar{\beta}_{t-1} \\ \delta_{t-1} \end{pmatrix} + \begin{pmatrix} 0 \\ I_k \end{pmatrix} \epsilon_t, \tag{4.1}$$

where $\epsilon_t \sim \text{NID}(0, \sigma^2 Q)$.

The associated measurement equation is of the form

$$y_t = z_t' \alpha_t, \tag{4.2}$$

where $z_t' = (x_t' x_t')$. Note that if all the elements of β_t are assumed to be dynamic, then, in terms of (3.1), $h_t = 0$ for all t, i.e. $\omega_t \equiv 0$. However, if a subset, Ω of the parameters are random and distributed independently of the dynamic parameters, the corresponding components of δ_t may be removed from the state vector and incorporated in ω_t. When the random parameters are distributed independently of each other

$$\text{Var}(\omega_t) = \sigma^2 h_t = \sigma^2 \sum_{j \in \Omega} X_{jt}^2 q_j, \qquad t = 1, \ldots, n,$$

where X_{jt} is the j-th element of x_t and q_j is the j-th diagonal element of Q. A further reduction in the length of the state vector may also be effected when some of the elements in β_t are fixed. Thus the number of elements of δ_t will, in general, only be equal to the number of *dynamic* parameters in β_t.

Given the MMSE's of $\bar{\beta}_t$ and δ_t for a particular value of t, the recursive equations (3.3) to (3.7) will eventually produce the GLS estimator of $\bar{\beta}$. In order to apply the recursions, therefore, 'starting values' are needed. In the recursive residual literature this problem is handled by forming an estimator of the coefficient vector from the first k observations. Exactly the same solution is possible in the more general case considered here. Provided the $k \times k$ matrix $X_k = (x_1, \ldots, x_k)'$ is of full rank, the MMSE of $\bar{\beta}$ based on the first k observations is given by

$$b_k = X_k^{-1} Y_k, \tag{4.3}$$

where $Y_k = (y_1, \ldots, y_k)'$. The associated covariance matrix is

$$E[(b_k - \bar{\beta})(b_k - \bar{\beta})'] = \sigma^2 X_k^{-1} V_k (X_k^{-1})', \tag{4.4}$$

where V_k is a $k \times k$ matrix with elements given by (2.5) for $t, s = 1, \ldots, k$.

Following the development at the end of the previous section, the starting value for d_k, the estimator of δ_k, is a vector of zeros. This has a covariance matrix, $E(\delta_k \delta_k') =$ $= \sigma^2 \Gamma_0$. Thus the MMSE of α_k is $a_k = (b_k' \; 0_k')'$, and the associated matrix, P_k is

$$P_k = \sigma^{-2} \begin{pmatrix} E\{(b_k - \bar{\beta})(b_k - \bar{\beta})'\} & -E\{(b_k - \bar{\beta})\,\delta_k'\} \\ -E\{\delta_k\,(b_k - \bar{\beta})'\} & E\{\delta_k \delta_k'\} \end{pmatrix}. \tag{4.5}$$

The off-diagonal blocks in (4.5) may be evaluated using (2.3) and (2.4) to give

$$-\sigma^{-2} E[(b_k - \bar{\beta})\delta_k'] = -X_k^{-1} \begin{pmatrix} x_1'\Gamma_{k-1}' \\ \cdot \\ \cdot \\ \cdot \\ x_k'\,\Gamma_0 \end{pmatrix} \tag{4.6}$$

where $\Gamma_s = \Phi\Gamma_{s-1}$ for $s = 1,2,\ldots$

Thus a_k and P_k may be calculated for given values of Φ and Q, and conditional on these values the Kalman filter will yield the GLS estimator of $\bar{\beta}$ and the MMSE of δ_n. When Φ and Q are constrained to be diagonal, the computations involved in evaluating P_k are simplified considerably, since the matrix Γ_τ is diagonal for all τ. The j-th diagonal element in Γ_τ is given by $\phi_j^\tau q_j/(1 - \phi_j^2)$, where q_j and ϕ_j are the j-th diagonal elements in Q and Φ respectively. In addition, diagonality of Φ and Q permits some simplification in the filtering equations and this may be taken into account in programming.

4.2 Generalized Recursive Residuals

As a by-product of the recursions used to compute b_n and δ_n, a set of $n - k$ prediction errors are produced for $t = k + 1, \ldots, n$. Conditional on Φ and Q, these prediction errors are normally distributed with mean zero and variance $\sigma^2 f_t$. They are also independent, a result which may be demonstrated by linking the material presented in this section with standard results on recursive residuals. This is done in the next section, where at the same time it is shown that the likelihood function (2.6) may be decomposed in terms of the prediction errors.

Since the standardized prediction errors – or 'generalized recursive residuals' – are NID(0, σ^2), *conditional* on Φ and Q, they may be used for 'diagnostic checking' of the model in the sense of *Box/Jenkins* [1970].

4.3 Forecasting

For given values of Φ and Q, the Kalman filter may also be used to forecast future values of y_t. This is done simply by extending the prediction equations, and the resulting forecast l steps ahead, $\hat{y}_{n+l/n}$, will be the MMSE of y_{n+l}. Thus

$$\hat{y}_{n+l/n} = z_{n+l}' a_{n+l/n} = z_{n+l}'\, T^l a_n, \quad l = 1,2,\ldots \tag{4.7}$$

where T is the transition matrix defined by (4.1), and x_{n+l} is assumed to be known.

The mean square error (MSE) of $\hat{y}_{n+l/n}$ *conditional* on Φ and Q may also be computed by extending the covariance matrix prediction equation (3.4).

4.4 Computational Considerations

It may sometimes be the case, particularly with economic data, that the explanatory variables in (2.1) are highly correlated. In these circumstances rounding errors may build up in the Kalman filter. This may be guarded against by carrying out the recursions using a numerically stable 'square root algorithm' as described, for example, in *Kaminski/Bryson/Schmidt* [1971].

A second computational point concerns the evaluation of a_k and P_k. Rather than calculate these explicitly, it may often be more convenient to start the recursions at $t = 0$ with an initial estimator $a_0 = 0$, and an associated matrix

$$P_0 = \begin{pmatrix} \kappa I & 0 \\ 0 & \Gamma_0 \end{pmatrix}, \tag{4.8}$$

where κ is a large, finite number. After k recursions the state estimate and the associated covariance matrices will be approximately equal to the corresponding quantities obtained by an exact procedure when a_k and P_k are computed directly. The first k prediction errors must be discarded as they depend on the arbitrary starting values at $t = 0$, but the remaining prediction errors correspond to those calculated using the exact a_k and P_k, and will be approximately equal to them. The results reported in *Harvey/Phillips* [1979] suggest that this type of approximating procedure can be made extremely accurate.

5. Maximum Likelihood Estimation

5.1 The Likelihood Function

The prediction errors obtained from the Kalman filter recursions for the return to normality model be standardized to give

$$\tilde{\nu}_t = (y_t - z_t' a_{t/t-1})/f_t^{1/2}, \qquad t = k+1, \ldots, n. \tag{5.1}$$

Conditional on Φ and Q, these residuals are NID$(0, \sigma^2)$, and furthermore they may be used to construct, $\hat{\sigma}^2$, the maximum likelihood estimator of σ^2, as

$$\hat{\sigma}^2 = n^{-1} \sum_{t=k+1}^{n} \tilde{\nu}_t^2. \tag{5.2}$$

The proof that these properties hold follows by noting that the inverse of the covariance matrix of the disturbances in (2.3)$'$ may be decomposed into the product of a lower triangular matrix, L, and its transpose, i.e. $L'L = V^{-1}$. Premultiplying (2.3)$'$ through by L then yields a transformed model obeying the classical assumptions. The recursive residuals obtained from this model may then be shown to be equivalent to the residuals defined by (5.1) and so the required results follow. The full argument is set out in Appendix A.

Once $\hat{\sigma}^2$ has been obtained it may be used to form the concentrated log-likelihood function

$$\log L_c\,(y;\,\Phi,Q) = -\frac{1}{2}n\,(\log 2\pi + 1) - \frac{1}{2}n\log\hat{\sigma}^2 - \frac{1}{2}\log|V|. \tag{5.3}$$

This may then be maximized with respect to Φ and Q by means of a numerical optimization procedure which does not require analytic derivatives.

5.2 Auxiliary Recursions

One problem remains in connection with (5.3), namely the evaluation of det $\{V\}$. Contrary to what might be expected this quantity cannot be obtained from the one-step prediction error variances resulting from the GLS filter described in the previous section. However, it may be calculated from the prediction error variances corresponding to the model

$$\tilde{y}_t = x_t'(\beta_t - \bar{\beta}), \qquad t = 1, \ldots, n. \tag{5.4}$$

This model would be appropriate of $\bar{\beta}$ were *known*, since in terms of (2.1), (2.2), $\tilde{y}_t = y_t - x_t'\bar{\beta}$. Its state space formulation is a special case of (4.1), (4.2), but the state vector is simply δ_t. Since this contains no fixed components, the recursions can be started at $t = 0$ with $a_0 = 0$ and $P_0 = \Gamma_0$. It then follows from the likelihood decomposition results of *Schweppe* [1965] that

$$\log|V| = \sum_{t=1}^{n} \log\tilde{f}_t \tag{5.5}$$

where $\sigma^2\tilde{f}_t$ is the variance of the t-th prediction error.[2]) The computation of (5.5) only requires that the recursions for the P_t and $P_{t/t-1}$ matrices be programmed. These are known as *auxiliary recursions*. The additional calculations involved in evaluating (5.4) in this way are not great as Γ_0 must be computed in any case as part of the main recursions.

5.3 Starting Values

Even if Φ and Q are constrained to be diagonal, the likelihood function is still non-linear in $2k - 1$ parameters, $\phi_1, \ldots, \phi_k, q_2, \ldots, q_k$, when all the elements in β_t are dynamic. Hence good starting values are important.

Considering (2.3), with Φ and Q diagonal, we have

$$E(\zeta_t^2) = \sigma^2 \sum_{j=1}^{k} X_{jt}^2\, q_j/(1 - \phi_j^2), \tag{5.6}$$

where $q_1 = 1$ and $X_{1t} = 1$, while

$$E(\zeta_t\zeta_{t-1}) = \sigma^2 \sum_{j=1}^{k} X_{jt}X_{j,t-1}q_j\,\phi_j/(1 - \phi_j^2). \tag{5.7}$$

---

[2]) This suggests an alternative method of carrying out ML estimation, based on evaluating the likelihood function for given values of β. However, the disadvantage of this approach is that the concentrated likelihood must then be maximized numerically with respect to β, as well as Φ and Q.

This suggests that preliminary estimates of $\phi_1, \ldots, \phi_k, q_2, \ldots, q_k$ may be obtained by computing the OLS residuals $e_1, \ldots, e_n$, and regressing e_t^2 on $X_{1t}^2, \ldots, X_{kt}^2$ and $e_t e_{t-1}$ on $X_{1t}X_{1,t-1}, \ldots, X_{kt}X_{k,t-1}$; c.f. *Rosenberg* [1973].

6. Two-Step Estimation Procedure

The general conditions under which the properties of the ML estimator may be derived should be sufficient to enable the consistency of the 'starting values' of the previous section to be established; see *Pagan* [1977]. Thus the first stage of the two-step procedure consists in estimating $\phi_1, \ldots, \phi_k, q_2, \ldots, q_k$ using the OLS residuals in regressions based on (5.6) and (5.7). A feasible GLS estimator of $\bar{\beta}$ is then computed by a single pass of the Kalman filter.

7. Monte Carlo Experiments

The Monte Carlo experiments were based on a simple linear model of the form

$$y_t = \bar{\beta}_1 + \beta_{2t} X_t + \epsilon_{1t}, \qquad t = 1, \ldots, n, \tag{7.1}$$

where $\epsilon_{1t} \sim \text{NID}(0, \sigma^2)$ and

$$\beta_{2t} - \bar{\beta}_2 = \phi(\beta_{2,t-1} - \bar{\beta}_2) + \epsilon_{2t}, \tag{7.2}$$

with $|\phi| < 1$ and $\epsilon_{2t} \sim \text{NID}(0, \sigma^2 q)$. The disturbances ϵ_{1t} and ϵ_{2t} are independent, i.e. $E(\epsilon_{1t}\epsilon_{2s}) = 0$ for all t and s. Equation (7.1) is therefore a classical linear regression[3]) model, except that the coefficient of the explanatory variable, X_t, is dynamic.

The state space measurement equation is

$$y_t = [1 \; X_t \; X_t] \begin{pmatrix} \bar{\beta}_{1t} \\ \bar{\beta}_{2t} \\ \delta_{2t} \end{pmatrix} + \epsilon_{1t}, \qquad t = 1, \ldots, n, \tag{7.3}$$

where $\delta_{2t} = \beta_{2t} - \bar{\beta}_2$. The transition equation is

$$\begin{pmatrix} \bar{\beta}_{1t} \\ \bar{\beta}_{2t} \\ \delta_{2t} \end{pmatrix} = \begin{pmatrix} 1 & 0 & 0 \\ 0 & 1 & 0 \\ 0 & 0 & \phi \end{pmatrix} \begin{pmatrix} \bar{\beta}_{1,t-1} \\ \bar{\beta}_{2,t-1} \\ \delta_{2,t-1} \end{pmatrix} + \begin{pmatrix} 0 \\ 0 \\ 1 \end{pmatrix} \epsilon_{2t}. \tag{7.4}$$

Starting values may be computed using the first two sets of observations, and for given values of ϕ and q the Kalman filter yields the MMSE of $(\bar{\beta}_1, \bar{\beta}_2)$.

The experiments were carried out with $X_t = t$, $t = 1, \ldots, n$, and $n = 20$. Letting X_t follow a time trend imparts very strong heteroscedasticity into the model, and it could be

---

[3]) In terms of (2.1) we could write $\beta_{1t} = \bar{\beta}_1 + \epsilon_{1t}$, thereby indicating that β_{1t} could be regarded as a *random* coefficient.

argued that it is an extreme case. However, the advantage of such a formulation is that it highlights the differences between the different estimators very clearly.

For each replication independent normal disturbances, ϵ_{1t} and ϵ_{2t}, were generated using the NAG library subroutine, E04CDF. Values of the dependent variable, y_t, were constructed using (7.2) and (7.1). In all cases we set $\bar{\beta}_1 = \bar{\beta}_2 = 5$, but various values of q and ϕ were employed as shown in Table 1. The number of replications for each experiment is between 329 and 350. The figures vary, firstly, because there was a time limit on the duration of each run and secondly, because estimation procedures 'failed' in some cases. The computations were carried out on the University of London CDC 7600 and 6600 machines.

ϕ	$\sqrt{q}$	Estimation Procedure	Bias				MSE			
			$\bar{\beta}_1$	$\bar{\beta}_2$	ϕ	$\sqrt{q}$	$\bar{\beta}_1$	$\bar{\beta}_2$	ϕ	$\sqrt{q}$
		OLS	−0.038	0.004	–	–	10.619	0.038	–	–
0.5	0.316	Two-step	−0.031	0.003	−0.072	−0.158	1.807	0.017	0.060	0.046
		ML	0.005	0.001	−0.070	1.629	0.378	0.012	0.028	6.158
		OLS	0.145	−0.003	–	–	53.216	0.197	–	–
0.8	0.316	Two-step	−0.080	0.008	−0.071	−0.189	13.431	0.103	0.056	0.061
		ML	0.018	0.007	−0.083	1.472	1.482	0.062	0.023	5.483
		OLS	0.027	−0.008	–	–	105.145	0.375	–	–
0.5	1.0	Two-step	0.085	−0.010	−0.078	−0.550	16.889	0.166	0.065	0.572
		ML	0.057	−0.009	−0.066	0.717	3.636	0.117	0.027	2.819
		OLS	−0.440	0.022	–	–	505.289	1.939	–	–
0.8	1.0	Two-step	−0.498	0.028	−0.070	−0.627	126.001	1.001	0.052	0.681
		ML	0.120	−0.019	−0.082	0.640	12.493	0.756	0.021	3.455

Tab. 1: Bias and MSE for Estimators in Various Models with $X_t = t$ and $n = 20$

The following estimation procedures were examined:

(i) OLS – estimates of $\bar{\beta}_1$ and $\bar{\beta}_2$ were obtained simply by regressing y_t on X_t.

(ii) Two-step Estimator – estimates of q and ϕ were first computed from the OLS residuals using the method described in Section 5. These estimates were then used to compute feasible GLS estimates of $\bar{\beta}_1$ and $\bar{\beta}_2$ by a means of a single pass of the Kalman filter.

(iii) ML – full ML estimates of the parameters were obtained by maximizing the concentrated log-likelihood function, (5.3), with respect to q and ϕ. This was carried out using the quasi-Newton method of *Gill/Murray/Pitfield* [1972] which is available in the NAG library. The two-step estimates of q and ϕ were used as starting values in the iterations. Negative estimates of q were avoided by carrying out the numerical optimization with respect to the variable $\hat{\hat{q}}$, which is defined by the relation $\hat{\hat{q}}^2 = \hat{q}$. Inadmissible estimates of ϕ show up for model (7.1) when a value of f_t is less than unity. When this was detected a high penalty was attached to that particular (invalid) concentrated likelihood function, thereby forcing the estimate of ϕ back into the range $[-1, 1]$.

On a number of occasions the routine failed to converge within the permitted number of replications. When this occurred, the results from that particular replication were not included in the summary statistics reported.

The figures in Table 1 show the biases and mean squared errors (MSE's) of the estimates of $\bar{\beta}_1$ and $\bar{\beta}_2$ obtained in each set of experiments. The biases are very small in each case. This is to be expected in the case of the OLS estimator which is easily shown to be unbiased. However, in Appendix B, it is shown that the two-step and ML estimators are also unbiased, provided that their respective first moments exist. The results of the sampling experiments appear to indicate that this is indeed the case, but it must be borne in mind that certain decision rules must be adopted for rejecting or, at least modifying, 'unacceptable' estimates. In the case of the two-step procedure this amounts to constraining the estimate of ϕ to have modulus less than one, and the estimate of q to lie in the range $[0, \infty]$. (In fact neither of these constraints was violated in any of the runs we carried out).

The sample biases in both the two-step and ML estimators of ϕ are relatively small, and of roughly the same order of magnitude. However, there is a clear tendency to underestimate ϕ for both $\phi = 0.5$ and $\phi = 0.8$.

Since the estimators of $\bar{\beta}_1$ and $\bar{\beta}_2$ are unbiased in all cases, the MSE's may also be regarded as estimators of the respective variances. There is a clear gain in using the full ML both over OLS and the two-step procedure. However, the latter shows a substantial improvement over OLS. The relationship between the MSE's is fairly constant over the four combinations of values of ϕ and q. For $\bar{\beta}_2$, the MSE of the two-step estimator is about half that of the OLS estimator. The ML estimator in turn has a MSE which is around forty percent below that of the two-step estimator. The differences are even more marked in the case of $\bar{\beta}_1$.

The sample skewness and kurtosis measures for all the estimates of $\bar{\beta}_1$ and $\bar{\beta}_2$ were both close to zero in all cases, indicating a reasonable approximation to normality. A similar result was found for the estimates of ϕ, but not for q. The sample frequency distribution tended to be strongly skewed to the left (recall that estimates were constrained to be non-negative), with a long tail. This strong positive skewness and high kurtosis was much more apparent in the ML case where on a number of occasions estimates greater than ten were encountered. In order to make a more meaningful comparison between the two-step and ML estimators of q, therefore, the summary statistics for estimates of the standard deviation, $\sqrt{q}$, were computed[4]) and it is these which are presented in the Table. A rather surprising feature of these results is that the two-step estimates of $\sqrt{q}$ have a lower MSE than the ML estimates. (The discrepancy was even larger between the MSE's of the estimates of q). However, the MSE's of the ML estimates of ϕ are smaller than the corresponding two-step estimates. This leads to the conclusion that the efficiency of the estimators is sensitive to the accuracy with which ϕ is estimated, but relatively insensitive with regard to q.

---

[4]) The estimate of $\sqrt{q}$ corresponds to the variable $\hat{q}$ defined earlier which was used in the numerical optimization routine.

8. A General Stationary Time-Varying Parameter Model

The model generating the parameters may be generalized from the first-order vector autoregressive process set out in (2.2) to a stationary multivariate ARMA process of the form

$$\Phi_p(L)\{\beta_t - \bar{\beta}\} = \theta_q(L)\{\beta_{t-1} - \bar{\beta}\}\,\epsilon_t \tag{8.1}$$

where

$$\Phi_p(L) = I - \Phi_1 L \cdots - \Phi_p L^p, \tag{8.2}$$

and

$$\theta_q(L) = I + \theta_1 L + \cdots \theta_q L^q, \tag{8.3}$$

where the Φ_i's and θ_j's are $k \times k$ matrices of parameters, and $\epsilon_t \sim \text{NID}(0, \sigma^2 Q)$.

The multivariate ARMA model (8.1) may be reduced to a first-order vector autoregressive process by constructing a vector, δ_t, of length kr, where $r = \max(p, q + 1)$, such that

$$\delta_t = \left(\begin{array}{c|c} \Phi_1 & \\ \cdot & \\ \cdot & \\ \cdot & I \\ \cdot & \\ \cdot & \\ \hline \Phi_r & 0' \end{array}\right)\delta_{t-1} + \begin{pmatrix} I \\ \theta_1 \\ \cdot \\ \cdot \\ \cdot \\ \cdot \\ \cdot \\ \theta_{r-1} \end{pmatrix}\epsilon_t; \tag{8.4}$$

Note that unless $p = q + 1$ some of the Φ_j matrices or, alternatively, some of the θ_i matrices will be null. By repeated substitution it may be shown that the first k elements in δ_t obey exactly the same process as $\beta_t - \bar{\beta}$ in (8.1).

This model may be cast in state space form by defining the state vector $\alpha_t = (\bar{\beta}_t' \delta_t')'$. The transition equation is a generalization of (4.1), while the measurement equation is of the form (4.2), but with z_t defined as the $r \times 1$ vector $z_t = (x_t' x_t' 0')'$.

The starting value for the state vector is given by $a_k = (b_k' 0')'$, where b_k is as defined in (4.3). The associated matrix P_k is of the form (4.5). This may, however, be complicated to evaluate, and it will usually be more convenient to start the recursions at $t = 0$ with $a_0 = 0$ and P_0 defined by (4.8). The matrix Γ_0, which is needed both for (4.8) as well as for the auxiliary recursions may be evaluated without too much difficulty; see, for example, *Gardner/Harvey/Phillips* [1980].

All the remaining results on the properties of the generalized recursive residuals and on maximum likelihood estimation follow by a straightforward extension of the results established previously.

Finally note that if all the parameters are constant, except for the one associated with the constant term, then the model reduces to a regression model with ARMA errors. ML estimation of this model is discussed in *Harvey/Phillips* [1979].

9. Conclusion

This paper has developed a method of estimating regression models with coefficients generated by first-order autoregressive processes. The approach adopted is to compute the exact likelihood function by the Kalman filter, and then maximize this with respect to the parameters of the process generating the time-varying regression coefficients. The computational feasiblity of this method has been demonstrated by the Monte Carlo results reported in Section 7.

A simpler two-step estimation procedure is also proposed. This is asymptotically efficient, but the experiments of Section 7 show it to be less satisfactory than the full ML estimator.

However, this may be a reflection of the small sample size examined, and the nature of the exogenous variable. The gain in using the two-step estimator over OLS is considerable, and with a moderate sample size, say fifty or one hundred, it could well attain a similar level of efficiency as full ML.

Finally, in Section 8, it was shown how the ML technique could be extended to handle coefficients modelled by any stationary ARMA process.

Appendix A: Generalized Recursive Residuals

Consider a linear regression model

$$y = X\beta + u, \tag{A.1}$$

in which the disturbance vector, u, has a multivariate normal distribution with mean zero and covariance matrix $\sigma^2 V$, where V is a known $n \times n$ matrix and σ^2 is an unknown scalar. Since V will be positive definite (p.d.), there exists an $n \times n$ nonsingular lower triangular matrix, L, such that $L'L = V^{-1}$. Pre-multiplying the observations y and X by L yields a transformed regression model in which the disturbances are NID$(0, \sigma^2)$. A set of $n - k$ 'recursive residuals' denoted by $\tilde{v}_t$, $t = k + 1, \ldots, n$, may, in principle, be obtained by applying recursive formulae, which are special cases of (3.3) to (3.7). These residuals are NID$(0, \sigma^2)$, and it may be shown that

$$\begin{aligned}\sum_{t=k+1}^{n} \tilde{v}_t^2 &= (Ly - LX\hat{\beta})'(Ly - LX\hat{\beta}) \\ &= (y - X\hat{\beta})'V^{-1}(y - X\hat{\beta}),\end{aligned} \tag{A.2}$$

where $\hat{\beta}$ is the GLS estimator of β; see *Brown/Durbin/Evans* [1975] or *Phillips/Harvey* [1974].

The t-th recursive residual in the transformed model will be equal to a fixed quantity multiplied by the prediction error

$$\bar{v}_t = \bar{y}_t - \hat{\bar{y}}_{t/t-1}, \tag{A.3}$$

where $\bar{y}$ is the t-th transformed observation and $\hat{\bar{y}}_{t/t-1}$ is the MMSE of $\bar{y}_t$ based on the first $t - 1$ tranformed observations. However, in view of the triangular nature of L,

$\hat{y}_{t/t-1}$ depends only on the first $t-1$ untransformed observations, while $\bar{y}_t$ is equal to y_t multiplied by the t-th diagonal element of L, which is fixed, plus a linear combination of $(y_{t-1}, \ldots, y_1)$. Therefore the prediction error for the original observation y_t, given $(y_{t-1}, \ldots, y_1)$, is

$$\bar{v}_t^* = y_t - g_t(y_{t-1}, \ldots, y_1), \qquad t = k+1, \ldots, n, \tag{A.4}$$

where $g_t(y_{t-1}, \ldots, y_1)$ is a linear function of $(y_{t-1}, \ldots, y_1)$. Now $g_t(y_{t-1}, \ldots, y_1)$ must be the MMSE of y_t based on $(y_{t-1}, \ldots, y_1)$, since, if it were not, it would be possible to construct a better estimator of y_t than the one implied by (A.3).

Suppose that the disturbances in (A.1) are such that the GLS estimator of β may be obtained by applying the Kalman filter with starting values computed from the first k observations. This will yield a set of $n-k$ prediction errors,

$$\nu_t = y_t - z_t' a_{t/t-1}, \qquad t = k+1, \ldots, n. \tag{A.5}$$

The quantity $z_t' a_{t/t-1}$ in (A.5) is the MMSE of y_t and so it must be identical to $g_t(y_{t-1}, \ldots, y_1)$. Therefore $\nu_t = \bar{v}_t^*$ for $t = k+1, \ldots, n$, and since each $\bar{v}_t^*$ is equal to the t-th recursive residual multiplied by a fixed quantity, it follows that when the ν_t's are standardised they will be identically equal to the recursive residuals in the transformed model. Hence they are NID$(0, \sigma^2)$, and they may be used directly to compute the quantity (A.2).

Appendix B: Unbiasedness of Estimators

Unbiasedness of the two-step and ML estimators of $\bar{\beta}$ may be demonstrated by a development of the argument originally used by *Kakwani* [1967].

In view of the normality of ϵ_t, the disturbance term, ξ_t, in (2.3) is symmetrically distributed. If $\hat{\beta}$ denotes the GLS estimator of $\bar{\beta}$ for a given V, then

$$\hat{\beta} - \bar{\beta} = (X'V^{-1}X)^{-1}X'V^{-1}\zeta, \tag{B.1}$$

and since ζ is symmetrically distributed about a null vector, so is $\hat{\beta} - \bar{\beta}$.

That the two-step estimator is symmetrically distributed then follows by observing that the estimate of V remains the same when ζ is replaced by $-\zeta$. This may be seen by noting that the OLS residual vector simply changes sign when ζ is replaced by $-\zeta$, and so e_t^2 and $e_t e_{t-1}$, the dependent variables used in the regressions based on (5.6) and (5.7), are unchanged.

As regards the ML estimator, the concentrated log-likelihood function, (5.3), remains unchanged when ζ is replaced by $-\zeta$. Since a numerical optimization procedure operates directly on the concentrated likelihood function, the values of the elements of Φ and Q produced at each iteration will be exactly the same when ζ is replaced by $-\zeta$. Hence, provided the starting values do not depend on the sign of ζ, the ML estimators of the elements in Φ and Q will be the same for ζ as for $-\zeta$. Thus, from (B.1), the final estimators of $\bar{\beta}$ produced by the iterative procedure will be symmetrically distributed about $\bar{\beta}$.

The two-step and ML estimators are therefore unbiased, provided that their respective first moments exist. This will almost certainly be the case provided that the restrictions placed on the elements of Φ and Q in Section 2 are not allowed to be violated by any of the estimates.

References

Box, G.E.P., and *G.M. Jenkins*: Time Series Analyis: Forecasting and Control. San Francisco 1970.

Brown, R.L., J. Durbin and *J.M. Evans*: Techniques for Testing the Constancy of Regression Relationships Over Time (with Discussion). Journal of the Royal Statistical Society, Series B, **37**, 1975, 149–192.

Cooley, T.F., and *E.C. Prescott*: Estimation in the Presence of Stochastic Parameter Variation. Econometrica **44**, 1976, 167–184.

Cooley, T.F., and *K.D. Wall*: Identification for Time-Varying Parameters. NBER Working Paper No. 127, 1976.

Duncan, D.B., and *S.D. Horn*: Linear Dynamic Regression Estimation from the Viewpoint of Regression Analysis. Journal of the American Statistical Association **67**, 1972, 815–821.

Gardner, G., A.C. Harvey, and *G.D.A. Phillips*: The Maximum Likelihood Estimation of Autoregressive-Moving Average Models by Kalman Filtering. Applied Statistics **29**, 1980, 311–322.

Gill, P.E., and *W. Murray*: Quasi-Newton Methods for Unconstrained Optimization. Journal of the Institute of Mathematics and Its Applications **9**, 1972, 91–108.

Harvey, A.C.: The Estimation of Time-Varying Parameters from Panel Data. Annales de l"INSEE, Special Issue on the Econometrics of Panel Data **30–31**, 1978, 203–226.

Harvey, A.C., and *G.D.A. Phillips*: Maximum Likelihood Estimation of Regression Models with Autoregressive-Moving Average Disturbances. Biometrika **66**, 1979, 49–58.

Kakwani, M.C.: The Unbiasedness of Zellner's Seemingly Unrelated Regression Equation Estimators. Journal of the American Statistical Association **62**, 1967, 141–142.

Kalman, R.E.: A New Approach to Linear Filtering and Prediction Problems. Transactions ASME Journal of Basic Engineering **82**, 1960, 35–45.

Kaminski, P.G., A.E. Bryson and *S.F. Schmidt*: Discrete Square Root Filtering: a survey of current techniques. IEEE Transactions on Automatic Control **AC-16**, 1971, 727–737.

Pagan, A.R.: An Approach to Estimation and Inference for Varying Coefficient Regression Models. Unpublished paper, 1977.

Phillips, G.D.A., and *A.C. Harvey*: A Simple Test for Serial Correlation in Regression Analysis. Journal of the American Statistical Association **69**, 1974, 935–939.

Rosenberg, B.: Random Coefficient Models: The Analysis of a Cross-Section of Time Series by Stochastically Convergent Parameter Regression. Annals of Economic and Social Meausrement, **2**, 1973, 399–428.

Sarries, A.H.: A Bayesian Approach to Estimation of Time-Varying Regression Coefficients. Annals of Economic and Social Measurement **2**, 1973, 501–523.

Schaefer, S., et al.: Alternative Models of Systematic Risk. International Capital Markets: an Inter and Intra Country Analysis. Ed. by E. Elton and M. Gruber. Amsterdam 1975, 150–161.

Schweppe, F.C.: Evaluation of Likelihood Functions for Gaussian Signals. IEEE Transactions on Information Theory, **11**, 1965, 61–70.

Theil, H.: Principles of Econometrics. New York 1971.

Games, Economic Dynamics, and Time Series Analysis. 1982 ©Physica-Verlag, Wien–Würzburg

Economic Time Series Analysis and Sample Survey Theory[1])

By *P.M. Robinson*, Guildford[2])

1. Introduction

Let P be a population in existence at time $t = 0,1, \ldots$ The units of P are labelled $i = 1,2, \ldots, N$. Associated with each unit is a vector of p measurements Y, which can change over time. We introduce the stochastic processes

$$\{Y_i(t),\ t = 0,1, \ldots\}, \qquad 1 \leqslant i \leqslant N.$$

In practice one has at most N time series, one per unit, but for the usual reasons it is convenient to refer to underlying stochastic processes.

At each time period t, one either observes a value of $Y_i(t)$ for all $i \in P$ (a census), or else one draws a probability sample of size $n_t < N$. In the latter circumstance there is interest in predicting such population measures as

$$\bar{Y}(t) = \frac{1}{N} \sum_{i=1}^{N} Y_i(t).$$

The sample drawn at time t can play an important role, but so also can the sample or census information at other points of time, when the $Y_i(t)$ are serially correlated and use is made of a time series model or a multiple equation dynamic econometric model.

A predictor which is based on only the sample at the current period is called an elementary predictor. Several suggestions have been offered as to how elementary predictors at different time points can be efficiently combined. *Patterson* [1950], *Narain* [1954], *Eckler* [1955], *Gurney/Daly* [1965], have derived best linear unbiased estimators, given a model such as a first order autoregression, sometimes in the presence of strict rotation sampling, where after initial random selection, each unit remains in the sample for the same number of time periods. Their analysis is appropriate to an infinite population, $N = \infty$. Also in an infinite population setting, *Scott/Smith* [1974], *Scott/Smith/Jones* [1979] propose the use of signal extraction theory of *Whittle* [1963] and modern time series methods of *Box/Jenkins* [1970]. Their approach offers considerable flexibility and has the advantage of not requiring successive samples to overlap. However, it also requires a longer time series than is sometimes available in survey work. For finite

[1]) This research was supported by Grant SOC78-05803, from the National Science Foundation.
[2]) *P.M. Robinson*, Department of Mathematics, University of Surrey, GU2 5XH Guildford, England.

N, and strict rotation sampling, *Rao/Graham* [1964] study the properties of a "composite" predictor which is a simple function of elementary predictors for the present and previous period. This predictor has been used in the U.S. Current Population Survey, [see *Hansen* et al.]. *Rao/Graham* [1964] show that it is design unbiased, that is it averages to $\bar{Y}$ over all possible samples. However, this composite predictor does not appear to be optimal with respect to any particular time series model, and does not allow much flexibility. *Gurney/Daly* [1956], *Graham* [1973] consider alternative composite predictors.

The use of models in survey work has been criticized by traditional sampling theorists who fear that model misspecification may produce bias. (For an excellent discussion of these issues see *Sarndal* [1978].) This suspicion is well-founded in view of the disappointing forecasting performance of many econometric models. In this paper we consider a class of predictors which is capable of incorporating *a priori* information in the form of complicated dynamic econometric models, but which is asymptotically design unbiased and consistent, as $N \to \infty$, even when the model is false. The predictor improves upon elementary predictors in respect of an asymptotic mean square error criterion when the model is true. Our predictor generalizes a predictor that has been considered by a variety of earlier authors, nearly always involving a simple linear regression model and without emphasis of time series aspects [see *Sukhatme; Tikkiwal; Sarndal,* 1978, 1979; *Robinson/Sarndal*, for example]. The conditions which we state for asymptotic theorems suggest that the predictor will be useful when the population size N is large. There is no requirement that the time series be long, however. Our analysis can be extended to the prediction of alternative population measures to $\bar{Y}$, such as population regression coefficients.

Some background material on sampling procedures is provided in the next section. In Section 3 we describe a class of models which will be familiar to econometricians. Subsequently the predictor is introduced and its asymptotic properties described.

2. Sampling Background

Denote by I_i, $1 \leqslant i \leqslant N$, binary random variables, such that $I_i = 1$ when unit i is included in the sample at time t and $I_i = 0$, otherwise. Each possible sample is of the same, non-random, size, n. Define the inclusion probabilities

$$\pi_i = \Pr(I_i = 1), \qquad 1 \leqslant i \leqslant N, \tag{2.1}$$

so

$$\sum_i I_i = \sum_i \pi_i = n. \tag{2.2}$$

When census information is available on $Y_i(t-u)$ for $u > 0$ the question of randomness due to sampling at time periods prior to t does not arise. Generally, matters will be considerably simplified if we condition on the sampling pattern prior to time t. We require $\pi_i > 0$, $i \in P$, thus excluding strict rotation sampling. However, such rotating schemes can be modified by giving every unit some chance, albeit small, of inclusion in the sample. Because we allow the π_i to vary over i, π_i can be a function of whether or not the unit i is in the sample at time $t-1$, and, if so, how long it has been present. *Kulldorff*

[1963], *Raj* [1965] mention simple versions of such schemes. Another motivation for allowing unequal π_i is the traditional one of giving larger units a greater chance of inclusion than smaller ones: take $\pi_i = nz_i / \sum_i z_i$, where z_i is a measure of size of unit i [see *Sarndal*, 1978, for example].

The π_i do not uniquely define the sampling scheme. Our results involve also the probabilities of including both units i and j in the sample, $i \neq j$,

$$\pi_{ij} = \Pr(I_i = I_j = 1).$$

The deviations $\pi_{ij} - \pi_i \pi_j$ are a measure of dependence; if $\pi_{ij} > \pi_i \pi_j$ the inclusion of unit i makes the inclusion of unit j more likely; if $\pi_{ij} < \pi_i \pi_j$, the reverse is true. The signs and magnitudes of the $\pi_{ij} - \pi_i \pi_j$ are of importance in classical sampling theory, and they also substantially affect our results. Thus it is of interest to note that *Sinha* [1973] proposes a scheme whereby almost any desired π_i, π_{ij} can be attained. We describe two sampling schemes used in practice, which we shall refer to subsequently.

Example 1. A simple method of accomplishing unequal π_i is stratified simple random sampling. One divides P into r subpopulations P_g, $1 \leqslant g \leqslant r$, where P_g comprises N_g units, so $N_1 + \ldots + N_r = N$. By simple random sampling n_g units are drawn from P_g, $1 \leqslant g \leqslant r$, so $n_1 + \ldots + n_r = n$. We have

$$\pi_i = \frac{n_g}{N_g}, \qquad i \in P_g, \tag{2.3}$$

$$\pi_{ij} = \frac{n_g(n_g - 1)}{N_g(N_g - 1)}, \quad i, j \in P_g \tag{2.4}$$

$$= \frac{n_g n_h}{N_g N_h}, \qquad i \in P_g, j \in P_h, h \neq g,$$

for $1 \leqslant g \leqslant r$.

Example 2. A method of *Sampford* [1967] (he calls it method (c)) works with arbitrary π_i. The sample is selected *with* replacement, but if it does not contain n different units it is rejected completely. This process continues until an acceptable sample is obtained. The first drawing is made such that the i-th unit has probability π_i/n of being selected; on subsequent drawings the i-th unit has probability proportional to $\pi_i/(1 - \pi_i)$. *Sampford* [1967] gives expressions for the π_{ij} and shows that they satisfy

$$\pi_i \pi_j > \pi_{ij}, \quad \text{all } i \neq j. \tag{2.5}$$

It is readily verified that (2.5) is true also for Example 1.

3. Time Series Models

The modelling of $Y_i(t)$ is complicated by the variation in sampled units over time.

Introduce the sets

$$O_i = \{u \mid 1 \leqslant u \leqslant t, \text{ unit } i \text{ is sampled at time } t - u\}.$$

For units that are unsampled prior to time t, O_i is empty and we define

$$Q = \{i \mid O_i \text{ is empty}\}.$$

Of interest is the conditional expectation

$$\mu_i(t) = E(Y_i(t) \mid Y_i(t-u), u \in O_i\}.$$

For $i \in Q$, the expectation is unconditional, $\mu_i(t) = E(Y_i(t))$. In general we can write

$$Y_i(t) = \mu_i(t) + X_i(t) \tag{3.1}$$

where

$$E(X_i(t) \mid Y_i(t-u), u \in O_i) = 0. \tag{3.2}$$

A general class of models for $\mu_i(t)$, $i \notin Q$, is

$$\mu_i(t) = \sum_{u \in O_i} \Gamma_i(u; \theta)\, Y_i(t-u) + \Delta_i(\theta) Z_i(t), \tag{3.3}$$

where:

$\Gamma_i(u; \theta)$ is a known $p \times p$ matrix function of an unknown parameter vector θ;
$\Delta_i(\theta)$ is a known $p \times q$ matrix function of θ;
$Z_i(t)$ is a $q \times 1$ vector of non-random exogenous variables, available for all $i \in P$. For example when $Z_i(t)$ represents an intercept, $Z_i(t) \equiv 1$.

The parameters θ are fixed constants. An alternative type of model that might be appropriate in the present circumstance uses a random θ, the sampling of a unit involving the occurrence od a particular outcome of θ [see *Robinson*, 1978].

It is assumed that, for any given value of u and θ, the matrices $\Gamma_i(u; \theta)$, $\Delta_i(\theta)$ take at most finitely many distinct values as a function of i, as $N \to \infty$. When the units are of heterogeneous sizes some differences in model form or parameters may be appropriate, just as differences in inclusion probabilities π_i may be appropriate. The variability in sampling over time may also lead to variation in model over i, as the following example suggests.

Example 3. A familiar model to econometricians is the reduced form

$$Y_i(t) = AY_i(t-1) + BW_i(t) + U_i(t) \tag{3.4}$$

where $W_i(t)$ is a $r \times 1$ vector of non-random exogenous variables and

$$E(U_i(t) \mid Y_i(t-u)) = 0, \quad u > 0.$$

Consider the sets

$$Q_1 = \{i \mid 1 \in O_i\}$$

$$Q_u = \{i \mid u \in O_i, \mathrm{v} \notin O_i, 1 \leqslant \mathrm{v} < u\}, 2 \leqslant u \leqslant t.$$

Thus Q_1 consits of all units sampled at time $t-1$, Q_2 consits of all units sampled at $t-2$ but not at $t-1$, and so on. The sets $Q_1, \ldots, Q_t$, Q are disjoint and have union P.
From the Markovian property of (3.4),

$$\mu_i(t) = A^u Y_i(t-u) + \sum_{\mathrm{v}=0}^{u-1} A^{\mathrm{v}} B W_i(t-\mathrm{v}), \tag{3.5}$$

for $i \in Q_u$, $1 \leqslant u \leqslant t$. Accordingly take θ to be the parameters in A and B, and

$$\Gamma_i(u;\theta) = A^u Y_i(t-u), \qquad i \in Q_u,$$
$$= 0, \qquad i \notin Q_u,$$
$$Z_i(t) = (W_i(t)', W_i(t-1)', \ldots, W_i(1)')',$$
$$\Delta_i(\theta) = (A^{u-1}B, A^{u-2}B, \ldots, B, 0, \ldots, 0), i \in Q_u.$$

4. Prediction of $\bar{Y}(t)$: I

Classical sampling theory introduces randomness only in the sampling design, and treats the $Y_i(t)$ as fixed constants. We follow the more recent "superpopulation" theory [see *Royall*, for example], to the extent of taking the $Y_i(t)$ to be random variables, to bring us into the familiar setting of time series analysis, and enable us to use models such as (3.4). However, we attempt to satisfy the classical theorist by requiring our predictor to be (approximately) design unbiased even when the model is mis-specified.
A predictor $T(t)$ is said to be design unbiased for $\bar{Y}(t)$ if

$$E(T(t) \mid Y_i(t), 1 \leqslant i \leqslant N) = \bar{Y}(t). \tag{4.1}$$

If we know $\mu_i(t)$ for all i, an obvious predictor of $\bar{Y}(t)$ uses $Y_i(t)$ when i is sampled, and $\mu_i(t)$ when i is unsampled, i.e.

$$T_0(t) = \frac{1}{N}\sum_{i=1}^{N} I_i Y_i(t) + \frac{1}{N}\sum_{i=1}^{N}(1-I_i)\mu_i(t).$$

This type of predictor was considered by *Royall* [1970], for example, with θ replaced by an estimate in (3.3). Now

$$E(T_0(t) - \bar{Y}(t) \mid Y_i(t), 1 \leqslant i \leqslant n) = \frac{1}{N}\sum_{i=1}^{N}(\pi_i - 1)(Y_i(t) - \mu_i(t)), \tag{4.2}$$

which is non-zero, so $T_0(t)$ is not design unbiased. If the model (3.3) is correct, we expect that under reasonable conditions (4.2) will converge stochastically to zero by a law of large numbers, whence $T_0(t)$ is asymptotically design unbiased. However, if (3.3) is misspecified an asymptotic bias is present, in general.
It is easy to find a predictor that is design unbiased irrespective of whether the model

(3.3) holds. From (2.1) the following vector form of the predictor of *Horwitz/Thompson* [1952]

$$T_1(t) = \frac{1}{N} \sum_{i=1}^{N} \frac{I_i}{\pi_i} Y_i(t) \tag{4.3}$$

is design unbiased. However, (4.3) makes no attempt to use the time series information.

The predictor $T_1(t)$ belongs to the class of generalized difference predictors [*Basu*]

$$T_2(t) = T_1(t) - \frac{1}{N} \sum_{i=1}^{N} \left(\frac{I_i}{\pi_i} - 1\right) \nu_i(t). \tag{4.4}$$

From (2.1), $T_2(t)$ is design unbiased for $\bar{Y}(t)$ for any choice of $\nu_i(t)$. One way of selecting the $\nu_i(t)$ is to introduce the time series model for $Y_i(t)$ and minimize mean square error after averaging both over the sampling design and over $Y_i(t)$. It is reasonable in many applications to assume that units behave independently of one another, specifically

$$EX_i(t) X_j(t)' = \Sigma_i \delta_{ij}, \tag{4.5}$$

where δ_{ij} is Kronecker's delta. The matrices Σ_i are nonnegative definite, and we allow

them to vary with i for the reasons explained in the previous section. From (3.1), (3.2), (4.5) we can write

$$\begin{aligned} &Y_i(t) - \nu_i(t) = X_i(t) + (\mu_i(t) - \nu_i(t)), \\ &E\{(Y_i(t) - \nu_i(t))(Y_j(t) - \nu_j(t))'\} = \Sigma_i \delta_{ij} + E\{(\mu_i(t) - \nu_i(t)) \\ &\quad \cdot (\mu_j(t) - \nu_j(t))'\}. \end{aligned} \tag{4.6}$$

Introduce the matrix norm $\| A \|_\Omega$,

$$\| A \|_\Omega^2 = \operatorname{tr}(AA'\Omega)$$

for any symmetric non-negative definite matrix Ω. As a criterion we consider

$$\text{MSE}_\Omega = E \| T_2(t) - \bar{Y}(t) \|_\Omega^2.$$

The metric Ω is inserted in case we are interested in predicting only a single element of $\bar{Y}(t)$, or some linear combination of the elements. Now from (2.1), (4.4), (4.6),

$$\text{MSE}_\Omega = E \left\| \frac{1}{N} \sum_{i=1}^{N} (Y_i(t) - \nu_i(t)) \left(\frac{I_i}{\pi_i} - 1\right) \right\|_\Omega^2$$

$$= \frac{1}{N^2} \sum_{i=1}^{N} \operatorname{tr}(\Sigma_i \Omega) \left(\frac{1}{\pi_i} - 1\right) \tag{4.7}$$

$$+ E \left\| \frac{1}{N} \sum_{i=1}^{N} (\mu_i(t) - \nu_i(t)) \left(\frac{I_i}{\pi_i} - 1\right) \right\|_\Omega^2, \tag{4.8}$$

where all expectations are over both the I_i and the $Y_i(t)$. It is apparent that MSE_Ω attains a minimum with respect to $\nu_i(t)$ when

$$\nu_i(t) = \mu_i(t), \quad i \in P,$$

producing the "ideal" predictor

$$T_3(t) = T_1(t) - \frac{1}{N} \sum_{i=1}^{N} \left(\frac{I_i}{\pi_i} - 1 \right) \mu_i(t), \tag{4.9}$$

which has MSE_Ω

$$\mathrm{MSE}_\Omega = \frac{1}{N^2} \sum_{i=1}^{N} \mathrm{tr}(\Sigma_i \Omega) \left(\frac{1}{\pi_i} - 1 \right). \tag{4.10}$$

It follows from *Godambe/Joshi* [1965] that (4.10) equals the minimum MSE_Ω of any design unbiased estimator, given the π_i.

For the model (3.4) of Example 3 we assume

$$E U_i(u) U_j(v)' = \Sigma \delta_{ij} \delta_{uv}, \tag{4.11}$$

so that residuals $U_i(t)$ are contemporaneously and serially uncorrelated. We have

$$X_i(t) = \sum_{v=0}^{u-1} A^v U_i(t-v), \quad i \in Q_u,$$

whence, from (4.11),

$$\Sigma_i = \sum_{v=0}^{u-1} A^v \Sigma A^{v'}, \quad i \in Q_u.$$

Thus $\Sigma_i - \Sigma$ is null for $i \in Q_1$, and non-negative definite for $i \in Q_u$, $u > 1$. It follows that (4.10) is minimized with respect to Σ_i when there is a census at time $t-1$ (in the case of model (3.4)).

The expression (4.10) suggests an objective choice of the inclusion probabilities π_i, namely one that minimizes (4.10) for given Σ_i, Ω. By the Schwarz inequality and (2.2)

$$\sum_{i=1}^{N} \mathrm{tr}^{1/2}(\Sigma_i \Omega) \leqslant \left\{ n \sum_{i=1}^{N} \mathrm{tr}(\Sigma_i \Omega) \frac{1}{\pi_i} \right\}^{1/2}$$

so that (4.10) is minimized when there is equality; i.e. when

$$\pi_i = \frac{n \, \mathrm{tr}^{1/2}(\Sigma_i \Omega)}{\sum_{i=1}^{N} \mathrm{tr}^{1/2}(\Sigma_i \Omega)}. \tag{4.12}$$

Brewer [1979] obtains a similar result for a different predictor. Referring again to Example 3, the implication of (4.12) is that units that have not been sampled recently should have higher inclusion probabilties than units which have.

5. Prediction of $\bar{Y}(t)$: II

Unfortunately, the "ideal" predictor (4.9) is often uncomputable, for two reasons. The first arises when Q is nonempty, so that P contains some units that are unsampled prior to time t. In that case we have, presumably, no knowledge of $\mu_i(t) = E(Y_i(t))$ for $i \in Q$, so we cannot take $\nu_i(t) = \mu_i(t)$ for all $i \in P$. Suppose we agree to take

$$\nu_i(t) = 0,\ i \in Q,\ \nu_i(t) = \mu_i(t),\ i \notin Q,$$

and thus consider

$$T_4(t) = T_1(t) - \frac{1}{N} \sum_{i \notin Q} \left(\frac{I_i}{\pi_i} - 1\right) \mu_i(t). \tag{5.1}$$

On applying a result in, for example, *Sukhatme* [1954, p. 71], (4.8) is then

$$\frac{1}{N^2} \Sigma' (\pi_i \pi_j - \pi_{ij}) E \operatorname{tr} \left\{ \left(\frac{\mu_i(t)}{\pi_i} - \frac{\mu_j(t)}{\pi_j}\right) \left(\frac{\mu_i(t)}{\pi_i} - \frac{\mu_j(t)}{\pi_j}\right)' \Omega \right\}, \tag{5.2}$$

where the sum is over all $i, j \notin Q$, $i \neq j$. We can compare the MSE_Ω of (5.1), that is (4.10) plus (5.2), with that of the Horwitz-Thompson predictor (4.3). Because $T_1(t)$ has the form $T_2(t)$ also, we conclude that the MSE_Ω of $T_1(t)$ is (4.10) plus

$$\frac{1}{N^2} \sum_{i=1}^{N} \sum_{j>i} (\pi_i \pi_j - \pi_{ij}) E \operatorname{tr} \left\{ \left(\frac{\mu_i(t)}{\pi_i} - \frac{\mu_j(t)}{\pi_j}\right) \left(\frac{\mu_i(t)}{\pi_i} - \frac{\mu_j(t)}{\pi_j}\right)' \Omega \right\}. \tag{5.3}$$

A sufficient condition for (5.2) $\leqslant$ (5.3) is (2.5). As earlier noted (2.5) is a property of the sampling schemes in Examples 1 and 2, and indeed it is also a property of other schemes that are used in practice. Therefore $T_4(t)$ will often do at least as well as $T_1(t)$.

The other obstacle to computing $T_3(t)$ concerns the units which are previously sampled, because even for these exact knowledge of the $\mu_i(t)$ is unlikely. We assume that the $\Gamma_i(u; \theta)$ and $\Delta_i(\theta)$ are known functions of θ, which is unknown but estimable. We insert an estimate, $\hat{\theta}$, of θ, in (3.3), and consider

$$T_5(t) = T_1(t) - \frac{1}{N} \sum_{i \notin Q} \left(\frac{I_i}{\pi_i} - 1\right) \hat{\mu}_t(t), \tag{5.4}$$

$$\hat{\mu}_i(t) = \sum_{u \in O_i} \Gamma_i(u; \hat{\theta}) Y_i(t-u) + \Delta_i(\hat{\theta}) Z_i(t).$$

The predictor (5.4) generalizes the regression predictor that has been considered by a number of authors, but usually for a simple linear regression model and when the predetermined variable is observed for all $i \in P$. If $\hat{\theta}$ is based purely on observations prior to time t, as may be possible if the model is time-invariant, then $\hat{\theta}$ is not a function of the I_i, and so $T_5(t)$ is design unbiased,

$$E(T_5(t) \mid Y_i(t), 1 \leq i \leq N) = \bar{Y}(t).$$

However, the mean square error calculations of the preceding section are affected, because $\hat{\theta}$ is function of random variables $Y_i(t-u), u > 0$. In any case $\hat{\theta}$ is rather likely to be a function of the $Y_i(t)$, and thus of the I_i also, and this will be unavoidable if $t = 1$. For the model of Example 3, a simple estimator $\hat{\theta}$ is given by

$$(\hat{A}, \hat{B}) = \sum_{i \in Q_1} I_i Y_i(t) \begin{pmatrix} Y_i(t-1) \\ W_i(t) \end{pmatrix}' \left[\sum_{i \in Q_1} I_i \begin{pmatrix} Y_i(t-1) \\ W_i(t) \end{pmatrix} \begin{pmatrix} Y_i(t-1) \\ W_i(t) \end{pmatrix}' \right]^{-1}, \tag{5.5}$$

the ordinary least squares estimator based on units sampled at both times t and $t-1$. It is apparent that not only will the mean square error be affected, but $T_5(t)$ will not be exactly design unbiased. The purpose of the following section is to give conditions under which $T_5(t)$ will, asymptotically, have the same properties as $T_4(t)$.

6. Asymptotic Properties

We let $N \to \infty$ and $n \to \infty$, but keep t fixed. Each n, N pair corresponds to a different set of I_i variables, but our notation suppresses reference to this fact. Likewise the π_i and π_{ij} are functions of n and N, although if n increases at the same rate as N they may remain roughly constant as $n \to \infty$ and $N \to \infty$ (see (2.3), (2.4)). The sets

$$\beta_i = \{j \mid 1 \leq j \leq N,\ j \neq i,\ \pi_{ij} > \pi_i \pi_j\}, \quad 1 \leq i \leq N,$$

in general depend on n and N, although because of (2.5) the β_i will always be empty for the sampling schemes of Examples 1 and 2. We define

$$\xi_N = \max_{1 \leq i \leq N} \sum_{\beta_i} (\pi_{ij} - \pi_i \pi_j), \tag{6.1}$$

$$\zeta_N = \min_{1 \leq i \leq N} \pi_i, \tag{6.2}$$

$$\epsilon_N = \frac{1}{N\zeta_N} \left(1 + \frac{\xi_N}{\zeta_N}\right), \tag{6.3}$$

$$Y = \{Y_i(u) \mid i = 1, 2, \ldots; 0 \leq u \leq t\}.$$

By the qualification "almost surely" we shall mean that the statement holds true for almost every realization of Y. By $\|\cdot\|$ we mean $\|\cdot\|_\Omega$ with Ω replaced by the identity matrix.

Theorem 1. Let

$$\sum_{i=1}^{N} \|Y_i(u)\|^2 = O(N), \quad 0 \leq u \leq t, \tag{6.4}$$

almost surely, and

$$\sum_{i=1}^{N} \| Z_i(t) \|^2 = O(N). \tag{6.5}$$

For any value of θ, let $\Gamma_i(u; \theta)$, $\Delta_i(\theta)$ take at most finitely many values as functions of i, as $N \to \infty$. Let there exist a sequence $\bar{\theta} = \bar{\theta}_N$, not depending on the I_i, such that, almost surely,

$$E(\| \Gamma_i(u; \hat{\theta}) - \Gamma_i(u; \bar{\theta}) \|^2 \mid Y) = O(\epsilon_N), 0 \leqslant u \leqslant t, \tag{6.6}$$

$$E(\| \Delta_i(\hat{\theta}) - \Delta_i(\bar{\theta}) \|^2 \mid Y) = O(\epsilon_N). \tag{6.7}$$

Then as $N \to \infty$, almost surely,

$$E(T_5(t) \mid Y) = \bar{Y}(t) + O(\epsilon_N), \tag{6.8}$$

$$\Pr(\| T_5(t) - \bar{Y}(t) \| > \eta \mid Y) = O(\epsilon_N^{1/2}), \text{ all } \eta > 0, \tag{6.9}$$

irrespective of whether the model given by (3.1) – (3.3), (4.5) is true.

We omit the lengthy proof because it combines features in proofs in *Robinson/Sarndal* [1980], *Robinson* [1980]. *Robinson/Sarndal* [1980] give a rigorous proof of asymptotic design unbiasedness and consistency (i.e. they prove (6.8) and (6.9) such that $\epsilon_N \to 0$) for the scalar linear multiple regression model. They do not give the rates of convergence ϵ_N and $\epsilon_N^{1/2}$, but these follow from the lemma in *Robinson* [1980]. We conclude from (6.1) – (6.3) that a sufficient condition for asymptotic design unbiasedness and consistency is $N\zeta_N \to \infty$, $\xi_N = O(\zeta_N)$. For Examples 1 and 2 we have $\xi_N \equiv 0$, and then indeed if the π_i are bounded away from zero the bias is $O(N^{-1})$, the same as that of the conventional ratio estimator under simple random sampling [*David/Sukhatme*]. The condition $\xi_N = O(\zeta_N)$ is a type of weak-dependence condition on the I_i, which would not be satisfied if, for example, the sampling scheme consisted merely of tossing a coin to decide whether the sample should be all units with odd labels, or all units with even labels. However for such schemes we would not expect a design consistent predictor of $\bar{Y}$ to exist.

The conditions (6.6), (6.7) generalize a condition used by *Robinson/Sarndal* [1980] which they show to be essentially a lack-of-multicollinearity condition when a multiple regression model is estimated by ordinary least squares. For the estimator $(\hat{A}, \hat{B})$ of (5.5), which pertains to Example 3, (6.6) and (6.7) are partly satisfied if for all large N, the smallest eigenvalue of

$$\frac{1}{n} \sum_{i \in Q_1} I_i \begin{pmatrix} Y_i(t-1) \\ W_i(t) \end{pmatrix} \begin{pmatrix} Y_i(t-1) \\ W_i(t) \end{pmatrix}'$$

is almost surely bounded away from zero, over all possible outcomes of the I_i (i.e. over all possible samples). Then the remainder of (6.6) and (6.7) may be verified in the same way that the rest of Theorem 1 is proved, if we agree to choose for $\bar{\theta}$,

$$(\bar{A}, \bar{B}) = \sum_{i \in Q_1} \pi_i Y_i(t) \begin{pmatrix} Y_i(t-1) \\ W_i(t) \end{pmatrix}' \left[\sum_{i \in Q_1} \pi_i \begin{pmatrix} Y_i(t-1) \\ W_i(t) \end{pmatrix} \begin{pmatrix} Y_i(t-1) \\ W_i(t) \end{pmatrix}' \right]^{-1},$$

and strengthen (6.4) and (6.5) to

$$\sum_{i=1}^{N} \| Y_i(u) \|^4 = O(N), \qquad u = 0, 1, \ldots, t, \text{ almost surely,}$$

$$\sum_{i=1}^{N} \| W_i(t) \|^4 = O(N).$$

Our second theorem confirms that, after suitable normalisation, $T_5(t)$ has the same MSE as $T_4(t)$, asymptotically.

Theorem 2. Let conditions (6.4) and (6.5) hold, and let the model given by (3.1) – (3.3) and (4.5) be true. Let

$$E(N \| \Gamma_i(u; \hat{\theta}) - \Gamma_i(u; \theta) \|^2 \mid Y_i(u), u < t, I_i, 1 \leqslant i \leqslant N) = O(1), \tag{6.10}$$

$$\xi_N = O(1), \quad \zeta_N^{-1} = O(1), \tag{6.11}$$

as $N \to \infty$, and let there exist σ such that

$$\mathrm{tr}(\Sigma_i) < \sigma < \infty, \quad i = 1, 2, \ldots$$

Then

$$NE \| T_5(t) - \bar{Y}(t) \|_\Omega^2 = NE \| T_4(t) - \bar{Y}(t) \|_\Omega^2 + O(N^{-1/2}),$$

as $N \to \infty$.

Again we give no proof but refer the reader to *Robinson/Sarndal* [1980], whose result is less general in the sense that they consider only the scalar multiple regression case, and give no rates of convergence, but more general in that they show what happens to the mean square error when the model is misspecified.

The condition $\xi_N = O(1)$ is satisfied by Example 1 and 2, and $\zeta_N^{-1} = O(1)$ is likely to be true if n increases as fast as N. Condition (6.10) is reasonable in view of the lack-of-correlation between units requirement (4.5): as far as the estimator (5.5) is concerned, it is readily seen that

$$E\left(\| \sum_{i \in Q_1} I_i (Y_i(t) - \mu_i(t)) \begin{pmatrix} Y_i(t-1) \\ W_i(t) \end{pmatrix} \|^2 \mid Y_i(u), u < t, I_i, 1 \leqslant i \leqslant n \right) = O(N)$$

whence the remainder of (6.10) can be checked so long as a multicollinearity requirement like that discussed in connection with (6.6), (6.7) is satisfied. We observe that the asymptotic mean square error of $T_5(t)$ is insensitive to the efficiency of estimation of θ ((5.5) is not in general efficient if some of the Q_u, $u > 1$, are non-empty). The practical interpretation of (6.10) is that one of the usual $\sqrt{N}$-consistent methods of estimation will suffice.

7. Summary

We have attempted to synthesize themes in time series analysis and econometric models on the one hand, and sample survey theory on the other. Much economic data are collected by sampling, and sample surveys are often carried out periodically over time. One wishes to make use of relationships between variables across time and contemporaneously in order to improve survey estimates. At the same time one wants the randomization in the sampling procedure to protect one against bias due to the common problem of model-mis-specification.

References

Basu, D.: An essay on the logical foundations of survey sampling, Part one. Foundations of statistical inference. Ed. by V.P. Godambe and D.A. Sprott. Toronto 1971, 203–242.

Box, G.E.P., and *G.M. Jenkins*: Time Series Analysis, Forecasting and Control. San Francisco 1979.

Brewer, K.R.W.: Ratio estimation in finite populations: some results deducible from the assumption of an underlying stochastic process. Aust. J. Statist. **5**, 1963, 93–105.

–: A class of robust sampling schemes for large-scale surveys. J. Amer. Statist. Assoc. **74**, 1979, 911–915.

David, I.P., and *B.V. Sukhatme*: On the bias and mean square error of the ratio estimator. J. Amer. Statist. Assoc. 69, 1974, 464–466.

Eckler, A.R.: Rotation sampling. Ann. Math. Statist. **26**, 1955, 664–685.

Godambe, V.P., and *V.M. Joshi*: Admissibility and Bayes estimation in sampling finite populations I. Ann. Math. Statist. **36**, 1965, 1707–1722.

Graham, J.E.: Composite estimation in two cycle rotation sampling designs. Comm. in Statist. **1**, 1973, 419–431.

Gurney, M., and *J.F. Daly*: A multivariate approach to estimation in periodic sample surveys. Amer. Statist. Assoc.: Proceedings of the Social Statistics Section, 1965, 242–257.

Hansen, M.H., et al.: The redesign of the census current population survey. J. Amer. Statist. Assoc. **50**, 1955, 701–719.

Horwitz, D.G., and *D.J. Thompson*: A generalization of sampling without replacement from a finite universe. J. Amer. Statist. Assoc. **47**, 1952, 663–685.

Kulldorff, G.: Some problems of optimum allocation for sampling on two occasions. Rev. Int. Statist. Inst. **31**, 1963, 24–57.

Narain, R.D.: The general theory of sampling on successive occasions. Bull. int. Statist. Inst. **34**, 1954, 87–89.

Patterson, H.D.: Sampling on successive occasions with partial replacement of units. J.R. Statist. Soc. B **12**, 1950, 241–255,

Raj, D.: On sampling over two occasions with probability proportionate to size. Ann. Math. Statist. **36**, 1965, 327–330.

Rao, J.N.K., and *J.E. Graham*: Rotation designs for sampling on repeated occasions. J. Amer. Statist. Assoc. **59**, 1964, 492–509.

Robinson, P.M.: Statistical inference for a random efficient autoregressive model. Scand. J. Statist. **5**, 1978, 163–168.

–: On the convergence of the Horwitz-Thompson estimator. Preprint, 1980.

Robinson, P.M., and *C.E. Sarndal*: Asymptotic properties of the generalized regression predictor in probability sampling. Preprint, 1980.

Royall, R.M.: On finite population sampling theory under certain linear regression models. Biometrika **57**, 1970, 377–387.

Sampford, M.R.: On sampling without replacement with unequal probabilities of selection. Biometrika **54**, 1967, 499–513.

Sarndal, C.E.: Design-based and model-based inference in survey sampling. Scand. J. Statist. **5**, 1978, 27–52.

–: On π-inverse weighting versus BLU weighting in probability sampling. Biometrika **67**, 1980, 639–650.

Scott, A.J., and *T.M.F. Smith*: Analysis of repeated surveys using time series methods. J. Amer. Statist. Assoc. **69**, 1974, 674–678.

Scott, A.J., T.M.F. Smith and *R.G. Jones*: The application of time series methods to the analysis of repeated surveys. Preprint, 1979.

Sinha, B.K.: Sampling schemes to realize preassigned sets of inclusion probabilities of first two orders. Bull. Calcutta Statist. Assoc. **22**, 1973, 89–110.

Sukhatme, P.V.: Sampling Theory of Surveys, With Applications. Ames, Iowa, 1954.

Tikkiwal, B.D.: On the theory of classical regression and double sampling estimation. J.R. Statist. Soc. B **22**, 1960, 131–138.

Whittle, P.: Prediction and Regulation by Linear Least-Square Methods. London 1963.

Games, Economic Dynamics, and Time Series Analysis. 1982 © Physica-Verlag, Wien–Würzburg

Strong and Weak Consistency of Instrumental Variable Estimates and Application to Dynamic Models

By *S. Heiler*, Dortmund[1])

1. Introduction

In recent contributions, *Anderson/Taylor* and *Cristopeit/Helmes* gave conditions for the strong consistency of least squares estimates in linear regression with stochastic regressors. *Willers* considered the weak consistency in this model setup. In all these papers autoregressive or the mixed autoregressive (AREX-) models are studied. Willers' assumptions are the weakest known so far.

In this paper we use a similar approach for instrumental variable estimates. We present two theorems on strong and weak consistency of instrumental variable estimates. For the theorem on weak consistency we give an application to an AREX-model with ARMA-residuals.

2. Instrumental Variable Estimators

We consider the regression model

$$y_t = \sum_{j=1}^{K} x_{tj} \beta_j + u_t, \qquad t \in \mathbf{N}$$

where the $\beta_1, \ldots, \beta_K$ are fixed parameters. All other variables are random, defined on a common probability space (Ω, A, P). Besides the regressors x_{tj} we observe the instrumental variables $p_{tj}, j = 1, \ldots, K$, also defined on the same probability space. For the observation period $\{1,2, \ldots, T\}$ we have the usual vector notation

$$\underline{y}_T = X_T \beta + \underline{u}_T, \tag{1}$$

and by P_T we denote the $T \times K$ matrix of instrumental variables p_{ti}, $t = 1, \ldots, T$, $i = 1, \ldots, K$.

In the sequel we call any solution $\widetilde{\beta}_T$ of

$$P_T' X_T \widetilde{\beta}_T = P_T' \underline{y}_T \tag{2}$$

an *instrumental variable estimate for* β.

[1]) *S. Heiler*, Abt. Statistik, Universität Dortmund, Postfach 500500, D–4600 Dortmund

Let $A_{t-1} := \sigma(p_{sj}, u_{s-1}; s \leqslant t, j = 1, \ldots, K)$ be the σ-subalgebra of A generated by the instruments up to time t and by the error terms up to time $t-1$ and let $g: \mathbf{R}_+ \to \mathbf{R}_+$ be a non-decreasing function with

$$\int_c^\infty g^{-2}(x)\,dx =: \bar{g} < \infty \tag{3}$$

for some $c > 0$. If A is a $m \times n$-matrix then with $\lambda_{\min} A$ ($\lambda_{\max} A$) we denote the square root of the smallest (largest) eigenvalue of $A'A$. $\lambda_{\max}$ is the so-called supremum or spectral norm of A.

Theorem 1; Under the following conditions (A) – (D) the instrumental variable estimate $\tilde{\beta}_T$ converges a.s. to β:

(A) $E(u_t \mid A_{t-1}) = 0$ a.s., $t = 1,2,\ldots$

(B) $u_t \in L_2(\Omega, A, P)$ and $\sup E(u_t^2 \mid A_{t-1}) = \bar{\sigma}^2 < \infty$ a.s.

(C) (a) $d_{Tj}^2 := \sum_{t=1}^T p_{tj}^2 \to \infty$ a.s., $j = 1, \ldots, K$ for $T \to \infty$

(b) $\lim_{T\to\infty} \lambda_{\min}(P_T' X_T) > 0$ a.s.

(D) The matrices $(P_T' X_T)^- D_T$ are a.s. uniformly bounded in T where by $(\;)^-$ we denote a generalized inverse and D_T is the diagonal matrix $D_T := \operatorname{diag}(g(d_{T1}^2), \ldots, g(d_{TK}^2))$.

Theorem 1 may be proved in a similar way as theorem 1 of Christopeit/Helmes. Our assumptions (A) – (Ca) correspond to the assumptions (A) – (C) there with the regressors replaced by the instruments. Following *Eicker* [1979] we slightly generalized the norming matrix D_T by introducing the diagonal elements $g(d_{Ti}^2)$ instead of d_{Ti}^2.

In practice the problem of finding instruments such that the above assumptions are met has to be solved. Assumption (D) might be the most difficult one to check. It implies that the terms

$$\sum_{t=1}^T p_{ti} x_{ti} \Big/ \sum_{t=1}^T g(p_{ti}^2)$$

are a.s. bounded away from zero, $i = 1, \ldots, K$, for a function g with property (3).

(D) is equivalent to the requirement that $(P_T' X_T) D_T^-$ is a.s. uniformly bounded away from zero. Now

$$\lambda_{\min}(P_T' X_T) D_T^- \geqslant \lambda_{\min} P_T \lambda_{\min} X_T \lambda_{\min} D_T^- = \frac{\lambda_{\min} P_T \lambda_{\min} X_T}{\lambda_{\max} D_T}$$

$$= \frac{\lambda_{\min} P_T \lambda_{\min} X_T}{\max\limits_{1 \leqslant i \leqslant K} g(d_{Ti}^2)}.$$

Thus the condition

(D′) $\lambda_{\min} P_T \lambda_{\min} X_T = 0\,(\max_{1 \leq i \leq K} g(d_{Ti}^2))$

is sufficient for (D).

On the other hand (D′) together with (Ca) imply (Cb).

According to assumption (A) $(u_t)_{t \in \mathrm{N}}$ is a martingale difference sequence pertaining to the increasing sequence of σ-algebras $(\mathrm{A}_t)_{t \in \mathrm{N}}$ induced by the instruments up to time t and the past values $u_{t-1}, u_{t-2}, \ldots, u_1$.

Assumption (A) is particularly met if the instruments p_{ti} are predetermined, i.e. measurable with respect to the σ-algebra $\mathrm{A}^*_{t-1} = \sigma(u_{t-1}, \ldots, u_1)$ for all $t = 1,2,\ldots$ with $\mathrm{A}_0 = \{\phi, \Omega\}$.

(A) implies that the u_t are uncorrelated. The following theorem 2 gives sufficient conditions for weak consistency of instrumental variable estimates also for cases where the error terms are correlated in some way.

For the consideration of weak consistency we assume that

$$x_{tj}, p_{tj} \in L_2(\Omega, \mathrm{A}, P), j = 1, \ldots, K, t = 1,2, \ldots$$

and introduce the notations

$$\Xi_T := E\,X_T, \qquad W_T := X_T - \Xi_T$$

$$\Pi_T := E\,P_t, \qquad V_T := P_T - \Pi_T$$

and $K \times K$-matrices M_T and N_T with

$$M_T' M_T := E\,X_T' X_T = \Xi_T' \Xi_T + E\,W_T' W_T$$

$$N_T' N_T := E\,P_T' P_T = \Pi_T' \Pi_T + E\,V_T' V_T.$$

With Var $(\underline{u}_T)$ the $T \times T$ covariance matrix of the error terms is denoted.

Theorem 2. Under the following conditions (I) – (IV) $\widetilde{\beta}_T$ converges to β in probability.

(I) (a) $E(\underline{u}_T) = 0$,
(b) $\lambda_{\max}$ Var $(\underline{u}_T) = 0\,(1)$.

(II) (a) $\lambda_{\min} E(X_T' X_T) \to \infty$,
(b) $\lambda_{\min} E(P_T' P_T) > 0$ for some $T \in \mathrm{N}$.

(III) $\lambda_{\min} (N_T'^{-1} P_T' X_T M_T^{-1})$ is bounded away from zero.

(IV) $\| N_T'^{-1} V_T' \underline{u}_T \|$ is bounded in probability.

Remark 1: Because of (II) M_T and N_T are invertible for almost all T. Conditions (III) and (IV) are thus reasonable. By (III) we mean that $\lambda_{\min}^{-1} (N_T'^{-1} X_T M_T^{-1})$ is bounded in probability.

Remark 2: The properties of instrumental variables are characterized by the conditions (IIb), (III) and (IV). The matrices M_T^{-1}, N_T^{-1} (and D_T in theorem 1) serve for norming purposes. Theorem 2 contains stronger restrictions for the regressors (IIa) as theorem 1. On the other hand condition (I) admits a fairly general structure of the residual process. If for instance the u_t are elements of a weakly stationary process which has a spectral density f that is uniformly bounded on $[-\pi, \pi]$, then condition (I) holds.

Proof of theorem 2. From the above equation (1) and (2) we have

$$P'_T X_T (\tilde{\beta}_T - \beta) = P'_T \underline{u}_T \tag{4}$$

or

$$N'_T N'^{-1}_T P'_T X_T M_T^{-1} M_T (\tilde{\beta}_T - \beta) = P'_T \underline{u}_T .$$

With

$$A_T := N'^{-1}_T P'_T X_T M_T^{-1}$$

and

$$g_T := \lambda_{\min}^{-1} M_T .$$

(4) may be written in the form

$$A_T g_T M_T (\beta_T - \beta) = g_T N'^{-1}_T P'_T \underline{u}_T . \tag{5}$$

From (IIa) it follows that $g_T \to 0$ for $T \to \infty$. With A_T^- we denote a generalized inverse of A_T. By virtue of (III) we have

$$\lim_{T \to \infty} P(\lambda_{\min} A_T > 0) = 1$$

or

$$\lim_{T \to \infty} P(A_T^- = A_T^{-1}) = 1 \tag{6}$$

and the difference

$$\lambda_{\max} A_T^- - (\lambda_{\min} A_T)^{-1} \tag{7}$$

converges to zero stochasticly.

We now multiply (5) with $(g_T M_T)^{-1} A_T^-$ from the left and denote the new lefthand side by Δ_T,

$$\Delta_T := (g_T M_T)^{-1} A_T^- A_T g_T M_T (\tilde{\beta}_T - \beta) =$$
$$= (g_T M_T)^{-1} A_T^- g_T N'^{-1}_T P'_T \underline{u}_T .$$

By virtue of (6) the difference

$$\Delta_T - (\tilde{\beta}_T - \beta)$$

converges to zero stochasticly with $T \to \infty$. Therefore the theorem is proved if we can show that $\Delta_T \to 0$ stochasticly. Now

$$\| \Delta_T \| = \| (g_T M_T)^{-1} A_T^- N_T'^{-1} P_T' \underline{u}_T \| g_T.$$

Since for any invertible square matrix B $\lambda_{max} B^{-1} = (\lambda_{min} B)^{-1}$ we have

$$\lambda_{max} (g_T M_T)^{-1} = g_T^{-1} \lambda_{max} M_T^{-1} = \lambda_{min} M_T / \lambda_{min} M_T = 1.$$

From (7) and assumption (III) it follows that $\lambda_{max} A_T^-$ is bounded in probability. We estimate the third factor in Δ_T:

$$\begin{aligned} \| N_T'^{-1} P_T' \underline{u}_T \| &= \| N_T'^{-1} (\Pi_T' + V_T') \underline{u}_T \| \\ &\leqslant \| N_T'^{-1} \Pi_T' \underline{u}_T \| + \| N_T'^{-1} V_T' \underline{u}_T \|. \end{aligned}$$

By virtue of (IV) the second term is bounded in probability. The first term has expectation

$$E (N_T'^{-1} \Pi_T' \underline{u}_T) = 0$$

and variance

$$\text{Var} (N_T'^{-1} \Pi_T' \underline{u}_T) = N_T'^{-1} \Pi_T' \text{Var} (\underline{u}_T) \Pi_T N_T^{-1}.$$

Now

$$\begin{aligned} 0 \leqslant \lambda_{max} \text{Var} (N_T'^{-1} \Pi_T' \underline{u}_T) &\leqslant \lambda_{max}^2 (N_T'^{-1} \Pi_T') \lambda_{max} \text{Var} (\underline{u}_T) = \\ &= \lambda_{max} (N_T'^{-1} \Pi_T' \Pi_T N_T^{-1}) \lambda_{max} \text{Var} (\underline{u}_T) = \\ &= \lambda_{max} (N_T'^{-1} [N_T' N_T - E(V_T' V_T)] N_T^{-1}) \lambda_{max} \text{Var} (\underline{u}_T) = \\ &= \lambda_{max} (I_K - N_T'^{-1} E(V_T' V_T) N_T^{-1}) \lambda_{max} \text{Var} (\underline{u}_T). \end{aligned}$$

Since $N_T'^{-1} \Pi_T' \Pi_T N_T^{-1}$ is positive semidefinite we have

$$\begin{aligned} \lambda_{max} (I_K - N_T'^{-1} E(V_T' V_T) N_T^{-1}) &= \sup_{\|x\|=1} x' [I_K - N_T'^{-1} E(V_T' V_T) N_T^{-1}) x \\ &\leqslant 1 - \inf_{\|x\|=1} \underbrace{x' (N_T'^{-1} E(V_T' V_T) N_T^{-1}) x}_{\geqslant 0} \leqslant 1. \end{aligned}$$

With assumption (Ib) we get therefore that

$$\lambda_{max} \text{Var} (N_T'^{-1} \Pi_T' \underline{u}_T) = 0 (1).$$

Since the expectations and the variances of the components of $N_T'^{-1} \Pi_T' \underline{u}_T$ are uniformly bounded in T it follows from Tschebyshev's inequality that the components are bounded in probability.

With $g_T \to 0$ for $T \to \infty$ we arrive at the result that $\Delta_T \to 0$ stochasticly. ∎

3. Mixed Autoregression with ARMA-Residuals

As an application we consider the model

$$y_t = \alpha_1 y_{t-1} + \ldots + \alpha_p y_{t-p} + z'(t)\beta + u_t \tag{8}$$

with

$$u_t = \sum_{i=1}^{m} \gamma_i u_{t-i} + \sum_{j=0}^{n} \delta_j \epsilon_{t-j}, \quad \delta_0 = 1, \tag{9}$$

where (ϵ_t) is white noise with expectation zero and variance $\sigma_e^2 > 0$, the z_{ti} are non-stochastic exogenous variables, the $\alpha_i, \beta_j, \gamma_k, \delta_l$ are fixed real numbers.

We assume that all roots of the equations

$$\text{(a) } 1 - \alpha_1 z - \ldots - \alpha_p z^p = 0$$

and (10)

$$\text{(b) } 1 - \gamma_1 z - \ldots - \gamma_m z^m = 0$$

are outside the unit disk.

The residual process (u_t) is assumed to be weakly stationary. This means that it is either defined for all $t \in \mathbf{Z}$ or that the initial distributions coincide with the stationary solution.

Remark: The following consistency considerations cover also cases where the exogenous variables have a lag structure provided the model is identifiable (i.e. the polynomials, describing the lag structure have no common roots with the polynomial (10a).

The residual process has the transfer function

$$H(z) = \frac{1 + \delta_1 z + \ldots + \delta_n z^n}{1 - \gamma_1 z - \ldots - \gamma_m z^m}, \; z \in \mathbf{C}$$

and the spectral density is given by

$$f(\omega) = \frac{|1 + \delta_1 e^{1\omega} + \ldots + \delta_n e^{in\omega}|^2}{|1 - \gamma_1 e^{i\omega} - \ldots - \gamma_m e^{im\omega}|^2} \sigma_e^2, -\pi \leqslant \omega \leqslant \pi.$$

Obviously $f(\omega)$ has a finite upper bound M and not more than n zeros. Later on we shall use the spectral representation of the autocovariances of the process (u_t),

$$\gamma(h) := E(u_t u_{t+h}) = \frac{1}{2\pi} \int_{-\pi}^{\pi} e^{ih\omega} f(\omega) d\omega.$$

We are interested in estimating the parameter vector $\alpha = (\alpha_1, \ldots, \alpha_p)'$ and β by an instrumental variable approach. For the exogenous part on the right hand side of (8) the $z(t)$ may serve as instruments themselves. Let us assume that we are able to find instruments $p_{t1}, \ldots, p_{tp}$ for $y_{t-1}, \ldots, y_{t-p}$ such that the assumptions (IIb), (III) and (IV) of theorem 2 hold.

We now investigate the other assumptions. It is easy to see that with the above model assumptions (I) holds. (I a) is obvious and for (I b) we have

$$\lambda_{\max} \operatorname{Var}(\underline{u}_T) = \sup_{\|x\|=1} x' \Sigma_T x,$$

where $\Sigma_T := (\gamma(t-s))_{t,s=1,\ldots,T}$. Now

$$\begin{aligned} x' \Sigma_T x &= \sum_{s=1}^{T} \sum_{t=1}^{T} x_t \bar{x}_s \gamma(t-s) \\ &= \frac{1}{2\pi} \sum_{s=1}^{T} \sum_{t=1}^{T} x_i \bar{x}_s \int_{-\pi}^{\pi} e^{i(t-s)\omega} f(\omega)\, d\omega \\ &= \frac{1}{2\pi} \int_{-\pi}^{\pi} | \sum_{s=1}^{T} x_s e^{is\omega} |^2 f(\omega)\, d\omega \\ &\leqslant \frac{M}{2\pi} \int_{-\pi}^{\pi} | \sum_{s=1}^{T} x_s e^{is\omega} |^2\, d\omega \\ &= \frac{M}{2\pi} \sum_{s=1}^{T} \sum_{t=1}^{T} x_s \bar{x}_t \int_{-\pi}^{\pi} e^{i(s-t)\omega}\, d\omega = M \| x \|^2 = M. \end{aligned}$$

The investigation of assumption (II a) is more tedious. Let Z_T be the $T \times K$-matrix of the exogenous variables.

Lemma 3.1: In the above model

$$\lambda_{\min} Z_T' Z_T \to \infty \tag{11}$$

implies

(II a) $\lambda_{\min} E X_T' X_T \to \infty.$

Proof: The solution of (8) with the (stochastic) initial values $y_. := (y_0, y_{-1}, \ldots, y_{1-p})'$ may be written in the form

$$\begin{aligned} y_t &= \sum_{s=0}^{t-1} c_s z'(t-s)\beta + \sum_{s=0}^{t-1} c_s u_{t-s} + \underline{c}_t' y_. \\ &=: \quad w_t \quad + \quad y_t^* \quad + y_t^0 . \end{aligned} \tag{12}$$

The coefficients c_s are given by the equations

$$c_0 = 1, c_{-1} = c_{-2} = \ldots = c_{1-p} = 0$$

$$c_s = \alpha_1 c_{s-1} + \alpha_2 c_{s-2} + \ldots + \alpha_p c_{s-p}$$

and the components of the vector $\underline{c}_t$ are given by

$$c_{t1} = c_t, c_{tj} = \sum_{k=0}^{p-j} \alpha_{j+k}\, c_{t-k-1}, \quad j = 2, \ldots, p$$

[see, e.g. *Schönfeld*].

The stability assumption (10 a) implies that

$$|c_t| = o(\lambda^t), |c_{t,j}| = o(\lambda^t) \tag{13}$$

for some λ with $0 < \lambda < 1$.

For (12) we introduce the notation

$$y_t := E(y_t) + v_t = (w_t + E y_t^0) + (y_t^* + v_t^0),$$

$$v_t^0 := y_t^0 - E y_t^0 \text{ for } t \geq 1 \text{ and } v_t^0 := y_t - E y_t \quad \text{for } 1 - p \leq t \leq 0.$$

We now decompose the matrix $E X_T' X_T$ as follows,

$$E X_T' X_T = \begin{pmatrix} S_T & \tilde{C}_T \\ \tilde{C}_T' & Z_T' Z_T \end{pmatrix}.$$

The elements of the $(p \times K)$-matrix $\tilde{C}_T$ are

$$(\sum_{t=1}^{T} E(y_{t-i}) z_{tj}); \; i = 1, \ldots, p, \; j = 1, \ldots, K,$$

and elements of the $(p \times p)$-matrix S_T are

$$\sum_{t=1}^{T} E(y_{t-i} y_{t-j}) = \sum_{t=1}^{T} (E y_{t-i})(E y_{t-j}) + \sum_{t=1}^{T} E(v_{t-i} v_{t-j}).$$

Correspondingly we decompose S_T further into $S_T = A_T + B_T$ and have

$$E X_T' X_T = \begin{pmatrix} A_T & \tilde{C}_T \\ \tilde{C}_T' & Z_T' Z_T \end{pmatrix} + \begin{pmatrix} B_T & 0 \\ 0 & 0 \end{pmatrix}$$

where both matrices are non-negative definite. The matrix B_T has the elements

$$\sum_{t=1}^{T} E(v_{t-i} v_{t-j}) = \sum_{t=a}^{T} E(y_{t-i}^* y_{t-j}^*) + \sum_{t=1}^{T} E(v_{t-i}^0 v_{t-j}^0)$$

$$+ \sum_{t=i+1}^{T} E(y_{t-i}^* v_{t-j}^0) + \sum_{t=j+1}^{T} E(v_{t-i}^0 y_{t-j}^*)$$

where $a := \max(i, j) + 1$.

With

$$F_T = (\sum_{t=a}^{T} E(y^*_{t-i} y^*_{t-j}))_{i,j=1,\ldots,p}$$

we write

$$B_T = F_T + G_T$$

and show that the elements of G_T are bounded.

With

$$\kappa_1 := \max_{1 \leqslant l \leqslant p} E(v^{02}_{1-l})$$

and

$$\sum_{t=1}^{T} E(v^0_{t-i} v^0_{t-j}) = \sum_{k=1}^{p} \sum_{l=1}^{p} \sum_{t=1}^{T} c_{k,t-i} c_{l,t-j} E(v^0_{1-k} v^0_{1-l})$$

where we put $c_{k,s} = 1/p$ for $s \leqslant 0$ we get the upper bound

$$| \sum_{t=1}^{T} E(v^0_{t-i} v^0_{t-j}) | \leqslant \kappa_1 \sum_{k=1}^{p} \sum_{l=1}^{p} \sum_{t=1}^{\infty} | c_{k,t} | \, | c_{l,t} | < \infty. \tag{14}$$

The last inequality follows from (13).

With

$$\kappa_2 := \sup_{\substack{t \in \mathbb{N} \\ 1 \leqslant l \leqslant p}} | \operatorname{cov}(u_t \, v^0_{1-l}) |$$

and

$$\sum_{t=i+1}^{T} E(y^*_{t-i} v^0_{t-j}) = \sum_{t=i+1}^{T} \sum_{s=1}^{t-i-1} \sum_{k=1}^{p} c_s c_{k,t-j} E(u_{t-i-s} v^0_{1-l})$$

we again conclude from (13) that

$$| \sum_{t=i+1}^{\infty} E(y^*_{t-i} v^0_{t-j}) | \leqslant \kappa_2 \sum_{k=1}^{p} \sum_{t=1}^{\infty} | c_{k,t} | \sum_{s=0}^{\infty} | c_s | < \infty$$

for $i, j = 1, \ldots, p$.

(14) and (15) yield that $\| G_T \|$ is uniformly bounded in T.

Since $\lambda_{\min} E X'_T X_T = \inf_{\|x\|=1} x'(E X'_T X_T) x$ we consider the quadratic form

$$x' E(X'_T X_T) x = (x'_1 \; x'_2) \begin{pmatrix} A_T & \tilde{C}_T \\ \tilde{C}'_T & Z'_T Z_T \end{pmatrix} \begin{pmatrix} x_1 \\ x_2 \end{pmatrix} + x'_1 B_T x_1, \; \| x \| = 1, \tag{16}$$

where the first term is non-negative and

$$0 \leqslant x_1' B_T x_1 = x_1' F_T x_1 + x_1' G_T x_1.$$

$x_1' B_T x_1 \to \infty$ for any $x_1 \neq 0$ and (11) imply $\lambda_{\min} E X_T' X_T \to \infty$. This follows from the fact if $x_1 \neq 0$, then in (16) the second term goes to infinity for $T \to \infty$. If $x_1 = 0$, then $\| x_2 \| = 1$ and the first term is given by $x_2' Z_T' Z_T x_2$, which goes to infinity by assumption (11).

Therefore we have to show that $x' B_T x \to \infty$ for any $x \neq 0$. Since $x' B_T x = x' F_T x + x' G_T x$ and since $\| G_T \|$ is uniformly bounded in T this is equivalent to

$$Q_T := x' F_T x \to \infty \text{ for any } x \in \mathbf{R}^p \text{ with } \| x \| = 1.$$

The elements of the nonnegative definite matrix F_T are

$$\sum_{t=a}^{T} E(y_{t-i}^* y_{t-j}^*) = \sum_{t=a}^{T} \sum_{s=0}^{t-i-1} \sum_{r=0}^{t-j-1} c_s c_r \gamma(s+i-r-j).$$

Taking the shifts into consideration this may be seen to be equal to

$$\sum_{s=0}^{T-i-1} \sum_{r=0}^{T-j-1} c_s c_r \gamma(s+i-r-j) [T - \max(s+i, r+j)].$$

Hence

$$Q_T = T \sum_{i=1}^{p} \sum_{j=1}^{p} x_i x_j \sum_{s=0}^{T-i-1} \sum_{r=0}^{T-j-1} c_s c_r \gamma(s+i-r-j) -$$

$$- \sum_{i=1}^{p} \sum_{j=1}^{p} x_i x_j \sum_{s=0}^{T-i-1} \sum_{r=0}^{T-j-1} c_s c_r \gamma(s+i-r-j) \max(s+i, r+j) =$$

$$=: Q_{1T} - Q_{2T}.$$

Introducing the spectral representation for the covariances we can write

$$Q_{1T} = \frac{T}{2\pi} \int_{-\pi}^{\pi} | \sum_{j=1}^{p} x_j e^{ij\omega} \sum_{s=0}^{T-j-1} c_s e^{is\omega} |^2 f(\omega) \, d\omega.$$

With

$$b_{jT}(\omega) := x_j e^{ij\omega} \sum_{s=0}^{T-j-1} c_s e^{is\omega}, \; b_T(\omega) := (b_{jT}(\omega))_{j=1,\ldots,p}$$

this is

$$Q_{1T} = \frac{T}{2\pi} \int_{-\pi}^{\pi} \| b_T(\omega) \|^2 f(\omega) \, d\omega.$$

The b_{jT} are sums of continuous and bounded functions. From (13) it follows therefore that they are uniformly convergent. Hence the limit function $b_j := \lim_{T\to\infty} b_{jT}$ is also continuous.

Since f is continuous, $f \geq 0$ and $f = 0$ for at most n points, the above integral can only vanish if b_j vanishes almost everywhere. This again is equivalent to

$$\lim_{T\to\infty} \int_{-\pi}^{\pi} \| b_T(\omega) \|^2 \, d\omega = \int_{-\pi}^{\pi} \| \lim_{T\to\infty} b_T(\omega) \|^2 \, d\omega = 0.$$

We show that the integrals $\int_{-\pi}^{\pi} \| b_T(\omega) \|^2 \, d\omega$ have a uniform lower bound greater than zero:

$$\begin{aligned}
\int_{-\pi}^{\pi} \| b_T(\omega) \|^2 \, d\omega &= \sum_{j=1}^{p} \sum_{k=1}^{p} x_j \bar{x}_k \sum_{s=0}^{T-j-1} \sum_{r=0}^{T-k-1} c_s \bar{c}_r \int_{-\pi}^{\pi} e^{-(s+j-r-k)\omega} \, d\omega \\
&= 2\pi \sum_{j=1}^{p} \sum_{k=1}^{p} x_j \bar{x}_k \sum_{s=0}^{T-j-1} c_s \, c_{s+|k-j|} \\
&= 2\pi \, x' H_T \, x,
\end{aligned}$$

where the element (j, k) of the nonnegative definite matrix H_T is given by

$$\sum_{s=0}^{T-j-1} c_s \, c_{s+|k-j|} \, .$$

Let L_T be the matrix

$$L_T := \begin{pmatrix} 0 & \dots 0 \\ & \vdots \\ I_{T-1} & 0 \end{pmatrix}$$

and let C_T be the matrix polynomial

$$C_T := \sum_{s=0}^{T-1} c_s L_T^s .$$

Then H_T may be seen to be the upper left corner of the matrix $C_T' C_T$. *Eicker* [1963] has shown that

$$0 < b_1 \leq \lambda_{\min} C_T' C_T, \; \lambda_{\max} C_T' C_T \leq b_c < \infty.$$

Hence a $b^* > 0$ may be found such that $x' H_T x \geq b^*$ for all T. From this it follows that

$$\lim_{T\to\infty} J_T := \lim_{T\to\infty} \int_{-\pi}^{\pi} \| b_T(\omega) \|^2 f(\omega) \, d\omega \geq b_0$$

for some $b_0 > 0$.

Hence $Q_{1T} \to \infty$ for $T \to \infty$.

We finally have to show that Q_{2T} is bounded above. We have

$$|Q_{2T}| \leqslant p^2 \gamma(0) \sum_{s=0}^{T} \sum_{r=0}^{T} |c_s| \, |c_r| \max(s+p, r+p)$$

$$\leqslant 2p^2 \gamma(0) \sum_{s=0}^{T} |c_s| \sum_{r \geqslant s}^{T} |c_r| (r+p) =$$

$$= 2p^3 \gamma(0) \sum_{s=0}^{T} |c_s| \sum_{r \geqslant s}^{T} |c_r| + 2p^2 \gamma(0) \sum_{s=0}^{T} |c_s| \sum_{r \geqslant s}^{T} |c_r| r.$$

From (13) we conclude that the first term is bounded. According to the ratio test the second term converges also, since $\lambda^{-r} r < 1$ for r large enough. Hence $Q_T = Q_{1T} - Q_{2T} \to \to \infty$ for $T \to \infty$. With this the lemma is proved. ■

References

Anderson, T.W., and *J.B. Taylor*: Strong consistency of least squares estimates in dynamic models. Ann. Statist. 7, 1979, 484–489.

Christopeit, N., and *K. Helmes*: Strong consistency of least squares estimators in linear regression models. To appear in Ann. Statist. 1980.

Drygas, H.: Weak and strong consistency of the least squares estimators in regression models. Z. Wahrscheinlichkeitsth. verw. Geb. 34, 1976, 119–127.

Eicker, F.: Über die Konsistenz von Parameterschätzfunktionen für ein gemischtes Zeitreihen-Regressionsmodell. Z. Wahrscheinlichkeitsth. verw. Geb. 1, 1963, 456–477.

–: Consistent parameter estimation in mixed autoregressions and in general linear stochastic regressions. Forschungsbericht 79/3, Abt. Statistik d. Univ. Dortmund, 1979.

Heiler, S.: Prediction of economic processes with linear regression part. Problems of time series. Schriftenreihe „Gesellschaft, Recht, Wirtschaft" der Universität Mannheim, Bd. 3, Mannheim 1980.

Lai, T.L., *H. Robbins* and *C.Z. Wei*: Strong consistency of least squares estimates in multiple regression. Proc. Natl. Acad. Sci. USA 75, 1978, 3034–3036.

Marcus, M., and *H. Minc*: A survey of matrix theory and matrix inequalities. Boston 1964.

Schönfeld, P.: Methoden der Ökonometrie, Band II. München 1971.

Willers, R.: Schwache Konsistenz von Kleinstquadrate-Schätzern für Regressions- und Streuungsparameter in linearen Modellen. Dissertation. Dortmund 1978.

Games, Economic Dynamics, and Time Series Analysis. 1982 ©Physica-Verlag, Wien–Würzburg

A Simple Regression Model with Trend and Error in the Exogenous Variable

By *H. Schneeweiß*, München[1])

1. Introduction

Consider the simple errors-in-the-variables model

$$\begin{aligned} \eta_t &= \alpha + \beta \xi_t \\ x_t &= \xi_t + v_t \\ y_t &= \eta_t + w_t \end{aligned} \tag{1}$$

where (x_t, y_t), $t = 1, 2, \ldots$, are the only observable variables, for which a sample $t = 1, \ldots, T$ is given. (v_t, w_t) are idd random variables distributed independently of $(\xi_1, \xi_2, \ldots)$ with expectation zero and with variances σ_v^2 and σ_w^2. With regard to the variables ξ_t two main cases have been treated in the literature [c.f. e.g. *Madansky; Kendall/Stuart; Johnston; Moran; Schneeweiß*, 1980b]:

- (FV) The functional variant: The ξ_t are nonstochastic and are considered as unknown parameters.
- (SV) The structural variant: The ξ_t are iid random variables with mean μ_ξ and variance σ_ξ^2.

Many more cases could be conceived of[2]). In fact (ξ_t) could be any stochastic process. In particular if (ξ_t) is a stationary process with the ergodicity properties

$$\lim_{T \to \infty} \bar{\xi} = \mu_\xi, \ \lim_{T \to \infty} s_\xi^2 = \sigma_\xi^2 > 0 \text{ (with probability 1)} \tag{2}$$

where $\bar{\xi} = (1/T) \Sigma \xi_t$ and $s_\xi^2 = (1/T) \Sigma (\xi_t - \bar{\xi})^2$, most of the properties of (SV) carry over to this case. On the other hand, if ξ_t follows a trend, the analysis of the model has to be adapted to this situation. It is this case which we want to study in greater detail, i.e. we are going to assume that

$$\xi_t = a + bt + \epsilon_t \tag{3}$$

---

[1]) Prof. Dr. *H. Schneeweiß*, Seminar für Ökonometrie und Statistik, Universität München, Akademiestr. 1/I, D–8000 München 40

[2]) One interesting variant which comprises (FV) and (SV) has been studied by *Dolby* [1976].

with a iid random variable ϵ_t, which is independent of all the (v_t, w_t) and which has expectation zero and variance σ_ϵ^2. Note that (3) and (2) cannot be reconciled unless one is willing to put $\mu_\xi = \infty$ and $\sigma_\xi^2 = \infty$.

In the next section a short review of some asymptotic results of the (FV) and (SV) cases is given in order to provide an appropriate background for the theory of the trend case to be considered thereafter.

In the case of (FV) we require the limits in (2) to exist, so that the quantities μ_ξ and σ_ξ^2 are implicitly defined by (2) for this case.

2. The Case of no Trend

In this section it is assumed that either (FV) or (SV) prevails where the latter case can be extended to comprise any stationary process satisfying (2). Most of the following results hold for both cases unless stated otherwise.

The most prominent result of the theory of errors-in-the-variables models is the inconsistency property of the least squares estimator

$$\hat{\beta}_{\mathrm{LS}} := s_{xy}/s_x^2.$$

In fact from (1) the following regression type equation can be deduced:

$$y_t = \alpha + \beta x_t + u_t \tag{4}$$

with

$$u_t := w_t - \beta v_t. \tag{5}$$

But as u_t and x_t are correlated, an important assumption of the regression model is violated and consequently $\hat{\beta}_{\mathrm{LS}}$ is inconsistent. The asymptotic bias is given by

$$p\lim(\hat{\beta}_{\mathrm{LS}} - \beta) = -\beta\frac{\sigma_v^2}{\sigma_x^2} \tag{6}$$

This result can be found in almost every textbook, but one can easily overlook the fact that it is based on (2) and does not hold in the case of trend.

Various consistent estimators have been suggested in the literature[3]), each depending on some additional piece of information.

a) If the exogenous error variance σ_v^2 is known and if $\sigma_{vw} = 0$

$$\hat{\beta}_{\mathrm{EV}} := \frac{s_{xy}}{s_x^2 - \sigma_v^2}$$

is consistent. It is the ML estimator if (SV) prevails and all variables are normal[4]).

---

[3]) See the above mentioned literature.

[4]) It may be interesting to note that the ML estimator for this case, if (FV) prevails, is not given by this formula and is, in fact, inconsistent [see *Schneeweiss*, 1980b].

b) If the ratio $\lambda = \sigma_w^2 / \sigma_v^2$ is known and $\sigma_{vw} = 0$

$$\hat{\beta}_\lambda := \frac{1}{2s_{xy}} [s_y^2 - \lambda s_x^2 + \{4\lambda s_{xy}^2 + (s_y^2 - \lambda s_x^2)^2\}^{1/2}]$$

is consistent. $\hat{\beta}_\lambda$ is the ML estimator in both cases (FV) and (SV).

c) If an instrumental variable z_t is known, which is independent of all the (v_t, w_t) and which is asymptotically correlated with ξ, then

$$\hat{\beta}_{IV} := \frac{s_{yz}}{s_{xz}}$$

is consistent.

For all these estimators an asymptotic variance can be computed. It turns out that $\sqrt{T}(\hat{\beta} - \beta)$ converges in distribution to $N(0, V)$ where V depends on the estimator considered. Even for the inconsistent estimator $\hat{\beta}_{LS}$ an asymptotic variance exists, but the center of the normal distribution has to be taken at a value β^* different from β. In the (FV) case the center is $\beta^* := \beta s_\xi^2 / (s_\xi^2 + \sigma_v^2)$ and in the (SV) case it is $\beta^* := p \lim \hat{\beta}_{LS} = \beta(1 - \sigma_v^2 / \sigma_x^2)$. Thus in both cases $\sqrt{T}(\hat{\beta} - \beta^*) \to N(0, V)$ where again V depends on whether (FV) or (SV) prevails. The asymptotic variances are given in the following table. For simplicity it is assumed that the error variables v and w are uncorrelated normal, and for $\hat{\beta}_{LS}$ in the case of (SV) that ξ is normal.

$\sqrt{T}(\hat{\beta}-\beta)$	V	references
$\hat{\beta}_{LS}$ (FV)	$(\sigma_u^2/\sigma_\xi^2)(1-e) - \beta^2 e^2 (3 - 4e + 2e^2)$	*Schneeweiss* [1980a]
$\hat{\beta}_{LS}$ (SV)	$(\sigma_u^2/\sigma_\xi^2)(1-e) - \beta^2 e^2$	*Rothenberg* [1972]
$\hat{\beta}_{IV}$ (Opt)	σ_u^2/σ_ξ^2	*Sargan* [1958]
$\hat{\beta}_\lambda$	$(\sigma_u^2/\sigma_\xi^2)/(1-e) - \beta^2 e^2/(1-e)^2$	*Malinvaud* [1966]
$\hat{\beta}_{EV}$	$(\sigma_u^2/\sigma_\xi^2)/(1-e) + \beta^2 e^2/(1-e)^2$	*Schneeweiss* [1976]
	$e := \sigma_v^2 / \sigma_x^2$	

$\hat{\beta}_{IV}$ (Opt) is an optimal IV estimator, where the instrumental variable z has maximum asymptotic correlation with ξ, i.e. where $\rho_{\xi z} := p\lim r_{\xi z} = \pm 1$. More generally, the asymptotic variance for any $\hat{\beta}_{IV}$ is $V = (\sigma_u^2/\sigma_\xi^2)/\rho_{\xi z}^2$. The estimators are arranged in the order of increasing V. Note that although all asymptotic variances differ from each other, they are all equal to σ_u^2/σ_ξ^2 if terms of higher order in σ_u^2/σ_ξ^2 or σ_v^2/σ_x^2 are neglected.

3. ML Estimation in a Model with Trend

When ξ follows a trend, i.e. when (3) is assumed, $\hat{\beta}_{LS}$ is consistent.

There is also a natural competitive estimator, viz. the IV estimator with instrumental variable t, i.e.

$$\hat{\beta}_{\mathrm{IV}} := \frac{s_{yt}}{s_{xt}},$$

which is consistent, too, but may have different sampling properties. In what follows we want to compare the large (and medium size) sample properties of $\hat{\beta}_{\mathrm{LS}}$ and $\hat{\beta}_{\mathrm{IV}}$.

When σ_ν^2 is known we can also construct $\hat{\beta}_{\mathrm{EV}}$ and investigate its properties as well. In the same way $\hat{\beta}_\lambda$ could be studied, but we shall restrict our investigations to $\hat{\beta}_{\mathrm{EV}}$ as an example of an estimator with additional information. Note that $\hat{\beta}_{\mathrm{LS}}$ and $\hat{\beta}_{\mathrm{IV}}$ do not use any additional information.

To start with, we shall find the ML estimator[5]) for the parameters α, β, and the error variances for our model (1,3).

(1) and (3) can be reformulated as

$$\begin{aligned} x_t &= a + bt + \upsilon_t \\ y_t &= c + dt + \omega_t \end{aligned} \tag{7}$$

with

$$\begin{aligned} \upsilon_t &:= \epsilon_t + \nu_t \\ \omega_t &:= \beta\epsilon_t + w_t \end{aligned} \tag{8}$$

and

$$\begin{aligned} c &:= \alpha + \beta a \\ d &:= \beta b . \end{aligned} \tag{9}$$

Let the covariance matrix of (υ_t, ω_t) be denoted by Ω, then

$$\Omega = \begin{pmatrix} \sigma_\epsilon^2 + \sigma_\nu^2 & \beta\sigma_\epsilon^2 + \sigma_{\nu w} \\ \beta\sigma_\epsilon^2 + \sigma_{\nu w} & \beta^2\sigma_\epsilon^2 + \sigma_w^2 \end{pmatrix}.$$

We also introduce the matrix

$$W = \begin{pmatrix} \overline{\upsilon^2} & \overline{\upsilon\omega} \\ \overline{\omega\upsilon} & \overline{\omega^2} \end{pmatrix},$$

where υ and ω are to be computed from (7) and where the bar denotes the arithmetic mean of the variable underneath. The log likelihood function (apart from a constant) is

---

[5]) See also *Goldberger* [1972] for the more general case of instrumental variables.

$$\log L = -\frac{T}{2}\log|\Omega| - \frac{T}{2}\operatorname{tr}(\Omega^{-1}W).$$

If there are no restrictions imposed on the elements of Ω the likelihood function can be maximized with respect to a, b, c, d conditional on Ω. Setting the derivative of $\log L$ with respect to a, b, c, d equal to zero we get the ML estimates

$$\hat{a} = \bar{x} - \hat{b}\bar{t}, \quad \hat{b} = s_{xt}/s_t^2$$
$$\hat{c} = \bar{y} - \hat{d}\bar{t}, \quad \hat{d} = s_{yt}/s_t^2 \tag{10}$$

and from these by using (19)

$$\hat{\alpha} = \bar{y} - \hat{\beta}\bar{x}$$
$$\hat{\beta} = s_{yt}/s_{xt} = \hat{\beta}_{\mathrm{IV}}. \tag{11}$$

Thus $\hat{\beta}_{\mathrm{IV}}$ is the ML estimate of β for the present model.

By setting $\partial \log L/\partial\Omega = 0$ we finally get

$$\hat{\Omega} = \hat{W}, \tag{12}$$

where $\hat{W}$ is the matrix W with a, b, c, d replaced by their ML estimates.

We can derive the same ML estimates (11) when certain restrictions are imposed on the elements of Ω, as e.g. $\sigma_{vw} = 0$, or $\sigma_\epsilon^2 = 0$, or $\sigma_{vw} = \sigma_\epsilon^2 = 0$, or when σ_v^2 is given a priori. In all these cases $\hat{\beta}_{\mathrm{IV}}$ is the ML estimate of β. (Note, however, that these estimates do not always take into account that the variances in $\hat{\Omega}$ should be non-negative. Thus, strictly speaking, they are not ML estimators in all cases.[6]) But since for $T \to \infty$ $\hat{\Omega}$ will converge to the true matrix Ω with nonnegative variances $\sigma_\epsilon^2, \sigma_v^2, \sigma_w^2$, these estimators will be asymptotically equivalent to the true ML estimators. We may call the estimators (11) and (12) ML estimators in a wide sense.)

It therefore seems that $\hat{\beta}_{\mathrm{IV}}$ is the optimal choice of an estimator in the present model. In the next section we shall see how its asymptotic properties compare with those of $\hat{\beta}_{\mathrm{LS}}$ and $\hat{\beta}_{\mathrm{EV}}$.

4. Asymptotic Normality

In order to derive the asymptotic normality property of $\hat{\beta}_{\mathrm{LS}}$ we write (see (7))

$$\hat{\beta}_{\mathrm{LS}} - \beta = \frac{s_{xu}}{s_x^2} = \frac{b\, s_{tu} + s_{vu}}{b^2 s_t^2 + 2b\, s_{tv} + s_v^2} \tag{13}$$

[6]) *Leamer* [1978] studied the ML-estimator of β in the context of a normally distributed instrumental variable. See also *Fuller* [1977].

$$T^{3/2}\,(\hat\beta_{\mathrm{LS}}-\beta)=\left(\frac{T^{3/2}\,s_{tu}}{b\,s_t^2}+\frac{T^{3/2}\,s_{vu}}{b^2\,s_t^2}\right)/F \tag{14}$$

where $F := 1 + (2s_{tv})/(b\,s_t^2) + s_v^2/(b^2\,s_t^2)$ tends to 1 in probability with $T \to \infty$. The second term in the brackets tends to 0 in probability with $T \to \infty$, while the first term tends to a normal distribution. In fact, introducing the standardized variable $t^* = (t - \bar t)/s_t$ the first term can be written as

$$\frac{1}{b}\frac{T}{s_t}\sqrt{T}\,s_{t^*u}$$

where according to a central limit theorem [see e.g. *Schönfeld*, p. 183 or *Malinvaud*, Chap. 6] $\sqrt{T}\,s_{t^*u}$ converges in distribution to $N(0, \sigma_u^2)$ and where $\lim\,(T^2/s_t^2) = 12$, because

$$s_t^2 = \frac{T^2-1}{12}. \tag{15}$$

Thus we have the result:

$$T^{3/2}\,(\hat\beta_{\mathrm{LS}}-\beta)\xrightarrow[(T\to\infty)]{} N(0,\,12\sigma_u^2/b^2). \tag{16}$$

By similar arguments we can derive

$$T^{1/2}\,(\hat\alpha_{\mathrm{LS}}-\alpha)\xrightarrow[(T\to\infty)]{} N(0,\,4\sigma_u^2) \tag{17}$$

Apart from the factor b, these results are the same as those found for the estimators of the parameters of a linear trend [see *Schönfeld*, p. 200].

For $\hat\beta_{\mathrm{EV}}$ we have

$$\hat\beta_{\mathrm{EV}}-\beta=\frac{s_{xu}+\beta\sigma_v^2}{s_x^2-\sigma_v^2}=\frac{b\,s_{tu}+s_{vu}+\beta\sigma_v^2}{b^2 s_t^2+2b\,s_{tv}+s_v^2-\sigma_v^2} \tag{18}$$

and for $\hat\beta_{\mathrm{IV}}$

$$\hat\beta_{\mathrm{IV}}-\beta=\frac{s_{tu}}{s_{tx}}=\frac{s_{tu}}{b\,s_t^2+s_{tv}}. \tag{19}$$

It turns out that the estimators $\hat\beta_{\mathrm{IV}}$ and $\hat\beta_{\mathrm{EV}}$ have the same asymptotic distribution as $\hat\beta_{\mathrm{LS}}$, and the same is true for the estimators of α. Thus from the point of view of asymptotic theory we cannot distinguish between these estimators[7]).

---

[7]) Note that because of (15) the asymptotic variance of $\hat\beta$ as given in (16) corresponds to the term σ_u^2/σ_ξ^2 which was found to be the leading term of the asymptotic variance of the estimators considered in section 2.

5. Bias for Medium Sample Size

So differences in the estimators can only show up when the bias or the variance is investigated in terms of powers of $1/T$. In this section[8]) we want to expand the bias of the various estimators in powers of $1/T$. We start with β_{LS} and rewrite (13) as

$$\hat{\beta}_{LS} - \beta = \frac{1}{b^2 s_t}\left(b\, s_{t*u} + \frac{s_{vu}}{s_t}\right)\left(1 - \frac{2s_{t*v}}{b\, s_t} + O\left(\frac{1}{s_t^2}\right)\right)$$

$$= \frac{1}{b^2 s_t}\left(b\, s_{t*u} + \frac{s_{vu}}{s_t} - \frac{2s_{t*u}\, s_{t*v}}{s_t} + O\left(\frac{1}{s_t^2}\right)\right). \tag{20}$$

Here $O(1/s_t^2)$ means a series of terms of the form Π/s_t^p with $p \geqslant 2$ where Π is any product of the covariances s_{t*u}, s_{t*v}, s_{uv}, and $s_{vv} = s_v^2$. Any such product has an expectation which is bounded as $T \to \infty$:

$$E(\Pi) = O(1)$$

It follows that $E(\Pi/s_t^p) = O(1/T^p)$. Now $Es_{t*u} = 0$ and

$$E\, s_{vu} = (1 - 1/T)\, Evu = -\beta\sigma_v^2 + O(1/T). \tag{21}$$

Finally $E\, s_{t*u} s_{t*v} = O(1/T)$. Putting all this together, we find that

$$E(\hat{\beta}_{LS} - \beta) = -\frac{\beta\sigma_v^2}{b^2 s_t^2} + O\left(\frac{1}{T^3}\right) \tag{22}$$

or, using (15),

$$E(\hat{\beta}_{LS} - \beta) = -\frac{12\beta\sigma_v^2}{b^2 T^2} + O\left(\frac{1}{T^3}\right). \tag{23}$$

The first term of the bias in (23) corresponds to the bias given in (6).

We next consider $\hat{\beta}_{EV}$. From (18) we derive a similar expression as (20) with the only difference that s_{vu} is replaced by $s_{vu} + \beta\sigma_v^2$. But this difference is crucial, because now we get instead of (21)

$$E(s_{vu} + \beta\sigma_v^2) = -\beta\sigma_v^2 + \beta\sigma_v^2 = 0$$

and therefore

$$E(\hat{\beta}_{EV} - \beta) = O\left(\frac{1}{T^3}\right). \tag{24}$$

[8]) See also *Robertson* [1974] for a similar expansion. It should be noted that the resulting formulae for the bias are to be considered as giving the bias of a distribution that approximates the exact distribution of the estimator.

Last let us consider $\hat{\beta}_{IV}$. From (19) follows

$$\hat{\beta}_{IV} - \beta = \frac{1}{b\, s_t}\left(s_{t*u} - \frac{s_{t*u}\, s_{t*v}}{b\, s_t} + O\left(\frac{1}{s_t^2}\right)\right)$$

and

$$E\,(\hat{\beta}_{IV} - \beta) = O\left(\frac{1}{T^3}\right). \tag{25}$$

So here, at last, we can see a difference in the properties of the estimators: $\hat{\beta}_{LS}$ has a bias of order $1/T^2$ whereas $\hat{\beta}_{EV}$ and $\hat{\beta}_{IV}$ have bias of order $1/T^3$.

The bias of $\hat{\alpha}$ can be reduced to the bias of $\hat{\beta}$. For any of the estimators we have

$$\begin{aligned}\hat{\alpha} - \alpha &= \bar{u} - (\hat{\beta} - \beta)\,\bar{x}\\ &= \bar{u} - (\hat{\beta} - \beta)\,(a + b\bar{t} + \bar{v}).\end{aligned} \tag{26}$$

Now $E\bar{u} = 0, E\,(\hat{\beta} - \beta) = O\,(T^{-2})$, and $|\,E\,(\hat{\beta} - \beta)\,\bar{v}\,| \leqslant \{E\,(\hat{\beta} - \beta)^2\, E\bar{v}^2\}^{1/2} = = O\,(T^{-3/2})\,O\,(T^{-1/2}) = O\,(T^{-2})$. Therefore

$$E\,(\hat{\alpha} - \alpha) = -\frac{bT}{2}\,E\,(\hat{\beta} - \beta) + O\left(\frac{1}{T^2}\right). \tag{27}$$

Specializing to the various estimators we get

$$\begin{aligned} E\,(\hat{\alpha}_{LS} - \alpha) &= \frac{6\beta\sigma_v^2}{bT} + O\left(\frac{1}{T^2}\right)\\ E\,(\hat{\alpha}_{EV} - \alpha) &= O\left(\frac{1}{T^2}\right)\\ E\,(\hat{\alpha}_{IV} - \alpha) &= O\left(\frac{1}{T^2}\right). \end{aligned} \tag{28}$$

6. Summary of Results

The results are summarized in the following two tables:

β	Bias B	Variance V	B^2/V
LS	$-\frac{12\beta\sigma_v^2}{b^2T^2} + O\left(\frac{1}{T^3}\right)$	$\frac{12\sigma_u^2}{b^2T^3} + O\left(\frac{1}{T^4}\right)$	$\frac{12\sigma_v^2}{b^2T\,[1 + \sigma_w^2/(\beta^2\sigma_v^2)]} + O\left(\frac{1}{T^2}\right)$
EV	$O\left(\frac{1}{T^3}\right)$	–"–	$O\left(\frac{1}{T^3}\right)$
IV	$O\left(\frac{1}{T^3}\right)$	–"–	$O\left(\frac{1}{T^3}\right)$

The variance is found from the asymptotic distributions of the estimators (see (16), (17)). It can also be computed along similar lines as the bias was derived. Actually by expanding

α	Bias B	Variance V	B^2/V
LS	$\frac{6\beta\sigma_v^2}{bT}+O\left(\frac{1}{T^2}\right)$	$\frac{4\sigma_u^2}{T}+O\left(\frac{1}{T^2}\right)$	$\frac{9\sigma_v^2}{b^2T[1+\sigma_w^2/(\beta^2\sigma_v^2)]}+O\left(\frac{1}{T^2}\right)$
EV	$O\left(\frac{1}{T^2}\right)$	–"–	$O\left(\frac{1}{T^3}\right)$
IV	$O\left(\frac{1}{T^2}\right)$	–"–	$O\left(\frac{1}{T^3}\right)$

to higher powers of $1/T$ it can be shown that the variance of $\hat{\beta}$ is correct up to terms of order $1/T^5$ for all three estimators, but we shall not follow this up here[9]). The last column of each table gives the square of the ratio of bias to standard deviation. It will be argued in the next section that this ratio should be of some adequate size if one wants to be able to detect the bias empirically. In computing the ratio the following relation was used

$$\sigma_u^2 = \sigma_w^2 + \beta^2\sigma_v^2$$

which follows from (5).

7. Shifts in the Regression Line

The asymptotic bias (6) of $\hat{\beta}_{LS}$ in the (SV) case shows up empirically if two samples of data (x_t, y_t) of sufficient size which differ in their values of $\bar{x}$ are compared. If we compute a regression line for each sample by least squares, the estimates of β will be attenuated according to (6), and because of the different $\bar{x}$ values this will result in a shift of one regression line with regard to the other line (see figure 1).

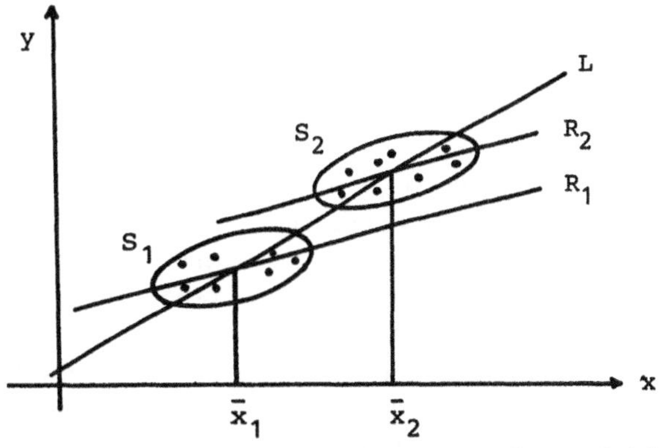

Fig. 1: Shifts in estimated regression lines: cross section samples. (S_i: sample i, R_i: regression line estimated from sample S_i, L: structural line $\eta = \alpha + \beta\xi$).

[9]) *Richardson/Wu* [1970] have derived exact formulae for the bias and variance of $\hat{\beta}_{LS}$ for the cases (FV) and (SV). In principle these formulae could be used to compute the bias and variance of $\hat{\beta}_{LS}$ for specific values of T and the other parameters. Richardson/Wu also give expansions of $B(\hat{\beta}_{LS})$ and $V(\hat{\beta}_{LS})$ in terms of powers of $1/T$, but with s_ξ^2 fixed or at least bounded. These expansions cannot be used in the present context.

Friedman's consumption function is a typical example of a regression with errors in the variables. The shift in regression lines can be detected indeed if cross section estimates are compared for different points of time [see *Friedman*].

In comparing cross section estimates the asymptotic theory of section 2 is appropriate. If however one tries to explain occasional shifts of the consumption function in a time series context one has to rely on the asymptotic theory of sections 4 to 6. This theory first of all says that $\hat{\beta}_{LS}$ is consistent, and consequently for very large T it should not be possible to detect a bias at all. A closer inspection of the estimators, as was carried out in section 5, reveals that there is at least a possibility for the shift to show up if the sample size T is not too large, but rather of a medium size. Indeed the formulae (23) and (28) for the bias were constructed so that they would cover the case of a medium sample size.

There is a fair chance for the bias to show up if the bias is approximately equal to the standard deviation. But if we want to be (almost) sure that the bias can be detected it must be of a size at least twice the standard deviation. Therefore we use as a criterion for a detectable bias the inequality.

$$B^2/V > 4. \tag{29}$$

According to the tables in section 6 the ratio B^2/V is much the same for $\hat{\beta}$ and $\hat{\alpha}$. (29) is satisfied for $\hat{\beta}_{LS}$ if

$$\sigma_v^2 \geqslant \frac{Tb^2}{6} + \left\{ \frac{Tb^2 \sigma_w^2}{3\beta^2} + \left(\frac{Tb^2}{6} \right)^2 \right\}^{1/2} \approx \frac{Tb^2}{3}, \tag{30}$$

it is approximately satisfied if

$$\sigma_v > \sqrt{\frac{T}{3}}\, b. \tag{31}$$

For $\hat{\alpha}$ the corresponding inequality is approximately

$$\sigma_v > \frac{2}{3} \sqrt{T}\, b.$$

Suppose $T = 30$, this means that the standard error σ_v should be about three times (or for $\hat{\alpha}$ three to four times) the average distance of consecutive ξ_t's. So only when the error variance of the exogenous variable is very large with respect to the average increase of this variable can one be sure to detect the bias of $\hat{\beta}_{LS}$ or of $\hat{\alpha}_{LS}$. In the opinion of the author, this means that structural shifts that are observed in real data regression lines are probably of a specific origin (like missing variables or changing behaviour of agents) rather than that they are the outflow of errors in the variables.

Of course the chance of detecting the bias is enhanced to some degree if two samples are compared that belong to time intervals which are very far apart. In order to study this situation more closely we change the model (1,3) by taking a to depend on the sample size in the sense that

$$a = (k-1)\, b\, \bar{t} + a'. \tag{32}$$

The modified model reduces to the one studied before if $k = 1$. For $k > 1$ the effect of (32) is that ξ_1, the first value of the ξ_t series, is placed at a larger distance from the origin O the greater the sample size. This will not change the properties of $\hat{\beta}$ but will change those of $\hat{\alpha}$. In fact by repeating former arguments and computations one can show that

$$B(\hat{\alpha}_{\mathrm{LS}}) = E(\hat{\alpha}_{\mathrm{LS}} - \alpha) = \frac{6\beta\sigma_v^2 k}{bT} + O\left(\frac{1}{T^2}\right) \tag{33}$$

$$V(\hat{\alpha}_{\mathrm{LS}}) = \frac{\sigma_u^2}{T}(1 + 3k^2) + O\left(\frac{1}{T^2}\right). \tag{34}$$

The same formula holds for the variance of $\hat{\alpha}_{\mathrm{EV}}$ and $\hat{\alpha}_{\mathrm{IV}}$, whereas the bias of $\hat{\alpha}_{\mathrm{EV}}$ and of $\hat{\alpha}_{\mathrm{IV}}$ is $O(1/T^2)$.

The ratio of the squared bias to the variance for $\hat{\alpha}_{\mathrm{LS}}$ is

$$B^2/V = \frac{12\sigma_v^2}{b^2 T(1 + \sigma_w^2/(\beta^2\sigma_v^2))(1 + 1/(3k^2))} + O\left(\frac{1}{T^2}\right). \tag{35}$$

It differs from the ratio for $\hat{\beta}$ found before by the factor $(1 + 1/(3k^2))^{-1}$, which for $k \geqslant 1$ increases from 3/4 to 1, which means that even for very large k there will – as before – hardly be any noticeable bias in $\hat{\alpha}$ unless σ_v^2 is extremely large.

The following figure depicts the situation of two samples of equal size being apart by a time interval of the same size, a situation, which corresponds to $k = 2$.

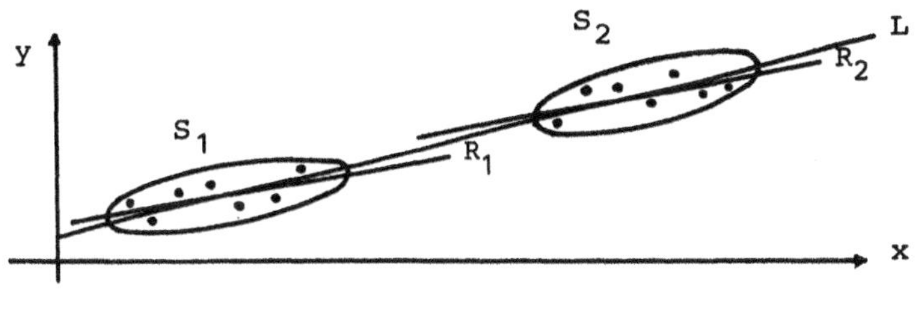

Fig. 2: Shifts in estimated regression lines: time series samples

References

Dolby, G.R.: The ultrastructural relation: A synthesis of the functional and structural relations. Biometrika **63**, 1976, 39–50.

Friedman, M.: A Theory of the Consumption Function. Princeton 1957.

Fuller, W.A.: Some properties of a modification of the limited information estimator. Econometrica **45**, 1977, 939–954.

Goldberger, A.S.: Maximum-Likelihood estimation of regressions containing unobservable independent variables. Int. Ec. Rev. **13**, 1972.

Johnston, J.: Econometric Methods. 1-st ed., New York–San Francisco-Toronto–London 1963.

Kendall, M.G., and *A. Stuart*: The Advanced Theory of Statistics. Vol. 2, 4th ed. London 1979.

Leamer, E.E.: Least-squares versus instrumental variables estimation in a simple errors in variables model. Econometrica **46**, 1978, 961–968.

Madansky, A.: The fitting of straight lines when both variables are subject to error. Journ. Am. Stat. Ass. **54**, 1959, 173–205.

Malinvaud, E.: Statistical Methods of Econometrics. 3rd ed. Amsterdam 1979.

Moran, P.A.P.: Estimating structural and functional relationships. Journ. Multivariate Analysis **1**, 1971, 232–255.

Richardson, D.H., and *De-min, Wu*: Least squares and grouping method estimators in the errors in variables model. Journ. Am. Stat. Ass. **65**, 1970, 724–748.

Robertson, C.A.: Large-sample theory for the linear structural relation. Biometrika **61**, 1974, 353–359.

Rothenberg, T.J.: The asymptotic distribution of the least squares estimator in the error in variables model. mimeo, 1972.

Sargan, J.D.: The estimation of economic relationships using instrumental variables. Econometrica **26**, 1958, 393–415.

Schneeweiß, H.: Consistent estimation of regression with errors in the variables. Metrika **23**, 1976, 101–115.

–: Different asymptotic variances for the same estimator in a regression with errors in the variables. Methods of Operations Research **36**, 1980a, 249–269.

–: Modelle mit Fehlern in den Variablen. Methods of Operations Research **37**, 1980b, 41–77.

Schönfeld, P.: Methoden der Ökonometrie. Vol. 1: Lineare Regressionsmodelle. Berlin–Frankfurt 1969.

Games, Economic Dynamics, and Time Series Analysis. 1982 ©Physica-Verlag, Wien–Würzburg

Econometric Specification Analysis – An Application to the Aggregate Demand for Money in the Netherlands

By *H.J. Blommestein* and *F.C. Palm*, Amsterdam[1])[2])

1. Introduction

Econometric analysis of money market relationships has nowadays its own tradition in applied econometrics. In order to get a flavour of the results that are available, the reader can look at the summary and the list of references given by *Fase/Kuné* [1974], [1975] and by *Laidler* [1969]. Among the money market equations, the demand function has received special attention by econometricians, perhaps partly because the specification of a money demand function requires less institutional knowledge than e.g. the specification of a money supply equation. Many of the recent empirical studies in econometrics can be characterized as attempts to statistically verify and test some of the assumptions underlying the econometric model. The demand for money function is not an exception. The recent study by *Hendry/Mizon* [1978] illustrates how one can ascertain an empirically verified money demand equation.

Our aim in this paper is similar, that is, we examine the validity and reliability of some assumptions underlying an econometric model. The starting point is an aggregate demand function for money specified and estimated by *Fase/Kuné* [1974] using Dutch quarterly data for the period 1952–1971. This model consists of a demand for money equation explaining desired holding of money by expected income and price level, an interest rate and a business cycle indicator. The assumptions of partial adjustment of nominal money balances to desired ones and of adaptive expectations for the real income and price variables complete the model. One interesting feature of the model is that the authors incorporate assumptions which are plausible from the point of view of economic theory. Nevertheless, it is worthwhile to investigate whether the specification of this theoretically meaningful model is in agreement with the information in the data. Therefore, we shall formally test several assumptions concerning the lag structure, the disturbance serial correlations and the restrictions on the structural parameters, using the same data as *Fase/Kuné* [1974]. We shall also investigate whether the model remains valid for the

[1]) *F. Palm*, Free University of Amsterdam, De Boelelaan 1105, NL-1007 MC Amsterdam.

[2]) The authors are indebted to Professor M.M.G. Fase, De Nederlandsche Bank, who has kindly provided them with the data used in this study and with helpful comments on a preliminary version of this paper, to Professors D.F. Hendry, G.E. Mizon and H. Visser for the useful suggestions. Some of the work reported in this paper was done by the second author during the Warwick Summer Workshop 1979.

years 1972–1976. In this way, we hope to get more insight into what we consider as being one of the major building-blocks of a monetary model and to end up with a specification that is theoretically meaningful and not contradicted by the information in the data.

In a recent study of the demand for money in the EEC countries, *Den Butter/Fase* [1979] follow a similar approach, by giving particular attention to the dynamic specification and the properties of the disturbances.

From a methodological point of view, one would ideally like to start the statistical investigation with a fully specified econometric model. In this way, the problem of "measurement without theroy" [see *Koopmans*] is avoided and the statistical properties of the econometric methods used can be ascertained. However as economic theory, especially on an aggregate level, does not yield a fully specified econometric model, it is necessary to make ad-hoc assumptions (e.g. the correlation properties of the disturbances). Empirical verification of some of these assumptions dominates the strategy of looking for escape in somewhat shaky and non-tested suppositions. Thereby we recognize the possibility that the main feature of the final model specification may be that of tracing the statistical regularities in the data.

In the approach adopted in this paper, we start with a fairly general specification, assumed to be invariant wherein the variables are included on grounds of considerations from economic theory and the structural equations of the model represent economic laws. Although in this paper we basically stick to a single equation model, the approach can be applied to a general linear simultaneous equation model (SEM). However, the SEM requires additional carefulness with respect to the choice of a parametrization and its implications for the estimation and testing procedures to be used. The models considered in this paper are log-linear in the variables. Any functional form is an approximation of the reality and may strongly influence the results of the empirical analysis. Of course, the functional form of a model can be tested. Recently, much work on comparing alternative functional forms has been done [see e.g. *Pesaran/Deaton*] and it is to be expected that the choice of the functional form will get growing attention in applied econometrics. With respect to the non-linearity in the variables, we should like to state that we agree with *Morgenstern* [1963, p. 94] that "Non-linearity is a great complication and is, therefore, best avoided as much as possible."

The dynamics of the starting model, i.e. the number of lags of the endogenous and exogenous variables, should be specified whenever possible on the basis of theoretical considerations. For instance, the partial adjustment and adaptive expectations' schemes determine entirely the dynamics of the model by *Fase/Kuné* [1974]. It will often be advisable to make the lag structure for the endogenous and exogenous variables in the starting model sufficiently large so as to guarantee the invariance of the maintained hypothesis over the sample period and to make the white noise assumption of the disturbances appropriate. This facilitates the estimation, testing and interpretation of the model. The white noise assumption on the disturbances of the starting model should be tested, using misspecification tests based on the residual autocorrelations, such as e.g. the Box-Pierce test or the Lagrange multiplier test. If the white noise assumption is rejected, the number of lags has to be increased or the possible autocorrelation in the disturbances has to be modelled explicitly (e.g. a moving average disturbance term). Several authors, see e.g. *Hendry/Mizon* [1978], *Sims* [1980] among others, advocate, partly for different reasons, to start with a general model. A major objective is to minimize the risk of misspecification due to the exclusion of variables and/or sufficiently long lags when there is little knowledge about the correct specification.

In the next step, overidentifying restrictions on the parameters of the model will be tested. One kind of restrictions are the common factor restrictions proposed by *Sargan* [1975] and tested by *Hendry/Mizon* [1978], [1980]. The advantage of this kind of restrictions is that they imply a model with simplified dynamics and autoregressive disturbances which can be easily estimated. Although restrictions such as the common factors lead to a statistically simplified model, the economic interpretation of the parameters under the restrictions is not always straightforward. Therefore, we prefer to consider first restrictions which have an interpretation in terms of economic behaviour. Restrictions implied by expectation schemes, e.g. adaptive expectations [see *Fase/Kuné*, 1974], the long run properties of the model [see e.g. *Davidson* et al.], the direction of causality will have to be investigated in many applications. In doing so, it will usually not be possible to formulate the tests of these restrictions as a uniquely ordered nest of tests as is done in the common factor approach. Therefore, the statistical properties of the sequence of tests applied to the initial model are not easily established, although those of a test in the sequence taken separately are known – at least in large samples.

Restrictions which are not rejected and which have a plausible ecnomic interpretation are imposed on the parameters of the model. Then the restricted model is checked using criteria such as its goodness of fit, the significance and plausibility of the restricted parameter estimates, the outcome of misspecification tests applied to the residuals, the stability of the specification over subperiods and the predictive performance. The implications of the dynamic specification for the properties of the transfer function form of a multi-equation linear model and of the final equations of a model in which the exogenous variables have an autoregressive-integrated-moving average representation have to be checked along the lines proposed by *Zellner/Palm* [1974] and by *Wallis* [1977] among others. Valuable insight can be obtained by trying to explain the results found by other investigators using similar data [see e.g. *Davidson* et al.]. In this way, we hope to end up with a model that is satisfactory from a theoretical point of view and in accordance with the information in the data.

In this context, it is important to emphasize what *Morgenstern* [1963, 94–95] writes about the process of modelling and the sources of errors inherent in it:

> "It must be understood that any such process, whatever its ultimate possibility, involves four steps: (1) the initial data, (2) the model, (3) the computations, and (4) the comparison of the numerical results with reality. Each one of them has its own sources of errors: the initial data are available only with a certain degree of accuracy (which it may be impossible to determine), the model is an idealization of reality, the computations can produce errors that are added to those existing at the start. The numerical result with all its cumulative errors will be compared with, and "checked" against, a "reality" that is again only revealed up to an (unknown) error factor. This is then hopefully called "verification"."

The four types of errors described by Morgenstern possibly affect the outcome of the specification analysis. Also, we should not expect the data to discriminate well between hypotheses which are not formulated with sufficient sharpness. On the other hand, testing of the model specification is possible to the extent that the empirical results are not falsified by errors of measurement in the data used to estimate the model or to check its predictive performance. The presence of seasonals or incorrect elimination of them may also have serious consequences for the modelling process. Treating ordinal data as if they were cardinal measurement can lead to difficulties when testing restrictions on the model and cause problems with the interpretation of the results of the specification analysis. While having these possibilities in mind, we shall analyse a demand for money function along the lines described above, using the same data as *Fase/Kuné* [1974].

In Section 2, we present the model used by *Fase/Kuné* [1974] and discuss the underlying assumptions. Section 3 is devoted to the results of the econometric analysis of the model for the period 1952–76. We report results on estimation, on tests of theoretically meaningful restrictions and on residual analysis. Finally, in Section 4 we give the major conclusions of our analysis and point of problems that will be analysed in future work.

2. A Model for the Aggregate Demand for Money in the Netherlands

Fase/Kuné [1974], hereafter F & K, have specified and estimated several models for the demand for money. The most general specification in their study will be presented here. In order to facilitate the interpretation of their model, we rewrite it as follows (all variables are in natural logarithm)

$$M_t^* = \alpha_0 + \alpha_1 Y_{t+1}^* + \alpha_2 R_t + \alpha_3 P_{t+1}^* + \alpha_4 C_t \tag{2.1}$$

where

M_t^* = desired amount of liquidities (nominal) in period t

Y_{t+1}^* = expected income for period $t+1$, with the expectations formed in period t

R_t = an interest rate

P_{t+1}^* = the expected price level for period $t+1$

C_t = a business cycle indicator in period t.

For the unobservable variables M^*, Y^*, and P^*, F & K postulate a partial adjustment equation for M_t^*

$$M_t - M_{t-1} = \theta(M_t^* - M_{t-1}), \qquad 0 < \theta \leqslant 1, \tag{2.2}$$

and an adaptive expectations' mechanism for Y^* and P^*, which we rewrite as

$$Y_{t+1}^* - Y_t^* = \lambda(Y_t - Y_t^*), \qquad 0 < \lambda \leqslant 1, \tag{2.3}$$

and

$$P_{t+1}^* - P_t^* = \kappa(P_t - P_t^*), \qquad 0 < \kappa \leqslant 1. \tag{2.4}$$

We can write the expressions (2.2), (2.3) and (2.4) using the lag operator L, defined as $Lx_t = x_{t-1}$,

$$\theta M_t^* = M_t - (1-\theta) L M_t \tag{2.5}$$

$$Y^*_{t+1} = \lambda \sum_{i=0}^{\infty} (1-\lambda)^i L^i Y_t = \frac{\lambda Y_t}{1-(1-\lambda)L} \tag{2.6}$$

$$P^*_{t+1} = \kappa \sum_{i=0}^{\infty} (1-\kappa)^i L^i P_t = \frac{\kappa P_t}{1-(1-\kappa)L} \tag{2.7}$$

and substitute the results for the unobserved variables in (2.1), which yields

$$M_t = (1-\theta) L M_t + \alpha_0\theta + \frac{\alpha_1\theta\lambda Y_t}{1-(1-\lambda)L} + \alpha_2\theta R_t + \frac{\alpha_3\theta\kappa P_t}{1-(1-\kappa)L} + \alpha_4\theta C_t. \tag{2.8}$$

Premultiplying expression (2.8) by the polynomials in L in the denominator gives us the final expression, which F & K write as

$$\widetilde{M}_t = \alpha_0\theta\lambda\kappa + (1-\theta)\widetilde{M}_{t-1} + \alpha_1\theta\lambda Y'_t + \alpha_2\theta\widetilde{R}_t + \alpha_3\theta\kappa P'_t + \alpha_4\theta\,\widetilde{C}_t, \tag{2.9}$$

where a variable (say X_t) with a (~) is defined as

$$\widetilde{X}_t = [1-(1-\lambda)L][1-(1-\kappa)L]X_t,$$

$$Y'_t = [1-(1-\kappa)L]\,Y_t \text{ and } P'_t = [1-(1-\lambda)L]P_t. \tag{2.10}$$

Finally F & K add a disturbance term u_t to the equation (2.9). They implicitly assume that u_t has expectation zero, constant variance, zero serial correlations, an assumption which they relax later on in favour of a first order autoregressive process for u_t, and that the disturbance and the explanatory variables in (2.9) are independent.

At this stage, the model deserves some comments.

1) Along with many authors, F & K assume that the model is log-linear. Economic theory has little to say about the functional form of a demand for money equation. In the present study we assume a log-linear functional form, an assumption that could be formally tested.
2) Economic theory of the demand for money generally explains the demand for real balances [see e.g. *Friedman*]. F & K specify their relationship in terms of nominal balances. Provided the price variable measuring the real value of money is predetermined, we can transform the model into a relationship for real balances without affecting the statistical properties of the model. *Den Butter/Fase* [1979] investigate demand functions for the nominal and real money balances in EEC countries and conclude that the latter are to be preferred – for empirical reasons – to the results for nominal balances.
3) F & K analyse the specification (2.9) as a single regression equation. Therefore, identification and simultaneity are only incidentally considered. Within the framework of the monetary approach to balance of payments [see e.g. *Johnson*], one can substantiate the assumption of independence between the explanatory variables in (2.9) and the disturbance term. Under a regime of fixed exchange rates, a small country's price and interest rate levels are assumed to be closely related to world prices and interest rates

and therefore predetermined. Changes in the real sector, e.g. in real income and the business cycle indicator C_t in (2.9), are assumed to be exogenous to the monetary sector, while the supply of money is instantaneously adjusted to the money demand, implying that $\theta = 1$. The sample used by F & K largely covers a period of fixed exchange rates. The transition to flexible exchange rates implies a structural change and offers a possible explanation as to why the model F & K does not necessarily remain valid for the recent years. The assumptions made in the monetary approach to the balance of payments determine the direction of the causality in the money demand function and give theoretical support to considering the money demand function as a reduced form and also as a transfer function equation.

4) In a final stage, the disturbance term is added to equation (2.9). Assuming that one or several of the behavioural equations (2.1) – (2.4) are stochastic would lead to serially correlated disturbances in the final expression (2.9), so that the correlations of the disturbances would be functions of the structural parameters. In any case, estimation and statistical testing in the presence of serial error correlations and lagged endogenous variables require special carefulness, a point of which Fase/Kuné are also aware. In the next section we shall pay attention to the specification of the disturbances.

5) The specification of the model (2.1) – (2.4) implies six restrictions on the parameters of equation (2.9). We can write equation (2.9) as a regression equation with 13 explanatory variables

$$\begin{aligned} M_t &= \beta_0 + \beta_1 M_{t-1} + \beta_2 M_{t-2} + \beta_3 M_{t-3} + \beta_4 Y_t + \beta_5 Y_{t-1} + \beta_6 R_t \\ &+ \beta_7 R_{t-1} + \beta_8 R_{t-2} + \beta_9 P_t + \beta_{10} P_{t-1} + \beta_{11} C_t + \beta_{12} C_{t-1} \\ &+ \beta_{13} C_{t-2} + u_t \end{aligned} \tag{2.11}$$

where the 14 parameters β_i are assumed to be nonlinear functions of the 8 structural coefficients $\alpha_0, \alpha_1, \ldots, \alpha_4, \theta, \lambda$ and κ.

$$\underset{14\times 1}{\beta} = \begin{bmatrix} \beta_0 \\ \beta_1 \\ \beta_2 \\ \beta_3 \\ \beta_4 \\ \beta_5 \\ \beta_6 \\ \beta_7 \\ \beta_8 \\ \beta_9 \\ \beta_{10} \\ \beta_{11} \\ \beta_{12} \\ \beta_{13} \end{bmatrix} = \begin{bmatrix} \alpha_0 \theta \lambda \kappa \\ 3 - \kappa - \lambda - \theta \\ -(1-\kappa)(1-\lambda) - (2-\kappa-\lambda)(1-\theta) \\ (1-\lambda)(1-\kappa)(1-\theta) \\ \alpha_1 \theta \lambda \\ -\alpha_1 \theta \lambda (1-\kappa) \\ \alpha_2 \theta \\ -\alpha_2 \theta (2-\kappa-\lambda) \\ \alpha_2 \theta (1-\kappa)(1-\lambda) \\ \alpha_3 \theta \kappa \\ -\alpha_3 \theta \kappa (1-\lambda) \\ \alpha_4 \theta \\ -\alpha_4 \theta (2-\lambda-\kappa) \\ \alpha_4 \theta (1-\lambda)(1-\kappa) \end{bmatrix} . \tag{2.12}$$

This implies 6 restrictions on the β_i's written as

$$\underset{6\times 1}{\phi(\beta)} = \begin{bmatrix} \beta_{13}\beta_6 - \beta_8\beta_{11} \\ \beta_{11}\beta_7 - \beta_6\beta_{12} \\ \beta_{10}\beta_4\beta_{11} + \beta_5\beta_9\beta_{11} - \beta_9\beta_4\beta_{12} \\ \beta_3\beta_6\beta_7 - \beta_2\beta_6\beta_8 - \beta_8^2 \\ \beta_4\beta_8\beta_9 - \beta_5\beta_6\beta_{10} \\ \beta_1\beta_9\beta_4\beta_8 + \beta_{10}\beta_4\beta_8 + \beta_5\beta_9\beta_8 - \beta_3\beta_6\beta_4\beta_9 \end{bmatrix} = 0 \tag{2.13}$$

where ϕ is a 6×1 vector of implicit functions of the β_i's. F & K choose several pairs of values for λ and κ.
For each pair, they compute the variables $\widetilde{M}_t, \widetilde{R}_t, \widetilde{C}_t, Y'_t$ and P'_t defined in (2.9) and regress $\widetilde{M}_t$ on the four remaining variables. As can be seen from (2.9), there is a one-to-one relationship between the coefficients of this linear regression equation and the structural parameters $\alpha_0, \ldots, \alpha_4, \theta$. In this way, F & K impose the restrictions (2.13) on the β_i's in (2.11) for given values of λ and κ. In the next section we shall investigate which values for λ and κ maximize the likelihood function under normally distributed disturbances and fixed initial values. For the model (2.9), maximizing the likelihood function is equivalent to maximizing the R^2. We shall also test the set of restrictions (2.13) imposed by F & K on their model. The assumption of normally distributed disturbances, which we do not test in this paper, is handy when testing for restrictions and for mis-specification in an econometric model. Furthermore, due to the presence of the lagged endogenous variable and other stochastic regressors, we have to rely on the asymptotic distributions of the test statistics to be used in the next section.

3. Results of the Empirical Analysis

In this section we present some estimation results of the F & K model (2.9) and its unrestricted version (2.11), and analyse the results in the light of the expected sign, the significance of the parameters, the stability of the parameter estimates over the sample period and the values of the elasticities. We test the restrictions formulated in (2.13) and analyse the residuals of the models (2.9) and (2.11) with the aim to empirically validate the demand function for money.

F & K assign a priori values to the parameters λ and κ, and make a final choice on the basis of two selection criteria, maximizing R^2 and a price elasticity of about one. This procedure leads to the values $\lambda = \kappa = .5$. Estimation results of the model (2.9) for $\lambda = \kappa = .5$ by OLS using seasonally adjusted data (except for the interest rate) are reported in Table 1. The figures between brackets are t-values (in absolute value). The estimate of the constant in model 1 differs from the result reported by *Fase/Kuné* [1974]. This is due to a different choice of units. For the period 1952–76, III the model has been estimated by *Blommestein/van Dijk* [1978] (see model 3 in Table 1). We also report estimates for the period 1972–76, III (see model 2). The long-term elasticities reported in Table 1 measure the percentage variation in equilibrium money holdings with respect to a percentage variation in an exogenous variable. The equilibrium situation in a stationary economy is characterized by the equality of realized values to desired and expected values, i.e. $M_t = M_t^*$, $Y_t = Y_t^*$ and $P_t = P_t^*$.

Period	λ	κ	constant	$\tilde{M}_{t-1}$	Y'_t	$\tilde{R}_t$	P'_t	$\tilde{C}_t$	D.W.	R^2	DF	$\ln L$	$\hat{\alpha}_1$	$\hat{\alpha}_2$	$\hat{\alpha}_3$	nr.
1952, I – 1971, IV	.5	.5	–.20 (1.88)	.69 (8.70)	.13 (2.41)	.06 (1.68)	.17 (2.26)	.03 (2.72)	2.31	.99	71	248.1	.84	–.20	1.09	1
1952, I – 1971, IV	.9	.7	–.31 (2.28)	.91 (23.2)	.08 (1.75)	–.04 (1.95)	.09 (1.67)	.02 (3.25)	1.92	.99	71	254.7	1.03	–.46	.14	1'
1972, I – 1976, III	.5	.5	1.14 (1.50)	.64 (3.64)	–.30 (1.51)	0.93 (1.77)	.53 (3.53)	–.24 (2.42)	1.5	.96	12	59.4	–1.66	2.55	2.94	2
1952, I – 1976, III	.5	.5	.02 (.23)	.68 (7.91)	.06 (1.5)	.02 (.48)	.22 (3.53)	.01 (.95)	2.41	.99	90	288.6	.37	.06	1.37	3

$\ln L$ = the value of the log-likelihood

Tab. 1: Ordinary least squares estimates of equation (2.9)

Period	Constant	M_{t-1}	M_{t-2}	M_{t-3}	Y_t	Y_{t-1}	R_t	R_{t-1}	R_{t-2}	P_t	P_{t-1}	C_t	C_{t-1}	C_{t-2}	D.W.	R^2	DF	$\ln L$	nr.
1952, I – 1971, IV	-.245 (1.43)	1.34 (10.2)	–.554 (2.7)	.162 (1.3)	.072 (1.1)	–.042 (.61)	–.073 (1.8)	.096 (1.6)	–.056 (1.3)	.054 (.48)	.064 (.62)	.006 (.37)	.006 (.24)	–.001 (.066)	2.02	.99	63	257.3	4
1952, I – 1976, III	–.160 (1.03)	1.35 (11.8)	–.443 (2.32)	–.004 (.03)	.039 (.55)	.020 (.28)	.0005 (.01)	.040 (.79)	–.047 (1.35)	–.011 (.09)	.126 (1.10)	–.009 (.49)	.016 (.55)	.004 (.21)	2.05	.99	82	299.4	5
1952, I – 1971, IV	.082 (.70)	1.423 (11.5)	–.603 (2.91)	.152 (1.18)	.044 (.68)	–.082 (1.27)	–.062 (1.55)	.086 (1.37)	–.034 (.82)	.044 (.40)	.080 (.79)				2.01	.99	66	253.3	6
1952, I – 1976, III	.055 (.51)	1.432 (12.8)	–.470 (2.43)	–.014 (.116)	.042 (.61)	–.038 (.58)	.007 (.19)	.034 (.66)	–.038 (1.16)	–.034 (.28)	.128 (1.13)				2.05	.99	85	295.7	7

Tab. 2: Ordinary least squares estimates of equation (2.11)

The parameters α_i in equation (2.9) are thus long-run elasticities. The compounded parameters in equation (2.9) are short-run elasticities. Conditionally on $\lambda = \kappa = .5$, F & K test for a structural change in model 1. The null hypothesis of no structural change could not be rejected by means of the Chow test: $F = .627$, $\nu_1 = 6$ and $\nu_2 = 65$, $T_1 = 38$ and $T_2 = 39$, $T_1 + T_2 = T$. F & K conclude that their model is satisfactory as the estimated coefficients are significant and have the expected sign, the price elasticity is close to one, R^2 is high and the D.W. value is acceptable. A D.W.-statistic close to two is not surprising as it is biased towards non-detection of possible autocorrelation in the disturbances when lagged endogenous variables are present. The Farrar-Glauber test indicates the presence of correlation among the explanatory variables, mainly caused by the significant dependence between $\widetilde{M}_{t-1}$ and P'_t. We take this as a warning that the data probably will not give us very precise information on the parameter values. According to the criteria used by F & K, the estimates for the periods 1952–76, III and 1972–76, III are quite unsatisfactory. For model 3 (Table 1) the coefficients of $\widetilde{R}_t$ and $\widetilde{C}_t$ are not significantly different from zero. The estimated coefficient of $\widetilde{R}_t$ does not have the expected sign, although the 90 per cent confidence interval for the coefficient of $\widetilde{R}_t$, [–.0468, .0868], covers negative values. For period 1972–76, III, the parameters are estimated with greater precision, but the estimates of the coefficients for $Y'_t, \widetilde{R}_t$ and $\widetilde{C}_t$ have a "wrong" sign. Also for the models 2 and 3, the Farrar-Glauber test indicates significant multicollinearity. The long-term price elasticity α_3 does not differ significantly from one. An estimate of the large sample variance of $\hat{\alpha}_3$ is given by var $(\hat{\alpha}_3) = 1.529$ (using a first order Taylor series approximation). Conditionally on $\lambda = \kappa = .5$, the hypothesis of no structural change for the periods 1952–71 and 1972–76, III has to be rejected (the Chow test is $F = 4.64$, $\nu_1 = 6$, $\nu_2 = 84$). This finding is not surprising as the second part of the sample covers a period of flexible exchange rates, of great changes in international money markets, high inflation and interest rates ... Recently, *Kuipers/Wilpstra* [1978, p. 1932] investigated the stability of the demand function for money using quarterly data on narrowly and broadly defined nominal balances for the period 1952, I – 1976, IV. One of their conclusions is that the post-war demand function for money in the Netherlands should be unstable.

Next, we look more closely at the choice of the values for $\lambda = \kappa = .5$. A first question is whether this pair of values gives an overall maximum of the likelihood function if we assume that the disturbance to be added to (2.9) is a normally distributed white noise. The shape of the log-likelihood function for the periods 1952–71 and 1952–76, III for different combinations of λ and κ is given in Figures 1 and 2. For the first sample period the likelihood function attains its maximum at $\lambda = .9$ and $\kappa = .7$ (see model 1′, Table 1), while for the entire period the ML-estimates are $\lambda = 1.$ and $\kappa = .5$. These values are higher than the values $\lambda = \kappa = .5$ retained by F & K, suggesting that the expectations with respect to the income and the price level adapt quickly. A value $\lambda = 1.$ indicates that the expected income is equal to the realized income. We should also notice that the equality $\lambda = \kappa$ implies that there is a common factor $(1 - \lambda L)$ in equation (2.9). We can now test the hypothesis $H_0: \lambda = \kappa = .5$ against $H_1: \lambda \neq .5$ and/or $\kappa \neq .5$, using a likelihood ratio test with 2 ln of the likelihood ratio = 13.16 for the years 1952, I – 1971, IV and equal to 13.128 for the period 1952, I – 1976, III. These likelihood ratio test statistics are χ^2-distributed in large samples with two degrees of freedom (= the number of restrictions imposed in H_0) so that for both periods we have to reject the null hypothesis at a 1% level of significance.[3])

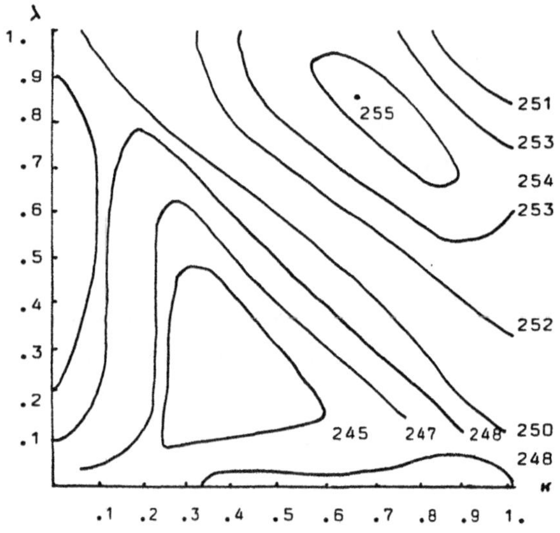

Fig. 1: Contours of the log-likelihood function for the period 1952, I – 1971, IV

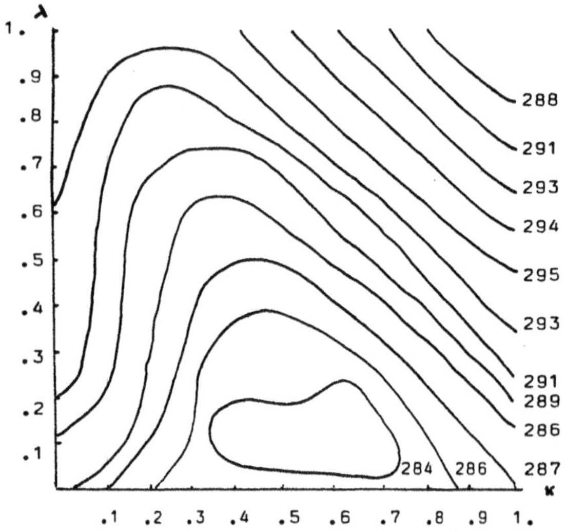

Fig. 2: Contours of the log-likelihood function for the period 1952, I – 1976, III

[3]) The use of the Bonferroni inequality in multiple comparisons implies smaller levels of significance for the individual comparison. We leave it to the reader to choose his own significance level.

It is also interesting to investigate whether the restrictions (2.13) formulated by F & K through the specification in (2.1) – (2.4) are in accord with the information in the data. For this reason, we estimate the unrestricted model (2.11). The results for the unrestricted model are reported in Table 2 (nr. 4 and 5). As expected, they are not very satisfactory. Few coefficients are significantly different from zero. The estimates do not always have the sign expected on the basis of theoretical considerations. As the restrictions have not been imposed on the models 4 and 5, there are several ways to compute "estimates" for λ and κ. We now test the null hypothesis $H_0: \phi(\beta) = 0$, where $\phi(\beta)$ is the vector of 6 nonlinear restrictions (2.13) on the regression coefficients of the model (2.11), against the alternative hypothesis $H_1: \phi_i(\beta) \neq 0$, some $i = 1, 2, \ldots, 6$. The test statistic, 2 ln of the likelihood ratio, is equal to 5.2 for the years 1952–71 and 8.506 for the years 1952–76, III. It is χ^2-distributed in large samples with six degrees of freedom. For the first and second sample, we cannot reject H_0 at a 10% level of significance. It is worthwhile to mention that the WALD-test [see e.g. *Sargan*],

$$W = T\phi(\hat{\beta})' V_{\phi}^{-1}(\hat{\beta})\,\phi(\hat{\beta}) \text{ with } V_{\phi}(\hat{\beta}) = \frac{\partial\phi}{\partial\beta} V_{\hat{\beta}}(\beta) \frac{\partial\phi'}{\partial\beta}\bigg|_{\beta=\hat{\beta}} \text{ and } V_{\hat{\beta}}(\beta)$$

being the large sample covariance matrix of $\hat{\beta}$, has the same asymptotic properties as the likelihood ratio test provided the $\hat{\beta}$'s are ML estimates of the unrestricted model. The Wald-test only requires estimates of the unrestricted model (2.11). Therefore, it is especially appropriate for testing hypotheses for which it is cumbersome to compute the maximum of the restricted likelihood function or when it is difficult to get fully efficient estimates of the unrestricted model. The Wald-statistic, which is approximately χ^2-distributed with 6 degrees of freedom under $H_0: \phi(\beta) = 0$ in (2.13), is equal to 1.935 for the years 1952, I – 1971, IV, and 1.8340, for the period 1952, I – 1976, III, so that for the period 1952–76 we cannot reject the hypothesis at conventional levels of significance. Notice that the OLS estimator for model (2.11) is also the maximum likelihood estimator.

Now we shall pay attention to the structure of the disturbances. For the models 1 and 3, the assumption of spherical disturbances tested by means of the Goldfeld-Quandt test is not rejected at a 5% level of significance. However the empirical evidence in the residuals is not in favour of the assumption of zero error correlations.

In Table 3 we report the estimated residual autocorrelation (ACF) and partial autocorrelation (PACF) functions for several regression models[4]). Estimated large sample standard errors for the ACF and the PACF are given in the column SE [see e.g. *Box/Jenkins*]. It is obvious that there are significant correlations in the residuals of models 1, 3 and 4. Given that the significant residual autocorrelations for these models are positive, one might suspect that the formula $s^2(X'X)^{-1}$ underestimates the variance of the OLS estimator, implying that the t-values for the regression coefficients are overestimated. For model 6, the third and eight autocorrelation coefficients and the third and ninth partial autocorrelation coefficients are significantly different from zero at a 5% level. Simple autoregressive moving average (ARMA) models have been fitted to the residuals of the regression models 1 and 3 using a nonlinear least squares estimation method.

[4]) The computations were performed using a computer program developed by C.R. Nelson, University of Washington, Seattle.

nr/T	period		1	2	3	4	5	6	7	8	9	10	11	12	SE	13	14	15	16	17	18	19	20	21	22	23	24	SE
1	52, I –	A	–.15	–.21	.33	–.15	–.14	.17	.04	–.24	–.14	.31	–.18	–.09	.11	.19	–.25	–.11	.21	–.09	–.05	–.03	.04	.01	–.06	.13	–.16	.16
T = 77	71, IV	P	–.15	–.24	.28	–.12	–.05	.01	–.12	–.20	–.27	.23	–.07	.00	.11													
1'	52, I –	A	.03	–.23	.15	–.13	–.14	.21	–.01	–.23	–.10	.21	–.08	–.06	.11	.07	–.24	–.13	.13	.01	.07	.04	.05	.11	.02	.04	–.10	.11
T = 77	71, IV	P	.03	–.23	.18	–.22	–.03	.13	–.05	–.15	–.19	.25	–.16	.01	.11													
3	52, I –	A	–.20	–.04	.24	–.26	–.04	.14	–.18	–.05	–.06	.06	–.03	–.07	.10	.07	–.06	–.07	.08	–.07	–.05	.04	–.02	.12	–.14	.09	–.06	.12
T = 96	76, III	P	–.20	–.08	.23	–.18	–.11	.06	–.06	–.13	–.19	.12	–.00	–.14	.10													
4	52, I –	A	–.02	–.16	.22	–.14	–.16	.16	–.03	–.18	–.10	.22	–.11	–.08	.11	.07	–.21	–.16	.10	.04	.04	.07	.12	.07	.02	.07	–.14	.14
T = 77	71,IV	P	–.02	–.16	.22	–.18	–.09	.08	–.01	–.13	–.20	.26	–.12	–.03	.11													
5	52,I –	A	–.04	–.05	.07	–.19	–.09	.12	–.12	–.10	.01	.10	–.06	–.03	.10	.08	–.07	–.02	.04	–.04	.00	.01	–.06	.07	–.08	.01	–.05	.11
T = 96	76, III	P	–.04	–.06	.06	–.19	–.10	.09	–.11	–.13	–.06	.14	–.08	–.11	.10													
6	52, I –	A	–.01	–.15	.23	–.12	–.18	.13	–.07	.23	–.12	.19	–.16	–.10	.11	.09	–.19	–.13	.14	.06	.09	.11	.12	.06	.01	.04	–.14	.14
T = 77	71, IV	P	–.01	–.15	.23	–.16	–.11	.06	–.06	–.17	–.23	.21	–.17	–.06	.11													
7	52, I –	A	–.04	–.04	.11	–.19	–.08	.10	–.17	–.14	–.06	.06	–.08	–.05	.10	.07	–.07	–.02	.07	–.01	.04	.05	–.01	.13	–.04	.04	–.03	.11
T = 96	76, III	P	–.04	–.04	.11	–.18	–.08	.08	–.14	–.18	–.14	.10	–.11	–.15	.10													
8	52, I	A	.00	–.15	.24	–.14	–.22	.15	–.09	–.28	–.14	.16	–.14	–.06	.11	.09	–.19	–.09	.18	.07	.12	.09	.07	.08	–.01	.03	–.09	.15
T = 77	71, IV	P	.00	–.15	.24	–.18	–.14	.08	–.10	–.21	–.29	.19	–.15	–.08	.11													

Tab. 3: Estimated autocorrelation (A) and partial (P) autocorrelation for the residuals

nr.	period	(p, q)	RSS	DF	RSS/DF	AR_1	AR_2	MA_1	MA_2	$Q(12)$	DF	$Q(24)$	DF	$Q(36)$	DF
1	52–71	(2,0)	.00706	75	.000094	–.193 (1.719)	–.243 (2.166)			17.2	10	27.6	22	38.4	34
1	52–71	(2,1)	.00659	74	.000089	–.721 (3.37)	–.372 (3.39)	–.593 (2.71)		12.9	9	20.9	21	31.6	33
3	52–76	(2,0)	.08996	94	.000956	1.887 (.1E+6)	–.885 (19.56)			72.0	10	94.2	22	101.9	34
3	52–76	(2,1)	.01267	93	.000136	–.813 (2.554)	–.283 (2.772)	–.599 (1.847)		10.6	9	15.7	21	21.4	33

Tab. 4: Estimated ARMA models for the residuals from the regression models

The results are given in Table 4. Values for the Q-statistic associated with ARMA models are also reported where $Q(k) = T \sum_{\tau=1}^{k} r_\tau^2(\tilde{\epsilon})$, with $r_\tau(\tilde{\epsilon})$ being the estimated τ-th autocorrelation coefficient of the residuals for the ARMA (p, q) models. In regression models with ARMA (p, q) disturbances and no lagged endogenous variables among the regressors, Q is χ^2-distributed with k-p-q degrees of freedom and independent of the explanatory variables in large samples [see *Pierce*]. Here we take high values for Q as a warning against a possible misspecification. The figures in Table 4 are not consistent estimates of non-zero disturbance autocorrelation parameters because there are lagged endogenous variables in the regression equations, but it ought to be clear that the evidence in the residuals is not supporting the white noise assumption for the disturbances. The empirical results in Table 3 suggest that imposing the restriction $\lambda = \kappa = .5$ strengthens the residual autocorrelation. A different picture of the serial correlation structure of the residuals is obtained by looking at the spectra. The estimated spectra[5]) for the residuals of the models 1 and 4 are given in Figures 3 and 4 respectively. Although the residual autocorrelations of the two models are quite different, the residual spectra have a similar shape with a minimum at the frequency of .25 (a period of one year) and peaks at the frequencies .04, .20, .30. The spectrum for ΔM, where Δ is the difference operator, given in Figure 5 has a very similar shape at and around the seasonal frequencies. The minimum at the frequency of .25 and the two peaks at the frequencies of .16 and .30 are probably the result of the seasonal adjustment of the series.

In conclusion, the model specified by F & K does not seem to be entirely in agreement with the information in the data. Also adding a white noise disturbance to equation (2.1) with its implication of a second order moving average error term in equation (2.9) and restrictions between the transfer function parameters and those of the error process does not yield satisfactory results. The unrestricted version of the F & K model (2.11) is acceptable as a maintained hypothesis by residual serial correlation standards. We select it as a starting point for our strategy which consists in specifying a model that is sufficiently general to be a safeguard against missing explanatory variables and autocorrelated errors and then to look for restrictions on the parameters that will not be rejected by the data.

First one may question the presence of the business cycle indicator C in equation (2.11). The coefficients of the variable C are not significantly different from zero in the unrestricted models 4 and 5. Part of its effect on the demand for money is expected to be explained by variations in the variable Y_t. Excluding the business cycle indicator from the unrestricted specification (2.11) does not lead to a substantial loss of explanatory power of the equation (see the models 6 and 7 in Table 2). The value of the likelihood ratio is 7.968 for 1952, I – 1971, IV, and 7.398 for 1952, I – 1976, III (number of degrees of freedom = 3), so that at a 5% level we reject the null hypothesis for the first period but not for the entire sample period. As the restrictions (2.13) imposed by F & K and their empirical finding that $\lambda = \kappa$ imply one common factor restriction on the model, we next investigate whether we can reduce the dimensions of the parameter space by im-

[5]) The spectra have been computed using a computer program developed by C.P.A. Bartels and E. Vogelvang, using the Tukey-Hanning window. The number of lags employed to compute the spectra is 24.

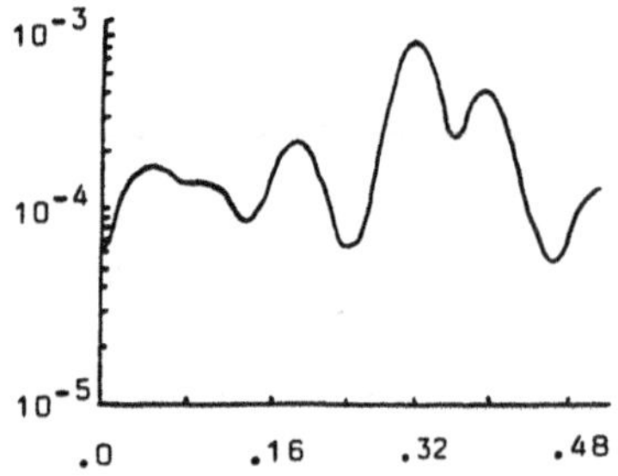

Fig. 3: Estimated spectrum for the residuals of model 1, 1952, I – 1971, IV

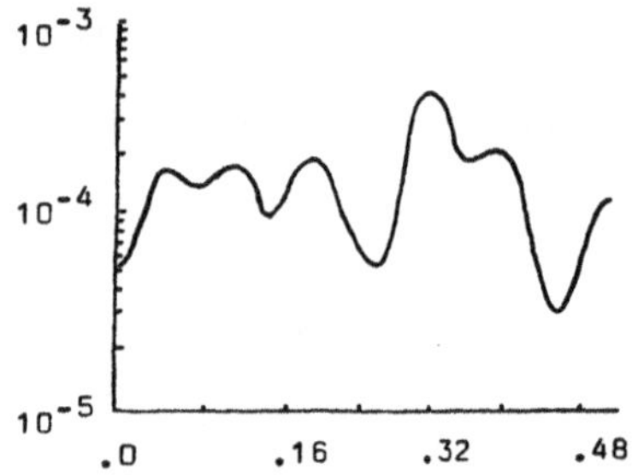

Fig. 4: Estimated spectrum for the residuals of model 4, 1952, I – 1971, IV

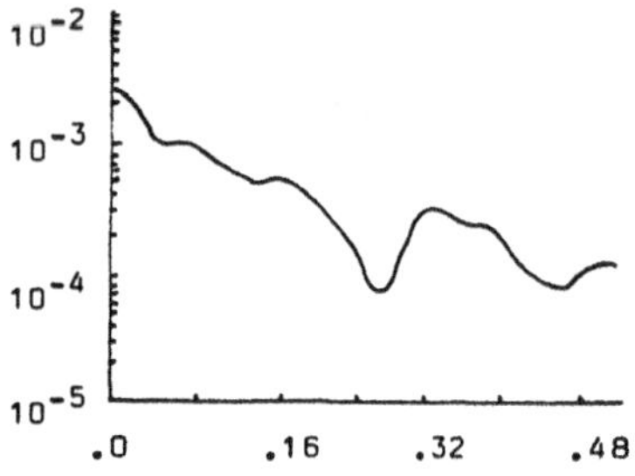

Fig. 5: Estimated spectrum for ΔM, 1952, I – 1976, III

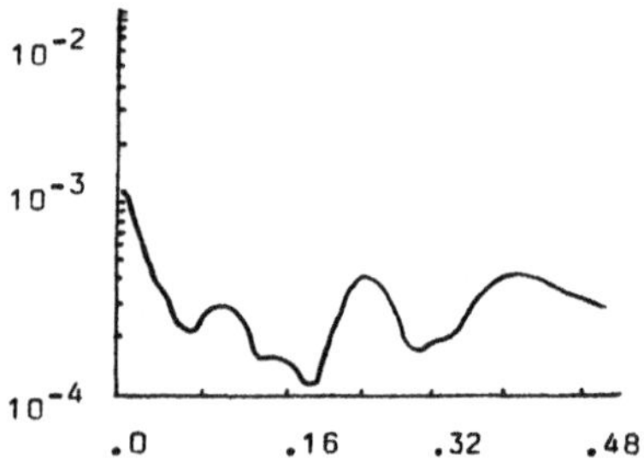

Fig. 6: Estimated spectrum for ΔP, 1952, I – 1976, III

posing a common factor restriction. Along the lines of *Hendry/Mizon* [1978] we test for the presence of common factors in the unrestricted model (2.11) with and without the business cycle variable. Imposing one common factor on the model (2.11) leads to a specification like

$$M_t = \gamma_0 + \gamma_1 M_{t-1} + \gamma_2 M_{t-2} + \gamma_3 Y_t + \gamma_4 R_t + \gamma_5 R_{t-1} + \gamma_6 P_t + \gamma_7 C_t + \gamma_8 C_{t-1} + \frac{u_t}{1-\rho L}. \tag{3.1}$$

As there are lagged endogenous variables and autocorrelated errors present in model (3.1), we estimate its parameters by the Hildreth-Lu method which yields ML estimates of the parameters in (3.1). The estimates are reported in Table 5. The likelihood ratio (LR) statistics for testing the presence of one common factor are given in the following table:

Model	Period	*C* included	2 ln LR	DF
4	1952–71	yes	2.680	4
5	1952–76	yes	3.848	4
6	1952–71	no	4.058	3
7	1952–76	no	3.282	3

From the outcome of the test, we have to conclude that we cannot reject the common factor restriction. It is worthwhile to notice that the estimated common factor for model 6* is equal to zero and that the common factor in model 7* ('*' denotes that the common factor restriction has been imposed) is not significantly different from zero. Non-rejection of the common factor hypothesis leads us to a simpler model.

The models for which the estimates are reported in Table 5 can be rewritten as relationships between variables expressed in growth rates and in levels.

For example, model 6* (Table 5) can be approximately written as

$$\Delta M_t = -.017 + .24\,\Delta M_{t-1} - .04\,M_{t-2} + .002\,Y_t - .071\,\Delta R_t$$

$$- .002\,R_t + .085\,P_t + \frac{\hat{u}_t}{1-.2L}\,.$$

Period	const.	M_{t-1}	M_{t-2}	Y_t	R_t	R_{t-1}	P_t	C_t	C_{t-1}	ρ	R^2	D.W.	T	$\ln L$	nr.
1952, I – 1971, IV	–.432 (2.165)	1.001 (8.063)	–.090 (.773)	.093 (1.966)	–.079 (2.101)	.050 (1.330)	.104 (1.399)	.010 (.712)	.005 (.357)	.30 (2.759)	.999	1.944	77	255.5	4*
1952, I – 1976, III	–.098 (.747)	1.426 (15.142)	–.520 (5.606)	.052 (2.170)	.010 (.349)	–.010 (.339)	.116 (2.456)	–.012 (.807)	.020 (1.426)	.10 (.985)	.999	1.984	96	297.5	5*
1952, I – 1971, IV	–.0174 (.1367)	1.204 (10.88)	–.243 (2.130)	.002 (.067)	–.071 (1.901)	.069 (1.849)	.085 (1.349)			.2 (1.791)	.999	1.924	77	251.3	6*
1952, I – 1976, III	.055 (.536)	1.443 (15.405)	–.494 (5.078)	.006 (.362)	.020 (.681)	–.014 (.485)	.085 (1.988)			.0 (0.0)	.999	2.009	96	294.0	7*

Tab. 5: ML estimates of the model (3.1) (one common factor)

However it is difficult to interpret the implications of these results for the demand for money along a steady state growth path. As an alternative to the models with the common factor restriction, we write the estimated regressions 6 and 7 in Table 2 in terms of the levels and the first differences of the variables. For the period 1952, I – 1971, IV we have approximately

$$\Delta M_t = .08 + .45\,\Delta M_{t-1} - .15\,\Delta M_{t-2} - .03\,(M_{t-1} - Y_{t-1} - P_{t-1})$$

$$+ .04\,\Delta Y_t - .08\,\Delta R_t - .03\,R_{t-2} + .04\,\Delta P_t + \hat{u}_t \tag{3.2}$$

with a steady state solution given by

$$M = A + Y + P - R, \tag{3.3}$$

where

$$A = 33\,(.08 - .70\,\Delta M + .04\,\Delta Y - .08\,\Delta R + .04\,\Delta P),$$

after taking antilogs

$$m = \alpha\, r^{-1} p\, y$$

with $\ln \alpha = A$ and m, r, p and y being the antilogs of M, R, P and Y respectively. Equation (3.2) explains the growth rate of nominal money balances as a function of the lagged money growth rates, an error learning mechanism $(M_{t-1} - Y_{t-1} - P_{t-1})$ being equal to minus the logarithm of the velocity of money in $t-1$ with respect to the transactions, the growth rate of expenditures in constant prices, the change in the interest rate, the lagged interest rate and the rate of change in prices. In the steady state the nominal demand for money as in (3.3) is homogeneous of degree one in nominal expenditures and of degree minus one in the interest rate. The error correction term, which has been used successfully by *Hendry* [1978], implies that the growth rate of money in period t decreases (increases) when money holdings in $t-1$ have been to high (too low) with respect to nominal expenditures, in other words, the growth rate of money depends on the past value of the transactions velocity of money. The specification in (3.2) of the demand for money function is a restricted version of the model 6. The restrictions imply a unit elasticity of money with respect to transactions in the steady state and a velocity which depends on the interest rate. Estimation of the restricted model yields the following results for the period 1952, I – 1971, IV (model 8):

$$\begin{aligned} \Delta M_t = &- \underset{(1.215)}{.078} + \underset{(3.712)}{.441}\,\Delta M_{t-1} - \underset{(1.264)}{.155}\,\Delta M_{t-2} - \underset{(1.057)}{.019}\,[M_{t-1} - Y_{t-1} - P_{t-1}] \\ &+ \underset{(.887)}{.053}\,\Delta Y_t - \underset{(1.449)}{.057}\,\Delta R_t + \underset{(.781)}{.007}\,R_{t-2} - \underset{(.186)}{.018}\,\Delta P_t + \hat{u}_t \\ &\ln L = 251.3 \qquad R^2 = .38, \qquad \text{D.W.} = 1.95. \end{aligned} \tag{3.4}$$

The spectrum for the residuals is given in Figure 8.

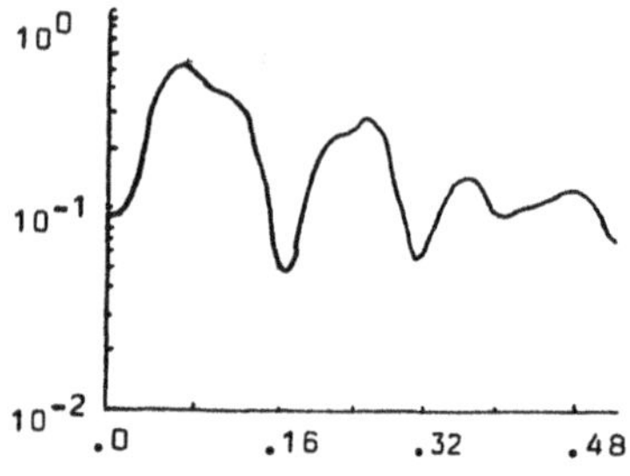

Fig. 7: Estimated spectrum for Δr, 1952, I – 1976, III

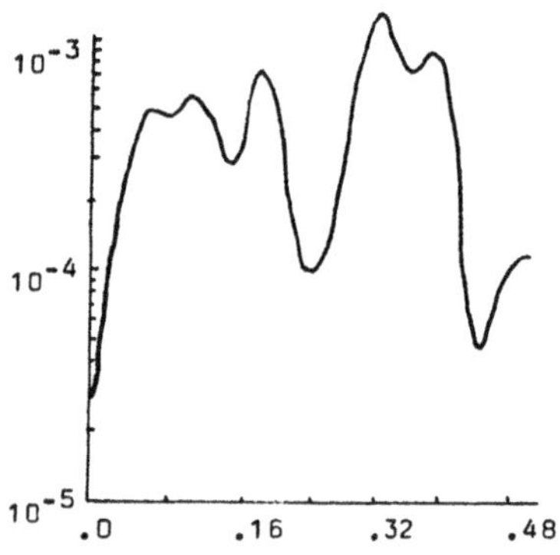

Fig. 8: Estimated spectrum for the residuals of model 8, 1952, I – 1971, IV

The estimates of the constant term and of the coefficient of R_{t-2} have signs different from those in (3.2) although the latter one is not significantly different from zero. The likelihood ratio test statistic for comparing (3.4) and model 6 is equal to 5.984 and has an asymptotic χ^2-distribution with 3 degrees of freedom under the null hypothesis that equation (3.4) is the correct model. We cannot reject the model (3.4) at conventional levels of significance. The decrease in the R^2 is partly due to the decrease in the variance of the left-hand side variable in (3.4). The increase in the residual variance of (3.4) compared to that of model 6 is not sufficient to reject (3.4) when using a likelihood ratio test. The sample autocorrelations for the residuals of model 8 are reported in Table 3. The 3rd, 5th and 8th autocorrelations and the 3rd, 8th and 9th partial autocorrelations are significantly different from zero, still pointing towards a possible misspecification of the model. The results in (3.4) also imply a positive, possibly zero, interest rate elasticity of the demand for money in the steady state. A slightly different specification is given by

$$\Delta M_t = -\underset{(2.860)}{.115} + \underset{(3.838)}{.458}\,\Delta M_{t-1} - \underset{(.979)}{.112}\,\Delta M_{t-2} - \underset{(3.109)}{.030}\,(M_{t-1} - Y_{t-1} - P_{t-1})$$

$$+ \underset{(1.051)}{.062}\,\Delta Y_t - \underset{(2.034)}{.076}\,\Delta R_t + \underset{(.319)}{.012}\,\Delta R_{t-1} - \underset{(.051)}{.005}\,\Delta P + \hat{u}_t$$

$$\ln L = 251.1, \qquad R^2 = .38, \qquad \text{D.W.} = 1.96. \qquad (3.5)$$

It is interesting to note that the point estimates of several parameters are insensible to changes of specification, suggesting that we are able to decompose with some accuracy the constant term in the steady state money demand function but that it is more difficult to accurately determine the effects of variables such as the interest rate on the steady state transactions velocity of money. Three possible explanations are straightforward. First, besides a long-term interest short-term interest rates are relevant for explaining the level of liquidities in an economy. In a recent study using U.S. data, *Heller/Khan* [1979] show that one can improve the explanatory power of the demand function for money by taking into account the entire term structure of interest rates. They avoid the problem of possibly high multicollinearity between interest rates through characterizing the term structure of interest rates by a few parameters. Second, the long-term interest rate used by F & K, which is one of the variables explaining the velocity of money, is not seasonally adjusted while the remaining variables are seasonally adjusted. In a situation like that, the estimated relationship can differ substantially from the true relationship as

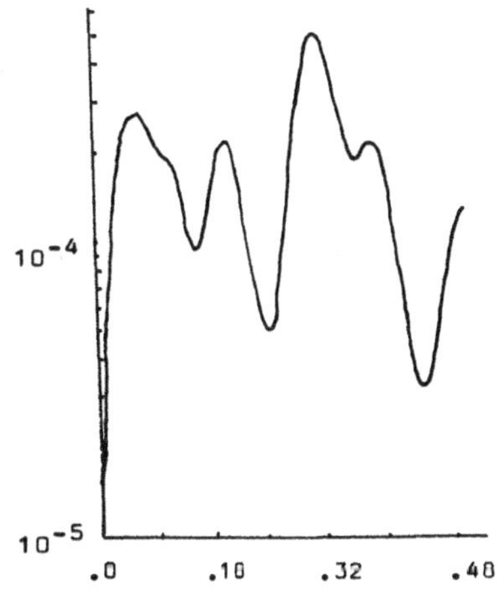

Fig. 9: Estimated spectrum for the residuals of model 11, 1952, I – 1971, IV

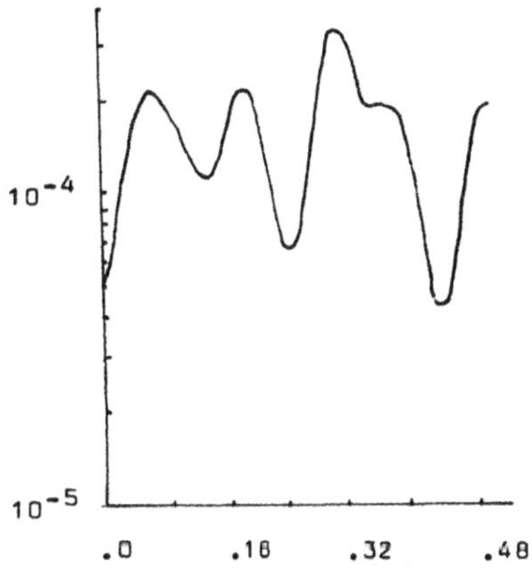

Fig. 10: Estimated spectrum for the residuals of equation (3.11), 1952, I – 1971, IV

has been illustrated by *Wallis* [1974], so that it can be worthwhile to investigate the relationship between seasonally unadjusted series, thereby modelling explicitly the seasonal variations in the data. Third, the quarterly data for income have partly been derived from annual figures [see e.g. *Driehuis*]. The estimates for the money demand equation using this income series may substantially differ from the estimates for a money demand equation using actual quarterly income.

A look at the estimated spectra for some of the variables (see Figs. 5–7) shows that the seasonality has not been entirely removed. The spectrum of ΔM has a peak at the frequency .32 implying a period of about 3 quarters, while the spectrum for ΔP shows a peak at the frequency of .25 with a period of one year. The spectrum of the differenced interest rate series has several peaks, one of which is at the frequency of .25 (a period of one year) pointing towards the presence of seasonality in the interest rate series [see also *Porsius*]. For the period 1951, I – 1976, III, we can write the model 7 (Table 2) approximately as

$$\begin{aligned}\Delta M_t = {} & .055 + .485\,\Delta M_{t-1} + .015\,\Delta M_{t-2} - .04\,[M_{t-1} - Y_{t-1} - P_{t-1}] \\ & + .04\,\Delta Y_t + .007\,\Delta R_t + .04\,\Delta R_{t-1} + .001\,R_{t-1} + .035\,\Delta P_t \\ & + .12\,P_{t-1} + \hat{u}_t \end{aligned} \tag{3.6}$$

with a steady state solution given by

$$M = A + Y + 4P + .025\,R,$$

where

$$A = 25\,(.055 - .5\,\Delta M + .047\,\Delta R + .035\,\Delta P + .04\,\Delta Y).$$

After taking antilogs, the inverse of the steady state transactions velocity of money can be written as a function of the price level p and interest rate r:

$$\frac{m}{py} = \text{constant}\; r^{.025}\, p^3. \tag{3.7}$$

The steady state velocity varies inversely with the interest rate and price level, a finding that one would not expect from theoretical considerations. Re-estimating the restricted specification (3.6) yields the following result

$$\begin{aligned}\Delta M_t = {} & -\underset{(.991)}{.074} + \underset{(4.449)}{.482}\,\Delta M_{t-1} - \underset{(.478)}{.056}\,\Delta M_{t-2} - \underset{(.167)}{.003}\,[M_{t-1} - Y_{t-1} - P_{t-1}] \\ & + \underset{(.411)}{.015}\,\Delta R_t + \underset{(1.258)}{.041}\,\Delta R_{t-1} - \underset{(.158)}{.002}\,R_{t-1} - \underset{(.905)}{.103}\,\Delta P_t \\ & + \underset{(1.466)}{.017}\,P_{t-1} + \underset{(.099)}{.006}\,\Delta Y_t + \hat{u}_t \qquad R^2 = .45 \quad \text{D.W.} = 2.04. \\ & \qquad\qquad\qquad\qquad\qquad\qquad\quad \ln L = 294.1 \end{aligned} \tag{3.8}$$

The likelihood ratio test statistic for comparing model (3.8) with the unrestricted model

7 is equal to 3.128 and has an asymptotic χ^2-distribution with one degree of freedom under the null hypothesis that (3.8) is the correct specification. The point estimates of (3.8) imply that the steady state velocity varies inversely with the price level. They also differ from those obtained in (3.4) for the period 1952 – 1971, IV.

Again the use of seasonally adjusted data together with a seasonally unadjusted long-term interest rate may have distorted the point estimates to the extent that we cannot interpret them as estimates of the structural parameters in a demand for money function. In order to compare the predictive performance of model 1 with that of model 8 in (3.4), we compute the multi-step-ahead "predictions" of nominal money balances for the period 1972, I – 1976, III using the realized values of the exogenous variables. The results are given in Figure 11. The "predictions" from model 8 are more accurate than those from model 1 for which the forecasted values are systematically greater than the realized values. Theil's inequality coefficient $u = [\Sigma u_t^2 / \Sigma r_t^2]^{1/2}$, where u_t is the prediction error and r_t is the realized value of the nominal money balances is equal to .20081 for model 1 and .09224 for model 8.

As a yardstick for the predictive performance of the models 1 and 8, we have fitted univariate ARIMA models to the nominal money balances M_t (logarithmic transformation). The analysis of the autocorrelation and partial autocorrelation functions for M_t suggested a second order autoregressive model with a low order, possibly a second order moving average error term.

The following model has been fitted to the data:

$$\Delta M_t = \underset{(139.7)}{.932}\,\Delta M_{t-1} + \underset{(6.346)}{.069}\,\Delta M_{t-2} + \hat{\epsilon}_t - \underset{(2.966)}{.297}\,\hat{\epsilon}_{t-1} - \underset{(6.528)}{.615}\,\hat{\epsilon}_{t-2}$$

$$R^2 = .324, \quad \text{RSS} = .007, \quad \text{DF} = 75, \quad \text{RSS/DF} = .0001, \qquad (3.9)$$

$$Q(12) = 13.5, \quad \text{DF} = 8$$
$$Q(24) = 19.6, \quad \text{DF} = 20$$
$$Q(36) = 26.0, \quad \text{DF} = 32$$

Theil's inequality coefficient = .11098.

Up to 19-step ahead forecasts have been calculated with this model and are plotted in Figure 11. Notice that model 8 reduces to a univariate ARIMA model if we approximate the error learning term and the exogenous variables by a moving average error. If the model given in (3.9) is correctly specified, its structure puts restrictions on the processes for the exogenous variables in model 8 (assumed to be correctly specified). The analysis of the autocorrelation function of the exogenous variables suggests random walk models for the income and the price variable and a first or second order autoregressive model for the interest rate variable. These univariate models and the model (3.9) for the endogeneous variable are not entirely compatible with model 8, a point that will be investigated more extensively in the future along the lines proposed by *Zellner/Palm* [1974]. Finally, notice that a random walk model for income and the price variable rules out a rational expectations interpretation of the adaptives expectations schemes formulated by *Fase/Kuné* [see e.g. *Sargent*].

Although the model 8 has been extensively tested and its predictive power is fairly good, the point estimates of the parameters are not entirely satisfactory. In particular,

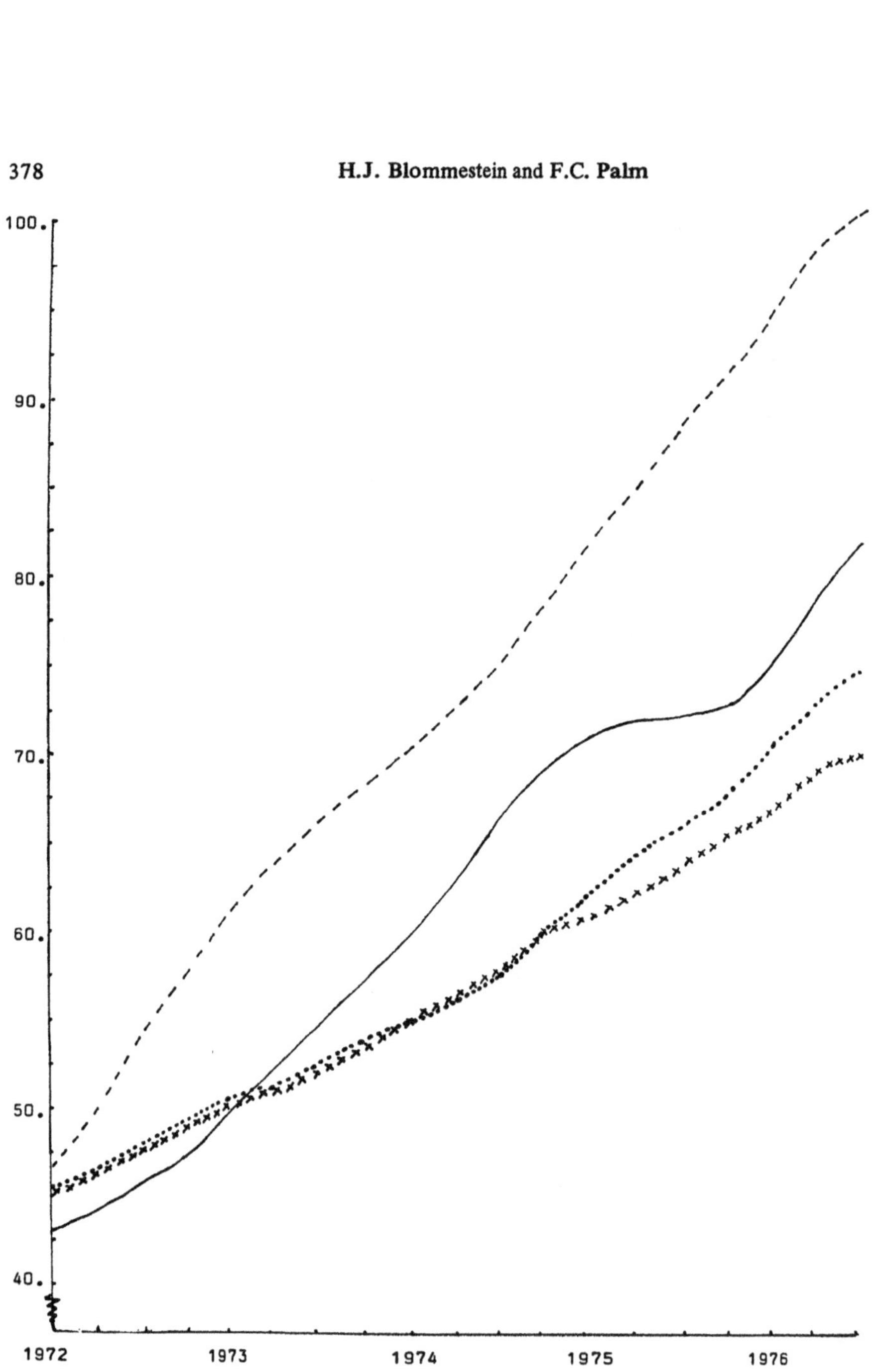

Fig. 11: Nominal money balances in millions of Dfl. (——), forecasts using model 1 (– – –), forecasts using model 8 (. . .), forecasts using model (3.9) (× × ×), 1972, I – 1976, III

the sign of the estimated coefficient of R_{t-2} implies that the steady state velocity of money with respect to transactions decreases when the interest rate increases. In order to see how the seasonal adjustment of the variables affects the estimation results, we have fitted the models 4, 6 and 8 to the seasonally unadjusted data. The results are given in Tables 6 and 7. Models 9 and 10 correspond to the model 8. The D_i's in model

10 are seasonal dummies with $D_i = 1$ in quarter i and zero otherwise. In model 11, all the variables have been filtered using the annual difference operator $1 - L^4$. The point estimates for model 11 are similar to those for model 8. However, the estimated coefficient of R_{t-2} is negative. This implies that the steady state velocity of money increases with the interest rate. Using a likelihood ratio test, we come to the conclusion that model 9 has to be rejected when compared to models 10 or 12. Model 11 is rejected when we test it against the model 14, but the model 14 is not rejected when compared with model 13 at the conventional 5% significance level. It should be clear that the method of seasonal adjustment of the data used in our analysis affects the outcome of the model comparison and the point estimates of the parameters. A more detailed analysis of the seasonally unadjusted data is presently under way.

According to the portfolio theory, the whole spectrum of interest rates is relevant for the amount of money demanded by agents in the economy. For the econometrician, it may be a difficult task to measure the effects of changes in the term structure of interest rates, because of the well-known problem of multicollinearity between the interest rates. However approximating the influence of the term structure of interest rates on the demand for money by including one interest rate in the demand equation may lead to a misspecification, a point, we shall briefly investigate now. In order to deal with the collinearity between interest rates with a different maturity period, we impose along the lines of *Heller/Khan* [1979] a priori restictions on the term structure of the interest rates by assuming that at each period t, the term structure can be described compactly by a quadratic function

$$\ln R_{it} = \alpha_t + \beta_t \tau_i + \gamma_t \tau_i^2, \qquad i = 1, 2, \ldots, n, \tag{3.10}$$

where R_{it} is the i-th interest rate and τ_i is its maturity period.

We estimate the parameters of equation (3.10) for each time period t and substitute them into the demand function for money. The parameter α_t can be viewed as a shift parameter of the term structure, β_t and γ_t determine the slope and the curvature of the entire term structure at time t. For a detailed discussion, we refer the reader to *Heller/Khan* [1979]. After substitution of the three term structure parameters for the interest rate, model 8 leads to the following results for the period 1952 – 1971, IV

$$\begin{aligned} \Delta M_t = &- \underset{(1.10)}{.083} + \underset{(3.75)}{.446}\, \Delta M_{t-1} - \underset{(1.71)}{.195}\, \Delta M_{t-2} - \underset{(1.26)}{.025}\, (M - Y - P)_{t-1} \\ &+ \underset{(1.07)}{.634}\, \Delta Y_t - \underset{(2.11)}{.063} \Delta\alpha_t - \underset{(1.22)}{.529}\, \Delta\beta_t - \underset{(.72)}{5.277}\, \Delta\gamma_t - \underset{(.11)}{.001}\, \alpha_{t-2} \\ &- \underset{(.38)}{.078}\, \beta_{t-2} - \underset{(.30)}{1.158}\, \gamma_{t-2} + \underset{(.44)}{.044}\, \Delta P_t + \hat{u}_t \end{aligned} \tag{3.11}$$

$R^2 = .43$, D.W. $= 1.94$, $\ln L = 254.5$, DF $= 65$.

The plot of the spectrum of the residuals is given in Figure 10.

Heller/Kahn show that the partial derivatives of M_t with respect to the parameters of the term structure of interest rates should be negative, except for values β_t and $\gamma_t < 0$ simultaneously. In equation (3.11), the point estimates of the interest rate variables have

Data transformation	constant	ΔM_{t-1}	ΔM_{t-2}	$(M\text{-}Y\text{-}P)_{t-1}$	ΔY_t	ΔR_t	R_{t-2}	ΔP_t	D_1	D_2	D_3	D.W.	R^2	DF	$\ln L$	nr.
–	.032 (.23)	.194 (1.56)	–.500 (4.34)	.009 (.30)	–.089 (2.31)	–.045 (.74)	.265 (1.84)	–.022 (.16)				2.08	.31	69	211.8	9
–	–.134 (1.12)	.18 (1.48)	–.081 (.65)	–.021 (.87)	.027 (.35)	–.079 (1.53)	.008 (.65)	.045 (.38)	.028 (2.25)	.030 (4.77)	.026 (4.04)	2.02	.55	66	228.6	10
$1-L^4$	.001 (.44)	.317 (2.55)	–.142 (1.08)	–.017 (.427)	.037 (.49)	–.071 (1.61)	–.012 (.54)	–.233 (1.80)				2.02	.23	65	202.1	11

Tab. 6: Ordinary least squares estimates of equation (3.4) using seasonally unadjusted data, 1952–1971, IV

Data transformation	constant	M_{t-1}	M_{t-2}	M_{t-3}	Y_t	Y_{t-1}	R_t	R_{t-1}	R_{t-2}	P_t	P_{t-1}	C_t	C_{t-1}	C_{t-2}	D.W.	R^2	$\ln L$	DF	nr.
–	–.13 (.45)	1.09 (8.3)	–.47 (2.52)	.32 (2.58)	–.09 (2.06)	.08 (1.93)	–.10 (1.66)	.01 (1.03)	–.32 (.50)	.14 (.93)	.05 (.35)	–.01 (1.97)	.01 (2.91)	.005 (1.06)	2.0	.99	223.4	63	12
$1-L^4$	.01 (2.16)	1.16 (8.86)	–.40 (2.05)	.08 (.60)	.04 (.48)	–.08 (1.05)	–.06 (1.47)	.07 (1.05)	–.03 (.57)	–.11 (.83)	.19 (1.40)	–.0002 (.04)	.007 (1.81)	.001 (.27)	2.0	.84	210.8	59	13
$1-L^4$	.01 (2.17)	1.17 (9.23)	–.38 (1.95)	.05 (.40)	.04 (.49)	–.12 (1.66)	–.05 (1.21)	.05 (.79)	–.19 (.43)	–.11 (.85)	.22 (1.62)				2.0	.83	208.7	62	14

Tab. 7: Ordinary least squares estimates of equation (2.11) using seasonally unadjusted variables, 1952–1971, IV

the expected sign. Those for the remaining variables are similar to the estimates for model 8 in (3.4). The steady state velocity of money implied by equation (3.11) increases with the interest rate variables.

In conclusion, model 8 seem to be appropriate to describe the short-run behaviour of the data and to predict future developments. The point estimates and the dynamic specification are sensitive to the method of seasonal adjustment and to the choice of interest rate variables. Therefore, it may be somewhat risky to take the point estimates of model 8 as estimates of the structural parameters in the demand function for money. Rather, our analysis suggests that model 8 is a transformation of a structural equation for the demand for money.

4. Some Final Conclusions

In the present paper we have analysed a model for the demand for money in the Netherlands. We have formally tested some of the assumptions and restrictions formulated by *Fase/Kuné* [1974]. In particular, the choice of the estimates $\kappa = \lambda = .5$ has to be rejected. Although the restricted model 1' is not rejected when compared with the unrestricted model 4 and that its residual correlation properties are acceptable (see Table 3), it had to be disregarded for at least two reasons: first, the point estimate of θ is equal to .088 implying a very slow adjustment of nominal money balances to desired ones; second, its predictive performance is very bad.

It predicts a decrease of money balances during the period 1972–1976, III. The unrestricted version of the model formulated by Fase/Kuné is sufficiently general to be taken as a starting point for our specification analysis. The value of the likelihood ratio test statistic for comparing model (2.11) with a general unrestricted regression equation with the endogenous variable M_t lagged up to four quarters and the current and past values of the explanatory variables Y_t, P_t, R_t and C_t, all lagged up to four periods, is equal to 11.3 (the nr. of degrees of freedom = 10), so that for the period 1952–1976 the model (2.11) is not rejected at the conventional significance level. Restrictions such as a unit elasticity of money with respect to income and prices in the steady state are not rejected by the data and are therefore imposed on the model (2.11). In this way we obtain a model, that is theoretically meaningful and that predicts rather well. For the years 1972–1974, its predictive properties are similar to those of the ARIMA model (3.9), while for 1975 and 1976 the predictive performance of the former model is superior.

The specification of the model and the point estimates are affected by the choice of a method for seasonal adjustment (the X-11 method or the annual difference operator) and by the choice of the interest rate variables. This aspect and the problem of simultaneity between variables such as M_t, P_t and R_t have to be investigated more extensively. The conclusion by *Jager* [1978] that the monetary approach to the balance of payments in the form of the global monetaristic version has to be rejected for Dutch data for the period 1967–1976 points to a possible problem of simultaneity. Some work in progress on testing for the direction of causality indicates that there is a feedback relationship between money and income in the Netherlands.

Finally, in line with the conclusion by *Kuipers/Wilpstra* [1978], that the demand for money in a narrow sense is better explained than the demand for broadly defined money, investigated by Fase/Kuné and in this paper, the definitions of the variables and the quality of the quarterly data also require more attention.

Appendix: The Data

A more detailed description of the data is given by F & K. The data are quarterly seasonally adjusted (except for the interest rate) observations on:

M_t = total domestic liquidities (M2) in hands of the public averaged over the quarter.
Y_t = gross national expenses in quarter t, measured in 1963 prices.
R_t = average of 18 rates of return on long-term government bonds.
P_t = price index of gross national expenses (basis = 100 in 1963).
C_t = quarterly average of unemployed males in percentage of total male employees.

The interest rates used to compute the parameters of the term structure are averages of monthly treasury bill rates with maturity periods of three, twelve, twenty four, thirty six and sixty months and the rates of government loans with maturity periods between six and thirty years. For the period 1962 to 1971 we also included the three months Euro-guilder deposit rate. The data have been collected by De Nederlandsche Bank.

References

Blommestein, H.J., and *G. van Dijk*: De vraag naar liquiditeiten in Nederland. Mimeo, Econ. Fac., Vrije Universiteit, Amsterdam 1978.

Box, G.E.P., and *G.M. Jenkins*: Time Series Analysis, Forecasting and Control. San Francisco 1970.

Den Butter, F.A.G., and *M.M.G. Fase*: The Demand for Money in EEC Countries. De Nederlandsche Bank N.V., mimeographed, 1979.

Davidson, J.E.H. et al.: Econometric Modelling of the Aggregate Time Series Relationship between Consumers Expenditure and Income in the United Kingdom. The Economic Journal **88**, 1978, 661–692.

Driehuis, W.: Fluctuations and Growth in a Near Full Employment Economy, Rotterdam 1972.

Fase, M.M.G., and *J.B. Kuné*: De vraag naar liquiditeiten in Nederland 1951–1971. De Economist **122**, 1974, 326–356.

–: The Demand for Money in Thirteen European and Non-European Countries: A Tabular Survey. Kredit und Kapital 3, 1975, 410–419.

Friedman, M.: The Quantity Theory of Money. Studies in the Quantity Theory of Money. Ed. by M. Friedman, Chicago 1956.

Heller, H.R., and *M.S. Khan*: The Demand for Money and the Term Structure of Interest Rates. Journal of Political Economy **87**, 1979, 109–127.

Hendry, D.F.: Predictive Failure and Econometric Modelling in Macro-Economics: The Transactions Demand for Money. Discussion Paper, London 1978.

Hendry, D.F., and *G.E. Mizon*: Serial Correlation as a Convenient Simplification, not a Nuisance: A Comment on a Study of the Demand for Money Function by the Bank of England. The Economic Journal **88**, 1978, 549–563.

–: An Empirical Application and Monte Carlo Analysis of Tests of Dynamic Specification. Review of Economic Studies **XLVII**, 1980, 21–46.

Jager, H.: The Global Monetaristic Variant of the Monetary Approach to the Balance of Payments. An Empirical Study of the Netherlands. De Economist **126**, 1978, 342–369.

Johnson, H.G.: The Monetary Approach to Balance-of-Payments Theory. Journal of Financial and Quantitative Analysis **7**, 1972, 1555–1572.

Koopmans, T.C.: Measurement without Theory. The Review of Economic Statistics **29**, 1947, 151–172.

Kuipers, S.K., and *B.S. Wilpstra*: On the Estimation and Stability of Demand for Money Functions for the Netherlands. Economies et Sociétés, Cahiers de l'I.S.M.E.A., Série M0 **1**, 1978, 1917–1942.

Laidler, D.E.W.: The Demand for Money, Theories and Evidence. Scranton, 1969.

Morgenstern, O.: On the Accuracy of Economic Observations. 2nd ed. Princeton 1963.

Pesaran, M.H., and *A.S. Deaton*: Testing Non-Nested Nonlinear Regression Models. Econometrica **46**, 1978, 677–694.

Pierce, D.A.: Distribution of Residual Autocorrelations in the Regression Model with Autoregressive-Moving Average Errors. Journal of the Royal Statistical Society B, **33**, 1971, 140–146.

Porsius, P.: Seasonality in Interest Rates in the Netherlands. Mimeo, University of Amsterdam, 1976.

Sargan, J.D.: A Suggested Technique for Computing Approximations to WALD criteria with Application to Testing Dynamic Specification. Discussion Paper, London 1975.

Sargent, T.J.: Observations on Improper Methods of Simulating and Teaching Friedman's Time Series Consumption Model, International Economic Review **18**, 1977, 445–462.

Sims, C.A.: Macroeconomics and Reality. Econometrica **48**, 1980, 1–48.

Wallis, K.F.: Seasonal Adjustment and Relations between Variables. Journal of the American Statistical Association **69**, 1974, 18–31.

–: Multiple Time Series Analysis and the Final Form of Econometric Models. Econometrica **45**, 1977, 1481–1498.

Zellner, A., and *F. Palm*: Time Series Analysis and Simultaneous Equation Econometric Models. Journal of Econometrics **2**, 1974, 17–54.

GPSR Compliance

The European Union's (EU) General Product Safety Regulation (GPSR) is a set of rules that requires consumer products to be safe and our obligations to ensure this.

If you have any concerns about our products, you can contact us on ProductSafety@springernature.com

In case Publisher is established outside the EU, the EU authorized representative is:

Springer Nature Customer Service Center GmbH
Europaplatz 3
69115 Heidelberg, Germany

Batch number: 10732714

Printed by Printforce, the Netherlands